Disaster Policy
and Politics

Third Edition

To my grandchildren, Sienna, Logan, Michaela, and Aaron J.,
and in fond and respectful memory of two "guiding lights,"
William R. Cumming, Esq., former FEMA Office of General Counsel, and
Joe Scanlon, professor emeritus Carleton University, School of Journalism, Ottawa, Canada

Disaster Policy and Politics

Emergency Management and Homeland Security

Third Edition

Richard Sylves
University of Delaware
(Emeritus Professor of Political Science)

Los Angeles | London | New Delhi
Singapore | Washington DC | Melbourne

FOR INFORMATION:

CQ Press
An Imprint of SAGE Publications, Inc.
2455 Teller Road
Thousand Oaks, California 91320
E-mail: order@sagepub.com

SAGE Publications Ltd.
1 Oliver's Yard
55 City Road
London EC1Y 1SP
United Kingdom

SAGE Publications India Pvt. Ltd.
B 1/I 1 Mohan Cooperative Industrial Area
Mathura Road, New Delhi 110 044
India

SAGE Publications Asia-Pacific Pte. Ltd.
18 Cross Street #10-10/11/12
China Square Central
Singapore 048423

Acquisitions Editors: Charisse Kiino,
Scott Greenan
Editorial Assistant: Lauren Younker
Production Editor: Jane Martinez
Copy Editor: Sheree Van Vreede
Typesetter: Hurix Digital
Proofreader: Barbara Coster
Indexer: Judy Hunt
Cover Designer: Candice Harman
Marketing Manager: Jennifer Jones

Printed in the United States of America

Library of Congress Cataloging-in-Publication Data

Names: Sylves, Richard, author.

Title: Disaster policy and politics : emergency management and homeland security / Richard Sylves.

Description: Third edition. | Los Angeles : Sage; CQ Press, [2020] | Includes bibliographical references and index.

Identifiers: LCCN 2018042766 | ISBN 9781506368689 (pbk. : alk. paper)

Subjects: LCSH: Emergency management—United States. | Intergovernmental cooperation—United States.

Classification: LCC HV551.3 .S95 2020 | DDC 363.34/5610973—dc23 LC record available at https://lccn.loc.gov/2018042766

This book is printed on acid-free paper.

19 20 21 22 23 10 9 8 7 6 5 4 3 2

BRIEF CONTENTS

DETAILED CONTENTS

TABLES, FIGURES, AND BOXES

Tables

Figures

"Tell Me More" Boxes

PREFACE

In his 1993 book, *Natural Disasters*, Professor David Alexander advised, "Objective analysis requires that the sensational aspects of disasters be played down and that we assume a sober, responsible attitude toward them. This also means that anecdotal and purely descriptive approaches should be avoided; case studies should be used only where they genuinely demonstrate or illustrate fundamental principles. Hence a rigorous approach to natural disasters requires that we look for the common regularities in each event, however unique it may at first seem. In this way it will be possible to improve our understanding of the phenomenon of natural catastrophe."[1] Alexander's advice is still appropriate today. However, the current political climate in America and around much of the world makes objective analysis of the political realm of disaster difficult in the extreme.

Today multidisciplinary disaster study reveals that disasters or emergencies rarely stem from natural forces alone. Humans help to manufacture or aggravate the calamities "Mother Nature" allegedly inflicts on them. Many have knowingly or obliviously placed themselves and their loved ones in harm's way. They often do this in choosing where to reside, in selecting the houses or structures they inhabit, and in surrendering to hazard vulnerabilities in their quest for comfort, convenience, personal gain, or social satisfactions.

As Alexander maintains, case studies should be used to demonstrate fundamental principles. Through two previous editions, and now this third one, the author has used short case studies to make larger points or to delve more deeply into subjects raised in the book. Moreover, some case studies, even though they may be criticized for being anecdotal or descriptive, help to "humanize" disasters for those who read studies of emergency management and disaster policy. The author stands in agreement with Alexander's insistence that we "look for the commonalities in each event."[2]

This book is written for those interested in disaster policy, politics, and emergency management. Disasters affect people and society in a great many ways. Disaster sociologist Dennis Mileti tells us that disasters stem from more than simply "unexpected events." Disasters result from somewhat predictable interactions of the physical environment (earthquakes, hurricanes, floods, drought, tornadoes, and so on), the social and demographic characteristics of the localities that experience them (population, population density, education levels of inhabitants, economic level of development, social systems in place, and the like), and the durability and resilience of the constructed or built environment (such as buildings, bridges, roads, housing, and utility infrastructure).[3] Disasters also challenge the operation, resilience, competence, and responsiveness of governments and political systems.

In the United States, disaster, whether produced from natural forces or human causes, has long had its own public policy and politics.[4] The roots of this nation's disaster law and policy in part reside in the U.S. Constitution itself. Likewise, disasters for America have long had political implications for its government leaders, up to and including the current president. As mentioned, what is more difficult to grasp is that humans are capable of producing disasters. Terrorism, other criminal acts, failures of technology, and tolerated vulnerabilities to natural forces mean that disaster may in whole or in part be the result of human behavior. Second, the national security relevance of disaster, stemming from public and official concerns emanating from the atomic age (1945–) threat of nuclear attack[5] and the modern era threat of terrorism over the last 30–40 years, continues. Add to this, political leaders and officials shape people's conceptions of what a disaster is. That is, government officials and policymakers are in many respects coming to define, sometimes in concert with news and social media, what disasters are and what constitutes a disaster or emergency threat.

Consequently, in some ways, disasters and emergencies are politically and socially "constructed" in the minds of the public, facilitated by those who influence and shape public opinion and public perceptions.[6] Complicating this further is that global forces evident in climate change, as well as the threats posed by better understood geological forces such as plate tectonics, earthquakes, and volcanic activity, are confronting humankind with new types of survival challenges.[7]

One reason why disaster policy and politics defy simple explanation is because disasters and emergencies impact almost every domain of public policy: defense, health, social welfare, housing and urban development, labor, agriculture, commerce, education, environmental protection, transportation, energy, criminal justice, and others. Since the era of deadly terror attacks began, disaster policy and emergency management have been fused to, and some claim subsumed under, homeland security policy and national defense.[8]

Policy study,[9] so often conducted in other policy domains, furnishes a useful tool one may use to make sense of the politics and management of past disasters.[10] It helps one to anticipate and predict government's response and reactions in the aftermath of disasters. The long-term evolution of the field of emergency management in general, and the rise of homeland security, has attracted the attention of scholars and students. Teachers and researchers have been drawn to the subject by an apparent upturn in the frequency and intensity of disasters, as well as by an explosion of information about disaster phenomena of many types. On top of this, the growth of a keenly interested audience comprising both the general public and higher education students has not escaped notice. Many among the general public anticipate that if they have not already been through a disaster, they may well be in the future. Many have elected to become better informed and prepared for these risks. Recent generations of students are also drawn to the subject of disaster by their interest in worthy humanitarian service and/or potential employment as an emergency management professional working in the public, nonprofit, or private sectors.

This third edition contains new and updated facts, analyses, and theory material. Authors of every good textbook seek to both educate and present facts and ideas. Good texts elicit thought, criticism, discussion, interpretation, and creation of new knowledge by their readers. This author hopes the third edition evokes these responses and that the facts presented here will be a basis for idea building. This study may serve as a crucible in which the perspectives, experience, insightfulness, and expertise of readers, including teachers and students, launches discussion, debate, exchange of ideas, and invitation to further study. This text is "not" a manual of practice doctrine, but it does present information about U.S. disaster policy and emergency management, and how each has changed over time. Similarly, it is about some of the operational side of emergency management. Much of disaster policy and politics is imbued with political, social, ethical, and economic values. In many, although not all, respects, values are open to individual and group interpretation. This study will make this apparent, but it will also allow readers to reason out problems such that they are invited to draw their own conclusions, which of course to some degree may vary from individual to individual.

Because emergency management fundamentally involves coordinated activity, and because much of this coordination work involves oversight and operational management of officials working at different levels of government and in different public and private settings, intergovernmental relations theory and analysis are most appropriate in disaster study. In addition, the framework of intergovernmental relations helps one appreciate that the definition of disaster is dynamic and is particularly influenced by political and managerial actors and forces.

I thought much had changed in the field of disaster policy and politics between my first edition and my second. However, I never anticipated how radically disaster policy and politics would change between my second edition and now this third one. Having won re-election to a second term in 2012, President Barack Obama continued in his second term to confront one of the nation's worst and longest economic downturns since the Great Depression of the 1930s. The failure of huge banks and investment firms, and the collapse of the U.S. housing market, helped drive up unemployment and poverty levels while it undermined investor confidence. This environment had an effect on President Obama's approach to the management of disaster. He was predisposed to approve a great many governor requests for major disaster and emergency declarations, and aware of this, many governors became skilled at assembling the information they needed to win declarations for calamities big and small. The Obama second term was after January 2015 hobbled by Republican majorities in the Senate and House; both bodies were led by leaders who vowed to thwart or undo every Obama administration initiative or achievement. Moreover, President Obama was a skilled campaigner but a poor political negotiator. Obama carried forward many G. W. Bush administration policies, including advancing the integration of all arms of the terrorism-focused U.S. Department of Homeland Security. However, with the possible exception of housing mistakes made after Superstorm Sandy in 2012, President Obama did take care to avoid disaster mismanagement gaffes, unlike his predecessor.

Then came the presidential campaign of 2016. The raucous and rancorous in-party and between-party battles of both Democrats and Republicans set a new low standard in American presidential campaigning. Although favored to win in many opinion polls before the November 2016 general election, Democratic Party presidential nominee Hillary Clinton lost the Electoral College vote but won the popular vote. Republican presidential nominee Donald J. Trump thereby won the presidency and was inaugurated the 45th President in January 2017. President Trump set as one of his main goals the reversal of nearly all Obama legislative and executive actions. Enjoying ever larger Republican majorities in the Senate and House, Trump and a Republican Congress were able to eviscerate most of Obama's Affordable Care Act.

President Trump's management style and public statements, many merely "tweets" posted on Twitter, sometimes alienated even lawmakers of his own political party. White

House staff turnover was fierce, and the pace of Trump's appointee selections and their Senate confirmations were remarkably slow when compared with previous new presidents. FEMA was led by an acting administrator from January to June 2017.

President Trump became a leader who unapologetically advanced the causes and interests of those who supported him. There was no place for those who did not support him. Years before the Trump presidency, partisanship divisions between America's two mass political parties had escalated to hyper-partisan extremes. The political center has shrunk to a tiny numerical minority, and bipartisanship is at this writing an endangered species. A January 2015 article reviewed factors that contributed to hyper-partisanship: partisan bias in redistricting (aka gerrymandering) by governors and state legislatures of a great many states had the effect of converting previously partisan contested legislative districts into safe ones. Because Republicans held a preponderant number of governorships, this gave their incumbents an electoral advantage. More than this, both the Democrats and Republicans stridently advanced opposing politically ideologies that saw them purge their membership of moderates.[11] In effect, the Democrats became more liberal and the Republicans became more conservative. Liberals and conservatives had different lifestyles, different worldviews, and somewhat different value systems. Add to this an accelerating urban–rural divide, worsening racial and ethnic tensions in part owing to disputes about immigration, fractures caused by slanted or biased news media coverage carried out by organizations now publicly perceived as rightist or leftist, lawmaker preoccupation with fund raising and cosseting the interests of their largest campaign funding donors, and diminished social interaction of lawmakers of opposing parties.[12] Clearly, the American political world has changed since the second edition went to print in August 2014.

MAJOR THEMES OF DISASTER POLICY AND POLITICS

All new cases have been added, and all outdated cases have been replaced. The third edition has three central purposes. First, the volume takes us far into 2018 but in a manner that does not overlook the importance of disaster policy and emergency management from 1950 onward. Second, this edition incorporates essentials of published political, administrative, and theory works conducted to mid-2018. Third, this version builds from work I prepared for graduate courses I taught at George Washington University (GWU, 2010–2015) and the University of Delaware (UD, 1977–2010). Moreover, colleagues at other universities who read and used the second edition were kind in offering feedback and suggestions that made possible improvements in this third edition.

My approach to disaster research taken in this book draws from the study of public policy, public management, and presidential leadership. The book carries forward several themes. It is also intended to guide students through a wealth of new material, aided by examples and simple-to-complex analytic frameworks.

There are a variety of introductory emergency management and homeland security texts now in print. Some flow from edition to edition and are assembled from successive scouring of official government websites. Many of these seek to provide the latest information about changes in federal (yes, almost always federal) disaster policy and emergency management. Some intro texts are crafted from pedagogical material used to teach in-person and online emergency management courses. Some are pitched as "practical guides" exploring both emergency management and homeland security. A few are not much more than training manuals. Yet, to their credit, others ambitiously take on international and comparative analysis of emergency management, homeland security, or both. Something nearly all of these texts have in common is that they are written to make emergency management, disaster policy, and homeland security seem as if they are "apolitical" when, in fact, each is political. Unfortunately, many of these textbook authors are aware of the political nature of their subject but choose to avoid mention of "politics" for fear that their tracts are pejoratively labeled as partisan, ideological, or propagandistic.

The problem is that emergency management, homeland security, and disaster policy are intrinsically political. They are the product of laws enacted by elected representatives of the people. These laws, and the legislative process that produces them, emanate under a democratic republic whose foundation is the U.S. Constitution. To ignore the political environment that produces emergency management, homeland security, and disaster policy is to think naively. It also advances the fiction that emergency management, disaster policy, and homeland security policy are merely products of what administrators and bureaucrats decide in their offices and meetings with one another.

Not to be overlooked are a smattering of books in print that are autobiographical or biographical studies of top emergency managers. A few of these are informative and worthwhile, although most are not written for academic audiences, are not particularly objective, and are under-researched. In some respects, they represent "hero studies" that are personal self-promotions. The best of this lot are books that provide insight into how disaster management was carried out in specific incidents and where improvements can be made.

What this book contributes is a "public affairs" perspective plus an analysis that considers "politics." The working assumption is that disaster policy and politics significantly affect the public management of disasters and emergencies. This book is not a political polemic that argues only one side of issues. For 40 years, I worked as a professor of political science. I taught graduate and undergraduate students at three major universities. I am proud to say that I never taught my personal agenda, nor did I simply tell students what I thought they wanted to hear. What I endeavored to do was to educate them about the facts, issues, and politics of the American political system. For any single class session, I would press my students to think about political issues and to be aware of their own biases. One of my goals was to help them understand how in this nation politics generates laws, policies, oversight, public spending, public taxation, and outcomes—good, bad, or somewhere in between. Students who have taken my courses know that I regularly "shake things up" by taking the "devil's advocate" position. When the entire class agreed on a position, I knew it was my job to go to work on helping them understand the opposing position. A second goal I embraced was to not only teach the field and bring the textbook to "life" but also help them develop the capacity to think critically and independently about what we were covering. The goal was to empower them to think for themselves in a balanced, reasonable, and logical way. I had the same goals in crafting this third edition text for students and other readers.

An early first theme concerns emergency management in the United States. Most people associate disaster policy with the emergency responder occupational groups they have come to know and trust: firefighters, law enforcement, and emergency medical personnel. Public emergency management continues to rely on the support and contributions of these essential occupational specialties, but emergency management both includes and extends well beyond these occupational specialists. Emergency management appears to be the "application" side of disaster policy. Although this is true, emergency managers also contribute to problem identification, agenda building, policy formulation, and policy evaluation.[13]

One of the very best books about what emergency management is, and what emergency managers do, was authored by Lucien G. Canton as *Emergency Management: Concepts and Strategies for Effective Programs*.[14] A second edition of this book will soon be published. Canton, who in his career worked as a federal and municipal emergency manager, understands the field in professional and academic terms. What I have attempted to do is to draw from some of Canton's wisdom to explain and show what emergency management is about. Emergency management is clearly an important part of U.S. homeland security, but emergency management and disaster policy should not be judged as a sideline homeland security topic. A key theme in this book is that emergency management and disaster policy serve important public purposes. Moreover, whether others believe America does disaster management well or poorly, there is little doubt that the United States contributes to the advancement of disaster management globally.

A second theme is that disaster policy and politics constitute a worthy field of academic study. Disaster research has long been part of many academic disciplines. This book draws from political science and public administration. It also pulls from disaster sociology and economics theory to demonstrate how disaster research has become a force in shaping disaster policy. Disaster researchers have become part of the politics of disaster in the United States. Disaster researchers continue to make both major and minor contributions to our understanding of disasters as political, social, economic, and physical phenomena. They have also advanced knowledge and understanding of human-caused, and natural disaster, forces. They have helped prevent or mitigate the effects of forces capable of producing disasters, and they have used science and technology to forecast, monitor, track, and measure natural forces so that people in America and around the world are given advanced warning of disaster threats. Scientific, engineering, and particularly communications advances since 2000 have been remarkable. Emergency management continues its maturation into a profession, and those seeking to learn the profession are pressed to master it through interdisciplinary and multidisciplinary education. Just as in the first and second edition, this much-revised third edition has been developed for educational purposes more than "training" purposes. As a product of academic inquiry, information and observations offered in this book are intended to begin, not end, discussion, research, and knowledge creation.

The third theme involves management again but at the level of the elected executive. Presidents, governors, mayors, county executives, and city managers are major players in times of disaster and emergency. In many respects, disasters produce crises that leaders must address in some fashion. Arjen Boin, Paul t'Hart, Eric Stern, and Bengt Sundelius have produced an exquisite study of *The Politics of Crisis Management: Public Leadership under Pressure*.[15] They deliver a great many insights and lessons in their concise book. While they mention American leadership crises, their focus is mainly on European parliamentary democracies. This limits the applicability of their lessons for the United States. European parliaments operate under shifting coalitions of governing majorities, sometimes comprising far more than two political parties. For better or for worse, the U.S. political system, unlike parliamentary systems, does not feature "votes of no-confidence" or snap elections that can bring down prime ministers. American presidents, unless House impeached and found criminally guilty in a Senate trial, serve fixed terms of office until the next presidential election, regardless of whether their political party holds a majority in the House, Senate, or both.

Presidents and the presidency itself occupy a central position in U.S. disaster policy and politics. How presidents lead, manage federal officials, cope with the news media, address federal–state relations, act on governors' requests for disaster and emergency assistance, define policy agendas, and choose political appointees for responsible posts, all contribute to their ability to address the demands imposed by disasters and catastrophes. In many respects, political, policy, and managerial decisions made by presidents and their administrations before a disaster significantly affect the ability of federal, state, and local government to mitigate, prepare for, and respond to disasters and emergencies. An overview of the tools of federal, state, and local interchange in disaster management is presented, as are several theories that provide a suggested course for analyzing the president–governor relationships that underlie presidential decisions to declare disasters. Since 2008 when the first edition went to press, the roles of presidents and governors in disaster politics and policy have been the subject of considerable academic and professional inquiry. This third edition extracts and blends in the findings of this executive focused scholarship.

The fourth theme of the book involves civil–military relations and homeland security. In the United States, the military is an instrument of federal and state government and has long played a role in disaster management, usually in the emergency preparedness and response phases. Since 1950, when modern-era American emergency management arguably got its start, disaster policy and politics have overlapped, been periodically dominated by, and paralleled U.S. national defense policy. The Cold War era (approximately 1946–1990) of U.S.–Soviet conflict was a time when American federal, state, and local emergency managers had to work on matters of civil defense against nuclear attack. Civil defense of the Cold War era sometimes complemented, but often confounded, emergency management aimed at natural disasters and nonwar human-caused calamities. During the 1970s and 1980s, as emergency managers (at all levels) matured in their ability to address natural disasters and as the perceived need for civil defense against nuclear attack diminished, military dominance of disaster management waned. However, the rise of terrorism internationally, particularly the possibility that terrorists would strike inside the United States and that they might use massively destructive weapons, set the stage for the era of homeland security. The terrorist attacks of 9/11 made at least part of the envisioned nightmare a reality. Today, once again, U.S. disaster policy and politics, as well as American emergency management, cannot be fully understood apart from their relationship with national security and defense policy. However, the nation has dedicated great attention and resources to counterterrorism for well over a decade. At this writing, the U.S. Department of Homeland Security (DHS) is beginning to move into its late-teenage years. The Federal Emergency Management Agency (FEMA) has been part of DHS under three presidents to date. Although critics of the FEMA submersion into DHS still deserve a hearing, disaster policy and politics have in various ways "married up" with DHS offices tasked with counterterrorism and other homeland security–related missions.[16]

ORGANIZATION OF THE BOOK

Chapter 1 reviews some of the essentials of emergency management and disaster policy. It contemplates the status of emergency management as a profession. It explores disaster stakeholder groups, furnishes a brief overview of disaster as a field of scientific research, emphasizes the low issue salience of disaster as a public and political phenomenon, and describes some of the federalization of government responsibility for disaster management. Also considered are the difficulties local governments face in addressing emergency management, the political aspects of disaster, the multifaceted problem of disaster insurance, and the challenge of training and educating emergency managers for a field that is ever more technically complex and highly multidisciplinary. Disasters have a political side, but as later chapters show, the politics of disaster should never be oversimplified or pejoratively labeled. Disaster politics in America emanate from the nation's federal system of democratic governance. Americans do not want to completely entrust disaster management to an unelected set of bureaucratic officials working on the federal or state level. Deciding "what a disaster or emergency is" in the American system is a political and policy determination, something that over the past 60 to 70 years has been entrusted to elected executives, the president, and governors foremost. Relatedly, disaster policy and politics are also about "public money" and disaster insurance.

Chapter 2 takes up theory and methods. It asserts that theories hold out the potential to continually advance emergency management as a profession. People new to the field may draw from this chapter's theories and concepts to independently analyze disaster policy as a domain of public policy analysis or policy study. The chapter presents three simple normative theories: Jeffersonian, Hamiltonian, and Jacksonian. Arguably, Hamiltonian theory and assumptions were adduced to be the best of the three for professionalizing the work of emergency management. Jacksonian theory, first added in the second edition, is a tool that helps explain the current polarized and politicized environment. Chapter 2 also covers principal-agent theory, network theory, and theories of federalism, proposing each as tools for both analyzing and conducting emergency management. In addition, the chapter includes topics ranging from emergency management customer satisfaction to a disquisition about how emergency management knowledge is produced and how it is learned by others. Furthermore, there is a section about methods: specifically, the emerging role of "big data analytics" in the field of disaster study and management.

Chapter 3 covers history but in terms of 13 common threads or issues, each addressed in order. The chapter is also an overview of almost 70 years of disaster policy history. We are reminded that FEMA's portfolio has always included civil defense against nuclear attack. After the terror attacks of 2001, FEMA was also expected to serve the homeland security mission in a variety of ways. Although FEMA has a unique ability to expand and contract its workforce to cope with multiple disaster management demands, plus a massive funding backstop in the form of the Disaster Relief Fund, it continues to remain dependent on sitting presidents, on an understanding Congress, and since 2003 on a tolerant and supportive DHS hierarchy. Moreover, the chapter makes clear that FEMA must work cooperatively with governors and locally elected or appointed executives, satisfy a wide assortment of hard-to-please stakeholders, meet the needs of new disaster victims, and all the while protect the national taxpayer's dollar.

Chapter 3 also incorporates an administrative history. Presidents from Truman to Carter conducted disaster policy implementation through an assemblage of various federal organizations. Some of these resided in the White House, some operated as major or minor arms of federal departments, and some toiled in obscurity as back offices of independent agencies with very different core missions. The chapter tells us that it was not until year three of the Carter administration (1979) that U.S. disaster policy was granted a formal organizational and functionally integrated home in the form of the Federal Emergency Management Agency. FEMA was for 23 years a small, independent agency whose workforce was unrealistically capped at about 3,000. FEMA's top officials have always understood that they survived and succeeded politically largely as a result of how the agency was perceived and used by the president. Chapter 3 covers the major defining federal laws of U.S. disaster policy and the forms of federal disaster relief made available to state and local governments, as well as to victims of disaster.

Chapter 3 is also the story of emergency management's relationship with civil defense against nuclear attack. Part of this is the "yin and yang" of emergency management's civilian side and its national security side. Chapter 3 highlights the growing importance of television and social media news coverage of disasters on a national and international scale. It elucidates how successive modern presidents have perceived and used FEMA as a tool of their executive power. Beyond this, it explains how a tiny agency gained heft as a federal coordinating organization capable of yoking up nearly every federal department in matters of major disaster or catastrophe. It explains the evolution of "all-hazards" disaster management and why it became a modern "doctrine" of emergency management at all levels of government. Included as well are post–9/11 homeland security era matters important to understanding emergency management as it is being conducted in the 21st century. No less important is the rise of disaster mitigation as a policy priority.

Chapter 4 takes us into the world of presidential declarations of major disaster and emergency; here public policies, politics, process, programs, decisional power, and spending of public money are all in play. Over time, the U.S. Congress both granted and tolerated widening presidential discretion in deciding what constituted a declarable emergency. The declaration system has become more politicized than lawmakers in 1950 ever expected. Also, in presidential judgments about the deservedness of governors' requests, the system tolerates a degree of subjectivity and sometimes political bias. Owing to this freedom to decide, some presidents have created new categories of disaster agents (toxic waste incidents, chemical spills, relatively small-scale terror bombings, water main breaks, etc.), thus, setting precedents governors have been able to exploit in their quest for future declarations and federal help. On top of this, the availability of the Disaster Relief Fund furnishes presidents a convenient pool of spending authority to pay the federal costs of major disasters and emergencies they choose to declare.

Chapter 4 demonstrates that homeland security law and policy has augmented presidential authority and responsibility. These laws and policies have expanded the range of presidential declarations to include terrorism or even terrorist threats (see National Special

Security Events, NSSEs). They threaten to bond conventional Stafford Act declaration issuance for nonterror disasters with a president-led declaration system preoccupied with terrorism and terrorism threat in its many forms. Regardless, the U.S. disaster declaration process is in many ways the "Main Street" of American emergency management. This is made necessary by American federalism; a complex marriage of federal, state, and local interdependencies; and public policies advancing national endurance, resilience, burden sharing, and human compassion.

Examining the process and record of presidential declarations of major disaster is a useful way to learn about disaster management in the United States, an insightful way to investigate the geographical and historical record and statistics of U.S. disaster experience, and an illuminating way to grasp some of the politics of disaster. Thomas A. Birkland is correct in his assertion that disaster policy in the United States is driven by event-related policy change.[17] Disaster declarations are a good compendium of disaster events. The record of disaster declarations also reveals in some respects how presidents have coped with disasters and emergencies during their terms in office.

Chapter 4 is also a "cold hard facts" chapter. It explains what the terms *major disaster* and *emergency* mean in presidential declaration parlance. It provides people answers to questions such as the following: What can I expect to receive if I am a survivor of disaster? What help might my family receive? How do I qualify for government help? How do I make application? Chapter 4 describes the White House "machinery" in place to help the president consider governor requests for major disaster and emergency declarations. It explores each president's freedom to decide what is or is not a disaster or emergency. Chapter 4 takes up the hotly debated issue of "paying for presidential disaster declarations" via federal borrowing. FEMA sets thresholds of eligibility for states and counties, although each president is free to follow or ignore these thresholds case by case.

Chapter 5 observes that expensive "big science" applications necessary to conduct many forms of disaster scientific research require federal government funding, something only obtainable through subtle forms of political lobbying of lawmakers. Disaster study, particularly in scientific and engineering terms, informs but also transcends emergency management. Chapter 5 also posits that different types of disaster agents are of interest to different types of scientific and engineering clientele groups. In addition, communities of practice (CoPs) sometimes conflict with one another when they seek to secure government support and funding of their respective scientific endeavors. However, these groups also have a great deal in common. They often form alliances, or at least tolerate their differences, in the interest of showing a united front to policymakers.

Chapter 5 reminds us that in U.S. disaster management, most of the federal government's scientific and engineering agencies, offices, and programs important to emergency managers are neither in FEMA nor in the U.S. Department of Homeland Security (DHS). Some of these organizations are capable of making predictions of disaster frequency and magnitude, some design various countermeasures or advance disaster mitigation research and engineering, some work to improve government disaster preparedness and response, and some are capable of facilitating disaster recovery. In addition, the public works engineering side of emergency management is critical in disaster policy's intergovernmental relations. In many homeland security realms, research involves sizable pools of government contractors and universities working on security-related technologies. This has moved emergency management deeper into the world of national security and defense-related contracting.

Chapter 5 says much more about disaster researchers. They are people working in the physical, social, and biological sciences. Disaster sociologists have pioneered and enriched the study of disaster in ingenious ways. Disaster policy and emergency management are in some respects codependent on natural science and defense science researchers. Engineers have a major presence across the entire realm of disaster policy and emergency management for reasons this study will explore. Chapter 5 updates through 2018 federal research agency activity in disaster policy and management. The chapter provides a brief overview of social science contributions to the study of disaster.

Chapter 6 addresses the intergovernmental relations (IGR) of disaster management. Those relationships are extremely complex. Since the 9/11 terror attacks of 2001, U.S. IGR has become much more centralized at the federal level, much more security focused, much more obsessed with colossal framework building to advance national preparedness and to yoke every component of DHS into its planning factory. Chapter 6 devotes much attention to state and local government, particularly with respect to how the matters of federal homeland security and emergency management have shaped both kinds of work organizationally at the state level, and secondarily, at the local level.

Chapter 6 includes consideration of nonprofit organizations active in disaster as well as the impact of privatization of more services previously provided by government. Among major worries are ensuring that the homeland security induced transformation of FEMA does not alienate or drive away the universe of nonprofit altruistic organizations and volunteering individuals; that for-profit contractors do not come to monopolize disaster recovery and mitigation work; and that the tremendous burden of cross-cutting federal grant requirements does not reduce the pool of FEMA contract bidders to a handful of gigantic corporations.

Chapter 6 outlines various formal instruments of federal–state, state-to-state, and local-to-local emergency response agreements. The National Response Plan (NRP) and its 2008 successor, the National Response Framework (NRF), as well as the National Incident Management System (NIMS), make up the administrative superstructure of disaster policy and law that emergency managers collectively carry out. Within NIMS is the Incident Command System (ICS), a tactical instrument of response, multiagency coordination, and management. Also, within NIMS is multiagency coordination systems useful in addressing disasters that have expansive and/or multiple damage zones. Chapter 6 updates FEMA organization as well as NRF and NIMS organizational issues. Chapter 6 also takes us into the jungle of new and old national frameworks, of which there are now five: Prevention, Protection, Mitigation, Response, and Recovery. The Response and Recovery frameworks pre-date the other three, but the so-called "suite of frameworks" is now a driving force within both DHS and FEMA. These frameworks tether FEMA people, particularly grants managers, to nearly all other directorates and offices of DHS.

Chapter 7 is the civil–military chapter. It concerns the role of the U.S. military in disaster management domestically. Posse Comitatus restrictions on using federally directed armed forces as law enforcers is again considered. Relatedly, the chapter adds an analysis of the federal active duty forces and the state National Guard forces. This third edition's discussion of the military better explains the duty status of each of these military forces than was done in earlier editions. Chapter 7 introduces the dual status commander, which has proven so far to be a useful and constructive solution to military coordination of state National Guard (governor-directed forces) and federal military forces (directed by the president and under Pentagon control) in response to domestic disasters.

Chapter 7 also investigates major homeland security grant programs, nearly all of them geared to aligning state and local counterpart organizations into a more unified and more easily coordinated whole. In addition, the chapter demonstrates that many of these programs have imposed tremendous planning and information management burdens on state and local governments, which may offset the benefits of heavy DHS and FEMA subsidization.

Furthermore, Chapter 7 looks at the role of the National Guard in disasters and emergencies. U.S. military actions taken before, during, and after the hurricanes of 2017 are explored. This third edition incorporates emergency management duties of the U.S. Army Corps of Engineers (USACE), the U.S. Coast Guard, and the U.S. Northern Command (USNORTHCOM). Moreover, this edition briefly examines the National Terrorism Advisory System (NTAS). Included is an overview of how anti- or counter-terrorism federal programs under homeland security have affected the nation's system of disaster management. The Urban Area Security Initiative (UASI), the State Homeland Security Program (SHSP), Law Enforcement Terrorism Prevention Program (LETPP), Operation Stonegarden, and Emergency Management Performance Grants (EMPGs) are all programs briefly summarized in Chapter 7.

Chapter 8 is about globalization. As in the second edition, the U.S. system of international disaster assistance is compared and contrasted with the UN system of disaster aid. In the second edition, great attention was given to how the United States handled offers of help from other nations in the wake of Hurricane Katrina. That material was replaced in this edition with a study of U.S.–Canada disaster management relations and experience for provinces and states, as well as their subunits, located along the U.S.–Canada international border. In the course of this work, Canadian emergency management is compared and contrasted with U.S. emergency management. Several judgments and observations are made about how Canadian intergovernmental relations differ from U.S. intergovernmental relations in matters of disaster management.

Chapter 8 tells us about how FEMA and supporting federal agencies, most particularly the U.S. Department of the Interior, handle disaster management for U.S. trust and commonwealth partners. The U.S. Department of State, through the U.S. Agency for International Development (USAID), the Office of U.S. Foreign Disaster Assistance (OFDA), and its U.S. ambassadors posted in nations around the world are shown to be integral to U.S. foreign disaster assistance. Similarly, the U.S. Department of Defense (DOD) also plays a very meaningful and impactful role in America's post-disaster aid to other nations. Near the end of the chapter, FEMA and OFDA are compared and contrasted with one another.

Chapter 9, new for the third edition, explores the 2017 hurricane trio of Harvey, Irma, and Maria. A host of issues are raised. In Texas, for Hurricane Harvey, search and rescue, flood control, and property loss were priority concerns. In Florida, for Irma, evacuation, sheltering, storm surge and wind damage, and reconstruction were paramount issues. Although flaws and perceived errors in hurricane disaster response and recovery garner news and social media attention, it is also true that for Harvey and Irma, there were many success stories. Conversely, Puerto Rico had the misfortune of having been partially struck by Hurricane Irma only a week or so before it was ravaged by Hurricane Maria. Owing to Maria, Puerto Rico and the U.S. Virgin Islands suffered epic damage. The vast assortment of responding federal agencies, including FEMA and the U.S. military, could not easily cope with the sea of needs they encountered. The failure of Puerto Rico's entire electrical grid, requiring many months to repair and replace, confounded relief efforts there in every way possible. Puerto Rico had little electrical power and even less political power, particularly when compared with the mega-states of Texas and Florida, each of which suffered its own hurricane woes. Multiple catastrophes posed a tremendous disaster management challenge for American emergency managers of all stripes in 2017.

Finally, Chapter 10 reminds us that the political definition of disaster flows from law; judgments of previous presidents; a sitting president's previous actions modulated by the political circumstances of the time when his or her judgments were made; the strategic behavior of governors seeking federal assistance; and the pressure imposed by elected representatives at the federal, state, and local levels. Understanding disaster policy and politics is worthwhile, although it demands work, focus, and as much as possible, objectivity. Disaster policy and emergency management have made and will continue to make a difference both inside and outside the United States.

Today, a cardinal concern of the U.S. emergency management community must be whether the field will be supplanted and marginalized by homeland security leaders, agencies, and political forces or whether it can sustain itself by preserving its identity, professional norms, and values. The openness, humanitarian values, and public-mindedness of emergency management does not comport well with the secrecy, national security/military values, and the people-targeting surveillance of homeland security.

Chapter 10 includes a brief set of special issue and "gap" questions. Do Americans expect too much when disaster befalls them? Who are the winners and losers under U.S. disaster policy? How has government disaster relief become more politicized over time? Do we appreciate the importance of volunteers when disasters strike, particularly in this age of social media? Can the United States succeed in building its own disaster resilience? How healthy is it for FEMA to work under the yoke of DHS? The chapter offers some observations about the likely future of disaster policy and politics.

SPECIAL FEATURES

This book provides readers with boldfaced key words in the text that are also listed at the end of each chapter. The Glossary at the end of the book defines or explains these key terms. All the chapters provide source citations, which are listed in the Notes at the end of the book. Also helpful to readers, students, teachers, and researchers are the master bibliography and index that appear at the end of the book. Unlike previous editions, this one will include a more elaborate set of ancillaries helpful to both teachers and students. Half of Chapter 8 in this edition is devoted to a Canada–U.S. comparative study of provincial and state disaster management along the International Border shared by the United States and Canada.

This edition employs only one type of boxed feature, and boxed sections appear in all chapters. Each "Tell Me More" box elaborates on something in the preceding text. Some "Tell Me More" boxes provide real world examples to drive home a point. Others present facts and figures in a way that allows the reader to focus and learn more about a preceding point or claim. Several "Tell Me More" boxes spotlight human interest stories about the plight of disaster victims. The boxes help highlight facts drawn from accounts of specific disasters or provide more detailed documentary evidence from the field of disaster policy and emergency management. Boxed material complements textual material.

A disappointing and disturbing problem is that the integration of federal emergency management with federal homeland security is combining to produce vast quantities of planning and preparedness documents. This third edition will demonstrate that when the second edition went to print, there were two major and mushrooming "frameworks," a National Response Framework and a National Disaster Recovery Framework. Today there are three more frameworks: one for Prevention, one for Protection, and one for Mitigation. These documents grow like predator-less invasive species. Worse still, the "suite of frameworks" connects all five with one another. This makes it the job of your textbook author to simplify and make sense out of a vast and growing body of planning information. Furthermore, owing to homeland security primacy, FEMA and all other offices of the DHS now operate on the basis of "missions and capabilities." The mitigation –prepared–response–recovery phases or cycle model of emergency management, at the federal level, is barely hanging on. Finally, the massive changes transpiring under the "suite of frameworks" approach has profound implications for the National Incident Management System.

The purpose of this book is to provide an introductory, although substantial, understanding of disaster policy and politics. This work synthesizes the ideas, methods, and approaches used by other scholars of the subject and offers my own observations and insights as well. I can say with high confidence that both liberals and conservatives, and correspondingly, Democrats and Republicans, will find things to criticize in this textbook. Nevertheless, with great difficulty, I have tried to be fair to all sides. My reasoning is that by appreciating both the political and the policy side of disaster, one will achieve a better understanding of how government forms, shapes, and conducts emergency management. Where I may have temporarily left the path of objectivity comes, as readers will see, in my concern about the current fate of federal emergency management. For this, I make no apology.

I support emergency managers and what they do. I am thoughtfully concerned about, but not necessarily an opponent of, military and national security involvement in disaster policy and emergency management. This work concedes that disaster policy and emergency management, like any field of public policy, has flaws and deficiencies. Government manages many disasters capably. However, some have been very poorly managed. Occasionally, often in catastrophic circumstances, government disaster management has been abysmal. This edition, more than the first or second, gives much more attention to the politics side of *Disaster Policy and Politics*. The field of disaster policy and politics is ever changing, yet like America itself, is a perfectible experiment.

ACKNOWLEDGMENTS FOR THE THIRD EDITION

One major reason I so much wanted to write this third edition is because there are very few textbooks exclusively on U.S. disaster policy and politics.[18] Owing to the success of the first and second editions of *Disaster Policy and Politics,* and because the world of U.S. disaster policy and politics has changed dramatically in a variety of ways, it made sense to produce a third edition.

I am grateful to colleagues at GWU and UD and to professors and students at other universities and colleges where I have guest-lectured. As always, my wife Claire has been unflaggingly helpful and patient in giving me time and encouragement to work on this edition. Too many times I denied her day-trips or nights out so I could work on this manuscript. Also, many ideas in this work I owe to conversations with my friend and fellow long-distance hiker Dr. Malcolm Watts, retired from AstraZeneca International.

I owe much to now departed longtime colleagues and friends, among them the late William R. Cumming, retired FEMA Office of General Counsel attorney. Bill C. read draft chapters of my first and second editions offering wonderful help. He was for decades the History Division that FEMA never had. He collected and protected for posterity documents and papers circulating through the agency. When others at FEMA lived for the day, Counselor Cumming saw the big picture. He was a former Air Force missile man; he held security clearances responsibly but always knew when to bring to public attention newly declassified items important to those in the disaster study field. I last spoke to him March 27, 2018, only days before his passing. Bill had his quirky side, but if you got to know him, you understood his love for all things FEMA and his respect for his public servant federal colleagues.

I have an older debt to repay to the late Joseph (who insisted on "Joe") Scanlon, professor emeritus, Carleton University School of Journalism. In 2015, he passed at age 82 in his much beloved home city of Ottawa, Canada.[19] My dear friend Professor William L. Waugh, Jr., and I edited two books together in the 1990s. Joe contributed work to each one, and he referred other Canadian disaster studies scholars to us through the years. Joe was utterly capable, journalistically gifted, likeable, and charming. He was a dedicated and demanding teacher who not only drew the best out of his students, but he was someone who consistently attracted the best students.

I would also like to acknowledge the late Dr. William Anderson of the National Academy of Sciences and before that NSF. I am also deeply thankful for the years of help and support provided to me by the late Professor Thomas Pavlak of the University of Georgia's Carl Vinson Institute. I have not forgotten Tom's humor, kindness, affableness, and ethical dedication.

Although I did not impose on them to read this project work, I wish to thank Claire B. Rubin of Rubin Associates and formerly with GWU; Professor Rutherford H. Platt, University of Massachusetts at Amherst; Professor Sandra Sutphen, emerita at California State University, Fullerton; Professor James F. Miskel, formerly with the Naval War College; Professor David A. McEntire, formerly of North Texas State University and now dean of the College of Aviation and Public Services at Utah Valley University; Professor Linneal Henderson, University of Baltimore; and Dr. Dennis E. Wenger, retired, of the National Science Foundation (NSF).

I wish to acknowledge my lifelong thanks to my undergraduate mentor, Professor Henry Steck, State University of New York, Cortland, and to my University of Illinois at Urbana-Champaign graduate adviser and mentor, Professor Barry Rundquist, emeritus of the University of Illinois at Chicago.[20]

For this third edition, I want to thank Dr. and Professor Bruce Lindsay of the U.S. Congressional Research Service (CRS), my former student, doctoral advisee, and friend who is now a disaster researcher with the CRS. He has been extremely helpful and con-structively critical in his aid to me through the years. CRS disaster experts Francis X. McCarthy (retired) and Keith Bea (retired) have through their own work and through our interchanges helped me immensely. Professor Patrick S. Roberts, of Virginia Technical University Old Alexandria and Blacksburg, has kindly read and offered comment on each third edition chapter, much as Dr. Lindsay has. I am grateful to Patrick for his friendship and professionalism. He is a most gifted political scientist.

My friend and longtime fellow editor William L. Waugh, Jr., professor emeritus Georgia State University, has as always been a tremendous help in my work and previous manuscripts. I owe him a debt that is lifelong.

I wish to again thank Dr. B. Wayne Blanchard, former director of the FEMA Higher Education Program at its DHS-FEMA Emergency Management Institute in Emmitsburg, MD. The two voluminous "instructor guides" I prepared for him titled *Political and Policy Basis of Emergency Management*—one in the 1990s and a second a decade later—have helped countless educators and trainers, and they live on, like old television reruns, through the Internet. Wayne, although a demanding taskmaster, was a great help to me and to scores of scholars of emergency management through the years. Barbara Johnson, also of the FEMA Higher Education Program at the FEMA National Emergency Training Center, has continued in the tradition of Dr. Blanchard providing me and others excellent help and guidance. Wendy Walsh continues in the tradition of Dr. Blanchard as well. I also owe much to Richard Buck, a brilliant and highly experi-enced career FEMA official who is now retired and living in Washington State.

Dr. Kenneth Brevoort of the Consumer Financial Protection Bureau (CFPB), and previously of the Board of Governors of the Federal Reserve System, has been my go-to person for disaster economics for more than 15 years. Dr. Len Clark, a professor and emergency manager at Philadelphia's St. Christopher Hospital, has been a friend and trusted adviser. Professor Gavin Smith of the University of North Carolina at Chapel Hill conducted a PERI and NSF-sponsored workshop on disaster recovery in fall 2010 that was an inspiration for me.

Also helpful were Professor Naim Kapucu, University of Central Florida; Professor Linda Kiltz, Walden University; Professors John J. Kiefer and Alessandra Jerolleman, University of New Orleans; Professor Thomas Husted, American University; and Professor David Nickerson, Roosevelt University and the CFPB. Professor Howard Kunreuther of Pennsylvania University's Wharton School of Business, through his published research and our professional interactions, has helped me better understand the economics of disaster. Professor Kathleen Tierney, who directed until her retire-ment the University of Colorado Hazards Research Center, and Professor Emerita Joanne Nigg of the UD Disaster Research Center (DRC) have been colleagues I have respected for many years. DRC co-directors Jim Kendra and Tricia Wachtendorf have been a pleasure to work with, as has been DRC Professor Joseph Trainor. Former

Region 9 (Oakland) FEMA official, Lucien G. Canton, has contributed mightily to my understanding of emergency management and will have a second edition of his own book in print soon.

From 2010 through 2014, I entered semiretirement and taught one graduate course each semester at GWU. I am deeply indebted to now retired Professor Greg Shaw, former director of the Institute for Crisis, Disaster, and Risk Management at GWU, and Professor Joseph Barbera, MD, who is the codirector.

There is a sizable subset of students I would like to thank, in particular, GWU students Nicole Borland (now of FEMA), Nellie Darling, Jennifer Dorrance, James Holloway, Jessica Kratchman, Flora McKnight, Col. Les Moton, Meg Nash, Jeff Rubini, and Mark R. Sheridan. It is fair to say that all of my GWU and UD graduate students have helped me and my efforts in this endeavor.

I owe thanks as well to my former students Jason McNamara, of Obsidian Analysis and former FEMA chief of staff, and to Dan LoFaro, of the U.S. Soil Conservation Service and formerly of the FEMA Disaster Recovery Directorate and a former official of the National Flood Insurance Program (NFIP). I remain indebted to Dr. Zoltan Buzas, who worked with me when he was a graduate student at UD and who is now a political science professor at Drexel University in Philadelphia. I am grateful to the following GWU graduate students: Todd Abraham, Austin Brett, Carlos Castillo Lainez, Charlotte Fallon, Nicholas Furnari, Megan Hopkins, Trisha Jantzen, Michael Kahle, Gabrielle Lyon, Mike Manetti, Elizabeth Meserve, Phillip Owen, August Pabst, Christina Riebandt, Mark Rohan, Miriam Sangiorgio, Spencer Scharagorodski, Nathan Schoenkin, William Scott, Matthew Somers, Michael R. Sommerville, and Soala Whyte. At UD I owe much to graduate students Ray Chang, Robert Coons, Alex Greer, Andrew Hellwege, Ben Walker, Eva Wilson, and Daryl Yoder-Bontrager.

I want to thank my longtime colleagues and friends Professors Frances Edwards and Dan Goodrich,[21] San Jose State University, and Professor Thomas A. Birkland, North Carolina State University. Also, I want to make special mention of my friend and accomplished colleague Professor Louise K. Comfort, University of Pittsburgh. Professor Thomas E. Drabek, also a longtime friend, has been for me a mentor of sorts.

In addition, I need to acknowledge Dr. William Hooke, associate executive director of the American Meteorological Society and former director of the National Academy of Sciences Disasters Roundtable. My friend George Haddow, who has his own coauthored, highly successful, multiedition emergency management textbook series, warrants a thank you again in this edition. Professor William C. Nicholson, North Carolina Central University; Professor Michael K. Lindell, director of the Hazard Reduction & Recovery Center at Texas A&M University; Professor James F. Miskel, formerly of the Naval War College; Professor Beverly Cigler, Pennsylvania State University, Harrisburg; David M. Neal of Oklahoma State University; and Arts & Sciences Dean Brenda Phillips of Indiana University at South Bend have been helpful supporters of this author and his work.

A portion of Chapter 7 draws from the excellent work of Ryan Burke, whom I knew for a time when he was a graduate student at UD, and my long-time friend, UD Professor Sue McNeil. Their study of the dual status commander and the position's use during and after Superstorm Sandy in 2012 provided by far the clearest exposition on the origin, development, and use of dual status command authority.

A portion of Chapter 8, "Globalization of Disasters," was originally coauthored with UD doctoral student and former Villanova University assistant professor Cedric S. Sage and president of USAFrance Financials, to whom I am grateful. I want to also thank the first doctor of disaster studies and management at UD, Dr. Yvonne Radamacher, of the United Nations Development Programme, who was terrific in offering her advice on how to improve globalization in Chapter 8 for the second edition. Half of Chapter 8 in this third edition is a comparative U.S.–Canada state/province border study of disasters and their management. This work was made possible by an August 26–27, 2016, workshop, "Security Policy Coordination in North America and the European Union: Authors' Workshop Organized by the Centre for the Study of Security and Development (CSSD) and the European Union Centre of Excellence (EUCE) at Dalhousie University in Halifax, Nova Scotia, Canada. I am grateful to Professors Brian Bow and Ruben Zaiotti of the CSSD. Members of the workshop offered helpful comments on the Canada–U.S. case study.

I am especially fortunate to have had tremendous and able help from the following people at SAGE CQ Press: Charisse Kiino, publisher and co-acquisitions editor; Sheree Van Vreede, copy editor; and Jane Martinez, production editor. The cover photo for this edition shows the Santiago wildland/urban interface fire of 2007 in Orange County, California. Ironically, the fine people of SAGE working in the Thousand Oaks area northwest of Los Angeles were evacuated from their offices by the Hill Fire in November 2018 while they were engaged in production of this book. I also thank the adopters and reviewers of my second edition, all respected scholars and teachers of the field in their own right, for their sound advice and constructive criticism.

SAGE and the author are grateful for the input from the following reviewers:

Natalie D. Baker, Sam Houston State University

Larry C. Baucom, Regent University

David B. Cohen, The University of Akron

Rick C. Mathews, University at Albany, SUNY

John C. Mero, Campbell University

Christine Pommerening, George Mason University

Joseph L. Richmond, Arkansas State University

Barbara R. Russo, University of Mississippi

ABOUT THE AUTHOR

Richard Sylves is an emeritus professor of political science at the University of Delaware (UD), where he worked from September 1977 to September 2010, earning promotions from assistant to associate with tenure in 1982 and associate to professor in 1989. From 1975 to 1977, he was an assistant professor of political science at the University of Cincinnati. He was a senior research scientist and professor at the George Washington University (GWU) Engineering Management and Systems Engineering Department from 2009 to 2014. His previous books include *The Nuclear Oracles: A Political History of the U.S. Atomic Energy Commission General Advisory Committee, 1947–1977; Disaster Management in the United States and Canada* (edited with William L. Waugh, Jr.); *Cities and Disaster: North American Studies in Emergency Management* (edited with William L. Waugh, Jr.); and *Disaster Policy and Politics,* first (2008) and second editions (2015), in addition to many journal articles and book chapters. His BA is from the State University of New York at Cortland, his master's was earned at the State University of New York at Albany's Rockefeller School, and his PhD in political science is from the University of Illinois at Urbana–Champaign. From 1971 through 1972, he was employed as a policy analyst for the Senate Finance Committee of the New York State Legislature, in Albany, NY.

He conducts research and has taught courses in emergency management, disaster policy, environmental hazard management, energy policy, public budgeting, public administration, organization theory, and public policy. In 1988, he developed and taught until his UD retirement, "Politics and Disaster," one of the first such courses offered in political science; all three editions of this book had their origins in his UD and GWU experience. Dr. Sylves has held two post-doctorates, one as an associate producer for WHYY TV-12 Public Television News, which serves the greater Philadelphia metroplex, and another as a fellow of the UD Center for Advanced Study. He has served on a National Academy of Sciences, National Research Council panel, "Estimating the Costs of Natural Disaster," and he received research funding from the Public Entity Risk Institute (PERI), as well as from the FEMA Higher Education Program both before and after the FEMA transfer into the U.S. Department of Homeland Security (DHS). From 2002 to 2005, he served as an appointed member of the Executive Committee of the National Academy of Sciences Disasters Roundtable, where he participated in or helped organize with others workshops on various disaster-relevant topics, including 9/11, floods, earthquakes, and disaster prevention. He also helped cofound, with Professor William Petak, in the mid-1980s, the Section on Emergency and Crisis Management (SECM) of the American Society for Public Administration. From 2004 until his UD retirement in 2010, he and David Racca of the UD School of Urban Affairs and Public Policy created and maintained the website All about Presidential Disaster Declarations, previously found at www.peripresdecusa.org. Dr. Sylves was honored to receive the 2016 Wayne Blanchard Award for Academic Excellence in Emergency Management Research at FEMA's Emergency Management Training Institute. He is proud to know he is commonly referred to as "the presidential disaster declarations guy."

Lompoc Firefighter Chris Martinez, who is with a Search and Rescue Regional Task Force, scouts Montecito Creek at the East Valley Road crossing near Parra Grande Lane on Wednesday, March 21, 2018, in Montecito, California, where people lost their lives in the January mudslide.

Al Seib/Los Angeles Times via Getty Images

1

DISASTER MANAGEMENT IN THE UNITED STATES

THE MONTECITO DEBRIS FLOW DISASTER

At about 4 a.m. (PST) on Tuesday, January 9, 2018, a heavy downpour falling on the recently fire-ravaged hills of Santa Barbara County, California, triggered a massive debris flow that tumbled downhill and over-topped the banks of several creeks. It sent "car-sized" boulders and a deluge of muddy water smashing through homes, businesses, and other structures in the small community of Montecito. Those impacted had little or no advance warning of what would befall them.

The next day, a reporter for *The New York Times* recounted, "Rescue workers scoured mud-swollen riverbeds in the wealthy Southern California enclave of Montecito on Wednesday (January 10, 2018), clutching to the hope that they might find some of the more than a dozen people missing after mudslides swept away about 100 houses." Initial reports claimed that "at least 17 people were killed in mud flows so powerful that some one-story ranch homes in the area were covered up to their gutters. The devastation, sudden and violent, struck early Tuesday after a winter storm drenched and destabilized hillsides stripped bare last month by the largest wildfire (by total burned acreage) in California history."[1]

"Hundreds of people have been rescued and evacuated, many of them having to be hoisted out of the area by our aircraft," Bill Brown, the Santa Barbara County sheriff, said Wednesday afternoon. After surveying the affected area by aircraft, the sheriff said it was "very stunning to see the extent of the devastation, to see the breadth of the area that has been impacted so terribly by this."[2]

The authorities said 28 people were injured, four of them critically. Early estimates were that least 300 houses were damaged in the Montecito area and many more were listed by authorities as "threatened." Montecito is located northwest of Los Angeles and is tucked between the Pacific Ocean and the Los Padres National Forest south of the Santa Ynez mountain range.[3]

Search and Rescue

Authorities said late Thursday (January 11) that roughly 43 people were unaccounted for after heavy rains pounded the Thomas Fire burn scar this week and unleashed a torrent of mud, boulders, and debris that destroyed scores of homes. The number of missing had grown, officials said, after authorities combed through **social media** posts and message boards at evacuation shelters. Many of those people since have been reported safe, according to Chris Elms, a spokesman for the California Department of Forestry and Fire Protection (Cal DFFP), but the number of people missing remains fluid. Elms said, "We're starting to get to the phase where people are calling in and saying, 'If you're looking for me, I'm OK.'"[4]

On Friday, January 12, two *Los Angeles Times* reporters provided further information. "The number of people killed in the Montecito mudslides increased to 18 Friday as rescuers continued searching for seven missing people."[5] The Santa Barbara County Sheriff's Office today released an updated list of the names of the 18 dead, all of whom were Montecito residents. "They ranged in age from 3 to 89 years old." The county coroner has listed the cause of death for each victim as "multiple traumatic injuries due to flash flood with mudslides due to recent wildfire."[6] By January 16, the death toll reached 20 as two more bodies were found.[7]

Rescue efforts continued Friday (January 12) in the ravaged community. Chris Elms, of Cal DFFP, said emergency crews are still trying to fight their way through roadways made inaccessible by mudflow in the hopes of locating more people. Santa Barbara County Sheriff Bill Brown said Thursday (January 11) that officials were expanding mandatory evacuation zones because pedestrians and traffic are hindering rescue and repair operations. Rescue teams tried to sound an optimistic note—hoping for the best, bracing for the worst—as they used an arsenal of tools, technology, and specially trained dogs to probe debris piles more than 15 feet deep at the southern end of Romero Creek in the heart of the upscale community for signs of human remains—and survivors.[8]

"It's as exhausting, frustrating and tedious as looking for a needle in a haystack," Battalion Chief Mark Akahoshi said, while hunched over a topographical map of surrounding terrain studded with ranches and mansions offering panoramic views of the Pacific Ocean. "There is still a large area to be searched," he said. The mud and the debris have hindered progress. "It's just slow going out there. It continues as a search and rescue mission."[9]

Mike Eliason, a spokesman for the Santa Barbara County Fire Department, said, "We are still in the hopeful, optimistic mode that we can find survivors." His unit had rescued six people since the hillsides gave way. Canine units worked their way along the Montecito and San Ysidro Creeks, where many houses were swept away. The area near the creeks was the most treacherous, Mr. Eliason said, as creeks swelled with the sudden torrents of water mixed with ash from the fires, rocks, and dirt. "Some single-story homes were obliterated, just wiped off the foundation," he said. "Others had holes blown through from boulders."[10]

The mud also hid some dangers from rescue workers. "We've gotten multiple reports of rescuers falling through manholes that were covered with mud, swimming pools that were covered up with mud," Anthony Buzzerio, a Los Angeles County fire battalion chief, told The Associated Press. "The mud is acting like a candy shell on ice cream. It's crusty on top but soft underneath, so we're having to be very careful."[11]

A Wednesday, January 17, a news story disclosed that "at least 20 people were killed by the Jan. 9 debris flows, and another three were still missing as of that night. Twenty-eight people were treated at Santa Barbara Cottage Hospital with storm-related injuries, and five remained hospitalized, two in critical condition, as of Wednesday." An official update "listed 128 destroyed single-family residences and another 307 homes as damaged, six destroyed commercial structures and 17 damaged commercial structures."[12]

Highways, Hospitals, Water, and Power

Five highways remained closed on Wednesday (January 10, 2018), including rural, two-lane roads, said Tim Weisberg, a spokesman for the California Department of Transportation. The main north–south roadway, the heavily traveled 101 freeway, will be closed until at least Monday. "There are some portions that look like a riverbed," Mr. Weisberg said of the 101. "It's a mixture of dirt, debris, boulders, rocks. In some areas it can be six inches or a foot deep." Ron Werft, president of Cottage Health, a hospital in Santa Barbara that has treated those injured in the mudslides, said the hospital had to shuttle personnel by boat and by air as a result of the closing of the 101, a crucial north–south artery.[13]

Under blue skies Wednesday (January 10), rescue workers made progress, clearing roads that had trapped residents in the area around Romero Canyon, northeast of Montecito. But the longer-term consequences were also becoming evident, including damage to water mains and smaller pipes that provide the area with water.[14] "We have no water currently in storage," said Nick Turner, general manager of the Montecito Water District. The water district instructed those residents still receiving tap water to boil it before using it for cooking or drinking.[15]

Using bulldozers and other heavy equipment, workers cleared trees, boulders, downed power lines, household items, and building material that had been swept onto the roads. "A little bit of everything you could imagine, including a kitchen sink," Mr. Eliason said. "Literally a kitchen sink was found."[16]

Causes and Contributing Factors

Ironically, "the Thomas Fire, which set the stage for (Montecito's) devastation, was declared 100% contained Friday morning [January 12, three days after the debris flow disaster], officials said. The fire burned for more than a month, though its spread was contained several weeks," before it was completely extinguished. "In the end, the blaze burned 281,893 acres."[17]

How did it happen? "Although the disaster in Montecito has been described as a 'mudslide,' the scientific term for the event is a '**debris flow**.'" Debris flows launch massive quantities of rocks, boulders, trees, and mud downhill. They are typically triggered after wildfires on steep mountainsides, when heavy rains wash away the soil.[18]

"Big debris flows are relatively rare," said Ed Keller, a professor of earth science at University of California at Santa Barbara. He observed, "They don't occur after every fire in any one stream. The Thomas Fire was huge, and there are only a couple of places with really damaging debris flows. Montecito and San Ysidro creeks were primed for one." In catastrophic debris flows such as the one in Montecito, narrow canyons chock full of boulders start to flood and landslides may occur. Rocks and brush form temporary dams, then break through and roar downhill on thick slurries of mud. Car-sized boulders bob along like corks. In Montecito, the wall of mud and debris was 15 feet high in some locations.[19]

"You may get pulses of flows rushing out of canyons in the mountains," said Larry Gurrola, a Ventura-based consulting geologist who is on Keller's research team. "That material reaches the base of the foothills, chokes the streams, flows out over the banks and moves towards the ocean, dragging trees, brush, cars, utility poles and parts of homes along with it."[20]

Keller commented, "Through the millennia, debris flows have shaped the terrain of the South Coast. Almost all of Montecito and most of Santa Barbara is built on top of flows that occurred here over the past 125,000 years." He remarked, "Just look at the boulder field at Rocky Nook Park. That's evidence of a catastrophic flow out of Rattlesnake Canyon in prehistoric times." During the past 50 years, the South Coast has seen a few destructive but not catastrophic debris flows.[21]

The stage was set for catastrophe after the Thomas Fire burned 440 square miles in December 2017, largely in the backcountry of Ventura and Santa Barbara counties, becoming one of the most destructive wildfires in California history (it was surpassed a year later by the Camp Fire that engulfed the town of Paradise in late 2018). The Camp Fire burned less acreage but killed far more people and 18 times more structures than did the Thomas Fire.[22] It scorched the chaparral that anchors the soil to the bedrock and created a "hydrophobic" layer in the ground—a kind of crust that repels water like glass. In an era of year-round fire seasons, the Thomas Fire had not been fully contained when the rainy season got under way in earnest.[23]

"It was just kind of the perfect storm, when all the bad factors line up together," said Jon Frye, a Santa Barbara County engineering manager. "There was no time whatsoever between the fire and the winter." The trigger for the catastrophic debris flow in Montecito, geologists say, was several bursts of extreme rainfall, beginning at 3:34 a.m. One of these was a 200-year event—more than half an inch of rain falling in 5 minutes. That's a quarter of the total amount of rain, 2.1 inches, that was recorded in Montecito during the nine-hour storm.[24]

A U.S. Geological Survey (USGS) debris flow hazard map that was widely circulated before the January 9 storm showed the high probability of debris flows originating in the mountains above Mountain Drive in Montecito on the heels of the Thomas Fire. However, residents living in the hazard zone were neither asked to evacuate before the mudslide, nor did they receive a warning as the event transpired. The slopes there are on a "hair trigger," said Dennis Staley, a USGS research geologist who helped prepare the map. "The harder the rainfall, the bigger the flow," he said. "We knew that if it rained very hard, there could be very significant debris flows . . . and if you plug in the intensities that were received, our prediction aligns with what we saw." In any given year, there is only a half-percent chance that half an inch of rain will fall on Montecito in five minutes, said Jayme Laber, a senior hydrologist with the National Weather Service in Oxnard.[25] These were the heaviest short-term, high-intensity rainfalls recorded during the entire storm from Redding to San Diego, Laber said. He added, "It was horrible that it was right on top of the Thomas Fire burn area."[26] The first reports of the debris flow came in to the Weather Service shortly before 4 a.m.

A problem with this incident is that experts were aware of the threat of debris flows above Montecito, but they could not gauge how much rainfall it would take to cause a major debris flow. Moreover, they could not ascertain until after the rainstorm how intense and significant precipitation would be. It is unclear as to whether a system of stream gauging would have been possible or would have made a difference in this disaster. However, global positioning system mapping of the hydrology of the areas in and around Montecito, and other types of measurements, should make it possible to identify debris flow high-risk areas, and this would be helpful in the planning and rebuilding of homes and businesses.

Recovery Operations and Relief

Reporter Lindsey Holden disclosed, "Santa Barbara County communities affected by recent mudslides and flooding will be getting additional federal disaster relief funds to help offset emergency response and recovery costs. California Gov. Jerry Brown announced on Thursday the Federal Emergency Management Agency (FEMA) granted [it was actually granted by President Donald Trump] California's request to expand the disaster declaration already in place in areas affected by the Thomas Fire, according to a news release from the Governor's Office of Emergency Services."[27]

The declaration will now include damage from the flooding and mudslides that struck Montecito and other Santa Barbara County communities after heavy storms hit areas scorched by the December (2017) wildfire. President Trump had approved Governor Brown's original request for "California Wildfires, Flooding, Mudflows, And Debris Flows (DR-4353)" on January 2, 2018. The Montecito debris flow disaster of January 9 was also approved by the president as an addition to DR-4353 (DR stands for "major disaster" and 4353 is FEMA's numeric declaration designator).[28]

Holden adds, "The Governor's Office of Emergency Services activated the State Operations Center in Mather to help manage the federal, state and local response to the flooding and mudslides. State Emergency Services urban search and rescue teams and emergency management staff have been assisting local crews in Santa Barbara County.

California National Guard water vehicles and helicopters are also on hand, in addition to Caltrans crews and California Highway Patrol officers."[29]

In a statement released, California's Governor Brown offered consolation, "Our hearts break for the communities first ravaged by fires and now devastated by these mudslides." He vowed, "We will push for every available resource to help Californians recover from these tragedies."[30]

U.S. House member Salud Carbajal represents California's 24th Congressional District, which includes Montecito. On Friday (January 12), he sent a letter to President Donald Trump endorsing [the governor's request for] FEMA individual assistance funds to provide residents with housing assistance, access to the **Disaster Unemployment Assistance (DUA) Program**, and crisis counseling.[31] "The devastation from the Thomas Fire and subsequent mudslides have taken the ultimate toll on our community, claiming dozens of lives, destroying hundreds of homes, and hurting small businesses on the Central Coast," Carbajal said in a statement. He also declared that FEMA's "Individual assistance funding is critical to supporting the victims of the tragedies as our community rebuilds and recovers."[32]

David Passey, a FEMA representative who spoke Tuesday (January 16) at a community meeting in Santa Barbara, said state partners and federal and county agencies are dedicated to restoring Montecito and surrounding communities. Passey said that people who suffered losses not covered by insurance may be eligible for disaster financial assistance or low-interest loans. Even if people did not have property damage, they could be eligible for help with things like hotel costs if their home is within a mandatory evacuation area. Consistent with FEMA's Individuals and Households program, and under major disaster declaration DR-4353, Passey told the audience, "If you suffered loss—renters, homeowners or business owners—you are now eligible to apply for federal and state disaster assistance. We go from disaster to disaster helping people prepare for, respond to, recover from, and hopefully protect from future losses."[33]

Passey advised, "If people are worried about asking for help in their language of choice, or because of immigration status, FEMA wants them to know the agency wants to help as many people as it can." Santa Barbara County opened a Local Assistance & Recovery Center Wednesday with representatives from FEMA and other agencies to answer questions and help residents apply for various kinds of assistance.[34]

FEMA currently allows for a case-by-case review of those affected by flood and has exemptions for property affected by flooding on federal land, where flooding is caused or exacerbated by post-wildfire conditions on federal land (including Los Padres National Forest), and flood insurance was purchased within 60 days after the wildfire containment date, according to Carbajal's office. Residents can search the FEMA Flood Hazard Map to see if their home or business is in a flood zone.[35]

Closing Comments about the Disaster

This incident is remarkable in several respects. First, the disaster agent, a mudslide/debris flow, was generated by at least two disaster agents: the burned ground remains of a mammoth wildfire and extremely heavy rainfall. There had been geological precedents for this type of disaster in the Montecito area, but most of the biggest mudflows occurred tens of thousands of years ago. Nonetheless, experts and authorities were aware of the risk of mudslide and had even mapped out high-hazard zones in the days before it struck.

Residents of Montecito may have been aware of the danger before the mudslide, but they were not advised to evacuate because no one could predict precisely when, or even if, a debris flow would be triggered. Other Southern California communities situated below Thomas Fire burn lands, and which also got significant rainfall, did not experience mudflows.

There is also a patently false but common assumption that wealthy neighborhoods do not experience disasters, only poor ones. This case demonstrates that wealth does not necessarily insulate one from disaster. However, it might be reasonable to ask whether flood victims in other parts of the nation would be allowed to buy National Flood Insurance "after a flood" with the insurance coverage applied retroactively, as Montecito victims were invited to do.

There is also a "blame the victim" mentality. It arrogantly assumes that Montecito residents freely chose to make themselves vulnerable to a debris flow by residing near creeks known to have experienced mudflows in the very distant past. But ask yourself, how can Montecito residents be blamed for "making themselves vulnerable to a debris flow?" The Thomas Fire burn scar, the soil geology of the area, record rainfall in a short period, and a middle-of-the-night mudslide and flood were not things potential homebuyers could take into account years before when they bought or built their homes in the town.

If you resided in Montecito before the mudslide, what could you have done to be prepared? Would flood insurance be enough? Can one buy property insurance for mudslides or landslides? How culpable is the federal government given that the debris flow began on federal national forest land and barreled into a community of private homes? Did the elected officials mentioned in the case do right by their disaster-suffering constituents? If you lived in Montecito and survived the disaster, would you rebuild and resettle in the same spot or move elsewhere?

THE FUNDAMENTALS

From the nation's earliest days, coping with disasters and emergencies stemming from natural forces or from nonattack human causes was left to individuals, to secular or religious charitable organizations, or to voluntary actions of groups at the community level.[36] For more than a century the prevailing social and legal view was that disasters were "acts of God."[37] As such, it was up to surviving disaster victims—perhaps aided by altruistic individuals, family members, or organizations—to recover from such dire circumstances. As the nation developed economically, as business and industry grew, as capital formation advanced, and as people came to perceive the world with more scientific rationality, Americans began to understand disaster in a different and more logical way. Earthquakes, volcanic activity, mudslides, landslides, and avalanches were explained in geoscientific terms. Severe storms, tornadoes, hurricanes, and their ensuing manifestations—floods, straight-line winds, storm surges, erosion, droughts, and the like—were examined and largely analyzed by meteorologists, atmospheric scientists, hydrologists, and climate researchers. Disaster research scholar David Alexander tells us, "The concept of 'Acts of God' now has little relevance to natural disasters: regardless of who caused them, in the final analysis they are recurrent, broadly foreseeable events that are a function of human vulnerability patterns. However, it is not easy to determine when a victim should be held responsible for damage patterns and when, conversely, these are the responsibility of society in general."[38]

The private sector sought to adapt to the possibility and risk of disasters through the use of insurance and reinsurance systems. By distributing the risk through private insurance, those suffering losses from a disaster had a better chance to rebound economically. Property casualty insurance protected business owners as well as homeowners and owners of other property, such as cars and boats, but not everyone could afford the amount of insurance thought prudent.[39] However, the forces of disaster sometimes overwhelm insurance schemes put in place by the private sector or by governments. Various types of disaster agents pose various types of insurability problems.

In the past, when a disaster inflicted damage upon a region and its economy on a seemingly random and irregular basis, private insurers calculated that they could profitably sell policies to cover such things as fire, theft, and wind damage only as long as thousands of policyholders did not file claims for loss all at once and as long as a great many more people bought the insurance than filed claims on it. Major earthquakes, hurricanes, and floods that devastate highly developed and heavily populated areas often generate a colossal number of claims in a very short time. In the late 1940s and early 1950s, private insurers discontinued selling flood insurance. In addition, the insurance industry found it profitable to market commercial earthquake insurance but less so to sell residential earthquake insurance. And only days after the terrorist attack on New York and the Pentagon on September 11, 2001, private insurance companies eliminated provisions of their policies covering acts of terrorism.[40] The failure of insurance to cover various types of disasters represents a market failure that by default demanded government action. An insurance market can fail to operate as desired in basically four ways: through lack of capital, lack of cover, inability to pay claims, or failure to contract.[41] In short, lack of capital refers to an inability to sell enough insurance to be a viable business enterprise. Lack of cover refers to inadequate insurance coverage of risk across a market. Inability to pay claims applies when an insurer is unable to pay claims filed by policyholders. Failure to contract means that too few vulnerable parties purchase insurance adequate to indemnify themselves against a possible loss.

Government disaster relief in America is in many ways partnered with nonprofit organizations—some of them secular and some of them religious. For many decades, charitable organizations ministered to those who could not recover from disaster through private insurance. However, inadequate social giving and deficiencies in the methods of relief allocation used by some charities often failed to meet the full range of human needs created by disaster losses. Today, federal, state, and local governments sponsor a host of programs that rely tremendously on volunteers and altruistic organizations to do the work of ministering to those in need.[42] Sports celebrity has become a force in disaster relief in recent decades. For example, in the case of 2017's Hurricane Harvey, National Football League player J. J. Watt established a charity aimed at directing contributed funds via online YouCaring solicitation to various established altruistic organizations responding to the victims of Hurricane Harvey in the greater Houston, Texas, area.[43] Watt's efforts represent **celebrity-branded post-disaster online fund raising for survivors** facilitated by GoFundMe, or other, online brokers. Such altruistic activity is becoming more commonplace in the realm of private and charitable disaster victim assistance.

Because the United States is a democratic republic with a national constitution, and because it is composed of three countervailing branches of government, responsibility for protecting the polity from great harms posed in both pre-defined and novel emergencies falls largely upon government institutions operating in accord with the U.S. Constitution and established law. The U.S. Constitution clearly entrusts the president and Congress with the job of providing for the common defense. Preventing, repelling, responding to, and recovering from the effects of attacks on the American homeland by other nations or by terrorists who are stateless have always been a cardinal responsibility of the federal government.

When the citizenry generally accepted that disasters were not simply acts of "God," and when the American private sector conceded that the insurance industry could not cope with the complete panoply of disasters, it was time to press for government action. The creation and maintenance of public emergency management agencies is a product of public policymaking. Post–World War II recovery involved massive U.S. assistance to war-ravaged democratic nations of Europe through programs such as the Marshall Plan. This impelled many Americans to ask why the United States had no similar programs for disaster recovery at home. Congress answered their concerns with passage of the Disaster Relief Act of 1950, a law that, although unrecognized at the time, created the architecture of modern U.S. disaster assistance and emergency management.

As in many domains of public policy, disaster policy emerged at the local level first. Neighborhoods, local communities, and local governments were often forced to provide for both public safety needs and their own disaster recovery.

Governments, too, are property owners. Local and state governments not only own and operate public schools, public hospitals, and government office buildings but also often own and operate essential public utilities, roads, bridges, ports, bus and light rail systems, airports, and other public infrastructure. Most local and state governments do not buy private insurance to protect themselves against damage caused by disasters. Consequently, local governments have often petitioned their state governments to provide financial help after disasters, in lieu of raising local taxes in a time of suffering to pay for their disaster recoveries.

Governors, as well as mayors, city managers, or other local executives, have the power to declare or proclaim disasters or emergencies in their respective jurisdictions. Local and state taxes have been used to pay for significant shares of local and state government disaster loss. Owing to the damage caused by catastrophic multistate disasters and disasters that cover huge portions of single states, the federal government has gradually been expected to provide disaster relief to disaster victims and to local and state governments themselves. Since 9/11, disaster management has been more tightly linked to what is called "terrorism consequence management." Even before 9/11, under **all-hazards emergency management**, all levels of government had been in the business of preparing for and responding to acts of terrorism inside the United States. The so-called "Nunn-Lugar-Domenici Act" (Title XIV of the 1996 Department of Defense Authorization Act) through amendments approved in 1999 mandated that the federal government furnish major metropolitan jurisdictions with training and equipment that could be used to help local authorities thwart terrorist attacks of various types or respond to such attacks that do occur.[44]

The evolution of disaster policy across all levels of American government has helped create the field of emergency management. This chapter explores what emergency management is as an occupation, as a field of study, and as policy and politics. It elucidates the fundamental challenges of emergency management; it highlights the need for effective intergovernmental relations; and it introduces the phases and cycle of emergency management.

EMERGENCY MANAGEMENT AS A PROFESSION

Disaster management is seemingly an oxymoron.[45] A disaster is by definition a destructive, calamitous, and often deadly or injurious event, so how is it possible to conceive of managing one? Some insist that disasters cannot be "managed" at all.[46]

From a U.S. perspective, disaster management has its roots in **civil defense**. This is not necessarily the case for other nations. Damon P. Coppola observes, "While emergency management structures vary from country to country, having formed largely independent and irrespective of each other, patterns do exist. Many countries developed their disaster management capabilities out of necessity and their government's subsequent acceptance of the need to formalize both the authority and budget for an agency to address their risk. Other countries formed their disaster management structures not for civil defense, but after being spurred into action by popular criticism for poor management of a natural disaster."[47] Coppola adds that many nations have yet to develop emergency management agencies.[48] In 2010, the World Bank and the United Nations jointly sponsored publication of the book *Natural Hazards and Unnatural Disasters* with the aim of convincing key ministers in developed and developing nations to establish public and private entities to advance the "economics of disaster prevention."[49] America practiced various forms of civil defense at least as long ago as World War I and perhaps as far back as the War of 1812. Civil defense was part of the domestic realm of the U.S. experience during World War II. After World War II, as America's Cold War with the Soviet Union emerged, local communities were pressed to continue civil defense. When the Soviet Union detonated its first atomic bomb in 1949, President Harry S. Truman, and later President Dwight D. Eisenhower, sought to mobilize the nation to prepare for civil defense against nuclear attack. To this day, U.S. local emergency managers, whether they like it or not, owe the origin of their positions to civil defense work.

Over the years, civil defense work moved through a very long "dual use" phase, in which federal support to state and local civil defense provided overlapping benefits and costs to emergency management of natural disasters. Emergency management as a profession underwent gradual "civilianization." Preparedness and response to domestic natural disasters gradually supplanted and replaced a civil defense focused on national security.[50]

However, the civil defense component of emergency management remains in place today; consider the January 13, 2018, nuclear attack false alarm issued by Hawaii's emergency management agency. According to Alex Wellerstein of the *Washington Post*, "at 8:07 a.m. Saturday, 13 January 2018, the Hawaii Emergency Management Agency activated its civilian early warning system with a message sent to smartphones in the state: BALLISTIC MISSILE THREAT INBOUND TO HAWAII. SEEK IMMEDIATE SHELTER. THIS IS NOT A DRILL. The one part of the message that was correct was that it was indeed not a drill. It was an accident. No missile was incoming, and the warning was, according to the agency, the result of simple human error. As part of a routine test of readiness, a staffer selected 'live alert' rather than 'test alert.' That was all that it took for panic and fear to spread. Hawaiian officials scrambled to tell the public that it was a false alarm, but it still took 38 minutes for the same system to broadcast a message of safety."[51]

Certainly since 1950 and the Cold War era of civil defense against nuclear attack, emergency management has matured despite the 2018 Hawaii false alert mishap. **Emergency management** is the discipline and profession of applying science, technology, planning, and management to deal with extreme events that can injure or kill great numbers of people, do extensive property damage, and disrupt community life. Efforts are made to limit losses and costs through the implementation of strategies and tactics reflecting the full life cycle of disaster: preparedness, response, recovery, and mitigation.[52] For Haddow, Bullock, and Coppola, "emergency management is a discipline that deals with risk and risk avoidance."[53] They offer that emergency management "is integral to the security of everyone's daily lives and should be integrated into daily decisions and not just called out in times of disaster."[54]

An **emergency manager** is someone who has the day-to-day responsibility for emergency management programs and activities.[55] They marshal and distribute resources to mitigate (lessen the effect of or prevent) hazards, and they prepare for, respond to, and recover from the effects of all types of **hazards**. They work in every level of government. Some work in the private sector for businesses and corporations, and some may labor on behalf of nongovernmental altruistic organizations. Because disasters have the potential to affect almost every government agency or program, people with various emergency management duties can be found in almost every type of government agency. In the United States, local emergency managers may hold the title "emergency manager," but it is more likely that they hold a different title, such as director of public safety, sheriff, fire chief, police chief, or city or county manager. In some local areas, the job of emergency manager might be assigned people with these job titles:

- Civil Defense Manager

- Civil Emergency Preparedness Official

- Business Continuity Planner (also, Crisis or Consequence Manager, Contingency Planner, Business Resumption or Recovery Manager, or Professional Continuity Practitioner)[56]

- Disaster Management or Disaster Services Director

- Emergency Services Director

- Hazard Manager

- Risk Manager

- Police Chief

- Fire Chief

Some local emergency managers are paid, and some are not. State and federal emergency managers are paid civil servants, and those in the highest positions may be politically appointed to their posts. Many federal, state, and local emergency managers are salaried, full-time professionals. However, in many rural or low-population counties, towns, villages, and municipalities, emergency managers are part-time volunteers, some of whom may have professional education or training.[57]

Owing to the breadth and complexity of many disasters, the field of emergency management requires multidisciplinary and cross-disciplinary approaches. It requires a wide variety of expertise and technical skills: social welfare, public health, community and land-use planning, civil engineering, public works management, environmental science, supply chain management, and information technology, to name a few. Many emergency managers come from emergency responder occupations vital in emergency management: the fire services, law enforcement, and emergency medicine. Most emergency managers must understand elements of public law, public management, environmental policy, and disaster sociology. At the local level, emergency support services are usually within the departments of local government. These units are expected to be staffed in a way that enables them to respond to emergencies 24 hours a day. Their workers typically come from jobs in law enforcement, fire protection, rescue operations, environmental protection, and public works, and they are the backbone of local emergency response.

There are several different certification programs for emergency managers. There is the FEMA Professional Development Series (PDS) Certificate, the Advanced Professional Series (APS) Certificate, and the **International Association of Emergency Managers (IAEM)** Certified Emergency Manager (CEM)[58] and Associate Emergency Manager (AEM) Certificates. The CEM is considered by many to be the top certification in emergency management. Created as a joint venture by FEMA and the IAEM, the CEM was developed as a standard to recognize professional competency in emergency management across the nation. Since the creation of the CEM, it has spread worldwide and CEMs number in the thousands.[59]

Advancing Emergency Management as a Profession

The organizations that are presented next represent a share of those with strong interest in emergency management. These organizations have helped make emergency management a full-fledged profession, but their variety connotes just how multidisciplinary and interdisciplinary the field of emergency management is.

- *IAEM.* The IAEM (www.iaem.com) is a nonprofit educational organization dedicated to promoting the goals of saving lives and protecting property during emergencies and disasters. IAEM is primarily composed of local emergency managers. It operates a Certified Emergency Manager program.[60]

- *National Emergency Management Association (NEMA).* NEMA (www.nemaweb.org) is the professional association of and for state emergency management directors.[61]

- *American Public Works Association, Council on Emergency Management.* The American Public Works Association (www.apwa.net) is an international educational and professional association of public agencies, private-sector companies, and individuals dedicated to providing high-quality public works goods and services.[62]

- *American Planning Association.* The American Planning Association (www .planning.org) is a nonprofit public interest and research organization. Members are involved, on a day-to-day basis, in formulating planning policies and preparing land-use regulations that will meet the needs of people and society more effectively.

- *International City/County Management Association.* The International City/County Management Association (www.icma.org/main/sc.asp) is the professional and educational association for appointed local government administrators throughout the world.

- *American Society for Public Administration, Section on Emergency and Crisis Management.* The American Society for Public Administration (www .aspanet.org/scriptcontent/index.cfm), established in 1939, is the largest and most prominent professional association in the field of public administration. The Section on Emergency and Crisis Management (SECM) was formed in 1985 largely through the efforts of William Petak of the University of Southern California. SECM has some 200 to 300 members, and most of them are professors, students, or practitioners of the field.

- *International Sociological Association (ISA), Research Committee, Sociology of Disasters.* The ISA is a nonprofit association for scientific purposes in the field of sociology and social sciences. The ISA was founded in 1949 under the auspices of the United Nations Educational, Scientific and Cultural Organization (UNESCO). The goal of ISA is to represent sociologists everywhere—regardless of their school of thought, scientific approaches, or ideological opinion—and to advance sociological knowledge throughout the world. Its members come from 109 countries. The ISA Research Committee on Sociology of Disasters has made many contributions to both the study and the field of emergency management.[63]

- *The International Emergency Management Society (TIEMS).* TIEMS (www .tiems.org) has worldwide membership that includes emergency managers and social science researchers.[64]

- *International Association for Disaster Preparedness and Response (DERA).* DERA is a membership organization founded in 1962 as a nonprofit association linking professionals, volunteers, and organizations active in all phases of disaster preparedness and emergency management. DERA is an independent, nongovernmental organization (NGO) with dual missions of professional support and disaster service.[65]

Table 1-1 lists emergency management associations organized at the state and tribal levels. These bodies often advance the education and training of emergency managers employed within the respective jurisdiction. They serve not only state workers but often local government workers and nonprofit organization employees or volunteers as well.

TABLE 1-1 ■ Professional Organizations of Emergency Management

- Alabama Association of Emergency Managers
- Arizona Emergency Services Association
- Arkansas Emergency Management Association
- California Emergency Management Association
- Colorado Emergency Management Association
- Connecticut Emergency Management Association Inc.
- Florida Emergency Preparedness Association
- Emergency Management Association of Georgia
- Emergency Management Professionals of Hawaii
- Illinois Emergency Services Management Association
- Emergency Management Alliance of Indiana
- Iowa Emergency Management Association
- Kansas Emergency Management Association
- Kentucky Emergency Management Association
- Louisiana Emergency Management Association
- Maine Association of Local Emergency Managers
- Maryland Emergency Management Association
- Association of Minnesota Emergency Managers
- Mississippi Civil Defense Emergency Management Association
- Missouri Emergency Management Association
- Montana Association of Disaster and Emergency Services Coordinators
- Nebraska Association of Emergency Management
- Nevada Department of Public Safety Association
- New Jersey Emergency Management Association
- New Mexico Emergency Management Association
- New York State Emergency Management Association
- North Carolina Emergency Management Association
- North Dakota Emergency Management Association
- Emergency Management Association of Ohio

- Oklahoma Emergency Management Association

- Oregon Emergency Management Association

- Keystone Emergency Management Association (Pennsylvania)

- Rhode Island Association of Emergency Managers

- South Carolina Emergency Management Association

- South Dakota Emergency Management Association

- Emergency Management Association of Tennessee

- Emergency Management Association of Texas

- Utah Emergency Management Association

- Virginia Emergency Management Association

- Washington State Emergency Management Association

- West Virginia Emergency Management Council

- Wisconsin Emergency Management Association

- Wyoming All-Hazards Association

- National Tribal Emergency Management Council

Source: North Dakota State University, Emergency Management Professional Organizations at https://www.ndsu.edu/emgt/professional_development_resources/professional_organizations/

The **Emergency Management Accreditation Program (EMAP)** also advances the profession. EMAP maintains a voluntary assessment and accreditation process for state or territorial, tribal, and local government emergency management programs. EMAP conducts baseline assessments of all state and territorial emergency management programs. EMAP combines self-assessment in accord with accepted national standards; steps in the process include documentation of compliance, independent evaluation by trained assessors, and—for accreditation—committee and commission review. These reviews provide the following information:

- Evaluation of a jurisdiction's emergency preparedness and response system against established national standards

- Structure for identifying areas in need of improvement and benchmarking progress

- Methodology for organizing strategic planning and corrective actions and accountability in prioritizing resources

- Catalyst for improved interoperability and continuity

- Strengthened state, territorial, and local preparedness[66]

The standards used in emergency management are collectively called the **EMAP Standard**, and these are based on the National Fire Protection Association (NFPA) 1600 standards (recognized as the national preparedness standard for the private sector) and were developed by state, local, and federal emergency management practitioners.[67]

DISASTERS AS A FIELD OF SCIENTIFIC RESEARCH

Copious scientific research has been dedicated to identifying the causes of hazard threats. As Keith Smith offers, we define "hazard" cause as "a potential threat to humans and their welfare arising from a dangerous phenomenon or substance that may cause loss of life, injury, property damage and other community losses or damage," whereas **risk**, the likely consequence, is "the combination of the probability of a hazardous event and its negative consequences."[68]

Disaster research has been pursued in many disciplines and fields. Meteorology, seismology, volcanology, engineering, architecture, and a host of other fields routinely contribute scholarship to the study of emergency management. The social sciences, particularly through sociology, political science, and economics, have also contributed to knowledge creation in emergency management. Today, a wide array of institutes, research centers, and clearinghouses, many working through universities and colleges, conduct research that advances knowledge in disaster studies and emergency management.

Peer-reviewed journals like the *International Journal of Mass Emergencies and Disasters*, *Natural Hazards Observer*, the *Journal of Contingencies and Crisis Management* (Europe), the *Journal of Emergency Management*, *Natural Hazards Review*, *Crisis Response*, *Disasters*, *Risk Management*, and the *Journal of Homeland Security and Emergency Management* (an e-journal) have been platforms for presenting new research in the field. Mainstream academic journals have also published an increasing amount of hazards research and emergency management scholarship. The National Science Foundation (NSF), FEMA, the U.S. Army Corps of Engineers (USACE), the U.S. Geological Survey (USGS), the National Oceanic and Atmospheric Administration (NOAA), the U.S. Environmental Protection Agency (EPA), the U.S. Public Health Service, the National Institute of Standards and Technology (NIST), and other federal agencies have contributed research and research support to the field of emergency management as well. Today there is a profusion of slick-printed or online magazine publications about emergency management: *Emergency Management Magazine*, *IAEM Bulletin*, *Journal of Emergency Management*, and others.

The United Nations sponsored the International Decade for Natural Disaster Reduction during the 1990s and has assigned emergency management study and work to several of its component offices and organizations (see Chapter 8). The Organization for American States, serving almost the entire Western Hemisphere, has taken a keen interest in emergency management and disaster research. The World Meteorological Organization serves as an umbrella organization linking meteorologists around the world. The World Health Organization (WHO) seeks to prevent the spread of disease globally, and it too serves as a nexus of interchange for physicians and medical researchers worldwide. In 2005, the Hyogo World Conference on Disaster Reduction met in Kobe, Japan, and produced the Hyogo Framework for Action that was adopted by 168 nations, each of which promised to take actions from 2005 through 2015.[69]

Scientists now make daily contributions to emergency management. Earth observation satellites now track the advance of drought across West Africa. They make this information available to humanitarian relief organizations, which in turn pre-position food supplies in storage facilities in communities likely to experience drought six months to a year in the future. National Aeronautics and Space Administration (NASA) satellite telemetry supplies U.S. Forest Service scientists with terrestrial data that make it possible for them to project the likely path of forest fires moving through mountainous terrain. The information they supply is used by smoke jumper teams to plan drop zone locations where the teams, once on the ground, can safely and effectively combat the advancing conflagration. USGS scientists staff tsunami research centers in Alaska and Hawaii that use deep ocean sensors and seismologic equipment to detect sub-oceanic earthquakes likely to trigger sea waves, referred to as *tsunamis*, capable of traveling thousands of miles across the Pacific, ultimately smashing coastlines where they strike. They quickly broadcast their findings to governments and news organizations to provide an alert or disaster warning. The National Severe Storm Center uses Doppler radar, among other technologies, to detect the formation of tornadoes. It then notifies the National Weather Service (NWS) and media organizations like the Weather Channel to forewarn people in the danger zones. Similarly, the National Hurricane Center tracks tropical depressions, tropical storms, and hurricanes wherever they occur in the world. Its ability to forecast points of likely hurricane landfall has done much to spur successful coastal evacuations and hurricane preparation.

Emergency management is usually associated with public service and government work. However, corporations have entered the field for a variety of reasons. Insurance firms consider disaster probabilities in their models and calculations. Disasters and emergencies affect many lines of insurance, often in profound ways, such that insurers have a vested interest in studying and promoting new ways to reduce disaster risk and loss. Almost every business or corporation needs to consider how disasters and emergencies will affect their workers, their physical assets, their rates of production or service deliveries, and their profitability. Consider, for example, how Hurricane Harvey's impact on the Gulf Coast's oil platforms and onshore oil facilities drove up U.S. and world oil and gasoline prices for a time. Major "disaster industry" trade shows and exhibits are now common, demonstrating the growth of a disaster services industry. The private sector has been drawn to what disaster research promises and to the needs of emergency managers seeking commodities, products, and services that help them in their work.

PRESIDENTIAL DISASTER DECLARATIONS

Presidential declarations of major disaster or emergency are now so commonplace that they are becoming a routine mode of president–governor interchange. They are also evolving into a major conduit of interaction between federal, state, and local governments. Increased nationwide media coverage of disasters and emergencies of all types became the norm by the late 1980s.[70] This, along with other factors, may have discouraged presidents after Ronald Reagan from turning down gubernatorial requests for major disasters at the rate that earlier presidents did.

The rise of emergency management as a profession and changes in information technology have coincided with increased state and local administrative capacity to document disaster losses. In turn, this may be a factor in the greater number of presidential disaster declarations and subsequent policies and programs.[71] Improved disaster information management since the mid-1980s has aided FEMA in the past, and the U.S. Department of Homeland Security (DHS) FEMA today, in ascertaining the worthiness of each gubernatorial **major disaster declaration** request sent to the president.[72] With advances in information technology, state emergency managers can document disaster loss more accurately through more expert damage assessments, and thus governors now have a stronger factual basis for requesting declarations of major disaster than they did earlier. In other words, governors have become better able to prove need before they request declarations.

Some disaster researchers have maintained that U.S. disaster policy is becoming more federalized, this ironically in an era of devolution and decentralization in many other realms of public policy.[73] **Counterterrorism** initiatives may portend a complete nationalization of disaster management, but it is more likely that they indicate a much-expanded federal role in the intergovernmental relations of emergency management and disaster policy with DHS-directed counterterrorism paramount.[74]

FUNDAMENTAL CHALLENGES OF EMERGENCY MANAGEMENT

Emergency managers must face many challenges in crafting emergency management policies and programs and in responding to potential disasters. They need to understand the challenges of **issue salience**, **federalized government responsibility**, and technical expertise.[75]

Issue Salience

Issue salience, or the importance of the issue to the public and to their elected leaders, is a perennial political problem of emergency management. Disasters are high-risk, low-probability events. Their infrequency makes it difficult for responsible people to justify pre-disaster expenditures of money in view of seemingly more pressing, ongoing needs and issues. Moreover, in the aftermath of a major disaster, emergency managers, for a time, enjoy a high political profile and may be able to influence the public and their political representatives to undertake certain essential emergency preparedness, recovery, or disaster mitigation efforts or projects. However, their power to influence policymakers and ensuing policy is usually short-lived once the jurisdiction returns to a collectively perceived condition of normalcy.

Some mega-disasters, Hurricanes Harvey, Irma, and Maria in 2017 for example, not only open a "policy window"[76] to allow new issues to move on to government policy agendas but also blow down walls, "and through the resulting hole" comes "a raging stream of policy proposals."[77] Policy windows represent the confluence of three separate streams: problem, policy, and politics. Policy windows represent periods when solutions are coupled to problems, and both solutions and problems are connected to favorable political forces.[78] For example, the three mega-disaster hurricanes of 2017 stand as compelling events in which pronounced problems occurred; various solutions were available to address the problems highlighted by these events; and these events propelled the identified problems and solutions to the top of the policy agenda, whereby political officials acted on them. For example, H.R. 4667: Making Further Supplemental Appropriations for the Fiscal Year Ending September 30, 2018, for Disaster Assistance for Hurricanes Harvey, Irma, and Maria, and Calendar Year 2017 Wildfires, and for Other Purposes, introduced in December 2017 with disaster-related amendments, wended its way through the House and Senate and was signed into law by President Trump on February 9, 2018.[79] A two-month turnaround for this measure is extraordinarily fast and denotes the urgency of federal lawmakers and the president in responding to the plight of states, localities, and citizens impacted by these hurricanes.

One way to measure issue salience is through public opinion polling.[80] Disaster policy suffers from what is called the **issue-attention cycle**.[81]

This issue-attention cycle is rooted both in the nature of certain domestic problems and in the way major communications media interact with the public. The cycle itself has five stages, which may vary in duration depending on the particular issue involved but which almost always occur in the following stages:

1. *The pre-problem stage.* This is manifested when some highly undesirable social condition exists but has not yet captured much media or public attention, even though some experts or interest groups may already be alarmed by it. Usually, objective conditions regarding the problem are far worse during the pre-problem stage than they are by the time the public becomes interested in it.[82] For example, this was true of the U.S. vulnerability to terrorist attacks before 9/11, despite the bombing of the World Trade Center by terrorists in 1993. America's coastal vulnerability to hurricanes was understood by many experts before 2005 but poorly appreciated by the public until Hurricane Katrina and Superstorm Sandy spotlighted tremendous flood and storm surge vulnerability. Puerto Rico had been intermittently hit by hurricanes in the past, although it had been many years since a Category-5 strength hurricane had plowed a massively wide path directly through the center of the island as it did in 2017. Equally concerning is that too few Californians own residential earthquake insurance. The California Earthquake Authority, a state public entity, retains various private insurance firms to sell its earthquake insurance policies to cover private residences, condos, apartments, and manufactured homes. CEA reported in 2018, that with over 1,036,391 policyholders, it is one of the world's largest providers of residential earthquake insurance.[83] Since 1996, CEA has been encouraging California homeowners and renters to reduce their risk of earthquake damage and loss through education, mitigation, and insurance. Yet, in 2014, two NBC news reporters pondered, "Why Do So Few California Homeowners Have Earthquake Insurance?"[84]

2. *Alarmed discovery and euphoric enthusiasm.* As a result of some dramatic event, like Hurricane Katrina in 2005, the 9/11 terrorist attack, Superstorm Sandy of 2012, Hurricanes Harvey, Irma, and Maria of 2017, as well as a result of mass murder shooter attacks such as those in Parkland (FL) (2018: 17 dead), Las Vegas (2017: 58 dead), Orlando (2016: 49 dead), Blacksburg (VA) (2007: 32 dead), Newtown (CT) (2012: 27 dead), and Sutherland Spring (TX) (2017: 26 dead),[85] or others, the public suddenly becomes both aware of and alarmed about a particular problem. This alarmed discovery

is invariably accompanied by euphoric enthusiasm about society's ability to "solve this problem" or "do something effective" within a short period of time. There is strong public pressure in America for political leaders to claim that every problem can be solved. This outlook is rooted in the great American tradition of optimistically viewing most obstacles to social progress as external to the structure of society itself.

The implication is that every obstacle can be overcome and every problem solved without any fundamental reordering of society itself if we only devote sufficient effort to it. In some cultures, an underlying sense of irony or even pessimism springs from a widespread belief that many problems cannot be "solved" in any complete sense. In American social and political culture, pessimism about seemingly intractable problems like natural disasters and mass murder shootings are on the rise, but nevertheless, after every major disaster, most Americans expect, and often demand, that government officials do something to both address the incident and its causes as well as ensure it never happens again.[86] Sometimes there are great ironies even during the alarmed discovery stage. While concerned or enraged Americans make demands of their policymakers, and do so aided by news media coverage, many policymakers move against them. The public screamed for improved flood control and coastal protection even as federal lawmakers negated many flood mitigation provisions of the Biggert-Waters Flood Insurance Reform Act of 2012.[87]

3. *Realizing the cost of significant progress.* The third stage consists of a gradual collective realization that the cost of "solving" the problem is very high indeed. Really doing so would not only take a great deal of money but would also require major sacrifices by large groups in the population. The public, thus, begins to realize that part of the problem results from arrangements that are providing significant benefits to someone—often to millions. For example, Americans begin to realize that it will cost huge sums of money and vast resources to rebuild Puerto Rico to withstand another Category 5 hurricane or to bring back Houston so the flooding of Hurricane Harvey will not soon be repeated. They may also come to understand the high cost of replacing Puerto Rico's power grid as well as subsidizing recovery of its agriculture, tourism, and commercial sectors. They may also appreciate the astronomical cost of relocating homes and mitigating flood vulnerability in the San Jacinto basin around and through Houston. However, Americans, especially many residents in the damage zone, are likely to insist on resettling the same hurricane-vulnerable damage zones they occupied before. They will demand that all of the public infrastructure they relied on before the hurricane be rebuilt in the same location as before.

Similarly, in 2012, the governors of New Jersey and New York championed rebuilding, fueled by billions in federal funding, along still highly flood-vulnerable, low-lying coastal areas pounded by Superstorm Sandy. Another example comes in the wake of the Marjory Stoneman Douglas High School mass shooting by a lone gunman in Parkland, Florida, on February 14, 2018. Seventeen students were killed, and another 17 were wounded.[88] Students of the high school, aided by students and parents from across the nation, demonstrated in major cities, including in Washington, DC, near the Capitol. They advocated greater gun control and other measures to afford students added protection from gun-toting assailants while they are at school. The effort triggered a major blowback by the gun lobby, the National Rifle Association, hunters, and a massive share of America's political conservatives and their supporters in the news and commentary media. While limited reforms were made law by Florida governor Rick Scott and the legislature in Tallahassee, movement in the U.S. Congress and Trump administration on this subject has been either nonexistent or retrograde (i.e., arming the teachers with guns in the classroom).

In certain cases, technological progress may eliminate some of the undesirable results of a problem without requiring any major restructuring of society or any loss of present benefits by others. In the optimistic American tradition, such a technological solution is initially assumed to be possible for nearly every problem. Our most pressing social problems, however, usually involve either the exploitation, whether deliberate or unconscious, of one group in society by another or the prevention of one group from enjoying something those others want to keep for themselves.[89] For example, before Hurricanes Harvey and Maria in 2017, many of those who lived in hurricane-vulnerable zones and who had the means to purchase national flood insurance to protect their homes but elected not to buy it, nevertheless demanded that the national taxpayer bail them out through generous disaster relief.[90] Correspondingly, in the case of Hurricane Katrina, development policy, both at the federal and state levels, gave priority to dredging the Mississippi River and maintaining canal and channel navigability in the interests of commerce and water freight in the lower Mississippi and around New Orleans. This came at the expense of levee protection and wetland preservation that would have mitigated some of Katrina's devastating effects. There was in fact a trade-off between economic priorities and public safety.[91] The increasing recognition that this type of relationship exists between the problem and its "solution" constitutes a key part of the third stage.

After Superstorm Sandy, officials of the Port Authority of New York and New Jersey (PATH) went to work devising various technological fixes that might prevent flooding of its auto and train tunnels in Lower Manhattan. Many of the proposed "fixes" are colossally expensive: building a storm surge barrier with retractable doors spanning the Hudson River near the Verrazzano Bridge; surrounding Lower Manhattan with a tall break wall; and perhaps most feasible, fabricating giant tunnel plugs that might act like temporary stoppers in a sink when the waters rise again.

4. *Gradual decline of intense public interest.* The previous stage becomes almost imperceptibly transformed into the fourth stage: a gradual decline in the intensity of public interest in the problem. As more and more people realize how difficult, and how costly for them, a solution to the problem would be, three reactions set in. Some people just get discouraged. Others feel positively threatened by thinking about the problem, so they suppress such thoughts. Still, others become bored by the issue. Most people experience some combination of these feelings. Consequently, public desire to keep attention focused on the issue wanes. And by this time, some other issue is usually entering stage 2, so it exerts a more novel and thus more powerful claim upon public attention.[92]

Returning briefly to the California earthquake insurance mentioned earlier, the *Los Angeles Times* reported, "Earthquake insurance coverage changed radically after the 1994 Northridge temblor. Until then, companies that wrote homeowners insurance in the state were also required to offer earthquake coverage. After Northridge, most insurers refused to write either, saying the $12.5 billion in insurance claims from the quake was far higher than expected—higher, in fact, than the total of all earthquake insurance premiums ever collected in California."[93] The story continues, "But the state finally responded to homeowners' howls by offering more quake insurance options through CEA, including lower deductibles and greater contents coverage, for somewhat higher premiums. Two private companies, Pacific Select and GeoVera (now both owned by St. Paul Cos.), also began to offer more comprehensive earthquake policies. CEA now says demand for its enhanced policies is greater than anticipated: Nearly 34,000 homeowners have purchased the additional coverage in the first year it was available, compared with 917,000 who have the bare-bones CEA policies. That still leaves nearly five out of six homeowners with no quake coverage, however." Moreover, some Californians who managed to collect on their claims for earthquake damage have been known to then cancel their policies, reasoning that the chances of a similar or worse earthquake in their lifetimes were so slim that it was not worth the cost of maintaining their residential quake policies.

5. *The post-problem stage.* In the final stage, an issue that has been replaced at the center of public concern moves into a prolonged limbo—a twilight realm of lesser attention or spasmodic recurrences of interest. However, the issue now has a different relation to public attention from that which prevailed in the pre-problem stage. For one thing, during the time that interest was sharply focused on this problem, new institutions, programs, and policies may have been created to help solve it. These entities almost always persist and often have some impact even after public attention has shifted elsewhere.[94] For example, the president and Congress established a Gulf Coast Recovery Authority to help victims of Hurricanes Katrina and Rita recover from those 2005 disasters. Billions of federal dollars were funneled to the region through a variety of federal and state programs. This was repeated in the 2012–2013 Superstorm Sandy disaster recovery. Similarly, Congress passed, and President Trump signed into law, a battery of measures to address public needs in the aftermath of the three hurricanes of 2017. This helps assuage public concern but gives the public and a few vocal pundits the false impression that the problem of hurricane vulnerability has been addressed. As other problems come to the fore, hurricane disaster preparedness and mitigation tends to draw less news media, public, and policymaker attention.

Any major problem that once was elevated to national prominence may sporadically recapture public interest. Certain aspects of it may become attached to some other problem that subsequently dominates center stage. Coastal shoreline erosion, often compounded by major storms of hurricanes, has come to be a major concern in the realm of sea level rise along coasts. The SARS epidemic of the past, something made worse by the ease of international air travel, highlighted similar concerns in the 2014–2016 West Africa Ebola outbreak.[95] Therefore, problems that have gone through the cycle almost always receive a higher average level of attention, public effort, and general concern than do those still in the pre-discovery stage.[96]

Federalization and Government Responsibility

The United States apportions government responsibility for disaster management over at least three tiers of government: national (federal), state (including District of Columbia and U.S. Trust and Commonwealth Territories), and local (which encompasses a wide variety of sub-state governments: counties, cities, other municipalities, special district governments, etc.). America has a highly decentralized, federal system of government, which under the U.S. Constitution affords the national government a range of authority. Some powers are reserved for the states under the Tenth Amendment. Similarly, in some states, local governments, although legally vestiges of their respective state government, possess certain powers under home rule provisions approved by their states, by their state constitution, or through enabling statutes. The federal system of layers of governments creates a form of vertical fragmentation among national, state, and local governments.

Moreover, there is also horizontal fragmentation, owing to a multitude of competing agencies with overlapping jurisdictional prerogatives on each level of government. Effective decision making and program coordination among all these agencies is difficult in the extreme. Here is one view of the system:

> Disaster relief is a system of complex and interdependent programs that work well most of the time. When it succeeds, the disaster relief system does so not because of the inspired operational leadership at the federal level, but because it is a system whose pieces have been built beforehand, over time in response to public preparedness policies, state and local government initiative, and private sector response to market incentives and regulation, as well as the dedication of private voluntary organizations, and the acumen of individuals and families.[97]

This underlines the need for multiagency and multijurisdictional coordination concerning emergency and disaster issues. The former **National Response Plan (NRP)**, which was replaced in 2008 by the **National Response Framework (NRF)**, is predicated on the need for such coordination. When a response to a major disaster or emergency is necessary, the **National Incident Management System (NIMS)**, the implementation component of the NRF, represents the epitome of multiagency and multijurisdictional coordination.

Vertical fragmentation occurs when federal, state, and local officials fail to coordinate their respective actions with one another. For example, this happens when federal officials act independently or without consultation of their state and local counterparts. It may also occur when local or state officials fail to act in concert or when one or more fails to properly apprise federal authorities of their actions. The over-centralization of decision making on the federal level, so often alleged by state and local emergency managers and their professional organizations, also promotes vertical fragmentation.[98]

Disaster policy and emergency management both inherently involve intergovernmental relations. **Intergovernmental relations** involve the interaction and exchanges of public and private organizations across all layers of government. The growth of societal interdependence, in economic and technological terms, has created a webbed and networked world that depends on both the support and the regulation of government.

In the summer of 2004, a major electric power blackout hit the Northeast and part of the Province of Ontario, Canada. The cause turned out to be inadequate tree pruning around the power lines of a small private electric utility in northeastern Ohio. That company was in a financial pinch, and it sought to save operating expense money by foregoing the pruning. As tree limbs dropped on powerlines, a cascade effect was produced that knocked out huge portions of the power grid of New York State, Ohio, Pennsylvania, and part of Canada in the Niagara region. Millions were without power for a period of several days. To rectify the problem, private and public utilities had to cooperate and rebuild or repair portions of the grid, and power pool managers (those who manage the flow of electricity from utility to utility and over a regional power network) had to work in synchronization to revive the grid; state and local emergency managers meanwhile had to swing into action to direct traffic when no signals operated, rescue people trapped on elevators, and work with public and private nonprofit social welfare agencies, making sure people would not die of heat stroke in their un-air-conditioned residences. The Federal Energy Regulatory Commission (FERC) launched months of investigations. FERC sought to ascertain the source of the outage and to determine liability for costs of the power failure. President G. W. Bush even issued disaster declarations to New York, Ohio, and Pennsylvania, among other states. How could inadequate tree pruning in Ohio produce such dire consequences? The answer is "**tightly coupled interdependence**,"[99] a concept put forth by organization theorist Charles Perrow. This power loss calamity was repeated for large swaths of greater Houston during Hurricane Harvey, for extensive areas of both northern and southern Florida during Hurricane Irma, and perhaps most tragic of all, for the entire island of Puerto Rico, a territory of the United States, which lost power owing to Hurricane Maria and to a dilapidated pre-existing system of power distribution. Maria struck as a Category 4 hurricane and plowed a path directly through the center of the island.

Communities of Stakeholders

Emergency management (EM) has communities of **stakeholders**. Stakeholders are persons, groups, or institutions with interests in a project, program, or policy. Primary stakeholders are those ultimately affected by the policy or program, either positively or negatively. Key stakeholders are those who can significantly influence, or are important to the success of, the policy, program, or project. Stakeholders with political clout have often been influential in determining which state or local agency has lead jurisdiction during emergencies and disasters. In some states and localities, the political power of paid (some unionized) or volunteer fire service people, a key stakeholder group, dominates emergency management. In some states and localities, law enforcement agencies have been entrusted with emergency management authority and responsibilities. In some local governments, the medical community, another key stakeholder, has assumed lead jurisdiction in emergency management through the services it provides in public and private hospitals, in emergency medicine, and in local public health. In about half of the states, top emergency management is a quasi-military responsibility led by the state adjutant general, an official who heads the state's National Guard. Because National Guard units are under the control of governors in each respective state, adjutant generals often have close working relationships with their respective state governor (see Chapter 7).

State and local governments have moved into the realm of disaster policy and emergency management in different ways. Through the 1950s and 1960s, some have nurtured emergency management as an extension of their civil defense work. Some have had poor experience in managing previous disasters—often with highly negative political repercussions for those in office—with the result that emergency management is moved closer to the mayor or county executive. In the past, for some localities disaster management has been a "political football" fought over by police and firefighters, both of whom wanted primary jurisdictional authority over EM. Some of the common audiences, partners, stakeholders, and customers of concern to policymakers and emergency managers are presented in Table 1-2.

TABLE 1-2 ■ Audiences, Partners, Stakeholders, Customers

Groups with Disaster Interests	Characteristics
General public	Largest audience (i.e., citizens and non-citizens, taxpayers, consumers, etc.)
	Composed of subgroups: age groups, economic classes, education levels, employment status, property owners, racial and ethnic minorities, religious affiliations, physically or psychologically impaired, etc.
	All subgroups are potential customers or clients of emergency management programs and resources.
	Some members of the general public will be inside disaster damage zones, some will be in host communities serving disaster victims, but many in the general public will be far from the damage zone, although affected in some way nonetheless.
Disaster victims	Individuals, families, households
	Includes corporations and other types of businesses
Business community	Executives and employees
	Owners and/or shareholders
	Proprietors, small business owners, franchisees, self-employed people
	Bankers, realtors, developers, investors, etc.
	Interdependent business enterprises, vendors, suppliers, etc.
Media	News media are potentially an audience and a partner in emergency management
	News media come in many forms (i.e., print, television, radio, Internet based, social media, citizen journalism, etc.)
Elected officials	The president, governors, mayors, county executives, federal, state, or local legislators, other elected office holders
Community officials	City, municipal, county managers, heads of local departments (i.e., public safety, public works, transportation, public health, water and wastewater management, housing, power authorities, etc.)
	Community officials include operators of life line service utilities, public or private owned (i.e., water and sewer services, electric power, phone and fiber-optic infrastructure, natural gas service, sanitation, etc.)
First responders	Police, fire services, emergency medical, volunteer responders
Volunteer and altruistic groups	Formally organized disaster response and recovery proficient groups (i.e., American Red Cross, Salvation Army, Save the Children, United Way, and more organizations of the National Volunteer Organizations Active in Disaster, etc.)
	Includes self-organizing, emergent volunteer groups.

Source: Adapted from George D. Haddow, Jane A. Bullock, Damon P. Coppola, *Introduction to Emergency Management,* 4th ed. (Boston: Elsevier, Butterworth-Heinemann, 2011), 139.

Who Has Jurisdiction over Emergency Management?

As in most municipalities, mayors rely heavily on emergency managers. Mayors need notification about local emergencies and disasters for at least two reasons. First, certain emergency circumstances require mayor-level executive decisions. Second, owing to the newsworthiness of local disasters and emergencies, mayors need to be apprised of these events at least as early as the news media if not sooner. In emergencies and disasters, the mayor's public image may be at stake. Moreover, a mayor is the personification of the municipality she or he leads, and people expect their mayor to respond to the calamities their city experiences.

Jurisdiction over some realms of emergency management is occasionally a subject of bureaucratic and political conflict, managerial infighting, or profession rivalries. In many ways, disputes over emergency management jurisdiction epitomize the bureaucratic politics model of decision making discussed in Chapter 2. Government reorganizations are often manifestations of ongoing "battles" between different leaders, public departments, agencies, and offices. Sometimes emergency management is the object of reorganization. State and local emergency management involves so many different subjects and concerns that seldom can a single state or local government agency claim complete dominion over it. This, too, adds to political and administrative disputes over who will have control of what in emergency management. The post–9/11 emergence of homeland security, introduced with massive levels of federal funding, triggered waves of state and local reorganization—much of it involving emergency managers and emergency management.

Local Governments and Decentralization Issues

Vertical Fragmentation and Competing Values

Albeit with some glaring exceptions (i.e., mega-earthquakes, explosive super-volcanic eruptions, hurricanes, tsunamis, major floods, major snowstorms and ice storms, etc.), disasters are usually spatially localized in terms of their immediate physical effects. Therefore, county and municipal authorities most often assume primary responsibility for emergency management of local incidents, unless precluded from doing so by an overhead government. However, the policymaking, administrative, and fiscal capacities of many American local governments vary tremendously. Owing to competing demands and cross-pressures, many local officials, executives and legislators, are reluctant, unwilling, or unable to design, implement, and support with local funds effective disaster preparedness and response programs. As mentioned, vertical fragmentation occurs when federal, state, and local authorities fail to coordinate their emergency management work with one another, when they act independently of each other, when they duplicate their efforts or work at cross-purposes, or when one level of government fails to carry out its obligations. Successive national response plans, the latest being the National Response Framework, have endeavored to prevent vertical fragmentation. So too has the National Incident Management System put to work on specific incidents. Combatting fragmentation means promoting intergovernmental and interagency coordination and cooperation. Inducements to achieving cooperation and coordination have come through law, policies, joint-planning, consultation, and most importantly conditional grant money paid out by overhead governments to local jurisdictions (see "Tell Me More" 1-1 box on page 32).

Multiagency and multigovernmental jurisdictions challenge emergency managers. Disasters and emergencies often do the following: change the division of labor and resources in an organization; compel a sharing of tasks and resources among organizations; involve the crossing of jurisdictional boundaries both in terms of geography and responsibility; require completion of non-routine tasks under abnormal circumstances; damage, make unavailable, or overwhelm normal emergency response tools and facilities; and necessitate new organizational arrangements to meet the problems posed.

Emergency management is always conducted within a political culture. Political culture "is a set of shared views and normative judgments held by a population regarding its political system. The notion of political culture does not refer to attitudes toward specific actors, such as a president or prime minister, but rather it denotes how people view the political system as a whole and their belief in its legitimacy. American political scientist Lucian Pye defined political culture as the composite of basic values, feelings, and knowledge that underlie the political process. Hence, the building blocks of political culture are the beliefs, opinions, and emotions of the citizens toward their form of government."[100] American emergency management is often challenged by some people's fundamental distrust of government planning efforts, strong grassroots resistance to land-use and construction regulation, and many people's tendency, especially at state and local levels, to focus only on recent disasters. Levels of hazard risk and disaster vulnerability are also difficult to measure. Cause-and-effect relationships are elusive as well. Unfortunately, in some places there remain people and government officials who continue to believe that waiting for emergencies to occur and then dealing with their effects is more sensible than preparing for and mitigating potential effects before a disaster strikes.

Emergency management, like almost every domain of public policy in a democracy, is rife with competing values. What seems logical in one value system is often judged illogical or unfair in a different value system. Consider this example: two economists, Sutter and Simmons, studying the economics of tornado losses concluded that the largest segment of dollar loss in tornado disasters they examined stemmed from opportunity costs resulting from "how long the tornado alert was in effect," not from the total cost of actual damage inflicted by the tornadoes themselves.[101] They calculate that about two-thirds of the largest segment of tornado losses come from the opportunity cost of time spent under tornado warnings. So, the economic activity foregone by people heeding a tornado warning was costlier than the damage generated by the effects of the tornadoes. The longer the tornado warning was in effect, the more the warning's economic effects exceeded actual tornado damage costs. As heartless as this may sound, in terms of economic values and calculations, these economists are probably correct in their findings. However, policymakers operating in a world of humanitarian and/or political values would never accede to foregoing or shortening tornado warnings because the warnings are uneconomic in their net effects. Valuation of life concerns, as well as the logic of electoral accountability, may impel lawmakers to disregard the economic logic of this case and maintain a robust system of tornado warning.

Correspondingly, government relief assistance is politically popular and desired, whereas mitigation and preparedness are seldom politically popular. Regardless of public pronouncements by emergency management leaders, "Mitigation is still not the sole or even the primary goal of federal disaster policy."[102]

In great measure, the federal system's division of powers accords local and state governments the lead role in responding to most types of hazards and disasters. The national government has assumed a facilitating role through FEMA, which was an independent agency from 1979 to 2003 and which has been positioned within DHS since then. State and local governments also develop emergency management procedures. America has a decentralized and elaborate array of emergency management procedures in which local emergency management is the base. Yet the NRF and the NIMS have sought greater consistency and conformity among state, local, and even federal emergency management. There are also some exceptions to this power-sharing among levels of government. For some types of incidents—civil defense against nuclear attacks of any type, nuclear accidents, bioterrorism, and counterterrorism—the federal role in policymaking and administration remains dominant.

Horizontal Fragmentation under Shared Governance

Horizontal fragmentation may be reduced if adjacent or nearby states and local jurisdictions establish mutual assistance agreements with one another "before" disasters and emergencies transpire. This also applies to nation-states that border each other (see Chapter 8). These agreements alleviate some of the jurisdictional confusion. Vertical and horizontal fragmentation complicates emergency management. Such fragmentation is not easily overcome even though "shared governance" holds some potential for achieving improvements in emergency management.[103] Vertical and horizontal fragmentation often contributes to the problems of insufficient technical expertise, inadequate fiscal resources, and unclear statutory mandates. Because so many laws are passed by legislators through coalition building that require various forms of trade-off or political side-payments (often favors or promises), legislative language appearing in many enacted laws is deliberately vague, muddled, or open to varying interpretations.

Over the past four decades, decentralization in government has become a mantra of elected leaders on either side of the partisan aisle. **Decentralization** of decision making, with sound coordination, is how many authorities define successful emergency management. As noted, emergency management has fundamentally been a local obligation, in the past and often in the present undertaken with the help of private charitable organizations. Local governments in most states are either considered "creatures" of their respective states or they are accorded certain "independent powers" by their states, sometimes under "home rule" laws or policies. States themselves enjoy limited areas of "reserved powers" under the U.S. Constitution, but the range of federal powers over the states is vast. Thus, although many people consider emergency management a "bedrock" local responsibility, both the state and federal government officials are now key actors, often with public endorsement, in local emergency management. Simply put, local officials may have recognized their own jurisdiction's limitations in addressing disaster. Since FEMA was established, and since federal post-disaster relief programs have been broadened and handsomely funded, local officials have become accustomed to seeking state and federal financial assistance after disasters. Even in states that manifest anti-federal political cultures, local communities and their elected officials have come to expect federal disaster assistance through an assortment of programs, not all of which are administered by FEMA.

Federal and state policymakers and public managers often cannot easily grasp the emergency management organizational complexity of some 3,500 county governments[104] and thousands more municipal and special district governments. In fashioning disaster policy, federal and state authorities have endeavored to promote where possible consistency and, to a degree, professionalism in local emergency management. Part of this effort is evident in all-hazards emergency management. The essence of this concept is that common sets of emergency preparedness and response procedures and practices are applicable in any locality regardless of differences in geography or demography. It also posits that an economy of scale can be reached by planning and preparing for disaster in generic terms (thus, "all hazards") rather than by planning or preparing for each unique type or classification of disaster agent(s).

Disaster management also requires strong cooperation and coordination among public, nonprofit, and private organizations. Emergency management is conducted in a fluid and often chaotic environment. Local government officials must interact ably with other local government officials and with people representing private or nonprofit organizations. A county government may offer assistance under a previously arranged mutual aid agreement. Private construction companies that have experience in meeting building code rules may offer emergency rebuilding or repair assistance. Area chemical companies may volunteer their services to clean up and detoxify hazardous substances accidentally released by others during the disaster. A host of local, state, or national charitable organizations may offer human services aid that local governments cannot be expected to offer. Help from the private and nonprofit sectors often augments successful emergency management, sometimes meeting needs or filling gaps that government is unable to address fully.

Disaster policy and management, despite the all-hazards precept, recognizes the need to consider and differentiate types or categories of disaster. Each category or kind of disaster embodies different types of duties and responsibilities for disaster managers. These duties and responsibilities are not always compatible across categories of disaster incidents. For example, a terrorist attack, such as the September 11, 2001, attacks on New York's World Trade Center and the Pentagon in northern Virginia, mobilized fire service personnel, police officers, emergency managers, law enforcement officials, military personnel, and many others. The sites attacked were scenes of human carnage, a crime scene, and a national security locus. Search and rescue, public safety, firefighting, crime scene investigation, forensic and coroner work all had to be pursued at the same site. In such situations, conflicts are likely to occur over who is to do what and when. Part of the work of emergency management is to harmonize this activity. Top emergency managers are sometimes assigned tasks they might not have imagined. This author's highly respected friend, Richard Buck, a now retired FEMA official, was, in the aftermath of 9/11, assigned to "the pile" where the Twin Towers and other WTC structures collapsed. One of his duties was to supervise teams of workers scraping mangled steel in search of human DNA from victims who had not yet been identified.

Similarly, a coastal flood, such as the flooding that often occurs after nor'easters in New England and along the Mid-Atlantic, may be a human disaster and an environmental issue. Some authorities will press for rebuilding damaged onshore structures or replenishing lost beach sand, whereas others will seek to protect natural habitats and coastal marine resources by discouraging rebuilding and instead recommending ways to accommodate the changes produced by the storm. Different types of disasters embody different sets of stakeholders, political figures, public managers, and interest groups.

The Politics of Disaster

Disasters have political features. Natural disasters and emergencies, in particular, provide excellent windows of opportunity for public officials.[105] Often these officials use disasters or emergencies to demonstrate their leadership capabilities and their willingness to tackle difficult problems. Their actions on these occasions usually draw media publicity and instant public notice. Moreover, it is extremely difficult to oppose or criticize an official who steps in and gives the appearance of taking charge to help disaster victims. Disasters often temporarily shift power from legislatures to elected or appointed executives.

Natural disasters also produce conditions that allow political leaders to show their concern for citizens' needs and demands. Disaster victims often encounter problems that they have never before experienced and which they may be unprepared or ill equipped to handle on their own. Public officials are in a position to highlight needs and channel resources to help those in distress. Disaster gives elected or appointed leaders a perfect opportunity to demonstrate their responsiveness to the needs of the people.

An entire subfield of research has emerged on the subject of **crisis leadership**. Building from past case examples about the behavior and decision making of specific heads of state, crisis leadership examines how presidents and prime ministers have performed during crises and in the aftermath of crises. The conception of "crisis" is somewhat broader than the subject of disaster management.[106] While many crises emerge from disasters and emergencies triggered by natural forces or by human causes that result in mass casualties and/or mass destruction, crisis leadership researchers draw a wider circle than this. In their masterwork, Boin, t'Hart, Stern, and Sundelius explain, "Crisis generally refers to an undesirable and unexpected situation: when we talk about crisis, we mean something bad threatens a person, group, organization, culture, society, or, when we think really big, the world at large. Something must be done, urgently, to make sure this threat will not materialize."[107] Crises can occur in many different realms. In a political realm, "crisis refers to a situation in which political elites and institutions are at risk of being replaced by an alternative set of actors and arrangements."[108] Owing to fixed terms of presidential office, with the exception of a presidential impeachment (in the U.S. House) followed by a two-thirds or greater guilty vote in a U.S. Senate trial, U.S. presidents are not subject to being replaced on account of their handling of a crisis as may be the case in parliamentary systems headed by a prime minister. Nevertheless, presidential bungling of response to a publicly perceived catastrophic disaster or crisis does indeed raise the possibility that the mismanaging president will be voted out of office in the next presidential election.

Disasters may create tremendous opportunities for elected officials, including presidents, to provide service to their constituents. Government leaders who successfully address disaster-related problems are likely to be rewarded politically, whereas those leaders who are unwilling or unable to act may suffer negative political repercussions.[109]

Disasters embody "political dangers" for elected executives and for senior public managers. Bungle a disaster, and political executives will pay a political price. Perceived incompetence during disasters often comes at a high price for political officials.[110]

The United States is arguably in an era of **hyper-partisanship**. For better or worse, most Republicans have moved to the political far right, and almost correspondingly, most Democrats have moved to the political far left. Centrist politics and candidates seldom emerge any longer. Public opinion polls show that most Americans tend to subsume their personal political ideology under the banner of their political party's position. In other words, when asked political questions, Americans tend to define their personal political beliefs in terms of where their own political party stands on the issue raised in the question. Thus, sitting presidents and state governors often tend to be prejudged by their political party. Those people in the same party as the president or state governors tend to provide those leaders the benefit of the doubt in times of crisis and disaster. They are likely to dismiss critics of their party's elected executives as merely opposition party enemy attackers. Conversely, those in the opposing party of a president or various state governors tend to immediately assume that the president and these governors are incompetent or foreordained to fail on account of their party affiliation and what that stands for. With the nation so partisanly divided, more and more disaster management is imbued with party politics and partisan bias.

There are countervailing forces that work against this hyper-partisanship. The American federal system of government comes with federal, state, and local layers. It is rarely the case that a major disaster or emergency does not include at least a mix of Republican and Democratic executives. Moreover, many disasters, owing to their geographic magnitude, span political borders. This sometimes brings together coalitions of elected officials who for a time work cooperatively across party lines to meet public needs created by the incident.

This study will introduce many more examples of disaster politics than is covered here. Regardless of hyper-partisanship, America remains a democratic republic operated under a constitution and other laws and with three separate but equal branches of federal government. Perhaps more worrisome is the rise of nativism in American politics. "America First" advocates are reluctant to support foreign aid programs, a portion of which are directed to humanitarian response to disasters and complex emergencies outside the United States. Nativism undercuts American support to disaster victims living in American trust or commonwealth territories.

The Problem of Disaster Insurance

It became apparent to policymakers as early as the 1950s that private-sector insurance companies were either unwilling to provide residential **disaster insurance** against flood or incapable of doing so. This created a major unmet need in several respects. Federal disaster relief programs only gradually came to extend relief directly to individuals and families, and much of this relief was at the time wholly inadequate to help victims who suffered losses from flooding or from any other disaster agent (see the "Tell Me More" 1-1 box).

A massive share of presidential disaster declarations from 1950 through 2017 covered flood disasters—many associated with hurricanes, storm surges, tornadoes, severe storms, seasonal snow melt, ice jams, and more. Presidents and lawmakers seemed constantly to revisit the problem of inadequate help for those individuals and families suffering flood loss.[111]

TELL ME MORE 1-1

THE MATTER OF DISASTER INSURANCE

Owing to a 1958 study by the late geographer Gilbert F. White[112] and his colleagues titled "Changes in Urban Occupancy of Flood Plains in the United States," and due to the public education and advocacy efforts of White and others, many policymakers and others were made aware that land-use pressures and the failure to keep development out of potential flood zones were putting more people and structures in jeopardy.[113] The study even alleged that a condition of **moral hazard** was emerging because post-flood federal disaster relief led many people to believe that should flood disaster occur, the federal government would be there to set things straight and make them whole again. Moral hazard in the realm of insurance refers to an increase in the probability of loss caused by the behavior of a policyholder.[114]

Another way to look at this is that federal disaster assistance does the following:

Creates a type of **Samaritan's dilemma:** providing assistance after a catastrophe reduces the economic incentives of potential victims to invest in protective measures prior to a disaster. If the expectation of disaster assistance reduces the demand for insurance, the political pressure on the government to provide assistance after a disaster is reinforced or amplified.[115]

By 1960, the final year of Eisenhower's presidency, Congress had amended the Flood Control Act and authorized the USACE to compile and disseminate information on floods and flood damages at the request of a state or responsible local agency. As a result of the act, the USACE established a Flood Plain Management Service, a body that promoted flood mitigation and supplied advisory flood maps to local communities.

One of the reasons that the National Flood Insurance Program (NFIP) was established in 1968 was to encourage individuals who resided in hazard-prone areas to purchase flood insurance.

The insurance was low priced—remember, a government insurance program is not necessarily required to show a profit—and policymakers hoped that the availability and low cost of this insurance would reduce the need to supply so much federal disaster grant and loan assistance after future floods. However, after this occurred, the following happened:

[F]ew individuals voluntarily bought this coverage so that when Tropical Storm Agnes in June 1972 hit the Northeast causing over $2 billion in damage, only 1,583 claims totaling $5 million were paid under the NFIP. Even though flood coverage has been required since 1973 as a condition for a federally insured mortgage, it has been estimated that less than 40 percent of the victims of Hurricane Katrina in Mississippi and Louisiana had flood insurance to cover their losses.[116] Fast forward to Hurricane Harvey, which massively inundated the greater Houston area in 2017. According to an article in *Forbes*, "In Houston's Harris County only 15% of homes have flood insurance. And in the coastal Corpus Christi vicinity, only 20% are covered. Simply put, many people currently being affected by Hurricane Harvey who were not required by mortgage lenders to buy flood insurance chose not to, despite the subsidies."[117] The article adds, "Homeowners' losses in Houston will be particularly high because, like no other U.S. city, Houston is famous for its lax building codes and permissive zoning laws. Homes are not required to have proper flood elevation, and neighborhoods are not planned to minimize flooding. It is this combination—lack of flood-prevention and of flood-insurance—that may account for the magnitude of uninsured property losses the region is now experiencing."[118]

Presidents and Congress slowly and hesitantly moved toward the creation of the NFIP, a program that would invite localities to join if they promised to meet federal standards aimed at limiting development in floodplains and if they promoted flood-proof construction. People living in the communities that joined the NFIP would then be eligible to buy low-cost flood insurance from the federal government. In effect, the federal government would use insurance as a key form of post-disaster assistance and as a tool of flood mitigation.

The NFIP was supposed to be a premier instrument of both disaster mitigation and disaster recovery. The program that continues today has been modestly successful. Many local governments participate in the program and generally abide by its flood mitigation rules. Through the years, however, NFIP has only weakly penalized localities that disregarded its rules, owing to understaffing and limited authority to punish noncompliant local governments. Worse still, too few property owners purchase and maintain NFIP policies. People who refuse to buy national flood insurance, even those who experience recurring flood loss through the years, are rarely denied federal disaster relief after a federally declared flood disaster damages their property. The Homeowner Flood Insurance Affordability Act of 2014 (HFIAA) repealed certain parts of the Biggert-Waters Act of 2012. It restored grandfathering of structures in map-identified high flood zones shielding them from NFIP rate hikes that would have better approximated their actuarial risk, and it put limits on certain rate increases and updated the approach to ensuring the fiscal soundness of the fund by applying an annual surcharge to all NFIP policyholders.[119]

On top of all of this, private insurers continue to cover wind damage (but not that caused by floodwater) in their homeowner insurance policies. NFIP covers floodwater damage but not wind-caused damage. There is a **"wind" versus "water" dispute** between FEMA and private insurers that does not serve policyholder or public interests. Consequently, many homeowners have fallen into insurance limbo as private insurer claims adjusters contest claims for damage they believe is caused by flooding, and NFIP claims adjusters deny claims for damage they conclude was caused by wind. For example, a vast number of NFIP policyholders in Katrina damage zones ended up having their claims denied by both NFIP and their private insurer. At this writing, this insurance "policy" has been only partially resolved. In 2013, a FEMA Federal Insurance & Mitigation Administration official signed a memorandum agreeing to FEMA's participation in state non-binding mediation of wind versus water damage disputes.[120]

The Challenge of Building and Maintaining Technical Expertise

Emergency management is conducted within a complex political, economic, and social environment. In part, this explains why emergency management has so long lacked a coherent, coordinated policy framework. Designing and implementing comprehensive emergency management procedures is easier said than done, principally because of the obstacles to effective action created by problems stemming from low political salience, over-federalized and fragmented government responsibility, and lack of emergency manager technical expertise.

Insufficient technical expertise and confusion about the kind of expertise that is needed are other impediments to effective emergency management. The technical expertise needed to identify and assess hazards adequately, predict the occurrence of disasters, and provide the requisite technical information for the design and implementation of effective programs is crucial to effective emergency management. Moreover, even when hazards have been identified, it is often unclear just how much risk is involved.

Today, emergency managers need to acquire a specialized body of knowledge, often involving many different academic or professional disciplines. Accounting and budgeting skills are important. Public relations expertise and political savvy are necessary. Computing ability, for information management, decision support, geographic information system (GIS), social media,[121] and so on, has become more a part of routine emergency management work. A working knowledge of disaster-related laws, regulations, and programs is vital. The FEMA Emergency Management Institute regularly conducts training sessions, conferences, and workshops that consider the knowledge, skills, and abilities (KSAs) needed to do emergency management.[122] There is a growing consensus about the general skill sets needed. A substantial list of institution-based and online courses is available today. As mentioned, EMAP, a private voluntary consortium, has been working to set forth qualifications and credentials needed for a person to be classified as a "qualified emergency manager."[123] A great many universities and colleges offer coursework and degrees or certificates in emergency management.[124] Moreover, some state and local governments offer in-house EM training and education programs for their employees. A few have formal government academies where government workers can train and study in a quasi-academic atmosphere.

Decision making in disaster planning and management encompasses the following assumptions:

- Disaster planning is a continuous process. It should not be based on a single emergency but instead on several. Such planning must allow for the constant incorporation of new findings.

- Disaster planning should attempt to reduce uncertainty in crises by anticipating problems and projecting possible solutions.

- Disaster planning stipulates that the appropriateness of response is more important than speed of response.

- Disaster planning is based on what will probably happen; procedures need to address what people are likely to do in emergencies, not on preconceived myths or common nostrums about human behavior.

- Disaster planning involves the education of response and recovery people. Managers need to know that emergency procedures exist and that it is important that they understand and follow these procedures.

- Disaster management needs to be "sold" effectively to communities to be taken seriously.

- Disaster management requires exercises and practice, or otherwise the best plans tend to become worthless.

Wise decision makers consider many sources of information, especially those which give them greater "situational awareness." Today, they need methods and help in filtering but taking into account information posted in social media.

PHASES OF EMERGENCY MANAGEMENT

The four phases model of emergency management encompasses mitigation, preparedness, response, and recovery. It makes sense to divide recovery itself into two phases: short- and long-term. A major reason for this is because **short-term recovery** often involves addressing immediate needs, which tend to be quite different from needs associated with **long-term recovery**. Short-term recovery may overlap some of the disaster response phase. It routinely includes "search and rescue, damage assessments, coroner and mortuary work, public information, temporary housing, utility restoration, and debris clearance."[125] Moreover, the people and organizations that tend to address short-term recovery over time begin to be replaced or supplanted by a much broader pool of people and organizations in long-term recovery. Long-term recovery "addresses the basic dimensions of a community's existence: permanent housing, economic conditions, the environment, the infrastructure (e.g., roads and bridges), and lifelines (e.g., water, power, telephone service)."[126] Each dimension of long-term recovery may be affected by social and psychological conditions that impact individual and group ability to advance through the long-term recovery period.

Mitigation

Mitigation involves deciding what to do where a risk to the health, safety, and welfare of society has been identified and devising a risk reduction program. It is sustained action to reduce or eliminate risk to people and property from hazards and their effects. The recovery phase of disaster also offers opportunities for mitigation actions.[127] Mitigation aims to cost-effectively reduce the potential for damage to a facility from a potential hazard or disaster agent. This includes identifying, measuring, and addressing hazard vulnerability. Mitigation steps undertaken after a disaster to reduce the likelihood of future disasters, caused by both physical and social phenomena, are also recommended.[128]

The formation of FEMA spotlighted hazard mitigation and preparedness, and by the 1990s, FEMA gave impetus to a proactive, rather than a reactive, approach to emergency management. Instead of merely doing disaster recovery work, FEMA emphasized keeping people out of hazard-prone, high-risk areas through local land use and regulatory instruments such as zoning laws, building codes, and land-use rules. In effect, FEMA began to encourage or induce local officials and individuals to adopt mitigation policies.[129] Mitigation work opened up a perennial, highly political difference of opinion between FEMA and various local officials, developers, and citizens.[130] As subsequent chapters explain, federal efforts to promote local disaster mitigation activity, especially through grant conditions and NFIP requirements, often ran afoul of local economic development interests, who countered with accusations that the federal government was interfering with local land use and building code powers. FEMA officials attempted to persuade community people to proactively protect themselves through hazard mitigation activities.

Tools for mitigation include the following:

- Hazard identification and mapping (e.g., by the NFIP, the USGS, the states, GIS, Hazards U.S.-Multi-Hazard [HAZUS-MH] software program).

- **Design and construction applications** (e.g., code development, model codes, geographic sensitivity, retrofit ordinances, elevation of homes, removal of flammable vegetation around homes, landscaping).

- **Land-use planning** (prevents development in floodplains or high-hazard zones, relocates structures), zoning rules, property acquisition.

- **Financial incentives** (special tax assessments in the interest of mitigation or relocation aid), use of other federal program monies to pay for property acquisition and relocation.

- **Insurance** (e.g., NFIP, federal subsidization of some other forms of insurance, such as terrorism insurance), indemnification requirements as a condition of loan approvals by the U.S. Department of Veterans Affairs (VA), the U.S. Department of Housing and Urban Development (HUD), or the Federal Housing Administration (FHA) or other federal mortgage aid. The federal government provides insurers with maps of high-hazard zones. The Community Rating System rewards good performers with lower NFIP premiums for their people.

- **Structural controls** (e.g., public works, flood works, levees, dams, flood channels, shoreline structural protection).[131]

Preparedness

Preparedness involves developing a response plan and training first responders to save lives and reduce disaster damage, identifying critical resources, and developing necessary agreements among responding agencies, both within the jurisdiction and with other jurisdictions. Preparedness also entails "readying for expected threats, including contingency planning, resource management, mutual aid . . . [and] public information."[132] It is a functional aspect of emergency management that contributes to sound emergency response and recovery from a disaster.

Emergency management has to rely on academic or analytical processes, especially those resting on a systems approach to management. Preparedness relies heavily on a systemic conceptualization. Some of the standards flow from the EMAP Standard; many are based on the NFPA 1600 standards (recognized as the national preparedness standard for the private sector domestically and internationally) and were developed by state, local, and federal emergency management practitioners.[133]

Response

Response entails providing emergency aid and assistance, reducing the probability of secondary damage, and minimizing problems for recovery operations. In an emergency situation, emergency managers rarely direct actual response operations. There are exceptions, as when management of a crisis falls to a senior elected official or to the lead emergency services agency.[134] Disaster response objectives include protecting lives, limiting property loss, and overcoming the disruptions that disasters cause.[135] The response phase of disaster is often the most dramatic, visually stunning, and newsworthy phase of the disaster cycle.

The National Incident Management System, its Incident Command System, and its multiagency coordination procedures have become the nation's "game plan" for managing specific incidents about to transpire, transpiring, or ending their acute impact stage.

Recovery

Recovery involves providing the immediate support during the early post-disaster period necessary to return vital life-support systems to at least minimum operational levels and continuing to provide support until the community returns to normal.[136]

Recovery is the most expensive phase of the disaster cycle. It involves restoration, rebuilding, and return to normalcy. The pool of players involved in recovery is huge and far exceeds the number of players usually involved in disaster response. Late stages of disaster recovery may involve only small numbers of emergency managers but vast numbers of officials working in functional, financial, and regulatory agencies. Decisions regarding disaster recovery are fundamentally made at the local level of government.[137]

Summary

In several respects, disasters are socially and politically constructed phenomena. Who could imagine that the influx of Cuban immigrants from Fidel Castro's Mariel boatlift in 1980 would induce President Jimmy Carter to issue a disaster declaration for this event? How could the breakup of the NASA space shuttle *Columbia* in 2003 impel President George W. Bush to invite governors of states in the debris zone to request presidential disaster declarations to pay reimbursement of the costs related to their shuttle disaster response? In 2013, President Obama issued an emergency declaration to Massachusetts to help that state, the city of Boston, and other localities impacted by the **Boston Marathon bombing** and its aftermath. As Chapter 4 will demonstrate, presidents have at times used their power to declare disasters in ways that have expanded the definition of disaster in political and public administrative terms.

Disasters sometimes cause shifts in national priorities and significant changes in policy domains that are only tangentially linked to disaster policy. For example, the August 2007 spectacular collapse of the Minneapolis-St. Paul area

I-35W Mississippi River Bridge, a dramatic infrastructure disaster, pressed national policymakers to shift a portion of federal defense spending to the replacement, repair, and improved maintenance and inspection of the nation's bridgeworks.[137] The 9/11 terrorism disaster of 2001 induced policymakers to move federal emergency management into a terrorism-focused holding company of agencies implementing policies ranging from immigration control, border security, coastal maritime work, aviation security, public health, domestic intelligence collection, right up to Secret Service protection of government leaders.

Boin et al. add that crises can sometimes "trigger situational leadership," meaning that extreme and rapidly unfolding contingencies may compel "people both inside and outside government" to "take actions, make decisions, and assume authority roles unforeseen in formal plans and regulations."[138]

This chapter examined some of the essentials of emergency management and disaster policy. It covered emergency management as a profession. It explored stakeholder groups in the domain of disaster policy. It also furnished a brief overview of disaster as a field of scientific research, something examined more thoroughly in Chapter 5. Additionally, the chapter outlined some of the major challenges facing both emergency management and emergency managers. Among these challenges are the perennial low-issue salience of disaster as a public and political phenomenon, the fragmentation of government responsibility for disaster-related concerns, the difficulties local governments face in addressing emergency management, the political aspects of the disaster phenomenon, the problem of disaster insurance, and the challenge of training and educating emergency managers for a field that is technically complex and highly multidisciplinary. It provided a cameo of the four-phased cycle of emergency management: mitigation, preparedness, response, and recovery. These essentials will be developed more fully in subsequent chapters. Disaster policy and politics are intriguing, often controversial, teachable, relevant, complex, and yet largely comprehensible.

Key Terms

All-hazards emergency management 9
Boston Marathon bombing 37
Celebrity-branded post-disaster online fund raising for survivors 9
Civil defense 10
Counterterrorism 18
Crisis leadership 30
Debris flow 4
Decentralization 28
Disaster insurance 31
Disaster management 10
Disaster Unemployment Assistance (DUA) Program 6
EMAP Standard 16
Emergency management 11
Emergency Management Accreditation Program (EMAP) 15
Emergency manager 11

Federalized government responsibility 18
Hazards 11
Horizontal fragmentation 28
Hyper-partisanship 31
Insufficient technical expertise 33
Intergovernmental relations 23
International Association of Emergency Managers (IAEM) 12
Issue-attention cycle 19
Issue salience 18
Long-term recovery 35
Major disaster declaration 18
Mitigation 35
Moral hazard 32
National Emergency Management Association (NEMA) 12

National Incident Management System (NIMS) 23
National Response Framework (NRF) 23
National Response Plan (NRP) 23
Preparedness 36
Recovery 37
Response 36
Risk (in the context of hazards) 16
Samaritan's dilemma 32
Short-term recovery 35
Social media 2
Stakeholders 24
Tightly coupled interdependence 24
Vertical fragmentation 23
"Wind" versus "water" dispute 33

This GOES-16 geocolor image, taken in the afternoon of September 25, 2017, shows Hurricane Lee in the open Atlantic Ocean to the east and Hurricane Maria off the eastern coast of the United States.

NOAA

2

THEORIES AND APPROACHES OF PUBLIC POLICY AND MANAGEMENT HELPFUL IN DISASTER STUDIES

Scholars have developed theories and concepts to help them and us understand and explain governance and public policy generally. Theories and concepts have also been used to help understand and explain specific domains of public policy, such as health care, social welfare, environment, defense, and education. Disaster policy, although a somewhat new domain of public policy, is also amenable to analysis through the development and application of theories and concepts. Theories and concepts often serve as tools one can apply to the study of specific subjects or problems.

Emergency management (EM) has evolved into a profession and an academic field of inquiry. As such, EM relies on theories, concepts, and abstract knowledge as well as on experiential learning and experimental research. Emergency management work increasingly demands the mastery of a body of professional knowledge, although such work also depends on the skills and abilities of generalist managers, including those who may have been politically appointed to their posts. Emergency managers need to understand their role in the policy process. They need to grasp the significance of political and managerial theories relevant to their job.[1] Emergency managers need to appreciate that government involves various officials and organizations intended to serve express public purposes as well as to facilitate the effective operation of democracy and political accountability.

This chapter presents a selected set of theories and concepts, many produced by scholars of political science, public administration, sociology, and economics. These theories, concepts, and methods are applicable in disaster policy and emergency management. Where does theory knowledge fit within the realm of emergency management? How can those new to the field use theories and concepts to analyze disaster policy and its management?

The chapter opens with three simple normative theories: Jeffersonian, Hamiltonian, and Jacksonian. This is followed by a section on the role of theory in emergency management and why theory knowledge is important in any profession. Matters of decision-making theory, bureaucratic politics, and administrative culture are then considered. After this we revisit matters of public management and we look into the role of "best practice" contributions to the field. From here we briefly consider social constructivism's contributions, most particularly in leadership studies. Then comes a brief introduction to network theory, principal-agent theory, and intergovernmental relations theory followed by consideration of disaster recovery theory. We conclude with a section on "Big Data Analytics and Emergency Management." "Big data analytics" is more about methods than theory, but it deserves attention because it is a promising tool for disaster managers. Finally, we consider how emergency management and homeland security knowledge is produced and how it is learned by others.

NORMATIVE POLITICAL THEORIES

Consider three simple normative political theories that emanate from the political contributions of three important American forefathers: Thomas Jefferson, Alexander Hamilton, and Andrew Jackson.[2] The models derived from the approaches of these three historical figures are designed to explain and characterize features of public management in general. The models are immensely useful in thinking about emergency management. Laurence E. Lynn, Jr., deserves credit for developing the first two of these models. These models serve two purposes. First, they provide a way to categorize presidential behavior in the realm of policymaking, including disaster policymaking. Second, the models allow for self-reflection on the part of serving emergency managers, students, and others. One could ponder, which of the three models seems most appropriate for emergency management officials? Where models stand in conflict, which one should be selected as the best guide to decision making? These determinations are in many respects "value judgments," more than they are products of scientific analysis and methods. Nevertheless, they raise issues of effectiveness, efficiency, public accountability, public responsiveness, and fairness. Some elements of each model stand in conflict with elements of one or two other models. Moreover, it is not enough to claim that because public policy flows out of established "law," there is little room for public officials and managers to exercise personal discretion in choosing how to act or behave. U.S. law, particularly in emergency management, is not overwhelmingly regulatory or rule-bound, with the exception of provisions that seek to prevent corruption, the mismanagement of public funds, unfair biases, and dereliction of public duty. In many respects, America's disaster management laws and policies are deliberately intended to allow flexibility and a range of discretion in times of disaster and emergency.

The Jeffersonian Model

Thomas Jefferson, the major author of the Declaration of Independence and the nation's third president, has been generally understood to insist that the job of public managers was to try to obtain "popular and stakeholder guidance" through political consultation or public deliberation before the fact. In other words, public managers should make their decisions as the product of grassroots public consultation and the consensus of interest group recommendations. This gives a public manager's decisions greater legitimacy for public purposes.

This so-called **Jeffersonian approach** requires that public managers possess not only skill in consultation, negotiation, and communication but also deftness in probing for public understanding and consent. Good **Jeffersonian public managers** are educated **generalists** (gentlemen [or gentlewomen], as Jefferson might put it) who know and understand personal relationships that exist between agents (workers) and their assigned tasks (their duties). Jeffersonian public managers are strictly accountable to the public and to their elected overseers. As communities bear the effects of a disaster, Jeffersonian managers must use their sociotechnical skills to meet the expressed needs of those in their communities. Strong community participation would be a hallmark of emergency preparedness and planning for Jeffersonian emergency managers.

Recent thinking about emergency management indirectly stresses the importance of Jeffersonian behavior at the local government level. One scholar's explanation of what emergency managers do captures the Jeffersonian approach superbly well:

> Emergency managers are public servants who help communities prevent and prepare for disasters. They issue warnings, oversee evacuation, and communicate with responders. They also assemble statistics on damages, share disaster knowledge with citizens through the media, and work with those in charge of shelters. Emergency managers also acquire resources. They make sure that departments are working together to address response and recovery challenges. They gather information about expenses. They help determine response and recovery priorities. Their contributions are crucial to post-disaster operations.[3]

Local emergency managers must serve local executives and other overseers, but at the same time they must respond to the needs of people in their jurisdiction. Should they fail badly on either or both counts, they risk losing their appointed posts or harming their careers in civil service. In addition, they risk harming the reputation and welfare of their agencies. However, to most elected and appointed local officials who control budgets and staffing allocations, emergency management is usually a secondary concern.

Emergency managers working in government agencies are today facing a growing challenge from crowdsource fund-raising operations, many of which have expanded into post-disaster public solicitations aimed at helping an individual, family, or community recover from their misfortune. Several private firms have become highly expert in posting online the stories of selected disaster victims, in print, photos, or video (see the "Tell Me More" 2-1 box). Some of these firms charge donors a contribution fee and a processing

TELL ME MORE 2-1
GOFUNDME AND YOUCARING AS EXAMPLES

Jeffersonian emergency managers would most likely embrace the emergence of Internet-based "GoFundMe" or "YouCaring" sites often used to aid highly unfortunate or suffering disaster victims. Both organization names are registered trademarks. Their websites allow the public to make direct financial contributions to specific disaster victims or their families. Such fundraising indirectly aids emergency managers in that gaps in help offered by the government, by insurance and by other parties, may in part be filled by crowdsource fundraising. Sometimes these solicitations are made by or through nonprofit charitable organizations. GoFundMe is a private company that collects modest fees from donors who contribute money through their fund-raising campaigns. YouCaring is also a private firm that solicits voluntary contributions with a recommended fee percentage from donors. Because many charitable nonprofits have at times been able to successfully fund raise through crowdsourcing firms such as these and others, they have generally acquiesced to the fundraising competition they pose.

According to an article by Ainsley Harris in Fast Company's online newsletter posted December 8, 2017, "Today, disaster victims have an additional, more personalized option available to them: crowdfunding. In the past few months, the seven-year-old GoFundMe, which hosts campaigns for everything from college tuition to veterinary bills, has emerged as something of a leading disaster-relief organization—minus the bureaucracy. In the two months following Hurricane Harvey, GoFundMe and its sister site, CrowdRise, managed to funnel $65 million to victims and charities. (The Red Cross, by way of comparison,

authorized $190 million in direct financial assistance over roughly the same time frame.) Millions more have been raised through hundreds of GoFundMe campaigns for people affected by Hurricane Maria, and the site is home to dozens of campaigns focused on rebuilding efforts in the Caribbean and Florida after Hurricane Irma tore through in early September."[4]

"As GoFundMe's influence increases, so too does [GoFundMe CEO Rob] Solomon's interest in making campaigns go viral. 'We're focused on growing the platform in such a way that it helps campaign organizers raise the most money possible. That's what they want: the highest yield. In order to do that you have to have a Silicon Valley mind-set: the best people, the best technology, the best process.' To build 'category-defining companies in this day and age'—as Silicon Valley investors expect and GoFundMe intends to do—'you need the best,' he says. Together, they're starting to change how society responds in times of crisis. But what does it mean to entrust care for the needy to platforms that reward the most compelling, shareable content?"[5]

"During [Hurricane] Harvey, rival crowdfunding site YouCaring became a Houston favorite, thanks to the NFL Texans' defensive end J. J. Watt, who used the platform to raise more than $37 million for flood relief in just two weeks. 'We want to grow and to become the largest, most loved, and most trusted crowdfunding site in the world,' says YouCaring CEO Dan Saper. When YouCaring launched in 2011, its founders were motivated by the belief that crowdfunding sites taking 5% or more 'out of the pockets of the people who are in dire need' were 'just wrong.'"[6]

fee, both deducted from their contribution. Other soliciting firms forgo a mandatory fee and instead ask donors to voluntarily make an added contribution of some percentage to cover their costs of business.

For Jeffersonian emergency managers, their work and the success of their agencies reside in maintaining community support from senior-elected and appointed officials, the news media, and the public.[7] Local emergency managers often rely on **local emergency management committees (LEMCs)** or local stakeholder groups. An LEMC is a disaster-planning network that increases coordination among local agencies.[8] LEMCs succeed when they effectively receive and respond to community information requests, when they establish and maintain good working relationships with people of the news media, when they earn and maintain local support, and when they retain the confidence and backing of local officials.[9]

LEMCs are often composed of volunteers from their respective municipal agencies; local people who volunteer and are appointed; and those representing various local non-profit or private-sector organizations. LEMCs routinely include representatives of police, fire, and emergency services organizations, as well as local people working in hospitals, public works, nursing homes, land-use departments, schools, building inspection agencies, environmental organizations, public health agencies, and local industries, to name a few.[10] This broad inclusiveness is necessary because local emergency managers need to consult with representatives of these stakeholder organizations as they draft emergency plans and proposals. Securing consensus or support of the LEMC may help them win the broad pluralistic consent and support they need to ensure political and administrative approval of their plans and proposals. Consultation and community participation are at the heart of Jeffersonian-type local emergency management.

In the United States, some LEMCs have been established under a legal mandate, as is the case for those required by the Emergency Planning and Community Right to Know Act (also known as the Title III of the Superfund Amendments and Reauthorization Act of 1986—SARA Title III) to inform and prepare their communities for accidental releases of toxic chemicals by various local industries. However, some emergency managers have established similar organizations outside of a legal mandate—calling them disaster preparedness committees, disaster planning committees, emergency management advisory committees, and so on.[11]

Jeffersonian principles apply at the state government level as well but less so than at the local level. Successful state emergency management depends on the active and sustained interest and support of the governor. However, state emergency management is conducted more in a world of bureaucratic politics, state legislative oversight, and intergovernmental relations such that this work is often far removed from direct public interaction. In federal emergency management, detachment from the general public is even greater and public participation in emergency management at that level is very circumscribed and frequently heavily co-opted. In federal emergency management, presidential support is vital, and the collective public perception of emergency management is of great political and managerial importance.

The Hamiltonian Model

Alexander Hamilton, who was a Revolutionary War hero and the first secretary of the U.S. Treasury, believed that public managers must put emphasis on "getting results." Hamilton was an immigrant to the United States, a college graduate, a lawyer, a Revolutionary War soldier, and a trusted friend of George Washington. After the United States achieved independence, Hamilton consistently pressed for a stronger federal government under a new Constitution. In 1787, while serving as a New York delegate, he met in Philadelphia with other delegates to discuss how to fix or replace the Articles of Confederation, which were so weak that they could not keep the Union intact much longer.[12] During the meeting, Hamilton insisted that a reliable ongoing source of revenue would be crucial to developing a more powerful and resilient central government. Hamilton did not have a strong hand in writing the Constitution, but he did heavily influence its ratification by the states. Also, in collaboration with James Madison and John Jay, Hamilton wrote 51 of 85 essays under the collective title "The Federalist" (later known as *The Federalist Papers*). In the essays, he artfully explained and defended the newly drafted Constitution prior to its approval. More than two centuries after his passing in 1804, Hamilton has won the attention of modern popular culture owing to the Tony Award–winning American musical, *Hamilton*. The extremely popular and ingenious play is sung and rapped through with music and lyrics by Lin-Manuel Miranda, who also authored a book emanating from his research for the play. Miranda was inspired to take on these projects by the 2004 biography of Alexander Hamilton by historian Ron Chernow.[13]

In a **Hamiltonian approach**, public managers expect others, especially strong elected executives, to judge them by whether their efforts produce the desired results. They work under after-the-fact accountability, and their concerns are performance and evaluation under public law and policy. **Hamiltonian public managers** strive to be expert decision makers who are also students of organization. They endeavor to cultivate executive talents in formulating plans and carrying out duties. Hamiltonian public managers know the substance, tools, and processes of their work.

A Hamiltonian public manager is today in many ways a **technocrat** who possesses special knowledge and expertise most average citizens do not have. She or he works under norms of objectivity and political neutrality. The rise of a professionalized U.S. civil service system of government employment during the Progressive Era (1880–1920) and its perpetuation today demands well-educated public managers. A landmark law of this era was the Pendleton Civil Service Act of 1883. Enacted after the assassination of President Garfield by someone who believed he was unfairly denied a patronage job in government, the measure established the tradition and system of permanent federal employment based on merit rather than on political party affiliation under the spoils system.[14] Another goal of the "science of public administration" movement in the first half of the 20th century was a separation of politics and administration.[15] Civil service has inculcated this goal into the public workforce so thoroughly that today almost every public servant working in emergency management can be expected to deny that his or her government work involves politics, partisanship, or anything other than complete political neutrality. Achieving public consensus, consultation, consent, or participation, if attempted at all, is never considered "politics" by modern emergency managers.

Moreover, the complexity and vast array of public problems and governmental responsibilities demand that managers possess specialized knowledge and technical abilities. Emergency management is time and knowledge sensitive. Thus, Hamiltonian emergency managers can be trusted to act independently and with dispatch. Time pressures raised by the acute needs of emergencies and disasters often make it difficult and inefficient for

Hamiltonian managers to work exclusively through a community- or public-participation model of consultation and decision making.

Hamiltonian-type forces have, over the past 50 or more years, converted emergency management into an intellectual and scientific public service enterprise. Significant advances in hazards research coincided with, and often were made possible by, major technological innovations: the emergence of the Internet and the World Wide Web advances in high-speed computing; broadband fiber-optic and Wi-Fi communications; a massive increase in data storage; the development of personal computers, laptops, and smartphones; sophisticated computer software; civilian use of satellite telemetry of data about the atmosphere and surface of the earth; social media; geographic information system (GIS) technology: and "big data analytics" (see ahead in this chapter), to name a few.

Modern technologies automated emergency planning, response, recovery, and mitigation. The combination of GIS software and global positioning system tools, including remote sensing, empowered emergency managers to do things they could only imagine decades before.[16] Much of the field today involves hyper-accurate geo-coding and spatial mapping of real property, buildings, infrastructure, and physical features of the land itself. Geographers and automated mapping software have revolutionized many types of emergency management work.[17] Advances in communications technology and the rise of social media means that in mere seconds countless people have the capacity to use their PCs, laptops, smartphones, and tablet computers to produce and disseminate to the web pictures, video, and audio of what they are witnessing or experiencing. No longer must emergency managers rely exclusively on their in-house communications resources or the news media to provide them with a stream of disaster information.[18]

The social sciences also made major contributions to the field through the work of disaster sociologists, political scientists, economists, social geographers, demographers, and urban planners. Sociologists expanded knowledge about how people behave in disaster circumstances. They helped identify "myths" and incorrect assumptions many people hold about how individuals and groups behave before, during, and after disasters. They advanced understanding about how people receive, comprehend, and respond to warnings and alerts.[19] Political scientists explained how disaster was emerging as a new domain of public policy, flush with major political actors, interest groups, and a political process. They demonstrated how emergency management involves politics, law, and governance. This highlighted the importance of public executives, most particularly for the U.S. case, presidents, governors, and mayors. Public administration scholars honed in on the public management realm of emergency management.[20] They helped produce and compile a wide assortment of disaster case studies, as have many historians, sociologists, and geographers.

Economists took on the task of studying and measuring the economic effects of disasters. They produced a copious body of work on how insurance may or may not be used as a tool of disaster mitigation.[21] They explored emergency management and disaster preparedness in terms of public finance and public budgeting as well. Social geographers, demographers, and urban planners produced many studies that promoted practical knowledge of emergency management.[22] Owing to their contributions, new communities and residential developments could be better designed and built to be more disaster resilient and better able to prevent people from occupying unsafe areas.[23]

Emergency management advanced as a Hamiltonian-style area of expertise in other ways too. In the 1990s, the Federal Emergency Management Agency (FEMA) aided by contractors developed **Hazards U.S. (HAZUS)**, an earthquake simulation applicable and adaptable to most of the nation, and **Hazards U.S.-Multi-Hazard (HAZUS-MH)**, a powerful risk-assessment software program for analyzing potential losses from earthquake, hurricanes, and more. FEMA distributed it free of charge on the Internet, thus making a huge contribution to seismic engineering science and disaster loss estimation. HAZUS-MH also models loss from wind and flood.[24] Modern emergency managers are routinely well educated and professional. They acquire knowledge, skills, and abilities that average citizens could not be expected to have. Moreover, they are often trusted to make independent judgments and decisions drawing on their authority of expertise. This is the epitome of Hamiltonian-style emergency management.

However, emergency managers in the course of their work cannot easily behave as both a good Jeffersonian and a good Hamiltonian simultaneously. The two theories point to at least two fundamentally different ways to approach public management work. Although the two theories may be compatible in some rare circumstances, they ordinarily stand in basic counterpoise to one another. In his pioneering work of 1948, Dwight Waldo argued in his book *The Administrative State* that public administration scholarship revolved around a core set of beliefs, one of which was that "efficiency and democracy were compatible."[25] In many respects they are not. Jeffersonians press for making public administration advance democracy. Hamiltonians advocate a public administration that rests on efficiency, or in modern parlance, state-of-the-art professional expertise. Also criticized in Waldo's 1948 book were those who would advance a science of administration geared to maximizing efficiency. A "science of administration," the author said, tends to overlook and ignore the political ramifications of public administrative work.[26] Emergency managers have much to learn from these two management approaches. Sometimes they need to behave in a Jeffersonian manner and at other times they must perform as a Hamiltonian. If managers understand these theories, they may better understand their roles and thus make more informed and responsible decisions in the course of their work. They also may be better able to cope with the competing demands of their work. The key is to know when each behavior, Jeffersonian or Hamiltonian, is called for. However, today a third model of public management has emerged in U.S. emergency management.

The Jacksonian Model

Andrew Jackson[27] was a military hero of the War of 1812 and a two-term U.S. president first elected in 1828. Born in Tennessee, he was the first president whose birth state was outside the original 13 states. He is known for founding the Democratic Party (which left the then-Republican Party), and he was dubbed the "people's president" because of his respect for the common man.[28] Andrew Jackson is a highly controversial historical figure today, owing to his indifference to slavery and to his inhumane treatment of Native American tribes and peoples. It is fair to say that Jackson was a charismatic figure, but he was not as intellectual a person as Jefferson or Hamilton were.

Jackson's preferred type of government organization was one of loose federal structure with power concentrated at the state and local level. Jackson's vision of America was, indeed, a continental empire of autonomous local communities, suggesting that simple and direct governance achieves better results.[29] The Jacksonian tradition was also to promote a strong executive. Jackson distrusted Congress and believed most entrenched politicians were untrustworthy and likely to produce corruption and inefficiency. The Jacksonian model was added to the 2015 second edition of this book because the author believed that there was a chance that a Jacksonian-type figure might be elected president of the United States. The impact of such an election outcome would be profound for all realms of federal public management. Furthermore, there have been charismatic individuals who have ascended to very high politically appointed positions in the emergency management of federal, state, and local agencies, who can be characterized as Jacksonian on a variety of scales.

Jackson respected the political and moral instincts of the common man, and he advocated allowing the average citizen greater political participation.[30] He is also known for abiding by the adage, "To the victor go the spoils." Jackson sought to replace as many government workers as possible with people loyal to himself and his political party. This practice was not uncommon in the era, but it was carried to an extreme by Jackson and many of his successor presidents until the Progressive Era and 20th-century civil service reform. In sum, the **Jacksonian approach** is:

- Highly populist

- Highly partisan in governance

- Very nationalistic and, in some respects, nativist

- Pro-decentralization with qualifications

- In favor of greater local government autonomy with direct governance, some of this at the expense of state governments

- Concentrates authority in elected executives, with distrust of legislatures at all levels

- Minimizes legislative interference in public management

- Allows elected executives to appoint their political partisans and allies to many government jobs

Andrew Jackson and President Donald J. Trump have parallel, although not identical, governing styles. Today Jacksonian management typifies much of the management style of President Trump, elected in November 2016 and inaugurated on January 20, 2017. President Trump, like President Jackson, is highly partisan, a populist, and is in many ways nativist in his pronouncements. Also, like President Jackson, Trump makes heavy use of presidential appointment and dismissal powers to ensure that those who work in his administration are loyal to him. Trump does not trust federal bureaucrats and regularly trumpets this distrust in his public comments and speeches. Like Jackson, Trump is suspicious of legislatures, although he understands arguably better than Jackson the need to work cooperatively with them at times. Jackson championed the causes of the so-called "common-man," while Trump champions the causes of his supporters, many of whom are of modest means and many of whom feel marginalized by how they have been treated by their employers over time. President Trump, like Jackson, tends to distrust many governors, particularly governors in the opposition party.

Now consider Jacksonian public management. **Jacksonian public managers** are characterized as self-reliant, bold, individualistic, and entrepreneurial. Modern Jacksonian public managers may emerge from local and state patronage systems under which political supporters of elected executives win appointments to government offices. Jacksonian public managers tend to see themselves as prominent figures who assert their personality while siding unconditionally with their own beliefs.[31] They articulate what they judge to be public desires sometimes in defiance of political elites to whom they are profoundly suspicious. Individualistic and entrepreneurial, the Jacksonian public manager will take the initiative and pursue new directions in light of what they judge as government slowness or inefficiency.[32] Jacksonian emergency managers who are civil servants cannot be overtly partisan in their work. However, for those lacking civil service employment protection, achieving work successes that redound favorably for appointed overseers and elected executives is a sensible way to promote one's job security.

Jacksonian emergency managers sometimes do well as intermediaries between state and local governments and responders who must carry out the modern Incident Command System (ICS). Jacksonian emergency managers address state and local concerns while coping with friction among officials and agencies at the federal level even as they advocate for greater public participation.[33] They tend to use the force of their personalities to win cooperation and trust. Jacksonian public managers often succeed on account of their generally daring and entrepreneurial spirit, their strong belief in public participation, and their impatience with federal-level delay or inaction. Some possess political and public media savvy that serves them well in public relations. They attempt to champion public causes, even if this is in conflict with the wishes of certain bureaucratic or organizational elites.

The Jacksonian model overlaps but is not identical to the Jeffersonian model. Jackson, like Jefferson, touts the benefits of state and local government though Jackson provides for a state government role that is at least as important as the local government role. Jackson, unlike Jefferson, views government employment as requiring personal, political, partisan, and public commitment more so than education and refinement. If anything, Jackson views government workers of previous administrations as effete and indifferent to the public they were expected to serve. Jackson, unlike Jefferson or Hamilton, thinks corruption and inefficiency flow from legislative interference in administration. For Jackson, emergency managers should work to both represent common people and to aid elected or appointed executives they work under. Jackson and Hamilton both favor strong executives; however, Jackson would despise Hamiltonian federal technocrats who impose their practices and intellectual approaches on state and local officials (see Table 2-1).

In an era when government financial problems have undercut portions of emergency management capability at all levels and at a time when disasters have been perceived by many as more political and partisan than in the past, the Jacksonian model may today have a place among the Jeffersonian and Hamiltonian models of emergency management. As claimed, Jacksonian emergency managers are likely to be charismatic figures intensely loyal to their executive supervisors but who champion the cause of their agencies in a very public way. They would be well attuned to public sentiments and today probably avid users of social media.[34] They would be more politically motivated than their Hamiltonian or Jeffersonian counterparts in part because they would recognize how disaster management has become considerably more political. Top Jacksonian emergency managers, although very likely politically appointed to their posts, would be generalists, or sometimes former practitioners in the field, able to perform well under pressure.

TABLE 2-1 ■ Public Management Models				
	Character Profile	**Focused On**	**Key Constituency**	**Animating Principle**
Jeffersonian model	Educated generalists adept at tuning in to public concerns	Management at the local level	The grassroots public and their elected officials	Democratic process, guided by educated elites
Hamiltonian model	Technocrats with executive skills and understanding of the bureaucracy	Management at the state and federal level	The elected officials who hold them accountable *ex post facto*	Bureaucratic efficiency, focused work that achieves measurable goals
Jacksonian model	Strong, charismatic executives with an orientation toward the public and a practitioner background	Management that is concentrated at state and local level	The common public and in aid of appointed executives they work under	Entrepreneurial democracy, advances partisan and nationalist interests

Note: The author would like to thank Elise Frasier of SAGE CQ Press for her development of this table.

In closing, be warned that the three models have been derived from the political and management philosophy and reasoning of the three principal characters. The models are not meant to be biographical representations of these men. Moreover, presidents of modern era emergency management, from Truman to Trump, may demonstrate thinking or behavior at various times associated with one or more of these models. It is fair to say that every president has used powers of appointment to build staffs who would be loyal to them. Each president holds views and opinions on federal–state relations, nationalism, partisanship, grass roots democracy, and government administrators and administration.

THE ROLE OF THEORY IN EMERGENCY MANAGEMENT

Another way to explore how political theory may contribute to the study and application of emergency management is to consider its contributions to organization studies and theories of public management.

But before considering these theories, first think about what defines something as a **profession**. A profession is an occupation that is esoteric, complex, and discretionary. It requires theoretical knowledge, skill, and judgment that others may not possess or cannot easily comprehend. Theory-grounded knowledge is the basis of most professions and it is acquired through higher education. A profession embodies self-directing work, occupies a position of legal or political privilege, or both, that protects it from competing professions.[35] Professions sanction theory and application, something emergency managers must fully appreciate. Furthermore, a profession is regulated by a **professional body** that sets examinations of competence, acts as licensing authority for practitioners, and enforces adherence to an **ethical code**.

Regulation enforced by statute distinguishes professions from **occupations** represented by technocratic groups that aspire to collective bargaining or professional status for their members. For example, medical doctors in the United States and elsewhere work in a profession that requires them to master a vast body of complex knowledge, to train and practice the application of that knowledge, to pass licensure examinations, to agree to uphold an ethical code, and to submit to oversight by professional boards of their profession in the course of their medical practice.

To enter a profession, one needs education at the college or university level and/or training in some type of accredited and intellectually rigorous professional program. Such education and training help one achieve mastery of the necessary abstract concepts. Professions often rely on universities and colleges since people at these institutions are expert at imparting and creating abstract knowledge. Almost every profession confronts competition and encroachment by other professions, often through the special knowledge systems, abstractions, and accepted methodologies unique to the profession. Once people master a profession's abstractions, they enjoy more autonomy in the work they do. People in most professions must be suitably credentialed, and universities or colleges are often able to convey these credentials. Many people find it worthwhile to become a member of a profession, because along with greater freedom of action, they come to assume higher-paying, higher-status, and often socially or politically powerful positions.[36]

If those working in the field of emergency management want to establish their work as a profession, they have to do so by building and enriching theoretical knowledge in emergency management. Lack of theory or weak theory undercuts emergency management's authority of expertise and contributes to its marginalization: something dangerous in an era of competition among professions, including in the realm of competing homeland security-related professions or disciplines.[37] As Drabek shows, some in the broad homeland security field insist that emergency management is merely a category of "security science."[38] The longer it takes for emergency management to fully form a mature profession, the more it risks being suffused within a more aggressive management-related profession, as perhaps in national security, law enforcement, border control, immigration, transportation security, or various civil-military professions.

Why is abstraction important in a profession? **Abstract reasoning** helps produce testable propositions and knowledge that is generalizable and applicable in many contexts. **Generalized knowledge** furnishes reasoning tools or conceptual lenses. In other words, generalized knowledge has explanatory power within or across a wide variety of cases and circumstances.

Abstraction and generalized knowledge help individual researchers transcend the world of single case studies. Disaster research is rife with case studies. Many case studies provide extraordinary historical information about specific events in time.[39] However, many case studies imply that each disaster is a unique event. Abstract reasoning and theory developed from the study of many cases provides disaster researchers and managers with some degree of predictive power about future disaster events. Such broad-gauged work also advances hazard risk and vulnerability analysis. However, case studies should not be the sole engine of disaster research and EM professional development.

Abstraction enhances the value of experiential learning and case studies by enabling those with field experience to collect empirical evidence amenable to analysis by themselves and by others, most particularly those experts working to add predictive power to the theories they are developing and testing. Abstraction provides a basis for improved qualitative and quantitative examinations of social and physical phenomena; this includes disaster phenomena. The logic and rationalism supporting abstract reasoning facilitates the co-production and exchange of knowledge between people of different scientific disciplines, something essential in emergency management work.

Emergency management as a field achieves greater academic legitimacy when its core theories and concepts have currency in the physical and social sciences. Conversely, physical and social scientists are likely to contribute to the theory and conceptual growth of emergency management and disaster studies if they conclude that emergency management is a knowledge-driven, research-conducive realm.

The outcome of disputes regarding who may officially accredit emergency management education programs and who may certify people as qualified emergency managers has profoundly affected emergency management's evolution as a profession.[40] Theories and concepts are engines of knowledge creation, but in emergency management the matters of developing and testing theories and deciding what constitutes knowledge may well be determined by the authorities and interests that win accreditation and certification powers (see the "Tell Me More" 2-2 box).

TELL ME MORE 2-2
TO BE OR NOT TO BE A PROFESSION

Some tend to judge emergency management as a body of unsophisticated skill sets imparted to others through simplified, one-directional training. Worse still is that some might assume "anyone could do emergency management because the field is so ill-defined, diffuse, or based on easily learned behaviors."[41] People might then conclude that emergency managers are interchangeable functionaries who carry out simple tasks with clerk-like efficiency during episodic periods officially defined as disasters or emergencies.

This conceptualization may appeal to Jeffersonians because it rests on simplification, facilitates mobilization and participation of unskilled volunteers, and maximizes political control and grassroots political responsiveness. However, there is not much use for Jeffersonian emergency managers between disasters. Jeffersonian emergency managers have little or no role in mitigating disasters or reducing hazard vulnerabilities in any sophisticated way; and these emergency managers are neither well suited to address the causes of disaster nor likely to understand the complex, multifaceted ramifications of disasters and emergencies.

It would be reasonable to expect the recommendations of *professional* emergency managers presented to top political officials, including the president and White House officials, to be respected and taken seriously. Ideally, such recommendations would be objective, meaningful, ethical, and scientifically appropriate. They would be prepared by those with acknowledged EM expertise (possessing extensive education, training, and experience). If political officials do not consider emergency managers as part of a specialized, knowledge-based profession, or if they consider emergency management skill

(Continued)

(Continued)

sets interchangeable or indistinguishable from that of other professions, those political officials might conclude that their own judgments about disasters and emergencies are just as valid as those of their emergency managers.[42] In other words, emergency managers would lack an "authority of expertise," and (generalist) emergency managers might then be supplanted by political appointees who have little or no emergency management training or experience. For example, President Obama assigned federal lead agency status in Superstorm Sandy disaster recovery to officials of the U.S. Department of Housing and Urban Development (HUD) rather than to DHS-FEMA, much to the chagrin of FEMA officials.

DECISION MODELS FROM POLITICAL SCIENTIST GRAHAM ALLISON

The political scientist Graham Allison used the Cuban missile crisis as a case example to demonstrate that there were differing or alternative explanations for political events.[43] Much of the logic behind Allison's groundbreaking thesis is that government decision making can be differentiated by highest level central authority, by the second-level interactions of very senior federal department officials, or by third-level lower ranking officials empowered to act. Allison's work had a dramatic effect in clarifying and differentiating a bureaucratic politics conceptualization (the second level). Recently, Allison published *Destined for War: Can America and China Escape Thucydides's Trap?*[44] Much of the argument in that book adapts his Cuban missile crisis models to the current state of affairs between the United States and China.

Each of Allison's models can be adapted to help explain presidential decisions to declare disasters in a different way. *First*, the **rational actor model** holds that the president decides largely on his or her own, as a unitary actor, on behalf of the entire federal government. It also assumes that individual rationality surrounds that decision making. The rational actor model assumes that each president, or national leader in the case of other nations, decides largely on his or her own what their respective national government should do. Consider, in the case of U.S.

disaster law and policy, the president has authority to approve or reject a governor's request for a presidential declaration of major disaster or emergency. The president is free to consider any factors or conditions involved and can, under law, decide which FEMA programs will apply under the declarations they issue.

Second, under Allison's **bureaucratic politics model,** decisions at the presidential level are a product of the outcome of negotiations between senior political appointees (various agency heads, cabinet-level secretaries, and so forth) and elected executives (governors, mayors, and the like). Allison refers to these players as *elites*. Their bargaining and negotiation activities among themselves may or may not culminate in convincing the president (or national leader) to make a decision. In rare cases, the chief executive, under this concept, may delegate authority to decide to a group of these elites. In the disaster policy realm, the bureaucratic politics model posits that whether or not a president issues a declaration of major disaster or emergency is largely based on the recommendations of a group consensus of these major political actors. Certainly, in asking, a governor presses the president to approve the governor's request by convincing the president of the worthiness of his or her request. Presidents might also be advised by top FEMA and DHS officials, executive branch groups, by their White House staffs, by their confidants, as well as by lawmakers.

Third, and alternatively, Allison's **organizational process model** assumes that presidential decisions are intentionally left to lower ranking officials, perhaps those working a problem in the field. In the organizational process model the executive has either largely delegated decision authority to someone else or rubber-stamps the official recommendation of his or her functionaries. Again, referring to the example of a president's handling of a governor's request for a disaster or emergency declaration, under this model, the president would essentially defer to FEMA's recommendation on approval or denial as a routine administrative determination. In this case, a stovepipe-connected assortment of federal, state, and local disaster management officials would be involved, with DHS-FEMA entrusted to make the final decision. The organizational process model contends that emergency management professionals compile disaster damage information and then use it to review gubernatorial requests for declarations (similarly, the governor's request itself would be assumed the product of state emergency management agency activity).

In summary and staying with disaster policy, one would expect presidents to decide and act on very major, even catastrophic, disasters or emergencies under the rational actor model, at least in the acute stage. Allison and others suggest that all too often outside observers assume that every chief executive decision is made under rational actor assumptions (as in the political realism school).[45] He maintains that this is not always the case and that his two alternative models may better explain how a decision or decisions were made.

Because disasters or emergencies sometimes pose unusual, complex, multifaceted, or unanticipated political and management problems, it is reasonable to assume that chief executives sometimes rely on the bureaucratic model type of decision making.

Under the bureaucratic politics model, it is often assumed that public officials seek to protect or promote their own agency's special interests (as they compete with other agencies).

This may be a major motivating factor in shaping the timing and the content of their decisions. "Bureaucratic politics are conducted quietly, behind the scenes, in skillful ways, with strategic reversals possible, caution, and contentment with sharing credit for good results. A person needs these attributes in order to exhibit good statecraft."[46] The statecraft of political administration is how effectively people fulfill the obligations of the office they hold and how much they advance the welfare of the entire polity and state from the official position they hold.[47] Statecraft is defined as "using and risking political power through action."[48] It is political leadership multiplied by bureaucratic power.

In other words, heads of government departments, divisions, programs, or offices continually strive to maximize their budgets and authorized workforce, as well as protect or extend their operating autonomy and discretion in decision making in the area of their assigned responsibilities. Often this can be most readily accomplished by lobbying for an expansion of their unit's responsibilities. So, the policies and policy recommendations generated in the executive branch of government and passed on to the chief executive (and often the legislature) are often the by-product of bureaucratic turf wars, interoffice competition, and expedient compromises between administrative chieftains rather than products of reasoned analysis about how to most effectively and efficiently carry out the law and policy commitments of the elected chief executive so as to serve the public interest.

Finally, organizational process model has its own place. In disaster policy, very routine disasters and emergencies (seasonal flooding, winter storms, metropolitan power outages, minor earthquakes in seismically active zones, and the like) that are neither mega-disasters nor catastrophic and that involve few political costs or benefits for a president might encourage the chief executive to simply rely on the organizational process model decision. He or she would trust lower-level officials to make the routine decisions necessary to address and resolve the problems posed.

Public Management Theory

Remember, the essence of modern emergency management is "management." More precisely, it is "management" that is based on contemporary principles of organization theory and administration. The ethos of U.S. emergency management in a nutshell is:

- Emphasis on grassroots local emergency management in emergencies and disasters with overhead governments providing help but not necessarily taking command or control of local emergency response and recovery operations

- Emphasis on the four-phased cycle of emergency management: mitigation, preparedness (and prevention), response, and recovery (short- and long-term) with acknowledgment that the phases may overlap and that recovery needs fulfillment should be linked to mitigation (so the cycle has a feedback loop)

- Emphasis on contracting out services and eschewing direct delivery of services where possible because most public emergency management agencies are limited in what their workers can do for disaster victims directly

- Emphasis on best practices, after-action reports, and continual reform

- Emphasis on working under conditions of flexible regulation with a high tolerance for risk taking and adaptation (note: U.S. disaster management embodies modest regulation; most regulation stems from rules and conditions specified in federal grants to state and local governments; an exception is the case of local land-use, zoning, and building regulation, all heavily regulated and usually local government responsibilities)

- Emphasis on leadership that is entrepreneurial and adept at drawing in free or inexpensive help through co-production (public agency reliance on unpaid temporary volunteers from the public who augment the government workforce) efforts and public–private partnerships

- Emphasis on facilitating change and creating public value, most particularly through disaster mitigation and preparedness activity;[49] best-practices approaches often create public value and facilitate reform or change.

The Best Practices Approach

At the intersection of public management and bureaucratic politics, we find what is referred to as best practices. The **best-practices approach** is a method of producing knowledge by observing (or recounting) field experience and then creating applicable principles. This is often described as "practice as the basis for scholarship," not scholarship as the basis for practice, and reflective practitioners are needed to make the best-practices approach work.[50] Here, public management study becomes a kind of art form. The practitioner draws the picture for the observer. James Lee Witt, Admiral Thad Allen, David Paulison,[51] and Craig Fugate,[52] all former or current FEMA leaders, stand as good examples of people who advocate best-practice knowledge and who appreciate emergency management reflective practitioners.[53] Reflexive practitioners serve at least two purposes. First, by writing and publishing information about their experiences in a constructive and even self-critical way, they point the way for other practitioners to learn and adapt. They facilitate insider learning and reforms so as to help emergency managers avoid repeating mistakes they and others have made in the past. Second, by publishing works for broader audiences outside of the nexus of their emergency management realm, reflexive practitioners help add to emergency management scholarship, research, and teaching. This serves instructors, researchers, and students within schools and institutions of higher learning. Moreover, by writing for public audiences, reflexive practitioners promote public education about emergency management, sometimes inspiring people to begin careers in the field.

Another best-practices approach is to create knowledge based on empirical validations of useful propositions derived from models—in other words, building practice wisdom as a social scientific approach to scholarship and as a basis for professional practice. This is the **applied heuristics approach**. Such **analytical approaches** help public managers deal with a messy reality. These approaches and models allow for experimentation, trial, and error; they were the early basis of policy analysis. For public managers, heuristics are verbal explanatory sketches or conceptual frameworks, which help them to produce adequate explanations for puzzling things. Heuristics embody propositions subject to confirmation or disconfirmation; in other words, one can test the usefulness of the proposition. For example, one can test the proposition that increased federal funding to a state's terrorism preparedness program will improve its terrorism response capability. This can be measured in part by evaluating the performance of state emergency managers via unannounced terrorism drills and exercises.[54]

Some studies alleged to represent best practices in public management have been criticized because they are often not good guides to scholarship, teaching, or practice. However, some open-minded studies of cases, especially those showing how public executives shape the institutional frameworks for policymaking and execution, have been praised for their contributions to theory knowledge.[55] Government executives who share their experiences help influence public policy in both the short and long runs. Best practice research flows in part from public executive leadership, which draws from classic works on executive leadership inspired by practice.

One recent example of DHS use of the best practices approach is its publication, *Best Practices for Incorporating Social Media into Exercises*, Social Media Working Group for Emergency Services and Disaster Management and DHS Science and Technology First Responders Group.[56] The best practices approach has carried through in preparedness training evident from FEMA's efforts to train citizens through forming a Community Emergency Response Team (CERT). This program educates people about disaster preparedness by training them in response skills that include fire safety, light search and rescue, team organization, and disaster medical operations. This training is designed to help local volunteers in the community assist in their neighborhood or workplace in the event that professional responders are not immediately available to help. CERTs are especially helpful in meeting the demand for supporting emergency services personnel following a disaster where the extenuating factors such as numerous victims, communication failures, and road blockages can impede and overwhelm normal resources.[57]

The author's late youngest brother was for many years a commercial airline pilot. At the peak of his career, he flew jumbo passenger jets from American cities to European cities and return. He would occasionally show me or mail me certain NOTAMs, short for "Notices to

Airmen" (men and women), which were regularly issued to the aviation community by the Federal Aviation Administration. A NOTAM is a notice filed with an aviation authority to alert aircraft pilots of potential hazards along a flight route or at a location that could affect the safety of the flight.[58] Aviation is an industry composed of high-reliability organizations in which pilots are expected to maintain safety (under risk management), proficiency, preparedness, training, licensure, and regular simulation testing (you fail, you're fired). NOTAMs are a great example of the best practices approach. Many NOTAMs are reported by pilots seeking to help other pilots. Mistakes, when they occur, should not be repeated under a forthright NOTAM system. Many NOTAMs involve counter-intuitive decision outcomes or combinations of hazards likely to jeopardize the life and welfare of aviators and their passengers. The NOTAM system inheres in emergency management best practices. NOTAM-like practices should not be judged as simply preparedness measures; they embody mitigation, response, and, in many respects, recovery features.

Analytical Approaches and Social Constructivism

Within subfields of various physical and social scientific disciplines, there is an incredible range of analytical approaches to the study of disaster (e.g., meteorology, climate science, seismology, volcanology, sociology, policy studies, economics, physical geography, epidemiology, emergency medicine, engineering). Those advancing the analytical approach to the study of disaster have benefited from advances in high-powered computing and the development of sophisticated software programs (computer-based data analysis, GIS, HAZUS, and others).[59] Emergency managers and students of emergency management would be wise to embrace analytic approaches and tools to perform their work more effectively and to advance disaster study and research.

However, the generalization sought in analytical approaches overlooks the assumption, "Reality is a social construction rather than an objective construct that is the same for all observers."[60] Those following **social constructivism** might argue that it is the actions and persuasiveness of people, perhaps amplified through mass communications, that defines what is or is not a disaster. In other words, the "reality" of some disaster phenomenon may be more an issue of how people have conceived of and conveyed the "idea" that a disaster has occurred. Consider the following claim: "Whether an event constitutes a disaster, how probable and how damaging disasters are, and what can be done to reduce their impacts, are socially produced through organized claims-making activities."[61]

Some social constructivist scholars working in the disciplines of sociology or political philosophy maintain that organizations (including government organizations) are systems of socially constructed and cognitively ordered meanings.[62] This author once heard a respected and brilliant economics professor glibly inquire, "So FEMA makes disasters?" What he was inferring was that the mere fact that the government has established FEMA, presumably composed of disaster management experts, suggests that those experts will look for opportunities to apply their skills and expertise. As FEMA officials they would have great incentive to find more and more phenomena they could persuade the president to declare as disasters or emergencies so their agency could prove its worth, serve public needs, and win more authority and larger budgets.

In contrast, empiricism is the collection of information about the physical and social "real" (existential) world, which is so essential to analytical approaches. Empirical research and the social constructivist approach often clash. This is because social constructivists are, at least until recently, likely to discount empirical information and scientific "facts" as mere products of individual or group constructions of social "reality" and personal belief systems. "A constructivist theory of social problems explains problems and policy issues by focusing on people's actions rather than on the putative 'conditions' that are the object of those actions."[63] "Conditions" are alleged to exist and to have harmful qualities owing to what issue advocates and claims makers say and do. Shanahan et al. see the Narrative Policy Framework (discussed below), and discuss a "bridge" between empirical research employing scientific methods and a social construct of reality. They maintain that "narratives both social construct reality and can be measured empirically."[64]

For example, television news reporters disclose certain important human needs that they allege or infer must be addressed by government. Also, political actors representing what they perceive to be the needs of various individual people or aggregations of people and interests issue clarion calls for action. Some of these people may be elected government officials, some may be officials representing an interest group, and some may be independent social advocates. Social media have added yet another mammoth layer of perceivers, constructivists, and claims makers. The concern here is how issue advocates and claims makers define problems and their policy solutions and how they are able to persuade others to take their concerns seriously, even to the point of getting them to act on those problems.

Today, constructivist theory is widely popular in many academic realms, including disaster sociology[65] and political study.[66] Social constructivist research has an important place in the intellectual sphere of emergency management.[67] There is a growing body of scholarship, international in scope and predicated on social constructions of the disaster phenomenon. Much of it is insightful, and much of it is relevant to political officials and their advisers. Political officials need to understand how people comprehend safety and danger, how people formulate judgments of risk and vulnerability, and how people gauge the effectiveness of disaster management (particularly given their role in a disaster: disaster victim, unaffected observer, emergency responder, and so forth).

One excellent work that employs considerable social constructivist reasoning is *The Politics of Crisis Management*, authored by four professors of political science and/or government. Crisis management in the realm of public leadership can be examined artfully in social constructivist terms, as done in *The Politics of Crisis Management*.[68] The book provides almost a handbook guide for leaders. It makes a good case that crisis management is an emerging profession in its own right.[69] Topics such as "meaning making," "sense making," "framing contests," and others are insightfully employed in examining actual crises leaders have had to manage. Although largely written for a European audience and context, the work is appropriate for U.S. leaders, as well as for leaders of democratic nations anywhere.

Another contribution comes in the form of "The Narrative Policy Framework" (NPF), "which seeks to answer questions about the role of policy narratives in the policy process."[70] Narratives themselves consist of setting, characters, plot, and moral of the story.[71] Under the NPF, there must be at least one character and some policy referent. Important in this approach is that policy narratives often surface in policy debates in which two or more narratives clash or compete. Many narratives appear in the news media, in social media, and in the expressed claims and arguments of stakeholders. The NPF considers the policy narratives (story lines and expressed beliefs) that are communicated by actors within specific policy subsystems and does so "not to uncover" the veracity of any specific policy narrative but to capture policy realities, "or what exists in the world as presented by people."[72] The NPF can work on both grand and meso-level scales. NPF has many features, among them it examines narratives in empirical terms. Essentially the goal of NPF is to answer the question, "Do narratives play an important role in the policy process?"[73] In simple terms, NPF assumes that policy is made or shaped or left unchanged as the outcome of a battle (policy debate) of ideas expressed as stories. Shanahan et al. present the origins of NPF, define the NPF, review the works of scholars who have used it in their research, and demonstrate how policy narratives can be studied empirically. Although he does not claim to be using the NPF in his 2006 book, Thomas A. Birkland's highly regarded *Lessons of Disaster: Policy Change after Catastrophic Events* employs many elements of the NPF approach.[74] He asks, how do disaster policymakers learn? He considers public opinion, often expressed in a narrative form.

Social constructivism and its variants, however, do not represent the only intellectual paradigm or theory tool through which to conduct disaster research. Several alternative theories and paradigms—such as scientific rationalism,[75] empirical study, management theories, institutional studies, public policy analysis, and some interdisciplinary theories that link the physical and social sciences—also offer instrumental and application usefulness for emergency managers.

Network Theory

The modern world of organization, including the world of government public organizations, is increasingly built and maintained through networked intelligence. **Network theory** is a field of computer science and network sciences. It is often a method used to characterize and model complex networks. Network theory has also been applied to logistic networks, gene regularity networks, metabolic networks, the World Wide Web, ecological networks, epistemic communities,[76] and social networks. It is applied in many disciplines, including sociology, biology, computer science, business, economics, particle physics, and operations research.[77]

The use of networked information systems is critical in modern emergency management. As organization theorist Gareth Morgan observes, "Information systems that can be accessed from multiple points of view create a potential for individuals throughout an enterprise, even those in remote locations, to become full participants in an evolving system of organizational memory and intelligence."[78] Networking through organizational information systems creates the possibility of achieving a shared organizational mind.[79] Today cloud-computing services, computer-sharing software, screen-sharing software, video conferencing, Skype, and file sharing, to name a few, have allowed people in many organizations to achieve a shared organizational mind.

Extensive "between disaster" emergency management work involves preparedness activities including planning, simulations, and exercises. Facilitated by the Internet and the World Wide Web, government emergency managers have established immensely rich, and sometimes unnecessarily complicated, emergency plans and preparedness tools devised through elaborate networked intelligence exchanges among themselves and with others, including nongovernmental nonprofit and private-sector partners and to a lesser degree the general public. Networked intelligence was championed very much by advocates of the New Public Management of the 1990s.

Networked intelligence in disaster management is both a blessing and a curse. It makes needs more obvious and does so quickly, it facilitates interorganizational coordination, it helps mobilize aid providers in a more coordinated and sensible fashion, and it expands the pool of participants in ways that may well serve the needs of disaster-stricken citizens and subnational governments. Conversely, networked intelligence is extremely difficult for organizational leaders to manage. Elected government executives and lawmakers are often hard-pressed to hold networked organizations and people accountable for failures. Networked organizations rely on technical resources (e.g., uninterrupted electricity flows, undamaged telecommunications infrastructure or infrastructure that can sustain colossal usage demands in emergencies, durable software, interoperability) that may not always be available when needed. Moreover, disaster victims may be unable to access the Internet for long periods or they may lack the ability to use modern computer-based information technologies required to make application for help.

Yet sometimes the failure of one communications technology may be addressed with another one. After the Moore, Oklahoma, tornado disaster in May 2013, FEMA dispatched to the damage zone a set of trained volunteers, as a Disaster Survivor Assistance Team, equipped with tablet computers. These people aided the tornado damage victims they encountered by helping them make online application for aid using prestored forms that, once completed, could be e-mailed immediately to the appropriate government disaster assistance offices. "FEMA officials are registering individuals on site with iPads."[80]

Consider this claim: "From geotagging photos to taking notes, purpose-built tablet computers are paving the way for emergency managers to work faster, effectively, and more safely. Here are twelve ways that . . . tablets are changing the game."[81]

1. *Digital documents.* With technology quickly replacing paper-based systems of record-keeping, it may be necessary to skip paper records entirely. Tablets can make it easier to write reports and update files, no transcription necessary.

2. *Updated maps.* This can be necessary after storms, fires, or natural disasters. Geotagged photos and map-marking can make it easy to locate where damage has occurred.

3. *Real-time weather updates.* Weather tracking can be necessary, especially for emergency management personnel. Whether it's tracking winds during a wildfire, giving updates on a storm, or mapping flooding, a reliable source of information can be crucial.

4. *Monitored social media.* Keeping official accounts updated, communicating with coworkers, and assessing public reaction can be done anywhere from the palm of your hands.

5. *Information backlogs.* Carry and open important files, documents, photos, and videos with ease, so they can be accessed at any time, no matter the situation.

6. *Durability.* Where laptops and smartphones are in grave danger when it comes to drops, falls, and water damage, rugged tablets are designed to take the heat.

7. *Improved communication.* With 4G LTE connectivity, tablets can help people keep in touch with one another, no matter where they are in the world. Warning systems, emergency calls, and rapid-fire messaging has never been easier.

8. *Productivity.* With an on-hand device, there doesn't have to be any wasted time. Printing maps, filing reports, and walking back to desktop computers to send emails is a thing of the past.

9. *Long-term investment benefits.* [Sturdy], purpose-built tablets are designed to last, both technologically and physically. Where they can handle physical stresses with ease, they are also protected against obsolescence; reliably operating for many years.

10. *Versatility.* Whether the tablet is being mounted in a car, carried in-hand, put in a bag, or being passed around a group, their slate-design and lightweight build makes them perfect for any situation.[82]

For better or worse, networked intelligence will be a dominant feature of public administrative organizations for many years to come.

Principal-Agent Theory

Principal-agent theory assumes that managers function in an environment in which they cannot observe whether their agents in fact carried out the instructions they issued as principals. In addition, it assumes that agents hide information from principals and that agents may use the information to act in ways contrary to what principals intended. Principal-agent theory gives rise to performance-based government contracting studies.

For example, the study and use of principal-agent theory would not only help government emergency managers better understand the realm of contracting and grants management but would also press elected and appointed officials to work jointly toward achieving legal and policy goals. Thus, they would better be able to oversee and steer contractors to do what they are expected to do. Principal-agent theory may also help them oversee and influence the behavior of their grantees working in state and local emergency management organizations.

Principal-agent theory helps merge normative noneconomic concerns with structured economic analysis. This approach involves refining situational logic.[83] Principal-agent theory seems quite appropriate in the world of emergency management.[84] Government emergency managers work in a universe of federal, state, local, and private-sector agencies.[85] An immense amount of government emergency management work is contract management, involving private contractors and nonprofit organizations. In a sense, government officials are principals who retain agents, in this case contractors, who in turn carry out various duties, functions, and tasks. Information flows between agents and principals. This information is used by policymakers and government officials and influences their decisions in matters of public spending, budgeting, planning, program administration, and management in general. Emergency manager principals might be well served by using normative factors (i.e., Was the public happy with the job the contractor performed? How quickly was work completed and how satisfied were clients or customers with the products and services they received from the contractor?). They may use structured economic analysis to help ensure that contractor agents addressing disaster-related needs are better guided toward achieving the goals emergency manager principals are legally and officially obligated to meet.

"Working the seams" is part of principal-agent theory. Public managers must know how to work the edges of administrative-legislative interaction, intergovernmental relations, agencies, and interest groups.[86] Seams are gray zones. They are areas in which there is legal and administrative flexibility. Disasters and emergencies often require that emergency managers behave adaptively, bend or ignore rules that confound or delay their work and establish new and often unusual modes of interaction with people and organizations they do not often encounter in normal periods. They need technical and analytical knowledge to do this. Their world is composed of agents, seams, and a technical core.

Intergovernmental Relations Theory

Three types of authority models have helped classify U.S. intergovernmental relations. They are the coordinate-authority, overlapping-authority, and inclusive-authority models.[87]

The **coordinate-authority model** assumes a sharp and distinct boundary between separate national and state governments. National and state governments appear to operate independently and autonomously, and they are linked only tangentially. Moreover, in the coordinate-authority model, local governments are somewhat dependent on their respective state governments.[88] Before 1950, intergovernmental public management in the United States generally conformed to the coordinate-authority model of **federalism** and **dual federalism**. The *Stanford Encyclopedia of Philosophy* defines *federalism* in the following way:

> Federalism is the theory or advocacy of federal political orders, where final authority is divided between sub-units and a center. Unlike a unitary state [system], [in a federal system] sovereignty is constitutionally split between at least two territorial levels so that units at each level have final authority and can act independently of the others in some area. Citizens thus have political obligations to two authorities. The allocation of authority between the sub-unit and center may vary, typically the center has powers regarding defense and foreign policy, but sub-units may also have international roles. The sub-units may also participate in central decision-making bodies.[89]

The period from 1789 to 1901 has been called the "era of dual federalism," which is "characterized as an era during which there was little collaboration between the national and state governments." However, in the period from 1865 to 1901, the national government began to move into several policy areas that had previously been the purview of the states.[90]

In the coordinate-authority model, local governments often handled major disasters and emergencies on their own with only intermittent state government help and with very little federal help. When local governments could not cope, they sought state government help, usually petitioning the governor or state legislature. State governments coped with disasters and emergencies that largely affected state government assets, infrastructure, and interests. U.S. policy has long assigned the responsibility for disaster management to the government jurisdiction(s) that experienced the disaster. As Clinton-era FEMA director James Lee Witt used to say, "All disasters are local."[91] The responsibility for public safety is a local government role under American federalism.

In the **overlapping-authority model**, areas of autonomy or single-jurisdiction independence and full discretion are small. Power and influence for any one jurisdiction is substantially limited and authority patterns involve heavy bargaining.[92] As Chapter 3 will show, major federal disaster laws passed in 1950 significantly changed intergovernmental authority relationships in major ways. This meant that from 1950 to about 2003, U.S. disaster management could be categorized as an overlapping-authority model. In the overlapping-authority model, substantial areas of governmental operations involve national, state, and local governments simultaneously.

Consequently, a new set of relationships emerged under the disaster declaration process. If a disaster or emergency exceeded the response and recovery capacity of the local government, the local government executive officer (mayor, city manager, county executive, or the like) and the city or county council declared a "local disaster." This was often followed by a local request for state and federal assistance. The governor may respond to the request by issuing a state declaration of disaster or emergency. Once the governor declares a state of emergency, the local government may then receive personnel, goods, services, and funding from the state to deal with the disaster. If the governor believes that the disaster may overwhelm the capacity of the state to manage the emergency effectively, the governor then sends the president a request for a presidential declaration of major disaster or emergency. A presidential declaration of major disaster mobilizes a multidepartmental, multiprogram federal response conducted in coordination with state and local officials and agencies.

This overlapping, layered approach to local, state, and federal relations is consistent with the overlapping-authority model of intergovernmental relations. In this model, no one level of government is dominant, and no level intervenes in the affairs of another without the permission of that government.

The era of overlapping authority in U.S. disaster policy came to an abrupt end after the 9/11 terrorist attacks on the United States. The legal manifestation of this change came in the enactment of the Homeland Security Act of 2002, the establishment of the U.S. Department of Homeland Security (DHS) in early 2003, and a succession of G. W. Bush administration presidential homeland security directives.

These changes—including the creation of a National Response Plan and later National Response Framework (NRF) and National Incident Management System (NIMS)—brought on an era of inclusive authority. Under the **inclusive-authority model** of intergovernmental relations, each level of government has a diminishing proportion of responsibilities, from the national to the state to the local government level.[93] Under the inclusive-authority model the federal government plays a key coordinating role as the states and federal government cooperate and interact in certain critical areas. The inclusive-authority model assumes the sharing of power and responsibility, with the various participants working toward shared goals.[94] The authority model also conveys the essential hierarchical nature of authority. In some respects, most particularly in state-sponsored or foreign agent terrorism, the homeland security paradigm has made states and localities "mere minions of the national government." The role of the state as the "service delivery arm" continues as it has since 1950. However, the federal government provides "its vast resources" as a new backstop for state and local governments.

In the inclusive-authority eras of presidents George W. Bush and Barack Obama, homeland security presidential directives, several new federal laws, and a battery of new federal grant programs were introduced. Collectively, these measures dictated to local governments the necessary steps they were expected to take in emergency management. These measures placed terrorism preparedness above preparedness for all other types of disaster agents. The effect of these reforms was to move both emergency management and homeland security toward "nation-centered" federal dominance within an inclusive-authority model. DHS authorities told states and localities that they would be heavily consulted and welcomed "partners." Yet the profusion of "top-down" directives and the vast sums of federal money used to steer states and localities in various directions have left little space for state codetermination and even less local freedom of action.[95] In the Barack Obama era, the inclusive-authority model remains paramount, although tempered by extensive efforts to include state and local interests in formulating disaster mitigation and disaster recovery plans and projects for emergency management. As in the previous administration, federal pre- and post-conditional disaster assistance has a major impact on how state and local government participates. In the era of President Donald J. Trump, national security and anti-terrorism remain twin priorities. However, W. Brock Long, President Trump's FEMA administrator at the time of this writing, has pressed for states and local governments to become more self-reliant in matters of smaller scale disasters and emergencies. After several presidentially declared mega-disasters, a few state governments have been entrusted with more authority to dispense federal post-disaster funds under FEMA programs as either co-administrators or as parties working under delegated federal authority. In some respects, U.S. disaster policy has begun moving gradually away from the inclusive-authority model and back toward the overlapping-authority model. How far this will progress depends on several factors:

- Whether federal budgetary constraints and an improving national economy beneficial to state and local fiscal health weans the states and localities away from their dependence on federal post-disaster largesse

- Whether the major national disaster planning frameworks will allow sufficient flexibility for states and localities to customize their respective disaster management systems to best suit their needs, less encumbered by a one-size-fits-all imposition of uniformity by the federal government

- Whether state and local disaster management capacity, combined with appropriate public–private partnerships (popular with President Trump), improve to the point that DHS-FEMA is encouraged to loosen its grant condition reins

THEORY IN DISASTER RECOVERY[96]

Disasters are often outside the realm of whatever defines "normalcy" (itself a controversial subject) and disasters are experienced differently by different individual people, be they as individuals, in families or groups (be they social, political, or economic in nature), or as formal elected or administrative officials of some type. Disasters transpire in several different environments or contexts: natural, personal, familial, community/social, political/governmental, economic, cultural, ecological, geographical, physical/structural, news/communication, and more. It is not possible to examine all of these environments here, but the political and governmental realms represent a start and the problem of **disaster recovery** is a worthy subject.

There are many theoretical approaches from which to examine disaster recovery. However, it is both difficult and controversial to set forth common "principles" of disaster recovery, elucidate ways to measure recovery and the course it takes, and chart ways to model future recovery. However, it is possible to build theories that help those on the "public management and public policy side" of the disaster phenomena.

After many months of preparation, in 2010, FEMA, in consultation with a great many state and local stakeholder groups, established a **National Disaster Recovery Framework (NDRF)** (see the "Tell Me More" 2-3 box).[97] The NDRF promotes management and consultation schemes by which FEMA and its stakeholders can plan disaster recovery long before disasters occur. Officials leading this effort emphasized consultation with the public and with many public and private groups. The aim was to help people in local governments, communities, and neighborhoods across the nation facilitate, improve, and refine pre-disaster recovery planning. This work has the potential to produce conceptual tools, variables, and datasets that may advance broad development and application of disaster recovery theory. Such theory creation may help emergency managers and disaster researchers better measure, model, and generalize about how local people as individuals or as part of **communities of interest (COI)** plan and make possible their disaster recovery.

A community of interest is a gathering of people assembled around a topic of common interest. Its members take part in the community to exchange information, to obtain answers to personal questions or problems, to improve their understanding of a subject, to share common passions, or to play. Their synergy cannot be assimilated into that of a formal group motivated by a common goal. Communities of interest have a variable lifespan. Some appear and disappear soon after their creation, while others thrive for years. Often, they divide into smaller communities.[98]

Theory tools usable in disaster recovery are in high demand for several reasons. First, as mentioned, they help transcend the case study realm by positing that all disasters are "not unique." In other words, disasters and disaster recovery often embody certain identifiable commonalities. If these commonalities are understood such that generalizations are possible, a worthwhile disaster recovery tool may be forged that will allow for improved disaster recovery planning and ultimately implementation. Second, theories that offer broad explanatory power often facilitate knowledge creation and application that is less ethnocentric or single-nation centered and more international, culturally sensitive and diverse, and teachable. Third, they provide a bridge for the healthy interchange of academic knowledge and practice knowledge.

Exploring Disaster Recovery in Theory Terms

Is disaster recovery an "end state" or a "dynamic"? For democratic nations, disaster recovery should be considered a dynamic which can succeed in varying degrees or fail in varying degrees. It does so in empirically measurable terms as well as in terms of media, public, and/or political opinion. The notion of an "end state" for disaster recovery is arbitrary because to identify a fixed "end state" is to form individual value judgments in subjective ways about a condition of finality. Also, governments and sub-governments of almost every nation, democratic or otherwise, are constantly undergoing change, sometimes gradually and subtly or other times comprehensively and dramatically.

TELL ME MORE 2-3
NATIONAL DISASTER RECOVERY FRAMEWORK

According to FEMA, the NDRF[99] is a guide that enables effective recovery support to disaster-impacted states, tribes, and territorial and local jurisdictions. It provides a flexible structure that allows disaster recovery managers to operate in a unified and collaborative manner. It also focuses on how best to restore, redevelop, and revitalize the health, social, economic, natural, and environmental fabric of disaster-stricken communities, cumulatively making the nation more disaster resilient.

The NDRF fulfills a portion of President Obama's 2011 Presidential Policy Directive 8 (PPD-8): National Preparedness, which directs FEMA to work with interagency partners to publish a recovery framework. The framework puts various sets of agency partners to work on building core recovery capabilities through setting forth operational plans that seek to improve the National Preparedness System. As PPD-8 requires, the NDRF expects participants to work toward a shared understanding and a common, integrated perspective across all mission areas—prevention, protection, mitigation, response, and recovery. The aim is to achieve unity of effort and to make the most effective use of the nation's limited resources. The NDRF is also the product of efforts to meet requirements of the Post-Katrina Emergency Management Reform Act (PKEMRA) of 2006, which called for FEMA to develop a National Disaster Recovery Strategy.[100] The NDRF incorporates the following:

- Core recovery *principles*

- *Roles* and *responsibilities* of recovery coordinators and other stakeholders

- A *coordinating structure* that facilitates communication and collaboration among all stakeholders

- Guidance for pre- and post-disaster recovery *planning*

- The overall *process* by which

communities can capitalize on opportunities to rebuild stronger, smarter, and safer[101]

The NDRF created three positions to provide focal points for incorporating recovery considerations into the decision-making process. People in these posts monitor the need for adjustments in assistance whenever necessary and feasible during the recovery process. Those positions are:

- Federal Disaster Recovery Coordinator (FDRC)

- State or Tribal Disaster Recovery Coordinator (SDRC or TDRC)

- Local Disaster Recovery Manager (LDRM)

People holding these new positions will have flexibility, and they will be assigned to some of the hardest hit areas, so that as a community and a team, the federal government and its partners can ensure a speedy and smooth disaster and emergency recovery process.

FEMA calls the NDRF a conceptual guide designed to promote coordination and recovery planning at all levels of government "before a disaster transpires." It defines how six federal agencies will work together (see below), following a disaster, to best meet the needs of states, local and tribal governments and communities, and individuals during their respective recoveries. People using the framework establish coordination structures, define leadership roles and responsibilities, and endeavor to guide coordination and recovery planning across all levels of government before a disaster occurs. It aims for better use of existing resources; faster and trouble-free application for government assistance; local consensus about how, what, and where a community will rebuild after a future disaster; and pre-disaster consultation with all communities of interest and stakeholders.

(Continued)

(Continued)

Recovery Support Functions

NDRF includes six Recovery Support Functions (RSFs) that are led by designated federal coordinating agencies. The RSFs comprise the coordinating structure for key functional areas of assistance. Their purpose is to help support local governments by aiding in problem solving; improving access to resources; and fostering coordination among state and federal agencies, nongovernmental partners, and stakeholders. The RSFs and respective six designated federal coordinating agencies are:

- Community planning and capacity building: FEMA

- Economic: U.S. Department of Commerce

- Health and social services: U.S. Department of Health and Human Services (HHS)

- Housing: Housing and Urban Development (HUD)

- Infrastructure systems: U.S. Army Corps of Engineers (USACE)

- Natural and cultural resources: U.S. Department of the Interior[102]

Each RSF is led by a designated federal coordinating agency. These coordinating federal agencies support state, local, tribal, and private-sector groups with community planning and capacity building. Goals include regaining economic stability, rebuilding infrastructure, restoring health and social services as well as natural and cultural resources, and meeting the housing needs of residents displaced by disasters.

The effective implementation of the NDRF, whether or not in the context of a presidential disaster declaration, requires interagency cooperation and engagement across all levels of government and support from NGOs, COIs, and the private sector. NDRF concepts also present an opportunity for emergency managers and others to increase collaboration and coordination of recovery resources. To clarify, under the NDRF, recovery work is continuous, not simply something done in the aftermath of a disaster or emergency.

The NDRF presses for a clearer system under which partners can better align resources and work together to support recovery in a holistic, coordinated manner.

Consequently, it makes sense from a governmental perspective to approach disaster recovery as if it were a dynamic and evolutionary phenomenon. Governments in nations with established systems of emergency management tend to form and implement disaster recovery in accord with pre-disaster adaptable plans and processes. However, it would be a mistake to categorize any national government's disaster recovery approach or condition as merely composed of organized processes. Also, the "recovery process" should not be the exclusive focus of those who build disaster recovery theory. The NDRF (see the "Tell Me More" 2-3 box) sees matters of disaster mitigation, preparedness, and response as part of sound disaster recovery.

Is recovery "replacement or compensation for an acute loss in a defined area"? Is it a matter of addressing needs, distributing resources, or reducing conflict? Is "recovery" intended to redress or correct an imbalance? These are all broad questions to which the general answer is "yes."

Is there such a thing as "holistic recovery"? Holistic recovery, or in federal emergency management parlance "whole community" recovery, may be a worthwhile and even admirable social and political goal in the sense that such recovery seeks to address the needs, and sometimes losses (see Chapter 9), of those negatively affected by a disaster. Ideally, whole community recovery should be pursued in a broadly equitable, fair, democratically responsive, and compassionate way. However, holistic recovery is something that is not yet accepted public policy in nations of the world, and this includes the United States. Equity, fairness, and compassion are, in the language of international relations, "soft norms" subject to interpretation that varies by one's personal and cultural values. Moreover, holistic recovery in emergency management is aspirational and not easily measured.

Should a theory or theories of disaster recovery be customized for specific forms of hazard? From a governmental perspective the answer is "arguably" affirmative. While an all-hazards approach to governmental emergency management has many attractive features, different types of hazards require different, though perhaps often overlapping, types of theory. There are different sets of rational/scientific theories used to study the destructiveness of various types of disaster agents (i.e., the geosciences for seismology, and meteorology for atmospheric phenomena). To draw from these theories in disaster recovery studies requires differentiation by type of hazard.

Why include the NDRF in a chapter about disaster theory? Because the NDRF grew out of theory scholarship, academic workshops are asked to ponder a theory of disaster recovery, and through theory work of reflexive practitioners (i.e., many of who have a foot in their government work and a foot in academia as part-time professors and instructors). One would hope that important government policies are not fashioned and approved thoughtlessly.

We exist in a world of complex systems. There are social, economic, and political systems, as well as engineered systems, to name a few. Even our homes represent systems. Buckminster Fuller long ago sought "a house that would function like a machine to improve the quality of life for its inhabitants,"[103] as well as to maintain the health and safety of the occupants. Many such systems are joined or interlinked. A theory is a "relational statement."

This being said, it is also true that different types of hazards have different sets of political clientele groups and communities of interest. Theory about disaster recovery might well be shaped by the interests and motives of those preoccupied with the nature of the hazard that may be imputed to have caused the disaster. From the perspective of government and governance, theories of disaster recovery should take into account the type of hazard and the type of damage associated with that hazard. Birkland has demonstrated that certain types of hazards have identifiable sets of political interests.[104] Few who work in the emergency management field would dispute the claim that in the United States, there is an "earthquake" COI, a "flood" COI, a "hurricane" COI, and an "urban-interface wildland fire" COI, to name a few. Add to this, certain types of hazards have their own **communities of practice (CoPs)**. These are groups of people who share a concern or a passion for something they do, and they learn how to do it better as they interact regularly. A major difference between a COI and a CoP is that members of a CoP are practitioners.[105]

Communities of interest have a social, rather than spatial, definition. This stems from fragmentation of their memberships owing to people's interest in various specialized topics. COIs form in both the in-person world and in the online virtual world, and sometimes simultaneously. For example, there is the COI that formed around the issue of safe room protection for children while at school in the aftermath of the Moore, Oklahoma, area tornado in 2013. More recently, in the realm of crisis events, communities of interest have proliferated around the subject of mass murder shootings inside American K–12 schools. "Sandy Hook Promise," an organization formed by parents of children who died in the 2012 Newtown, CT, school shootings, works to train schools in threat assessment.

In special sessions, teachers learn to identify and address concerns. The organization also works with students to encourage speaking up when peers contemplate harming themselves or others in a campaign called "Say Something." Another, "Everytown for Gun Safety," is a group that advocates for more restrictive gun laws. It compiles incidents in which "a firearm discharges a live round inside a school building or on a school campus or grounds," including on the campuses of colleges and universities. That count includes suicides and incidents that did not result in injuries, like the accidental discharge of a security guard's weapon.[106] Perhaps most remarkable is the high school student community of interest formed as a result of the February 14, 2018, mass shooting of students and faculty at Stoneman Douglas High School in Parkland, FL. Across the nation, a succession of national student walkouts have resulted. A massive coalition of student-led COIs marched on Washington, DC, in mid-March 2018.[107]

There is a "hurricane" COI, a "flood" COI, and a "tornado" COI, to name a few. Likewise, each of these has a CoP. Moreover, for human-caused hazard agents there are "nuclear," "hazardous material," and "terrorism" COIs and CoPs (and terrorism itself is fragmented into a variety of sub-interest communities—border security, immigration control, bioterror, cyberterrorism, intelligence gathering, infrastructure protection, etc.), as well as several more.

Conversely, some existing theories, risk analysis theory, for example, may be appropriate and applicable regardless of hazard type. Some theories from economics, including from public finance, public budgeting, and welfare economics, may have suitable applicability regardless of the type of hazard agent that caused or initiated the disaster. Certain, if not most, sociological and communications theories may have all-hazard utility as well.

Regardless, some differentiation of type of hazard and location of damaging effects seems necessary in order that recovery theory break out the categories of intermediate theory. These may become nested theories within a broader master theory or they may stand independent. There are different social scientific theories—positivist (scientifically objective and behavioral) or normative (incorporating values)—which offer varying degrees of explanatory power when applied to different types of hazards that carry disaster potential. Theories of bureaucratic politics, social choice, principal-agent, network, and democratic theory may all have a place. Policy process theories also deserve mention: the multiple stream framework, punctuated equilibrium theory, the advocacy coalition framework, the institutional analysis and development framework, the social-ecological systems framework, and others.[108]

What are the barriers to recovery? There are an immense number of barriers in disaster recovery: government versus private-sector disputes over property rights versus the public interest, legal liability issues, cost incidence (to whom will the costs of recovery ultimately be shifted and ultimately be absorbed and what recourse do other parties have in escaping these costs?), migration of individuals and families away from the zone of damage, the permitting required to undertake major capital reconstruction whether public or private, and so on.

Disaster Recovery Theory and Local Economics

There are both formal and informal economies in communities. These are affected by disasters and often deserve reconstitution in some form in the wake of disaster. Also, social conditions may shape economic recovery. Not to be overlooked is that informal economies may be an essential part of a local community.

Disasters affect household economics, sometimes in profound ways. Those who provide disaster relief to households must understand how household economics were managed before the disaster, as well as how they are managed, or were managed, after the disaster. It is important in the sequencing of aid that the correct form of relief is offered at the correct time. Recovery is a measurement of household losses and disaster costs. Recovery involves planning of, and appropriate design and application of, policy instruments that equitably and fairly facilitate household recovery.

Disaster recovery researchers often overlook "quality of life issues" for those affected by disasters. What does it mean when a neighborhood loses a beloved public school, recreation center, a library, or a public horticulture institution? Disaster recovery theory also needs to grapple with the issue of valuing the services that the environment produces in natural ways for humankind. Major damage to the natural environment may affect local businesses and livelihoods, the local real estate market, flood abatement, agriculture, forestry, potable water sources, as well as local plant and animal life.

Recovery resources and activities inside an impacted community must be harmonized and reconciled with the recovery resources and activities introduced to the impacted community from the outside.

There is also the matter of "public economics." Governments affect the climate or environment of business by providing incentives and disincentives for various types of business activity. Governments establish laws and rules that regulate business and trade. Governments use taxes as much as direct public spending to encourage or discourage various business behaviors as well as to regulate private markets on behalf of both consumers and business in general.[109] All of this is directly relevant to a theory of disaster recovery for households. Taxation, particularly through broad-gauged measures like property, sales, and income taxes, is a way in which "the many may subsidize the few." Ideally, the economic sacrifice imposed on the many should be light while the benefits disbursed to the few (say those in disaster-ravaged communities) may be substantial. However, economic recovery within any governmental jurisdiction depends on "willingness-to-pay" and "ability-to-pay" questions. Many state governments lack a "willingness to pay" for and create state disaster relief programs that parallel those of FEMA—even when those states have the means or money to do so. Yet it is also true that many states and localities lack "ability to pay" for their own disaster recoveries or for pre-disaster mitigation endeavors that would serve a public interest.

In these economic terms, what is a successful disaster recovery, and will we know it when we see it? A successful disaster recovery may be one that redresses historical issues. Consider the Tennessee Valley in the United States. Before the 1930s, the valley was long vulnerable to repeated major flooding. The Tennessee Valley Authority (TVA), a federal regional agency, engineered and built flood control projects, which were fundamentally structural flood mitigation solutions, that helped advance the entire regional economy of the valley. Construction of the massive system of flood works and hydroelectric generation stimulated local businesses and created tens of thousands of jobs in a region then economically depressed. Economic revival was one of President Franklin D. Roosevelt's express TVA purposes: the TVA projects produced major public goods and foremost improved flood abatement and hydroelectric power that generated low-cost electricity in abundance and new recreational lakes from water impoundments created by the dams.

Disasters create economic winners and losers. Some economic sectors lose while others gain. Disasters often redistribute wealth such that impacted communities are poorer while nearby unaffected communities gain at the damaged community's expense. In another sense, the economic stimulation that outside funding, investment, and in-kind contributions provide often has a beneficial economic multiplier effect for the recovering locality.

Yet government officials are challenged to appropriately read market signals, even those emanating from celebrity-driven altruism pursued through social media. In certain periods, outside direct cash and in-kind assistance is essential in both response and short-term recovery. However, it is also true that sometimes outside cash and in-kind assistance offered for too long seriously slows the revival of the local economy as people will tend to prefer the "free" goods offered as disaster relief over paying for locally produced products as they did before the disaster. Government disaster recovery needs to be adept at gradual scale-down and disengagement.

Local (and sometimes even regional and national) economics are affected by public perception. People want reassurance that public safety is being maintained.

Few businesses are more interlaced with matters of disaster and disaster recovery than is the business of private insurance. Almost every line of insurance involves risk from disaster-induced loss at primary, secondary, or tertiary levels. However, insurance involves matters of valuation and indemnification. How much is a life worth? How much insurance does one need to purchase to be adequately covered against exigencies; remember that "adequately covered" relates significantly to the ability to recover from disaster economically, whether a large or small business, a public entity, a nonprofit, or a family.

Disasters may entice businesses to relocate from a damage zone. Another economic dilemma for businesspeople in disaster recovery is deciding whether or not to let a business fail after a disaster. Often if the business was already failing "before" the disaster, the decision to cut losses via shutdown or relocation may seem appropriate. Some businesses are too marginal to properly insure themselves against the costs and losses a disaster can impose. Perhaps a theory of disaster recovery needs to embed a triage system in which the following occurs:

- Businesses that would have most likely failed and that have little chance of recovery regardless of financial assistance should be left to declare bankruptcy if they so choose.

- Businesses that were "not failing" before the disaster but that would surely fail without post-disaster financial aid would deserve and receive public assistance.

- Businesses that were healthy, adequately insured, and likely to rebound without financial aid should receive little or no public financial aid.

The scale of the disaster needs to be compared to and contrasted with the scale of the firm affected. Government post-disaster aid to business is often conditional: it may come in the form of loans, loan guarantees, tax abatement, etc. Insurance claims filed for physical loss, business interruption, worker's compensation, and so forth, may assist firms that were covered by these policies before the disaster.

Few would contest that for-profit firms play major roles in disaster economic recovery but so, too, do nonprofit organizations (see Chapter 6). To what extent do results and findings of disaster recovery hypotheses testing reveal unmet needs of disaster recovery? Because nongovernmental organizations (NGOs) often work to address unmet needs created by gaps in conditions of governmental disaster relief, a sound theory of disaster recovery should examine the record of NGO performance in disaster recovery.

Sound recoveries involve hazard risk management and hazard risk reduction, such as **resilience in disaster management**. Resilience in economic terms involves pre-disaster surpluses and shortages. Resilience also relates to actions taken during recovery. There is a burgeoning scholarly literature on resilience to disaster.[110]

Several variables are key in developing metrics of disaster recovery, including rules, systems, values, scales, interest, time frames, infrastructure, and process. These involve a variety of dimensions and contexts. A sound theory of disaster recovery would be one that compiles information about these variables in an integrated way. If disaster recovery is very much a matter of correcting imbalances, what barriers affect the variables important in disaster recovery? How can the identified imbalances be corrected? Did a recovery succeed because it was conducted rapidly (time, time frames)? Was the recovery well conceived methodologically (process, scaling)? Was recovery made possible by properly engineering rebuilding (infrastructure)? Was the recovery achieved because it manifested sustainability features (systems, process, values)? Did it succeed because it was not obstructed by regulation (rules)? Or did it triumph owing to its responsiveness to the needs of disaster victims of all types and circumstances (values, interests)?

Is disaster recovery radical and transformative, or is it inherently conservative, as determined by insurance payouts and relief aid that returns disaster zones to their near exact pre-disaster economic conditions? Disaster recovery in some places may rest on a conservation strategy of "pick up the pieces" and let's figure out how to keep going. Deciding whether a recovery is radical, transformative, conservative, or minimalist is a matter best left to local people and local authorities in a damage zone.

The work invested in developing a worthwhile theory, or set of theories, about disaster recovery promises important long-term payoffs.

Disaster Victims and Clients as Customers

This chapter opened with a review of Jeffersonian-oriented emergency management. Owing to the professionalization of emergency management, the Hamiltonian perspective was shown to be gaining ascendance over the Jeffersonian approach. Regardless, the rise of the **reinventing government movement** in the 1990s and the modern management consultant conclusion that organizations need to rediscover the importance of customer satisfaction have given Jeffersonian and Jacksonian emergency management reinvigoration.

Increasingly, customer satisfaction has become a focus of emergency management.[111] The Clinton-era reinventing government effort offered low-level administrators more power. However, low-level administrators must have the training and experience necessary to assume more responsibility. Under James Lee Witt, FEMA assiduously embraced the reinvention movement. Customer satisfaction in government work has a ring of Jeffersonianism and is something relished by Jacksonian emergency managers as well. Clearly, no agency or profession can afford to ignore customer satisfaction very long without losing credibility, clients, and positive public reputation. However, although customers may help professionals identify unmet needs, in no profession do customers define the nature of professional work.

Still, if emergency managers are judged to have failed in meeting the legitimate needs of people seeking post-disaster government aid, then they have also failed in the criterion of customer satisfaction. Policy analysts have been slow to recognize the utility of customer satisfaction studies in measuring the effectiveness of government disaster assistance programs. Catastrophic disasters, such as Superstorm Sandy in 2012 and Hurricanes Harvey, Irma, and Maria in 2017 produced a vast array of citizen (and subnational government) needs. Meeting those victim needs expeditiously and competently is a daunting challenge for all government emergency managers.

KNOWLEDGE CODIFICATION AND KNOWLEDGE DIFFUSION ISSUES

How do people learn emergency management and how can the government's roles in disaster study be understood? The experience and actions of any organization are based on a blend of tacit, or uncodified (unwritten), knowledge and structured, or codified, knowledge. **Tacit knowledge** (acquired by observation, practice, experience, mentoring, etc.) is vague and ambiguous and depends on sharing expectations and values through social relationships. **Codified knowledge**, meaning written knowledge, is impersonal and learned through thinking and reasoning, not social relationships. To manage well, do emergency managers need to operate in face-to-face forums (that are consensual, democratic, Jeffersonian, and based on tacit knowledge)? Or might they achieve their goals by imparting technocratic knowledge, which is produced from data analysis, repeated experimentation, scientific study, Hamiltonian behavior, and codified knowledge?

This may depend on whether codified knowledge is diffused or undiffused knowledge.[112] Diffused codified knowledge is written down and openly available so that audiences outside government can use it. If knowledge is codified but not diffused, it sits contained within the bureaucracies. Someone could master this knowledge only if he or she worked inside the bureaucracy and learned internal rules and unique types of information. If knowledge is diffused but not codified, those entering public management positions from the outside stand little chance of coordinating the work of others, unless they receive help from those inside or they have the time to learn the uncodified information as government employees. To succeed under conditions of diffused, tacit knowledge, a public manager needs to "learn the agency." Managers would have to learn from mentors. Table 2-2 provides a tabular comparison of tacit versus codified knowledge along two dimensions: diffused and undiffused.

Unfortunately, a considerable share of federal emergency management knowledge, if recorded at all, is partially codified but not sufficiently diffused beyond the agency. This said, a qualification is needed. One underappreciated arm of most major federal agencies is "the history division or office." This organization is responsible for soliciting, collecting, and managing a vast assortment of the respective department's or agency's day-to-day information and records. History units filter out unnecessary or trivial information and seek to build a long-term repository of essential department or agency records. In some respects, history units contain the institutional brain cells of short- and long-term memory. Frequently, history unit officials are asked to conduct briefings within various

TABLE 2-2 ■ Written vs. Unwritten Knowledge and Diffused vs. Undiffused Information		
	Diffused	**Undiffused**
Tacit Knowledge— unpublished or unwritten knowledge acquired by observation, practice, experience, and mentoring	If knowledge is diffused but not codified, those entering public management positions from the outside stand little chance of coordinating the work of others, unless they receive help from those inside or they have the time to learn the uncodified information as government employees. Verbal story legacies and in-house training are common.	Administrative fiefdoms. Mostly oral, ad hoc, and unwritten basis for practice knowledge. Extremely difficult for government employees to master independently. Unavailable to outsiders, including academic researchers, the media, and even potential future employees. "Need to know" restrictions may apply under security clearance strata regarding certain protected and largely unwritten information.
Codified Knowledge— written knowledge that is impersonal and learned through thinking and reasoning	Diffused codified knowledge is written down and openly available so that audiences inside and outside government can use it. Promotes transparency and public accountability, as well as education and research.	If knowledge is codified but not diffused, it sits contained within the bureaucracies. Someone could master this knowledge only if he or she worked inside the bureaucracy and learned internal rules and unique types of information. Common under state secrecy restrictions.

offices of their home institution. Sometimes this work guides current workers who do not have a long-term perspective on their institution's past decisions and actions. Sometimes the counsel and information provided by history offices saves officials from repeating mistakes and from unproductive or wasteful public spending. Among federal agencies with exceptional history divisions or offices is the U.S. Department of Energy, the U.S. Nuclear Regulatory Commission, NASA, and the U.S. Department of State. The U.S. Department of Homeland Security has a History Office, which may help FEMA better save its key records, codify and make publicly available more of its reports and documents, and promote the education and training of its present and future employees based on the agency's written reports, documents, and records.[113]

The *U.S. Code of Federal Regulations* sets forth the core rules of federal emergency management, but it does not elucidate the essence of what emergencies and disasters are and it does not explain how to do emergency management work.[114] Some federal emergency managers have codified their expertise, but much of this information resides within the bowels of various agency offices; a possible exception is the National Emergency Training Center within DHS-FEMA, which disseminates codified emergency management knowledge and trains state and local authorities and managers. However, according to former FEMA attorney William Cumming, "the real disaster tradition was oral, not in writing, and ad hoc rather than procedural."[115]

A fiefdom or cult of personality results when management knowledge is both uncodified and undiffused (inaccessible) or kept secret by government classification. Such may have been the case in J. Edgar Hoover's Federal Bureau of Investigation (FBI) many years ago. Management control then becomes highly personalized, unreviewable, and not appealable. Some fear that the advancement of emergency management largely depends on high-profile, charismatic figures chosen to lead agencies like FEMA or state and local emergency management agencies. If emergency management know-how depends heavily on a cult of personality, there is little hope emergency management will be professionalized.

In uncodified but diffused situations, clans are the norm and people learn by being socialized. Those selected to join the U.S. diplomatic corps face this type of situation. Diplomatic histories are many but inadequate to train potential diplomats. Before they are officially entrusted to do U.S. diplomatic work, new diplomats must be socialized to the State Department's way of doing things.[116] Certain first responder emergency management occupational specialties (fire services and law enforcement), too, put great emphasis on socialization and mastery of tacit knowledge and of codified knowledge not widely diffused to those outside the occupational specialty.

If emergency management is basically learned through apprenticeships within emergency management agencies, few in the academic profession will be drawn to the field. If that is the case, the growth of the field of emergency management will be a function of in-house training, not of broadly based advancement of emergency management education and published research.

BIG DATA ANALYTICS AND EMERGENCY MANAGEMENT

In a May 11, 2016, public lecture, Gary King, a named university professor and director of the Institute for Quantitative Social Science at Harvard University declared, "Today it is much easier to engage in data intensive social science research than it has been in the past."[117] He offered that owing to massive IT improvements, the commoditizing of knowledge, and huge data production increases over time, it is now possible to conduct research on colossally large data sets. He advised, "What is important is not 'big data' per se. The value is in the "analytics."[118] How is it possible to make the data actionable? King then answered his own question: "Modern analytics allow you to customize output. Moore's Law holds that computers double in speed and power every 18 months. Today this doubling occurs in a much shorter period of time."[119] Moreover, advances in computing software, like Microsoft Excel and Tableau Software, have been scaled up to enable researchers to analyze significantly larger scale data sets than most data processing software could handle even five years ago.

Information storage in the **cloud**, which refers to software storage and service run on the Internet, has also enabled researchers to save and analyze prodigiously large volumes of information.[120]

But the cloud has deficiencies too. Without an Internet connection, or with a poor connection, people are basically locked out of accessing their data and cloud-based programs. The same applies if there are any technical issues or outages on the server side. Also, because one's information lives online, there is always the risk of it getting into the wrong hands. All cloud companies have security measures in place to protect one's data from hackers, but they are not foolproof, so it is always a good idea for people to be judicious about what they choose to store in the cloud versus what they elect to store locally on their respective computers.[121]

In regard to emergency management, Akter and Wamba claim, "As the number of disasters has increased over the years, a concern has grown worldwide about how to extend critical knowledge and innovation to prevent, mitigate, and manage disaster operations."[122] Drawing from a 2013 article by Zheng et al., Akter and Wamba add, "The techniques to efficiently discover, collect, organize, search, and disseminate real-time disaster information have become national priorities for efficient crisis management and disaster recovery tasks."[123] In addition, they argue, "emerging technological innovations including social media, location-based systems, radio frequency identification, and big data analytics (BDA) are considered as powerful tools that may help all stakeholders during the disaster management cycle."[124] BDA is defined as a "holistic process to manage, process, and analyze 5 Vs (i.e., volume, variety, velocity, veracity, and value) in order to create actionable insights."[125] Akter and Wamba reason that BDA can assist in creating the next generation of emergency response technologies in part because big data analytics may provide important real-time information about disasters as they transpire, thereby helping decision makers during a crisis.[126]

Returning to Prof. King's lecture, he explained that he and his students were recently given a problem. "The choice was to buy a $2 million computer to conduct a complex analysis or [instead] invest two hours of work in developing an algorithm design capable of running on an average laptop. Obviously, the two hours invested in **algorithm** design, able to be run on an average laptop, was the preferred and cost-effective option. His point was that innovative analytics was 'way better' than relying on expensive off-the-shelf hardware. The ability to draw inferences and from this make predictions is today better than ever."[127]

In mathematics and computer science, an algorithm is a step-by-step procedure for calculations and it is a procedure or formula for solving a problem, based on conducting a sequence of specified actions. Algorithms are used for calculation, data processing, and automated reasoning. In fact, operations performed on one's personal computer consist of algorithms. Furthermore, an algorithm is a well-defined procedure that allows a computer to solve a problem.[128] Another way to describe an algorithm is a sequence of unambiguous instructions. "The first step in developing the standard algorithm requires that one shows each step in the process. Next, write out the process in a vertical form, called the partial products algorithm."[129] Finally, as an example consider "the standard multiplication algorithm; it is a short-cut method for writing partial products."[130]

Put more simply, an algorithm is a fancy to-do list for a computer. Algorithms take in zero or more inputs and give back one or more outputs. A recipe is a good example of an algorithm because it tells you what you need to do step by step. It takes inputs (ingredients) and produces an output (the completed dish). A flowchart is a type of diagram that represents an algorithm, workflow, or process, showing the steps as boxes of various kinds, and their order by connecting them with arrows. As a diagrammatic representation it illustrates a solution model to a given problem. A **programming algorithm** is a computer procedure that is a lot like a recipe (called a *procedure*) and tells your computer precisely what steps to take to solve a problem or reach a goal. The ingredients are called *inputs*, while the results are called *outputs*. The characteristics of a good algorithm are:

- Precision—the steps are precisely stated (defined).

- Uniqueness—the results of each step are uniquely defined and only depend on the input and the result of the preceding steps.

- Finiteness—the algorithm stops after a finite number of instructions are executed.[131]

An algorithm is a method for solving a problem. The quadratic formula is an algorithm, because it is a method for solving quadratic equations. Algorithms may not even involve mathematics; however, formulas almost exclusively use numbers. A **computer program** is a sequence of instructions that apply the rules of a specific programming language, written to perform a specified task with a computer. Algorithms are general and have to be translated into a specific programming language.[132]

Dr. King promotes **computational social science**, which is a specific subcategory of work in big data analytics. "Computational social science" is an approach to social inquiry defined by

1. the use of large, complex datasets, often—although not always—measured in terabytes or petabytes;

2. the frequent involvement of "naturally occurring" social and digital media sources and other electronic databases;

3. the use of computational or algorithmic solutions to generate patterns and inferences from these data; and,

4. the applicability of social theory in a variety of domains from the study of mass opinion to public health, from examinations of political events to social movements.[133]

King offered examples. "If one were doing a study of how often people exercise, would it be better to conduct an individual exercise survey of 500 people or would it be better to analyze the exercise record of 500,000 people drawing from their cell phone accelerometer data?"[134]

"Political scientists collect and compile interview data from which they draw conclusions about what people were thinking in the past—at the time of the interview. Today it is possible to collect billions of political opinions available and expressed in yesterday's social media posts. At present there are about 650 million social media posts every day [this was said in 2016]."[135]

"Sociologists often study human social networks by asking people, like their students, to identify their daily contacts over the course of a day. By this they seek to identify each individual's five best friends. An alternate and perhaps far superior method would be to track individuals' continuous record of emails, text messages, Bluetooth address book use, and activity in social media. However, this would involve informed consent, avoiding violation of privacy laws, and highly accurate classification of the data."[136]

"Demographers have great difficulty ascertaining the economic development levels of many lesser developed nations. Relying on the official government statistics of those nations is often a mistake because of problems in the respective nation's information collection, distortions caused by its political activities, limited capacity to compile information, etc. Big data analysis may provide a better option. Earth orbiting satellites could track levels of night light in the country visible from space. Daytime satellite observation may reveal the extensiveness of a nation's road networks or the sophistication and pervasiveness of its essential critical infrastructure—dams, bridges, ports, power grid, phone lines or Wi-Fi towers, and so on."[137]

Prof. King warned that "without new analytics, the data collected is often worthless." He maintained that the social sciences can now be used to solve problems rather than merely document or study them. However, a typical challenge of this era is how to read 1 trillion social media posts. He referred to the problem of tracking disease. He said doctors' "verbal autopsies" were mostly useless. Instead, next of kin or caretaker interview transcriptions were more promising. He advocated "sentiment analysis" by word count (as in counting the use of various words in tweets). By doing an audit account of the word *malaria* in social media in a particular region, for example, one may get a better sense of the scale and spread of malaria in that region.[138]

Sentiment analysis refers to the use of natural language processing, text analysis, and computational linguistics to identify and extract subjective information in source materials. Sentiment analysis is also the process of determining whether a piece of writing is positive, negative, or neutral. It's also known as **opinion mining**, deriving the opinion or attitude of a speaker. A common use case for this technology is to discover how people feel about a particular topic. "In essence, it is the process of determining the emotional tone behind a series of words, used to gain an understanding of the attitudes, opinions and emotions expressed within an online mention."[139]

Through **Twitter sentiment analysis** one can learn why people think something is good or bad, often by extracting the exact words that indicate why people did or didn't like some particular thing.[140] In some ways, this is the kind of insight one seeks to find through market research, but, he asked, "why devote enormous budgets and countless man-hours to conducting surveys and cold calling? Data analytic text mining tools promise answers in seconds."[141] In the 1990s, when the New Public Administration was popular, public and private firms labored to determine client satisfaction with their services and products. FEMA, under President Clinton-appointee James Lee Witt, embraced the idea and sought to measure at various times disaster victim satisfaction or dissatisfaction with FEMA.[142] This was examined previously in the customer satisfaction section of this chapter.

King asked the audience to consider the issue of unemployment, something of considerable significance in the study of disaster impacts. Instead of relying on government tabulations of unemployment, one could, if the search were refined enough, count the use of the word *job* as an indicator of unemployment.

Unrelated substantive problems often have the same analytic solution. Methods rely on classification and goals. Classification, whether it be for deaths, illness, joblessness, or social media posts, only works if we're perfect at it. The key to achieving goals is yielding answers that give us estimated percentages or that take us where we want to go. Sometimes we must estimate a percentage of a category. Big data analytics may give us a much broader base from which to make estimations.

Prof. King explained that the business he established from his research was born while searching for a way to deal with challenging health care data sets in the developing world. He said, "We quickly realized that it could be applied on a grander scale: distilling meaning from the vast amounts of data in the social media landscape." King went on, "In Jorge Luis Borges' short story, *The Library of Babel*, an infinite expanse of hexagonal rooms filled with books contained every possible arrangement of letters. For every important, beautiful, or useful book in this library there existed endless volumes of gibberish. The only way to navigate this vast sea of meaningless information was to locate the Crimson

Hexagon, the one room that contained a log of every other book in the library—a guide to extracting meaning from all the unstructured information." Like Borges's Crimson Hexagon, he said his firm's aim was to be a key to the world of social data, guiding others in their attempt to find actionable information.

According to King, humans are "horrible" at selecting keywords and even worse at remembering keywords. He referred to "a study of 10,000 Twitter posts [that] counted the number of times the place name 'Boston' and the word 'bombing' were used in the days after the Boston Marathon bombing. Searches for the word 'Boston' alone and searches for 'bombing' alone rarely take one to the subject 'Boston Marathon' bombing. Studies show that humans tend to recognize keywords well but have poor recall of them."[143]

King indicated that **Thresher** is a new technique to discover the right keywords for what you want to find in net searches. It suggests keywords to you as you advance. King asked the audience, "What university research has had the biggest impact on you?" Prof. King maintains that "quantitative social science" should be on the list. Quantitative social science has in recent years:

- Transformed Fortune 500 companies [e.g., corporate data mining of customers]

- Created massive numbers of "friendship networks" [e.g., Facebook]

- Amplified greatly human expressive capacity [ability of tweets to reach the world]

- Transformed public health, crime control, policing, sports [e.g., Billy Bean's Oakland A's "money ball"]

- Been used to evaluate the success or failure of health policies

- Has reinvented the discipline of economics

- Has set scientific standards by which to evaluate public policy[144]

King asked, "How do we infer meaning from language?" Humans communicate complex information. Data analytics are very much about what to ignore in communication. Computer-assisted conceptualization helps our working memory. Our short-term memory often leaves much to be desired. King is probably alluding to human-machine verbal communication. When can advanced technology delicately remind us of something we need to know or do? Your car tells you to stay-in-lane. Your refrigerator pings to let you know its door is ajar. Computer-assisted conceptualization has been of immense help to those attempting to learn a foreign language. At this writing, Amazon's Echo and Alexa, Apple's Siri, Microsoft's Cortana, and Google's Google Home serve as intelligent personal assistants in the homes of millions of Americans.[145]

The data sharing which facilitates big data analytics saves us from the biases of working alone on problems. However, "access to data" is essential. He said almost all the data in the world is either data held by governments or data held by corporations. Many governments engage in limited sharing of their data. International treaties help increase this data sharing among nations and the world in general. Corporations do not generally share their data. To encourage data sharing, companies must get protection of their proprietary rights or derive some benefit from sharing.

Predictive risk modeling employing data analytics has been used in criminal justice for improving child protection services. This type of modeling raises bias and surveillance issues. Big data is more and more intrusive but it also provides a good. He said there are ways to use private data to everyone's advantage. People need to understand that sharing or giving up data is in the interest of science.

People are being trained to serve as social scientists at large. Data analytics have advanced the psychological study of organizations. Data analytics is changing the methodological basis of academic disciplines.

Consider what big data analytics has added to research: the emergence of cleo-metrics in history; the rise of econometrics in economics; the evolution of psycho-metrics; and advances in polling used in political science, to name a few.

Working with big data is challenging owing to "issues of generalizability, ethics, and theory."[146] Also, acquisition, archiving, and analysis of these types of data are not easily processed using conventional database applications.[147] However, massive increases in storage capacity, boosts in processing power, and the availability of analytic systems have dramatically expanded the ability of social scientists to collect and use these sorts of data. What previously required access to networked computing cores in a dedicated facility can now be handled by a small server cluster housed in the corner of an office, or alternatively, "in the cloud" through a distributed computing system.[148]

Moreover, the acquisition and archiving of complex data systems, let alone their manipulation, often involve collecting personally identifiable information. This raises the issue of data privacy and de-identification, all at a time when people are worried about increased tracking and limits on their freedom to engage in confidential expression of their views. Some of this is evident recently in public criticism of Cambridge Analytics, a firm which used data analytics to guide the 2016 presidential campaign of Donald Trump, and which allegedly misused the Facebook data of some 50 million users.[149]

Big data analytics has its critics and skeptics. Shah, Cappella, and Neuman advocate that researchers employ both conventional methods and computational social science, and they argue against "abandoning established methods in favor of data science" exclusively.[150] Add to this, "Given the extraordinarily large sample sizes in much of this research, nearly everything is statistically significant in big data analytics. As such, researchers must use inferential statistics carefully, recognizing the risk of 'false discoveries'—Type I errors, or the assertion of a relationship that is not present."[151] They go on to allege that huge samples may make insignificant findings seem meaningful "because they achieve conventional thresholds of statistical significance" so easily. In effect, data science may appear superior to conventional social science owing to how easy it is for computational social science methods to achieve "statistically significant" findings.[152]

Dr. King's lecture pointed to many computational social science achievements, including advancing various public goods. However, in the case of social media users, it is often a daunting task to classify the data correctly, partition it appropriately, filter it, and then attribute veracity to what has been posted. Datasets outside of social media may be easier to work with if the basis of their information is verified and generally more objective. Prof. King was captivated by the "possibilities of computational social science" but less concerned about the "perils" of this new instrument of data science.

Summary

This chapter furnished a sampling of theories and theory knowledge for the purpose of suggesting ways in which theory could be used, or has been used, to research various dimensions of disaster phenomena. Theories hold out the potential to continually advance emergency management as a profession. People new to the field can draw from this chapter's theories and concepts to independently analyze disaster policy as a domain of public policy.

It opened by summarizing three simple normative theories: Jeffersonian, Hamiltonian, and Jacksonian. Hamiltonian theory and assumptions hold out the best prospect for professionalizing the work of emergency management. However, Hamiltonian emergency management embodies an authority of expertise for emergency managers. They must learn and apply a growing body of knowledge—some of it practical knowledge and some of it academic knowledge. Hamilton's managers would be chosen on the basis of their education and qualifications without discrimination on the basis of gender, race, ethnicity, or LGBTQ status. Jeffersonian theory has many laudatory features in that it rests on public participation, public assent, democratic principles, and local priorities. However, arguably, Jeffersonianism is somewhat unsuited for the modern, complex, automated, highly networked world of today. Jacksonian theory has a place insomuch as it applies well to the current polarized and politicized environment of disaster politics. Jacksonianism emphasizes state and local participation and demands a highly politically responsive emergency management leadership. However, it tends to project populism via a set of particularistic values. Many of these values do not promote diversity in the public workforce, are suspicious of newly arrived immigrants, and advance strident nationalism as a counter to globalization in its many forms. Jacksonianism today spotlights the plight of the undereducated workers, men and women, who have very few champions of their causes in positions of political power.

Bureaucratic politics and matters of administrative culture permeate emergency management and disaster policy in the United States. Understanding models and concepts of bureaucratic politics helps one analyze power relationships in disaster policy and management. Also, hugely important is intergovernmental relations theory (see Chapter 6). Owing to the U.S. system of relations between federal, state, and local governments and because other parties outside of government are heavily involved in "governance" of this policy domain (for example, nonprofit organizations active in disasters, corporately owned utilities, special district governments, and armies of trained volunteers), intergovernmental relations is one of the most critical components of disaster policy. This is true both in the formulation and implementation of that policy.

Principal-agent theory, network theory, and public management theory were briefly examined as potential worthwhile theory tools for both analyzing and conducting emergency management. The chapter also included a review of topics ranging from the best practices approach and customer satisfaction to a commentary about how emergency management knowledge is produced and how it is learned by others. Included as well was a section about methods: specifically, the emerging role of big data analytics in the field of disaster study and management.

Key Terms

Abstract reasoning 50
Algorithm 75
Analytical approaches 55
Applied heuristics approach 55
Best-practices approach 54
Bureaucratic politics model 52
Cloud 74
Codified knowledge 72
Communities of interest
  (COI) 64
Communities of practice
  (CoPs) 67
Computational social
  science 76
Computer program 76
Coordinate-authority model 61
Disaster recovery 63
Dual federalism 61
Ethical code 50
Federalism 61
Generalists 41

Generalized knowledge 50
Hamiltonian approach 44
Hamiltonian public
  managers 44
Hazards U.S. (HAZUS) 46
Hazards U.S.-Multi-Hazard
  (HAZUS-MH) 46
Inclusive-authority model 62
Jacksonian approach 47
Jacksonian public
  managers 47
Jeffersonian approach 41
Jeffersonian public
  managers 41
Local emergency management
  committees (LEMCs) 43
National Disaster Recovery
  Framework (NDRF) 64
Network theory 58
Occupations 50
Opinion mining 77

Organizational process
  model 53
Overlapping-authority
  model 61
Principal-agent theory 60
Profession 49
Professional body 50
Programming algorithm 75
Rational actor model 52
Reinventing government
  movement 71
Resilience in disaster
  management 71
Sentiment analysis 77
Social constructivism 56
Tacit knowledge 72
Technocrat 44
Thresher 78
Twitter sentiment analysis 77

A plaque commemorating the dedication of the National Fire Academy in 1979 resides at FEMA's National Emergency Training Center, located in Emmitsburg, Maryland.

Photo by Jocelyn Augustino/FEMA News Photo

3

A SHORT HISTORY OF U.S. DISASTER POLICY

History matters. Decisions and actions of presidents, governors, lawmakers, and public administrators have made disaster policy and management what it is today. Ordinarily in nations that are democracies, chief executives and legislators recognize or identify a problem. If they choose to define it as a "public problem," lawmakers, sometimes at the behest of the chief executive, begin a process of policy formation in which various solutions to the problem are considered and put forward, often in the form of legislative bills or measures. Various political interests establish positions on these measures and begin to lobby both the legislature and the executive to craft bills that protect or benefit their interests, and a process of coalition building ensues among legislators. There are a great many interests engaged in politics; some of them are serving public interests. Therefore, lawmakers may sometimes be responsive to public needs not necessarily backed by private lobbying. Legislators are obligated to serve the public. They also want to maintain and increase their popularity and win re-election. Consequently, lawmakers must decide how they want to serve both public and/or private interests. They come to office through the help and support of their political party. By aligning with and voting along party lines, lawmakers of the majority or minority party in a legislative body may seek to build winning or blocking coalitions on that basis. The president and various officials of the executive branch may engage in the policy formation and policy adoption process by exercising political influence on their own or by contributing to the legislative hearing process. Legislators ultimately vote on proposed measures to address the problem, and once a policy is adopted, often through enactment of a law, institutional resources and spending authority are provided to implement the law. This is the idealized "textbook" version of the policy process. Usually, chief executives play a key role in the enactment of laws inasmuch as they are included in the legislative process; nonetheless, their vetoes of any specific bill may be overridden by supermajorities in the legislature. A share of federal disaster laws have emerged by way of this general process over the years.[1]

However, history demonstrates that in the U.S. case, the president and other policymakers regularly have to decide how to manage disasters in general, and different types of disaster specifically, under severe time pressures. In the United States, most federal disaster laws are passed as a reaction or response to a recent mega-disaster. Such laws are often necessary because they convey vitally needed federal funds (usually through federal borrowing by the U.S. Treasury).

Many of these post-disaster measures have shaped the role of the federal government in disaster management. In the United States before 1950, whenever a major disaster occurred that captured or involved the national interest, it would be Congress that would respond, with the president as a secondary respondent. This system proved to be slow, ineffective, and cumbersome. Disaster impacted states, localities, and victims had to wait for legislative enactments that often took many months to be worked out. Consequently, in a major 1950 law, Congress entrusted presidents with authority to decide if a governor's request for federal disaster assistance was justified and whether a national interest would be served in approving the request. In the terminology of economists, decision-making costs fell from "535" (100 U.S. Senators and 435 U.S. House members) to "1," the president of the United States.

Relatedly, presidential executive orders sometimes provide the president and the federal government a high-speed, highly responsive alternative to the conventional policy process. The president also holds the constitutional authority to declare national emergencies; however, this is usually reserved for truly profound problems that seriously threaten the entire nation. The president's disaster declaration authority, conferred by Congress in a 1950 law, is another important and available tool; this is particularly so when the president wants the federal government to offer help in managing a disaster, emergency, or crisis for incidents that he does not think meet the gravity of a "national emergency."

Thus, presidents often have the power to lead in the formulation and legitimation of disaster policy if they so choose. Presidents are chief executives, and many presidents have either by choice or by the press of emergency circumstances used their executive authority to move the federal government to address new emergencies, disasters, and exigencies.

TABLE 3-1 ■ Common Issues or Threads in U.S. Disaster Politics, Policy, and Management since 1950 by Institution Type				
Issues and/or Threads Institutions	Presidents	Congress	Federal Agencies	State & Local Govt
National security and disaster	High	Moderate	Moderate	Low
Civil-military relations in disaster policy and management	High	High	Moderate	Moderate
Defining federal–state–local relations in disaster policy and management	High	Moderate	High	High
Presidential power vs. congressional power in disaster politics and policy	High to moderate	Moderate	Low	Low
Presidential leadership and prerogatives in disaster	High	Low	Moderate	Low
International concerns and disaster	High	Moderate to low	Moderate	Low
How emergency management is conducted	Moderate	High	High	High
How emergency management is funded	Moderate	High	Moderate	High
Stakeholder and community of interest activity in disaster politics and policy	Moderate to low	High	Moderate	High
Increasing frequency and magnitude of disaster as a problem	High	High	Moderate	High
Broadening the definition of disaster	High	Moderate	Moderate to low	Moderate
Rising public expectations about disaster assistance as a problem	High	High	Moderate	High
Natural disaster vs. human-caused disaster: What is the government role in each? Liability, insurance, mitigation?	High	Moderate	Moderate	Moderate

Expected degree of influence on the issue area: High, Moderate, Low.

There are a variety of ways to examine U.S. disaster politics, policy, and management over time. It makes sense to set time boundaries on this history; otherwise this chapter could easily balloon to book-length. In 1950, Congress passed, and President Harry S. Truman signed into law, a measure that granted the president authority to issue presidential declarations of major disaster to states. Hence, we begin our history in 1950. Table 3-1, devised by this author, furnishes a thumbnail grouping of issues and threads running through the history of U.S. disaster politics, policy, and management since 1950. Opposite the issues or threads are four columns composed of major institutions. Clearly, many other institutions besides these could have been added. Each issue or thread is arrayed against each of the four columns of institutions for the purpose of comparing relative degree of influence each institution has in the matter of each issue or thread.

The rankings of high, moderate, and low were determined by this author and should therefore be considered open to debate. The rankings connote both potential degree of influence and actor interest in the issue, albeit in generic terms for presidents, Congress, and state and local governments. The point of Table 3-1 is to encapsulate the major issues within or surrounding disaster politics, policy, and management from 1950 to the present. Certainly, not included in the table are many sub-issues that have emerged within nearly every issue or thread over time.

Not every issue or thread in Table 3-1 is explored in this chapter because many are taken up in other chapters (i.e., Chapter 4 takes up presidents and their disaster declarations; Chapter 6 delves into intergovernmental relations; Chapter 7 addresses civil military relations; Chapter 8 covers the international realm of disaster; and Chapter 9 scrutinizes 2017 post-hurricane disaster relief to individuals and families, in part addressing the matter of public post-disaster expectations). Regardless, this chapter does discuss the milestone actions of presidents and the Congress in the formation and implementation of federal disaster policy since 1950. Specific disaster-related laws and policy trends, as well as actual major disasters that have been factors in the enactment of these laws or contributors to these policy trends, are examined. The theme of federal–state and intergovernmental relations in disaster issues, as well as civil defense and civil–military relations, runs through this chapter as well. In many ways, the continuum set forth in this chapter reveals the antecedents of 21st-century homeland security and emergency management.

THE COLD WAR AND THE RISE OF CIVIL DEFENSE

Continued testing of atomic weapons by the United States after the end of World War II and the Soviet Union's successful test of an atomic bomb in 1949, the Soviet occupation of Eastern Europe, and a growing rivalry and competition between the United States and the Soviet Union opened the Cold War, which lasted about 44 years. Over much of the 1950s and early 1960s, civil defense against nuclear attack became a principal focus of U.S. disaster management. President Harry S. Truman's administration (Apr. 1945–Jan. 1953) and congressional lawmakers prepared Americans for the possibility that the nation might be attacked by atomic weapons, and they pressed for improved civil defense preparedness. One reason they did so is because Premier Joseph Stalin and subsequent leaders of the U.S.S.R. were at the time attempting to prepare their own population for nuclear attack by the United States. Ironically, the escalation of the Cold War drew federal policymakers to the issue of disaster preparedness for the civilian population. Several landmark federal disaster laws and policies originated, for better or worse, from the Cold War and the need for civil defense against nuclear attack.

The Civil Defense Act of 1950

Congress and President Truman enacted the Civil Defense Act of 1950, a measure that placed most of the nation's civil defense burden on the states. The act created the Federal Civil Defense Administration (FCDA), which was to formulate national policy to guide the states' efforts.[2] Congress assigned the states a central role in civil defense not as punishment, but instead to ensure that the federal government would not dominate civil defense as might be expected in a "coordinate-authority" model of intergovernmental relations. Civil defense by definition involves the local population and state's rights advocates did not want state and local governments pushed aside or bypassed under the dictums of a federal civil defense leviathan.

Congressional resistance to paying for a new comprehensive program, and concerns about establishing public dependency on government, led to adoption of a doctrine of **self-help**: individual responsibility for preparedness to minimize (although not eliminate) risk. The idea of decentralized, locally controlled, volunteer-based civil defense was not new at the time; in fact, it had been the foundation of Britain's civil defense effort in World War II. Even during World War I, over 1917 and 1918, the United States had mobilized civil defenders to watch for enemy activity along coastlines and borders. Still, the decision to make self-help the basis of civil defense was a political compromise and a way to balance conflicting views over the size, power, and priorities of the emerging postwar nation.

The Civil Defense Act of 1950 allocated significant funding to a shelter initiative. The FCDA-led shelter-building programs also spurred improvements in federal and state coordination, established a national and state attack warning system, stockpiled supplies, and started a well-known national civic education campaign.

Over the 1950s and for years beyond, political, fiscal, and emotional disputes mounted about the feasibility of civil defense against nuclear attack, and this came to be reflected in reduced civil defense funding. Despite ambitious funding requests, actual appropriations to civil defense remained low throughout the Truman administration and far into the 1950s.[3]

The Federal Disaster Relief Act of 1950

The **Federal Disaster Relief Act of 1950 (FDRA)**, enacted with the FCDA, represents a major milestone in America's history of disaster policy and management. As typical after major disasters that grab national attention, the Disaster Relief Act of 1950 was passed as a limited federal response to a flood in the Midwest. However, this law was anything but "typical." The new law set forth a framework and process that carried the nation through many decades of disaster experience. Much of that framework and process is embedded in a succession of federal disaster laws that followed. Many provisions of this law, albeit in amended form, remain in force today. The FDRA of 1950 provided "an orderly and continuing means of assistance by the Federal government to State and local governments in carrying out their responsibilities to alleviate the suffering and damage resulting from major disasters,"[4] including floods. It created the first permanent system for disaster relief without the need for congressional post-disaster action. The new law made federal disaster assistance more immediately accessible because it no longer required specific congressional legislation to address each new disaster but instead simply allowed the president to decide when federal disaster assistance was justified and necessary. It also stated for the first time that federal resources could and should be used to supplement the efforts of others in the event of a disaster.

Policymakers of the era did not envision that the Disaster Relief Act of 1950 would have profound ramifications. They saw the measure as a standard congressional response to disaster. Only years later did congressional lawmakers begin to recognize this 1950 law as a "game changer." It came to be a landmark in the history of federal disaster policy. Moreover, it represented a major shift of decision-making power from Congress to all future presidents (see Table 3-1, item 4). Almost every issue or thread category of Table 3-1 was affected. Disasters and emergencies on the domestic level were gradually drawn into the spheres of national security, civil military relations, the globalization of disaster, and more.

The Disaster Relief Act of 1950 set forth a standard process by which governors of states could ask the president to approve federal disaster assistance for their respective states and localities. The law helped create a legal basis for an ever-evolving federal policy regarding post-disaster relief; it made abundantly clear national government responsibilities in disasters; and, it transformed the intergovernmental relations of disasters (see Table 3-1, item 3). The FDRA of 1950 founded a federal system that entrusted presidents with broad authority to define and declare disasters as they saw fit. The law also moved responsibility and accountability for meaningful disaster response and recovery to the president. However, Canton reminds us that preparedness (FCDA of 1950) and disaster relief (FDRA of 1950) were considered as two separate functions, not as parts of a system.[5] He observed that it took about another 40 years before each were judged to be linked components of a disaster management system.

Dual-Use Preparedness Programs

Through the 1950s, **civil defense preparedness** continued to evolve. Civil preparedness emergency management and the policy options associated with it were in great measure influenced by foreign policy and nuclear weapons technology matters. Certain foreign policy conflicts between the United States and the Soviet Union that came to diplomatic or military boiling points pressed American presidents to take various civil defense countermeasures on the home front. Many nations allied with the United States, most under defense treaties with America, helped form a bulwark against the perceived spread of Communism in its many forms. Moreover, as atomic weapons of the 1940s became thermonuclear weapons of the 1950s and beyond, their destructive capacity increased by many orders of magnitude. Over the years, nuclear weapons became smaller and more easily delivered to their targets by ever more sophisticated and faster ballistic missiles carried on submarines, in military aircraft, or launched from hidden land-based silos.[6] Over time, more and more civil defense options proved ineffective or infeasible even though new ones were regularly proposed.

President Dwight D. Eisenhower (in office from Jan. 1953 to Jan. 1961) advanced a mass evacuation policy instead of the shelter program initiated under Truman.[7] Mass evacuation measures only succeed, if they succeed at all, if there is sufficient advance warning of an impending nuclear attack and if presumed targets prove to be actual targets. The enemy of mass evacuation schemes are time limitations and the demands of mass population movement. President John F. Kennedy (serving from Jan. 1961 to Nov. 1963 when he was assassinated) emphasized the importance of home, school, or workplace fallout shelters as a means to save lives.[8] Kennedy's approach was shelter-in-place in a hardened structure. The Cuban Missile Crisis of October 1962 came close to triggering a nuclear exchange between the U.S.S.R. and the United States. Later, owing to escalation of the war in Vietnam, President Lyndon B. Johnson (in office from Nov. 1963 to Jan. 1969) put civil defense against nuclear attack on a back burner.[9] Attention to civil defense in the Johnson administration was also displaced by a series of major natural disasters that rattled the nation. Hurricane Hilda struck New Orleans in October 1964, and Hurricane Betsy devastated the American southeast in August 1965; a catastrophic Alaskan earthquake transpired in 1964, and a long-track tornado swept through Indiana on Palm Sunday in 1965. Johnson may have realized that some of the progress of his Great Society program was being undercut by domestic natural disasters. From 1950 under Truman to the mid-1960s under Johnson, federal post-disaster aid to states and localities largely involved government-to-government help and most of that repair and replacement of damaged public infrastructure. Nearly all presidential declarations of that interval were issued for floods, earthquakes, hurricanes, and severe storms of various types.

In 1965, Sen. Birch Bayh, D-IN, responded to the needs of his constituents in the wake of the "Palm Sunday tornado" disaster by championing legislation that granted emergency federal loan assistance to disaster victims. The bill passed in 1966, and Bayh urged Congress over the next few years to provide even more disaster assistance to citizens. The concept of all-hazards assistance was gaining adherents at the expense of civil preparedness for attack.[10]

In the late 1960s, President Richard M. Nixon (in office from Jan. 1969 to Aug. 1974) introduced National Security Decision Memorandum (NSDM) 184.[11] It recommended a **dual-use approach** to federal citizen preparedness programs and the replacement of the Office of Civil Defense with the Defense Civil Preparedness Agency (DCPA). Nixon implemented these recommendations, placing the new DCPA under the umbrella of the U.S. Department of Defense (DOD). Congress played a role in formulating dual-use policy through the Disaster Relief Act of 1966, a measure that linked civil defense warning systems with threats from natural disasters.[12] In 1973, the DOD determined that civil defense activities could also be used to prepare for natural disasters, "and the parallel tracks of civil defense and natural disaster management merged," into what became known as dual-use policy.[13]

After President Richard M. Nixon resigned from office in August 1974, his vice president, Gerald R. Ford, replaced him (Ford was president from Aug. 1974 to Jan. 1977). Ford initially supported the dual-use approach to disaster preparedness.[14] However, after only seven months in office, he rescinded (a means by which a president can cancel appropriated spending for a specific purpose during a federal fiscal year. Congress must vote majorities in favor of the proposed rescission within 45 days or else the rescission fails and the spending authority is reinstated)[15] the Defense Department's use of civil defense funding for natural disaster mitigation and preparedness.[16] Civil defense returned to what it was in the Truman and Eisenhower years, primarily a nuclear attack preparedness program.[17]

Ford was told about Soviet progress in civil defense against nuclear attack. It compared poorly with modest American efforts and so contributed to his belief that the United States was falling behind. Developments in Cold War diplomacy also contributed to the temporary suspension of all-hazards planning. Gradually the idea of limited nuclear strikes against strategically important military and industrial targets, rather than population centers, replaced earlier notions. Table 3-1 posited that international concerns would at times intersect U.S. disaster policy as it did at this time.

By 1978, with President James E. Carter's (Jan. 1977–Jan. 1981) assent, Congress amended the Civil Defense Act of 1950 so that it again authorized funding on a dual-use basis: "to prepare for the threat of enemy attack *and* for natural disasters."[18] For the first time in the history of U.S. civil defense, federal funds previously allocated for the exclusive purpose of preparing for military attacks could be shared with state and local governments for natural disaster preparedness. This dual-use initiative assumed that preparations for evacuation, communications, and survival were common to both natural disasters and enemy military attacks on the homeland.[19] From a practical perspective, the dual-use approach allowed planners to prepare for a broader range of disasters and emergencies. It also altered civil-military relations in matters of the nation's disaster management. The 1978 law also refashioned how emergency management would be conducted and funded.

Through the 1970s the concept of dual-use gained acceptance as the public perception of nuclear threats changed and as modest increases of federal funding to states, with shares passed through to local governments, spurred states and localities to increase their disaster planning and response efforts. In public management parlance, this infusion of federal funding helped build and grow state and local emergency management "capacity." This is something often overlooked by those who insist that the federal government should have little to no role in local and state emergency management.

Over the 1970s and 1980s, owing to advances in nuclear weapon miniaturization and new delivery systems by both the United States and Soviet Union, flexible targeting and limited retaliation evolved into the policy of "flexible response." Flexible response was based on the idea that both the Soviet Union and the United States had the ability to carry out small-scale nuclear attacks that could be answered by similarly sized acts of retaliation by the other side. Theoretically, instead of massive retaliation against population centers, targets would be specific, highly strategic sites. Since some of these sites could be civilian in nature, some level of civil defense and nuclear attack preparedness was deemed necessary. So again, U.S. policymakers again emphasized civil defense as a means of protecting against targeted highly strategic attacks.[20]

One result was a new initiative called the **Crisis Relocation Plan (CRP)**. CRP evacuation planning was to be done by state officials receiving federal funds. CRP work encompassed all of the necessary support for relocation, food distribution, and medical care. Under the CRP, urban residents would be relocated to rural host municipalities and counties. According to Corbett, "In 1982 President Reagan (in office from Jan. 1981 to Jan. 1989) proposed a seven-year, $4.3 billion program to upgrade national civil defense capabilities."[21] The revitalized civil defense program emphasized crisis relocation, or the evacuation of populations from as many as 400 high-risk target areas to locations of alleged safety. Proponents of crisis relocation argued it reduced the threat of war by reducing the vulnerability of population centers, and that it increased the prospects for survival of the urban population in the event war occurred.[22]

Vocal critics in Congress and among the public challenged the feasibility of such large-scale evacuations as they envisioned horribly bottlenecked transportation routes and grossly inadequate provision for food, housing, and other vital resources at the destinations of evacuees. However, as in previous administrations, civil defense still competed for funding against more traditional military expenditures, and the 1975 Ford increases were nullified the following year in favor of spending on offensive military capabilities. As a harbinger of things to come, in June 1976 the Working Group of the Cabinet Committee to Combat Terrorism called for the Federal Preparedness Agency to assume responsibility for coordination of federal and federal–state responses to terrorism.[23]

NATIONWIDE EMERGENCY MANAGEMENT

When President Nixon was inaugurated in January 1969, public and government interest in civil defense had fallen precipitously from its peak in the early 1960s. The Nixon administration helped "redefine civil defense policy to include preparedness for natural disasters."[24] After only seven months in office, Nixon himself was profoundly affected by his administration's poor experience in managing the Hurricane Camille disaster of August 1969. The haphazard and bungled federal response to Camille and its aftermath was a public relations nightmare for the new president. Nixon recognized that he had failed to meet rising public expectations about what the federal government could offer in post-disaster response and recovery, and he came to understand that how disaster management was conducted and funded was politically significant.

During the Nixon era and over the course of the 1970s, the basic governmental approach to disasters began to shift from an exclusive preoccupation with **structural hazard mitigation** (e.g., building flood works, coastal infrastructure, dams, and other "hard" engineered structures) to greater emphasis on the use of **nonstructural hazard mitigation** (e.g., using wetlands to buffer against flooding, protecting coastlines and barrier islands from erosion and development, encouraging the use of landscaping that protects structures from flooding or wildfires, and using other "soft" engineering approaches). Keith Smith posits that there are three eras of disaster mitigation history. He dubbed the first the "structural era," running roughly from 1930 to 1950, "hard" structures dominated mitigation.[25] Reservoirs, levees, sea walls, channelization, dams, stormwater collection and diversion systems, and other structures were typical of this era. He observed that "schemes were assessed on civil-engineering criteria and cost benefit grounds but little thought was given to community acceptance or environmental side-effects."[26]

In Smith's second era, from about 1960 to 1980, he tells us that non-structural measures gained acceptance in public policy. There was a mix of both "soft" and "hard" mitigation tools. Improved flood warning, stream gauging, land use planning, insurance, better management and preservation of wetlands as flood control, and other "soft" measures were "designed to reduce human vulnerability to floods." Matters concerning financial and ecological sustainability were introduced into debates about the worthiness of proposed or existing "hard structures."

In the late 1960s and early 1970s, the American environmental movement was widely popular among the public and many federal policymakers. Conserving wetlands, reducing humanity's impact on the natural environment, protecting natural habitats, and removing human structures and pollution contamination from areas where they were producing environmental damage were all tenets of American environmentalism. In many ways, American environmentalism and disaster mitigation complemented one another. Often, political alliances between environmental and disaster mitigation interests produced mutual victories. For example, the U.S. Environmental Protection Agency (EPA), which began operation in 1970, had an environmental emergency response division, conducted land and water environmental research that helped reduce disaster effects, and carried out an elaborate environmental impact statement process that was relevant to disaster mitigation efforts. For example,

> The Coastal Zone Management Act of 1972 gave states a great deal of authority to get involved in hazard mitigation planning and spawned a slew of state-enabling statutes, which required the adoption of hazard mitigation plans at the local level.[27]

Federal policy shifted from merely initiating projects designed to build physical barriers to emphasis on keeping people and structures out of hazard-prone, high-risk areas by encouraging states and their local governments to develop improved disaster mitigating zoning laws, building codes, and land-use regulations. Thus, national environmental and disaster policies combined to press more people and officials of state and local government to assume greater responsibility for where and how people lived.

In K. Smith's third era, running from the 1990s onward, more and more local communities have been encouraged to live safely with floods and other hazards in more sustainable ways.[28] Softer defense works in the era not only help reduce human vulnerability, but are used to limit ecological damage and visual blight. In a later phase, measures were advocated that improved or grew disaster resilience. In the third era, micro-protection of homes, businesses, and other structures against various hazard agents is considered in building and zoning laws.[29] Also, in the era more people have come to realize that retrofitting structures could help those edifices better withstand hazardous natural forces. Retrofitting was encouraged and, in some cases, subsidized. Acknowledgment of climate change-induced hazards, such as more temperature and precipitation extremes and sea level rise, have encouraged bolder hazard mitigation measures. These include a retreat in development or post-disaster rebuilding along many coastlines; many proactive insurance companies now press their policyholders to engage in improved hazard mitigation; and a great many public officials are becoming more aware of how long-term capital infrastructure will be impacted by natural forces, climate extremes, and sea level rise in the future, thus guiding their investment and development decision making.

Such lifestyle-changing policies, however, often created disputes between levels of government and between the government and the public. At one end of the intergovernmental spectrum is a growing sentiment among many federal, and a share of state, officials that their governments should not have to "bail out" localities that do not proactively protect themselves from known hazards through the reasonable use of improved zoning laws, building codes, and land-use restrictions. Besides the anti-bailout group, there were resentful local officials, aggrieved citizens, and various private interests who saw the mitigation conditions of federal flood insurance and federal disaster relief as unnecessarily burdensome and federal regulatory overreach. Citizens and private interests sometimes argued that federal rules intended to mitigate disaster restricted their personal freedom, diminished their private property rights, and were costly for them to obey. Many state and local officials remain steadfast in their belief that land-use is a traditional state and local government duty to be protected from federal encroachment. Many also think that land-use authority was one of those powers reserved to the states under the U.S. Constitution. A perennial worry of American local government officials has been fear of **federal zoning**, whereby federal officials enforcing such things as endangered species laws, coastal preservation, watershed management, air quality, transportation planning, public housing rules, certain realms of public eminent domain authority, flood hazard management, government mortgage rules, and more effectively preempt local control of land-use and building regulation.

Local people have often noticed that federal involvement in what was before state and local jurisdiction tends to gradually, or sometimes spectacularly, increase over time. Local control over land-use, zoning, and building regulation is often diminished or supplanted by both the federal and the state governments. Consequently, federal and state government policymakers have had to find inducements and uncontroversial ways to convince local publics and their government officials to recognize hazard vulnerability as a local collective "public duty" and to act responsibly to address it. For example, when local governments ignore the need to regulate certain forms of private construction or building maintenance that pose hazards to the public, they risk being sued for negligence by plaintiffs who allege in lawsuits that they have been harmed by both the private defendant's irresponsibility and by the municipality's failure to regulate in the interest of public safety. For example, if a municipality fails to regulate building fronts vulnerable to collapse onto public sidewalks, or if it claims to regulate that problem but fails to carry out inspections to enforce the regulations, and if a pedestrian is hurt or killed by a collapsing building front, both the building owner and the municipality may be subject to litigation by the plaintiff or her representatives.

Besides disputes between level of government over emergency management, there was also confusion among pre-FEMA federal-level organizations about who was to do what in handling disasters (see the "Tell Me More" 3-1 box).

TELL ME MORE 3-1
THE EVOLUTION OF FEDERAL EMERGENCY MANAGEMENT ORGANIZATIONALLY OVER TIME

From the 1950s to about 1979, problems arose because many federal disaster management responsibilities were parceled out to different federal agencies and offices. Disaster policy implementation duties resided in an assemblage of federal agencies, many of which were nested in different Cabinet-level departments. These bodies vied for control, jurisdiction, and budget money. Their powers often overlapped; there was frequent duplication of effort; and they occasionally worked at cross-purposes. These organizations worked under different laws and often

(Continued)

(Continued)

served policy purposes tangential to emergency management. This organizational jumble often generated complaints and criticisms, especially whenever mega-disasters challenged federal authorities to act. Moreover, there ensued a lack of leadership and coordination because respon-sibility for various types of disaster relief at the federal level seemed to bounce from one agency to another, especially after a new president took office. These problems and inconsistencies often complicated and confounded the work of state and local emergency managers.

TABLE 3-2 ■ Federal Emergency Management Organizations

Organization	Dates
Housing and Home Finance Administration	1951–1953
U.S. Small Business Administration (SBA)	1953–
Federal Civil Defense Administration (FCDA)	1953–1958
Office of Civil Defense and Mobilization	1958–1961
Office of Emergency Planning (renamed Office of Emergency Preparedness)	1961–1973
Federal Disaster Assistance Administration, Defense Civil Preparedness Agency (DCPA), and Federal Preparedness Agency	1973–1979
Federal Emergency Management Agency (FEMA) (independent agency)	1979–2003
U.S. Department of Homeland Security (DHS), FEMA	2003–

Between 1951 and 1973, disaster assistance and relief activities were at times a responsi-bility of five different federal agencies (see Table 3-2). From 1950 to 1979, elements of the federal emergency management portfolio included several federal offices and agencies not included in Table 3-2. For example, early public warning systems, federal agricultural disaster insurance, certain emergency trans-portation programs, emergency food and water programs, emergency temporary housing, emergency public health, and much more were not tethered to pre-FEMA agencies on the list. From 1953 to 1958, FCDA worked in so-called partnership with the Defense Department's Office of Defense Mobilization until those offices were merged in 1958. Yet, the U.S. Army Corps of Engineers, a preeminent federal disaster response and recovery agency, worked apart from these bodies.

The **U.S. Small Business Administration (SBA)** has long provided low-interest disaster loans to disaster victims who qualify for them. "Through its Office of Disaster Assistance (ODA), SBA is responsible for providing affordable, timely and accessible financial assistance to businesses of all sizes, private non-profit organizations, home-owners, and renters following a disaster. Financial assistance is available in the form of low-interest, long-term loans. SBA's disaster loans are the primary form of federal assis-tance for the repair and rebuilding of non-farm, private-sector disaster losses. For this reason, the disaster loan program is the only form of SBA assistance not limited to small businesses. Disaster Assistance has been part of the agency since its inception in 1953."[30] See the "Tell Me More" 3-2 box.

TELL ME MORE 3-2
THE U.S. SMALL BUSINESS ADMINISTRATION (SBA)

"The U.S. Small Business Administration (SBA) is responsible for providing affordable, timely and accessible financial assistance to homeowners and renters located in a declared disaster area. Financial assistance is available in the form of low-interest, long-term loans for losses that are not fully covered by insurance or other recoveries."[31]

"Homeowners may apply for up to $200,000 to repair or replace their primary residence to its pre-disaster condition. The loan may not be used to upgrade the home or make additions to it, unless as required by building authority/code. In some cases, SBA may be able to refinance all or part of a previous mortgage (not to exceed $200,000) when the applicant does not have credit available elsewhere, has suffered substantial disaster damage not covered by insurance, and intends to repair the damage. SBA considers refinancing when processing each application. Loans may also be increased by as much as 20 percent of the verified losses (not to exceed $200,000) to protect the damaged real property from possible future disasters of the same kind. Secondary homes or vacation properties are not eligible for home disaster loans; however, qualified rental properties may be eligible for assistance under the business disaster loan program."[32]

"Disaster survivors must repay SBA disaster loans. SBA can only approve loans to applicants with a reasonable ability to repay the loan and other obligations from earnings. The terms of each loan are established in accordance with each borrower's ability to repay. The law gives SBA several powerful tools to make disaster loans affordable: low fixed interest rates, long-terms (up to 30 years), and refinancing of prior real estate liens (in some cases). As required by law, the interest rate for each loan is based on SBA's determination of whether an applicant has the ability to borrow or use their own resources to overcome the disaster."[33]

Remember, currently, "the SBA can provide up to $200,000 to homeowners to repair or replace their primary residence. Homeowners and renters are eligible for up to $40,000 to help repair or replace personal property. There are no upfront fees or early payment penalties charged by SBA.[34] Because several sub-programs of FEMA's Individual and Households Assistance (see Chapter 4) are "means tested" (meaning, if one's income or cumulated personal wealth exceed a certain amount, one is ineligible for financial assistance) and because FEMA assistance to rebuild or replace homes or other residences is capped at a sum often far less than what many structures are worth, SBA loans provide a financial alternative for a vast number of disaster victims.

Also, renters and homeowners alike may borrow up to $40,000 to replace damaged or destroyed personal property such as clothing, furniture, appliances, automobiles, etc. As a rule of thumb, personal property is anything that is not considered real estate or a part of the actual structure. This loan may not be used to replace extraordinarily expensive or irreplaceable items, such as antiques, collections, pleasure boats, recreational vehicles, fur coats, etc.[35]

By 1969, the Nixon administration began making a host of organizational changes in federal disaster management.[36] In total, Nixon's emergency management bureaucratic structure parceled out responsibility for disaster relief among more than 100 federal agencies.[37] All these shifts of administrative authority may seem trivial and confusing. What is important is that there was no central administrative identity for federal emergency management over the Nixon, Ford, and half of the Carter years. Table 3-2 shows that from 1973 to 1979, three different federal agencies directly handled disaster management in some way. Various stakeholders and interest groups associated with policies other than natural and human-caused disaster policy managed to keep their respective pieces of disaster policy where they wanted them and did so ostensibly with White House and congressional consent. Housing, defense, insurance, business regulation, transportation, and other interests jealously retained control of their disaster-relevant jurisdictions.

Clearly, before 1979, federal emergency management was fragmented and lacked an integrated identity. When President Carter created the U.S. Federal Emergency Management Agency by executive order in 1979, an assortment of federal offices and agencies with EM-related duties were folded into the new FEMA. Miskel adduces that those units folded into FEMA were preparedness focused more than operational entities.[38] Nonetheless, this author and others have insisted that FEMA's "golden age" ran from its April 1979 start until its absorption into the new U.S. Department of Homeland Security in March 2003.

Some of the organizational mish-mash that occurred from 1951 to 1979 would be repeated after the 9/11 attacks in 2001, when fear of terrorism impelled policymakers to again reorganize emergency management. The enactment of the Homeland Security Act of 2002, a series of G. W. Bush administration presidential homeland security directives, and other policy changes squeezed a tiny FEMA into a giant "holding company" of big and small federal organizations, most of which handled some aspect of homeland security: border security, customs, immigration control, infrastructure protection, transportation security, coastal protection, national special security events, and so on.

In 2003, when FEMA, previously an independent federal agency for 24 years, was folded into the Department of Homeland Security (DHS), federal emergency management lost much of the integrated essence that it had acquired in the intervening years. It was not simply that FEMA was absorbed into DHS. In fact, FEMA was from 2002 until about mid-2007 hollowed out as top DHS officials tried to bind together and refashion all of the 22 DHS so-called "legacy agencies" into one administrative whole whose primary mission would be preventing or deterring acts of terrorism and helping the nation prepare for and respond to actual terrorist attacks. What G. W. Bush DHS administrators may have forgotten was that each of these agencies was never relieved of their original legal and program responsibilities.

From its start, FEMA embraced as its core mission disaster management in all of its phases and manifestations. By March 2003, the only DHS agency whose core mission was disaster management was FEMA. Moreover, FEMA was one of the few DHS agencies to have a long and deep history of relationships with state and local governments, especially through the fire service community. Many other DHS entities were accustomed to working exclusively at the federal level, internationally, or through links to state and local law enforcement authorities. Even the few organizations that had specialized links to state and local governments tended to work through geographic entities outside the ten standard federal region format that FEMA and so many other federal departments and agencies operated in.

Ironically, despite FEMA's much-maligned handling of the Hurricane Katrina disaster in 2005, Congress reinvigorated that DHS agency through the **Post-Katrina Emergency Management Reform Act (PKEMRA) of 2006.** What G. W. Bush administration DHS officials had taken from FEMA from 2003 to 2006 was largely replaced, re-entrusted, or strengthened under provisions of PKEMRA.

The Disaster Relief Act of 1974

In May 1974, President Nixon signed into law the **Disaster Relief Act of 1974**, a measure that sought to remedy the bureaucratic confusion created by the administration's earlier reorganizations. Also, the new law created a program that provided direct assistance to individuals and families following a disaster. From 1950 to 1974, federal post-disaster relief had been more generous to state and local governments than it had been to victims of disaster. Although preceding laws had provided temporary housing aid and other modest forms of in-kind individual assistance—food-water-clothing, etc.—the new **Individual and Family Grant (IFG) program**, renamed and refashioned as the Individuals and Households Program (IHP) in 2002, finally bridged the gap that had existed between public and individual assistance. Remember, "public assistance" here means government-to-government aid, not direct aid to the public. The IFG provision directed FEMA and its predecessor organizations to dispense directly, or through state agency workers, federal financial assistance to disaster victims when a presidential declaration of major disaster was in effect. The IFG program, and since 2002 the IHP, provides financial housing assistance that helps pay rent, alternative lodging expenses, home repair or home replacement, and certain other needs, all made necessary owing to a disaster or emergency of some type. Home replacement or repair covered by the homeowner's private insurer cannot be reimbursed under the program, but costs above the insurance claim payout may be eligible. Home replacement is means-tested such that many middle-class homeowners are ineligible for help under the home replacement part of the program, and so are steered to the Small Business Administration's disaster loan program. (See Chapter 4 for more about the IHP.)

Disaster's Public Money

Budgeted funding for these programs remained modest, however. The original Federal Disaster Relief Act of 1950 had the effect of minimizing congressional involvement in federal post-disaster relief. However, whenever a mega-disaster or accumulating smaller declared disasters tended to deplete the president's **Disaster Relief Fund (DRF)**, a main repository of federal post-disaster relief monies, Congress would be called upon to urgently approve emergency supplementary appropriations within a federal budget (fiscal) year to replenish the DRF. The fights in the House and Senate over the content of these supplemental appropriations often had the effect of re-politicizing disaster policy and implementation. Supplementals would arrive at each president's desk with non-germane riders that would never have won majority votes were they not appended to "must pass" disaster supplementals. These bills had the effect of ballooning federal spending and deficits, bypassing standard budget rules, and reminding everyone of why it had been wise to relieve the Congress of handling disasters on a case-by-case basis. The pattern of disaster supplemental appropriations has been maintained throughout the years. The most recent was in 2017 and 2018 when Congress appropriated over $136 billion to various federal agencies in response to the 2017 hurricane season.[39]

The Emergency Declaration Is Born

The Disaster Relief Act of 1974 brought state and local governments into all-hazards preparedness activities and provided matching funds for their emergency management programs. The act also authorized in law the **emergency declaration** category. This new declaration type was made necessary by the federal government's highly criticized 1972 experience with Hurricane Agnes.[40] Presidents Truman, Eisenhower,

Kennedy, and Johnson, who all served before 1974, could only issue declarations of major disaster. Now under emergency declarations, governors could ask the president to issue their state and localities an emergency declaration without having to have first conducted and completed a damage assessment, as is necessary when they ask the president to issue them a major disaster declaration. The emergency category was a great relief to governors because it made possible president-approved proactive federal mobilization for disasters that had not yet transpired but appeared imminent. If the president granted an emergency declaration, a governor could count on federal funding to help pay some of the costs of state and local pre-disaster mobilization. Yet, the emergency category also tempted presidents to issue declarations for events that would ordinarily not meet damage thresholds administratively set for major disaster declarations. However, it is essential to remember that emergency declarations do not ordinarily confer the range of federal disaster assistance available under major disaster declarations. In fact, FEMA must notify Congress if spending on an emergency declaration will exceed $5 million. This is why many mega-disasters are preceded by an emergency declaration and then followed up by a major disaster declaration. Emergency declarations sometimes allow presidents to appear proactive and compassionate in the time before a major disaster strikes.

Mitigation and Multi-Hazard Approaches

The 1974 law recognized the need for improved disaster mitigation. It required states and communities receiving federal disaster assistance to "agree that the natural hazards in the area in which the proceeds of the grants or loans are to be used shall be evaluated and appropriate action shall be taken to mitigate such hazards."[41] Despite lack of regulatory "bite," these provisions represented the first congressional call for hazard mitigation as a precondition for federal disaster assistance. Many hoped that the emphasis on disaster mitigation would save lives, protect both public and private property, and eventually suppress future disaster losses and costs.

The 1974 act was precedent setting in its own right. Among its features were the following:

1. Instituted the IFG program (mentioned above), which supplied 75 percent of the funding for state-administered programs providing cash help for furniture, clothes, and essential needs

2. Formalized efforts to mitigate, rather than simply respond to, disaster events

3. Mandated that local, state, and federal agencies develop strategies aimed at preventing disasters in the future

4. Stressed a **multi-hazard approach** to disasters, in which the government would manage all kinds of hazards, rather than maintaining unique and separated capacities to deal with different types of disaster agents[42]

The 1974 law also advanced multi-hazard, or all-hazards, approaches to emergency management. This inferred that before 1974 emergency management was fragmented and preoccupied with confronting individual disasters or specific types of disasters as if each disaster were unique or as if each category or type of disaster had its own independent set of response needs. An all-hazards approach would help reduce duplication and redundancy in emergency management. It would encourage cross-training of emergency responders, and it would encourage adaptability. It would also integrate functions and disaster types, providing more coherence for the field and the profession. Also, by emphasizing a multi-hazard approach, the Disaster Relief Act of 1974 signaled the diminution of civil defense issues, funding, and concerns in the realm of domestic emergency management. However, the bureaucratic rivalry between civil defense and emergency management officials would not end for 20 more years, when during the Clinton administration the Federal Civil Defense Act of 1994 was weakened and subsumed via amendment into Title VI of the Stafford Act.[43]

THE BIRTH OF THE FEDERAL EMERGENCY MANAGEMENT AGENCY

Few presidents are more associated with disaster policy than President James Earl Carter (Jan. 1977–Jan. 1981).[44] He is justifiably credited with establishing the Federal Emergency Management Agency (FEMA). As a former governor of Georgia, President Carter knew natural disasters well, and he was anxious to respond to the calls of many governors for improvements in the organization of federal disaster management.

FEMA had its origins in proposals put forward by the National Governors Association in the late 1970s and a 1978 working group formed by President Carter. In 1978, civil emergency management programs and activities were scattered among five principal federal departments and agencies. Using authority allowing him to reorganize the executive branch, President Carter presented Reorganization Plan No. 3 of 1978 to Congress for its approval in June.[45] Carter had specific aims in the plan:

1. To establish a single entity (FEMA), headed by an official directly responsible to the president that would serve as the sole federal agency responsible for anticipating, preparing for, and responding to major civil emergencies

2. To develop an effective civil defense system, integrated into the programs and operations of nonfederal entities, to improve communications, evacuations, warnings, and public education efforts to prepare citizens for a possible nuclear attack as well as for natural and accidental disasters (an all-hazards approach)

3. To rely on federal agencies to undertake emergency management responsibilities as extensions of their regular missions and on FEMA to coordinate these resources

4. To incorporate federal hazard mitigation activities, linked with state and local activities, into preparedness and response operations[46]

In the reorganization, FEMA absorbed the Federal Insurance Administration (FIA) (chiefly responsible for the National Flood Insurance Program [NFIP]), the National Fire Protection and Control Administration, the Federal Preparedness Agency of the General

Services Administration (GSA), and the Federal Disaster Assistance Administration that had resided in the U.S. Department of Housing and Urban Development (HUD). The DCPA at the Pentagon had its civil responsibilities transferred to FEMA as well.[47]

Carter moved civil preparedness programs, fire prevention and control, flood insurance, crime insurance, dam safety, earthquake hazard reduction, terrorism, and national emergency warning systems into the new FEMA and gave it primary responsibility for mobilizing federal resources, coordinating federal efforts with those of state and local governments, and where possible managing the efforts of the public and private sectors in disaster responses.[48] FEMA as a body was expected in times of disaster or emergency to act much like a symphony conductor seeking to unify performers playing "different instruments," setting the "tempo," executing "clear preparations and beats," "pacing the music," "listening critically," and "shaping the sound of the ensemble." Sometimes a conductor is expected to coordinate ensembles composed of a hundred performers. Admittedly, the conductor analogy is far-fetched in part because it entrusts FEMA with too much disaster response power. Regardless, the analogy evokes the need for multi-agency coordination (harmony), the need to keep pace (tempo or pacing) in the response and short-term recovery phase, the need for situational awareness and self-correction (listening critically), and the need to be prepared and practiced ahead of time.

Following congressional acceptance of Reorganization Plan No. 3, the new agency opened for business on the inauspicious date of April 1, 1979.[49] President Carter then issued an executive order in July that delegated most of the authority granted to the president under the Disaster Relief Act of 1974 to the director of FEMA. The order also transferred to FEMA various functions previously carried out by the DOD, HUD, and the General Services Administration (GSA), as well as by other federal entities. Also, the director of FEMA was delegated authority to establish federal policies for all civil defense and civil emergency planning, management, mitigation, and assistance functions of executive branch agencies. This continued the process of merging FEMA's national security duties with its civilian emergency management work (see "Tell Me More" 3-3 box). One section stipulated, "The Director shall be responsible . . . for the coordination of preparedness and planning to reduce the consequences of major terrorist events."[50] In August 1979, John Williams Macy, Jr., won Senate confirmation as the first FEMA director.[51] Macy had already compiled an impressive array of achievements in public service before President Carter tapped him to head FEMA. Macy had earned a BA, had done post-graduate study, and was a Rhodes Scholar nominee. Over his life, he held a two-year post in the Social Security Board and had served as a U.S. Army Air Corps captain for three years in the China theater during and after World War II. He held posts in the Pentagon. He also worked in and later directed the Los Alamos National Laboratory (1947–1953). Macy was the first director of the National Corporation for Public Broadcasting and, most significantly, he led the U.S. Civil Service Commission from 1953 to 1958 and again from 1961 to 1969. Macy was one of those individuals freely appointed or re-appointed by Democratic and Republican presidents alike. He stepped down from his post as FEMA director in late 1980 as Carter's term approached its end.[52]

FEMA itself ultimately absorbed civil defense, certain elements of national emergency preparedness, fire prevention and assistance, federal disaster relief, national flood insurance, earthquake hazards reduction, and dam safety. Under Carter, the new FEMA did not assume control of all federal disaster and emergency functions and programs. Consequently, a bevy of federal agencies continued to compete for jurisdiction over certain realms of disaster and emergency management. For example, disaster loan programs operated by the U.S. Small Business Administration and by the U.S. Department of Agriculture (USDA) Farmers Home Administration were not transferred into FEMA, and both continue operation today.

By May 1980, FEMA had adopted a fund-matching policy that required state and local governments to agree to pay 25 percent of the eligible costs of public assistance programs; however, emergency housing IFG remained fully federally funded. Prior to this time, the required nonfederal contribution was subject to negotiation between FEMA and the affected state and local governments. From 1950 to this writing, presidents have been free to waive all or part or the "state–local" match under any disaster declaration they issue, despite the 25 percent fund-matching rule (see Chapter 4). Waiving the state and local match fully or partially usually requires extraordinary circumstances. For example, when it appears that owing to the magnitude of disaster loss, a state and its local governments are overwhelmed and judged incapable of raising the money to pay their match-shares, the president may waive the matching share in full—thus committing the federal government to pay 100 percent of the eligible response and recovery costs. Also, in rare instances when the federal government itself has caused, is liable for, or has a significant federal interest in a disaster, the president may approve a full waiver of state and local match.

TELL ME MORE 3-3

"CIVILIANIZING" THE FEDERAL EMERGENCY MANAGEMENT AGENCY?

An intriguing political issue that arose during FEMA gestation involved the transfer of civil preparedness activities from the Pentagon to FEMA. Many questioned how important civil defense would be within FEMA. If civil defense were to be under the umbrella of the new FEMA, how would national security aspects of civil defense, particularly preparedness for nuclear attack, be addressed? Nuclear attack civil defense officials and domestic emergency management officials regularly fought or disagreed over management, funding, operations, transparency, matters of state secrecy, and personnel issues. At times, the FEMA public image suffered as various lawmakers and journalists alleged that the agency maintained an overly large and influential "secret" side: a side dedicated to certain national security concerns, such as continuity of government, national emergency communications, and maintenance of a set of secret underground facilities to be made available to the president and Congress during national emergencies.[53]

In combining national security work and traditional domestic emergency management work, each interacting awkwardly, the young FEMA gravitated toward an all-hazards approach to emergency management in a somewhat schizophrenic way. Because national security responsibilities were included in the job of Carter's new FEMA, most of the agency's personnel were required to apply for and hold certain security clearances. Sometimes these requirements extended out to state and local authorities, including various emergency responders.

Nuclear Power and Civil Defense

The month-long nuclear accident that began on March 28, 1979, at Metropolitan Edison's Three Mile Island Unit 2 nuclear power plant, located south of Harrisburg, Pennsylvania, changed federal emergency management and nuclear power regulation. Although the incident did not result in a presidential declaration of a major disaster, it did

(Continued)

(Continued)

persuade President Carter to quickly put FEMA into operation. The slow response, miscommunications, lack of decisive leadership, and poor coordination of the federal Nuclear Regulatory Commission (NRC) with the utility, the state of Pennsylvania, and affected localities demonstrated to policymakers the need to improve nuclear power incident response, coordination, and planning. Carter, reacting to vociferous criticism of the NRC by the news media and the public, entrusted FEMA with some of the NRC's emergency planning duties for areas surrounding nuclear power plants.[54] Remember, FEMA began its operations on April 1, 1979, three days into the TMI crisis.

At the time, the creation of FEMA represented the single largest consolidation of civil preparedness efforts in U.S. history. Federal emergency plans of the period continued in the vein of traditional civil defense, although Carter's executive order did urge FEMA to direct more of its attention to addressing peacetime disasters. Evacuation continued to be the focus of federal planners, and Carter's secretary of defense Harold Brown continued work on crisis relocation strategies. When FEMA assumed responsibility for citizen preparedness, the agency called on civil defense planners nationwide to create area-specific Crisis Relocation Plans (CRPs). The Carter administration's focus on evacuation

was very much affected by Cold War diplomacy of the late 1970s. The continuing Strategic Arms Limitation Talks with the Soviet Union created a conflict between the president's desire to advance U.S. civil defense and his desire to avoid upsetting the delicate strategic balance required for successful threat-reduction negotiations. President Carter continued to support evacuation policies, believing that this offered the best option for the nation.[55]

Given civil defense against nuclear attack concerns and the Three Mile Island nuclear power plant accident, President Carter concluded that it made sense to allow the new FEMA to include nuclear attack and nuclear power plant incident response and preparedness in its mission. However, FEMA was at its heart a civilian agency that included a variety of national security duties and responsibilities. As noted, many FEMA officials were required to hold security clearances that allowed them to do double duty. In other words, they could work in both civilian and national security realms. Sometimes natural disasters would pull the FEMA national security program staff into handling necessary civilian tasks. Conversely, sometimes national security incidents or crises would pull the FEMA security-cleared civilian workers into working for the agency's national security programs.

DISASTER DECLARATION ISSUES

From 1981 through 2001, the federal government increased its subsidization of state and local disaster response and recovery costs. Federal disaster outlays spiraled upward from the late 1980s to the present; some of this was attributable to ever-more expensive catastrophes over time, and some of this can be explained by a host of other factors.[56] Chapter 4 will examine presidential declarations of major disaster and emergency in greater detail.

A Disaster Metric for State Deservedness

In April 1986, FEMA proposed changing the process of declaring disasters, the criteria for eligibility for federal assistance, and the nonfederal responsibility for major disasters.[57] The suggested regulations would have decreased the federal share of disaster costs to 50 percent from 75 percent. Furthermore, states would have been required to meet certain economic criteria before they would be eligible to receive federal assistance, and they were expected to increase their cost-sharing responsibilities, along with that of their local governments, for disaster assistance. Due to strong opposition in Congress, FEMA subsequently withdrew the proposed rules.[58] In 1993, Congress amended the Stafford Act of 1988 to expressly prohibit FEMA from using only mathematical formulas in advising the president about the worthiness of a governor's request for a presidential declaration of major disaster. Lawmakers in Congress feared that if economic calculations of disaster loss were compared against a FEMA metric of presumed worthiness, and if this became the definitive basis for issuance of presidential disaster declarations, too many subjective factors would be overlooked and they would be screened out of making their case for a declaration to the president (see Chapter 4 for more about this).

However, FEMA does continue to employ criteria to evaluate a state or tribal nation's request for major disaster assistance. One such criteria measures economic impact in terms of damage costs calculated in per capita terms, which is damage costs to public infrastructure in total dollars compared to the state's population.[59] (See Chapter 4.) This information is included in the White House package FEMA conveys to the president as he decides on whether to approve or turn down the governor's request for a major disaster declaration. It is important to note that the per capita threshold amount, while very important, it is not the sole determination for a declaration. It is one of several factors evaluated by FEMA to make major disaster declarations. FEMA also evaluates other factors such as the amount of insurance coverage the area has, the impact the incident has had on special needs populations, and whether the area has had repeated disasters.

The Dual Use Dance and Fear of Federal "Big Foot"

Because disaster management is so centrally linked to the institution of the presidency, and because preparations for the destructiveness of a possible nuclear attack in some ways corresponds with preparedness for catastrophic natural or non-war disasters, it was not unreasonable to expect presidents from Truman through G. H. W. Bush to make one purpose also serve the other. Although formal dual-use policy had to await "official" approval in law in the 1970s, Presidents Truman, Eisenhower, Kennedy, and Johnson all found ways to make their civil defense programs, which were interlocked with state and local emergency management, provide some form of double duty as disaster management activities.[60]

The jumble of federal disaster agencies that operated from 1950 until 1979 connoted presidential and congressional failure to recognize the need for cohesiveness and sound organization in federal disaster management. Yet the limited range of federal disaster relief available to subnational governments and disaster victims in 1950 was gradually expanded, usually owing to controversial experience with mega-disasters, escalating disaster losses over many areas of the nation, and political pressure to increase federal government involvement in disaster response and recovery. More than this, emergency management itself was a nascent idea that took time to get traction, application, and refinement in conceptual terms and in practice terms.[61]

DISASTER LAW, POLICY, AND PUBLIC RELATIONS FROM REAGAN TO CLINTON

Disaster policy, regardless of laws and rules in force, has been very much a function of what each president and his appointed leaders wanted to do in this field. For President Ronald Reagan, FEMA was, for a few months, an uncomfortable holdover and remnant of the Carter administration.[62] Regardless, Reagan backed away from his campaign pledge to close FEMA and once in office he soon recruited FEMA into his strategic and tactical battle with Soviet communism. He also quickly discovered that FEMA was needed to help him handle disasters and emergencies of many types. Moreover, the Reagan administration operated in an era when worldwide 24-hour news coverage was beginning to flourish. Disasters and emergencies, big or small, got national television news coverage—often with riveting video images of the calamities and tragedies as they transpired. The 1980s were a time when the CNN example seemed to become pervasive for all major television network news organizations (see the "Tell Me More" 3-4 box).

TELL ME MORE 3-4
THE CNN EXAMPLE

President Reagan and future presidents had to learn to cope with a new stressor in emergency management: improved television news coverage of disasters and emergencies. In the early 1980s, Ted Turner's CNN showed that television news had achieved the ability to cover disasters and emergencies quickly, owing to major technological advances in electronics, satellite communications advances, miniaturization of cameras, and other equipment. News commentators could do voice-overs of live video from the field and could ask questions like, "What is the president doing about this?" or "Why isn't the president doing something?" Camcorder politics and **video journalism** came to be a television news staple. Television news now covered cities, states, or any region of the nation. Broadcasts could go global and take live feed of reportage and video from almost anywhere in the world. Spotlighted by media coverage, the major and minor disasters of the era were often quickly politicized—or at the very least political officials were expected

to be more immediately visible and responsive to them. In an era when the Internet and cell phone did not exist as they do today, network television news was a very dominant media. Many newspaper and radio station owners scrambled to establish their own TV stations to mimic CNN-type news coverage in their local markets after 1980.

In 1981, CNN, owing to its around-the-clock news broadcasting, was the first to break the story that a would-be assassin had shot President Ronald Reagan. In 1986, millions were watching CNN when the space shuttle *Challenger* exploded shortly after liftoff. CNN had been the only network carrying the launch live. "By then, some were calling the channel the 'Crisis News Network,' and it consistently pulled in large audiences when major stories broke."[63] CNN coverage of the *Challenger* disaster drew President Reagan into weeks of official pronouncements; he impaneled the Rogers Commission to investigate the incident and was filmed by CNN in several commemorations. Reagan, and each later president, learned to cope with, and sometimes use to their political advantage, CNN coverage. Owing to CNN and other 24-hour TV news channels (i.e., Fox News Channel, MSNBC, ABC News 24, Bloomberg Television, and many more), disaster and emergency video and reportage came almost immediately to the White House just as it did to the homes of millions of TV viewers. Other nations launched their own public and private news channels, many broadcasted in English and were available in the United States (i.e., formerly Al Jazeera English, BBC News and BBC World News, CBC News Network [Canada], DW-TV [Germany], France 24, NHK World-TV [Japan], RT [Russia], and more). Other private news channels outside the United States emerged as well (i.e., Times Now and NDTV Profit [India], Sky News [United Kingdom, Australia, New Zealand], Sky TG24 [Italy], Global News Network [Philippines], Dawn News [Pakistan], etc.).[64]

In the Reagan years, state and local government officials, recognizing the rising importance of emergency management and seeking to find ways to stretch dual-use civil defense to the limit, began to establish their own state and local variations of FEMA. Moreover, nonprofit organizations active in disaster, the nation's fire services, private property insurers, the nation's public safety and police officials, and others began to lobby on behalf of government emergency management interests as stakeholder groups.

From 1981 to 1989, President Reagan gave civil defense against nuclear attack priority in his disaster policy. He succeeded in convincing the nation to build up its defense against nuclear attack by Soviet intercontinental ballistic missiles (ICBMs) through an expensive antiballistic missile program. Reagan refused to take a vow of "no first use of nuclear weapons," thus reserving the right to use limited or medium-scale nuclear weapons (neutron bombs, tactical nuclear weapons, or the like) to confront or rebuff a conventional Soviet military attack or invasion of Western Europe. Through all of this, his administration tapped FEMA for help, and his FEMA directors were happy to oblige the president. Population sheltering and crisis relocation again became FEMA priorities. During this build-up, a Pentagon official created a public relations gaffe for the Reagan White House when he publicly remarked that Americans should be prepared to dig holes in their backyards and cover them with boards to survive a Soviet nuclear attack.[65]

Civil defense issues were moved to a back burner in the late 1980s as U.S.–Soviet relations improved. Both presidents Reagan and George H. W. Bush (1989–1993) built improved relations with the Soviet leader Mikhail Gorbachev, as they and the world watched Soviet communism collapse.[66] Yet in counterpoise, the threat of terrorism grew during the 1980s as the United States grappled with successive and sometimes tragic airliner hijackings and other terrorism incidents that sometimes killed or injured Americans. The civil war in Lebanon and a deadly suicide bomber attack on the U.S. Marine barracks in that nation in October 1983 was a harbinger of future terrorist attacks on American forces abroad.[67]

The Stafford Act of 1988

In November 1988, President Reagan signed into law the Robert T. **Stafford Disaster Relief and Emergency Assistance Act of 1988**, amending the Disaster Relief Act of 1974. The Stafford Act, as it came to be called, added many wholly new provisions, superseded many old ones, and revised others. The effects of the Stafford Act were so profound for emergency managers that this law came to demarcate the beginning of modern-era national disaster management. (The Stafford Act is examined in more detail in Chapter 4.) In the United States, new federal disaster laws are customarily cobbled together in the immediate aftermath of a mega-disaster of some type. The Stafford Act did not follow this pattern. It was crafted over many months when lawmakers were not rushed by the need to address a recent disaster. Many hearings were held and the Reagan administration, FEMA, and many other stakeholders were consulted. The new reform law sought to modernize federal emergency management. For example, under Stafford, the FEMA director (or after 2002, the secretary of Homeland Security and the FEMA administrator) recommends to the president appointment of a Federal Coordinating Officer (FCO).[68] The person appointed "is a senior FEMA official trained, certified, and well experienced in emergency management," and specifically charged with coordinating federal support in the response to and recovery from emergencies and disasters.[69] FEMA FCOs, when deployed, have authority to act as FEMA's primary representative in the field. FCOs play a very major role in disaster response and recovery. They are asked to achieve unification of myriad federal agency activity, to work cooperatively with their State Coordinating Officer counterparts (including tribal officials), and to interact with local authorities.[70]

Also, the Stafford Act reauthorizes the president to issue major disaster and emergency declarations, set broad eligibility criteria, and specify the type of assistance conferred. In the matter of emergency declarations, *emergency* refers to:

> Any occasion or instance for which, in the determination of the president, federal assistance is needed to supplement state and local efforts and capabilities to save lives and protect property and public health and safety, or to lessen or avert the threat of catastrophe in any part of the United States.[71]

As mentioned previously, this refinement of the definition of *emergency* clearly affords the president a great deal of latitude in determining what is or is not an emergency. In March 1989, an executive order issued by President George H. W. Bush delegated Stafford Act authority, with some exceptions (principally major disaster and emergency declarations), to the director of FEMA. The Stafford Act, much like the original Federal Disaster Relief Act of 1950, authorizes the president to issue major disaster declarations when an incident overwhelms state and local resources. See Chapter 4 for more about Stafford's effects on presidential declaration authority.

Regarding federal–state relations, President Reagan's record of approvals and turn-downs of governor requests for declarations of major disasters and emergencies says much about his philosophy of federal–state relations. A tough judge of declaration deservedness, to date Reagan turned down a larger share of gubernatorial requests for major disaster and emergency declarations than "almost" any other president from Truman to Trump. The exception was, ironically, President Jimmy Carter. He matched Reagan in the percentage of turndowns of governors' requests for major disaster declarations, but Carter approved a much larger share of emergency declaration requests than did Reagan (see Table 4-3 in Chapter 4). Emergency declaration requests do not require that governors submit damage estimates, as do their requests for major disaster declarations. Governors may have calculated that they could avoid Carter's high standard for major disaster qualification by seeking an emergency declaration at the outset. Later, Reagan proved to be nearly as tough on emergency declaration requests as he was on major disaster requests.

Yet, President Reagan was fortunate because the nation experienced few mega-disasters and no catastrophic disasters during his eight years in office. Nevertheless, disasters outside the United States, such as the 1984 poison chemical release in Bhopal, India,[72] and the 1986 Chernobyl nuclear power plant disaster[73] in the Soviet Ukraine, induced American policymakers to make changes in U.S. law and disaster policy that would avoid similar incidents at home.

George H. W. Bush, serving only one term in office, suffered through a series of mega-disasters both at the beginning and at the end of his administration. The Northern California Loma Prieta earthquake and Hurricane Hugo (which devastated much of the Carolinas), both transpiring in 1989, plus Hurricane Andrew in 1992, disclosed FEMA's limitations under George H. W. Bush and revealed significant flaws in the nation's system of disaster management.

The Federal Emergency Management Agency as an Instrument of Presidential Power

From 1950 onward, presidents were empowered to do something when disasters struck. Besides offering expressions of spiritual or symbolic support, presidents could sign disaster declarations, often while being filmed doing so in the Oval Office of the White House. As time passed, the number of federal agencies dispensing assistance to subnational governments and their eligible disaster victims grew. One of the effects of these changes was that pre-FEMA agencies working declarations, and later FEMA itself, would come to be appreciated as instruments of presidential power. The fortunes of the agency, for better or for worse, depended greatly on who the president chose to run it, how the president perceived its effectiveness and competence, and what types of incidents the president used it to address.

The president's Disaster Relief Fund authorized in 1950 provided the president a useful emergency spending account. Presidents could and did use it to fund unexpected problems not otherwise anticipated or not adequately funded in other programs established by Congress (see Chapter 4).[74] Thus, the Disaster Relief Fund is, in effect, a first-layer financial safety net open to the president; under the DRF, FEMA reimburses other federal agencies for costs associated with events the president chooses to declare as disasters or emergencies[75] under a disaster mission assignment, defined in the next paragraph. Note, in some cases, a federal agency may already have an account dedicated to emergency and major disaster recovery work (such as the Federal Highway Administration Emergency Relief program). Consequently, those agency disaster or emergency accounts should be fully obligated or expended before FEMA issues mission assignment spending authority to these organizations.

In other words, FEMA possesses authority, funding, and limited assets that enable it to do some disaster management work independently. However, it must depend on other federal departments and agencies to provide additional work and resources to ensure a complete federal response. Under a presidential declaration, FEMA may make DRF money available to other federal departments or agencies through "**mission assignment (by FEMA)**" authority. This funding may be conferred by the FEMA head, the associate director, or a FEMA region director. Mission assignment work orders usually direct a federal agency or office to complete a specified task using the approved funding and subject to managerial controls and guidance. Mission assignment work orders do not always involve DRF reimbursement.[76]

There are reasons why FEMA has been and remains deeply beholden to each president. It has a small, often politically weak, and occasionally divided set of clientele and communities of interest. FEMA has a base of support in Congress, but that base is usually only stimulated to act after disasters in which large sums of federal money need to be dispensed to meet a great many needs—needs often championed by lawmakers whose states and districts are impacted. Congress often exhibits great ambivalence toward the agency; they need it to do what it does, but they sometimes feel compelled to criticize it when their constituents complain about slow or inadequate disaster relief has been. If FEMA officials are highly responsive to presidential and congressional wishes and if they succeed in maintaining a positive image in the minds of most of the public, FEMA leaders judge this as successful management.

From 1979 to 2002, FEMA was an independent federal agency with few regulatory powers.[77] With some exceptions, the organization came to be exceptionally good at mobilizing contractors and temporary volunteer workers to meet most of the nation's fluctuating but routine disaster management needs. The FEMA full-time workforce from 1979 to 2003 rarely exceeded 3,000, as the agency relied on paid reservists and unpaid volunteers, various paid disaster-knowledgeable private contractors, and certain nonprofit organizations when circumstances dictated.[78] Moreover, FEMA's public assistance (government-to-government) program relied on heavy interaction with state and local emergency management or disaster recovery officials. Several of FEMA's individual assistance programs compensate states for program implementation, meaning that federal financial assistance is distributed by state offices and administrators. FEMA was also sometimes aided by state National Guard units deployed by the respective state governor and paid by the Department of Defense or the respective state government itself. Besides this, the independent agency's emergency response and recovery capabilities were dramatically enhanced by its ability to mobilize and work cooperatively with the people and resources of other federal agencies, including working under various emergency response plans in effect between 1981 and 2003. By federal fiscal years 2011 and 2012, FEMA told Congress it had a total full-time federal workforce of 5,645 and 5,101, respectively.[79]

Once FEMA became part of the DHS, it experienced major fluctuation in the size of its full-time workforce. In 2010, its full-time employee total, including paid volunteers, was 7,838 and by 2011 it rose to 10,054.[80] These totals included Disaster Assistance Employees (DAEs) and Cadre of On Call Response/Recovery Employees, shortened to CORE by FEMA (specialists for specific types of disasters retained for the full budget year, neither of which can be considered full-time federal civil servants). Conversely, FEMA has dramatically augmented its temporary workforce capacity by drawing from full-time employees of other agencies and offices of DHS when needed. In 2015, the Government Accountability Office reported that FEMA's combined workforce had grown from 7,558 in 2005 to 18,449 employees in September 2014. However, this figure includes a surge workforce composed of about 4,000 people outside of FEMA but in other DHS units who volunteered to be deployed to work specific disasters. It also includes about 1000 AmeriCorps volunteers, plus DAE workers and CORE employees also assigned to work individual disasters.[81] FEMA's FY 2018 budget request to Congress discloses that the agency had 8,806 full-time equivalent (FTE) workers in FY 2017 and sought only 1 additional FTE worker for FY 2018[82] (Oct. 1, 2017–Sept. 30, 2018). The 8,806 figure is under "Mission 5: Strengthen National Preparedness and Resilience." FEMA shows an additional 1,023 FTE workers for FY 2017 under the separate mission to "Mature and Strengthen Homeland Security." So, it is safe to report that FEMA had about 9,829 FTE workers during FY 2017.

It was somewhat difficult for the agency to maintain a high profile in the White House of both presidents George W. Bush and Barack Obama because, in 2003, it was emplaced in a department of some 220,000 full-time federal workers led by a secretary holding permanent cabinet rank. Over its first three years in DHS, FEMA was headed by a succession of disaster-inexperienced G. W. Bush political appointees (Joseph Allbaugh and Michael Brown) who held the title of undersecretary. When Hurricane Katrina struck in 2005, FEMA still only comprised 3 to 5 percent of the total full-time federal employee workforce of DHS. Despite criticisms of its performance in the hurricane, FEMA won a reprieve from a benevolent Congress. It was reconstituted by the Post-Katrina Emergency Management Reform Act (PKEMRA) of 2006. The title of FEMA's head was converted from undersecretary to administrator. More importantly, the FEMA administrator was by law ensured direct access to the president during very major disasters and emergencies. After Hurricane Katrina, Presidents G. W. Bush, Obama, and Trump made a habit of appointing only well-qualified and experienced emergency managers to lead FEMA.[83]

Stakeholders in Disaster Policy

Any history of American emergency management must consider stakeholders. There are many sets of stakeholders in U.S. disaster policy and emergency management. Stakeholders are persons, individually or in a group, who have, or think they have, something to gain or lose in a policy domain. In emergency management, they are people and organized interests of people affected by the decisions of policymakers and emergency officials. Some stakeholders unselfishly seek benefits or protections for the people or groups whose interests they champion.

The nation's pool of emergency managers, public safety directors, and firefighters, working mostly at the state or local level, usually supports FEMA strongly.[84] Less committed but still likely to promote federal emergency management are many of the nation's governors, mayors, and county executives. In addition, the people of nonprofit organizations active in disasters, who often work shoulder to shoulder with FEMA temporary workers and whose organizations often qualify for FEMA funding in declared disasters or emergencies, can usually be counted on to back the agency as a stakeholder and clientele group. FEMA has a considerable training component that helps it build friendships and working relationships with others, but it does not usually conduct its own research and it only indirectly supports higher education research and teaching in emergency management. Occasionally FEMA supports academic research projects of various types, but owing to highly competitive contract bidding rules, sole source contracts are rare and so Beltway contractors are likely to swallow up the small amounts FEMA offers in its requests for proposals.

Additionally, property insurance officials are also stakeholders. They are almost uniformly enthusiastic about federal efforts in disaster loss reduction but always suspicious that the federal government might nationalize certain lines of their private insurance. Regardless, private insurers have often found it advantageous to promote government emergency management.[85] Another set of stakeholders include major construction firms, the building trades, and economic development interests, who have all benefited from post-disaster, federally subsidized reconstruction. However, these same groups sometimes perceive FEMA as a de facto regulator or inhibitor of development and construction in times between disasters, *particularly when the agency advances disaster mitigation or presses local governments to restrict building or rebuilding in hazard zones.*

FEMA trainers list these as stakeholders in disaster recovery:

- Local, state, and federal government agencies

- Citizens (as disaster victims)

- Media (all types)

- Businesses and corporations

- University and research institutions

- Nonprofit agencies and emergent community organizations

- Contractors

- Associations and collaborative partnerships[86]

These sources of support are vital in the maintenance of FEMA's political life. Remember, it was a set of unhappy governors and a concerned ex-governor elevated to the presidency that chiefly helped create FEMA in the late 1970s. Regrettably, the collective political power of FEMA stakeholders is not strong when compared with the political clout of special interest and clientele groups supporting many other long established federal departments and agencies. For example, consider health policy and the program offices of the U.S. Department of Health and Human Services (HHS). Clearly, HHS stakeholders such as the American Medical Association, the American Hospital Association, health maintenance organizations, major pharmaceutical companies, health insurance companies, and others have vastly greater political influence, and lobbying power, in Congress than FEMA backers do.[87]

Disasters, as prevalent as they may seem nationally, are by definition intermittent and, at least for any specific locality, infrequent. People who survive disasters and who receive aid from FEMA, or from any government agency at any level, do not necessarily go on to champion emergency management. Disasters unquestionably affect the perceptions of voters, regardless of whether or not they directly experienced a disaster themselves.[88] A growing number of Americans have come to respect, admire, and praise emergency responders. However, disasters rarely affect how people cast their votes in elections, and even more rarely do disasters influence election outcomes. According to political scientists Kevin Arceneaux and Robert M. Stein, "Whether citizens blame the government depends on their level of political knowledge" and how severely the disaster affected their lives. "Although many individuals attribute blame to the government, it does not affect their voting decision for mayor unless they blame the city in particular."[89] Still, there have been some notable exceptions in a few states and cities, as when elected or appointed government officials bungle management of a disaster and an election looms a few weeks or months in the future.[90]

U.S. Emergency Management and Federalism

When examining the evolution of emergency management from 1981 through 1992, one is inevitably led to ask, why does it seem that disaster management is moving away from being a function that is state and locally centered to one that is federally centered?

How was it that the president and Congress expanded the federal role in disaster management and how was it that governors, as well as state and local authorities, were willing to submit to this accretion in the federal role?

Over the 1980s, President Reagan, a former two-term California governor, espoused a **New Federalism** policy. His philosophy assumed that states too often relied on the federal government for help in matters they could easily address on their own. Reagan insisted that the federal government needed to be less intrusive in matters traditionally left to state and local government. A catchword of the Reagan era was "devolution" of certain federal responsibilities back to the states and localities.

However, from 1989 through 1992, when President George H. W. Bush held office, the number of disasters increased and the scale of disaster devastation for several of them bordered on catastrophe. Thus, on average, more presidential disaster declarations were issued than in the Reagan years. Natural and human-caused disasters challenged the government's system of disaster management. Governors grew accustomed to regularly requesting declarations for major and minor disasters and emergencies. In addition, Bush and federal policymakers themselves seemed more receptive to greater federal involvement in emergency management, a realm long understood to be a local and state responsibility.

In April 1992, the **Federal Response Plan (FRP)** was issued. It established a process and structure that promised more systematic, coordinated, and effective delivery of federal assistance to address major disasters or emergencies declared by the president. The central goal of the FRP was to better organize federal agencies in pre-disaster planning for the work they would be expected to undertake in disasters. The plan laid out emergency support functions in which certain federal agencies (not always FEMA) would be assigned lead-agency role. The FRP also directly stated that sometimes a major disaster or emergency may affect the national security of the United States.[91]

Owing to the 9/11 attacks, to formation of DHS, and to President George W. Bush's issuance of Homeland Security Presidential Directive-5 (HSPD-5) in early 2003, an NRP was developed to replace the FRP. It was to "align federal coordination structures, capabilities, and resources in a unified, all-discipline, and all hazards approach to domestic incident management."[92] In many ways, the trend toward "nationalizing disaster" management and toward creating a National Response Plan (NRP), as introduced in Chapter 1, under which ideally federal, state, and local authorities worked in unison, was something well under way before the 9/11 attacks and before the era of homeland security. By 2008, the NRP was replaced with a more collaborative National Response Framework (NRF) geared to better consultation with state and local governments, and greater flexibility.

The NRF so-called third edition took effect in 2017. The third edition of the National Response Framework advocates a "whole community" approach in which all participants work together. Response efforts are related to other parts of National Preparedness. The NRF is at this writing one of five documents in the suite of **National Planning Frameworks**. Each covers one preparedness mission area: Prevention, Protection, Mitigation, Response, or Recovery.[93] All of these frameworks have many features and elements that cannot be reviewed in detail here. The third edition NRF reiterates the principles and concepts of the 2013 version of the NRF and sets forth the new requirements and terminology of the National Preparedness System. By fostering a holistic approach to response, this NRF version emphasizes the need for the involvement of the whole community. Along with the National Planning Frameworks for other mission areas, this document now describes the all-important integration and interrelationships among the mission areas of Prevention, Protection, Mitigation, Response, and Recovery. In many respects, this multiple framework's approach, seeking to be all-inclusive and "whole community," broadens planning vertically and horizontally. It pulls in several new partners: science and technology offices tasked with addressing cybersecurity, public health organizations pitched to handle disease and pandemic outbreaks, and logistics and supply chain management, etc. Fire Management and Suppression is now listed as a core capability. Other purposes, such as law enforcement, police on-scene security and protection, and services offered in health organizations, emergency medicine (including pre-hospital care provides), and fatality management, also have joined the National Planning Framework community.[94]

Famous disaster sociologists have warned against making disaster plans that are too complex, too vast for any single individual to master, and too large and unwieldly to use as a guide under acute emergency response conditions. By growing disaster planning into a jungle of documents everyone can seemingly contribute to (from individuals and households, to governors, to the FEMA head, and to the president), the entire effort risks production of "fantasy documents." Time will tell.

Terrorism Displaces Civil Defense

On November 18, 1988, the Reagan White House issued an executive order No. 12656 titled "Assignment of Emergency Preparedness Responsibilities," which defined a national security emergency as any occurrence that seriously degraded or threatened the national security of the United States.[95] Terrorist incidents were not directly addressed but only listed as Department of Justice responsibilities. The National Security Council (NSC) was assigned responsibility for developing and administering this national security emergency policy. The director of FEMA was to assist in the management of national security emergency-preparedness policy by coordinating with other federal departments. FEMA was also to be responsible for coordinating, supporting, developing, and implementing civil national security emergency preparedness and response programs, continuity of government functions, and civil-military support. This executive order was in effect for five years.[96]

However, by the very late 1980s and early 1990s, civil defense against nuclear attack proved less essential as the Cold War came to a rapid and surprising end. Consequently, civilian emergency management that addressed other hazards in the United States benefited accordingly. Federal, state, and local emergency managers were gradually freed of the restraints imposed by civil defense dual-use requirements—in which civilian use of federal emergency management funding had to have an acceptable civil defense justification—that had previously confounded and frustrated emergency managers at all levels.

Ironically, by the 1990s a countermovement was under way. Homeland security governance began to evolve. In 1998, the Hart-Rudman Commission on national security called for creation of a National Homeland Security Agency.[97] Simultaneously, the DOD began to use the term *homeland defense*. Homeland security governance was to rest on emergency management, civil defense, resource mobilization, and counterterrorism.[98] This movement originated years in advance of the 9/11 attacks; even so, terror attacks at home—the 1993 bombing of the World Trade Center and the Murrah Federal Building bombing in Oklahoma City in 1995—were harbingers of the threat terrorism would pose for the United States domestically.

The Clinton–Witt FEMA Era

President William Jefferson Clinton's administration (in office from Jan. 1993 to Jan. 2001) represented a watershed in U.S. disaster policy history.[99] Clinton had twice been governor of Arkansas, and he had had good and bad experiences with FEMA through the years. Clinton was governor when President Carter issued a major disaster declaration to help Florida address the influx of fleeing Cubans during the so-called Mariel boatlift in 1980. Arkansas was selected as a place to host a type of detention facility to house many of these evacuees. FEMA and other federal agencies were to separate average Cubans from the convicted criminals Fidel Castro had funneled in among evacuees. Long processing times and poor living conditions impelled some of those in detention camps to riot, thus producing a political headache for both President Carter and Governor Clinton.

Arkansas, like many states, experienced its own share of floods, tornadoes, severe storms, and other disasters through the years. Clinton knew what federal help meant to states and their governors. Clinton was also keenly aware of President George H. W. Bush's disaster management failures and problems with both Hurricane Andrew and Hurricane Iniki, both produced widespread human suffering. Andrew and Iniki took place a mere two months before the 1992 presidential election, and this gave presidential contender Bill Clinton the opportunity to use FEMA mismanagement and slow response under G. H. W. Bush as a strategic weapon in his campaign. Hurricane Andrew cut a devastating path across south Florida just below Miami, which itself sustained damage. The mid-August Category 5 storm "was blamed for 61 deaths and an estimated $27 billion in damage, or $47.8 billion in 2017 dollars, according to the National Oceanic and Atmospheric Administration. At the time it was the costliest hurricane in United States history; it has since been passed by Katrina in 2005 and Sandy in 2012."[100] Andrew destroyed or damaged some 125,000 homes, left 160,000 homeless, and displaced a quarter million people.

Iniki was a Category 4 tropical cyclone carrying windspeeds of 140 mph. On September 11, 1992, it struck the state of Hawaii, causing the heaviest damage on the island of Kauai. It killed six and generated about $3.2 billion (1992 USD) in damage, including destruction of some 1,500 homes and significant damage to some 14,000 homes and buildings.[101]

Between 1993 and 2001, several other mega-disasters and a great many smaller disasters transpired, including the great Midwest flood (1993), California's Northridge earthquake (1994), and a series of highly destructive hurricanes. Also, as mentioned, the World Trade Center truck bombing of 1993 and the Murrah Federal Building bombing in Oklahoma City in 1995 signaled an escalation in the scale of terrorist attacks inside the United States.

Under the Clinton administration, FEMA enjoyed its "golden years," although agency staff probably did not realize it at the time.[102] Under President Clinton, FEMA was directed by an experienced emergency manager, his Arkansas friend James Lee Witt. FEMA continued as an independent agency but always beholden to presidential support. President Clinton and Director Witt did much to phase out FEMA civil defense activities. Witt created three functional directorates within FEMA, corresponding to the major phases of emergency management: mitigation; preparedness, training, and exercises; and response and recovery. The shift in emergency preparedness toward an all-hazards approach allowed FEMA to focus on addressing natural disasters without having to fear negative political reactions from advocates of civil defense. The agency's mitigation directorate, for example, concentrated many of its early initiatives on such hazards as flooding and earthquakes.

At the same time, however, recognition of the threat of terrorist attacks inside the United States became tragically obvious. In 1993, Congress included a joint resolution in the National Defense Authorization Act that called for FEMA to develop "a capability for early detection and warning of and response to potential terrorist use of chemical or biological agents or weapons; and emergencies or natural disasters involving industrial chemicals or the widespread outbreak of disease." As evidenced by this resolution, Congress was becoming increasingly concerned about the threat posed by terrorist organizations and technological disasters. Much of this concern resulted from the World Trade Center bombing earlier that year, an attack committed by a group of radical Islamic fundamentalist terrorists (later determined to have been led by Osama bin Laden), in which 6 people were killed and 1,042 were wounded, most by smoke inhalation during their escapes from the towers. The blast left a five-story-deep crater inside the complex and caused $500 million in damages.[103] The attack had been an obvious attempt to collapse one or both of the Twin Towers of the World Trade Center.

By early 1993, President Clinton and Congress helped divest FEMA of many of its responsibilities in planning and preparing for nuclear attack by Russia, which had shed Communism in the early 1990s. In November 1994, the National Defense Authorization Act for fiscal year 1995 stipulated that the policy of the federal government was for FEMA to provide necessary direction, coordination, guidance, and assistance so that a comprehensive emergency preparedness system would emerge for *all* hazards in the United States.[104]

In January 1994, the FEMA National Security Steering Group, chaired by a FEMA national security coordinator, was established to serve as the focal point for intra-agency and interagency coordination of national security–related activities. It was to ensure that national security matters were integrated into the FEMA "all-hazards" approach to emergency management. Nonetheless, there was "pushback" by FEMA Director James Lee Witt. According to Morton, "James Lee Witt did not want his agency to be in the counter-terrorism business, a preparedness tasking that would compete for funds with its mitigation and disaster assistance functions."[105]

In November 1994, under a National Defense Authorization Act, the old Civil Defense Act of 1950 was repealed and all remnants of civil defense authority were transferred to Title VI of the Stafford Act. The all-hazards approach to preparedness, much favored by state and local emergency managers, had finally broken free of the confines of "civil defense against nuclear attack" dual-use restrictions. FEMA now had the statutory responsibility for coordinating a comprehensive emergency preparedness system to deal with all types of disasters. Title VI also ended all Armed Services Committee oversight over FEMA and significantly reduced the priority of national security programs within FEMA. Money authorized by the Civil Defense Act was reallocated to natural disaster and all-hazards programs, and more than 100 FEMA defense and security staff members were reassigned.[106]

Support for traditional civil defense declined, but in the 1990s terrorism by non-state actors was increasing. FEMA had just undergone a complete reorganization early in the Clinton administration, and so FEMA leadership had no appetite for additional responsibilities and obligations in matters of terrorism.[107]

Among his many achievements as director of FEMA, James Lee Witt approved a Federal Coordinating Officer Professional Cadre (FCOPC) initiative in 1999. This provided a training and promotion ladder for FEMA officials who were, or desired to be, appointed as federal coordinating officers for disasters. As FEMA announced in 1999,

> Recent Congressional legislation authorized the establishment of a FCO Professional Cadre (FCOPC) to manage disasters and emergencies. This legislation in conjunction with the attached Credentialing Plan will provide consistency in disaster response operations and is necessary for optimizing Federal support to the states. This Credentialing Plan establishes rigorous requirements involving training, experience, evaluation of demonstrated knowledge, skills & abilities and professional development. The intent of the plan is to have FCOs progress through a series of challenging requirements to prepare them for their critical role in various levels of disasters.[108]

The Rise of Terrorism as a Cause of Disaster

During the Reagan, G. H. W. Bush, and Clinton administrations, terrorism abroad and at home gradually emerged as a new and major concern of federal emergency management. The United States has a long history of dealing with terrorists and terrorism, but the first presidential disaster declaration for a terrorist-caused incident occurred only after the 1993 truck bomb attack on the World Trade Center in New York City early in the Clinton first term.

This attack was followed in 1995 by a much deadlier truck bomb attack, committed by domestic terrorist Timothy McVeigh and his co-conspirators, on the Murrah Federal Building in Oklahoma City, killing more than 168 people, 19 of whom were children, and injuring about 500 others.[109] The Oklahoma City bombing was the first disaster in which FEMA officials had to work closely with FBI officials. The attack, although committed by Americans, drew FEMA further into the business of managing the consequences of terrorism.

The Oklahoma City bombing impelled the president and other policymakers to seek clarification of the FEMA role in terrorism consequence management.[110] Also, this was one of the very few times that a president had used his authority under the Stafford Act of 1988 to issue an emergency declaration before a governor requested one.[111] Ordinarily, presidents do not issue an emergency or major disaster declaration in the absence of a governor's request unless the disaster or emergency involves a direct federal concern.

A presidential decision directive issued by Clinton in June 1995 stated that it is the policy of the United States to use all appropriate means to deter, defeat, and respond to all terrorist attacks on our territory and resources, both people and facilities, wherever they occur. It assigned main responsibility for crisis management to the Department of Justice and main responsibility for consequence management to FEMA.[112]

So even before September 11, 2001, domestic disaster management began to be eclipsed by the nation's growing concerns about terrorism.[113] Some policymakers and emergency management professionals worried that the devastation from human-made disasters, particularly terrorist-caused disasters, would match or exceed the scale of damage caused by natural disasters.

In 1994, amendments to the Title VI of the Stafford Act of 1988 told FEMA to provide the necessary direction, coordination, guidance, and assistance to create a comprehensive emergency preparedness system based on all-hazards emergency management, including terrorism. FEMA was tasked with devising federal response plans and programs for the emergency preparedness of the United States, in cooperation with state and local emergency preparedness efforts. The FEMA director could request reports on state plans and operations for emergency preparedness as may be necessary to keep the president, Congress, and the states advised of the status of emergency preparedness in the United States.

As part of the effort, Emergency Management Assistance Compacts (EMACs) were negotiated via agreements of various state governments and approved in federal law by Congress and the president. They were pre-disaster interstate compacts aimed at facilitating cross-border mutual aid among signatory state governments. The compacts also sought consistency with federal emergency response plans and programs. They were fundamentally intended to help states and their respective localities assist adjacent states and localities experiencing disaster in some form. Most compacts called for reciprocal state emergency preparedness legislation advancing mutual aid and assistance between states and in cooperation with the federal government.[114] Such initiatives promised signatory states cross-border help in times of disaster, and the agreements helped avoid problems of legal liability, cost reimbursement, and regulatory misunderstandings common whenever responders from one state cross over into another state.

Disaster Mitigation Becomes Law and Policy

Disaster mitigation is defined as sustained action to reduce or eliminate risk to people and property from hazards and their effects. The recovery phase of disaster offers opportunity for mitigation actions. In December 1993, following the great Midwest flood of the previous summer, the **Volkmer Amendment** contained within the Hazard Mitigation and Relocation Assistance Act of 1993 amended some parts of the 1988 Stafford Act. The Volkmer Amendment increased FEMA funds dedicated to community assistance disaster funding for relocation or hazard mitigation activities from a subsidy of 10 percent (in the original Stafford Act of 1988) to 15 percent.[115] What this means is that once FEMA has paid out a sum total of federal disaster relief to a state under a presidential declaration of major disaster, the state then is entitled to receive additional federal money equivalent to 15 percent of the total funds the state received from the federal government under the declaration. The state may use this additional federal money to subsidize state and FEMA-preapproved disaster mitigation projects. Such projects pay for relocating buildings vulnerable to flooding, improving stormwater systems in various municipalities, bridge retrofitting, seismic reinforcement of public structures, or other purposes.

The Volkmer Amendment also increased from 50 percent to 75 percent the federal share of the cost of specific mitigation activities or projects. This increase greatly benefited states and localities that put forward worthy mitigation projects and that were willing to come up with the remaining costs. The amendment also stipulated federal rules and conditions under which FEMA could "buy out" damaged homes and businesses vulnerable to recurring disaster loss owing to their presence in high-hazard zones; it required the complete removal of such structures in certain circumstances; and it dictated that the purchased land be dedicated "in perpetuity for a use that is compatible with open space, recreational, or wetlands management practices."[116] One reason why so many U.S. cities today have open space, bikeways, river walks, parks, and other recreational amenities adjacent to rivers and streams running through their jurisdictions is because of their disaster mitigation efforts, many of these subsidized by FEMA mitigation funding.

President Clinton, Director Witt, and many thousands of Southern Californians had to endure a major earthquake that tested the competence of FEMA and the California Office of Emergency Services, as well as almost countless emergency response organizations in and around Los Angeles. "On January 17, 1994, at 4:31 a.m., a magnitude 6.7 earthquake struck the San Fernando Valley region of Los Angeles, killing more than 60, injuring more than 9,000, and causing widespread damage. Freeways crumbled, gas mains burst and caught fire, apartment complexes collapsed, and power was lost to vast sections of the city. Thousands of buildings were either destroyed outright, or declared unsafe to enter, and later demolished."[117] Under Witt's leadership, FEMA confronted the Northridge quake's effects by expediting relief payments to homeowners whose houses were believed to be near the temblor's epicenter; set out a "Fast Track" system of housing assistance; fielded crisis counseling helpers; and maintained an automated process for handling victim claims that ran full tilt for more than 11 weeks. If anything, FEMA was criticized for doing too much too soon rather than too little, too late.[118] Northridge was in the early 1990s the nation's most expensive disaster.

By early 1995, Witt's vision for FEMA was to strive for a cooperative effort among the three levels of government and their respective agencies, through the Partnership for a Safer Future for America. The initiative included a wide assortment of FEMA stakeholders. Witt wanted to ensure that more people were dedicated to protecting their families, homes, workplaces, communities, and livelihoods from the sometimes devastating effects of disasters. FEMA wanted builders and developers to construct hazard-resistant structures located out of harm's way. The agency's leaders hoped that governments and private organizations would set forth plans, compile necessary resources, and rigorously train and exercise for disaster responses. Another goal was community preparation and planning for recovery and reconstruction before disasters struck.

Central to Witt's vision was an increased emphasis placed on disaster mitigation. FEMA had housed a collection of modest mitigation programs before Witt's regime, but Witt made mitigation the foundation of emergency management and the primary goal of the agency.[119] The reasoning was that mitigation activities and strategies may substantially reduce the impact of disasters and, in some cases, prevent disasters altogether.

Through highlighting mitigation efforts and securing more program resources, FEMA could substantially enhance its capacity and presence in intergovernmental relations on a continuous basis, rather than merely after a disaster. Whether such invigorated FEMA mitigation efforts would elicit adequate state and local responses, however, was uncertain. Local officials sometimes assume that they have little to gain from mitigation efforts, because in the event of a disaster, the federal and state government will pay the major share of their local disaster losses.[120] Moreover, mitigation efforts often have to compete with the far more alluring concerns of economic growth and development on the local level. Because local officials, developers, and citizens often view mitigation efforts as financially costly and restrictive of personal freedom, mitigation efforts were bound to become politically controversial.

In October 1997, the Clinton-Witt FEMA launched **Project Impact**, an effort that sought to build disaster-resistant communities through public-private partnerships.[121] The endeavor included a national public awareness campaign, the designation of pilot communities, and an outreach effort to community and business leaders. FEMA encouraged communities to assess the risks they faced, identify their vulnerabilities, and take steps to prevent disasters. The first three pilot communities were Deerfield Beach, Florida; Pascagoula, Mississippi; and Wilmington, North Carolina. Soon after, communities in the states of California, Maryland, Washington, and West Virginia joined Project Impact. The FEMA goal was to have at least one Project Impact community in every state by September 30, 1998. The program resonated well with U.S. lawmakers, and Congress appropriated $30 million for Project Impact for the federal fiscal year 1998 and $25 million for fiscal year 1999. Ten years later, Project Impact communities such as Tulsa, Oklahoma; Seattle, Washington; Miami-Dade County, Florida; and Jefferson County, West Virginia, among others, continued to sustain their disaster mitigation initiatives.[122]

Project Impact was a small-scale but widely popular "distributive" politics program. It was distributive in the sense that "benefits" were allocated narrowly to an interested pool of local government applicants aided by their respective states. The "costs" of the program were shouldered broadly by the national taxpayer, but the funding amounts were so modest relative to the size of the federal budget that any single national taxpayer was spending only a fraction of a cent on the program. The logic behind the project was that the small federal subsidy could leverage ambitious local and community-level mitigation activity while at the same time raising community awareness of disaster vulnerability.

Project Impact paved the way for enactment of the **Disaster Mitigation Act of 2000 (P.L. 106-390) (DMA 2000)**, a law that amended the 1988 Stafford Act and gave FEMA authority to establish a program of technical and financial assistance for enhanced pre-disaster mitigation to state and local governments. FEMA was to help state and local governments develop and carry out pre-disaster hazard mitigation measures that were cost effective and designed to reduce injuries, loss of life, and damage to and destruction of property, including damage to critical services and facilities under the jurisdiction of the states or local governments.

DMA 2000 also upgraded the 1974 requirement for post-disaster mitigation plans by requiring that states prepare a comprehensive state program for pre-disaster emergency and disaster mitigation before they could receive post-disaster declaration mitigation funds from FEMA. It also required local governments to identify "potential mitigation measures that could be incorporated into the repair of damaged facilities" before being eligible for pre- and post-disaster funding. The aim of this policy was to encourage local governments to engage in such mitigation activities as "hazard mapping, planning, and development of hazard-sensitive building codes."[123] The pre-disaster mitigation efforts that grew out of Project Impact built community partnerships and sought to increase community support for actions proposed. By 2001, more than 200 local governments were participating in Project Impact.[124]

Nevertheless, the success of the DMA 2000 and Project Impact has been modest at best. It is difficult for the federal government to compel county and municipal governments to take mitigation steps.[125] Disaster mitigation work at the local level is often difficult and controversial. Community opposition to mitigation may result from the costs mitigation imposes on residential and commercial property owners, from countervailing local development pressures, from a lack of political will or funding needed to retrofit existing government-owned facilities, and from controversy surrounding private property rights and government "takings" issues.

THE 9/11 ATTACK REMAKES U.S. DISASTER MANAGEMENT

On September 11, 2001, foreign terrorists stormed the flight decks, killed the pilots, copilots, and others, and so hijacked four large commercial jetliners to carry out suicide attacks. The first aircraft struck the upper floors of the North Tower of New York's World Trade Center (WTC). Within minutes a second was flown into the South Tower of the Trade Center. Meanwhile, in the skies above the mid-Atlantic area, terrorists piloting two more hijacked airlines prepared for their attacks. One of those planes was flown into the side of the Pentagon, penetrating through two outer rings. A fourth plane, United Airlines Flight 93, might have also struck a critical Washington target had it not been for the heroic efforts of passengers who fought to regain control of the plane. Hijackers of Flight 93, realizing they would be overwhelmed by a group of passengers, deliberately brought the plane down. Flight 93 crashed outside of Shanksville, Pennsylvania, killing all on board.

President George W. Bush (in office from Jan. 2001 to Jan. 2009) issued an emergency declaration to New York State immediately upon Governor George Pataki's request, and six hours later the president issued a major disaster declaration to the state for New York City (approximately six hours after the initial attack at 8:43 a.m. Eastern Daylight Time).[126] Soon after, Virginia (the Pentagon is in Arlington County, VA) and New Jersey (home for many of those who perished in the attack and which had under-Hudson commuter rail connections to the WTC) were issued major disaster declarations as well. On September 14, 2001, President Bush signed a declaration of national emergency, anticipating other possible terrorist attacks. By September 15, 2001, Congress had approved a $40 billion emergency supplemental appropriation to pay for 9/11-related disaster relief and further antiterrorism and counterterrorism actions.

Months later, several congressional leaders advocated creating a homeland security department. President Bush at first opposed the idea on grounds that another new, large federal bureaucracy was not the way to prevent or prepare for future possible attacks. However, he relented in the face of growing political pressure to establish the new department. Moreover, the G. W. Bush administration's White House-level Homeland Security Council, led by former Pennsylvania governor Tom Ridge, proved to be an awkward and powerless entity. The **Homeland Security Act of 2002** was passed by Congress late in that year and signed into law by President G. W. Bush. On January 24, 2003, the DHS began operation in accord with the new law.

The creation of the DHS was one of the largest federal reorganizations since President Truman created the DOD in 1947. As DHS was being formed, it incorporated all or part of 22 federal agencies, 40 different federal entities, and approximately 180,000 employees.[127]

The reorganization merged together agencies (or parts of agencies) with very different organizational structures, missions, and cultures, and, importantly, diverse ideas about the management of domestic threats and emergencies. In the emergency management arena, the overall effect of the reorganization has been to expand the role of defense- and law enforcement–oriented agencies concerned exclusively with terrorism while diminishing the role and decreasing the prestige of organizations conducting non-terror emergency management (see Figure 3-1).[128]

Homeland Security Presidential Directive-5

Profound events in U.S. history have often triggered major changes in the governmental process.[129] A great political impetus to act on terrorism was provided by the investigations and reports of the National Commission on Terrorist Attacks Upon the United States, commonly referred to as the 9/11 Commission.[130] From this, the George W. Bush administration was pressed to prepare a comprehensive and new National Response Plan (NRP).

On February 28, 2003, President George W. Bush issued HSPD-5.[131] Its purpose was to help the United States better manage domestic incidents "by establishing a single, comprehensive national incident management system." The secretary of DHS was given responsibility for implementing HSPD-5 by developing the NRP and a National Incident Management System (NIMS), which was introduced in Chapter 1.[132] To this end, HSPD-5 called for development of a "concept of operations" for disasters. It would incorporate all levels of government as well as crisis and consequence management functions within one unifying management framework to manage **domestic incidents**. Under HSPD-5, all federal agencies were required to adopt NIMS and to make its adoption a requirement for other governmental entities receiving federal assistance. Specifically, sections 3 and 4 revealed how the marriage of conventional disaster management and terrorism consequence management would work. Section 3 sets out the objectives of the department:

> To prevent, prepare for, respond to, and recover from terrorist attacks, major disasters, and other emergencies, the United States Government shall establish a single, comprehensive approach to domestic incident management. The objective of the United States Government is to ensure that all levels of government across the Nation have the capability to work efficiently and effectively together, using a national approach to domestic incident management. In these efforts, with regard to domestic incidents, the United States Government treats crisis management and consequence management as a single, integrated function, rather than as two separate functions.[133]

Section 4 summarizes the general responsibilities of the secretary:

> The Secretary of Homeland Security is the principal Federal official for domestic incident management. Pursuant to the Homeland Security Act of 2002, the Secretary is responsible for coordinating Federal operations within the United

FIGURE 3-1 ■ U.S. Department of Homeland Security, FEMA Organizational Chart in March 2018

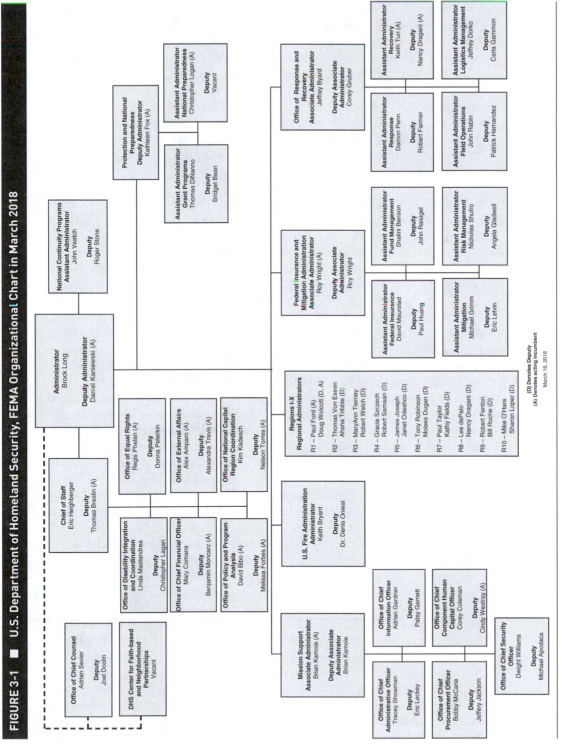

March 16, 2018

(D) Denotes Deputy
(A) Denotes acting incumbent

Source: Federal Emegerncy Management Agency, https://www.fema.gov/media-library-data/1530013746275-e64418b73bc6677e3153bf65ae6a7f64/FEMA.pdf.[134]

States to prepare for, respond to, and recover from terrorist attacks, major disasters, and other emergencies. The Secretary shall coordinate the Federal Government's resources utilized in response to or recovery from terrorist attacks, major disasters, or other emergencies if and when any one of the following four conditions applies: (1) a Federal department or agency acting under its own authority has requested the assistance of the Secretary; (2) the resources of State and local authorities are overwhelmed and Federal assistance has been requested by the appropriate State and local authorities; (3) more than one Federal department or agency has become substantially involved in responding to the incident; or (4) the Secretary has been directed to assume responsibility for managing the domestic incident by the President.[135]

Additionally, section 15 calls for a NIMS that is to include a core set of concepts, principles, terminology, and technologies covering the Incident Command System (ICS); multiagency coordination systems (MACs); unified command; training; qualifications; certification; and incident information collection, tracking, and reporting.

However, in calling for the development of a new NRP, HSPD-5 seemingly ignored the fact that the United States already had a plan for coordinating the federal response to major disasters. The existing Federal Response Plan (FRP), which had been developed in the late 1980s and used over the 1990s, had proved effective for coordinating "federal" resources in many major disasters and emergencies. It had even worked well in managing the effects of the 9/11 attacks. Although the NRP did not supplant that framework, it did make several important modifications. Under the NRP, the primary responsibility for managing domestic crises was now to rest with the secretary of homeland security. The plan also contained language strongly suggesting that the federal government would in the future assume more responsibility for directly managing some crises. State and local governments were included, but some alleged that subnational officials were poorly consulted in the design of the new plan. This significantly disregarded the "bottom-up" emergency management and "shared governance" policies that had existed before.[136] In effect, state and local governments were no longer completely free to independently devise their own emergency management systems. They now had to work in conformity with the national template largely fashioned by federal officials endeavoring to obey new federal law and presidential orders.

Owing to state and local emergency management resistance, federal lawmaker assent, and a dismal NRP experience during and after the Hurricane Katrina catastrophe, the plan was revised, updated, and reissued as the National Response Framework (NRF), which was introduced in Chapter 1, in early 2008. The NRF is constantly subject to revision. In the 2008 round, state and local emergency management partners were both included and consulted in the framework's development process. The NRF established a comprehensive all-hazards approach intended to strengthen and improve the ability of the United States to manage domestic incidents in cooperation with state, local, tribal, and territorial governments. In the NRP, **incidents of national significance** encompassed major disasters or emergencies declared by the president and/or the secretary of DHS. However, under the NRF the term *incidents of national significance* was eliminated.[137] Nonetheless, the secretary of the DHS could continue to "use limited predeclaration authorities to move initial response resources closer to a potentially affected area," and presidential authority to issue a variety of other types of disaster or emergency declarations, whether of national significance or not, was unaffected.[138] Simply put, the troublesome and often confusing incident of national significance designation appeared to both duplicate existing presidential authority as well as seemingly invest the DHS secretary with a special form of discretionary power that was largely symbolic.

On December 17, 2003, President G. W. Bush issued HSPD-8.[139] This directive gave the secretary of DHS broad authority in establishing **national preparedness** and implementing programs to improve "prevention, response, and recovery" operations. Although the directive explicitly calls for actions that address all hazards within a risk-based framework, its major focus is on preparedness for terrorism-related events. Similarly, although HSPD-8 was intended to address issues related to preparedness, a broad term that is generally conceptualized as an integrative and comprehensive process, the directive is mainly concerned with training and equipping emergency response agencies.[140]

In late August 2005, the Gulf Coast from southern Louisiana to the tip of Florida's panhandle experienced catastrophe. The following account concisely summarizes events surrounding Hurricane Katrina and the federal response for New Orleans in particular:

> Before Hurricane Katrina made landfall, Governor Katherine Babineaux Blanco declared a state of emergency in Louisiana on August 26, 2005, and asked President [G. W.] Bush to do the same at the federal level the next day, a request with which he complied. This authorized FEMA to organize and mobilize resources as it saw fit to help the residents of New Orleans (Office of the Press Secretary 2005). The same day, the mayor of New Orleans, C. Ray Nagin, declared a voluntary evacuation of the city. This evacuation became mandatory the very next day, August 28, the day before the hurricane hit the city. Many residents did not have the ability to leave the city, so the Superdome was opened as a site for residents to weather the storm (USC Annenberg 2005).
>
> The hurricane hit on August 29th. As a direct response, FEMA mobilized 1,000 Homeland Security workers to provide assistance to the city (USC Annenberg 2005). In an effort to organize the response, FEMA also asked that no firefighters or ambulance crew respond to areas hit by Hurricane Katrina without being first mobilized by local and state authorities, a declaration that undoubtedly slowed response to the disaster (FEMA 2005). FEMA seemed almost unwilling to accept help from non-government organizations. For example, the American Red Cross was not allowed into New Orleans following the disaster and was unable to supplement the government's response (American Red Cross 2005). By August 30th, the Superdome was packed past capacity, with at least 20,000 people residing in the building. The situation in the Superdome eventually became so bad that it had to be evacuated the next day (USC Annenberg 2005).
>
> As the situation unfolded, it became clear that the government's response was inadequate and inefficient. The federal government did not have adequate information concerning the true devastation that the hurricane had caused (White House). Despite the quantity of government workers in the area, the effects of the hurricane continued to wreak havoc on the city with people still stranded in New Orleans and looters robbing stores left and right. Firefighters from around the country were called to the region to help with the federal government's response.

Many of these firefighters were not able to put their skills to use in rescue operations, but instead had to spend time handing out flyers for FEMA to residents of New Orleans (USC Annenberg 2005). The organizations in charge of search and rescue, the Urban Search and Rescue and the Civil Search and Rescue, did not coordinate their efforts and lacked a strategy for their mission (White House).[141]

Hurricane Katrina immediately swallowed up $10.4 billion in federal aid, and Congress added after that an additional $51.8 billion.[142] From 2005 through 2008, congressional appropriations to address Hurricanes Katrina and Rita cumulated to $120 billion. In 2006, Congress passed and President G. W. Bush signed the Post-Katrina Emergency Management Reform Act (PKEMRA). Although discussed previously, it is worth adding, "PKEMRA significantly reorganized FEMA, provided it substantial new authority to remedy gaps in response, and included a more robust preparedness mission for FEMA."[143] This act:

- Establishes a disability coordinator and develops guidelines to accommodate individuals with disabilities

- Establishes the National Emergency Family Registry and Locator System to reunify separated family members

- Coordinates and supports precautionary evacuations and recovery efforts

- Provides transportation assistance for relocating and returning individuals displaced from their residences in a major disaster

- Provides case management assistance to identify and address unmet needs of survivors of major disasters[144]

Testifying before Congress in March 2004, former FEMA director James Lee Witt warned that the nation's ability to respond to disasters of all types has been weakened by some post-9/11 agency realignments. In written testimony regarding the loss of cabinet status for the FEMA undersecretary and the position of FEMA within DHS at the time, Witt stated, "I assure you that we could not have been as responsive and effective during disasters as we were during my tenure as FEMA director had there been layers of federal bureaucracy between myself and the White House."[145]

In January 2009, President Barack Obama was inaugurated. Interestingly, his inauguration ceremony was declared a national special security event by the U.S. Secret Service months before, and President George W. Bush had issued an emergency disaster declaration for the District of Columbia well in advance of the day. Both measures helped fund and organize security, law enforcement, and emergency management for the event. The new president nominated Craig Fugate, a highly experienced emergency manager and firefighter from Florida, as FEMA administrator.

President Obama confronted a series of national economic emergencies as massive banks and investment houses continued to fail and as the national housing market cratered. In some respects, Obama's great reluctance to turn down disputable governor requests for declarations of major disaster and emergency during his first term may have been a subtle effort to use federal post-disaster relief as a kind of economic stimulus for states and localities double hit by economic hard times and a calamity of some sort. In 2011, he set a record for issuing the largest number of presidential disaster declarations of any previous president. Obama was neither motivated to remove FEMA from DHS, nor was he interested in diminishing homeland security powers. He did support federal disaster mitigation targeted to help the states and their localities. He was proactive in preparing for and responding to disasters that befell the nation. Moreover, he is one of the first presidents to recognize the disaster-causing potential of climate change effects. In 2012, as he sought re-election, several competitors in the opposing political party, including the ultimate Republican presidential nominee, former Massachusetts governor Mitt Romney, alleged that the president had misused his disaster declaration authority and had been economically wasteful and political in doing so.[146] Some criticized FEMA and sought its termination.

Ironically, by late November 2012, President Obama appeared to have been vindicated on all counts. He won re-election and a second term. Soon after, he and his emergency management workforce had to respond to Superstorm Sandy, which ravaged nearly the whole of the New Jersey Atlantic coastline and extensive inland areas, produced a massive swath of damage across Long Island, New York, with barrier island areas hardest hit, and flooded significant portions of lower Manhattan, including two major under-river auto tunnels. Not to be forgotten, it also hit low-lying, populated areas of Staten Island, New York, causing fatalities. The president issued disaster declarations to Sandy-impacted states and visited damage zones, often with his FEMA administrator at his side. The Obama White House judged recovery from Sandy as largely a housing challenge, and to the chagrin of the emergency management community, Obama appointed the secretary of HUD to lead the federal recovery effort in cooperation with state and local authorities.[147] President Barack Obama completed his second term and left office in January 2017.

Not to be overlooked is that President Obama, even though he disliked the term and wanted it discontinued, supported and advanced the nation's "**war on terror**." Under Obama's watch, Osama bin Laden, the founder and first leader of the Islamist group Al-Qaeda, was killed in Abbottabad, Pakistan, on May 2, 2011, by U.S. Navy SEALs of the U.S. Naval Special Warfare Development Group. Bin Laden had been among the plotters of the 9/11 attack and was implicated in other terror attacks on American civilians and military people inside the United States and abroad.[148] Nonetheless, the Obama administration was plagued by a succession of deadly radical Islamist attacks at home and elsewhere. The American ambassador to Libya and three other Americans were killed when terrorists attacked and burned the U.S. diplomatic compound in Benghazi on September 11, 2012. On April 15, 2013, two radicalized terrorist brothers detonated two bombs near the finish line of the Boston Marathon, killing 3 people and injuring 260. In San Bernardino, California, a radicalized Islamic couple went on a shooting rampage, killing 14 and injuring 22 on December 14, 2015. On June 12, 2016, self-radicalized Omar Mateen opened fire at a gay nightclub, killing 49 and injuring 53.[149] These are just a few examples. Many other less spectacular but still deadly domestic terrorist attacks took place over Obama's two terms in office.

On January 20, 2017, Republican Donald J. Trump, having won more electoral college votes than his Democratic opponent, Hillary Clinton, in the November 2016 presidential election, was sworn in as the 45th president of the United States. Despite the turmoil he encountered in making cabinet-level department appointments and in staffing his White House, the Trump administration continued to process governor requests for declarations of major disaster and emergency much as previous administrations had done. Many declarations were approved, and as Chapter 4 will show, few governor requests to President Trump were turned down. There were two matters of recent history that stand out. First, President Trump was slow to appoint and win Senate confirmation of a FEMA administrator, but so too a succession of people moved through the DHS secretary post over 2017, among them, former DHS secretary and at this writing White House chief of staff, John Kelly. On June 20, 2017, Trump's pick, William Brock Long, who had been director of the State of Alabama's Emergency Management Agency, was finally confirmed as FEMA administrator in a 95–4 Senate vote.[150] Second, President Trump, and the nation as a whole, had the misfortune to experience three mega-disaster hurricanes—Harvey, Irma, and Maria—in 2017. Chapter 9 will be devoted to an analysis of these hurricane disasters from the vantage point of victim disaster relief.

The Trump administration has broadened the fight against terrorism. The following passage produced by the European Parliament Think Tank concisely encapsulates this change. "To improve the country's intelligence and homeland security apparatus, the presidential administrations of George W. Bush and Barack Obama implemented a series of legislative, organizational, policy, and personnel reforms. The new administration under Donald Trump is continuing these efforts and has put particular emphasis on restricting the entry of and tightening the vetting process for refugees and immigrants. The administration has released a series of documents that provide strategic guidance for the U.S. approach to national security and defense. Today, the U.S. domestic counter-terrorism strategy focuses on radical Islamic terrorist threats, stopping the movement of foreign terrorist fighters, and countering the spread of radicalization. In this context, cyberspace is of particular interest, since the internet provides opportunities for terrorists to inspire, radicalize and recruit followers; raise funds; communicate through encrypted apps; and supply guidance and instructions to followers for carrying out attacks. The European Union and the United States are key partners in the fight against terrorism, including through NATO."[151]

Summary

This chapter explored almost 70 years of disaster policy history. It revealed that presidents take their disaster declaration authority very seriously. Presidents from Truman to G. H. W. Bush, generally heeding limits set by Congress, tethered civil defense to a nascent and evolving state and local emergency management of non-war disasters and emergencies. The theme and thread of civil defense continued for decades, often confounding or complicating conventional emergency management.

Disaster policy is not simply emergency management shaped by presidents and other policymakers and carried out by government workers. Disaster policy is a mix of conventional all-hazards emergency management, civil defense, and since 2002, homeland security. Presidents from Reagan to Trump have counted on FEMA to manage a dizzying array of disasters stemming from natural or human causes. The agency was expected in the response and recovery phases to handle large, middle-sized, and small disasters and emergencies. Many expansive disasters included all or parts of many states, sometimes even spanning FEMA regions. Because declared major disasters and emergencies show up serially on FEMA's doorstep, the agency was often forced to manage several disaster responses and recoveries at the same time. FEMA's portfolio almost always included civil defense against nuclear attack. After the terror attacks of 2001, FEMA was also expected to serve the homeland security mission in a variety of ways. While FEMA has a unique ability to expand and contract its workforce to cope with multiple disaster management demands, plus a massive funding backstop in the form of the Disaster Relief Fund, it continues to remain dependent on sitting presidents, on an understanding Congress, and since 2002, on a tolerant and supportive DHS hierarchy. Moreover, FEMA must work cooperatively with governors and locally elected or appointed executives, satisfy a wide assortment of hard-to-please stakeholders, meet the needs of new disaster victims, and all the while protect the national taxpayer's dollar.

This chapter summarized the history of presidential domination of disaster policy formulation and implementation since 1950. Congress has afforded the president considerable and unfettered discretion to define for the nation what is or is not a disaster or an emergency. This chapter demonstrated that emergencies and disasters are in some ways "political" constructs. The president is even entrusted with a fund he can use to pay for various disaster-related costs for the declarations he issues. Congress periodically must replenish these funds with new spending authority under emergency supplemental appropriations, something increasingly controversial in the federal

budgetary environment since the economic downturn of 2008 and the tax cut of 2017.

Presidents from Truman to Carter conducted disaster policy implementation through an assemblage of federal organizations. Some of these organizations resided in the White House, some operated as major and minor arms of federal departments, and some labored in obscurity as back offices of independent agencies. It was not until year three of the Carter administration (1979) that U.S. disaster policy was granted a formal organizational and functionally integrated home. It came in the form of a small independent federal agency whose workforce for many years was unrealistically capped at about 3,000. FEMA officials have always understood that they survived and succeeded largely as a result of how the agency was perceived and used by the president. The agency lacked a strong pool of stakeholders that could assiduously lobby for it on Capitol Hill. It was too small to go toe-to-toe with the much larger departments like defense, HUD, justice, or transportation. Whatever clout FEMA possessed had to be reinforced by the White House and collegially supported by other federal agencies serving various emergency support function (ESF) arrangements in times of disaster.

Table 3-1 listed thread #10, the changing nature of disaster, and thread #11, rising public expectations in disaster. The nature of disaster needs to be considered a variable that changes over time. In many ways, the public, news and social media, and public officials, including presidents, have shaped the definition of disaster. Along with these changes also came a change in the metric of deservedness used to determine whether federal assistance will be part of a state and local disaster or emergency response and recovery (more on this in Chapter 4). Embedded in all of this are hazard vulnerability and increasing dependence on communications technologies that are today penetrating nearly all facets of modern life. Consider the range of technological and communication advance from 1950 to the present. Consider American population growth, economic development, land development, transportation, and medical advances since 1950. Included in all of this are international concerns: trade and interdependence, national security concerns (including ye old civil defense), globalization of many sectors of the U.S. economy, the rise of global environmental and resource concerns, and much more. A significant problem of emergency management, from the U.S. perspective, is that so many other policy areas seek to encroach upon or swallow up disaster management as a field. How long will it be before the knowledge, skills, and ability to be an emergency manager are too multi- and cross-disciplinary for a single individual to reasonably achieve? (See Chapter 5.)

History shows that certain catastrophes or unique disasters help produce new disaster laws.

Yet, presidents, in cooperation with Congress, have mostly fashioned and steered federal disaster policy. The theme of federal–state and intergovernmental relations is evident throughout the chapter and will emerge again with more detailed analysis in Chapter 6. Similarly, matters of civil defense and homeland security were chronicled in conjunction with maturing conventional all-hazards disaster management. Subsequent chapters delve more deeply into matters of presidential disaster declarations, the role of science and engineering in the field, how intergovernmental relations work in emergency management, how civil-military relations influence disaster policy, how disaster policy has global relevance, and what the hurricanes of 2017 have revealed about disaster politics and policy today. This chapter was an attempt to paint an accurate, although compressed, picture of America's disaster policy history.

Key Terms

Civil defense preparedness 88
Crisis Relocation Plan
    (CRP) 90
Disaster Mitigation Act of 2000
    (DMA 2000) 118
Disaster Relief Act of 1974 96
Disaster Relief Fund 97
Domestic incidents 120
Dual-use approach 89
Emergency declaration 97
Federal Disaster Relief Act of
    1950 (FDRA) 87
Federal Response Plan
    (FRP) 111
Federal zoning 93

Homeland Security Act of
    2002 119
Incidents of national
    significance 122
Individual and Family Grant
    (IFG) program 97
Mission assignment (by
    FEMA) 107
Multi-hazard approach 98
National Planning
    Frameworks 111
National preparedness 123
New Federalism 111
Nonstructural hazard
    mitigation 91

Post-Katrina Emergency
    Management Reform Act
    (PKEMRA) of 2006 96
Project Impact 118
Self-help 87
Stafford Disaster Relief and
    Emergency Assistance Act
    of 1988 105
Structural hazard
    mitigation 91
U.S. Small Business
    Administration (SBA) 94
Video journalism 104
Volkmer Amendment 116
War on terror 125

U.S. President Donald Trump visits residents affected by Hurricane Maria in Guaynabo, west of San Juan, Puerto Rico, on October 3, 2017.

Mandel Ngan/AFP/Getty Images

4

PRESIDENTIAL DECLARATIONS OF MAJOR DISASTER OR EMERGENCY

The U.S. Constitution grants the president special powers in times of catastrophic disaster and national emergency. Beyond this, enactment of the Federal Disaster Relief Act of 1950 gave then and future presidents the authority to officially declare, on behalf of the federal government, major disasters. Presidential authority in disaster policy was further augmented in the Disaster Relief Act of 1974, which provided presidents with the authority to issue emergency declarations that helped mobilize and fund federal, state, and local agencies when a disaster was imminent. At first, emergency declarations did not require that governors document need or furnish proof that their state and local governments were overwhelmed and therefore unable to handle the incident on their own, as major disaster requests customarily required. Emergency declaration requests from governors have always been scrutinized by presidents and their emergency management officials.[1] Sometimes these requests are turned down by the president, always with FEMA announcing the turndown in place of the president. In recent years, governors or other governor equivalent executives have submitted their emergency declaration requests with preliminary damage assessment data.[2]

Each president's declaration decisions reveal something about that president as a person, as a public servant, and as a political leader. The record of disaster declarations also says something about each president's view of federal-state-local relations, position with regard to disaster policy and emergency management, use of declarations as an instrument of political power, and understanding of disasters over the era each served.[3] In more recent decades, the threat of terrorism has also dramatically increased the range of presidential discretion in declaring events or circumstances as disaster or potential disaster. These events range from suspected small-scale bombings and threats to terror-caused catastrophes. The post-9/11 attacks of 2001, and escalating concern about the threats foreign terrorism may pose to the United States, impelled Congress to grant the president extraordinary power under the Homeland Security Act of 2002 to define disaster in terms of the threat posed and the possible consequences expected by a terrorist action. Ironically, warnings of experts and researchers about hazard vulnerabilities and their potential to cause disaster seem to have been heeded more in the realm of terrorism threat and prevention than in the context of natural or non-terror human-caused disasters.

This chapter explores six "P words" that will help elucidate facts and issues about presidential disaster declarations:

- "Policies" that inhere in declaration-relevant law, executive orders, and regulation, and the two types of disaster declarations: major disasters and emergencies

- "Process" by which declaration requests come to the president

- "Programs," under approved declarations, operated by FEMA that confer federal assistance (programs that help subnational governments and eligible nonprofits, individual and household assistance, and disaster mitigation)

- "Power" the president exercises in deciding whether to approve or reject specific governor requests for declarations, and the ramifications of these decisions in general terms

- "Politics" of disaster declarations, electorally, in partisanship, legislatively, intergovernmentally, etc.

- "Paying" for presidential declarations with public money (e.g., federal budgeting, the Disaster Relief Fund, emergency supplemental appropriations, obligations, pace of payouts, audits, etc.)

Presidents and Congress, often with state and local input, shape and influence disaster policy in general ways as well as in case-by-case decision making. A few new types of disaster agents the president approves for disaster declaration coverage set precedents that state governors pay close attention to. This is another way declaration policy is shaped. The state governors directly, and members of the U.S. Congress indirectly, play a role in the declaration process. Also, the federal emergency management agency (includes pre-FEMA agencies) has a role, is a major part of the process, and is a force in presidential declaration decision outcomes. Consequently, pre-FEMA (pre-1979) agencies, the independent agency FEMA (April 1979–March 2003), and the Department of Homeland Security FEMA (April 2003–present) will get attention in this chapter. FEMA directors, administrators, or undersecretaries who have headed FEMA through the years, will also be presented. The chapter concludes with a summary of findings.

THE U.S. CONSTITUTION AND EMERGENCY POWERS OF THE PRESIDENT

Under the U.S. Constitution, the president may invoke certain emergency powers in extraordinary circumstances: rebellion, epidemic, national labor strike, or disaster. The president's oath of office requires that he or she "preserve, protect, and defend" the Constitution and uphold its provisions. Although no specific emergency powers were included in the Constitution, principal authorization of emergency powers resides in Article II, Section 3, which states in part that the president "shall take care that the laws be faithfully executed," and Section 2, which grants the president power as commander in chief of the armed forces. In times of crisis, presidents can declare that the Constitution authorizes them to exercise powers usually granted to the legislative or judicial branches of government, thus fusing all governmental power in the executive branch for the duration of the crisis. President Abraham Lincoln justified the actions he took after the outbreak of the Civil War by claiming that the emergency made it necessary for him to exercise legislative powers until he could call Congress back into session. During World War II, President Franklin D. Roosevelt declared that unless Congress repealed a certain provision in a war-related economic measure, he would treat the law as if it had been repealed for the duration of the emergency, in effect threatening Congress with the loss of its legislative powers.[4]

Actual disasters and emergencies through American history have helped to develop, refine, and expand the range of presidential emergency powers under or beyond what is written about them in the U.S. Constitution.[5] In the mid-20th century and beyond, Congress enacted, with presidential assent, a series of new or revised disaster relief laws, and a great many of these have had the effect of expanding the president's role in disaster management and policy over time.

War as Disaster

One might notice that the word "war" is not mentioned in the preceding section. This is because under the Constitution's War Powers, Article I, Section 8, Clause 11, only Congress has the power to declare war. "The President derives the power to direct the military after a Congressional declaration of war from Article II, Section 2, which names the President Commander-in-Chief of the armed forces." Over time, and given the myriad ways in which the United States has been attacked or threatened with attack, including by parties using weapons of mass destruction, the presidency has accrued war-making authority in the absence of a formal declaration of war by Congress.[6] The term "weapon of mass destruction," in the parlance of social constructivism, has been subject to "reframing" over the past three decades. According to the U.S. Department of Homeland Security, "The United States faces a rising danger from terrorists and rogue states seeking to use weapons of mass destruction. A weapon of mass destruction is a nuclear, radiological, chemical, biological, or other device that is intended to harm a large number of people. The Department of Homeland Security works . . . to prevent terrorists and other threat actors from using these weapons to harm Americans."[7] The reframing comes in the "or other device" category. Other devices have come to apply to bombs of any type or size that terrorists, foreign or domestic, have detonated in locations where people have amassed, including on commercial aircraft.

Harold Koh observes, "In 1973, an irate Congress passed the War Powers Act in response to President Lyndon Johnson and President Richard Nixon's prosecution of the war in Vietnam without a congressional declaration. Under the War Powers Act, the president has 90 days after introducing troops into hostilities to obtain congressional approval of that action. It looks good on paper, but presidents have generally ignored the War Powers Act, citing Article II, Section 2 as their authority to send soldiers into combat."[8] For example, consider "the resolution used in 1991 to authorize action by President George [H. W.] Bush against Iraq prior to the Gulf War. That resolution authorized the president to 'use armed forces pursuant to the UN Security Council's resolutions passed in response to Iraq's invasion of Kuwait." The resolution (HR-77) went out of its way not to be a declaration of war. In fact, other than saying this constitutes authorization under the War Powers Act, it never used the word "war" at all. It did cite a UN resolution seeking to "restore international peace and security in that area," so it was only a declaration of war if you can assume that the opposite of peace is sort of war.[9]

Indeed, international factors also play a role in affording the U.S. president seemingly "extra-constitutional" war-making powers. Koh, writing only a few days after the 9/11 attack, asserts, "The U.N. charter was ratified by the Senate, and as such the president is bound by its terms. Nevertheless, the [2001] attacks on New York and Virginia are clearly war crimes under the U.N. definition. Moreover, Article 51 of the U.N. charter provides for the 'inherent right . . . of self-defense if an armed attack occurs.' NATO also took steps toward approving military action [shortly after the 9/11 attacks], by invoking Article 5 of the NATO charter, authorizing the use of force if it is determined that this was an attack from abroad against the United States."[10] Furthermore, after the September 11 attacks, "the United States Congress passed the Authorization for Use of Military Force against Terrorists (AUMF). While the AUMF did not officially declare war, the legislation provided the President with more authority upon which to exercise his constitutional powers as Commander in Chief. As the U.S. Supreme Court explained in *Youngstown Sheet & Tube Co. v. Sawyer*, Presidential Commander in Chief powers increase when Congressional intent supports the actions taken by the Commander in Chief. The AUMF served as that expression of Congressional intent. AUMF authorizes the President to use 'all necessary and appropriate force against those nations, organizations, or persons he determines planned, authorized, committed, or aided in the Sept. 11 attacks.'"[11]

The War Powers ambiguity continues. Twice in his first 16 months in office, President Trump authorized cruise missile attacks on targeted locations in Syria, both intended to thwart Syrian president Bashar Assad's capacity to prepare or deliver chemical and biological weapons he has used against his enemies.[12] Trump's first attack was in April 2017, directed at an airfield suspected to be the launch site of aircraft Syria used in chemical weapon bombing missions. A year later in April 2018, Trump, aided by British and French military forces, struck with more missiles, this time targeting suspected chemical weapon's production facilities. Neither of these attacks was approved as a formal declaration of war. President Trump is among an almost unbroken line of presidents since 1973 who have launched attacks on other nations, or against non-state actors abroad, outside of a formal congressional declaration of war.

Eric A. Posner claims, in reviewing a book by Benjamin Kleinerman,[13] that Hamilton, Madison, Jefferson, and Lincoln "all agreed that the president of the United States must have discretionary authority to disregard laws where necessary to address an emergency."[14] They disagreed about whether presidents have implicit constitutional authority to act outside the Constitution. The point is that presidential war-making authority, whether anchored in the Constitution or not, has commingled national security concerns with matters of natural- and human-caused disaster. Moreover, by embracing "all-hazards" emergency management as law, a doctrine of U.S. disaster management, and as a homeland security-emergency management organizing principle, America has recruited its emergency managers into the so-called "war on terrorism."

THE "POLICIES" AND LAWS THAT ESTABLISHED PRESIDENTIAL DISASTER DECLARATIONS

As mentioned previously, before 1950—when Congress considered unique relief legislation for each disaster—awkwardness, delay, pork barreling, and administrative confusion often resulted.[15] By 1950, lawmakers had decided that it made more sense to entrust declaration decision making to the president as an executive responsibility.[16] As Chapter 3 made clear, presidential authority to address domestic disasters won political support in 1950 because many Americans and their elected lawmakers grew concerned that there was no domestic equivalent of the post–World War II Marshall Plan, which sent U.S. aid and funding to countries ravaged by war and famine disaster.[17] Taxpayers complained that they were supporting rebuilding and recovery efforts abroad but not at home.

Ever since presidential disaster declaration authority was enshrined in law, the president has been afforded the discretion to decide on federal declarations of major disaster and emergency. Since the Stafford Act of 1988[18] and several of its predecessor laws, presidents are free, within certain limits, to interpret broadly or narrowly what is declarable as an emergency.[19] Requests for major disaster declarations get tight review. Presidents can pull requests through to approval even if FEMA, using its criteria and threshold system, recommends a turndown. However, experts have determined that such actions are extremely rare and that most requests for major disaster declarations are judged in accord with FEMA criteria and thresholds.[20] Each president makes declaration decisions on a case-by-case basis.[21]

Ordinarily, a governor must ask the president to declare a major disaster or emergency before a state can win a declaration. However, the Stafford Act of 1988 and several preceding laws empower the president to declare a major disaster (since 1950) or emergency (since 1974) "before" a governor asks for one or in the absence of a governor's request altogether. All governors have the authority to request a declaration. Sometimes in the interest of speeding mobilization a governor may submit an expedited request bypassing the usual process of submitting the request with damage estimates by asking the president and FEMA directly. In addition, federal law permits presidents to issue declarations of major disaster or emergency in the absence of a governor's request when there is a major federal interest (the federal government is a directly involved party in the event) or when a governor is unable officially to request a presidential declaration.

A presidential declaration of major disaster or emergency has far-reaching consequences because it opens the door to federal assistance and aid by legitimizing the disaster for affected populations.[22] The declaration specifies the state or territory and its eligible counties or county-equivalents, including tribal governments, and thereby delineates by location exactly who is eligible for federal relief. Each declaration is issued to a state or the District of Columbia or an American trust territory, commonwealth, or free-association partner. When a declaration identifies counties eligible to receive federal disaster assistance, unincorporated jurisdictions within the county will be eligible for assistance. Incorporated (often chartered) municipalities within a county may receive federal assistance passed through by the state or by the county, depending upon the procedures used in each state. Cities that are coincident with a county or counties (e.g., New York City comprises five counties) are treated as if they are stand-alone counties.

Some major disaster declarations issued by the president make every county in a state eligible for some form of federal disaster assistance. When every county of a state is included, that state's governor must have either asked for this in his or her original request or it must have been agreed to in governor–FEMA negotiations.[23] Unrequested but invited all-county emergency declarations are not unprecedented. In matters of "federal interest" disasters or for certain emergency declarations (e.g., President G. W. Bush's 2006 emergency declaration inviting almost all states, to take advantage of a preapproved emergency declaration that subsidized their respective state and local costs incurred in helping Hurricane Katrina victims who had resettled in their jurisdictions), presidents may in effect solicit emergency declaration requests from governors. This said, usually presidential declarations apply only to the counties that governors have asked them to cover. Moreover, FEMA may add counties to an already in-force presidential disaster declaration without the need for presidential preapproval. In such cases, the added counties must have met or exceeded the FEMA county per capita loss qualification threshold (see the "Process" section).

Presidential declarations of major disaster and emergency are intriguing because authority to make the essential decision rests only with the president. Most federal laws require implementation decisions by legions of government officials, many of whom operate some distance from the president.[24] Admittedly, once the president issues a declaration, federal agency and program officials, usually in concert with their state and local counterparts, undertake an elaborate and extensive assortment of implementing decisions. Yet the president's decision to push either the "approval button" or the "denial button" is often highly consequential.[25]

Every presidential declaration contains an initial statement about the kinds of program assistance people or subnational governments may be eligible to request. This is crucial because it determines whether disaster victims will receive direct cash grants, housing supplements, emergency medical care, disaster unemployment assistance, and so forth. It also specifies whether or not state and local governments themselves are eligible to receive federal disaster assistance to replace or repair public facilities and infrastructure. Certain nonprofit organizations may also qualify for federal disaster aid of various types. Moreover, public and privately owned utilities—electric, natural gas distribution, communications (cable service, Internet, Wi-Fi towers, and telephone), water purveyors, wastewater treatment services, certain transportation providers, etc.—may also receive federal assistance to cover repair or replacement of their disaster damaged infrastructure and equipment. As mentioned, federal disaster relief may flow to sub-county incorporated municipalities but only those that are located in counties included in the presidential declaration, and usually through a preset system of state and/or county pass-through.

A presidential declaration is vitally important to those directly affected by the disaster or emergency. It confers on them an "official" victim status needed to qualify for federal aid. Under the Individuals and Households Program, people may apply and qualify for various forms of federal disaster assistance under a declaration (see the "Programs" section). Many declarations also make aid available through the Public Assistance Program (FEMA) (again, see the "Programs" section), which provides government-to-government (federal-to-state or local) disaster relief to subsidize much of the cost of repairing, rebuilding, or replacing damaged government or utility infrastructure. Enactment of the Stafford Act in 1988 authorized presidential declarations of major disaster to include hazard mitigation funding calculated as a percentage of the total federal payouts to the state under the declaration.

To the public, including those not directly affected by the disaster, a presidential declaration of major disaster or emergency is significant for other reasons. At a basic level, a declaration signifies that a serious event has occurred, requiring the attention and resources of the federal government. The symbolism and content of the presidential declaration structures popular perceptions about the nature and scope of the disaster. Indirectly, a presidential declaration may encourage private charitable contributions from people and businesses near or far from the damage zone. It may also help to mobilize more responders and volunteers to serve in the response and recovery phases of the incident.

The increasing number and changing "variety" of presidential disaster declarations reveals in some respects the nation's history of disaster experience and its increasing vulnerability to disaster agents and forces. "Variety" refers to the types and causes of hazards and incidents granted presidential declarations of major disaster or emergency. Some declarations have little or nothing to do with natural hazards or natural disasters and nothing to do with terrorism. In some cases, a problem is sufficiently anomalous (see the "Tell Me More" 4-1 box on page 162) that a president is not guided by existing law, policy, or precedent, yet he or she (yes, in the near future "she") feels compelled to act and a presidential declaration of major disaster or emergency is an available action tool. The record of disaster declarations also connotes change in public, media, and official views about what "disaster" means, changes in federal–state relations, changes in various presidents' perception and use of disaster declaration authority, and changes in disaster law and management over time. Beyond this, there is speculation that new vulnerabilities and emerging threats (i.e., cyber-terror, bio-terror, failures in border security, massively dislocating economic crimes, etc.) may extend the "disaster declaration umbrella" to cover more and more problems or potential problems a president would be expected to address. Some of these mishaps or acts of sabotage may not fall within Stafford Act jurisdiction; however, incidents involving fire and explosion do.

Federal Disaster Relief Law and Declaration Authority

To understand presidential disaster declarations, it is necessary that we briefly revisit some of what was covered in Chapter 3. Congress passed the first permanent statutes authorizing federal disaster assistance in 1947[26] and 1950. The 1947 law provided surplus property and personnel as needed, and its 1950 counterpart gave the president authority to determine what type of aid was required. President Harry S. Truman issued several dozen disaster declarations, most of which were for flood and that conveyed technical assistance and mostly government surplus items (much from post-WWII stockpiles of military equipment) to the states impacted. Nonetheless, these two laws changed the nature and process of disaster relief in the United States. Only later did congressional leaders begin to see the 1950 act as precedent setting and as an early, general, national-level disaster policy model.

The Federal Disaster Relief Act of 1950 (Public Law 81-875) (DRA of 1950, for short) specified for the first time that federal resources could and should be used to supplement the efforts of others in the event of a disaster. The new law made federal disaster assistance more accessible since it no longer required specific congressional legislation to address each new disaster but instead simply empowered the president to decide when federal disaster assistance was justified and necessary. However, federal assistance was intended to supplement, not replace, state and local disaster management efforts. It was also directed to facilitate some disaster response and recovery efforts, more than to advance disaster preparedness and mitigation efforts. The DRA of 1950 provided "an orderly and continuing means of assistance by the federal government to states and local governments in carrying out their responsibilities to alleviate suffering and damage resulting from major disasters."[27]

An updated definition of "major disaster" under the Stafford Act of 1988 is as follows. Also, under the Sandy Recovery Improvement Act of 2013, Native American tribal governments were treated as states for the purpose of making disaster declaration requests directly to the president or through FEMA to the president:

> **Major disaster** means any natural catastrophe (including any hurricane, tornado, storm, high water, wind-driven water, tidal wave, tsunami, earthquake, volcanic eruption, landslide, mudslide, snowstorm or drought), or regardless of cause, any fire, flood, or explosion in any part of the United States that in the determination of the President, causes damage of sufficient severity and magnitude to warrant **major disaster assistance** under the Stafford Act to supplement the efforts and available resources of the States, Local Governments," (Native American Tribal Governments), and disaster relief organizations in alleviating the damage, loss, hardship, or suffering thereby.[28]

Congress built on the 1950 act by passing several laws in the 1970s that expanded the scope of federal government responsibility in disasters. For example, the Disaster Relief Act of 1974 (Public Law 93-288) created a program that provided direct assistance to individuals and families following a disaster. Importantly, the act gave the president the power to declare an emergency as well, whereas previously only a major disaster could be declared. The 1974 law's narrow "emergency" language was superseded by the Stafford Act of 1988, which conveyed broader authority to the president:

> **Emergency**: Any occasion or instance for which, in the determination of the president, federal assistance is needed to supplement state and local efforts and capabilities to save lives and to protect property and public health and safety, or to lessen or avert the threat of catastrophe in any part of the United States.[29]

An emergency is often of less magnitude and scope than a major disaster. However, the president may issue an emergency declaration to address an ongoing event that may later be declared a major disaster.

The Disaster Relief Act of 1974 also called on the president to:

- Establish a program of disaster preparedness using the services of all appropriate federal agencies

- Make grants for the development of plans and programs for disaster preparedness and prevention

- Declare a major disaster at the request of a governor

- Make contributions to state or local governments to help repair or reconstruct public facilities

- Make grants to help repair or reconstruct nonprofit educational, utility, emergency, and medical and custodial care facilities

- Purchase or lease temporary housing, and provide temporary mortgage or rent payment assistance

- Provide assistance to people unemployed as a result of the disaster

- Provide additional relief, including food coupons and commodities, relocation assistance, legal services, and crisis counseling

- Make grants to a state for the state to provide grants to individuals and families if assistance otherwise provided by the act is inadequate

- Make loans to local governments suffering a substantial loss of tax and other revenues[30]

Congress passed the Robert T. Stafford Disaster Relief and Emergency Assistance Act in 1988 (Public Law 100-707). This law slightly changed presidential declaration authority. In one provision it sought to restrict the president from using declaration authority to cover border penetrating immigration crises.[31] The Stafford Act maintained the president's right to issue major disaster declarations and empowered the president to confer these types of federal disaster assistance:

- General federal assistance for technical and advisory aid and support to state and local governments to facilitate the distribution of consumable supplies

- Essential assistance from federal agencies to distribute aid to victims through state and local governments and voluntary organizations, perform lifesaving and property-saving assistance, clear debris, and use resources of the U.S. Department of Defense (DOD) before a major disaster or emergency declaration is issued

- Hazard mitigation grants to reduce risks and damages that might occur in future disasters

- Federal facilities repair and reconstruction

- Repair, restoration, and replacement of damaged facilities owned by state and local governments, as well as private nonprofit facilities that provide essential services or commodities

In congressional language, the Stafford Act called on the federal government to set forth an orderly and continuing means of assistance to state and local governments as each endeavor to alleviate the suffering and damage that result from disasters. The law tasked the federal government, most particularly FEMA, with these obligations:

- Revising and broadening the scope of existing disaster relief programs

- Encouraging the development of comprehensive disaster preparedness and assistance plans, programs, capabilities, and organizations by the states and by local governments

- Achieving greater coordination and responsiveness of disaster preparedness and relief programs

- Encouraging individuals, states, and local governments to protect themselves by obtaining insurance coverage to supplement or replace governmental assistance

- Encouraging hazard mitigation measures to reduce losses from disasters, including development of land-use and construction regulations

- Providing federal assistance programs for both public and private losses sustained in disasters[32]

The Stafford Act also provides federal post-disaster relief assistance under fixed dollar limits and means-testing on relief to individuals and households (see the "Assistance to Individuals and Households Program" section examined ahead). Stafford also maintains federal to state and local government assistance (see the "FEMA Public Assistance Program" section). This subsidizes repair or replacement of disaster damaged state or local infrastructure or facilities and is done as a percentage of eligible costs, usually on a 75/25 federal/state and local cost share basis. In addition, the indistinctiveness of the federal definition of "emergency" has allowed presidents to add new categories of emergency. For more information about federal disaster assistance programs and vagueness of criteria, see the "Tell Me More" boxes later in this chapter.

The **Sandy Recovery Improvement Act of 2013** (P.L. 113-2) "authorizes the chief executive of a tribal government to directly request major disaster or emergency declarations from the President, much as a governor can do for a state."[33] Under the Stafford Act of 1988 "tribes were dependent on a request being made by the governor of the state in which their territory is located."[34] Tribal governments maintained that this requirement undermined their independence and sovereignty, keeping them from obtaining needed assistance. Moreover, some tribal lands overlap state borders. For the declaration process, the Sandy Act of 2013 has now made tribal governments the equivalents of state governments. Governors are still free to add major disaster or emergency impacted tribal lands (as local governments) in their respective state requests for presidential declarations. The benefit for tribal governments is that in the past it has been difficult for many state emergency management officials to assess disaster damage on tribal lands owing to language and cultural differences as well as to the physical isolation of many tribal areas and reservations. The new law includes a section that allows the president to waive the nonfederal contribution (same as state cost share) or to adjust the cost share to a more generous match for tribal governments under the FEMA Public Assistance Program.[35]

THE "PROCESS" FOLLOWED IN REQUESTING PRESIDENTIAL DECLARATIONS

Both the DRA of 1950 law and the Stafford Act of 1988 stipulate that the governor of an affected state must formally ask the president to declare a major disaster or emergency. If the request is granted, the federal government will then provide disaster assistance "to supplement the efforts and available resources of state and local governments in alleviating the disaster."[36] The governor must provide certain information on the severity and magnitude of the disaster and on the amount of state and local resources to be committed to the disaster or emergency. The president is given wide discretion to determine whether the disaster or emergency is of sufficient severity and size to warrant federal disaster or emergency assistance. The authority to declare a disaster carries with it the power to determine the types of federal disaster assistance that will be made available to state and local governments and to individuals, families, and households. Ever since they were entrusted with declaration authority, each president has labored to protect this authority from being eroded by Congress, and no president to date has advocated delegating this responsibility to an executive branch official.

As stated previously, the Stafford Act (§401) requires that "all requests for a declaration by the President that a major disaster exists shall be made by the Governor of the affected State." A State also includes the District of Columbia, Puerto Rico, the Virgin Islands, Guam, American Samoa, and the Commonwealth of the Northern Mariana Islands. The Marshall Islands and the Federated States of Micronesia are also eligible to request a declaration and receive assistance. Only governors, or when the governor is unavailable, their lieutenant governors, can request presidential declarations of major disaster or emergency.[37] Sub-state executives (i.e., mayors, county executives, city managers, etc.) seeking presidential declarations must ask for them through their governor and appropriate state offices. Legislators can advocate that the president confer such declarations, but they are not part of the official request process.

The governor's request is made through the regional FEMA office. State and federal officials conduct a **Preliminary Damage Assessment (PDA)** to estimate the extent of the disaster and its impact on individuals and public facilities. This information is included in the governor's request to show that the disaster is of such severity and magnitude that effective response is beyond the capabilities of his or her state and respective local governments and that federal assistance is necessary.[38] Normally, the PDA is completed prior to the submission of the governor's request. However, when an obviously severe or catastrophic event occurs, the governor's request may be submitted prior to the PDA. Nonetheless, the governor must still make the request.

"As part of the request, the Governor must take appropriate action under State law and direct execution of the State's emergency plan. The Governor shall furnish information on the nature and amount of State and local resources that have been or will be committed to alleviating the results of the disaster, provide an estimate of the amount and severity of damage, including the disaster impact on the private and public sector, and provide an estimate of the type and amount of assistance needed under the Stafford Act."[39] In addition, the governor will need to certify that, for the current disaster, state and local government obligations and expenditures (of which state commitments must be a significant proportion) will comply with all applicable cost-sharing requirements.

Based on the governor's request, the president may declare that a major disaster or emergency exists, thus activating an array of federal programs to assist in the response and recovery effort. Not all programs, however, are activated for every disaster. The determination of which programs are activated is based on the needs found during damage assessment and any subsequent information that may be discovered.[40]

Some declarations will provide only individual assistance or only public assistance. Since 1988, FEMA hazard mitigation funding is also made available to states, and their respective localities, for FEMA-approved mitigation projects in most cases.

The Texas Department of Public Safety, Division of Emergency Management, posted a set of slides online on June 2, 2015, that provides a clear picture of the general pathway followed in the declaration process. Although the process may slightly vary in other states, the graphic portrays the application process well. See Figure 4-1.

The Role of Governors

Many governors, as state chief executives, possess emergency powers applicable to disasters or emergencies within their respective states. They have at their disposal state emergency management agencies, other state agency assistance, and the state's National Guard (along with reserve and active-duty forces made available by the president, if needed).

Through state legislative work and often governor assistance, state governments enact emergency management laws. A variety of state agencies fashion codes and regulations subject to supervision by the governor and oversight by the state legislature. State government is a conduit through which extensive federal–local interchange takes place. In turn, state governments are responsible for implementing and enforcing a great many federal laws, among them federal emergency management laws. States are obligated to assist their respective local governments in development and maintenance of emergency management responsibilities.

FIGURE 4-1 ■ The Presidential Declaration Process⁴¹

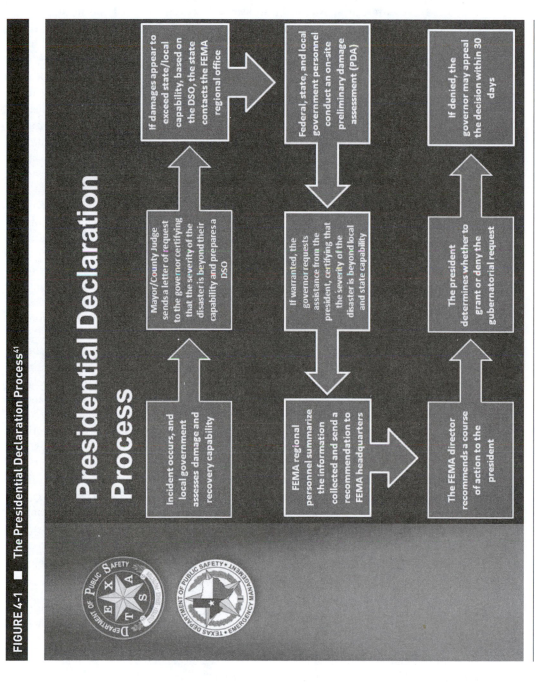

Presidential Declaration Process

Incident occurs, and local government assesses damage and recovery capability

Mayor/County Judge sends a letter or request to the governor certifying that the severity of the disaster is beyond their capability and prepares a DSO

If damages appear to exceed state/local capability, based on the DSO, the state contacts the FEMA regional office

Federal, state, and local government personnel conduct an on-site preliminary damage assessment (PDA)

If warranted, the governor requests assistance from the president, certifying that the severity of the disaster is beyond local and state capability

FEMA regional personnel summarize the information collected and send a recommendation to FEMA headquarters

The FEMA director recommends a course of action to the president

The president determines whether to grant or deny the gubernatorial request

If denied, the governor may appeal the decision within 30 days

Source: Texas Department of Public Safety, Division of Emergency Management, "TCEQ Regional Workshop: Emergency Response Preparing for Disasters and Emergency Incidents."

In this chart, a DSO is a Disaster Summary Outline. It is a document that local organizations need to submit under the Texas declaration process.

Governors play a key role in the presidential declaration process. They need to mobilize and supervise their state agencies as those agencies address the emergency or disaster. They need to ensure that disaster loss information has been compiled and included in their request to the president. They need to consult and work cooperatively with local elected executives and other local government officials who are in the areas affected by the disaster or emergency. When a disaster strikes, local authorities and individuals often request help from their state government as well as private relief organizations. Local governments sometimes seek federal disaster assistance, often with state encouragement. Customarily, the process begins when county or municipal leaders, or both, ask their governor to declare a state emergency. These same local officials may ask the governor to request a presidential declaration. Governors may issue, if they believe it is warranted, a state declaration of disaster. They typically do this through an executive order or proclamation. The order usually describes the nature of the emergency, where it occurred, and the authority under which the governor makes the declaration.

Often, governors request presidential emergency declarations when a disaster seems imminent and federal aid would help in the pre-event response stage of a disaster. Many of these emergency declarations cover events that do not later earn a presidential declaration of major disaster.

Although the president has legal authority to issue a declaration of major disaster or emergency in the absence of a governor's request, presidents have the authority to declare an emergency if the "emergency involves a subject area for which, under the Constitution or laws of the United States, the United States exercises exclusive or preeminent responsibility and authority." A good example is the *Columbia* space shuttle explosion of 2003. Since NASA is a federal program, the federal government is responsible for the cleanup and recovery. President George W. Bush invited governors of states thought to be within the debris field of the shuttle's remnants to take advantage of a preapproved emergency declaration he had offered them to cover state expenses incurred in searching for, collecting, and protecting astronaut remains and shuttle parts. (See "Tell Me More" 4-2 box on page 165.)

Governors almost always consult their respective state emergency management officials before requesting a presidential declaration. The governor may authorize a state-level PDA if state officials are not already assessing damage with local authorities. Sometimes, if the disaster appears to be beyond state and local response capacity, the governor can ask FEMA to join state and local personnel in conducting a PDA. On account of the vagueness of the criteria FEMA uses to judge governor requests to the president, plus each governor's keen awareness that under federal law the president can disregard any FEMA recommendation to deny a major disaster request that fails to meet the agency's criteria, governors must contemplate whether to request presidential declarations in an uncertain environment. They can consider previous presidential approvals and turndowns as precedents. They can gauge the degree of newsworthiness their state's calamity has drawn. However, the mere fact that their disaster request may not qualify for a declaration under FEMA criteria is seldom enough to deter them from asking the president to issue their state and its impacted localities a declaration (see the "Politics" section). The "Tell Me More" 4-2 box (page 165) encapsulates, from a governor's perspective, the twin issues of vague FEMA criteria and subjective presidential decisions.

Governors, in requesting emergency declarations, do not have to prove to the president that the emergency disaster is beyond state and local response capabilities. Instead, they have to demonstrate that federal assistance is needed to save lives, protect property and public health, or lessen or avert the threat of catastrophe. Under federal law, FEMA expenditures under an emergency declaration may not exceed $5 million.[42] However, when an emergency declaration is in effect and federal spending approaches the $5 million limit, the president need only notify Congress in a letter that the $5 million cap will be exceeded, and this allows spending on the emergency declaration to exceed the limit. Many events that have earned emergency declarations have exceeded $5 million, and the president has routinely notified Congress that spending would exceed the cap in these incidents. Governors appreciate presidential declarations of emergency because they supply federal funds and other assistance quickly, do not require the collection of state and local information to document need, and often furnish help when the full scope of the emergency or disaster is either not yet understood or is still unfolding.

The Federal Emergency Management Agency Director

The FEMA director/administrator is a politically appointed official who is often personally selected by the president, and is subject to U.S. Senate confirmation; typically that person is one of his political confidants or supporters. Since the creation of FEMA in April 1979, some FEMA directors/administrators have had previous experience in emergency management and some have not. Table 4-1 lists appointed and Senate-confirmed FEMA directors (1979–2002) or administrators/undersecretaries (2002–present). Table 4-1 does not include the names and terms of acting FEMA heads who are temporary appointees.

The head of FEMA is in effect the chief executive officer of the agency, although some who have been appointed to the post have been satisfied in delegating day-to-day management of the agency to the deputy administrator. Under the Post-Katrina Emergency

TABLE 4-1 ■ FEMA Directors and Administrators, 1979–2018, with Appointing President[43]

FEMA Directors/Administrators* and Period in Office	Appointing President
John Macy, August 1979 to January 1981	James E. Carter
Louis O. Giuffrida, May 1981 to September 1985	Ronald R. Reagan
Julius W. Becton Jr., November 1985 to June 1989	Ronald R. Reagan
Wallace E. Stickney, August 1990 to January 1993	George H. W. Bush
James L. Witt, April 1993 to January 2001	William J. Clinton
Joseph M. Allbaugh, February 2001 to March 2003	George W. Bush
Michael D. Brown, March 2003 to September 2005	George W. Bush
R. David Paulison, September 2005 to January 2009	George W. Bush
W. Craig Fugate, May 2009 to January 2017	Barack H. Obama
W. Brock Long, June 2017 to present	Donald J. Trump

Source: FEMA, "The Federal Emergency Management Agency," Publication 1, November 2010. At https://www.fema.gov/media-library-data/20130726-1823-25045-8164/pub_1_final.pdf.

* Does not include acting directors/administrators

Management Reform Act of 2006 (P.L. 109-295) (PKEMRA), introduced in Chapter 3, the FEMA administrator has been given a more direct line of access to the president, albeit with expected consultation of the DHS secretary, during periods of disaster response and when carrying out his or her responsibility to help in the processing of emergency and major disaster declaration requests submitted by governors. Several of the FEMA heads in Table 4-1 were discussed in Chapter 3, and they and others will come up in later chapters.

Typically, the route of a governor's request starts with the regional FEMA director, who receives a request, reviews it, and sends a recommendation to FEMA headquarters in Washington. There, a declaration processing unit prepares documents pertaining to the request, and the administrator of FEMA, after compiling information for the president about the event and, often, consulting with the governors who have requested the declarations, adds a memorandum recommending to the president a course of action: approve or reject. All the information FEMA sends to the president, including the director's recommendation, is protected by rules of executive privilege and therefore unavailable for public scrutiny. The president is neither bound by FEMA's recommendation nor obligated to follow the agency's declaration criteria. The president alone determines whether to approve or reject every governor's request.

Here are some common factors FEMA officials consider before they make their recommendation:

- Number of homes destroyed or sustaining major damage

- The extent to which damage is concentrated or dispersed

- The estimated cost of repairing the damage

- The demographics of the affected area

- State and local governments' capabilities

The Stafford Act does not prescribe exact criteria to guide FEMA recommendations or the president's decision. As a prerequisite to federal disaster assistance under the act, though, a governor must take "appropriate action" and provide information on the nature and amount of state and local resources committed to alleviating the disaster's impacts. Other relevant considerations include the following:

- The demographics of the affected areas with regard to income levels, unemployment, concentrations of senior citizens, and the like

- The degree to which insurance covers the damage

- The degree to which people in the disaster area have been "traumatized"

- The amount of disaster-related unemployment the event has produced

- The amount of assistance available from other federal agencies, such as the SBA and its disaster loans to homeowners and businesses

- The extent to which state and local governments are capable of dealing with the disaster on their own

- The amount of disaster assistance coming from volunteer organizations and the adequacy of that assistance given the magnitude of the disaster

- The amount of rental housing available for emergency occupancy

- The nature and degree of health and safety problems posed by the disaster and its effects

- The extent of damage to essential service facilities, such as utilities and medical, police, and fire services[44]

FEMA also evaluates the impacts of a disaster at the county, local government, and tribal levels. It considers the following:

- Whether critical facilities are involved

- How much insurance coverage is in force that could provide affected parties reimbursement for various losses

- The degree of hazard mitigation a state or local government has undertaken prior to the disaster

- Recent disaster history of the respective state and its localities

- The availability of federal assistance aside from that to be provided by a presidential declaration

Factors that reduce the chances that a governor's request for a presidential declaration of major disaster or emergency will be approved are several. Obviously, major infrastructure loss and widespread or intense human suffering advances deservedness, whereas ample insurance coverage that helps alleviate loss and advance recovery diminishes worthiness. Presumably, when it can be shown that the requesting government(s) failed to take reasonable steps to prevent a minor incident from occurring, deservedness goes down.

Sometimes other federal agencies besides FEMA host disaster programs that may sufficiently address the needs of the disaster in question, such that a presidential declaration of major disaster or emergency is unnecessary. Governors contemplating, or formally in the process of, filing requests for presidential declarations may be dissuaded from doing so by FEMA or White House officials. They may be advised that given the nature of their problem, other federal programs may provide help that is better suited to assist them. For example, when the I-35 bridge collapsed spectacularly in Minneapolis in August 2007, the Minnesota governor was advised that a presidential disaster declaration was unnecessary because the U.S. Department of Transportation (DOT), aided by the U.S. Army Corps of Engineers (USACE), the FBI, and other federal agencies, would make help and resources available such that a presidential disaster declaration was duplicative and so[45] unwarranted.[46]

When a governor seeks a presidential declaration for an incident that does not conform to standard eligibility requirements, FEMA may recommend to the president that the governor's request be denied. Presidents regularly turn down gubernatorial requests for major disasters or emergencies.[47] However, in rare cases, presidents approve requests for major disaster declarations when damage in the state is light and the state may have been able to recover from the event without federal assistance.[48]

Table 4-3 shows that a total of 789 turndowns for majors and 131 turndowns for emergency were announced between May 1953 and August 2017.[49] For all 12 presidents, Eisenhower to Trump, there is a one-in-four chance of a turndown of governor requests on major disasters and only slightly less than a one-in-four chance of turndown when governors request emergency declarations. Table 4-3 shows that pre-FEMA presidents Eisenhower, Kennedy, Johnson, Nixon, and Ford had, by modern standards, high rates of turndown on major disaster requests; Johnson rejected 53 percent and Nixon 53 percent. Eisenhower (34%), Kennedy (30%), and Ford (32%) reject about 3, or slightly more, requests of every 10 requests they receive. Oddly, Carter, the president who championed FEMA's creation, rejected 45 percent of all the governor requests for major disaster declarations he received. It may be that governors in the Carter years needed time to become accustomed to FEMA's per capita threshold Public Assistance criterion. As mentioned previously, Carter was tough on requests for majors but less strict in turning down requests for emergencies (39%). Reagan went easier on major requests (34% turndown rate) but was extremely tough on emergency requests (64%). A "sea change" occurred in turndowns after 1988. Presidents from G. H. W. Bush to Trump turn down only about one in five requests for majors, with G. W. Bush and Obama at very low rates of turndown (16.3% and 16.7%, respectively).

When numbers of major disaster declarations are considered for full two-term presidents, Eisenhower shows 106, Reagan has 184, Clinton has 380, G. W. Bush 458, and Obama 476. This is a very substantial rate of increase even given the long time span considered. Another way to consider change over time is that from May 1953 to Jan. 1993, a span of just under 40 years, a total of 976 major declarations were issued. From Jan. 1993 to Nov. 2017, a little less than 25 years, 1,368 majors were approved.

FEMA relies most heavily on how the assessment of a state's capability compares with the costs imposed by the disaster. Each governor requesting a declaration is expected to demonstrate to FEMA and the president that the state is "unable to adequately respond to the disaster or emergency," of whatever nature, and that federal assistance is therefore needed. The "unable to adequately respond" condition is often highly controversial. Some governors claim that state budget limitations make it impossible for them to "adequately respond." Some claim that they do not have reserve funds sufficient to pay for the costs of the response.

Some governors have explained that their state has no disaster relief programs in law to match FEMA's, and so in the absence of a presidential declaration many victims will be without government assistance. FEMA officials, and the president, may find it difficult to determine whether a state is "unable to adequately respond," drawing on their own resources. It is possible that DHS-FEMA officials advising the president on whether to approve or reject a governor's request for a declaration of major disaster may inform the president that the requesting state has not established state-funded disaster relief programs that parallel FEMA's programs. Weighing the merit of a request is often complicated by news media coverage of the event, political pressures imposed on both FEMA officials and the president by legislators and other officials in the damage zone, and the difficulty of measuring state (and local) disaster response and recovery capacity.

Under the Public Assistance (PA) program (the government-to-government aid) that pays for infrastructure repair and reimburses certain disaster expenses of nonprofit organizations, FEMA examines the estimated cost of the assistance, using such factors as the cost per capita within the state. Table 4-2 reveals that in FY 2018, FEMA, under its Public Assistance program, used a figure of $1.46 per capita damage costs as an indicator that the disaster is of sufficient magnitude to warrant federal assistance.[50] (See Table 4-2.) This figure is adjusted annually based on changes in the Consumer Price Index. So, in straightforward terms, in 2018 a state with a 2010 U.S. Census population of about 1 million (Montana and Rhode Island, for example) has to demonstrate that it has experienced damage costs (not covered by insurance) that meet or exceed $1,460,000 to hit FEMA's threshold of qualification. Remember, as ever, presidents are not bound by FEMA's criteria when they consider governor requests for major disaster declarations. Note as well that these must be eligible damages to public infrastructure and facilities, including public or privately owned utilities, and eligible nonprofit organizations.

Similarly, FEMA established for each county a cost-indexed threshold.[51] According to Table 4-2, a county must have experienced $3.68 per capita to meet FEMA's threshold of qualification. Let us assume that a county has a population of about 2 million in the 2010 U.S. Census. For example, King County in Washington State had a 2010 U.S. Census population of nearly 2 million (1,931,249). For King County, WA, to meet FEMA's county threshold of disaster loss, it would have to document eligible damage of $7,360,000 (about $7,106,996 if its actual 2010 Census population were used). At this writing, the formula uses population of the jurisdiction as determined in the 2010 official U.S. Census. Population is then divided into estimated damage cost.

Presumably, if any county is to be added to an in-force major disaster declaration, the county's disaster per capita loss figure should meet or exceed the FEMA county per capita loss threshold. When this happens, FEMA may approve the county as eligible for assistance without the need to ask the president. Still, both FEMA and the president may take into account factors beyond meeting or exceeding the county per capita loss threshold when county officials seek to be included in a major disaster declaration. Not to be forgotten is that per capita loss thresholds are NOT used in the Individual and Households Program (IHP). Consequently, if the president decides to issue a major disaster declaration on grounds that individuals and households deserve the assistance a declaration can provide, the declaration request may be approved. FEMA records show that sometimes declarations to states include IHP coverage but not PA coverage. Sometimes this is reversed. However, most declarations convey both IHP and PA assistance. Also, since 1988, the bulk of major disaster declarations include hazard mitigation assistance (Section 406 of the Stafford Act).[52]

Remember that there is a "county" track and a "state" track. For the state track, the estimated disaster costs for each county the governor includes in her or his request is cumulated and added to the state government's own disaster costs. The resulting figure is then divided by the population of the entire state in the most recent U.S. Census, thus yielding the state's per capita loss figure. If this amount exceeds the FEMA per capita loss threshold for the state (a total determined by FEMA administratively well in advance of the disaster in question), presumably the agency recommends that the president approve the governor's major disaster declaration request. State per capita loss totals that fail to meet the FEMA threshold usually are sufficient evidence to FEMA officials that the governor's request may warrant a presidential turndown.

However, it is difficult and sometimes impossible for FEMA officials to ascertain that an event is worthy of a presidential declaration unless PDAs are first conducted and analyzed (often through photographs or video recordings) or unless media coverage of the event makes it obvious a major disaster has occurred. Moreover, it is difficult to judge whether state and local areas are capable of recovering on their own if disaster damage has not been assessed beforehand. Consequently, sometimes the president issues declarations of major disaster without documentary evidence that the misfortunes have met FEMA qualifying criteria.

FEMA Declaration Request Processing

The federal declaration process usually follows these steps. See Figure 4-2 for a flow chart showing the path a governor request for a major disaster declaration usually follows. If the governor requests a major disaster declaration through FEMA, the agency prepares a **White House package**. The package contains documents prepared for the president's action on a governor's request. The package includes the governor's request and the FEMA director's memorandum, made up of the following items:

- Summary of significant aspects of the event

- Statistics relative to damage and losses

- Outlines of the contributions made by federal, state, local, and private agencies

- List of the unmet needs for which the governor seeks federal assistance

- Recommended course of action for the president

The package also contains appropriate letters and announcements related to the action, including the FEMA director's recommendation to the president regarding whether to approve or deny the governor's request.

In many cases the FEMA regional office initially receives the governor's request first; officials there prepare a regional summary, analysis, and recommendation. The summary contains only factual data concerning the disaster event, whereas the analysis and recommendation sections may contain opinions and evaluations. The FEMA regional office forwards the governor's request along with the regional summary, analysis, and recommendation to FEMA national offices. At headquarters, the director and senior FEMA staff evaluate the request, prepare the White House package, and then forward it on to the president accompanied by the FEMA director's recommendation. The president is free to accept or reject the governor's request. Finally, the president makes a decision to either grant or deny the request.

The White House Staff

The White House staff consists of key aides whom the president sees daily—the chief of staff, congressional liaison people, the press secretary, the national security adviser—and a few other political and administrative assistants. About 500 people work on the White House staff, most of whom see the president rarely but provide a wide range of services.[53] Some of these people, such as the White House chief of staff and the domestic policy advisor, are assumed to play a role in helping the president consider governors' requests for declarations of major disaster or emergency.

Most presidents rely heavily on their staffs for information, policy options, and analysis. Different presidents have different relations with, and means of organizing, their staffs. Different presidents also have different leadership and management styles. President Carter was a "detail man," toiling ceaselessly over memoranda and facts. President Reagan was the consummate "delegator," who entrusted tremendous responsibilities to his staff. President George H. W. Bush fell somewhere between the Carter and Reagan extremes and was considerably more accessible than President Reagan. President Clinton, like Carter, was a detail person but also someone who ran an open White House with fluid staffing.[54] President George W. Bush was a delegator who followed a chief executive officer model of management and who preferred a less open White House. President Barack Obama tended to focus "at high levels where there's disagreement at agencies or among advisors"—so he could then make an executive decision.[55] Obama preferred to let problems percolate up through his staff and senior administrators, often tolerating considerable disagreement, until he determined the right time to intervene. He was known as a regular mediator of disputes, and he was skilled at pacifying his administrators after conflicts. President Trump relies heavily on his own independent judgments but is aided by staffers he knows and trusts. Trump often has reservations about the validity of information and documents provided to him by senior federal civil servants. Perhaps reflecting his business background, President Trump sees loyalty paid to him as the first order requirement of an adviser, staffer, or senior public servant. Loyalty and trust convey credibility in the Trump White House. President Trump has entrusted certain of his close family members with high White House posts, although he does not always support or concur with their views or recommendations. The Trump White House and Cabinet has experienced very high turnover over in its first two years. Regardless, President Trump's record in approving or denying governor requests for major disaster declarations and emergencies, based on 2017 data, is very similar to that of his predecessor, Barack Obama (see Table 4-3).

When the White House package is delivered to the Office of the President by a FEMA official, from then on it is protected by **executive privilege**. "President Dwight Eisenhower was the first president to coin the phrase 'executive privilege' but not the first to invoke its principle: namely, that a president has the right to withhold certain information from Congress, the courts or anyone else—even when faced with a subpoena. . . . Presidents have argued that executive privilege is a principle implied in the constitutionally mandated separation of powers. In order to do their job, presidents contend, they need candid advice from their aides—and aides simply won't be willing to give such advice if they know they might be called to testify, under oath, before a congressional committee or in some other forum."[56]

In any disaster or emergency, many offices are likely to engage in facilitating the president's work. Clearly, the White House Political Affairs Office and the Communications Office would be tasked to help the president address a disaster or emergency, especially in cooperation with the White House press secretary and press office. The White House Homeland Security Council and perhaps the National Security Council (NSC) would also be involved.[57] The "Tell Me More" 4-3 box on page 169 about presidents and public relations underscores how presidents must be aware of and responsive to news media coverage of disasters or emergencies, transpiring or impending, as these rapidly ascend to national newsworthiness.

THE "PROGRAMS" OF FEDERAL EMERGENCY MANAGEMENT

What help do governments and people expect under the two post-disaster assistance programs from the Federal Emergency Management Agency (FEMA)?

FEMA Public Assistance Program

The **Public Assistance Program (FEMA)** provides grants to state and local governments and certain nonprofit entities to help them in their response to, and recovery from, disasters. Specifically, the program provides assistance for debris removal, emergency protective measures, and permanent restoration of infrastructure.[58]

Eligible Applicants: Eligible Public Assistance (PA) applicants include state governments, local governments, and any other political subdivision of the state; Native American tribes; and Alaska Native Villages. Certain private nonprofit

organizations may also receive assistance. Eligible private nonprofits include educational, utility, emergency, medical, temporary or permanent custodial care facilities (including those for the aged and disabled), irrigation, museums, zoos, community centers, libraries, homeless shelters, senior citizen centers, rehabilitation, shelter workshops and health and safety services, and other private nonprofit facilities that provide essential services of a governmental nature to the general public. It also extends to public-serving museums, zoos, horticultural institutions, as well as sport and recreational stadiums and facilities.

FEMA's PA Program general pathway consists of:

- Preliminary damage assessment
- Governor's or tribal chief executive's request

FIGURE 4-2 ■ Process Steps When a Presidential Disaster Declaration Is Approved and Includes Public Assistance Program Help to State and Local Governments[59]

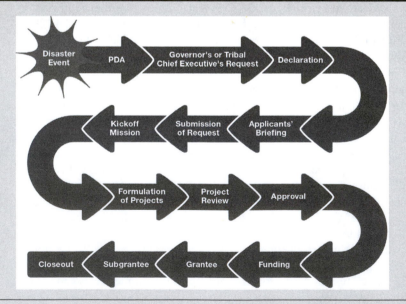

Source: FEMA, "IS-634 Introduction to FEMA's Public Assistance Program, Lesson 2: Steps in the PA Process," undated. At https://emilms.fema.gov/IS634/PA0102summary.htm.

- Declaration

- Applicants' briefing

- Request for public assistance

- Kickoff meeting

- Project formulation

- Project review:

  o Small projects

  o Large projects

- Project funding

- Program closeout[60]

Figure 4-2 may help explain the process visually.

Under the Trump administration as of January 2, 2018, FEMA now provides public assistance to "houses of worship," on grounds that they are community centers.[61] Community centers have long been eligible for public assistance. Churches, synagogues, mosques, and other houses of worship before this change were only eligible for assistance to cover the costs they incurred in operating disaster shelters or relief sites on their grounds. The policy change that opened houses of worship (HOWs) for public assistance program coverage was applied retroactively; HOWs could apply for PA if they sustained damage in an area covered by a federal disaster declaration after August 23, 2017.[62] This back-dating allowed HOWs damaged by 2017 hurricanes Harvey, Irma, Maria, or from other declared disasters after that date, to apply for FEMA PA. However, many conditions applied to HOWs. When HOWs were considered by FEMA to be non-critical private nonprofits, they had to first apply for a Small Business Administration (SBA) disaster loan, and if that loan was denied or if the loan obtained could not cover the full extent of repairs, the HOW could then be eligible for some amount of PA. Among other conditions, facilities owned by HOWs that were not used for worship or education, like recreation buildings, were not eligible for PA.[63] There has long been a church versus state controversy in federal disaster assistance, just as there has been in U.S. law. For example, religious bodies are ineligible for FEMA reimbursement of their sheltering and relief costs during declared disasters if they proselytize to those taking refuge in the shelter. Moreover, HOWs that offer sheltering and other post-disaster aid, and that carry out FEMA sanctioned functions, must obey anti-discrimination rules when people seek refuge in their facilities during disasters or emergencies. This change in HOW policy significantly benefits HOWs in the sense that disaster damaged or destroyed HOW buildings now may be eligible for FEMA PA, despite whether or not the HOW provided disaster assistance or shelter to the community.

Private nonprofits that provide "critical services" (power, water—including water provided by an irrigation organization or facility—sewer, wastewater treatment, communications and emergency medical care) may apply directly to FEMA for a disaster grant. All other private nonprofits must first apply to the U.S. SBA for a disaster loan. If the private nonprofit is declined for an SBA loan or the loan does not cover all eligible damages, the applicant may reapply for FEMA assistance.

Public Assistance Process: As soon as practicable after the declaration, the state, assisted by FEMA, conducts the Applicants' Briefings for state, local, and private nonprofit officials to inform them of the assistance available and how to apply for it. A Request for Public Assistance must be filed with the state within 30 days after the area is designated eligible for assistance. Following the Applicants' Briefing, a Kick-off Meeting is conducted. At that time damages are discussed, needs assessed, and a plan of action is put in place. A combined federal/state/local team proceeds with Project Formulation, which is the process of compiling and completing documents about the eligible facility, the eligible work, and the eligible cost for fixing the damages to every public or private nonprofit facility identified by state or local representatives. The team prepares a Project Worksheet (PW) for each project.

Public Assistance Projects Categories:

Emergency Work

- Category A: Debris removal

- Category B: Emergency protective measures

(*Continued*)

(Continued)

Permanent Work

- Category C: Road systems and bridges

- Category D: Water control facilities

- Category E: Public buildings and contents

- Category F: Public utilities

- Category G: Parks, recreational, and other items[64]

This list of categories may appear to be mundane, but for many local government officials confronting a disaster response and recovery, these categories open a path to highly generous federal funding, even when such funds come with a state and local cost share, as they normally do. In many disasters, including floods, hurricanes, earthquakes, tornadoes, and severe storms, "debris removal" tops out as a government expense category. Repairing or restoring roads, bridges, water and wastewater systems, lifeline service utilities, public buildings and offices, and so on, can run far into the millions. Those who closely examine presidential emergency declarations will discover that FEMA PA is this type of declaration's primary form of post-disaster aid, and that under some emergency declarations not all categories of PA apply.

Small Projects: Projects falling between the maximum and minimum thresholds of Table 4-2 are considered "small." The threshold is adjusted annually for inflation. For fiscal year 2018, the maximum small project threshold is $125,500 and minimum is $3,140, as Table 4-2 shows. For small projects, payment of the federal share of the estimate is made upon approval of the project, and recipients are required to notify FEMA upon completion of the project.

Large Projects: For large projects, payment is made on the basis of actual costs determined after the project is completed, although interim payments may be made as necessary. Once FEMA obligates funds to the state, further management of the assistance, including disbursement to subgrantees, is the responsibility of the state. FEMA will continue to monitor the recovery progress to ensure the timely delivery of eligible

assistance and compliance with the law and regulations. Large projects must have exceeded the small project maximums of Table 4-2.

The federal share of assistance is not less than 75 percent of the eligible cost for emergency measures and permanent restoration. The grantee (usually the state) determines how the non-federal share (up to 25 percent) is split with the sub-grantees (eligible applicants).[65] The state and local cost-share is almost always predetermined in state and local law or regulation. How states and their local governments apportion the burden of the cost-share among one another is pertinent. States that cover all or most of the cost-share reduce the burden for localities covered under a presidential declaration. This encourages maximum participation by local governments as they seek to document all of their legitimate losses to both their state and FEMA. Conversely, states that cover only a small fraction of the cost-share impose a significant burden on their respective local governments. Those local governments often must absorb 15 or 20 percent of the cost share. Moreover, regardless of the size of the local cost share, localities must shoulder the substantial bureaucratic burdens of documenting PA-covered losses, must retain and oversee contractors chosen to carry out rebuilding and replacement, and then await FEMA and state reimbursement. Often, local governments are "left holding the bag" if and when various construction costs prove to be ineligible for PA coverage. When this occurs, they must absorb 100 percent of the uncovered costs.

Assistance to Individuals and Households Program[66]

FEMA's **Individuals and Households Program (IHP)** provides financial help or direct services to those who have necessary post-disaster expenses or serious needs they are unable to meet through other means. Up to the IHP maximum is available in financial help (adjusted each year), although some forms of IHP assistance have limits. Effective October 1, 2016, the maximum amount of FEMA IHP paid to any individual or household cannot exceed $34,300.[67] By law, the maximum

TABLE 4-2 ■ Public Assistance per Capita Impact Indicator and Project Thresholds				
Fiscal Year (FY)*	Statewide Indicator**	Countywide Indicator***	Small Project Minimum	Small Project Maximum
2004	$1.11	$2.77	$1,000	$54,100
2005	$1.14	$2.84	$1,000	$55,500
2006	$1.18	$2.94	$1,000	$57,500
2007	$1.22	$3.05	$1,000	$59,700
2008	$1.24	$3.11	$1,000	$60,900
2009	$1.31	$3.28	$1,000	$64,200
2010	$1.29	$3.23	$1,000	$63,200
2011	$1.30	$3.27	$1,000	$63,900
2012	$1.35	$3.39	$1,000	$66,400
2013	$1.37	$3.45	$1,000	$67,500
2014	$1.39	$3.50	$1,000	$68,500
2014*	$1.39	$3.50	$3,000*	$120,000
2015	$1.41	$3.56	$3,040	$121,600
2016	$1.41	$3.57	$3,050	$121,800
2017	$1.43	$3.61	$3,100	$123,100
2018	$1.46	$3.68	$3,140	$125,500

Source: FEMA, "Public Assistance Per Capita Impact Indicator and Project Thresholds," October 11, 2017. At https://www.fema.gov/public-assistance-indicator-and-project-thresholds.

Note: FY 2018 figures are for all disasters declared from Oct. 1, 2017, through Sept. 30, 2018. State and countywide indicators are adjusted each year for inflation according to the Consumer Price Index.

*Federal fiscal years run from October 1 through September 30 each year.

**The statewide indicator sets the threshold that each state, DC (treated as a state), and trust, commonwealth, or free association partner is expected to meet or exceed in per capita damage costs to be eligible for FEMA PA. The president is free to disregard the threshold when acting on a governor's request for a major disaster declaration.

*** The countywide indicator sets the threshold each county or county equivalent of a state and DC (treated as a county), or each county or county-equivalent of a trust, commonwealth, or free association partner, is expected to meet or exceed in per capita damage costs to be eligible for FEMA PA.

is increased or left unchanged each federal fiscal year based on changes in the respective year's Consumer Price Index. The following forms of help are available: Public Housing Assistance (including temporary housing, repair, replacement, and semi-permanent or permanent housing construction) and Other Needs Assistance (including personal property and other items).[68]

(Continued)

(Continued)

Individual Assistance is provided by FEMA directly to eligible individuals and families who have sustained losses due to disasters. Here are some facts about what the program offers:

- Homeowners and renters in designated counties who sustained damage to their primary homes, vehicles, and personal property under a declared disaster may apply for disaster assistance.

- Disaster assistance may include grants to help pay for temporary housing to include rental and lodging expense, emergency home repairs, uninsured and underinsured personal property losses, and medical, dental, and funeral expenses caused by the disaster, along with other serious disaster-related expenses.

- Disaster assistance grants are not taxable income and will not affect eligibility for Social Security, Medicaid, medical waiver programs, welfare assistance, Temporary Assistance for Needy Families, food stamps, Supplemental Security Income or Social Security Disability Insurance.

- Low-interest disaster loans from the SBA may be available for businesses of all sizes (including landlords), private nonprofit organizations, and homeowners and renters. Low-interest disaster loans help fund repairs or rebuilding efforts and cover the cost of replacing lost or disaster-damaged real estate and personal property. Economic injury disaster loans are available to businesses and private nonprofits to assist with working capital needs as a direct result of the disaster.[69]

Housing Assistance

To be clear, housing assistance here refers to a sub-program of IHP. Also, in reviewing the information provided, remember that FEMA money cannot be used to duplicate what is paid out in claim settlements by insurers. Those with homeowner's insurance, car insurance, and other forms of property insurance are required to file claims under those policies. Homeowner's insurance that covers a home's contents, and alternative living expenses incurred when an individual, family, or household must temporarily leave their homes, for example, cannot also be covered by FEMA. However, various expenses left unreimbursed after insurance claims are settled may be eligible for FEMA assistance of some type.

FEMA temporary housing: This is money to rent a different place to live or a temporary housing unit (when rental properties are unavailable).

Repair: This is money for homeowners to repair damage from the disaster that is not covered by insurance. The goal is to repair the home to a safe and sanitary living or functioning condition. FEMA may provide up to the IHP maximum for home repair ($33,300 in 2018); then the homeowner may apply for an SBA disaster loan for additional repair assistance. FEMA will not pay to return a home to its condition before the disaster. In rare cases, FEMA may pay up to a maximum of $33,300 to "replace" a totally demolished home. Flood insurance may be required if the home is in a special flood hazard area. Repair and replacement items include the following:

- Structural parts of a home (foundation, outside walls, roof)

- Windows, doors, floors, walls, ceilings, cabinetry

- Septic or sewage system

- Well or other water system

- Heating, ventilating, and air conditioning system

- Utilities (electrical, plumbing, and gas systems)

- Entrance and exit ways from the home, including privately owned access roads

- Blocking, leveling, and anchoring of a mobile home and reconnecting or resetting its sewer, water, electrical, and fuel lines and tanks[70]

Replacement: Money to replace a disaster-damaged home, under rare conditions, if this can be done with limited funds. FEMA may provide up to the IHP maximum for home replacement. If the home is located in a special flood hazard area, the homeowner must comply with flood insurance purchase requirements and local flood codes and requirements. Note that under Other Needs Assistance, FEMA may cover the initial cost of the NFIP policy for the homeowner.

Semi-permanent or permanent housing construction: This is direct assistance or money for the construction of a home. This type of FEMA aid is conferred in very unusual circumstances, in locations specified by FEMA, and where no other type of housing assistance is possible. "Construction shall follow current minimal local building codes and standards where they exist, or minimal acceptable construction industry standards in the area. Construction will aim toward average quality, size, and capacity, taking into consideration the needs of the occupant. If the home is located in a special flood hazard area, the homeowner must comply with flood insurance purchase requirements and local flood codes and requirements."[71]

Other Needs Assistance

The **Other Needs Assistance (FEMA)** provision of the IHP provides grants for uninsured, disaster-related necessary expenses and serious needs. If the applicant resides in a special flood hazard area, they may be required to buy National Flood Insurance to cover their insurable items (personal property). Assistance includes the following:

- Medical and dental expenses
- Funeral and burial costs
- Repair, cleaning, or replacement of:
  - Clothing
  - Household items (room furnishings, appliances)
  - Specialized tools or protective clothing and equipment required for the applicant's job
  - Necessary educational materials (computers, schoolbooks, supplies)
- Clean-up items (wet/dry vacuum, air purifier, dehumidifier) and fuel for primary heat source (heating oil, gas)
- Vehicles in need of repair or replacement due to damage by the disaster, or reimbursement of public transportation or other transportation costs
- Moving and storage expenses related to the disaster (including storage or the return of property to a pre-disaster home)
- Other necessary expenses or serious needs (e.g., towing or setup or connecting essential utilities for a housing unit not provided by FEMA)
- Cost of a National Flood Insurance Program (NFIP) group flood insurance policy to meet the flood insurance requirements[72]

Conditions and Limitations of Individuals and Households Program Assistance

Federal disaster-related laws and policies embody rules, conditions, evidence, time limits, applicant rights and protections, and appeal rights. Cross-cutting rules set forth for other policy purposes regularly impact federal disaster assistance programs.

Non-discrimination: All forms of FEMA disaster housing assistance are available to any affected household that meets the conditions of eligibility. No federal entity or official (or their agent) may discriminate against any individual on the basis of race, color, religion, gender, age, national origin, disability, LGBTQ[73] status, or economic status.[74] The definition of a household now used by FEMA is highly relevant. "FEMA Individual Assistance (IA) is provided by 'household.' This is a broad term and includes everyone living in the residence at the time of the disaster. It does not refer to the nature of the relationship, therefore it is unnecessary to ask a couple if their relationship is legally recognized. Only one

(Continued)

(Continued)

person per household will complete the assistance form. The legal owner of the lost property should represent the household. All evacuees should be encouraged to reach out to FEMA for assistance."[75]

Patrick Roberts claims that FEMA, particularly from 1980 into the mid-1990s, had leaders and practices that were racially discriminatory. He adds that many FEMA leaders, and hiring policies, were biased against gays and lesbians. Roberts documents that some of this discrimination was apparent in personnel and security clearance policies as well as in emergency planning and quarantine preparedness.[76]

Residency status in the United States and its territories: To be considered for disaster housing assistance, applicants, or a household member, must provide proof of identity and sign a declaration stating that they are a U.S. citizen, a noncitizen national, or a qualified alien. The Disaster Housing Assistance Program (DHAP) is a joint HUD- and FEMA-administered program.[77]

Notable here is that "out of status" aliens are not eligible to apply for FEMA assistance; nonetheless, they may receive in-kind help distributed by FEMA or by those working on FEMA's behalf.

Supplemental assistance: Disaster housing assistance is not intended to substitute for private recovery efforts but to complement those efforts when needed. FEMA expects minor housing damage or the need for short-term shelter to be addressed by homeowners, condo owners, renters, or tenants. Furthermore, the DHAP is not a loss indemnification program and does not ensure that applicants are returned to their pre-disaster living conditions.[78]

Moreover, FEMA strongly advocates that both homeowners and tenant or civic associations purchase insurance that covers them for the hazards that may possibly befall them.

Household composition: People living together in one residence before the disaster are expected to continue to live together after the disaster. Generally, assistance is provided to the household unit in residence before the disaster. If, however, the assistance provided to the

household is not shared, or if the new residence proves to be too small or causes undue hardship, members of the household may request assistance separate from their pre-disaster household.[79]

Type of assistance: Generally, more than one type of IHP assistance may be provided to the household. Only FEMA has the authority to determine which type(s) of assistance is or are most appropriate for the household.[80] FEMA also decides how long the assistance will be provided.

Proper use of assistance: All financial assistance provided by FEMA should be used as specified in writing: to rent another place to live, to make the home repairs identified by FEMA, or to replace or repair personal property. Failure to use the money as specified may result in ineligibility for additional assistance.[81]

This rule is difficult for FEMA to enforce, and news or social media often reveal that some of those who received FEMA money did not use it as it was intended. All money provided by FEMA is tax-free.

Documentation: Applicants are responsible for providing all documentation necessary for FEMA to evaluate eligibility. Applicants may need to provide proof of occupancy, ownership, income loss, and/or information concerning their housing prior to the disaster. Applicants should keep all receipts and records for any housing expenses incurred as a result of the disaster. This includes receipts for repair supplies, labor, and rent payments.[82]

For disaster victims who seek FEMA assistance, documentation may be one of FEMA's most detested requirements. Victims, particularly those who have lost their homes, are often hard pressed or unable to supply FEMA with all of the documents the government requires. Sometimes the lack of a single document makes the applicant ineligible for FEMA Individual and Household Assistance. Conversely, by law FEMA must ensure that its payments are substantiated and legitimate. Disasters often tempt some people to commit fraud, deception, or misrepresentation—all at the federal government's expense. After working a disaster, FEMA is regularly investigated by federal auditors, inspectors general, and congressional oversight committees. FEMA overpayments are "grist" for news media people. Moreover, FEMA is often excoriated when it demands that money it paid out to victims be paid back on grounds that it was inappropriately obtained or awarded by mistake.

Insurance: If applicants have insurance, any assistance provided by FEMA should be considered an advance and must be repaid to FEMA upon receipt of an insurance settlement payment. If the settlement is less than the FEMA estimated cost to make the home habitable, applicants may qualify for FEMA funds to supplement their insurance settlement—but only for repairs relating to the home's habitability. FEMA does not provide replacement value amounts or assistance with non-essential items.[83]

Duration of assistance: Repair and replacement assistance is provided as a one-time payment. **FEMA temporary housing assistance** (or a manufactured housing unit) is provided for an initial period of one, two, or three months. To be considered for additional assistance, applicants must demonstrate that they have spent any previous assistance from FEMA as instructed and must demonstrate their efforts to reestablish permanent housing. Additional assistance is generally provided for one, two, or three months at a time. The maximum period for IHP assistance is 18 months.[84]

Appeal rights: Applicants who disagree with the FEMA determination of eligibility or the form of assistance provided have the right to appeal within 60 days of the date of the notification letter.[85]

This overview of FEMA assistance programs may appear overwhelming. However, those who study U.S. disaster management should familiarize themselves with at least some of the details of these programs. First, they may be asked questions about this information by future disaster victims. Second, there is never any guarantee that researchers and students of this field will not someday need to avail themselves of the benefits offered by these programs.

Moreover, once a disaster is declared by the president, individual and household assistance is not offered permanently. FEMA tracks the flow of applications for all IA programs under each in-force declaration. When application numbers dwindle, FEMA posts in the *Federal Register* a closeout date for the respective declaration's IA applications. Interestingly, the closeout date applies to Individual Assistance programs and not Public Assistance (government-to-government) aid. Sometimes when a proposed closeout date is posted for IA, protests ensue and lawmakers intercede with FEMA to extend the deadline for late filers. Sometimes IA closeout dates on a declaration are extended, but they eventually reach a termination date beyond which no more applications are accepted. The Public Assistance component of many declarations faces a tougher challenge in reaching closeout. The PA projects approved under each declaration must have been fully completed with final FEMA outlays made before FEMA can close the books (closeout) on the PA portion of a declaration. Depending on the size of the projects, the number of permits required to complete them, the pace of construction, the length of time inspection of work takes, and other factors, some PA projects are not completed for a period of years. In rare cases, some massive PA projects are not closed out for a decade or more.

A final observation about FEMA's Individual Assistance program is warranted. In those unfortunate locations that suffer back-to-back declared disasters, victims often believe that rather than request FEMA IA help for each declared incident they have endured, they can simply add the damage they suffered in the first declared event to the damage they suffered in the second declared event and then make application to FEMA. FEMA treats each declared disaster in isolation from preceding or subsequent declared disasters. In back-to-back declaration circumstances, applicants need to file for damage they sustained in the first disaster and then file separately for new damage they sustained in the second disaster. Aggregating damage costs from two disasters into one is, pun intended, a "recipe for disaster."[86]

THE PRESIDENT'S "POWER" TO DECIDE

Over most of the 20th century, natural and non-terrorism-related human-caused disasters were rarely considered matters of national security, with the notable exception of civil defense plans against nuclear attack. Owing to the September 11, 2001, terror attacks, the administration of President George W. Bush, with the assent of Congress, redefined presidential disaster declaration authority as a possible national security instrument, thus dramatically changing federal emergency management. The 9/11 disaster further centralized presidential authority, as war and several catastrophic disasters had done so before in the nation's history. Terrorism policy and disaster policy would be conjoined and in doing so presidential declaration authority would be significantly broadened.[87]

The G. W. Bush administration was asked to prepare a comprehensive national response plan by those who produced the *9/11 Commission Report*.[88] With the help of Congress, the Bush administration complied.

The Homeland Security Act of 2002 (P.L. 107-296), Homeland Security Presidential Directive-5 (HSPD-5), and the Stafford Act of 1988 justify and provide, according to the former National Response Plan (NRP) and since 2008 the current National Response Framework (NRF), a comprehensive, all-hazards approach to domestic incident management.[89] Disaster declarations in the post-9/11 era are now matters of domestic incident management. All major disasters, emergencies, and catastrophic events declared by the president are considered incidents. Under the NRF, and its NRF third edition, an incident is defined as "[a]n actual or potential high-impact event that requires coordination of Federal, State, local, tribal, nongovernmental and/or private sector entities in order to save lives and minimize damage."[90]

With the exception of a few federal emergency management officials, former FEMA official George Haddow,[91] and a few others, most disaster management experts did not immediately recognize that the merger of the terrorism mission and the disaster management mission would open the coffers of the Disaster Relief Fund for use by a range of federal security agencies. CRS Researcher Bruce R. Lindsay examines this issue in one of his recent reports.

Lindsay summarizes his report concerning terrorism and the Stafford Act:

> The Stafford Act has been used to provide assistance in response to terrorist attacks in the past including the 1995 bombing of the Alfred P. Murrah Building in Oklahoma City, the September 11, 2001, attacks, and the 2013 Boston Marathon attack. Nevertheless, the tactics used in recent incidents such as the 2015 San Bernardino, CA, and the 2016 Orlando, FL, mass shootings, and the 2016 Ohio State University vehicular and knife attack, have brought to light two main challenges that might prevent certain types of terrorist incidents from receiving the wider assistance provided under a major disaster declaration:
>
> - Major disaster definition lists specific incident types that are eligible for federal assistance. Past terrorist incidents were considered major disasters, in part, because they resulted in fires and explosions. Incidents without a fire or an explosion may not meet the Stafford Act of 1988 definition of a major disaster.
>
> - Federal Emergency Management Agency's (FEMA) recommendation to the president to issue a major disaster declaration is mainly based on damage

amounts to public infrastructure compared to the state's population. Terrorist incidents with a large loss of life but limited damage to public infrastructure may not meet this criterion. Some may argue that terrorist incidents warrant the wider range of assistance provided by a major disaster declaration, and advocate for changes to the Stafford Act and FEMA policies to make all acts of terrorism eligible for major disaster assistance. Others may disagree and argue that the Stafford Act should not be altered for the following reasons:

o   Regardless of cause, state and local governments should be the main source of assistance if damages are limited,

o   If the incident does not qualify for major disaster assistance, it could still be eligible for limited assistance under an emergency declaration.

Advocates of changing the Stafford Act may argue that emergency declaration assistance is too limited. For example, parts of FEMA's Individual Assistance (IA) program, which provides various forms of help for families and individuals, are rarely available without a major disaster declaration. Another concern is the limited availability of SBA disaster loans under an emergency declaration. Advocates might therefore argue that changes to the Stafford Act are needed to make it easier for certain terror attacks to qualify for major disaster assistance. These include

•   expanding the major disaster definition to include terror incidents that do not involve fires and explosions;

•   requiring FEMA to use additional metrics when making major disaster recommendations; and/or

•   extending the availability of certain IA programs and SBA disaster loans under an emergency declaration.[92]

Lindsay's report examines many of the problems encountered in declaring "all" terrorist incidents as major disasters or emergencies. For example, the Oklahoma City Murrah Office Building bombing in 1995, and the 9/11 attacks on the World Trade Center and the Pentagon in 2001, were all acts of terrorism, and each received a major declaration or emergency declaration or both. Interestingly, for the Boston Marathon bombing of April 2013, the governor of Massachusetts asked for and received from President Obama an emergency declaration to cover certain losses in that incident.[93] However, in 2016, in the aftermath of the Orlando Pulse Nightclub shooting, where at least 49 were killed plus the gunman, there was a different outcome. Florida governor Rick Scott asked President Obama for a declaration of emergency and was turned down. The president, advised by FEMA officials, told Governor Scott in his letter of denial that Florida was not eligible for the emergency declaration because it had not proven in its request that the state could not recover on its own from the incident.

Many types of incidents that are unique or original, and that involve governor requests for a presidential disaster declaration of some type, are at first denied by presidents. For example, President G. W. Bush denied then-Florida governor Jeb Bush's (the president's brother's) request for an emergency declaration after an anthrax poisoning incident at American Media Inc. in Boca Raton, FL, which began only six days after the 9/11 attacks of 2001. One person at American Media died in the incident days after he opened mail he received that contained the substance. By mid-October 2001, anthrax-laden letters began arriving in the incoming mail of two U.S. senators, a TV news correspondent, and others. The federal government spent billions screening for the substance at various key government offices in Washington, DC. Several U.S. Post Office mail processing centers were contaminated and numbers of postal workers were exposed to the substance and sickened. All told, another 5 people died and 17 were injured owing to anthrax exposure. This was investigated by the FBI as bioterror attack. An Army laboratory scientist who had worked on anthrax vaccines committed suicide, such that the FBI ended its investigation with the conclusion that this individual was the culprit.[94] The point is that the president and FEMA, working in cooperation with several other law enforcement, medical, and defense organizations, learned from this experience and now include bioterrorism on the list of potentially disaster- or emergency-declarable incidents.

Catastrophes and National Special Security Events Enter the Presidential Declaration Mix

The National Response Framework in place since 2008 includes a category of incident beyond major disaster and emergency. **Catastrophic incidents** are defined as

Any natural or manmade incident, including terrorism, that results in extraordinary levels of mass casualties, damage, or disruption severely affecting the population, infrastructure, environment, economy, and national morale and/or government functions. A catastrophic event could result in sustained national impacts over a prolonged period of time; almost immediately exceeds resources normally available to State, local, tribal, and private sector authorities; and significantly interrupts governmental operations and emergency services to such an extent that national security could be threatened.[95]

The word "catastrophe" is meant to elicit several responses. It aims to impel state and local governments to plan for disasters of catastrophic magnitude and deadliness. It also may serve to pull in a wider assortment of federal agencies than have been included thus far in standard federal emergency support functions. It may also be used as a trigger to press officials at the U.S. Department of the Treasury, and who implement major provisions of the Terrorism Risk Insurance Act (TRIA) of 2002, to certify that an act of terror has indeed occurred and that federal support to the private insurance and reinsurance industry will be made available under rules of the program.[96] Moreover, the Post-Katrina Emergency Management Reform Act (P.L. 109-295) offers a definition of catastrophic incident, but does not create catastrophic incident declaration authority. This may be a moot point since the president can use, and has in the past used, his Stafford Act major disaster declaration authority to address disasters meeting much of the definition of catastrophe.

National Special Security Events (NSSEs)

National Special Security Events (NSSEs) are in some respects under the umbrella of presidential declaration authority, although largely outside Stafford Act authority. On May 22, 1998, President William J. Clinton issued Presidential Decision Directive 62

(PDD 62)—Protection Against Unconventional Threats to the Homeland and Americans Overseas. PDD 62 established a framework for federal department and agency counter-terrorism programs, which addressed terrorist apprehension and prosecution, increased transportation security, enhanced emergency response, and promoted cybersecurity. PDD 62 also designated specific federal departments and agencies as the lead agencies in the event of terrorist attacks. The U.S. Secret Service (USSS), part of the Department of Homeland Security since 2003, was designated as the lead agency in the planning, implementation, and coordination of operational security for events of national signifi-cance—as designated by the president. Other lead agencies for counterterrorism activities included the Federal Emergency Management Agency, the Department of Defense, and the Department of Health and Human Services.[97]

On December 19, 2000, Congress enacted P.L. 106-544, the Presidential Threat Protection Act of 2000, and authorized the USSS—when directed by the president—to plan, coordinate, and implement security operations at special events of national signif-icance. The special events were designated National Special Security Events (NSSEs). Some events categorized as NSSEs include the following: presidential inaugurations, major international summits held in the United States, major sporting events, and presi-dential nominating conventions.[98]

NSSEs include "high-profile, large-scale events that present high probability targets" such as various summit meetings of world leaders inside the United States, the Republican and Democratic national political party conventions, inaugurations, and any other event the president believes may be vulnerable to terror attack. The U.S. Department of Homeland Security uses NSSEs to cover any potential target for terrorism or other crim-inal activity. These events have included meetings of international organizations. NSSE designation requires federal agencies to provide full cooperation and support to ensure the safety and security of those participating in or otherwise attending the event, and the community within which the event takes place, and is typically limited to specific event sites for a specified time frame. An NSSE puts the USSS in charge of event security; the Federal Bureau of Investigation (FBI) in charge of intelligence, counterterrorism, hostage rescue, and investigation of incidents of terrorism or other major criminal activities asso-ciated with the NSSE; and FEMA in charge of recovery management in the aftermath of terrorist or other major criminal incidents, natural disasters, or other catastrophic events.[99]

Prior to the establishment of DHS in January 2003, the president determined which events would warrant NSSE designation. Since the establishment of the depart-ment, the DHS secretary—as the president's representative—has had the responsibil-ity to designate NSSEs. NSSE designation factors include the following: anticipated attendance by U.S. officials and foreign dignitaries; size of the event; and significance of the event.

The secretary of DHS manages an NSSE grant program that provides reimbursement of eligible costs of organizations engaged in preparing and implementing an NSSE.[100] Even though NSSEs have been designated since 1998, Congress has only appropriated funding for a general NSSE fund since FY 2006. Since about 2000, presidents have used their authority to issue emergency declarations to cover NSSEs, thus tapping the Disaster Relief Fund rather than the USSS's modestly funded NSSE program budget.[101] Many may be surprised to learn that President G. W. Bush issued an emergency declaration to cover Barack Obama's inauguration in January 2009 and that President Obama issued one to cover Donald Trump's January 2017 inauguration. Also, the annual NFL Super Bowl routinely garners NSSE coverage.

The Significance of Post-9/11 Changes

Why are these post-9/11 changes important? Presidents now possess almost unencumbered authority to mobilize federal, state, and local resources if they conclude that an event of some kind represents either a terrorism threat or an assumed act of terrorism. When a terrorist event occurs, the NRF draws federal, state, and local agencies together to work under the National Incident Management System (NIMS). In addition, the Homeland Security Act of 2002, related laws, and a series of homeland security presidential directives created changes in FEMA and the domestic and international world of emergency management.

Because the president and DHS-FEMA officials define so many major disasters and emergencies of any type or cause as incidents of national importance, emergency management is today very much interwoven with national security at home and abroad. U.S. emergency managers on every level of government must now learn more about disasters and emergencies, especially those involving terrorism, that occur outside, as well as inside, the United States.[102]

TELL ME MORE 4-1
ANOMALOUS PROBLEMS INVITE NEW DECLARATION PRECEDENTS

Occasionally, certain anomalous events invite presidents to use the discretion they have in disaster declaration authority to issue declarations for unprecedented phenomena. An example is the presidential response to Cuban president Fidel Castro's Mariel boatlift of Cuban evacuees to the United States in 1980. President Jimmy Carter issued an emergency declaration to reimburse Florida for the costs incurred in working with Cuban refugees from the boatlift.[103] This action handed FEMA a unique management task that had to be performed in cooperation with various federal and state agencies, most particularly corrections agencies, which were assigned the job of separating convicted criminals from the pool of refugees.

Sometimes presidents single-handedly, or in conjunction with Congress, transform or expand what officially constitutes a disaster.

In 1979, President Carter issued a controversial presidential declaration of a major disaster covering the Love Canal hazardous waste incident in a neighborhood of Niagara Falls, New York. This action was one of the first to engage FEMA in buying out contaminated or endangered homes in the interest of public safety. The FEMA **buyout program** for houses and other properties became more common in future years, particularly for structures subject to recurring flood loss or from hazardous substance threats prohibitively expensive or technologically infeasible to correct.

In 1999, President Clinton's decision to approve New York governor George Pataki's West Nile virus emergency request (to cover pesticide spraying and public health costs) created a new category of federal emergency aid. Some analysts allege that federal activity in support of West Nile virus spraying was a precursor of modern anti-pandemic or bioterrorism federal preparedness initiatives.[104] These decisions set precedents that led governors to conclude that they could ask for presidential declarations to cover similar problems and calamities.

On February 1, 2003, the space shuttle *Columbia* disintegrated in the atmosphere upon reentry from space, killing its seven astronauts and scattering debris across several southwestern states. President George W. Bush exercised his disaster declaration authority and invited governors of the states engaged in searching for the remains of the astronauts and parts of the shuttle to request 100 percent federally funded emergency declarations that would reimburse their respective states and localities for the costs of searching for, protecting, and returning to the National Aeronautics and Space Administration (NASA) all physical and material remains. Texas, where most of the debris was eventually located, and Louisiana both applied for and received emergency declarations (EM 1371 and 1372, respectively) from the president for this purpose.

Federal emergency management is predicated on terrorism as a paramount threat, whereas other types of disasters or emergencies occupy diminished positions within the federal emergency management and homeland security community.[105] Until the mid-1980s, when concerns about terrorism arose within the Reagan administration, natural and non-war human-caused disasters have rarely been considered matters of national security.[106]

Owing to the president's and federal government's problems in the 2005 Hurricane Katrina catastrophe, presidents facing potential mega-disasters may be tempted to federalize the government's response to certain disasters under presidential declarations of "catastrophic disaster." However, the Stafford Act of 1988 and its amendments in subsequent measures remain law, and the process by which the president and DHS-FEMA consider gubernatorial requests for declarations of major disaster and emergency and the nature of what constitutes a disaster agent have been only slightly altered owing to terrorism concerns. Most of these changes reflect a shift toward homeland security and defense. This has produced some negative ramifications at the state and local levels. See Chapter 7.

THE "POLITICS" OF PRESIDENTIAL DECLARATIONS

Sometimes disasters, particularly those that are catastrophic in magnitude, profoundly affect presidents and their administrations. Hurricane Camille (1969), and an ensuing weak and highly criticized federal response to that disaster, impelled President Nixon to assign various emergency management duties to an archipelago of federal agencies. By furnishing a wide variety of federal departments and agencies small pieces of disaster management jurisdiction, Nixon hoped to broaden the congressional base of political support for disaster assistance in general. The federal–state debacle in managing the response in Florida to Hurricane Andrew in 1992 damaged President George H. W. Bush's image, and although he narrowly won the state's electoral votes in 1988, it may have contributed to his defeat in the November 1992 presidential election. Once in office,

President Clinton responded to the Hurricane Andrew failure by appointing a qualified and experienced state emergency manager to head his FEMA. In spite of controversial problems in some realms of his administration, Bill Clinton left office perceived as a president capable of managing domestic disasters, although perhaps less so terrorism. The terrorist attack disaster of September 11, 2001, moved President George W. Bush to quickly redefine his administration's primary mission as one of countering terrorism. Hurricane Katrina and the excoriated federal response to that disaster chastened President G. W. Bush and moved Congress to reconstitute FEMA as a full-service emergency management agency but one still embedded within the gigantic DHS. President Barack Obama confronted massively destructive Superstorm Sandy in November 2013, which generated major disaster declarations for twelve mid-Atlantic and northeastern states and caused property losses rivaling those of Hurricane Katrina in 2005.[107] In the spring of 2011, President Obama responded to a tornado outbreak and severe weather with seven major disaster declarations for southern states—Alabama hit the hardest with nearly three quarters of a billion dollars in damage, some for the deadly Tuscaloosa tornado.[108] President Trump, in office only some six months, had to confront three successive massively destructive hurricanes: Harvey in the greater Houston area of Texas, Irma along a south-to-north line of peninsular Florida, and Maria, which carved a path of mass destruction across the heart of the island of Puerto Rico and seriously impacted the American Virgin Islands (see Chapter 9).

Disaster policy and politics are very much **event driven**.[109] Politics permeate the realm of disaster and emergency; in nations that embrace democracy, politics and disasters have an ambivalent relationship that is very much time-related. Overtly political behavior in the immediate aftermath of a disaster is not only bad politics but self-defeating politics. However, disasters during campaign seasons usually benefit incumbents and hurt challengers. Disasters tend to suspend political campaigns and partisan competition. However, as time passes elected executive officials who are astute politically need to prove their mettle. They need to act and they need to know how to resolve problems that their disaster managers bring them. If the response and recovery seem to be moving forward satisfactorily, elected executives, including presidents, need to know when it is appropriate to visit a disaster site and its victims. It is only natural that elected executives claim political credit for well-managed emergencies and crises. However, whether deserved or otherwise, a disaster response judged to have been bungled or too slow will redound poorly for elected executive officeholders.

There is a tendency among policymakers to be influenced by, if not fixated upon, the latest memorable disaster or catastrophe. Certain disasters or catastrophes not only stress the nation's disaster management system but force massive reforms that produce a **new normal** in the domain of disaster policy and homeland security.[110] FEMA, whether independent or within DHS, is fairly good at managing "routine" disasters.[111] However, no single federal agency is invested with sufficient authority to adequately or proficiently cope with a catastrophe. It becomes the job of the president and his staff to orchestrate and oversee the work of many federal disaster agencies in catastrophic circumstances. Such work has to be carried out with the help and cooperation of governors, mayors, and other elected executives. A host of other players are involved as well, and these include state and local emergency managers, emergency responders, nonprofit organizations active in disasters, and private corporations, large and small.[112] This type of work is

TELL ME MORE 4-2
PRESIDENTS, NEWS, AND PUBLIC RELATIONS

Over the past 30 or more years, presidents have taken a greater interest in disasters, particularly major ones. Disasters have become targets of camcorder politics in which political officials seek opportunities to be filmed at disaster sites to exhibit compassion and at the same time demonstrate responsiveness to the public, actions that may yield them political benefits.[113] In 1980, President Carter issued a presidential disaster declaration in *Air Force One* while flying over the volcanic eruption of Mount St. Helens in Washington State. President Reagan was once photographed shoveling sand into a gunnysack on the banks of a flooding Mississippi River after issuing a presidential declaration of major disaster. President George H. W. Bush was filmed commiserating with victims of the Loma Prieta earthquake in a heavily damaged San Francisco neighborhood, weeks after having issued a declaration for the quake. Television cameras showed President Clinton at shelters and inspecting freeway damage in the days after he issued a declaration for the Northridge earthquake. Similarly, President George W. Bush visited the Pentagon and the World Trade Center "ground zero" in the days after the 9/11 terrorist attacks to exhibit compassion, concern, and resolve to prevent future attacks. He did likewise after Hurricane Katrina in September 2005 when he visited Louisiana and toured flood-damaged areas inside New Orleans. In late May 2013, President Obama personally toured the Enhanced Fujita Scale 5 tornado damage zone in Moore, Oklahoma, where 14 adults and 10 children perished and where an estimated 1,200 homes and 2 elementary schools were destroyed, to commiserate with affected families and individuals and to offer reassurance of ongoing federal relief aid.[114] Both President Trump and First Lady Melania Trump visited flood-ravaged Houston neighborhoods after Hurricane Harvey in early September 2017.[115] Today, Americans expect their president both to dispatch federal disaster help and to personally visit damaged areas. It is now customary for most of the president's cabinet, especially officials heading disaster-relevant departments, to visit major disaster sites.[116] Such visits and "photo ops" are an intrinsic part of modern presidential crisis management.

How presidents manage disasters and how responsive they are perceived to be to the needs of victims have far-ranging political and electoral consequences, which underline the importance of the role of the head of FEMA. How well the FEMA leadership manages the agency's response to disaster is of great political importance to the president and his staff.[117]

The Clinton administration appreciated the role of the news media in covering disasters. Both President Clinton and FEMA director James Lee Witt emphasized post-disaster public relations, in part because they believed the president's public image was at stake in disaster circumstances. The public requires reassurance that a president is doing all he can to help disaster victims. The need for the president to provide reassurance, backed by action, was underscored after Hurricane Katrina. Not only was President G. W. Bush perceived to have performed poorly in managing the early stages of the disaster, but he went on national television to apologize for his own behavior and for the failures of the government's disaster response. Again, there were political consequences. Heavy Republican losses in House and Senate races in the midterm elections of November 2006 were attributed to public dissatisfaction with the war in Iraq and with the Bush administration's poor performance in the Katrina catastrophe as well. Superstorm Sandy, which struck only days before the 2012 presidential election, may have affected some election outcomes in and around damage zones of New York, Long Island, and coastal areas of New Jersey.

How the FEMA director and staff manage the federal response, and how they portray this effort to the media, shapes public opinion of both the

(Continued)

(Continued)

presidency and the agency. Major disasters cus- tomarily, but not always, pull the nation together, encourage a centralization of authority, and often improve the president's approval ratings in pub- lic opinion polls.[118] Such activity promotes public awareness of the disaster across the state, nation, and world. It underscores the legitimacy of the gov- ernment's response and of the presidency, and it may convey a greater sense of urgency to respond- ers and to those considering the offer of help.

expected under the National Preparedness Plan, the NRF, and recently under the "five suites" frameworks: mitigation, preparedness, prevention, response, and recovery.

White House officials tend to keep their office televisions tuned to CNN, Fox News, MSNBC, or BBC World News, among others, all day long so as not to miss breaking news that may come to involve the president or that may require the president's attention or action. Often breaking news about disasters, emergencies, or other calamitous events gets priority attention in the White House and in the Oval Office.

The Domestic Policy Council and Office of Cabinet Liaison would most likely help the president address various emergency or disaster management activities. Within the White House staff, schedulers, speechwriters, and travel planners would also join in this effort, especially if the president were to make arrangements to visit the disaster area. Secret Service officials, military liaison, and medical personnel may also play roles, as would the Office of the Vice President.[119]

The Secretary, Department of Homeland Security

The DHS secretary is a member of the president's cabinet. The Homeland Security Act of 2002 authorized creation of DHS, a super department opening with some 180,000 employees.[120] It was formed by transferring some 22 federal agencies or offices into the new department. The DHS secretary and deputy secretary are managerial supervisors of the FEMA administrator. The DHS secretary has authority to consult with the FEMA administrator and may be shown the White House Package containing a governor's dec- laration request and other information compiled by FEMA, the respective state, and its localities. In the past, researchers perusing presidential libraries have documented that a list of congressional districts impacted by the incident accompanies (or is part of) the White House package. Presidents are routinely made aware of the U.S. senators and U.S. representatives whose constituents have been impacted by the incident.

Today, when health and safety are threatened, and a disaster is imminent but not yet declared, the secretary of the DHS may position department employees and supplies before the event. DHS monitors the status of the circumstances, communicates with state emergency officials on potential assistance requirements, deploys teams and resources to maximize the speed and effectiveness of the anticipated federal response, and, when necessary, performs preparedness and PDA activities.[121]

In the aftermath of a catastrophic event, the Department of Homeland Security turns to its Surge Capacity Force, a cadre of federal employees who are limited service volun- teers that help affected communities by supporting the Federal Emergency Management Agency's urgent response and recovery efforts. The Surge Capacity Force is made up of vol- unteer federal employees from within DHS outside of FEMA and from almost every federal department or agency that sends volunteers. In the immediate aftermath of Hurricanes Harvey, Irma, and Maria, Acting Secretary of Homeland Security Elaine Duke activated the Surge Capacity Force. DHS has deployed many Surge Capacity Force volunteers from throughout the federal government to support disaster survivors in Texas, Florida, Puerto Rico, and the U.S. Virgin Islands.[122] The Surge Capacity Force is a new initiative. It is functionally worthwhile and it builds a positive public image of both DHS and FEMA

The Role of Congress

Congress as an institution and congressional lawmakers themselves enter into the politics and policy of disasters in myriad ways. When a disaster or emergency is threatened or is imminent, lawmakers representing jurisdictions in the threatened zone often press the president to mobilize federal help or issue a declaration of emergency. Presidents considering a disaster declaration request submitted by a governor receive, as a matter of routine, a list of the names of the lawmakers whose districts are affected by a disaster event.[123]

Senators and representatives often petition the president as an entire state delegation to confer a declaration. Moreover, lawmakers frequently contact the White House about matters of disaster or emergency. Sometimes individual legislators seek audiences with the president or with White House staff to press for federal help.

FEMA has many overseers within Congress. Before FEMA was folded into the DHS, it had a wide variety of House and Senate committees and subcommittees with jurisdiction over its programs in whole or in part. Since FEMA entered the DHS, Congress has reorganized these committees such that there is now a House Committee on Homeland Security. Moreover, the former Senate Governmental Affairs Committee elected to expand its title to become the Committee on Homeland Security and Governmental Affairs. However, many of the federal agencies folded into DHS retain their traditional jurisdiction and so retain their original House and Senate committee and subcommittee overseers, the majority of which are not also members of the House or Senate homeland security committees. This significantly complicates management of DHS units and risks muddled congressional oversight.[124]

On top of this, some researchers allege that presidential and congressional political considerations affect "the rate of disaster declaration" conferral and the allocation of FEMA disaster expenditures across states.[125] A few researchers have shown that states politically important to the president have higher rates of disaster declaration request approvals than other states. They have also claimed that federal disaster relief expenditures are larger in states having congressional representation on FEMA oversight committees than in states unrepresented on FEMA oversight committees. Remarkably, one pair of political economists posited a **congressional dominance model**, which predicts that nearly half of all disaster relief is motivated politically rather than by need.[126] The same researchers assert that there is a possibility that political influence may affect the outcome of gubernatorial requests for presidential disaster declarations at two distinct stages: during the initial decision to declare a disaster or not and in the decision of how much money to allocate for the disaster.[127] Here they assume that bureaus, like FEMA, follow congressional preferences and that the responsible congressional committees, FEMA jurisdictional overseers, make sure that they do so. Here legislators are assumed to behave as wealth maximizers seeking to direct federal resources to their home states or districts.[128]

There are other researchers who insist that differences in major disaster declaration approval rates between presidential and non-presidential election years is slight and statistically insignificant. Sylves and Buzas quantitatively calculate that approval rates for major disaster (DR) and emergency (EM) requests only show slight upturns in the months before an incumbent president seeks re-election, and then only in battleground states of high electoral vote value.[129] Lindsay shows that from 1974 to 2016, turndowns in non-presidential election years average 16.0 per year, which is an average 25.3 percent of all DR and EM requests. In the same interval, for presidential election years, Lindsay shows that turndowns drop to 14.5 per year, which is 25.3 percent of all DR and EM requests.[130] These small differences may not be significant enough for one to draw polit-ical inferences. Whenever the president-governor nexus is considered, one must keep in mind that governors have their own motives, just as presidents do. It may well be that governors of battleground states, in presidential election years when an incumbent presi-dent seeks re-election, exploit these circumstances by asking presidents to approve decla-rations for incidents on the cusp of approvability.

However, the political geography of declaration issuance demonstrates that the alleged FEMA effort to "reward legislators" (Reeve's congressional dominance model) who serve on the agency's authorizations or appropriations oversight committees is both far-fetched and arguable. This is because the ultimate decision to approve or reject a governor's request for a declaration is made by the president, not by FEMA officials. In effect, FEMA officials have little leeway in matters of presidential declaration decision making.

FEMA heads assisted by their staffs (and region offices) have considered the worthi-ness of a governor's request in accord with estimated losses and with FEMA's thresholds of loss at the state and county levels. Since 2002, the administrator, in consultation with the DHS secretary, provides the president with FEMA's official recommendation regard-ing whether the president should approve or reject the governor's declaration request. It is highly unlikely, although difficult to prove, that any FEMA leader would engage in strategic behavior, aimed at placating the desires of lawmakers on FEMA oversight committees, by endorsing unworthy or undeserving requests for presidential approval. It is difficult to prove this because the FEMA director's memorandum to the president is a matter of executive privilege (discussed previously) and so is not open to public scrutiny.

In theory, presidents, on their own, may use their declaration discretion to reward states that are the political homes of key House and Senate legislators and to advance electoral strategies beneficial to themselves, to their fellow party members on Capitol Hill, and to other political actors they judge to be important, including the requesting governors themselves.[131] Presidents could use their declaration power to punish or reward governors, and in rare cases legislators, who support or oppose their policies. They may also want to "simply tarnish the image of opposing party governors or legislators in hopes of reducing their probability of reelection."[132] However, these claims are speculation. Any president's exercise of reward or punishment behavior in the aftermath of major or minor disasters is likely to be evident in how a president, and the White House, choose to use publicity, photo opportunities, and public relations in their dealings with elected officials from states and districts impacted by the event. It is not likely to be evident in their deci-sion to approve or reject a governor's declaration request.[133]

Soon after opening in 1979, FEMA developed a general set of criteria by which the president may judge gubernatorial requests for declarations of major disasters or

TELL ME MORE 4-3
VAGUE CRITERIA AND POLITICAL SUBJECTIVITY

For many years, the process and criteria of disaster declaration has been purposely subjective to allow the president discretion to address a wide range of events and circumstances. Beyond the annual statewide and county per capita damage thresholds set by FEMA to advise the president, governors and their state disaster officials have little to guide them in estimating whether to go ahead with a request for presidential declaration of major disaster or emergency. They have little basis for concluding in advance whether their petition for a presidential declaration will be approved or denied.

However, as long as a governor or other state officials know that the state can afford to shoulder the 25 percent share of the 75 percent/25 percent federal aid formula contained in a presidential disaster declaration, they have an incentive to request a federal declaration. State officials have an incentive to "cry poor" in petitioning for federal help, minimizing their own capacity and capability to address disaster.

Some argue for reducing presidential discretion in the review of governors' requests for disaster declarations and often point to the disaster declaration systems used by Canada and Australia. Canadian provinces and Australian states and territories rely less upon federal assistance during disasters than do U.S. states. In Canada and Australia (nations with federal systems), "there is no requirement for an explicit disaster declaration" by the prime minister, and "the decision to authorize federal reimbursement is essentially automatic."[134] Canadian provinces and Australian states and territories must pay out sums in disaster relief that exceed certain deductible levels before they qualify for their respective nation's federal assistance. It should be noted that the provinces, states, and territories of these two nations are expected to shoulder the brunt of disaster management and relief duties, in service to their local governments.[135]

Some recommend making declaration judgments more of an administrative determination under which states would have to experience preset thresholds of damage to qualify; states would be expected to pay an upfront deductible sum of money and pay a much larger share of the total cost than the 25 percent that is now the state share in the United States.

Such proposals are interesting, but they tend to overlook the fact that American states come in all population and land-area sizes. Some states cover immensely large tracts of land but contain few people (Alaska, Montana, New Mexico, Nevada, North Dakota, Utah, Wyoming, etc.); some have small populations and small land area (Delaware, New Hampshire, Rhode Island, Vermont). Moreover, there are heavily populated states that also cover massive land areas (California, Texas, etc.).

The issue here is that American demographics make it difficult if not arbitrary to impose disaster deductibles on states and territories. American disaster declaration history shows that presidential discretion may take the degree of human suffering into account even if losses are light and damage is confined to a small area. There are many examples of a presidential disaster declaration issued to a single county in a single state, the most notable perhaps being the declaration that went to New York State and New York City after the first World Trade Center bombing in 1993.[136]

Americans would be expected to oppose the idea of disaster deductibles for their states for a variety of reasons. First, using deductibles as thresholds for issuing federal declarations limits presidential flexibility to address disasters and emergencies. Second, it makes deservedness depend on loss accounting rather than on other indicators of need. Third, Americans, unlike a few of their elected representatives, probably do not generally perceive presidential disaster declaration

(Continued)

(Continued)

spending as redistribution of taxpayer monies from one state to another. Few would conceive of federal disaster spending as a zero-sum game in which one part of the nation gains unfairly at the expense of another part of the nation. Fourth, the massive economic integration of the nation and the pervasiveness of global trade and economic transactions create a national interdependence. A small disaster in Florida may have significant economic consequences for interests in California, Massachusetts, Michigan, or Texas.

Some may find it ironic that giant European reinsurance companies worry deeply about hurricanes threatening strikes along the U.S. Gulf or Atlantic coasts. A major earthquake in California could easily, albeit temporarily, wipe out the liquidity of American auto insurance firms, protracting the claim settlement of a fender bender

in Massachusetts. Some disasters affect entire regions of the United States, and it would be foolish to discriminate between states in a massive damage zone on the basis of a deductible payment system of loss.

Many emergency declarations, more than major disaster declarations, are likely to stretch the rule that states must lack the capacity to recover on their own to qualify for a presidential declaration. In times of tight state and local budgets, or when they are in deficit, an emergency offers governors a flexible path for securing federal help. FEMA records disclose that snowstorms, windstorms, minor flooding, and drought are the most common types of emergency declarations. Emergency requests, even more than for major disaster requests, allow politically subjective determinations to come into play.

emergencies. However, the president is not legally bound to use or follow those criteria. A governor's request for disaster or emergency relief is not necessarily granted. As mentioned, presidents can issue a **turndown**. A turndown is the action authorized by the president and signed by the director of FEMA that denies a governor's request for a major disaster or emergency declaration. Every president from Truman to Trump has turned down some requests for declarations (see Table 4-3). Presidents are as free to turn down emergency declaration requests as they are to turn down requests for presidential declarations of major disaster. Declarations, even if approved, may embody denial of certain kinds of assistance and may deny inclusion of certain areas. In other words, declarations stipulate approval and disapproval of certain requested program assistance.

In addition, sometimes presidents approve governors' requests submitted as emergencies but then go on to declare the events major disasters later. Presidents do not need a second gubernatorial request to elevate an emergency to a major disaster. The decision may flow logically from official recognition that the emergency phase of lifesaving and property protection is at an end and a major disaster declaration is needed to mobilize the additional federal agencies, spending, and resources necessary in disaster recovery.

Remember, governors may request that certain localities (usually counties or the state's equivalent of counties) be added to a presidential declaration already in force.[137] Since 1988, the federal coordinating officer (FCO) assigned to respond to the disaster, not the president, has possessed the authority to add counties to a presidential declaration of major disaster.[138] If the president denies a governor's request for a declaration, that governor has the right to appeal. In rare instances, a governor may win a declaration on appeal. Figure 4-3 provides a bar chart of major disaster declaration issuance by year from 1953 to 2014.

TABLE 4-3 ■ Presidential Approvals and Turndowns of Governor Requests for Disaster Declarations, May 1953 through December 2017

President	Time Span	Approvals			Turndowns			Turndown Percentage		
		Major[a]	Emerg[b]	Total	Major[c]	Emerg[d]	Total	Major	Emerg	Total
Eisenhower	5/2/53–1/21/61	106	0	106	55	0	55	34%	0%	34%
Kennedy	1/21/61–11/20/63	52	0	52	22	0	22	30%	0%	30%
Johnson	11/23/63–1/21/69	93	0	93	49	0	49	53%	0%	53%
Nixon	1/21/69–8/5/74	195	1	196	102	15	117	52%	94%	37%
Ford	8/5/74–1/21/77	76	23	99	35	7	42	32%	23%	30%
Carter	1/21/77–1/21/81	112	59	171	91	37	128	45%	39%	43%
Reagan	1/21/81–1/21/89	184	9	193	96	16	112	34%	64%	37%
G. H. W. Bush	1/21/89–1/21/93	158	2	160	43	3	46	21%	60%	22%
Clinton	1/21/93–1/21/01	380	68	448	103	13	116	21%	16%	21%
G. W. Bush	1/21/01–1/21/09	458	140	598	89	28	117	16.3	16.6%	16.4%
Obama	1/21/09–1/20/17	476	79	555	96*	12*	108*	16.7*	13.1*	16.2*
Trump	1/20/17–11/20/17	54	15	69	8*	N/A	N/A	N/A	N/A	N/A
Total		2344	396	2740	789	131	920	25.2%	24.9%	27.4%

Sources: (a) and (b) FEMA, Declaration Information System (DARISI), June 1997, and Federal Emergency Management Information System (FEMIS), December 2001, Department of Homeland Security, Emergency Preparedness and Response Directorate; FEMA, DFSR Obligations Summary—Grouped by Event and Year, Reporting Cycle through January 2013, Automated DFSR Report Export to Excel, database compiled by Bruce Friedman, Manager CFO-FST and (c) and (d) DHS Justification of Estimates fiscal year 04, March 2003; 9/11/01–9/22/05 turndown data: Sen. Thomas R. Carper, D–DE, to author. FEMA, Turndowns of Major Disaster and Emergency Governor Requests through December 2011, compiled by Dean Webster, February 14, 2012.

Note: Date of declaration checked for each administration to the day. Remember, turndown percentage is the number of turndowns as a percentage of total requests for the respective category, such that turndown requests and approval requests are summed in the calculation denominator. * Please note that in this table, President Obama's turndown data on major disaster requests begins January 21, 2009 and continues to December 11, 2011, has a gap of some four months, starts again on March 7, 2012, and ends January 20, 2017. An even larger gap appears in Obama's emergency declaration turndowns (from 11/3/2011 to 2/17/2014). There may have been turndowns in the two gap periods of Obama's Major Disaster and Emergency Totals. President Trump's turndown data was only available for the period January 20, 2017 (when he was inaugurated) to August 22, 2017, and it included only requests denied on major disaster declarations, not on emergency declarations. Also, President Trump's emergency declarations end August 22, 2017. Owing to gaps in both the Obama and Trump data, turndown percentages are listed as not available (N/A). Turndown data is nearly impossible to obtain even using the Freedom of Information Act. Turndowns are sometimes the subjects of newspaper articles but searches on this are difficult in the extreme.

a. Represents approved presidential declarations of major disasters, which began in 1953.

b. Represents approved presidential declarations of emergencies. Emergency declarations began in 1974.

c. Represents president's turndown of a governor's request for a presidential declaration of major disaster.

d. Represents president's turndown of a governor's request for a presidential declaration of emergency.

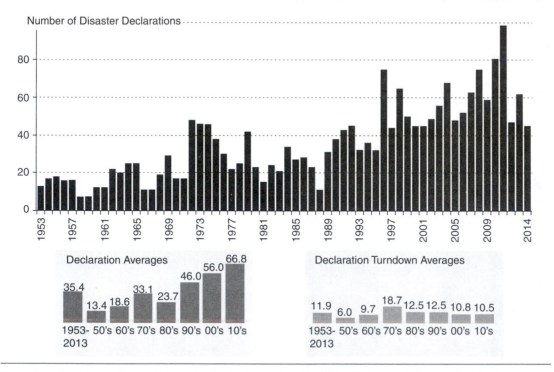

FIGURE 4-3 ■ Major Disaster Declarations from 1953 to 2014

Source: Bruce R. Lindsay and Francis X. McCarthy, "Stafford Act Declarations 1953–2014: Trends, Analyses, and Implications for Congress," Congressional Research Service, p. 8, July 14, 2015, https://fas.org/sgp/crs/homesec/R42702.pdf (accessed July 9, 2018).

According to Table 4-3, there has been a significant increase in the number of major disaster declarations issued since 1988, the final year of the Reagan administration. Over the 1990s, 2000s, and 2010s, the decadal averages, 46.0, 56.0 and 66.8, respectively, have exceeded the 35.4 average for the interval 1953 to 2013. Figure 4-3 shows that while total majors issued and decadal averages for majors issued have both increased since the 1980s, the decadal averaged for turndowns over the 2000s and 2010s drops slightly below the annual average of turndowns from 1953 to 2013. In effect, regardless of who has served as president since 1988, more major disaster declarations are being issued (with fluctuation), the decadal average number of majors has ramped up, and rates of governor request turndowns by each president has been flat or declining.

"PAYING" FOR PRESIDENTIAL DISASTER DECLARATIONS

Lawmakers are key players when it comes to furnishing federal money for disaster relief. The president's Disaster Relief Fund is the chief repository of funding authority to pay the federal share of disaster costs. It was administered by independent FEMA (April 1979–March 2003) and has been administered by DHS-FEMA since 2003. The DRF is replenished by "no-year" appropriations monies. *No year* simply means that there is no time limit attached to the spending authority of an appropriation law. The fund carries over unspent budget authority from previous disasters and receives an annual congressional appropriation, but it is often insufficient to cover federal payouts for declared disasters and emergencies during the federal fiscal year. Congress has the power to approve emergency supplemental appropriations to recapitalize the fund. Congress endeavors to never let the Disaster Relief Fund exhaust its spending authority. Even if the fund's budget authority was exhausted, presidents are legally permitted to borrow money from the Treasury to continue to pay federal expenses for ongoing declared major disasters and emergencies.[139]

In previous decades, the tendency was for each administration to ask for the maximum emergency supplemental appropriation they thought necessary. They reasoned that it is always better to estimate high rather than low, as no administration wants to have to return to Congress to seek an additional emergency supplemental for the same disaster (although this sometimes happens). Because these appropriations come with no spending expiration date, and because the disasters they are aimed at often end up costing the federal government less than the total spending authority conferred, spending authority in the fund often accumulates and so pays for other, smaller disasters and emergencies. However, great disasters or catastrophes on rare occasions swallow up all of the fund's spending authority. It is then that Congress goes to work on emergency supplemental appropriations.

In recent years, policymakers have changed tactics. Today the tendency is to request smaller amounts for the DRF through submitting a series of supplemental appropriations. This better protects the money from rescissions (laws that terminate budget authority) and transfers (which move appropriated amounts from one account to another). Also, since 9/11, when Congress changed budgeting rules in the wake of that disaster, the DRF has been regularly replenished and generally amply funded.[140]

The politics of congressional enactment of emergency supplemental appropriations often makes it obvious why Congress should continue to entrust the president with the bulk of routine declaration authority. **Emergency supplementals** must, like all legislation to be enacted into law, pass both the House and Senate. Whether or not an emergency supplemental is open to "riders" (non-germane legislation attached to a bill) in either body is often both controversial and consequential. Individual lawmakers often add riders to emergency supplementals that could never win majority support were they not attached to these "must pass" emergency supplementals for disasters.

Presidents have come to detest emergency supplementals because those measures often come to the Oval Office laden with riders that confer pork barrel or special interest benefits they would never otherwise approve were these not part of a "must pass" bill. As the president has no line-item veto to remove what he judges to be undeserved riders, he is more or less compelled to sign the emergency supplementals into law or otherwise be judged heartless and unresponsive to the needs of disaster victims who are awaiting the federal help the supplemental will provide. Emergency supplementals pose other problems. They often drive up the federal deficit and so may damage fiscal policy, potentially harming the health of the national economy. The legislative process is often slow and cumbersome, even if riders are not permitted on the emergency supplemental.

Some lawmakers, Democrats and Republicans, have come to view emergency supplementals for disaster as a form of **redistributive politics** in which a zero-sum game applies. One part of the nation gains at the expense of another part of the nation. Some have alleged that states with large congressional delegations that frequently experience disasters or emergencies have "gamed" the system in a way that funnels excessive federal resources to their post-incident redevelopment. Conversely, legislators from large population states maintain that FEMA's per capita threshold system of disaster cost measurement disadvantages large population states and their localities. This is because large population states must have experienced massively costly disasters to meet or exceed FEMA's threshold. For small population states, the threshold bar appears to be set far lower, making it easier for those states and their localities to qualify.

The Conservative Center for American Progress, drawing from annual federal departmental disaster spending records, concluded that for fiscal years 2011 through 2013 inclusive, a total $136 billion of taxpayer funds or "an average of nearly $400 per household"[141] had been expended. The center's article maintains that the federal Office of Management and Budget, as well as Congress, routinely underestimates federal disaster spending and so fail to budget adequate funds in advance of disaster, thus necessitating federal borrowing when budgeted funds are exhausted during a fiscal year.[142]

Over the years, federal disaster officials have attempted to establish definitive and quantitative requirements for disaster declaration eligibility. One such effort would have strictly tied declarations to damage translated into dollars per capita.[143] These efforts proposed rigorous declaration criteria, but presidents have resisted and Congress has vehemently opposed such measures.[144] Presidents do not want their range of declaration discretion further circumscribed or ceded to federal disaster officials.[145] Legislators want assurance that they may use their legitimate political influence to press the president for declarations directly when their home states and districts experience incidents or events they consider emergencies or disasters.[146]

Presidents, assisted by their staffs and top disaster agency officials, must judge each governor's request for a declaration based on need. However, both managerial and political factors may enter the president's judgment. Clearly, initial damage assessments, imminent disaster threat (e.g., a hurricane about to make landfall), news media coverage of an event, and the like may make it obvious to the president that a governor's request deserves approval.[147] There are also many instances when presidents, and perhaps their advisers, are unconvinced of the need or worthiness of the request. Still, the president makes these determinations in a political environment.[148]

When the requests are accepted, FEMA, not the president, decides how much money to allocate. Remember that a major share of FEMA funding to eligible parties under a major disaster or emergency declaration is through means-tested applicant-driven programs similar to entitlements. Conversely, a very substantial share of FEMA funding goes out under public assistance (government to government) aid, which requires formal application administered as project grants of various types. Proving disaster declaration worthiness and need is, for better or worse, often an issue of public money. The "Tell Me More" 4-4 box summarizes the problem of dollar loss estimation and ability to (financially) recover in the absence of a federal declaration of major disaster.

History demonstrates that from May 1953, the time of the first serially numbered presidential disaster declaration, until January 2013, the president has approved about three in every four (75 percent) gubernatorial requests for declarations of major disaster and emergency. Since 1989, following adoption of the Stafford Act, the chance that the president will approve a governor's request has risen to about a four in five (80 percent) (see Table 4-3).[149] Certainly, the broader authority to judge what is or is not a disaster under the Stafford Act has provided presidents since 1988 with more latitude to approve unusual or "marginal" events as disasters or emergencies. This may be one reason for the higher rate of gubernatorial request approvals since 1988.

During his four years in office, President George H. W. Bush averaged 39 disaster declarations annually. Over the seven years of the Clinton presidency that Reeves studied, Clinton averaged 72 disasters per year.[150] Table 4-3 shows that over his full two terms, eight years, Clinton approved a total 380 major disaster and 68 emergency declarations, thus averaging 47.5 a year for major disasters and 8.5 for emergency declarations a year over his two terms. In contrast, President G. W. Bush, also a two-term president, approved 458 major disaster and 140 emergency declarations. Both categories show a sizable increase in the number of major disaster and emergency declarations issued over Clinton years relative to G. W. Bush years. President G. W. Bush annually averaged 57.25 major disaster and 17.5 emergency declarations. In reading these declaration totals of Table 4-3, remember that many factors are in play: more recent presidents may have decided to issue fewer turndowns, thus prompting more governor requests that were eventually approved;

TELL ME MORE 4-4
OVERWHELMED OR OVER BUDGET?

The word *overwhelmed* is subject to different interpretations. It is extremely difficult to determine whether a municipality, county, or state is overwhelmed by a disaster or emergency. The word *overwhelmed* connotes "incapacity." A dictionary definition of *overwhelm* is to surge and submerge, to engulf, to overcome completely, either physically or emotionally, to overpower, to turn over or upset.[151] Presumably, if a municipality, county, or state can respond to and recover from a disaster or emergency using their own resources, they are not overwhelmed. However, the term *overwhelmed* is not easily defined within the realm of intergovernmental relations. Even the worst disasters seldom terminate or suspend the operation of state and local government. In many disasters, state and local governments suffer significant economic losses and government aid to disaster victims is fully justified and deserved, but state and local governments are rarely overwhelmed.

Therefore, *overwhelm* is a disputatious term. Some governors have requested presidential declarations of disaster on the grounds that they must maintain a balanced budget or because they have no "rainy day" money to pay for the recovery costs. Municipalities and counties have grown accustomed to having the huge costs of public employee overtime and debris removal paid for by the federal government under presidential declarations. As mentioned, governors are tempted to ask for declarations in advance of the onset of disaster because they reason that county and municipal disaster response will be more robust if federal subsidization of response costs is assured ahead of time. Senators and representatives have frequently pressured various presidents to approve declaration requests submitted by the governors of their home states.

A governor's temptation to "cry poor" before, during, or after some state-level misfortune is often, pardon the pun, "overwhelming." FEMA deservedness criteria could provide a guide for governors but only if the president makes declaration decisions in conformity with FEMA recommendations. As noted, the president is not compelled to do so.

the uptick in frequency of multistate, ever expansive disasters, means there are more declarations because more states are impacted by the same event. Superstorm Sandy, for example, in 2012 yielded no less than 12 major disaster declarations, demonstrating that it impacted 12 states; and increasing news and social media coverage over time creates a drumbeat of pressure on the White House to expeditiously and generously issue more declarations.

In his 2011 paper, Reeves reports that for presidential disaster declarations issued from 1981 through 2004, "electoral considerations have come to shade a policy," referring to presidential disaster declarations, "that should be firmly based on need"[152] but are not.

Reeves reports that prior to the Stafford Act (1988) there was no statistically significant correlation between the presidential electoral competitiveness of each state and its respective disaster declaration count.[153] He is referring to statewide presidential election contests in which an incumbent president is competing to win state electoral votes, especially in certain battleground states. He asserts that "voters react and reward presidents for presidential disaster declarations."[154] Sylves and Buzas find that in general election years when incumbent presidents seek a second term, there is statistically significant evidence that governors of battleground states important in the president's reelection calculus experience extremely low disaster declaration request turndown rates.[155] In other words, these governors appear to hold an advantage over other governors when seeking presidential declarations of major disaster. Yet this benefit is confined to the months of the year before the general election and then only when a sitting president is seeking a second term.

Political parties view particular states as "friends," "enemies," or "competitive," based on their likelihood of voting for the party's presidential candidate.[156] When it comes to disaster declarations and presidential political strategizing, "the size of the state (in terms of electoral votes) and whether the political parties view it as 'competitive' matters quite a bit."[157] Large states friendly to the president appear to be more successful in winning declarations than large, unfriendly states. Reeves shows, "The incumbent president (or his party) is rewarded by voters for providing relief in the wake of natural disasters to the tune of over 1.5 points in the statewide popular vote."[158]

For Reeves, "the Stafford Act transformed the disaster declaration process into a highly political exercise."[159] Studies by Reeves, Garrett and Sobel, and Dymon infer that the pattern of presidential declaration approvals is consistent with the "politically driven, **distributive politics**" model. When declarations are examined in terms of political geography and elections, it seems that presidents, at least since 1988, are acting "on the basis of political motives, political pressures, and political responsiveness more than they are issued on the basis of objective need."[160] Governors of large and heavily populated states enjoying a sizable number of electoral votes and previously supportive of the incumbent president may seek to capitalize on this advantage and ask for declarations more often than they normally would. From this perspective, we would expect political factors to influence the odds of receiving a presidential disaster declaration.

Assuming the president does generally follow the recommendations, governors may find that asking for declarations when losses or damage are less than the recommendations, and under FEMA per capita damage thresholds, runs the risk of having requests turned down. Yet most governors would not judge a turndown as a great embarrassment, particularly in an era when presidential disaster declarations seem to be more freely issued and when a request may provide significant federal benefits to the state. In fact, governors are likely to face severe criticism by news and social media, and by stakeholders, for "not asking" the president to confer their impacted areas a declaration of major disaster or emergency.

As mentioned, once the president approves a governor's request for a declaration, it is the job of FEMA, not the president, to officially determine how much money is to be allocated to states, counties, and other eligible entities under specified conditions (i.e., damage assessment), laws, and rules—all subject to audit by a variety of government offices, including congressional organizations like the Governmental Accountability Office. Political discretion may possibly be exercised by the president when gubernatorial requests are for low-damage, marginal incidents, involving low federal payouts. This means the relationship is an "inverse one." In other words, the lower the federal payouts are for various declarations, the higher the probability that political considerations at the presidential level played a role in a president's approval of a declaration.[161] Nonetheless, the federal government is not pushing disaster relief money out of planes. People must apply for it, must prove eligibility, must document their losses, must show that their insurance is not duplicating federal disaster relief, and must submit to inspection and audit. State and local governments are expected to do even more than that in securing federal funds to repair infrastructure. State and local governments also must shoulder a share of the cost of rebuilding under many disaster declarations.

Conversely, "politically driven, distributive politics" comes into play when governors and local public officials respond to disasters by attempting to exploit and maximize federal support to their jurisdictions when in fact their jurisdictions have the ability to respond and recover without federal help. Here state and local taxpayers unfairly gain at the national taxpayer's expense. On top of this, winning this undeserved federal aid helps to meet their political and constituent needs. These officials want to be re-elected and thus they wish to curry favor with their electorate by providing tangible benefits for which they can claim credit.[162] Elected local and state officials also attempt to shield their constituents from the costs of disaster response and recovery by funding these costs at the national level, thus diffusing the fiscal burden over the largest possible population and taking advantage of the federal government's easier borrowing powers.[163] Under this form of distributive politics, state and local government officials tend to shape their behavior to conform to federal criteria to secure as many resources as possible (a form of moral hazard.)

In the economics of declaration decision making, there is a two-track dilemma in president-governor relations. The first track, in economic parlance, involves the issues of "ability to pay" and "willingness to pay." If a state is judged "able to pay (afford)" the costs of its disaster response and recovery costs, should the governor's request then be denied by the president with concurrence by FEMA? Here the grounds for a turndown may be that the state (and its disaster-impacted localities) has an ability to recover using their own resources but an unwillingness to pay these costs. However, structural problems may impede a state's ability to pay (i.e., state balanced budget requirements, restrictions on state borrowing, inability to raise taxes sufficiently quickly to pay for disaster costs, etc.). States with an inability to pay must be differentiated from those states able to pay but unwilling to do so.

The second track involves human need (beyond dollar costs), governmental compassion, and astute behavior by elected officials who desire a positive political and electoral future. A **need-based, means-tested model** for declaration decisions, ones that meet established rules and proven qualification, are fundamental administrative, rather than political, determinations. Also, to use economic language, to prevent disasters from having negative economic spillover effects in other places and to ensure that all state and local governments possess emergency management capability that is at least consistent with a national minimum standard, the federal government can promote state and local emergency management through grants dispensed after disasters and between disasters. Federal disaster policy aims to "sustain or restore a community's pre-disaster condition, not to alter the distribution of wealth."[164]

Consequently, need-based disaster management applies if a state or local government's disaster response and recovery funding is largely self-generated and if those governments have no designs on exploiting national taxpayer money beyond the minimum needed to reestablish itself after a disaster or emergency. In turn, the national government must target its help so that it can keep disasters from producing unwanted, negative spillover effects in the regional or the national economies. The president and his or her disaster managers must avoid driving up federal borrowing to pay for disaster relief. Also, the federal government gains when research, technical advancement, disaster mitigation, and national standards development help state and local authorities prevent disasters or minimize their future damage.

Important politically subjective determinations also come into play in the case of "marginal" disasters. **Marginal disasters** are those events that are far less than catastrophic, that are not matters of national security, and that are near or within the response and recovery capacity of the state or states in which they occur.[165] Analysis of nearly 70 years of presidential disaster declarations discloses that there have been hundreds of marginal disasters, some granted a presidential declaration and some turned down. Specific case examples indicate that there are definite losers in the competition for presidential declarations. For example, in 1980, Florida experienced flooding after a dam failure, and President Carter denied the Florida governor's request for a declaration. In the same year, he turned down two requests from Oklahoma within a two-week period for a declaration to cover devastation from severe storms and flooding. In April 2013, the city of West in Texas experienced a large and deadly explosion at a fertilizer plant. President Obama, having previously issued Texas an emergency declaration for the explosion, denied Governor Rick Perry's request for a major disaster declaration to cover uninsured or underinsured government disaster losses.[166] However, Governor Perry appealed the turndown and eventually the president, in consultation with FEMA officials, approved his appeal and issued Texas a major disaster declaration for the incident. If President Obama year 2016 and President Trump year 2017 (Jan. 20, 2017 to Aug. 22, 2017) are compared with respect to turndown requests for major disaster declarations, Obama issued 18 turndowns over the full 2016 year and Trump issued 7 turndowns over his first seven months in office.[167] All but one of Obama's turndowns were for severe storm, flood, or both. The notable exception was the turndown Obama issued for Flint, Michigan, drinking water contamination.[168] Trump turned down major disaster requests for two winter storms, two severe storms, one drought, and one flood. He also turned down a North Dakota governor's request for a major disaster declaration that would have paid for police costs associated with handling protestors who opposed construction and routing of the Dakota Access Oil Pipeline.[169] In the period considered, both presidents have comparable turndown rates and the nature of the incidents turned down were not at great variance, albeit for Obama's water contamination case and Trump's police reimbursement case. Also, several of the turndowns of 2016 and 2017 are under appeal and may yet be reversed.

The record of approvals and turndowns raises questions about how gubernatorial requests for presidential declarations are considered, particularly for **marginal disaster request denials** and **marginal disaster request approvals.** Marginal disaster denials are cases in which the governor's request fell short of meeting FEMA's threshold criteria and the president denied it. Marginal disaster approvals are cases in which the governor's request fell short of meeting the threshold criteria but the president approved the request anyway. Records here show that some turndowns are issued by the president because what the governor wanted the declaration to address was too unconventional or was improper under federal law and policy. For many years, there have been no objective criteria governing approvals and turndowns, and as stated earlier, only the president who received the governor's request knows the basis upon which a request is approved or denied. Nor is it possible to ascertain statistically from government records whether or not fatalities played a role in a president's decision. FEMA does not keep records of fatalities and injuries sustained in declared disasters or emergencies.

Governors also play the game by seeking presidential declarations for drought, crop failures, minor wildfires, small floods, beach erosion, and a wide range of other calamities that cannot be considered catastrophes, major disasters, or emergencies under the "overwhelm" or "beyond the capability of the state/local government to adequately respond" condition.

Summary

"People look to the President for reassurance, a feeling that things will be all right, that the President will take care of his people."[170] This is an important management responsibility for presidents. As the nation has come to face increasing numbers, wider varieties, and often larger scale disasters and emergencies, changes in law seem to have given presidents more latitude in deciding what constitutes an emergency. Also, the line between what is and what is not a Stafford Act-type incident is getting blurred. Presidents seem to be issuing declarations for non-Stafford Act incidents and using the Disaster Relief Fund to pay for them.

This chapter explored presidential declarations of major disaster and emergency in terms of policies, process, programs, decisional power, politics, and payment of public money. It was crafted as a chapter, not a stand-alone book. A book-length study of presidential disaster declarations would be expected to examine in more detail how presidents from Truman to Trump have used their declaration authority. Plus, such a book would consider how successive U.S. Congresses have developed authorization and appropriations laws on this subject and how Congress has performed oversight and auditing of federal spending dispensed through presidential disaster declarations. A major analysis would examine in much more detail the leadership and inner workings of pre-FEMA disaster agencies, the independent FEMA (of April 1979–March 2003), and the DHS-FEMA that has continued on from April 2003 to the present. Furthermore, authors of a tome on this subject would have to cover the behavior and motives of several thousand governors who requested presidential disaster declarations from 1950 to the present. Not to be overlooked are the many beneficiaries of the federal disaster assistance programs activated by presidential declarations of major disaster and emergency. Clearly, this chapter could not go that far.

With this said, it is surprising that countless works purporting to be about disasters and emergencies in America seldom mention or scrutinize presidential disaster declarations. This is a most unfortunate omission. About a dozen or so excellent books do take up the subject of presidents and disaster declarations.

Because over time the U.S. Congress both granted and tolerated ever-wider presidential discretion in deciding what constituted a declarable major disaster or emergency, the system has become more politicized than lawmakers in 1950 ever expected. Also, in presidential judgments about the deservedness of governors' requests, the system tolerates a degree of subjectivity, and sometimes political bias. Owing to this freedom to decide, some presidents have created new categories of disaster type, thus setting precedents governors have been able to exploit in their quest for declarations and federal help. On top of this, the availability of the Disaster Relief Fund furnishes presidents a convenient pool of spending authority to pay the federal costs of major disasters and emergencies they choose to declare.

A tolerated political dilemma continues. U.S. disaster policy holds that the president should not be restricted in using declaration authority to address calamities or crises, some expected and others quite unforeseen. Presidents are accorded the freedom to disregard recommendations of FEMA, if they so choose, when they approve or deny governors' requests for presidential declarations of major disaster or emergency. Yet the president's freedom to decide encourages lawmakers and

taxpayers to suspect that political motives tempt presidents, perhaps in collaboration with elected state and local officials, to distribute various forms of post-disaster federal largess to undeserving states. There are those who posit that some governors and their state legislatures have created a type of "moral hazard" under which the respective state government intentionally under-funds, or rebuffs calls to establish a state "rainy day" fund, so as to convince FEMA and the president that the state lacks the financial resources to recover on its own from some misfortune. Some states forgo creating parallel FEMA disaster assistance programs because their governors and legislators believe they can then better argue "inability to respond and recover" when they request presidential declarations of major disaster. In the words of W. Brock Long, President Trump's current FEMA administrator, "FEMA's ability to provide support in disasters builds on, and is subject to, the capacity of state, territorial, tribal and local governments. This is not a new lesson or challenge, but one that we are constantly reminded of. If the state, territorial, tribal and local governments are well resourced, well trained, and well organized, the effectiveness of FEMA's assistance is great. If, on the other hand, a state, territorial, tribal or local government is not well resourced, well trained, and well organized—either due to ineffective preparations or due to the significance of the disaster itself—FEMA can help, but the response may not be as quick or as effective as we would like it to be."[171]

Homeland security law and policy has augmented presidential authority and responsibility. These laws and policies have expanded the range of presidential declarations to include terrorism or even terrorist threats (see the section on NSSEs). They threaten to bond conventional Stafford Act declaration issuance for non-terror disasters with a president-led or DHS-led declaration system preoccupied with terrorism and terrorism threat in its many forms. The addition of catastrophic incidents formally signifies that some disasters have national security implications and the potential to damage the nation's economy. Presidents, advised by homeland security and federal emergency management officials, today have the power both to decide what a catastrophe is and to declare such events catastrophic disasters. The addition of the "power to declare catastrophic incidents" has again embellished presidential powers and has again altered president-governor and federal–state relations.

For presidentially declared major disasters that are far less than catastrophic, particularly those that are on the margin of deservedness, and which often demonstrate statewide per capita damage totals less than or on par with the per capita FEMA threshold, political factors may come into play. As Miskel reasons, it is "the small disasters" that test measurements of need.[172] When presidents turn down gubernatorial requests for a declaration, the president may be meeting his legal obligation to ensure that if a state and its localities can reasonably be expected to recover from an incident drawing from their own resources, the state is unworthy of a federal declaration. However, the denial of such requests may produce negative political repercussions for the presidents who turn them down.

Clearly, news and social media coverage is highly important in the realm of disasters and emergencies, as is presidential participation or co-production in the making of disaster news. News media coverage of disasters has helped paint presidential disaster declaration decisions as more "political" than they usually are in fact. In addition, each president's relationship with his or her top federal emergency manager influences how that president handles emerging disaster circumstances and governor requests for federal assistance. A few previous top federal disaster managers owed their appointments to political spoils more than to qualified disaster management expertise. However, several of these people learned disaster management on the job and were guided by senior emergency managers in their agency; others failed miserably when they were needed most. Since enactment of the PKEMRA of 2006, a law that required the president to nominate for FEMA administrator only candidates with previous emergency management experience, the agency has been led by a succession of highly experienced emergency managers. The U.S. disaster declaration process is the Main Street of American emergency management. It is made necessary by American federalism, a complex marriage of federal, state, and local interdependencies, and by a quest for endurance, resilience, burden sharing, and human compassion.

Key Terms

Workers examine the damaged area below the Oroville Dam emergency spillway, located in Oroville, California, February 19, 2017.

Florence Low/California Department of Water Resources

5

THE ROLE OF RESEARCH, SCIENCE, AND ENGINEERING

Practitioners and scholars studying the physical and social dimensions of hazards and disasters have built and continue to build the foundations of disaster research. Engineers of almost every stripe have helped design and build the infrastructure that makes modern societies both possible and sustainable. Mechanical, civil, chemical, and electrical engineering comprised the major types of engineering one could study some 50 years ago. Each had sub-branches. Today geotechnical as well as management engineering have been added and they too have sub-branches. Besides those already mentioned, there are many more.[1]

Disaster research is conducted by a broad array of experts. Scientific and engineering communities that focus on such research exist within all levels of government, in academia, and in the private sector.[2] Meteorologists and atmospheric researchers are assiduously examining weather phenomena, among them hurricanes, tornadoes, severe storms, and drought, as well as global climate change.[3] Flood phenomena are the focus of many dedicated geoscientists, engineers, meteorologists, land-use, and physical geography experts.[4] Biomedical researchers are hard at work tracking the spread of disease, striving to prevent pandemics, and testing and developing new vaccines, some intended to protect people from bioterrorist attack.[5] Scholars researching social media are seeking to find more and better ways for emergency managers to make use of social media systems.[6] Researchers developing homeland security technology have made advances in high-speed computing and massive data storage, sophisticated computer software, facial recognition, and the use of satellite data and geographic information system (GIS) technology.[7]

This chapter covers scientific and engineering groups who study disaster and who are developing a body of theoretical and applied knowledge aimed at improved disaster prediction, mitigation, prevention, preparedness, response, and recovery. Additionally, the chapter includes discussions about how science and engineering inform and shape disaster policy and politics.

RESEARCHING HAZARDS AND DISASTERS

Spurred on by intellectual and technological advances over the 20th century, federal emergency management grew as an intellectual, scientific, and engineering enterprise. By the 1980s and 1990s, great advances in hazards research—most particularly in meteorology, seismology, and physical geography but also in the building sciences, climate change research, and environmental science—gave credibility to disaster research.[8] The 21st century has thus far dramatically accelerated the pace of scientific and technological advancement.

The **National Academies**—made up of the National Academy of Sciences, the National Academy of Engineering, and the Institute of Medicine, facilitated by their National Research Council—conduct numerous disaster-related research studies for various sponsors, among them federal agencies that contract with them to form panels and conduct studies.[9] The research reports of the National Academies have been known to greatly influence makers of public policy who are struggling to find solutions or policy approaches to the complex problems they must address. For example, in 2012, the National Research Council published a report titled, "Disaster Resilience: A National Imperative."[10] The report opened with the declaration, "The nation needs to build the capacity to become resilient, and we need to do this now. Such capacity building starts with individuals taking responsibility for their actions and moves to entire communities working in conjunction with local, state, and federal officials, all of whom need to assume specific responsibilities for building the national quilt of resilience."[11]

In 2000, the National Academies formed the Disaster Roundtable, a body led by a group of experts from academia, scientific professional societies, federal scientific research agencies, and private industry. The disaster-related workshops sponsored by the roundtable brought together many of the top authorities in the world. In some respects, these workshops were a peak association of disaster-interested science and engineering experts.

After the 9/11 attacks, the National Laboratories of the U.S. Department of Energy (DOE) began to dedicate more of their research endeavors to examining disaster threats posed by terrorism. The National Laboratories owe their origin largely to the Manhattan Project of World War II. Today they comprise an expansive system of research facilities in which university, government, and private-sector scientists and engineers grapple with basic and applied research endeavors, many intended to address defense, security, and other societal needs.[12] The Homeland Security Act of 2002 transferred a portion of DOE laboratory research expertise to the new U.S. Department of Homeland Security (DHS).

The intellectual and technological advances achieved over the past 30 years gave rise to a disaster services business sector composed of consultants, contractors, for-profit businesses, and nonprofit organizations. Many business executives recognized the importance of maintaining business continuity before, during, and after disasters. Some types of businesses recognized their increased importance in periods of disaster. Home Depot, Lowe's, Ace Hardware, and other home improvement and building supply firms have cultivated an ability to scale up their operations at times of need in areas where their stores could be used to help their customers prepare for impending hurricanes or tropical storms.[13] Such disaster services work is responsive to the post-disaster needs of customers and is at the same time good business. In the same respect, these and many other businesses able to survive disasters often donate many of their critically needed wares to disaster victims at no charge. Major store chains, franchise businesses, and other firms improved their capacity to help the owners and managers of disaster-ravaged firms in their respective networks reestablish themselves.

The need to improve port security and interdict shipments of cargo hiding weapons of mass destruction impelled policymakers to fund both conventional and exotic lines of screening devices. Aviation and airport security was another top post-9/11 policy priority. Major firms won federal contracts to x-ray baggage, to detect explosives being carried by passengers, to set forth massive computer databases that could be used to verify the identities of air travelers, to check passengers against "watch lists," and to match every item of a plane's checked luggage to an actual passenger on that plane. Not long ago, the Transportation Security Administration (of DHS) began inspecting the iPhones, laptops, and other devices of foreign nationals as they entered the United States through customs checkpoints. Disturbingly, such inspections have been reportedly performed on Americans flying domestically as well.[14]

Since the early 1990s, the threat of terrorism inside the United States persuaded presidents William Clinton, George W. Bush, Barack Obama, and Donald Trump, as well as Congress, to support and fund new types of security research and technologies. Data mining, improved intelligence collection via analysis of Internet traffic and transmissions, improved surveillance technologies, new forms of bomb disposal and explosives monitoring, computer-assisted visual identification technologies, x-ray and electromagnetic resonance technology to examine the contents of containers shipped through airports and seaports, technologies used in hardline and wireless telecommunications, and other innovations all gave rise to a **securitization** of the field of emergency management. For our purposes, securitization means that authorities take extraordinary measures in national security, defense, and intelligence gathering on account of real or perceived threats. Some of these measures may preempt existing laws or treaty agreements on grounds that national survival is at stake.[15] Furthermore, nations unfriendly to the United States have resorted to weaponizing artificial intelligence. Martin Giles, writing for MIT's *Technology Review* in early 2018, warned of more data breaches of massive data holdings stored by banks, stores, and other firms; increased ransomware attacks; the potential hacking of elections; cyber physical attacks on under-protected software of major utilities and even older aircraft; and mining Bitcoin and other crypto-currencies.[16]

The 9/11 attacks impelled American policymakers to support private-sector and government contractor research on new types of counterterrorism technologies. The anthrax mail package incidents (briefly discussed in Chapter 4) occurring within only weeks of the 9/11 attacks of 2001 impelled Congress and President G. W. Bush to dedicate great sums of federal funding to firms researching and producing vaccines that would be needed in the event of future bioterrorism attacks. Terrorists might use such weapons to contaminate, poison, or destroy food, water, medicines, and even the air we breathe.

DISASTER RESEARCHERS COMPETE FOR GOVERNMENT FUNDING

Disaster research serves emergency management but also generates funding needs policymakers are asked to address. To pursue many lines of disaster study, researchers need expensive technical equipment. Special types of military aircraft are needed to fly through hurricanes and tropical storms; uniquely outfitted ships must be used to deploy and maintain arrays of high-technology ocean buoys arranged in a network latticed over many thousands of square miles of sea—all this to monitor changes in water temperatures, ocean currents, and ocean water chemistry critical in measuring or detecting climate change and global warming; high-speed computing technology is needed to process and store prodigious information flows to thwart possible plots and attacks on the nation.

According to *The Economist*, Argo is a research network operated under international collaboration. Argo has a "regularly replenished fleet of nearly 4,000 untethered buoys which divide their time between the surface and the depths, drifting at the whim of the currents. Over ten-day cycles they sink slowly down to about 2,000 metres and back up, measuring temperature and salinity as they go."[17] Argo data has vastly improved oceanographic study and research. "But the network is still sparse—one float for every Honduras-sized patch of ocean." Regardless, every ocean on the planet has a share of Argo's 4,000, and growing, diving buoys.

Universities and research firms have won and employed funding to research methods of structural reinforcement against seismic shaking, often using giant and costly shake-beds supporting three-story-tall mock buildings. Research organizations analyzing wildland fire behavior must become ever more proficient in advising the U.S. Forest Service and many other firefighting organizations about the direction a fire is heading, how surface contours will affect the path and intensity of the fire, what aerial and satellite images reveal about the magnitude of the fire and the progress of suppression efforts, and what natural vegetative fuels lie just ahead of the fire, and more. All this advances knowledge and increases the safety of those in the field fighting the advance of the fire. Such information may also be used to help keep people in the path of the fire out of harm's way.

Big Science, Research Funding, and Foundations

Securing budget authority to pay for these needs requires many disaster researchers to enter the world of lobbying government. Thus, owing to the need for government funding to pay for expensive research equipment and facilities, some domains of disaster research engage what has been referred to as **big science**.[18] A great definition of "big science" appears in online *Encyclopedia Britannica*. Big science is a "style of scientific research developed during and after World War II that defined the organization and character of much research in physics and astronomy and later in the biological sciences. Big Science is characterized by large-scale instruments and facilities, supported by funding from government or international agencies, in which research is conducted by teams or groups of scientists and technicians. Some of the best-known Big Science projects include the high-energy physics facility CERN, the Hubble Space Telescope, and the Apollo program."[19] The world of big science has its own politics and policy.[20] Indeed, many segments of the nation's academic community, often in cooperation with scholars outside the United States, have received government support for their research through federal agencies such as the National Oceanic and Atmospheric Administration (NOAA), the U.S. Environmental Protection Agency (EPA), the U.S. Geological Survey (USGS), the National Institute of Standards and Technology (NIST), the U.S. Army Corps of Engineers (USACE), the National Aeronautics and Space Administration (NASA), the DHS, FEMA, and more.[21]

Additionally, the **National Science Foundation (NSF)** funds a great variety of academic research endeavors, a portion pertinent to disaster studies.[22] Many federal departments, agencies, and offices maintain research budgets, a portion of which may fund hazards and disaster research. The American Association for the Advancement of Science (AAAS) has called on its members to strongly protect the research they do, much of it dependent on government funding, from imminent budget cuts. Interestingly, the AAAS at its 2017 annual conference also pressed for better engaging policymakers. "For scientists to maintain our relevance in this post-expert world, it will be important for us to actively seek out and create conversations with communities around the nation."[23]

Many private foundations either subsidize disaster study or pursue this research using their own experts in-house. The Rockefeller Foundation has launched a program that will sponsor municipal positions in some 30 cities intended to advance local resilience in the face of future disaster threats. The Robert Wood Johnson Foundation and the Howard Hughes Medical Institute both support cutting-edge health research important in disease control, pandemic response, and emergency medicine. The Bill & Melinda Gates Foundation is famously seeking to eradicate childhood diseases often resulting from the human strife of disasters and complex humanitarian emergencies.

The Gates Foundation does more than this. The organization announced, "The Bill & Melinda Gates Foundation's Emergency Response program aims to reduce suffering, disease, and death in countries affected by natural disasters and complex emergencies. In addition to responding directly to emergencies, we work to help improve the speed and performance of first responders in the first critical hours of an emergency. We also invest in strengthening the ability of first responders, their organizations, and local institutions to help communities prepare for and cope with future shocks. In addition, we collaborate with other foundation programs to develop and introduce innovative products and approaches that can save lives and build community resilience before an emergency occurs. The emergencies we respond to, which often number in the dozens per year, have included the Ebola virus outbreak in West Africa, cholera outbreaks in Cameroon, floods and landslides in Kashmir and Nepal, Typhoon Haiyan in the Philippines, and conflict and displacement in the Central African Republic and South Sudan."[24] While some may think this passage belongs in Chapter 8, where globalization is discussed, the emergency response work to address these and other diseases ultimately protects people around the world, including Americans. The Gates Foundation is providing both help and information about the outbreak and spread of disease, thus complementing the work of UN health organizations and the U.S. Centers for Disease Control and Prevention.

Major corporations, including giant utility companies, and insurance firms routinely pursue research that investigates natural forces, hazards, and disasters. Twigg reminds us that in disaster circumstances private corporative behavior may be classified over five categories:

- Philanthropic/charitable (money and in-kind assistance donations)

- Contractual (providing goods and services under terms of an agreement of some sort)

- Collaborative (extending cooperation; advice; help to governments; nonprofits; or other entities via services supplied, donated paid labor, loaned expertise, etc.)

- Unilateral (internal response and assistance, perhaps to arms or divisions of the firm itself, to its franchisees, affiliates, associated partners, etc.)

- Adversarial (resistance to public responders, objections to post-disaster regulatory changes, indifference or insensitivity to the community's or labor's post-disaster strife, etc.)[25]

SOCIAL SCIENCES AND EMERGENCY MANAGEMENT

Besides engineers and natural scientists, there are social scientists who research disaster phenomena and work inside many of the previously mentioned organizations.[26] Disaster sociologists, political scientists, economists, social geographers, demographers, social psychologists, and urban planners, to name a few, have made major contributions to the study of hazards and disasters.[27] The disaster sociology community laid the foundations for much of the field of emergency management as we know it today.[28]

The social sciences play a key role in helping emergency managers understand human behavior and the phenomena of disaster. Sociologists have produced a sizable body of scholarship and research results about the community-level disaster experience. They have helped identify common misconceptions (myths) about how people behave in disasters.[29] Moreover, by taking into account cultural, age, ethnic, racial, and LGBTQ factors, they have helped explain human behavior before, during, and after disasters.[30] Social science researchers have also explored such questions as to whether human-made disasters are becoming indistinguishable from "natural disasters" and whether both types of disasters are being made worse by tolerated and growing disaster vulnerability.

Most Americans believe they understand risks and many believe they are behaving prudently in the face of risk.[31] However, according to disaster sociologist Dennis Mileti, everyone he's interviewed "always thinks they are safe."[32] It is only human for a person to assume that disasters happen to other people, never to them. Unsurprisingly, many Americans fail to anticipate or prepare for the possibility of disaster. Research analysis, some of which is conducted in the field at or near disaster sites, has been the stock-in-trade of the University of Colorado Hazards Research Center and the University of Delaware (UD) Disaster Research Center for decades.[33]

Social scientists who focus on disaster research appreciate that "policy makers have sought ideas to improve the nation's preparedness for and response to natural and other types of disaster," and they understand that the products of their work carry the potential to influence public policy in ways that may diminish disaster vulnerability and promote hazard mitigation and preparedness.[34] The NSF has supported the social science research community "to pursue a long term program of research on hazards and disasters, to train cohorts of graduate students, and to pursue strategies to disseminate knowledge."[35]

Social scientists working in academic settings have often been able to examine controversial dimensions of disaster study. For example, several social scientists have argued that Hurricane Katrina was a **social disaster** in which deeper forces of structural racism and social inequality caused the poor and people of color to suffer disproportionately.[36] Some social scientists contend that there is no such thing as a "natural disaster" but only a natural event for which humans have inadequately prepared.[37] This is a strong assertion intended to convey a lesson. Moreover, social scientists posit that disasters are very much defined as types of extraordinary social events experienced by people and often in a variety of ways. Several political scientists in Europe and the United States have artfully crafted a "Politics of Crisis Management" approach that examines in multidisciplinary terms how strategic leaders behave under pressure and how they must manage the public perception of what they are doing during and after crises.[38]

Social scientists have helped the field of emergency management as well. They have demonstrated that human-caused disasters and natural disasters logically require an all-hazards emergency management approach. Social scientists sometimes explore the political interests and legal issues associated with each type of disaster. In this respect, philosophers would hold that **volition** is important. A common assumption is that most people who experience natural disasters are innocent victims. These victims did not freely choose to put their lives and their loved ones' lives at risk. They were unfortunate victims of circumstance. However, both natural and human-caused disasters often involve some form or degree of culpability on the part of some party or parties, and they sometimes involve the assumption of **voluntary risk** by people who may become victims. Did those who chose to build homes on the periphery of known, fire-vulnerable dry-brush-covered or chaparral areas in California, Arizona, Colorado, New Mexico, and other locations knowingly assume a disaster risk before the destructive wildland fires over the years 2003 to 2018? Did those who reside in homes or residential complexes located in river floodplains or near very low-lying coastal shorelines freely elect to assume higher flood risk? Are people ever aware of their proximity to hazards? Would information supplied to them regarding their individual probabilistic hazard risk ever be enough to convince them to reside in a so-called "safer" location? Disaster sociologists remind us that there is a tendency to "blame the victim" for disaster calamities. Yet disaster researchers fully appreciate that human settlement patterns, commercial and government building decisions and infrastructure construction, and known geophysical and meteorological phenomena often combine to create a realm of **tolerated disaster vulnerabilities**. In 2017, Hurricane Harvey produced devastating flood impacts in the greater Houston area in part because water diversion projects and development in flood-vulnerable low-lying areas, combined with an extreme precipitation event, wreaked havoc on many thousands of homes and businesses.[39]

In 2006, a committee of the National Research Council of the National Academies published a major report on how over the past 25 years the social sciences have contributed to disaster research. Below is a short summary of its major findings:

- The origins, dynamics, and impacts of hazards and disasters [have] become much more prominent in mainstream as well as specialty research interests throughout the social sciences.

- Traditional social science investigations of post-disaster responses [have become] more integrated with no less essential studies of hazard vulnerability, hazard mitigation, disaster preparedness, and post-disaster recovery.

- Disciplinary studies of the five core topics [hazard vulnerability, hazard mitigation, disaster preparedness, emergency response, and disaster recovery] within the social sciences [have] increasingly become complemented by interdisciplinary collaborations among social scientists themselves and between social scientists and their colleagues in the natural sciences and engineering.

- There is continuing attention throughout the hazards and disaster research community on resolving interdisciplinary issues of data standardization, data management and archiving, and data sharing.

- There is continuing attention throughout hazards and disaster research on the dissemination of research findings and assessments by social scientists of their impacts on hazards and disaster management practices at local, regional, and national levels.

- Each generation of hazards and disaster researchers makes every effort to recruit and train the next generation.

- The funding of hazards and disaster research by social scientists, natural scientists, and engineers is a cooperative effort involving the NSF, its partner agencies within the National Earthquake Hazards Reduction Program (under NEHRP of 1977, P.L. 95-124), the DHS, and other government stakeholders.[40]

SCIENCE INFORMS THE POLICY AND POLITICS OF DISASTERS

Science and engineering play integral roles in mitigation, preparedness, response, and recovery. Although FEMA has many scientists and engineers, there are far more in other federal agencies whose jobs involve disaster in some form. The examples and cases that are presented within the discussions of each of the four-phase categories demonstrate the importance of science and engineering in disaster policy and politics.

Since the 1970s, emergency managers have sought to abate disaster loss, or prevent a disaster or emergency altogether, by identifying and attempting to reduce hazard risks and vulnerabilities capable of producing disasters or emergencies. This is known as mitigation and is seen by many as the cornerstone of emergency management. Mitigation involves "keeping homes away from floodplains, engineering bridges to withstand earthquakes, creating and enforcing effective building codes to protect property from hurricanes."[41] There are small armies of geoscientists and engineers across the nation and the world who are dedicating their expertise to the study of seismic events. Similarly, the U.S. Forest Service invests sizable efforts in researching wildland and other types of fire disasters. Such research leads to programs and plans for mitigation and informs policy.

From its origin to the present, FEMA has made great strides in examining the practice of, and in performing, disaster loss estimation.[42] The FEMA Federal Insurance Administration (FEMA-FIA) manages the **National Flood Insurance Program (NFIP)**, established by Congress in 1968. The administration's Unified Program for Floodplain Management laid out national goals and set strategies to shrink losses and to protect natural resources.[43] For property owners to qualify for NFIP low-cost flood insurance, their respective local government has to agree to participate in the program and abide by its rules, which includes instituting laws and ordinances to discourage unsafe construction in flood zones. Homeowners whose domiciles were subject to recurring flood loss sometimes petitioned FEMA to buy their properties or relocate them (at government expense) to safer locations. The subsequent era of FEMA residential home buyouts may have had its origins in assistance provided to those displaced by the **Love Canal, in Niagara Falls, New York, hazardous waste incident** and later to the relocation undertaken in the small Missouri community of Times Beach, which was affected by dioxin contamination and subsequently relocated using FEMA funds.[44]

The NFIP, mentioned in other chapters, is noteworthy here because the success of the program rests very much on the ability of FEMA-FIA officials to analyze the science and geography of flood risk. NFIP is in the business of calculating flood risk information and factoring findings into actuarial calculations that determine rates to be charged to those who seek to buy NFIP insurance on their homes and businesses. The basis of the NFIP program is to advance flood disaster mitigation through encouraging local governments to engage in sound land-use practices and in pressing NFIP buyers through the instrument of insurance to do the same thing.

Disaster mitigation has assumed increasing and enduring importance in emergency management across all levels of government. Disaster mitigation is recognized as important "between disaster" emergency management work. Emergency management officials continue to stress that disaster mitigation or prevention is everyone's responsibility. An important element in disaster mitigation is to motivate Americans to engage in disaster prevention activity in their homes, schools, and workplaces. In many ways, the diffusion of disaster mitigation knowledge has done much to advance public awareness of emergency management and catalyze public action. Nevertheless, it sometimes takes many years before the public and responsible authorities understand and act on the findings and recommendations of disaster's scientific and engineering experts.

Preparedness involves anticipating and developing a variety of resources for response and recovery.[45] For emergency managers at the local level, a preparedness strategy "is the mechanism by which the community builds its capacity to respond" to an emergency or disaster.[46] A preparedness strategy involves tactical planning in which plans and procedures are developed to support the strategy; logistics management, which examines resources needed, resources available, shelter planning, and how resource shortages will be addressed; and training of personnel.[47] Preparedness identifies key functions to be performed after a disaster. Preparedness also involves warning systems and pre-disaster actions taken to promote safety and facilitate community disaster response.[48] For example, flood forecasting and warning has saved many lives in the United States and elsewhere. Flood modeling achieved high levels of accuracy for heavy rainfall and flood flows.[49] Real-time stream gauge data can also be used to track volume and depth of water as it moves downstream through a watershed. This may slash damage costs by up to one-third on the floodplains of larger rivers.[50] This only helps when the communication piece is synchronized with the forecasted information. If there is breakdown in the dissemination of vital information to decision makers, then this method fails. Homeland security officials have long advocated that "prevention" be added to the four-phased disaster cycle of mitigation, preparedness, response, and recovery. The prevention example embodies, although focused on interdiction, features of preparedness, mitigation, and response.

The Fire Services, Research, Science, and Technology

Science and engineered technology play a major role in disaster response. Consider the example of firefighting. Because fires are a constant threat to homes, businesses, farms, and other structures, it has become a customary public safety and emergency management obligation of local governments. They must establish and provide for local fire services able to respond quickly and capably. The local emergency manager in cooperation with the fire department officials develops emergency response plans, and firefighters must be equipped and trained to carry out these plans so as to save lives and reduce damage.[51] They must respond to both routine emergencies and major disasters.[52]

First-responder groups, such as firefighters, emergency rescue, hazardous materials teams, and emergency medical technicians must have various kinds of specialized education and training to do their work.[53] Training shows new recruits what is expected of them, and training helps build unified teams. Firefighters must be trained and educated to grasp the problems they confront, to operate and handle equipment, to work in groups, and to help serve their community. Fire service people also work to educate the public on matters of fire safety and prevention. Regular fire safety inspections conducted by fire service people have helped prevent or mitigate countless fires in the communities, cities, and counties they serve.

Over the years, national policymakers in Congress have enacted laws, established organizations, and created programs that have facilitated local and state emergency response to fire disasters. The **U.S. Fire Administration (USFA)**, the National Fire Academy, **Fire Investment and Response Enhancement (FIRE) grants** programs, and the First Responder Initiative are key components of the federal contribution to the fire services. The USFA was developed out of the former Fire Prevention and Control Administration of 1974 and is now a part of FEMA.[54] "The mission of the USFA is to reduce life and economic losses caused by fire and related emergencies, through leadership, advocacy, coordination, and support."[55] Through public education, training, technology, and data initiatives, the USFA hopes fire calls will decline and that improved firefighting response operations will cut fire damage over time.

The USFA provides training to fire service personnel on a national level. By augmenting existing state and local fire service training programs, it hopes to improve and maintain high fire company standards of capacity and performance across the nation. Also, the USFA helps develop and promote proper use of the technologies that fire service people need to acquire and master to aid, facilitate, and modernize their work. The USFA assists state and local groups in collecting and interpreting data on fires in their respective areas; using this information, USFA scientists and researchers develop customized solutions and programs tailored to community needs. This work promotes a partnership between people at the community level and their local fire service people.[56]

The USFA director reports directly to the FEMA director. The USFA conducts hazardous materials training courses for emergency responders at its **National Fire Academy**, in Emmitsburg, Maryland.[57] The National Fire Academy provides firefighters sophisticated education and training, all intended to improve their expertise as emergency responders.[58]

Since early 2001, Fire Investment and Response Enhancement grants, also known as the Assistance to Firefighters Grant Program (AFG), have been awarded to local fire departments for equipment, protective gear, training, and prevention programs. As Table 5-1 shows, this congressionally approved FEMA program provided $100 million in small grants in its first year. By FY 2002, that amount had risen to $360 million, perhaps as a reaction to the 9/11 attacks that preceded the enactment. By FY 2003, Congress dedicated about $745 million to AFG and for FY 2004 a peak $746 million.[59] For FY 2005 (October 1, 2004 to September 30, 2005), when the **Staffing for Adequate Fire and Emergency Response (SAFER)** first received an appropriation, AFG declined to $650 million as SAFER opened with $65 million. AFG grants may be used to hire or train personnel, buy more equipment, or develop prevention plans, all aimed at improving response.[60] The SAFER federal grant program became law as an amendment to the National Defense Authorization Act of 2004 approved by Congress in late 2003, thus advancing local disaster preparedness and firefighting capacity at the local level.[61] (See "Tell Me More" 5-1 box.)

The National Fire Protection Association (NFPA), the consensus standards-making body of the fire service, and the Occupational Safety and Health Administration (OSHA) have both promulgated standards for the minimum number of firefighters needed to respond safely and effectively to emergencies. The fire service community endeavors to secure local, state, and federal support sufficient to meet staffing levels that at least meet these NFPA and OSHA standards.

Similarly, the AFG program provides funding that fire departments can use to purchase equipment and to cover the costs of training. Many small or budget-strapped departments may be unable to make these expenditures without the funds AFG provides. Equipment and training funded by the AFG program help firefighters do their jobs more safely and successfully by improving the effectiveness of fire department operations and by protecting the health and safety of local firefighters. Although FIRE and SAFER grants had been passably funded, congressional efforts to reduce the deficit have caused a gradual contraction in funding for SAFER and FIRE in recent fiscal years. Table 5-1 reveals that FIRE grants have gradually declined from their peak funding year high of FY 2004 of $746 million to $345 million in FY 2017 (Oct. 1, 2016 to Sept. 30, 2017). SAFER grants, which may have eaten into likely AFG funding after FY 2004, opened at $65 million in FY 2005, climbed to a maximum of $420 million in FY 2010, but started a steady downward track from then on, finally fluctuating between $340 million in FY 2014 and $345 million in FY 2017.

The **Assistance to Firefighters Grant Program (AFG)** promotes mitigation and preparedness in fire departments across the United States. The Assistance to Firefighters Grant Program, also known as the FIRE grants program, provides assistance to fire companies at state or local levels, enabling them to identify and obtain the necessary public safety resources. These one-year grants go directly to fire departments.[62] It is through programs and organizations such as the USFA, FIRE grants, and the Assistance to Firefighters Grant Program that state and local fire services are better able to respond to disasters or emergencies:

> The primary goal of the Assistance to Firefighters Grants (AFG) is to meet the firefighting and emergency response needs of fire departments and nonaffiliated emergency medical service organizations. Since 2001, AFG has helped firefighters and other first responders to obtain critically needed equipment, protective gear, emergency vehicles, training and other resources needed to protect the public and emergency personnel from fire and related hazards.[63]

Federal fire programs make a significant contribution in national preparedness and response to terrorism. Congress and DHS understand that firefighters will be called first once a terrorist attack occurs, and they must be ready. As much as $3.5 billion to $4 billion a year in federal spending has been devoted to the first responder community. Fire grants, as well as Urban Area Security Initiative funding, have subsidized equipment purchases and training costs for first responders preparing them for various forms of terrorist attack.[64]

TELL ME MORE 5-1
RESEARCHING FIRE/AFG AND SAFER GRANTS

According to a Congressional Research Service report published in 2017, "During the 106th Congress (about 1999-2000), many in the fire community asserted that local fire departments require and deserve greater support from the federal government. The Assistance to Firefighters Grant Program (AFG), also known as fire grants or the FIRE Act grant program, was established by Title XVII of the FY 2001 Floyd D. Spence National Defense Authorization Act (P.L. 106-398)."[65] It is administered by DHS FEMA. "The program provides federal grants directly to local fire departments and unaffiliated Emergency Medical Services (EMS) organizations to help address a variety of equipment, training, and other firefighter-related and EMS needs. Since its establishment, the Assistance to Firefighters Grant program has been reauthorized twice."[66]

"In November 2016, the National Fire Protection Association (NFPA) released its Fourth Needs Assessment of the U.S. Fire Service, which seeks to identify gaps and needs in the fire service and assesses the extent to which fire grants target those gaps and needs. According to the study, for respondent departments, fire service needs are extensive across the board, and in nearly every area of need, the smaller the community protected, the greater the need. While some needs have declined, many others have been constant or have shown an increase. Gaps remain across the board in staffing, training, facilities, apparatus, personal protective equipment, and health and wellness. Evidence of the need for staffing engines; training for structural firefighting, Hazmat and wildland firefighting; and updated SCBA and personal protective clothing is concerning. Roles and responsibilities of the fire service are expanding apparently at the same time it appears that resources are being cut. EMS and Hazmat are now common responsibilities while active shooter response, enhanced technical rescue and wildland-urban interface firefighting are

up and coming challenges for many departments. AFG and SAFER grant funds are targeted towards areas of need. As other resources are cut back, more departments turn towards these grants for support. If anything, these grant programs should grow in order to address the considerable multi-faceted need that continues in the fire service."[67]

"The AFG statute prescribes different purposes for which fire grant money may be used. These are training firefighting personnel; creating rapid intervention teams; certifying fire inspectors and building inspectors whose responsibilities include fire safety inspections and who are associated with a fire department; establishing wellness and fitness programs, including mental health programs; funding emergency medical services (EMS) provided by fire departments and nonaffiliated EMS organizations; acquiring firefighting vehicles; acquiring firefighting equipment; acquiring personal protective equipment; modifying fire stations, fire training facilities, and other facilities for health and safety; educating the public about arson prevention and detection; providing incentives for the recruitment and retention of volunteer firefighters; and supporting other activities as FEMA determines appropriate. FEMA has the discretion to decide which of those purposes will be funded for a given grant year."[68]

"This decision is based on a Criteria Development Panel, composed of fire service and EMS representatives, which annually recommends criteria for awarding grants." Since the program began, "the majority of fire grant funding has been used by fire departments to purchase firefighting equipment, personal protective equipment, and firefighting vehicles. Eligible applicants are limited primarily to fire departments (defined as an agency or organization that has a formally recognized arrangement with a state, local, or tribal authority to provide fire suppression, fire prevention, and rescue services to a population within a fixed geographical area). Emergency

(Continued)

(Continued)

Medical Services (EMS) activities (at least 3.5% of annual AFG funding) are eligible for fire grants, including a limited number (no more than 2%) to non-fire department EMS organizations not affiliated with hospitals. Additionally, a separate competition is held for fire prevention and firefighter safety research and development grants, which are available to fire departments; national, state, local, tribal, or nonprofit organizations recognized for their fire safety or prevention expertise; and to institutions of higher education, national fire service organizations, or national fire safety organizations to establish and operate fire safety research centers."

The FIRE (AFG) grant program is in its 17th year. Table 5-1 shows the appropriations history

TABLE 5-1 ■ Total Appropriations for Firefighter Assistance, FY 2001–FY 2018

	AFG	SAFER	SCG[a]	Total
FY 2001	$100 million			**$100 million**
FY 2002	$360 million			**$360 million**
FY 2003	$745 million			**$745 million**
FY 2004	$746 million			**$746 million**
FY 2005	$650 million	$65 million		**$715 million**
FY 2006	$539 million	$109 million		**$648 million**
FY 2007	$547 million	$115 million		**$662 million**
FY 2008	$560 million	$190 million		**$750 million**
FY 2009	$565 million	$210 million	$210 million	**$985 million**
FY 2010	$390 million	$420 million		**$810 million**
FY 2011	$405 million	$405 million		**$810 million**
FY 2012	$337.5 million	$337.5 million		**$675 million**
FY 2013	$321 million	$321 million		**$642 million**
FY 2014	$340 million	$340 million		**$680 million**
FY 2015	$340 million	$340 million		**$680 million**
FY 2016	$345 million	$345 million		**$690 million**
FY 2017	$345 million	$345 million		**$690 million**
FY 2018	$350 million	$350 million		**$700 million**
	$7.975 billion	**$3.885 billion**	**$210 million**	**$12.1 billion**

Source: Kruger, L. "Assistance to Firefighters Program: Distribution of Fire Grant Funding," Congressional Research Service, p. 5–6, March 27, 2018. https://www.senate.gov/CRSpubs/da0b22d9-fa21-4fdb-8559-ca965476cb57.pdf

a. Assistance to Firefighters Fine Station Construction Grants (SCG) grants were funded by the American Recovery and Reinvestment Act (P.L. 111–5).

for firefighter assistance displaying AFG, SAFER, and the Fire Station Construction Grants (SCG) monies provided for 18 fiscal years.

"The FIRE Act statute provides overall guidelines on how fire grant money will be distributed. Previously, the law directed that volunteer and combination departments receive a proportion of the total grant funding that is not less than the proportion of the U.S. population that those departments protect (34% for combination, 21% for all-volunteer). Reflecting concerns that career fire departments (which are primarily in urban and suburban areas) were not receiving adequate levels of funding, the Fire Grants Authorization Act of 2012 altered the distribution formula, directing that not less than 25% of annual AFG funding go to career fire departments, not less than 25% to volunteer fire departments, not less than 25% to combination and paid-on-call fire departments, and not less than 10% for open competition among career, volunteer, combination, and paid-on-call fire departments. Additionally, P.L. 112-239 raised award caps (up to $9 million) and lowered matching requirements for fire departments serving higher population areas."[69]

"There is no set geographical formula for the distribution of AFG grants—fire departments throughout the nation apply, and award decisions are made by a peer panel based on the merits of the application and the needs of the community. However, in evaluating applications, FEMA may take into consideration the type of department (paid, volunteer, or combination), geographic location, and type of community served (e.g., urban, suburban, or rural)."[70]

"On January 3, 2018, President Trump signed the United States Fire Administration, AFG, and SAFER Program Reauthorization Act of 2017 (P.L. 115-98)."[71] That law perpetuates "the SAFER and AFG authorizations through FY 2023; extends the sunset provisions for SAFER and AFG through September 30, 2024; provides that the U.S. Fire Administration [USFA, part of FEMA] may develop and make widely available an online training course on SAFER and AFG grant administration; expands SAFER hiring grant eligibility to cover the conversion of part-time or paid-on-call firefighters to full-time firefighters; directs FEMA, acting through the Administrator of USFA, to develop and implement a grant monitoring and oversight framework to mitigate and minimize risks of fraud, waste, abuse, and mismanagement related to the AFG and SAFER grant programs."[72]

The Medical Sciences and Disaster

Biological and chemical warfare has been a reality for years. In 1988, Saddam Hussein ordered the use of chemical weapons against Iraqi Kurds—5,000 people were killed in that attack. In March 1995, members of the Aum Shinrikyo cult, using **sarin nerve gas**, launched an attack on five different cars of three different subway lines in Tokyo. Twelve were killed, 50 were injured, and some 5,000 people experienced temporary vision problems. From 2012 well into 2018, Syrian military forces have used chemical weapons (usually chlorine gas canisters dropped by aircraft as barrel bombs) against its opponents and in doing so has killed or injured a great many civilians as well as rebel faction soldiers.[73] The United States had considerable experience dealing with hazardous materials incidents and chemical contamination from abandoned hazardous wastes well before 2001. However, the anthrax- or ricin-laced letter attacks of fall 2001, coming only weeks after the 9/11 terrorist attacks, deeply alarmed Americans and their elected representatives. The prospect of terrorist biological and chemical attacks inside the United States was becoming a reality.

At that time one expert said the United States was unprepared to respond to a chemical or biological attack at the state and local levels because the U.S. public health infrastructure had been "decimated" over the previous two decades. The public health community helps track the incidence of disease, maintains records of morbidity and mortality, helps combat the outbreak of epidemics, monitors the adequacy of local health services, and promotes food and drug safety. The anthrax incident in 2001 helped move public health to the top of the federal policy agenda for a time. In the years after 2001, the federal government, aided by state and local governments, went on to vastly rejuvenate the nation's system of public health services. However, Sam Klein, writing for the Center for International Maritime Security, contends that the United States' investment in bioterrorism research in recent years has been declining. He claims that in the "growing threat of biological weapons of mass destruction, there is reason for concern that future bioterrorism attacks may be more effective than incidents in the past, and disease control facilities in other countries may not be as robust as those in our own."[74]

As mentioned, the U.S. Public Health Service and a variety of other federal health response agencies enjoyed a major and sustained infusion of federal funding in the long-term aftermath of the anthrax attacks of 2001. This has helped overhaul the nation's public health system. The U.S. Public Health Service has helped seed state public health efforts to train and certify volunteers who wish to serve in either a medical or non-medical capacity after disasters. These volunteers are expected to help in standing up and operating various temporary disaster shelters.[75]

America's system of hospital mass emergency care after deadly and injurious events continues to improve every year, although unevenly and sometimes erratically. The Boston Marathon terror bombing on Massachusetts's Patriot's Day in April 2013 revealed how advantageous use of social media and extraordinary pre-hospital and hospital medical care made a lifesaving difference for many victims of the tragedy.

In March of 2011, an earthquake off the coast of Japan triggered a massively devastating tsunami. One consequence of the disaster was critical damage to the Fukushima Daiichi Nuclear Power Plant, which had profound health ramifications for both plant workers and the surrounding public. The U.S. Nuclear Regulatory Commission worked with the owner of the plant, Tokyo Electric Power Company (TEPCO), to identify precautions needed to protect Americans from similar incidents at its remaining 100 or so nuclear power plants.[76] (See "Tell Me More" 5-2 box on page 200.)

An emerging issue is health impact analysis and disaster. "Health Impact Assessment (HIA) is a fast-growing practice in the U.S. that provides practitioners and policymakers with a tool to measure the health outcomes of decisions."[77] The National Research Council of the National Academies defines HIA as "a systematic process that uses an array of data sources and analytic methods and considers input from stakeholders to determine the potential effects of a proposed policy, plan, program, or project on the health of a population and the distribution of those effects within the population."[78]

With support from the Health Impact Project, a collaboration of the Robert Wood Johnson Foundation and the Pew Charitable Trust, Rutgers University explored how the practice of HIA can be applied in the context of post-disaster recovery and resilience planning. The project examined how HIA might serve as a tool to address the themes outlined in the Hurricane Sandy Rebuilding Task Force Report as well as to more systematically integrate health consideration into pre-disaster resilience planning. Toward this end, Rutgers conducted two HIAs designed to inform ongoing disaster recovery and resilience planning decisions in two case study communities.[79]

Both case study HIAs:

- Fostered forward-looking consideration of the short- and long-term health outcomes that may result from implementation of specific resilience approaches

- Integrated quantitative and qualitative data and evidence to inform decision-makers on the potential consequences of proposed strategies

- Engaged community stakeholders and members of the public, including particularly vulnerable populations, in open public processes that were both transparent and inclusive[80]

A chief purpose of these HIA efforts was to improve public planning and decision making by having stakeholders consider the health implications of what is proposed in local disaster mitigation, preparedness, and recovery.

Disaster recovery, as introduced in Chapter 2, is often the most expensive and most protracted phase of the disaster cycle. Science and engineering issues permeate a vast array of disaster recovery issues. For example, a major environmental health issue surrounded disaster recovery for those affected by Hurricane Katrina. Flooded areas, especially in and around New Orleans, created toxic or viral collections of mold and mildew. As after many floods, owners of flooded structures face the often-daunting task of identifying all the areas of contamination. Those who seek to repair flooded structures must take care not to ignore the environmental health threats posed by mold and other contaminants.

Flood Recovery Research

Disaster recovery involves a host of other scientific and engineering problems emergency managers and policymakers can ill afford to ignore. From April to October 1993, the great Midwest flood covered nine states, ranging over the Mississippi and Missouri river basins. Each state suffered enough flood damage to warrant presidential declarations of major disaster. At one point every county in the state of Iowa was covered under a presidential declaration of major disaster owing to flooding. Direct federal assistance for all nine states exceeded $4.2 billion, plus an additional $621 million in disaster loans to individuals and businesses.[81] Estimates of the total damage ran as high as $16 billion. Only about 1 in 10 structures affected by the flood were covered by national flood insurance policies.[82]

FEMA was widely praised for its handling of the flood response. The disaster was one of the first major challenges of Clinton's revamped FEMA. Director Witt made sure FEMA people proactively addressed the disaster under his new policy of no longer waiting for states to ask for damage assessment teams. Before the flooding became a major disaster, Witt sent out FEMA regional staffs to help states apply for disaster assistance. In the Midwest flood disaster, FEMA responded quickly to requests from states and anticipated requests. FEMA handling of the Midwest floods won praise from both Republicans and Democrats in the Senate and House.[83] Still, the Midwest floods were predicted by weather forecasters almost 12 weeks in advance, thus giving Witt and FEMA considerable time to consult with governors and to mobilize federal response people and assets before the flooding climaxed.

Chapter 2 briefly examined the FEMA-encouraged National Disaster Recovery Framework (NDRF). A key finding of that review is that communities of stakeholders are today in many localities planning their disaster recoveries far in advance of the disasters that may someday befall them.

TELL ME MORE 5-2

NORTHEAST JAPAN'S GREAT TSUNAMI AND THE FUKUSHIMA DAIICHI NUCLEAR POWER PLANT AS A COMPOUND DISASTER (2011)[84]

The **Japan Meteorological Agency (JMA)** leads that nation's mitigation and prevention of natural hazards, particularly those capable of catastrophic consequences. This office is within the Ministry of Land, Infrastructure, and Transport and part of the Courts branch of government. The JMA shoulders duties similar to those carried out by at least three different U.S. government agency counterparts. It is responsible for tracking all weather-related phenomena as well as monitoring, predicting, identifying, and measuring seismic events associated with tsunamis, earthquakes, and volcanoes. The agency is charged with both detecting earthquakes and formulating earthquake warning messages communicated to appropriate audiences, including the prime minister, the Disaster Management Headquarters, the Emergency Team, local governments, the mass media, and in some directly to the general public.[85]

JMA established the Earthquake Phenomena Observation Center (EPOC) in Tokyo, which collects information from over 3,200 seismographs and seismic intensity meters situated across Japan. The JMA also employs 200 sensors capable of detecting primary waves (which travel at speeds approximating five kilometers [3.1 miles] per second). **Primary waves (P-waves)**, emanating from an epicenter, are the initial indicators an earthquake has been triggered. Even though these waves are almost imperceptible to humans, sensor detection of primary waves may be used to calculate the epicenter of a seismic event, its magnitude, and when more damaging **secondary waves (S-waves)** will arrive. Secondary waves travel about three kilometers (1.86 miles) per second.[86]

On March 11, the P-waves from the Great East Japan Earthquake of 2011 were detected at the closest inland sensor at 2:46:45 p.m. local time. That sensor functioned properly and recorded these P-waves, which activated the national earthquake warning system alerting people working at businesses, railways, factories, hospitals, schools, and nuclear plants. Remarkably, the public's cell phones were mass alerted in a mere three seconds (2:46:48 p.m. local time). After the warning went out, actual ground shaking struck Sendai along the northeast coast 30 seconds later and Tokyo to the south 90 seconds after that. This alert-to-impact interval may seem minuscule, but it provided a sufficient window for countless businesses to shut down production lines, doctors to stop medical procedures, schools to get children under desks, cell phone–attentive motorists to pull off to the side of the road, railway operators to turn on backup electric generators, and rail engineers to begin a full stop of their trains.[87]

Fukushima Daiichi Nuclear Power Plant Complex and Na-tech Disasters

"**Na-tech**" **disasters** occur when natural hazards result in dangerous technological spills or releases.[88] They involve event chains characterized by a domino effect or a cascading series of outcomes, and they are a serious threat in many parts of the world. Sometimes natural disasters cause cascading effects. The **Fukushima Daiichi nuclear power plant disaster** is an example of a nuclear accident caused by a tsunami caused by an earthquake.[89] In this respect, it is a **compound disaster,** because it is a disaster that triggered a secondary hazard. Compound disasters can occur simultaneously or sequentially.[90] Na-tech incidents involve a combination of natural and technological interactions. Most na-tech disasters begin from lightning strikes and floods.

The earthquake and tsunami that struck Japan on March 11, 2011, proved to be one of that nation's worst set of disasters since World War II. Owing to the highly regulated nature of the nuclear industry, the siting of nuclear power plants seeks to ensure that they are not situated near urban areas; however, what about natural hazards? Threats of this type may not have been adequately considered in siting nuclear facilities. Moreover, in Japan, just as in the United States, the shrinking number of new operating nuclear powerplants is being countered by utility efforts to extend the operating lives of many old nuclear plants by several decades. In 1967, when Japan's Tokyo Electric Power Company (TEPCO) began construction of the Fukushima Daiichi plant on the Pacific Ocean shoreline, a sizable and protective seawall was also erected adjacent to the complex. The plant was commissioned for operation in 1971. Unfortunately, TEPCO officials and government regulators may not have considered the possibility that decades later a strong earthquake would cause a great tsunami to far overtop the seawall and massively damage the reactors and facility. To briefly summarize what happened, the World Nuclear Association offers these points.

- Following a major earthquake, a 15-meter tsunami disabled the power supply and cooling of three Fukushima Daiichi reactors, causing a nuclear accident on March 11, 2011. All three cores largely melted in the first three days.

- The accident was rated 7 on the International Nuclear Emergency Scale (INES), due to high radioactive releases over days four to six, eventually a total of some 940 PBq (I-131 eq).

- Four reactors were written off—capable of generating a total 2719 MWe net.

- After two weeks, the three reactors (units 1–3) were stable with water addition but with no proper heat sink for removal of decay heat from fuel. By July, they were being cooled with recycled water from the new treatment plant. Reactor temperatures had fallen to below 80°C at the end of October, and official "cold shutdown condition" was announced in mid-December.

- Apart from cooling, the basic ongoing task was to prevent release of radioactive materials, particularly in contaminated water leaked from the three units. This task became newsworthy in August 2013.

- There have been no deaths or cases of radiation sickness from the nuclear accident, but over 100,000 people had to be evacuated from their homes to ensure this. Government nervousness delays their return.[91]

While many changes in the nuclear industry were made relating to design, operation, training, and regulatory activities, following the Three Mile Island (1979) nuclear power plant accident in central Pennsylvania and the Chernobyl Disaster (1986) in the former Soviet Union, they were not enough to prevent the Fukushima Daiichi disaster in Japan. TEPCO, owner and operator of the facility, had prepared the nuclear complex for a major earthquake but not a major earthquake and, soon after, a tsunami.[92]

Because Japan has few natural resources of its own, a high priority was given to energy sources able to reduce the nation's dependence on oil imports. Over the past 30 years, this has spurred on Japan's construction of nuclear facilities as energy providers. However, this strategy may be changing following the aftermath of Fukushima Daiichi. Japan is an island located in a seismically active area of the world. Due to its geographic location and heavily dense population, Japan's vulnerability to natural hazards such as typhoons, earthquakes, and tsunamis is greater than in many other countries. Today Japan is transitioning into greater use of renewable energy sources both in its power grid and in its home and building energy use.

Immediate lessons learned from the disaster include new safety measures such as "providing auxiliary power supply cars, fire engines with high-power water injection, installation of watertight doors for buildings containing important equipment, and alternative cooling systems for spent fuel pools,"[93] and better prediction and preparedness for "unforeseen" events. Kitamura claims that warning reports about the possibility of a tsunami were neglected by the nuclear community. Reports were issued by researchers at the National Institute of Advanced Industrial Science and Technology (AIST) and by civil engineering professors at Tohoku University that indicated the significant possibility of a tsunami recurrence in Japan since the last one had been 1,100 years ago.[94] This case demonstrates that even highly developed and technologically advanced nations have a hard time planning for events that are of very low probability but very high consequence. Yet it is the planning for such unexpected events that makes nations and their biggest utility companies more disaster resilient.

The Policy and Politics of Earthquake Research and Engineering

Earthquake engineering research and seismological study have long been core concerns of both U.S. and Japan disaster policy and emergency management. The steady and major decline in fatalities from earthquake in the United States over the last 50 years is in part a credit to significant public and private investment in the building sciences, better engineered structures, improved **seismic building codes,** and **earthquake retrofitting** of homes and businesses. Japan's experience with its March 11, 2011, earthquake and tsunami provide an amazing account of how advances in science, engineering, and telecommunications have contributed to the challenge of earthquake preparedness, warning, and alert.

Earthquake research and engineering issues overlap many dimensions of emergency management. In the United States, earthquake research receives considerable attention and regular political support. The earthquake research and engineering community is both mature and politically influential. The United States is dotted by large and small earthquake research centers.

Earthquakes, like other disasters, may temporarily overwhelm the emergency response and recovery capacity of individuals, businesses, and state and local governments. The human and economic losses inflicted by an earthquake and its consequences may be so great that people, businesses, and governments outside the damage zone must provide a great deal of help. Consequently, earthquake threat and destruction have been addressed in national policy and federal law for many years.[95]

Earthquakes often strike with few or no measurable precursors. In spite of major scientific advances in both the science and technology of seismology, it remains extremely difficult if not impossible for seismologists to provide accurate advance warning of the month, week, day, or hour a major earthquake will strike. Beyond their decadal or longer probabilistic timescales, it is difficult for them to provide the public with sufficient advance warning of when a major quake will hit. Regardless, seismic and geologic research has advanced dramatically over the past 50 years. Seismic research has led to **seismic mapping.** Those who engineer built structures, everything from one-story homes to skyscrapers, have made major lifesaving contributions to the field. They have helped design and build seismic-resistant structures, and they have disseminated model building codes appropriate for the seismic risk communities endure.

With the possible exceptions of Hawaii and Alaska, few American states are more prone to earthquake activity than California, the nation's most populated state. Consequently, much of the history of U.S. earthquake policy at the national level is intertwined with California's earthquake experience. In 2018, California had more than 39 million people, and the state's delegation to the U.S. House of Representatives totaled 53, more than 12 percent of the chamber. Thus, the state, along with a handful of earthquake-vulnerable states in the West and Midwest, have had considerable political influence in shaping U.S. earthquake policy.

In 1977, Congress, advised by seismic experts, determined that almost all 50 states are vulnerable to earthquakes and that a national policy was needed to address earthquake as a major natural hazard.[96] The culmination of this legislative work was the National Earthquake Hazards Reduction Act of 1977; its implementing arm is a program that supports federal, state, local, and private research and planning to attenuate earthquake losses in seismic risk areas.[97]

The **National Earthquake Hazards Reduction Program (NEHRP)** has provided the framework for a national earthquake policy, and FEMA, after its formation in 1979, was designated the lead agency charged with coordinating that program until 2003. Under the NEHRP, FEMA worked with other federal agencies—the USGS, NSF, and NIST—the states, academia, and the private sector to minimize risk to life and property from future earthquakes. The primary goals of the program have been to make structures safer, better inform the public of earthquake threat, and advance better seismic mitigation. This entails the following:

- Providing better understanding, characterizing, and predicting of seismic hazards

- Improving model building codes and land-use practices

- Learning risk reduction through post-earthquake investigation and analysis

- Developing improved design and construction techniques

- Promoting the dissemination and application of research results[98]

The NEHRP has external grant programs funded through FEMA, the USGS, NSF, and NIST. From 1979 to 2003 FEMA provided project grants through its state cooperative agreements program. The state matching requirement ultimately rose to 50 percent, and a share of federal–state funding had to be used for mitigation activities; some states used these funds to support seismic hazard loss reduction.

Measuring Earthquake Intensities, Size, and Damage

"There are a number of ways to measure the magnitude of an earthquake. The first widely-used method, the **Richter scale**, was developed by Charles F. Richter in 1934. It used a formula based on amplitude of the largest wave recorded on a specific type of seismometer and the distance between the earthquake and the seismometer. That scale was specific to California earthquakes; other scales, based on wave amplitudes and total earthquake duration, were developed for use in other situations and they were designed to be consistent with Richter's scale."[99]

"Unfortunately, many scales, such as the Richter scale, do not provide accurate estimates for large magnitude earthquakes. Today the **moment magnitude scale** is preferred because it works over a wider range of earthquake sizes and is applicable globally. The moment magnitude scale is based on the total moment release of the earthquake. Moment is a product of the distance a fault moved and the force required to move it. It is derived from modeling recordings of the earthquake at multiple stations. Moment magnitude estimates are about the same as Richter magnitudes for small to large earthquakes. But only the moment magnitude scale is capable of measuring M8 (read 'magnitude 8') and greater events accurately."[100]

Magnitudes are based on a logarithmic scale (base 10). What this means is that for each whole number you go up on the magnitude scale, the amplitude of the ground motion recorded by a seismograph goes up 10 times. Using this scale, a magnitude 5 earthquake would result in 10 times the level of ground shaking as a magnitude 4 earthquake (and 32 times as much energy would be released).[101]

Another way to measure the strength of an earthquake is to use the **modified Mercalli scale**. Invented by Giuseppe Mercalli in 1902, this scale uses the observations of the people who experienced the earthquake to estimate its intensity. The Mercalli scale is not considered as scientific as the Richter scale, though. Some witnesses of the earthquake might exaggerate just how bad things were during the earthquake and you may not find two witnesses who agree on what happened; everybody will say something different. The amount of damage caused by the earthquake may not accurately record how strong it was either. Some things that affect the amount of damage that occurs are:

- Building designs

- Distance from the epicenter

- Type of surface material (rock or dirt) the buildings rest on[102]

Different building designs hold up differently in an earthquake, and the further you are from the earthquake, the less damage you will usually see. Whether a building is built on solid rock or sand makes a big difference in how much damage it sustains. Solid rock usually shakes less than sand, so a building built on top of solid rock should not be as damaged as it might if it was sitting on a sandy lot.[103]

Based on their magnitude, quakes are assigned to a class, according to the U.S. Geological Survey. An increase in one number, say from 5.5 to 6.5, means that a quake's magnitude is 10 times as great. The classes are as follows:

- Great: Magnitude is greater than or equal to 8.0. A magnitude-8.0 earthquake is capable of tremendous damage.

- Major: Magnitude in the range of 7.0 to 7.9. A magnitude-7.0 earthquake is a major earthquake that is capable of widespread, heavy damage.

- Strong: Magnitude in the range of 6.0 to 6.9. A magnitude-6.0 quake can cause severe damage.

- Moderate: Magnitude in the range of 5.0 to 5.9. A magnitude-5.0 quake can cause considerable damage.

- Light: Magnitude in the range of 4.0 to 4.9. A magnitude-4.0 quake is capable of moderate damage.

- Minor: Magnitude in the range of 3.0 to 3.9.

- Micro: Magnitude less than 3.0. Quakes between 2.5 and 3.0 are the smallest generally felt by people.[104]

After an earthquake strikes, measurement of its magnitude is continuously revised. As time passes and more stations report their seismic readings, measurements are refined. Several days can pass before a final number is agreed upon.[105]

In the 1990s, FEMA developed an earthquake simulation applicable and adaptable to most of the nation. It was called Hazards-U.S. (HAZUS), and FEMA distributed it free on the Internet. HAZUS is a powerful risk assessment software program for analyzing potential losses from earthquake. Its successor, Hazards U.S.-Multi-Hazard (HAZUS-MH), also models losses from hurricane, wind, and flood hazards.[106] The results of this research were used to mitigate the effects of disasters and to improve preparation for, response to, and recovery from such events. FEMA also made available a third generation of HAZUS-MH software.[107]

One of the significant accomplishments of the NEHRP has been the development of seismic resistance standards for new construction and for strengthening existing buildings in earthquake-prone areas. FEMA work under the program facilitated creation of the Federal Response Plan (FRP). As mentioned, the FRP provided the basic framework for coordination of federal disaster relief work among the federal departments and agencies until it was replaced by the National Response Plan (NRP) in late 2004, and by December 2007 the National Response Framework (NRF).

The U.S. Geological Survey Earthquake Hazards Program operates an Earthquake Notification Service (ENS). It is a system that can be customized and it is provided free to everyone who signs up for it. New accounts receive, by default, notice of all earthquakes with magnitude 6.0 or greater; users can subsequently customize these settings to better fit their needs.[108] Users can receive earthquake notifications for any earthquakes located by the Advanced National Seismic System/National Earthquake Information Center (ANSS/NEIC) in the United States and around the world. Information for earthquakes in the United States is generally available within 5 minutes; information for earthquakes elsewhere in the world is generally available within 30 minutes. Within America, the U.S. Geological Survey locates earthquakes down to about M2.0, and about M4.0 for the rest of the world.

ENS is an informational tool and NOT a robust earthquake or tsunami warning system. The USGS does not produce tsunami warnings. For the information about tsunamis, please refer to the information given in the NOAA website http://tsunami.gov/. The Earthquake Hazards Program provides rapid, authoritative information on earthquakes and their impact to emergency responders, governments, facilities managers and researchers across the country. The ENS allows users to report shaking intensity of earthquake events and permits users to volunteer to have seismic instrumentation installed on their property.

Before its absorption into the DHS, FEMA had a National Earthquake Mitigation Program Office within its Mitigation Directorate. FEMA produced manuals, seismic safety provisions, and guidance documents that were the basis for U.S. seismic safety codes. For its part, the USGS produces earth science data, calculates earthquake probabilities, and supports land-use planning and engineering design, as well as emergency preparedness. The NSF promotes earthquake mitigating construction and siting, fundamental geotechnical engineering design, and structural analysis, in part through the Multidisciplinary Center for Earthquake Engineering Research (MCEER) housed at the State University of New York at Buffalo.[109] NIST and FEMA together work with state and local officials, model-building code groups, architects, engineers, and others to be sure that scientific and engineering research flows into building codes, standards, and practices.

The **NEHRP Reauthorization Act of 2004** (P.L. 108-360) reassigned NEHRP lead agency authority from FEMA to NIST, but the law continued to hold FEMA responsible for earthquake emergency response and management, estimation of loss potential, and implementation of mitigations actions.[110]

The Policy and Politics of Tornado Research

Tornadoes are extreme weather events that have killed many people and have destroyed or damaged a sizable amount of structures and property through the years. Much tornado activity is seasonal or is associated with severe storms, and tornado activity continues from year to year. The quest to provide threatened communities with reliable forecasts and longer intervals of advanced tornado warnings has been a goal of many atmospheric scientists.

Vast areas of the United States are vulnerable to tornadoes and severe storms. Government officials at the federal, state, and local levels are responsible for providing public warnings of tornado and severe thunderstorm threats. How they do this and how well they do this are matters of controversy. Also controversial is the role of government in tornado mitigation activity. Moreover, not all tornado-damaged jurisdictions win presidential declarations of major disaster or emergency. Such determinations are sometimes a function of damage assessment after the fact.

Most people can recall previous tornado disasters reported by the media. This gives tornado disaster events broad, but thin, public attention over the nation. Sometimes new laws or policies have stemmed from tornado disasters. Some have argued that there is a tornado politics, very much intertwined with matters of how science comes to influence politics.[111]

Three issues are paramount in tornado policy: the degree of preparedness; the definition of disaster; and the amount of federal aid that should go to individuals, state, and local governments after a tornado or severe storm disaster.[112]

Political and policy factors have influenced all three issues. Many state and local governments are not as prepared to meet the threat of tornadoes as they could be. Local elected officials have difficulty determining the costs and benefits of spending public funds on tornado preparedness measures. They often seriously discount the probability that a tornado will strike their jurisdiction.

Meteorologists rely on weather radar to provide information on developing storms (see the "Tell Me More" 5-3 box on page 209). The **National Weather Service (NWS)** strategically located **Doppler radar** facilities across the nation. Doppler radar is capable of detecting air movement toward or away from the radar. Early detection of increasing rotation aloft within a thunderstorm may allow authorities to issue lifesaving warnings before the tornado forms. Not all tornadoes, however, are detectable or traceable on radar, regardless of the type of radar technology used.

Nevertheless, the increased use of Doppler radar by the NWS and other organizations has done much to improve public warning time in advance of tornado strikes. It is ironic that improvements in the handling of tornado watches and in the timely broadcast of tornado warnings issued by federal agencies and by radio and television news organizations have inadvertently alleviated some of the burden of emergency notification handled by local governments. Local governments that do not maintain adequate tornado warning systems for their people because of overdependence on tornado tracking by others may be derelict in fulfilling their public responsibility.

According to the NWS, "the **Enhanced Fujita Scale** or EF Scale, which became operational on February 1, 2007, is used to assign a tornado a 'rating' based on estimated wind speeds and related damage. When tornado-related damage is surveyed, it is compared to a list of Damage Indicators (DIs) and Degrees of Damage (DoD) which help

TABLE 5-2 ■ Enhanced Fujita Scale Wind Speeds in Tornado Intensity Measurement[113]

EF Rating	3 Second Gust (mph)
0	65–85
1	86–110
2	111–135
3	136–165
4	166–200
5	Over 200

Source: Storm Prediction Center, NOAA, https://www.spc.noaa.gov/faq/tornado/ef-scale.htm.

estimate better the range of wind speeds the tornado likely produced. From that, a rating (from EF0 to EF5) is assigned."[114] (See Table 5-2.)

"The EF Scale was revised from the original Fujita Scale to reflect better examinations of tornado damage surveys so as to align wind speeds more closely with associated storm damage. The new scale has to do with how most structures are designed. The EF scale still is a set of wind estimates (not measurements) based on damage. It uses three-second gusts estimated at the point of damage based on a judgment of 8 levels of damage to the 28 indicators listed below [Table 5-3]. These estimates vary with height and exposure. Important: The 3-second gust is not the same wind as in standard surface observations. Standard measurements are taken by weather stations in open exposures, using a directly measured, 'one-minute mile' speed."[115]

Metrics of Tornadic Intensity

"The goal is to assign an EF Scale category based on the highest wind speed that occurred within the damage path. First, trained NWS personnel will identify the appropriate damage indicator (DI) [see list in the "Tell Me More" 5-3 box on page 209] from more than one of the 28 used in rating the damage. The construction or description of a building should match the DI being considered, and the observed damage should match one of the 8 degrees of damage (DoD) used by the scale. The tornado evaluator will then make a judgment within the range of upper and lower bound wind speeds, as to whether the wind speed [causing] the damage is higher or lower than the expected value for the particular DoD. This is done for several structures not just one, before a final EF rating is determined."[116]

An unusual problem facing many local governments in more rural areas has been the loss of local privately owned radio stations owing to consolidations, mergers, and acquisitions in the radio industry. As independent local radio stations have been absorbed by much larger radio broadcast corporations, many rural or remote localities have lost an avenue for issuing unique tornado warnings to their local populace. However, local emergency management officials may access and use radio broadcast facilities in their environs

TABLE 5-3 ■ Enhanced Fujita Scale Damage Indicators		
Number	**Damage Indicator**	**Abbreviation**
1	Small barns, farm outbuildings	SBO
2	One- or two-family residences	FR12
3	Single-wide mobile home (MHSW)	MHSW
4	Double-wide mobile home	MHDW
5	Apartment, condo, townhouse (3 stories or less)	ACT
6	Motel	M
7	Masonry apartment or motel	MAM
8	Small retail building (fast food)	SRB
9	Small professional (doctor office, branch bank)	SPB
10	Strip mall	SM
11	Large shopping mall	LSM
12	Large, isolated ("big box") retail building	LIRB
13	Automobile showroom	ASR
14	Automotive service building	ASB
15	School—1-story elementary (interior or exterior halls)	ES
16	School—junior or senior high school	JHSH
17	Low-rise (1–4 story) building	LRB
18	Mid-rise (5–20 story) building	MRB
19	High-rise (over 20 stories)	HRB
20	Institutional building (hospital, government, or university)	IB
21	Metal building system	MBS
22	Service station canopy	SSC
23	Warehouse (tilt-up walls or heavy timber)	WHB
24	Transmission line tower	TLT
25	Free-standing tower	FST
26	Free-standing pole (light, flag, luminary)	FSP
27	Tree—hardwood	TH
28	Tree—softwood	TS

Source: Storm Prediction Center, NOAA, https://www.spc.noaa.gov/faq/tornado/ef-scale.htm.

under the **Emergency Alert System (EAS),** a public warning system operated by the Federal Communications Commission in conjunction with FEMA and NOAA to allow the president to address the nation in emergencies and when needed to issue various types of alerts. EAS equipment is a core element of the country's first response effort. Clear Channel's senior vice president of engineering, Steve Davis, said the following:

> Our responsibility as a broadcaster is twofold—to deliver the equipment to local authorities (in many cases, we subsidize the equipment also), and to ensure that the EAS equipment at each of our stations is fully operational so that local or Federal authorities can automatically interrupt our broadcasts with public-safety messages.[117]

Local emergency management officials must now understand and be prepared to use EAS equipment residing at transmission facilities of private radio broadcasters. The NWS is the most frequent user of EAS equipment, for things like tornado warnings, but it is also available to all local and federal authorities.[118]

TELL ME MORE 5-3

THE NATIONAL OCEANIC AND ATMOSPHERIC ADMINISTRATION NATIONAL SEVERE STORMS LABORATORY

The **NOAA National Severe Storms Laboratory (NSSL)** is a federal research laboratory under the NOAA Office of Oceanic and Atmospheric Research. NSSL research spans weather radar, tornadoes, flash floods, lightning, damaging winds, hail, and winter weather. NSSL is located in the National Weather Center (NWC) in Norman, Oklahoma. The NWC houses a unique combination of University of Oklahoma, NOAA, and state organizations that work together to improve understanding of weather.

NSSL has a strategic research partnership with the University of Oklahoma's Cooperative Institute for Mesoscale Meteorological Studies (CIMMS), one of the NOAA joint institutes. CIMMS enables NSSL and university scientists to collaborate on research areas of mutual interest and facilitates the participation of students and visiting scientists.

The laboratory works under the following charge:

- We know that changing demographics will place more people in the path of natural hazards.

- We have a responsibility to continue exploration and discovery in new areas to lay the foundation for services of the future.

- We have a responsibility to translate discoveries into tangible benefits that can impact society for generations to come.

- We have a responsibility to enable the nation and society to make informed decisions in the decades to come to prevent loss of human life.[119]

Tornado Dynamics

NSSL researchers have created a computer model that simulates a tornado-producing thunderstorm in 3-D. This model is used to study what

(Continued)

(Continued)

changes in the environment cause a thunderstorm to produce a tornado and how the tornado and storm behaves as it encounters different weather conditions.

Most tornadoes come from rotating thunderstorms, called supercells. However, nearly 20 percent of all tornadoes are associated with lines of strong thunderstorms called "quasi-linear convective systems" (QLCS).[120] QLCS tornadoes frequently occur during the late night and early morning hours when the public is less aware of severe weather hazards. NSSL scientists are looking for ways to detect non-supercell tornadoes more effectively.

Tornado Detection

The NWS of NOAA is upgrading the national network of weather radars dual-polarization technology, contributing to its ongoing scientific and engineering development. NSSL researchers discovered dual-polarization radars can detect debris from a tornado, helping forecasters pinpoint a tornado's location even at night or if it is wrapped in rain.

NSSL has a research-phased array radar that can scan the entire sky for severe weather in less than a minute, five times faster than current weather radars. This phased array radar has been used to capture developing tornadoes both in QLCS and supercells. Researchers are hoping to collect more high-resolution data on these storms to look for clues on radar that a tornado is forming. Phased array radar has strong potential to aid the NWS in the forecast and warning decision process by providing new radar data more quickly.

Tornado Warning Decision Support and Forecasting

NSSL continues to work on an automated multi-radar, multi-sensor (MRMS) system that quickly integrates data streams from multiple radars, surface and upper air observations, lightning detection systems, and satellite and forecast models. The MRMS system was developed to produce severe weather and precipitation products for improved decision-making capability within NOAA.

NSSL On-Demand is a web-based tool that helps confirm when and where tornadoes may have occurred by mapping circulations detected by radar on Google Earth satellite images. NWS forecasters can quickly review warnings and check their accuracy with this system. Emergency responders and damage surveyors have also used On-Demand to produce high-resolution street maps of affected areas so they can more effectively begin rescue and recovery efforts and damage assessments.

NSSL and the NOAA NWS collaborate to streamline moving research into practical operations. NSSL has developed severe weather warning applications and decision support systems that will make the forecasters' job easier. The result will be improved NWS warning services for the public, increased detection accuracy, and longer lead times.

NSSL Warn-on-Forecast project aims to create highly detailed computer weather forecast models that predict what the atmosphere will look like in the future. These models are unique because they will use the latest weather observations and radar scans to continuously recompute forecasts. The lab wants these forecasts to accurately predict when and where tornadoes will occur in the first hour of their formation so forecasters can issue warnings based on that forecast and give people more time to find shelter.

Tornado Preparedness

NSSL is very involved in shaping a "Weather Ready Nation," a program to improve the public's preparedness for extreme weather. The lab is looking at ways to improve the forecast and warning system, communicate threats to the public more rapidly, increase community resilience, and identify gaps in our current understanding of planning, coordination and decision making in a community.[121]

Since tornado and severe storm disasters have such low probability, they do not have high political salience. People residing in areas recently hit by these disaster agents may for a time accord these agents high political importance. Still, the infrequency of tornado experience for each single locality encourages local governments collectively to underprepare for tornado disasters. Many state and local officials who have not had recent experience with a devastating tornado or tornado outbreak (which is a rash of many tornadoes over a region) have decided that the risk of a touchdown is simply not great enough to warrant allocating funds to better prepare for one.

There are some steps that local jurisdictions can take to prepare for and mitigate the effects of tornadoes and severe storms. They include installing siren-warning systems, building reinforced structures near mobile home communities, and supplying NOAA self-activating radios to residents.

According to the NWS, the most tornado-vulnerable structures are permanent homes and mobile homes. Some 77 percent of tornado fatalities are among those in mobile homes. One mitigation measure that would probably save lives is to limit the use of mobile homes. However, it is extremely expensive to provide alternate housing, and it is politically infeasible to win approval of such a measure in law. Nonetheless, many mobile homes cannot withstand the high winds associated with tornadoes. Despite the increased risk, the 5 to 6 percent of the population who live in mobile homes and the manufactured-housing industry would aggressively fight any attempt to limit the sale or location of mobile homes. As a result, much of the federal government's tornado mitigation policy rests on a program of public education. One of the options for local municipalities, as previously mentioned, is the building of reinforced shelters in mobile home neighborhoods where residents may go to better protect themselves in the event of a tornado.

The NWS, the NSSL, and the EAS, in cooperation with state and local emergency management agencies, shoulder much of the burden for providing public warning of tornado threat. Privately owned television and radio news organizations, particularly **The Weather Channel,** provide extensive tornado tracking, severe storm tracking, and public warning coverage. The NWS continuously broadcasts updated weather warnings and forecasts that can be received by the NOAA Weather Radios sold in many stores. The average range of the radios is 40 miles, depending on topography. The NWS recommends purchasing radios that have both a battery backup and a tone-alert feature that automatically alerts people when a watch or warning is issued. Inadequate advanced warning time, wind-vulnerable structures, and an unaware or heedless public may result in many people being unnecessarily exposed to tornado or severe storm threats. Public education, drills, practices, siren warnings, and feasible structural mitigation (there is no such thing as a perfectly windproof building) could all help in reducing the public's vulnerability to tornadoes. However, strong national, state, and local leadership is needed to reach such goals.

Critical scientific and technical issues in tornado disasters include effective forecasting, credible public announcements of tornado watches and tornado warnings, tracking the general path of sighted tornadoes, public evacuation in advance of tornado hazards, and appropriate sheltering of evacuees. The matter of demobilizing—that is, issuing of an all-clear notice—standing down responders, and facilitating the return of people to their homes and offices is an additional responsibility. As in most disasters, emergency response to damaged areas, search and rescue operations, emergency medical services, utility repair, business and residential insurance against wind and rain damage, disaster relief from public sources, and long-term recovery efforts may all be part of tornado emergencies and disasters.

PUBLIC INFRASTRUCTURE POLICY

If emergency management is becoming more federally centered, one might also ask if U.S. disaster policy has become a modern and growing **public works** subsidy program for state and local governments.[122] How is infrastructure defined, and who pays for its post-disaster repair? Are buyouts and relocations replacing engineered disaster mitigation (e.g., flood levees, flood control works)? The U.S. Army Corps of Engineers (USACE) is an agency with a very long history of work in construction, operation, and maintenance of infrastructural works (dams, levees, revetments, reservoirs, and the like) and nonstructural, disaster mitigation works. USACE also owns, operates, and maintains other massive infrastructure (lock systems, navigable waterways, bridges, ports, and the like). Consequently, USACE is an important player in the nation's system of emergency management.[123]

The federal government had been in the business of building flood control works since at least the 1920s; however, by the 1980s, U.S. emergency management became more extensively involved in restoring disaster-damaged public infrastructure.[124] Such infrastructure included highways, roads, streets, bridges, ports, airports, flood control works, utilities such as water and sewer systems, electrical systems, natural gas distribution networks, and telephone and cable systems, plus government-owned buildings.

Communications infrastructure became a huge new concern of emergency management. The astounding growth of the Internet and the World Wide Web made possible colossal advances in the range and depth of information technology. Maintenance of routers and hubs, protection of transmission vehicles (from hard lines, to fiber-optic cables, to cell towers, to wireless instruments), and most particularly perpetuation of connectivity all became concerns of emergency managers. This involvement by emergency managers, public and private, came about in part because so many had come to depend on the availability of the Internet before, during, and after disasters.

Economic and social dependence on these communications and information pathways convinced political leaders that **cybersecurity** was essential. Computer hackers who disrupted Internet usage came to be recognized as potential "terrorists" and purveyors of disaster. By the 1990s, disasters and emergencies that damaged or threatened to damage any of these critical systems and facilities became a growing concern and a new core area of responsibility for FEMA. The vulnerability of these systems and facilities to both terrorism and natural disaster forces encouraged policymakers to fund scientific and engineering endeavors aimed at advancing the fortification and resilience of these systems and structures. In 1997, a report by the Presidential Commission on Critical Infrastructure and Protection convinced Clinton of the need to issue a presidential directive (number 63) in 1998, pressing federal agencies to act on these vulnerabilities. George W. Bush went much further on this subject when he issued Homeland Security Presidential Directive-7 (HSPD-7) in 2004.[125]

In many respects, one of the main criteria by which disaster management effectiveness has been judged is how quickly government agencies restore lifeline services and public infrastructure after a disaster. Repairing or replacing damaged public infrastructure often costs millions if not billions of dollars. Americans have become accustomed to uninterrupted delivery of lifeline services. Interruptions of electricity service, even for only a period of hours, are considered "disasters" or "emergencies." Loss of Internet availability and connectivity has grown to have massive economic and social implications. Hence, the president, Congress, and all federal agencies engaged in public infrastructure operations or publicly subsidized construction have come to recognize government's key role in the aftermath of disasters.[126] Since the mid-1950s, state and local political executives and lawmakers have come to appreciate the importance of federal post-disaster subsidies to repair or replace public infrastructure.

Although disaster mitigation had become a policy goal set forth in law in 1974, it was not until the Northridge earthquake in Los Angeles in January 1994 that FEMA was authorized to fund public infrastructure repairs so that they were more than restoration of original structures.[127] For example, California freeway overpasses that collapsed owing to the Northridge quake and its aftershocks were rebuilt, at great public expense, to meet more powerful seismic shocks.[128] The U.S. Department of Transportation (DOT) funds a major share of the federal highway system and has programs and resources in place to repair or replace disaster-damaged segments of its national system, as became necessary after the tragic collapse of a bridge and a major segment of an elevated eight-lane interstate highway in Minneapolis in August 2007. FEMA also subsidizes state and local government post-disaster road repair, as well as repair of disaster-damaged utility infrastructure, even when utilities are privately or shareholder owned.

Summary

Science and engineering have helped grow and professionalize the field of emergency management. Moreover, the scientists and engineers who study hazards and disaster phenomena have found ways to engage the political process in order both to promote the public interest and to solicit the funding resources they need to do much of their work. Big science applications of disaster research especially require subtle forms of political lobbying of lawmakers. It is clear that disaster study informs but also transcends emergency management.

This chapter posited that different types of disaster agents are of interest to different types of scientific and engineering clientele groups.[129] The scientific and engineering interests dedicated to the study of earthquakes are not identical to the scientific and engineering interests focused on hurricanes. Those who focus on tornadoes and severe storms, as meteorological phenomena, lobby often as a group separate from the two just mentioned. In turn, the scientific and engineering groups concerned with flood control and water resources only partially overlap the other groups. However, improvements in earthquake engineering as well as advances in tornado and severe storm research have through the years saved lives. Successful mitigation is seldom newsworthy and attention grabbing; hence the contributions of both earthquake and tornado research often go unheralded.

This means is that these communities of practice (CoPs) sometimes conflict with one another when they seek to secure government support and funding of their respective scientific endeavors. However, these groups also have a great deal in common. They often form alliances, or at least tolerate their differences, in the interest of showing a united front to policymakers, who are often rapaciously looking for ways to reallocate government funding to purposes they judge more important than basic or applied scientific and engineering research. For example, each year the federal budget request for climate science research is fashioned as a joint package of requests cooperatively crafted by federal officials whose agencies are researching different features or aspects of climate change or global warming. This package is reviewed by various White House offices, including the Office of Management and Budget. The logic of this research budget request is that the package is better justified and defended as a whole rather than as separately and independently submitted budget requests.

An unfortunate aspect of U.S. disaster policy is that most of the government scientific and engineering agencies, offices, and programs important to emergency managers are neither in FEMA nor in the DHS. Some of these organizations are capable of making predictions of disaster frequency and magnitude, some design various countermeasures or advance disaster mitigation research and engineering, some work to improve government disaster preparedness and response, and some are capable of facilitating disaster recovery. The NOAA, the USGS, the NIST, NASA, the EPA, and the NSF all operate very much independently of FEMA and DHS. Scientists of the National Hurricane Center, the U.S. Tsunami Warning Center, the NSSL, the National Center for Earthquake Engineering, the Centers for Disease Control and Prevention, the National Center for Atmospheric Research, and the National Climate Data Center have major ongoing research responsibilities, only some of which draw them into disaster policy and management. Not to be overlooked is that in 2006 DHS-FEMA established a National Preparedness Directorate, which includes a technological hazards branch. However, many of the experts in this directorate are largely focused on terrorism prevention.

The public works engineering side of emergency management is critical in disaster policy's intergovernmental relations. In many homeland security realms, research involves sizable pools of government contractors and universities working on security-related technologies. This has moved emergency management deeper into the world of national security and defense-related contracting. Although the president is rarely personally involved in issues of disaster-related science and engineering, certain techno-scientific problems do percolate to the presidential level. For example, President Obama took an interest in climate science owing to a spate of coastal disasters, some suspected of being unusually destructive owing to the effects of sea level rise along the Gulf and Atlantic coastlines.

In a speech at Georgetown University on June 25, 2013, President Obama said the following:

> The 12 warmest years in recorded history have all come in the last 15 years. Last year, temperatures in some areas of the ocean reached record highs, and ice in the Arctic shrank to its smallest size on record—faster than most models had predicted it would. These are facts.
>
> Now, we know that no single weather event is caused solely by climate change. Droughts and fires and floods, they go back to ancient times. But we also know that in a world that's warmer than it used to be, all

weather events are affected by a warming planet. The fact that sea level in New York, in New York Harbor, are now a foot higher than a century ago—that didn't cause Hurricane Sandy, but it certainly contributed to the destruction that left large parts of our mightiest city dark and underwater.

The potential impacts go beyond rising sea levels. Here at home, 2012 was the warmest year in our history. Midwest farms were parched by the worst drought since the Dust Bowl, and then drenched by the wettest spring on record. Western wildfires scorched an area larger than the state of Maryland. Just last week, a heat wave in Alaska shot temperatures into the 90s.

And we know that the costs of these events can be measured in lost lives and lost livelihoods, lost homes, lost businesses, hundreds of billions of dollars in emergency services and disaster relief. In fact, those who are already feeling the effects of climate change don't have time to deny it—they're busy dealing with it.

Firefighters are braving longer wildfire seasons, and states and federal governments have to figure out how to budget for that. I had to sit on a meeting with the Department of Interior and Agriculture and some of the rest of my team just to figure out how we're going to pay for more and more expensive fire seasons.[130]

In stark contrast to this position stands President Trump and many of his top political appointees. According to POLITICO, few have been as publicly outspoken on the climate change issue as President Trump, who more than once has dismissed human-caused climate change as a "hoax" and claimed in January 2018 that polar ice isn't melting.[131] Trump has chosen at least 20 like-minded people to serve as agency leaders and advisers, according to a POLITICO review of his appointees' past statements on climate science. And they are already having an impact in abandoning former President Barack Obama's attempt to help unite the world against the threat of rising sea levels, worsening storms, and spreading droughts.[132]

Key Terms

Assistance to Firefighters Grant Program (AFG and FIRE) 194

Big science 187

Compound disaster 200

Cybersecurity 212

Disaster research 184

Doppler radar 206

Earthquake retrofitting 202

Emergency Alert System (EAS) 209

Enhanced Fujita Scale (EF Scale) 206

Fire Investment and Response Enhancement (FIRE) grants 193

Fukushima Daiichi nuclear power plant disaster 200

Japan Meteorological Agency (JMA) 200

Love Canal, in Niagara Falls, New York, hazardous waste incident 191

Modified Mercalli scale 204

Moment magnitude scale 203

Na-tech disasters 200

National Academies, The 184

National Earthquake Hazards Reduction Program (NEHRP) 203

National Fire Academy 193

National Flood Insurance Program (NFIP) 191

National Science Foundation (NSF) 187

National Weather Service (NWS) 206

Texas National Guardsmen assist residents affected by flooding caused by Hurricane Harvey onto a military vehicle on August 27, 2017 in Houston, Texas.

Lt. Zachary West/Army National Guard via Getty Images

6

INTERGOVERNMENTAL RELATIONS IN DISASTER POLICY

Local government provision for emergency response is critical, but responders are not the only players in emergency management and homeland security. There are those who engage in prevention, mitigation, preparedness, protection, and recovery. Many of them do not draw the spotlight of publicity that emergency responders do. Yet, their work is also vital. In the United States, government "management of major disasters" is done through intergovernmental relations or it is not addressed by government at all. One thing obvious to anyone who studies or researches U.S. disaster policy and politics is the tremendous degree of overlap, interdependence, and redundancy of American governmental jurisdictions. The U.S. Department of Homeland Security (DHS) and its Federal Emergency Management Agency (FEMA) labor to maintain emergency management partnerships with other federal agencies, state and local governments, non-profit organizations (many of which are staffed by volunteers), and the private sector, all to serve the public. DHS and its FEMA, in concert with state and local partners, strive to build and sustain a national emergency management system that is comprehensive, risk-based, and all-hazards in approach. Hazard mitigation was for many years touted as the foundation of the national emergency management system. The federal government, in combination with state and local government, is counted on to provide a rapid and effective response to, and recovery from, declared disasters. Strictly speaking, however, DHS-FEMA is not so much a disaster response organization as it is a short- and long-term recovery, preparedness, and planning body. Since 2003, when it was moved from independence to operating as a component of DHS, FEMA's portfolio of duties has expanded to include substantial terrorism security work. While mitigation continues to be an expressed goal, so too is prevention under the homeland security mantle. Thus, the federal government, in law and policy, also asks FEMA and its partnering federal agencies to help strengthen state and local emergency management and homeland security capacities.

What happens when people serving one level of government must work with people of another level of government to address a disaster or emergency? Emergency management is by its very nature intergovernmental and intercommunity—it requires government agencies and officials to coordinate and cooperate with each other on the same level (horizontally) and across hierarchical levels (vertically). It also requires that communities of people cooperate and coordinate in preparing for, and responding to, a disaster.

In the United States, many policies are implemented through intergovernmental relations. As a term, intergovernmental relations, as introduced in Chapter 1, define the interaction of federal, state, and local officials and officials of the private and nonprofit sectors, as they collectively implement public policy.[1] The term includes special district governments as well as general-purpose governments. General-purpose governments are cities, counties, towns, or other municipal jurisdictions that collect broadly based taxes to pay for a wide variety of public services. Special district governments, usually spun off from cities or counties, customarily operate to provide one or two special-ized services funded from an earmarked (dedicated) single tax or sometimes user fees.[2] Intergovernmental relations also encompasses the interaction of these bodies with groups and organizations of the nonprofit and private sectors.

On top of this, there are geopolitical factors; the United States comprises 50 states, Washington, DC (a federal district), as well as more than 3,000 county governments[3] and some 89,000 sub-state governments of every type.[4] There is even more than this.

In the Caribbean are two U.S. trust territories: Puerto Rico (since 1900) and the U.S. Virgin Islands (since 1936). Both of these will get further attention in Chapter 9, which is about the Caribbean and Gulf hurricanes of 2017.

As for the Pacific, in 1947, the United Nations created the Trust Territory of the Pacific Islands (TTPI) from former Japanese possessions given to them by a League of Nations Mandate. The TTPI was in effect from 1947 to 1986, an era when many Pacific island-ers achieved greater self-governance and so began to seek independence. The Northern

Mariana Islands is the only part of the TTPI that is still a U.S. territory. Included as a U.S. trust territory outside the TTPI is Guam (since 1898). American Samoa, possessing self-governance and a central government, is considered an "unorganized" U.S. trust territory. Since April 1983, the Marshall Islands have worked with the United States under a Compact of Free Association.[5] Palau is the smallest of the former TTPI countries. Palau declared independence in 1981 and signed a compact of free association with the United States in 1994. The Federated States of Micronesia (FSM) consists of four island groups: Yap, Chuuk, Pohnpei, and Kosrae. Like the Marshall Islands, the FSM declared independence in 1979 and signed a Compact of Free Association with the United States in 1986. The FSM compact of free association also gives Micronesians access to U.S. services and aid.[6]

To clarify, in 1986, the U.S. government declared that the Trust Territory agreements were no longer in effect (an action approved by a majority vote of the Trusteeship Council of the UN). The Federated States of Micronesia and the Republic of the Marshall Islands thus became sovereign, self-governing states with the United States responsible for their security and defense, and the Northern Mariana Islands formally became a commonwealth of the United States. As mentioned, the Republic of Palau entered into a compact of free association with the United States and became a sovereign state in 1994.[7] Almost all of these current or former U.S. trust territories retain, under terms of agreement with the United States, the right to request presidential declarations of major disaster and emergency.

ORGANIZATION OF THE CHAPTER

This chapter examines the interaction of people working within specific levels of government and between levels of government. This is a realm of intergovernmental relations (IGR) and program management. This chapter surveys the policy and politics of federal–state–local interchange. Disaster management in IGR is populated by mutual aid agreements, interstate assistance compacts, memorandums of understanding, and other preparedness and response protocols. The National Response Plan (NRP), recast in December 2007 as the National Response Framework (NRF), and its tactical application, the National Incident Management System (NIMS), are discussed.[8] In June 2016, building on the example of the 2013 National Disaster Recovery Framework (NDRF), FEMA announced the creation of a "suite of frameworks" for the National Preparedness System. Instead of two frameworks (NRF and NDRF), there would be five: protection, prevention, mitigation, response (NRF), and recovery (NDRF). Each of these were predicated on identifying reasonably expected state and local hazards and then pressing all parties to build or acquire the capabilities necessary to address them.

The suites approach is both momentous and ambitious because all five frameworks were to be integrated with one another rather than evolved as separate stand-alone planning measures. The suites approach also denotes the intricate marriage of homeland security and federal emergency management. Homeland security policy today manifests itself as a colossal intergovernmental, multiagency, multimission enterprise fueled by widely distributed, but often highly conditional, federal program grants to state and local governments. Planning in homeland security is more than simply reorganization or realignment of existing functions; it is a formal embodiment of the federal government's official response to the 9/11/01 terror attacks and to subsequent terror incidents domestically. The mash-up of counter-terror and emergency management missions under this national preparedness schema will have long-running implications for both homeland security and emergency management authorities.

Also considered in this chapter are two hugely important nongovernmental players in disaster management: voluntary organizations and government **contractors (for-profit)** and **contractors (nonprofit)** that engage in disaster management work. Many of these entities are retained and reimbursed for their work by federal, state, or local governments.

INTERGOVERNMENTAL PROGRAM MANAGEMENT

America has a highly decentralized federal system, which under the U.S. Constitution affords the national government a range of authority, with some powers reserved for the states under the Tenth Amendment.[9] America's federal and state governments share authority concurrently in some domains, such as in the regulation of business, education policy, health care, and corrections.

In U.S. emergency management, shared authority is not supposed to be a **top-down command and control system**[10] (see the "Tell Me More" 6-1 box).

TELL ME MORE 6-1
NATIONAL URBAN SEARCH & RESCUE RESPONSE SYSTEM)

A great example of American intergovernmental cooperation in disaster management is the National Urban Search & Rescue Response System, established under the authority of the Federal Emergency Management Agency in 1989. It is a basis for organizing federal, state and local partner emergency response teams as integrated federal disaster response task forces.

The system's 28 Urban Search & Rescue (US&R) Task Forces, complete with skilled and highly trained responders possessing necessary tools, equipment, and funding, can be deployed by FEMA to assist state and local governments in rescuing survivors of structural collapse incidents or to assist in other search and rescue missions.[11]

The 28 task forces are located across every region of the continental United States. Any task force can be activated and deployed by FEMA to a disaster area to provide assistance in structural collapse rescue, or they may be pre-positioned when a major disaster threatens a community. Each task force must mobilize all its personnel and equipment within four hours of activation if traveling by ground or arrive at the embarkation point within six hours of activation if being transported by air so that it can conduct life saving as quickly as possible.[12]

National Urban Search & Rescue Response System Task Forces

A Type I task force is made up of 70 multifaceted, cross-trained personnel who serve in six major functional areas. They are search, rescue, medical, hazardous materials, logistics, and planning. This task force also includes technical specialists such as physicians, structural engineers, and handlers for canine search teams. A task force is able to conduct physical search and heavy rescue operations in damaged or collapsed reinforced concrete buildings. Each task force can be divided into two 35-member teams to provide 24-hour search and rescue operations. The task forces can also be configured as a Type III US&R task force for searching lighter construction usually encountered in weather-related events such as hurricanes and tornados. Self-sufficient for the initial 72 hours, the task forces are equipped with convoy vehicles to support over-the-road deployments.[13] There are four categories of US&R task forces.[14]

Hurricane Harvey Deployment of US&R Teams

The Federal Emergency Management Agency activated over a dozen Urban Search and Rescue task forces in the wake of Hurricane Harvey's devastation in Texas. There was available a total of 27 US&R teams. In an article written at the time Harvey reportedly struck, "Texas Task Force 1 (TX-TF 1) was activated early last week as forecasters found that Harvey would cause extensive damage. On Friday, US&R assets from Missouri (MO-TF 1), Ohio (OH-TF-1), Tennessee 1 (TN-TF 1), and Utah (UT-TF 1) were activated to assist in south Texas. Eighty members of TN-TF 1 left Memphis just after midnight and a 47-person Type III team from MO-TF departed with over 100,000 pounds of equipment. All eight of California's Urban Search and Rescue Task Forces have been activated to respond to Texas."[15]

"Orange County Fire Authorities make up CA-TF5 and the Type-III Urban Search and Rescue team was activated Friday. Los Angeles City's CA-TF 1 and Oakland's CA-TF 4 deployed with 80 personnel each on Type-I State/National Urban Search & Rescue Task Forces. Forty-five members assigned to San Diego City's CA-TF 8 formed a Type-III State/National Urban Search and Rescue Task Force to respond to Texas."[16]

The article added, "New York Task Force 1, comprised of FDNY and NYPD members, set out to respond to a staging point in San Antonio early Sunday." It offered this quote: "We are set up for all types of rescues, including swiftwater rescue," said FDNY Battalion Chief and NY-TF 1 Task Force Leader Jack Flatley. "We have a compilation of tools that include boats, motors, dry suits, rescue equipment for collapsed structures, rope equipment for confined spaces, and a large compilation of Haz-Mat equipment and tools. We're also supplied with a large, self-sufficient cache of food and supplies that make us sustainable for up to 72 hours in a row. I believe we're ready to face any danger." Flatley added, "We are trained to save lives before patients are extricated from natural or man-made disasters. Our role in Texas is to provide medical care, to take care of civilians and the task force members," FDNY Rescue Paramedic Silvana Uzcategui said. "We're in the disaster zone. We're expecting torrential rains, winds, floods, and chaotic conditions. We're ready for it."[17]

A 45-person team from Pennsylvania Task Force 1 (PA-TF 1) was ordered to stage in Fort Worth Sunday. "The images coming out of Texas are heartbreaking and difficult to imagine," said Pennsylvania governor Tom Wolf. "We know that this will be a long-term response and recovery effort, and Pennsylvania stands ready to provide whatever help we can to citizens and first responders in Texas or any other state impacted by the storm."[18]

Fairfax County, VA, Fire Rescue Department will send a 14-person team with water rescue equipment as part of VA-TF 1. A 14-person National Incident Support Team from California was sent out Friday.[19]

DHS-FEMA cannot, and the previously independent FEMA before it could not, "command" state and local officials in matters of emergency management.[20] Instead, there is supposed to be a **bottom-up approach**, wherein local political subdivisions (cities, towns, villages, boroughs, and counties, etc.) are primarily responsible for emergency management, unless those governments have been overwhelmed by the disaster or emergency.

Moreover, in some states, local governments, although they are legally vestiges of their respective state governments, are sometimes accorded certain powers under **home rule** provisions under the state constitution, or through enabling statutes. This underscores the need for multiagency and multijurisdictional coordination in emergency management work. However, many presidential and DHS initiatives in this homeland security era have reintroduced **command and control strategies** under which federal officials get to assume top-down leadership positions, and state and local authorities are expected to submit.[21] Owing to competition between homeland "defense" interests and homeland "security" interests, both seeking political attention and resources, military command-and-control type organizational arrangements have found their way into many realms of emergency management.

A well-coordinated and well-managed intergovernmental approach to disaster often involves a vast number of government-to-government arrangements, agency-to-agency memorandums of understanding (MOUs), interstate compacts, and pre-disaster preparedness and response agreements. Coordination of all of these public, private, and nonprofit organizations is a core purpose of emergency management.

Federal–State Agreements

From 1979 to 2003, the FEMA relationship with states and localities was primarily through agreements with state offices of emergency management and then, by extension, with local emergency management offices. FEMA allocated certain program grant funds to state offices of emergency management, and those offices in turn passed some or most of this funding onto local offices of emergency management. States, for better or worse, were the chief points of contact for most local governments seeking federal emergency management funding. This remained so even after 9/11 and into the era of homeland security.

Today, much as in the past, FEMA success in carrying out its missions is directly related to its success in interagency and intergovernmental coordination. Today's FEMA has authority, funding, and some assets but must depend on other federal departments and agencies to provide additional resources to ensure a complete federal response. Many assume that it is the job of FEMA to physically deliver most or all forms of federal assistance in a president-declared major disaster or emergency. This is incorrect. The job of FEMA is to plan, prepare, and respond to disasters in a way that functionally coordinates, or helps to coordinate, the provision of federal resources, human-power, and equipment possessed by "other" federal departments, agencies, and offices. Relatedly, it is the job of FEMA to help harmonize the delivery of federal resources and services to state and local governments, as well as to participating nonprofit voluntary organizations and retained **private, for-profit contractors**, under the NRF and NIMS.

In the 1990s, FEMA generated many new **federal–state agreements** under the agency's response to the second-round National Performance Review, a Clinton administration effort spearheaded by Vice President Al Gore aimed at reinventing federal government so that it would work better and cost less. Director James Lee Witt declared, "A centerpiece of our reinvention is changing the way in which we do business with the States by empowering them through **Performance Partnerships**."[22] FEMA asked state officials to integrate disparate programs into multiyear, risk-based agreements signed by the president and their respective governors. FEMA funding to the states was to be consolidated into two streams, one pre-disaster and the other post-disaster. FEMA authorities expected this to reduce state agency reportage to the federal agency. State officials also hoped that this might reduce what they perceived as FEMA micromanagement of existing grant processes. Federal–state agreements continue to be part of major disaster or emergency declarations, and they are a necessary component of the FEMA-administered Fire Management Assistance Grant (FMAG) (see the "Tell Me More" 6-2 box).

With regard to the post-disaster stream of agreements, the FEMA-State Agreement is central. The FEMA-State Agreement is "a formal, legal document between FEMA and the affected state that describes the understandings, commitments, and binding conditions for assistance applicable as the result of the major disaster or emergency declared by the president. It is signed by the FEMA Regional Director and the Governor."[23]

TELL ME MORE 6-2
FEMA'S FMAG AGREEMENT WITH THE STATE OF NEW MEXICO

New Mexico, like many southwest states, has a mild, arid or semi-arid, continental climate with low annual rainfall amounts, low humidity, and abundant sunshine. This makes it vulnerable to wildland fires. Some of these become, or threaten to become, disastrous if they burn into neighborhoods, communities, and localities. Under such circumstances, the (Governor of the) state of New Mexico may request a Fire Management Assistance Grant (FMAG) by filing the request with the FEMA Region VI office (the FEMA region that includes the state of New Mexico). Below is an excerpt of a 2017 agreement between FEMA and New Mexico. This DHS-FEMA document was chosen because it is typical of many such FEMA-State agreements. Each FEMA region director has authority to receive, review, and ultimately approve or reject governor requests for FMAG funding. Unlike major disaster and emergency declarations, FMAG declaration requests do not require presidential approval.

According to FEMA, "Fire Management Assistance is available to States, local and tribal governments, for the mitigation, management, and control of fires on publicly- or privately-owned forests or grasslands, which threaten such destruction as would constitute a major disaster. The Fire Management Assistance declaration process is initiated when a state submits a request for assistance to the Federal Emergency Management Agency (FEMA) Regional Director at the time a 'threat of major disaster' exists. The entire process is accomplished on an expedited basis and a FEMA decision is rendered in a matter of hours."[24] The FMAG "Program provides a 75 percent federal cost share and the state pays the remaining 25 percent for actual costs. Before a grant can be awarded, a State must demonstrate that total eligible costs for the declared fire meet or exceed either the individual fire cost threshold—which it applies to single fires, or the cumulative fire cost threshold, which recognizes numerous smaller fires burning throughout a State."[25] Eligible firefighting costs may include expenses for field camps; equipment use, repair and replacement; tools, materials and supplies; and mobilization and demobilization activities.[26]

FEMA-STATE AGREEMENT-2017: FIRE MANAGEMENT ASSISTANCE GRANT PROGRAM

STATE OF NEW MEXICO

I. PURPOSE AND BACKGROUND

This is the annual FEMA-State Agreement for the Fire Management Assistance Grant (FMAG) Program (the Agreement) under Section 420 of the Robert T. Stafford Disaster Relief and Emergency Assistance Act (the Stafford Act), 42 U.S.C. § 5187; in accordance with Title 44 of the Code of Federal Regulations (44 CFR) § 204.25 (FEMA-State

(Continued)

(Continued)

Agreement for fire management assistance grant program). The State must have signed an up-to-date FEMA-State Agreement before receiving federal funding for grant assistance under approved requests for FMAG Declarations. This Agreement between the United States of America through the Regional Administrator, Federal Emergency Management Agency (FEMA), Department of Homeland Security (DHS), and the State of New Mexico (State or Recipient) through the Governor governs all federal assistance FEMA provides the State for all FMAG Declarations approved pursuant to 44 CFR Part 204 (Fire Management Assistance Grant Program) throughout the calendar year 2017 which will be incorporated by amendment to this Agreement.

II. GENERAL PROVISIONS

A. GRANT AWARD PACKAGE.

Any federal grant award package issued under this Agreement will consist of this Agreement, the incorporated FMAG Declarations, and the Application for Federal Assistance (Standard Form (SF) 424), including Assurances- Non-Construction Programs (SF-4248) submitted by the State for each approved FMAG Declaration.

B. FEMA RESPONSIBILITIES.

FEMA may provide to the State funds in the form of federal grant assistance to support FMAG Program activity as authorized under Section 420 of the Stafford Act (42 U.S.C. §5187), and FMAG Declarations approved under this Agreement.

C. STATE RESPONSIBILITIES.

1. The State agrees to comply with the Federal grant award terms and conditions set forth in the FMAG Declarations and this Agreement.

2. The State legislative authority for firefighting is found in Section 68-2-8 NMSA 1978.

3. The State agrees to be the Recipient for all federal financial assistance provided under Section 420 of the Stafford Act (42 U.S.C. § 5187), the FMAG Declarations, and this Agreement.

    a. The State is accountable for the use of the funds provided.

    b. Department of Homeland Security and Emergency Management (NM) will serve as the Recipient.

    c. All other State Agencies applying for federal assistance will be designated as subrecipients.

4. The State agrees to serve as the "pass-through entity" with respect to the State's role in providing subawards and administering grant assistance provided to subrecipients.

    a. Recipient and pass-through entity have the same meaning as "Grantee," as used in governing statutes, regulations, and FEMA guidance.

    b. A recipient is also a "non-federal entity" for grants administration purposes.

5. The State agrees to comply with, and will require all subrecipients to comply with, the requirements of all applicable laws and regulations, including the Stafford Act, Title 44 of the Code of Federal Regulations (C.F.R.) (Emergency Management and Assistance), 2 C.F.R. Part 3002 (implementing 2 CFR Part 200 (Uniform Administrative Requirements, Cost Principles, and Audit Requirements for Federal Awards)), and applicable FEMA policies and guidance. Subrecipients are defined the same as in 4a and 4b above.

6. The State is required to maintain a FEMA-approved State Mitigation Plan (SMP) in accordance with 44 CFR Part 20 I (Mitigation Planning) as a condition of receiving certain forms of Stafford Act assistance.

    a. The State must update its SMP every five years.

    b. The State must have a FEMA-approved SMP that addresses wildfire risks and mitigation as required by 44 CFR §204.5l(d)(2) to receive FMAG Assistance.

c. If the State does not have a FEMA-approved SMP as of the date of declaration of the FMAG Declaration, the State will submit its approvable SMP for FEMA review and approval within 30 days of the date of declaration. If the State fails to do so, FEMA will deny the State's application for assistance under the FMAG Declaration.

d. FEMA will not obligate funds until the SMP is approved. FEMA will cease obligating funds for open FMAG Declarations during any lapse period between expiration of the current SMP and approval of an updated SMP.[27]

FEDERAL ASSISTANCE

1. Federal assistance may be provided only for eligible costs incurred in the mitigation, management and control of a declared fire approved by FEMA for assistance and identified in a FMAG Declaration under an Attachment C Amendment to this Agreement in accordance with 44 CFR Part 204 (Fire Management Assistance Grant Program).

2. The [FEMA] Regional Administrator, in consultation with the Governor's Authorized Representative and the Principal Advisor (as appointed by the Forest Service, U.S. Department of Agriculture or the Bureau of Land Management, Department of the Interior), will establish the incident period for a declared fire. If the incident period for a declared fire extends into the next calendar year, federal assistance with respect to that fire is governed by the fire threshold and the FEMA-State Agreement in effect for the calendar year in which the incident period for the declared fire begins.

3. The State must meet the individual or cumulative fire cost threshold pursuant to 44 CFR § 204.51 (b) (Application and approval procedures for a fire management assistance grant - Fire cost threshold) prior to approval of the State's grant application (Standard Form (SF) 424, Request for Federal Assistance). The State must also have a current Administrative Plan and a FEMA-approved State Mitigation Plan (SMP) pursuant to 44 CFR Part 20 I (Mitigation Planning) and § 204.51 (d) (Application and approval procedures for a fire management assistance grant - Obligation of the grant) before FEMA approves the State's grant application.

4. Federal funding may be provided under the Stafford Act on a 75 percent Federal/25 percent non-Federal cost-sharing basis once the fire cost threshold is met.

5. The State agrees to make the non-federal cost share available.

6. All scopes of work and costs approved as a result of this Agreement, whether as estimates or final costs approved through subawards, project worksheets, or otherwise, will incorporate by reference the terms of this Agreement and must comply with applicable laws, regulations, policy and guidance in accordance with this Agreement.

As mentioned, this agreement is typical of many FEMA-State agreements. It formalizes the federal–state relationship and stipulates the legal responsibilities, duties, and obligations of each party. It also makes it easier for both FEMA and New Mexico because it sets forth understandings and obligations of each party in a pre-disaster environment. Such agreements pave the way for rapid FEMA approvals, and all such pacts are subject to annual renewal and revision by either or both parties. If one inspects the history of FMAGs, a sizable share has been issued on a precautionary basis and did not generate federal spending.

Governors and state emergency managers benefit from DHS-FEMA technical aid and financial help. However, governors and state legislators cannot afford to commit state resources to emergency management on an open-ended basis. Governors do have some degree of political influence in shaping the policies and operations of the federal government. Governors who believe they are being obligated by FEMA to do too much for too little support may press their arguments directly to the president or Congress. Moreover, in the 1990s, owing to insufficient "between" disaster grant funding, FEMA officials faced challenges in encouraging governors, state lawmakers, and state administrators to commit to growing and improving their state emergency management. The success or failure of FEMA programs before the 9/11 terror attacks rested on negotiated partnerships with states sweetened only by very modest infusions of federal funds "between" disasters for certain state and local preparedness and mitigation activities. However, if one examines presidential declarations of major disaster and emergency issued over any five-year interval since 1989, almost every state, including the District of Columbia, eligible U.S. Trust Territories, as well as Commonwealth and Free Association Compact states, has received at least one federal declaration over that time. Consequently, the federal-state agreements established under those declarations was another path of FEMA-State interchange.

The FEMA of April 1, 1979, through February 28, 2003, had, and the DHS-FEMA from March 1, 2003, through now has, specific intergovernmental relations goals. FEMA is expected to establish and maintain an emergency management partnership with other federal agencies, state and local governments, volunteer organizations, and the private sector (e.g., government contractors, corporate-owned public utilities, disaster service industry firms) to better serve their mission. Federal agencies are expected to establish, in concert with their state and local partners, a national emergency management system that is comprehensive, risk-based, and all-hazards in approach. They are expected to make hazard mitigation the foundation of the national emergency management system.[28] They are supposed to provide a rapid and effective response to, and recovery from, declared disasters. They are asked to strengthen state and local capacity to carry out emergency management duties. The original NRF, today one of the suite of five national frameworks under the National Preparedness System, plus the National Incident Management System (NIMS), has advanced these intergovernmental goals, principles, and doctrines. Collectively, state governments and their respective state emergency management and/or homeland security agencies, and a great many local governments with their own emergency management agencies, have immensely greater capacity to undertake emergency management work today than they did 20 or more years ago. Many of these subnational emergency management bodies have become better staffed, trained, educated, professionalized, equipped (often with cutting-edge technology), and funded thanks to more state and local budgeted dollars as well as infusions of federal homeland security and emergency management funding.

The Political Geography of FEMA

The FEMA of today, just as for the FEMA operating from 1979 to 2002, is divided geographically into 10 standard federal regions, and each region office is directed by a politically appointed (or acting) regional director. See DHS-**FEMA standard federal regions** in Figure 6-1.

FIGURE 6-1 ■ DHS-FEMA Ten Federal Regions with Respective Region Headquarters City

Source: Federal Emergency Management Agency, "Regional Contacts," https://www.fema.gov/fema-regional-contacts (accessed May 15, 2018).

Region offices allow DHS-FEMA to decentralize some operations geographically. Officials in these regional offices have an opportunity to become familiar with their respective set of state and local counterparts who engage in emergency management. Good working relationships of the individual directors and the governors in their respective regions often help facilitate emergency preparedness and response to disasters and emergencies.

Capable FEMA **regional administrators** and personnel sometimes contribute mightily to emergency management work in their regions, particularly when they work well with federal coordinating officers (FCOs) nominated by DHS-FEMA and appointed by the president to manage active major disasters and emergencies declared in their respective regions. Correspondingly, indifferent, inexperienced, or incompetent regional directors and officials sometimes muddle disaster management work. Some region directors who owe their appointment to their campaign support of the president and who have little disaster management experience encounter difficulties in their work. Region directors who make little effort to engage governors, mayors, and other key elected or administrative officials of their region, or who behave in a partisanly biased fashion, sometimes bungle federal response and sour federal relationships with state and local elected officials and emergency managers.

The Impact of 9/11 on Federal–State Relations

The terror attacks of September 11, 2001, had profound and surprising effects on FEMA federal–state relations. Under the new homeland security regime, FEMA both suffered and prospered. DHS, which began its formation in late 2002, was a major national policy response to 9/11. It poured 22 federal agencies (one of them FEMA) into a new department that would incorporate about 180,000 federal workers. By September 2017, DHS had grown to 240,000 workers.[29] Many of these federal organizations had vastly more personnel and much larger budgets than did FEMA.[30] When FEMA was plunged into a sea of larger and more politically influential federal agencies, it suffered and so did its relations with states.

The federal government recruited state and local governments into the war on terror.[31] This may have been done because the first official emergency responders to almost every disaster are state and local emergency responders. This was especially so on 9/11 when emergency responders, most particularly firefighters and police officers, turned out to confront explosive jetliner impacts at New York's World Trade Center, at the Pentagon in Arlington, Virginia, and at Shanksville, Pennsylvania.

In the United States, "registered fire departments are staffed by approximately 1,218,300 personnel. This includes career, volunteer and paid per call firefighters as well as civilian staff and nonfirefighting personnel. There was a total of 1,066,700 active career, volunteer and paid per call firefighters representing nearly 88 percent of the registered departments' personnel. Of the active firefighting personnel, 33 percent were career firefighters, 55 percent were volunteer firefighters, and 12 percent were paid per call firefighters."[32]

There are also some 900,000 sworn state and local police officers,[33] as well as a huge number and assortment of physicians, nurses, and other emergency medical personnel. The intergovernmental integration of these professionals and their agencies is being accomplished through massive federal, state, and local planning efforts, through information sharing, and through a profusion of heavily funded antiterrorism programs, a share of which involve FEMA.

In theory, many of the war on terror initiatives should have worked to the advantage of FEMA, in part because FEMA was one of the few DHS "legacy agencies" to have worked closely and often with governors and local leaders and with state and local emergency managers—many of the latter experienced in law enforcement, firefighting, emergency medicine, and public works. However, in its early DHS years, the rush to yoke and refashion all of the new department's component organizations into a massive antiterrorism assemblage had the effect of stripping FEMA of some of its most capable people. Many senior FEMA officials were reassigned, some by choice, to other posts in DHS, and some of these new but often prestigious jobs had little to do with emergency management.

When devising The Homeland Security Act of 2002, Congress and the first-term G. W. Bush administration did not fully consider the varied legally mandated **nonterrorism missions** of the agencies folded into DHS. Such mistakes are not without precedent. Many presidential administrations and Congresses have had a penchant for meeting new acute policy needs by re-tasking and realigning federal administrative entities. Policymakers give the impression that a new problem, need, or threat has been addressed but at "little or no additional cost" to the national taxpayer.[34] This tactic also supplies the public reassurance that the federal workforce will not have to grow to meet the challenge. Among the implications of this ploy are added work burdens for federal employees and an increase in government contracting to help meet new and old needs at the same time.

States and Their Homeland Security and Emergency Management Organizations

Before 9/11, federal and state emergency managers bonded through modestly funded "between disaster" federal grant programs and through their occasional, or sometimes regular, work on presidentially declared major disasters and emergencies (where federal funding and other aid was often substantial). After 9/11, many states found it advantageous to form their own state homeland security departments. These organizations typically competed for staff and funding with state emergency management offices and other state organizations. The National Guard or a state military department serves as the overhead organization for emergency management or homeland security, or both in some 14 states: Alaska, Arizona, Hawaii, Idaho, Kansas, Kentucky, Maine, Maryland, Montana, Oregon, South Carolina, Washington State, West Virginia, and Wisconsin (see gray shaded blocks of Table 6-1 to see states with HS and/or EM embodied in a military department). On account of this, emergency management in those states may, or may not, be dominated by military approaches. Therefore, some of these states may have been better prepared for military-oriented federal homeland security than were states whose emergency or homeland security managers worked outside the National Guard–dominant model. However, National Guard or Military Department-dominant states often incorporated fully civilian emergency management offices such that the only military link was at the top through the head of the state National Guard, ordinarily the state adjutant general. In addition, there has been a trend in many states to move emergency management and homeland security out of military departments. Some states embed EM and/or HS in their state police or public safety departments. Some states have combined HS and EM in different ways. Many give their EM agency HS responsibilities, or within their EM agency they set forth a section or branch that handles HS. A few others do the opposite and give their HS agency some EM duties. Many have attempted to fuse or link up their HS and EM components, occasionally as co-equal partners.

When all 50 states are considered three things are obvious. First, HS and EM are regularly targets of state reorganization and so are often in flux. Second, unsurprisingly there are disputes about which department (and which interest group) will house HS, EM, or both. Also, some governors insist on maintaining a direct organizational line to their emergency management and homeland security offices, evident when the agency's title begins "The Governor's Office of-." State legislators are also critically important in determining where and how HS and EM jurisdiction will be organized in their respective states. Senior lawmakers may not want a reorganization to weaken the jurisdictional scope of the committees they lead or serve on. Conversely, others may see an opportunity to pull more jurisdiction into their respective committees via creation of a new HS or EM department or agency. Third, for state governments collectively, there is a very gradual trend away from assigning state EM and HS duties to military departments. This change, however, only moves at the pace that state laws are passed and signed to effect reforms.

TABLE 6-1 ■ The 50 States and DC—Homeland Security and Emergency Management Organizations[35]

	State & DC as of 7/8/2018	Combined Homeland Security and Emergency Management State Department or Division (EM) (HS)	Stand alone Homeland Security Unit (HS=Homeland Sec.)	Stand alone Emergency Management Unit (EM=Emergency Mgt.)	Other key state agencies or overhead departments denotes State Military Dept. (PS=Public Safety)
1	Alabama		AL Dept of HS	Alabama EM Agency	HS in AL Law Enforce. Agency
2	Alaska	Alaska Div. of HS & EM			in Dept. Military & Vet Affairs
3	Arizona		AZ Dept of HS	AZ Dept of Military & EM	AZ Dept of Public Safety
4	Arkansas		ADEM handles HS	Ark. Dept of EM (ADEM)	
5	California		CA-OES has HS Office	Gov's Off. of Emer Svs.OES	
6	Colorado	Colorado Div HS & EM			both in Dept of Public Safety
7	Connecticut	CT-Div of HS & Div of EM			both in Dept of Emer Services
8	Delaware			DE-EM Agency (DEMA)	in Dept of Safety and HS
9	Dist. of Columbia	DC-HS & EM Agency			
10	Florida		FL Dept of Law Enf.	Florida Div of EM	
11	Georgia	Georgia EM & HS Agency			
12	Hawaii			Hawaii EM Agency	Hawaii Dpt of Defense, Adj Gen
13	Idaho			Idaho Office of EM	EM in Idaho Military Division
14	Illinois			IL EM Agency, also does HS	
15	Indiana	Indiana Dept of HS			Dept of HS has Emer Resp Div.
16	Iowa	Iowa Dept of HS & EM			
17	Kansas			KS Div of EM	in Adj Gen Dept.

18	Kentucky		KY Office of HS	KY Div of EM	EM in KY Dept of Military Affairs
19	Louisiana	LA Gov's Office HS & Emer Prep.			Part of State Police
20	Maine			Maine EM Agency	Dept Defense, Veterans, & EM
21	Maryland			Maryland EM Agency	in Maryland Dept of Military
22	Massachusetts		Mass. Div of HS	Mass. EM Agency	Div of HS part of State Police
23	Michigan	Mich. Div of HS & Div of EM			Divs HS&EM part of State Police
24	Minnesota	MN Div of HS & EM			HS&EM Div. in Dept Pub. Safety
25	Mississippi		Miss. Office of HS	Mississippi EM Agency	HS Office in Dept Public Safety
26	Missouri		Missouri-Office of HS	Missouri State EM Agency	EM & HS in Dept Public Safety
27	Montana			MT Disaster & Emer Services	in Dept of Military Affairs
28	Nebraska			Nebraska EM Agency	
29	Nevada			NV Div of EM has HS unit	in NV Dept of Public Safety
30	New Hampshire	NH - HS & EM Agency		NH-Bureau of EM in PS Dept	HS&EM in Dept of Public Safety
31	New Jersey		HS in NJ State Police (SP)	Office of EM in State Police	SP in Dept Law & Public Safety
32	New Mexico	NM Dept of HS & EM			
33	New York	NYS Div of HS & Emer Svs.		NYS Office of EM in DHSES	Off. of Counter Terror in DHSES

(Continued)

TABLE 6-1 ■ (Continued)

	State & DC as of 7/8/2018	Combined Homeland Security and Emergency Management State Department or Division (EM) (HS)	Stand alone Homeland Security unit (HS=Homeland Sec.)	Stand alone Emergency Management (EM=Emergency Mgt.)	Other key state agencies or overhead departments denotes State Military Dept. (PS=Public Safety)
34	North Carolina		NC Highway Patrol	NC Div. of EM	HS&EM in Dept of Public Safety
35	North Dakota		HS inside Dept EM Svs	ND Dept of EM Services	HS&EM divisions in NDDES
36	Ohio		Ohio. Div of HS	Ohio Div. of EM	HS&EM in Dept of Public Safety
37	Oklahoma		OK Office of HS	Oklahoma Dept of EM	
38	Oregon		OR has an HS Council	Oregon Office of EM	part of Oregon Military Dept.
39	Pennsylvania		Governors Off. of HS	PA EM Agency (PEMA)	
40	Rhode Island		State Fusion Center	RI-EM Agency	
41	South Carolina		Law Enforcement Div	SC-EM Division (SCEMD)	both part of Adj. Generals Off.
42	South Dakota		SD Homeland Security	South Dakota Office of EM	HS&EM in Dept of Public Safety
43	Tennessee		TN Office of HS	TN EM Agency	both in Dept. of Safety and HS
44	Texas		TX HS in PSC	Div. of EM Dpt. Pub Safety	HS in Public Safety Comm. (PSC)
45	Utah		Utah EM has HS Div.	UT Division of EM (D-E-M)	EM in Utah Dept of Public Safety
46	Vermont		HS Unit	Vermont EM	HS&EM in Dept of Public Safety
47	Virginia		VA-HS Division	Virginia Dept of EM	HS&EM in Secretariat PS & HS
48	Washington State			Wash. Div. of EM	in WA Military Department
49	West Virginia	WV Div. of HS & EM			in Dept of Military Affairs & PS
50	Wisconsin			Wisc. Div. of EM, does HS	EM in WI Dpt of Military Affairs
51	Wyoming		Wyoming Office of HS	WY HS handles EM work	

The lure of massive federal grants made available in the years after the 9/11 attacks of 2001, many tremendously larger than the between-disaster funding the federal government had offered in the past, impelled all governors and state legislatures to rethink their state disaster management organization. In their quest to take on more homeland security functions and to better qualify for DHS grants (i.e., some of which included FEMA), governors and state lawmakers had to decide how they wanted their state offices organized. How much priority would be given to state homeland security? How would state homeland security programs be organized? As is common when the federal government creates new departments and programs in the wake of a crisis, initial federal funding to state counterpart programs is generous but then begins a gradual decline, especially if the original crisis is unrepeated. Regardless, federal funding of state homeland security programs each year remains substantial and far larger than between-disaster emergency management funding to states in the decades before 2001.

It is remarkable that approximately 15 states operate combined HS and EM departments or divisions (see Table 6-1). Some 13 states house HS, EM, or both in their Public Safety Departments. Police, Highway Patrol, and/or law enforcement agencies assume a high profile in Florida's HS, Louisiana's HS and EM, Massachusetts's HS, Michigan's HS and EM, New Jersey's HS and EM, North Carolina's HS, and in South Carolina's HS. Presumably, departmental status represents the peak for a state government public administrative entity. Arkansas, Florida, Montana, North Dakota, Oklahoma, and Virginia have department-level state emergency management agencies. Similarly, Alabama and Arizona each have a Department of Homeland Security.

What is quite interesting is that collectively state HS and EM entities are an organizational menagerie. The threads of EM and HS flow through the 50-state assemblage. When HS and/or EM reside within a state department as divisions, offices, services, or agencies, two questions must be answered. First, how self-contained is the HS and EM unit? In other words, are these units largely independent of their overhead departments? Or, are they treated subserviently and largely put to work on matters outside their primary jurisdiction? Second, to what degree does the culture of the overhead department penetrate the embedded HS and EM units. This is not a trivial matter. For example, military dominated offices may look to staff their HS or EM offices with military veterans or state National Guard members.

Law enforcement and police overhead departments may deliberately favor lawyers (prosecutors) or retired police officers in their recruiting. Emergency medicine dominant departments may look for former public health or EMS workers. Several state Public Safety departments (PSD) give high priority to their fire service components and this is reflected in their recruitment and appointments. This may work to the advantage of current or former firefighters when they seek positions in the PSD's homeland security and emergency management units.

Outside of the personnel issue, equally important is state budgeting of HS and EM entities. When either or both of these appear far down in the overhead department's annual or bi-annual budget request, what are the ramifications? A perennial budgeting question of intergovernmental relations is, if the state HS, EM, or combined HS and EM entity received "no federal funding," would the state continue to fund it with its own revenue? In researching state HS and EM, it became apparent that many state HS and EM workers were 100 percent federally paid. If this is common, what does this infer about a state's commitment to HS and EM?

Table 6-1 shows state homeland security, emergency management, and other agencies for each of the 50 states and the District of Columbia. This research examined posted state government websites that pertain to state emergency management, state homeland security, or both. The research began by drawing from a DHS state government contact list but had to extend beyond that owing to errors or state governmental changes taking place since the DHS list was compiled. Care must be taken in interpreting Table 6-1 findings. Some states merely added "homeland security" to the title of their respective state emergency management agency. Others moved and fused various state offices to form their combined HS and EM organizations. The states that have organizationally fused homeland security and emergency management have mimicked the DHS-FEMA model of organization, albeit without necessarily subsuming emergency management under homeland security. Fused HS and EM entities also may not include all, or even most, of what DHS non-FEMA offices do.

A surprising 22 states have distinct homeland security organizations and 19 of these also had emergency management stand-alone organizations. Another way to look at findings is that 30 states had emergency management stand-alone organizations and of these 19 also had separate homeland security units. What is interesting here is that homeland security and emergency management are kept on two organizational tracks in nearly half of the states. Again, although organizationally distinct, many state HS and EM offices may work closely with one another, particularly in matters of grant application and management links to DHS and DHS-FEMA.

Nine states operate with only a state emergency management agency: Arkansas, Delaware, Kansas, Maryland, Massachusetts, Montana, Oregon, Rhode Island, and Washington State. Utah is the only state with an exclusive homeland security department and no other state emergency management unit or related office (other category). Not to be overlooked is that 11 states have entries in the "Other Key State Agencies" category. Moreover, Arizona and New Jersey host three homeland security/emergency management agencies or offices.

Some qualifications are necessary. States with "emergency management offices only" may have taken on homeland security duties related to emergency management. A Library of Congress report in 2007 disclosed that nine states and the U.S. Virgin Islands assign their respective state adjutant general with leadership of combined or separate HS and EM duties.[36] The same report reveals that in four states with separate HS and EM offices, those offices are led by the same director (civilian) director: Colorado, Georgia, Montana, and Oregon.[37] Chapter 7 will provide more information about state adjutant generals and their duties in homeland security and emergency management.

The Stakes for States

The absorption of FEMA into DHS in 2003 meant that the small, previously independent, federal agency had to find its place in a new department populated by many larger, as well as smaller, organizations—each of these with their own supportive political interests and clientele groups. FEMA also had to defend itself in **bureaucratic "turf wars"** with these sister DHS organizations. From 2003 to 2005, FEMA under DHS lost much of its jurisdiction over mitigation and recovery disaster management functions. However, the Post-Katrina Emergency Management Reform Act (PKEMRA) of 2006 ironically proved to be a godsend for FEMA. The 2006 law, and the assent of presidents George W. Bush and Barack Obama, enabled a reconstitution of FEMA. Several parts of its lost jurisdiction and staff were returned to the agency, most particularly, the authority to dispense its own program grants without having to work through a DHS grants clearinghouse unit outside of FEMA as it did from 2002 to 2006.

By January 2017, after President Trump's inauguration, DHS-FEMA was healthy, able to issue and administer many of its grant programs, and reinvigorated by many young new hires. Just as with every change of administration, the Trump White House went to work on replacing Obama DHS-FEMA appointees with Trump administration appointees. However, turnover and problems in Trump's transition team, combined with stalwart opposition from Senate Democrats, dramatically slowed Senate confirmation of his DHS and FEMA appointees. As indicated previously, W. Brock Long, Trump's nominee to head FEMA, and currently FEMA's administrator, was not confirmed by the Senate until June 2017, a full four months after Trump took office. Over 2017 and 2018, there has been a preponderance of Republican governors (33 R, 16 D, 1 Indep.), and inasmuch as candidate Trump narrowly beat Hillary Clinton in the 2016 presidential election, the new president may have thought it wise to continue approving governor requests for declarations at the pace his predecessor did. Moreover, Donald Trump is a self-avowed builder who sees great benefits and economic gain in both new and renovated commercial structures. This too may have motivated him to fast-track FEMA-recommended governor declarations to his Oval Office desk for his signature.

TELL ME MORE 6-3

A STATE AND LOCAL "WHO GETS WHAT" UNDER A PRESIDENTIAL DECLARATION

What can states and localities expect in the way of federal disaster relief? "The Stafford Act designates the universe of eligible applicants"[38] (e.g., states, and local governments, owners of certain private nonprofit facilities, individuals, families). However, not all persons or entities affected by a disaster are guaranteed federal disaster assistance when the president issues a declaration.

FEMA officials must recommend the categories of assistance to be made available before the president decides whether to issue a major disaster or emergency declaration. If any president decides to issue an approval, he or she may heed FEMA advice regarding aid categories or the president may add or deny FEMA-suggested aid categories, although this author has no evidence that any president has denied a FEMA-suggested

aid category but issued an approval anyway. However, presidential declarations are sometimes issued that deny governors one or more categories of assistance but that approve others.[39] Persons and organizations (including state and local governments) must make application to FEMA and other federal agencies for certain aid made available in the approved categories.

It is the job of FEMA and other federal agencies to ascertain that the applicant is eligible for the categorical aid for which they have applied. FEMA and other federal agencies accepting and processing applicant requests must determine that these requests are valid. FEMA, like many federal agencies tasked with issuing federal assistance on an expedited basis, is challenged to process applications as quickly as possible but

(Continued)

(Continued)

at the same time authenticate claims made so as not to issue funds to undeserving applicants or to applicants making **fraudulent claims**. Obviously, application is not necessary when FEMA and other federal agencies furnish directly to victims, or through voluntary organizations or contractors, such things as food, water, clothing, medicines, first aid, other in-kind commodities, emergency transport, and other services.

When victims seek compensation for their losses, certain rules apply. A family with adequate home or personal property insurance and alternative housing expense coverage might not be considered eligible to receive some forms of FEMA financial aid. A local government that suffers damages to some of its public facilities or infrastructure, but damage judged by FEMA officials to be insufficient under FEMA regulations and guidelines, might not receive federal funds to help subsidize rebuilding of those facilities and infrastructure. Certain non-profit organizations (e.g., owners or operators of educational or non-emergency health care facilities) may have to rely on Small Business Administration loans, not FEMA Stafford Act grants, to restore services."[40]

As Chapters 4 and 5 have made clear, the president is authorized to direct that the following types of federal disaster assistance be provided under a declaration of major disaster:

- General federal assistance for technical and advisory aid and support to state and local governments to facilitate the distribution of consumable supplies

- Essential assistance from federal agencies to distribute aid to victims through state and local governments and voluntary organizations, perform life- and property-saving assistance, clear debris from roadways, and use resources of the U.S. Department of Defense (DOD) before a major disaster or emergency declaration is issued

- Hazard Mitigation Program Grants to reduce risks and damages that might occur in future disasters

- Federal facilities repair and reconstruction

- Repair, restoration, and replacement of damaged facilities owned by state and local governments, as well as private nonprofit facilities that provide essential services, or contributions for other facilities or hazard mitigation measures in lieu of repairing or restoring damaged facilities

- Debris removal through the use of federal resources or through grants to state or local governments or owners of private nonprofit facilities

- **Individual and Household Assistance,** including financial grants to rent alternative housing, direct assistance through temporary housing units (mobile homes), limited financial assistance for housing repairs and replacement, and financial assistance for uninsured medical, dental, funeral, personal property, transportation, and other expenses

- Disaster Unemployment Assistance, as introduced in Chapter 1, to individuals out of work as a result of the major disaster, for up to 26 weeks, as long as they are not entitled to other unemployment compensation or credits

- Food coupons and food distribution for low-income households unable to purchase nutritious food

- Food commodities for emergency mass feeding

- Legal services for low-income individuals

- Crisis counseling assistance and training grants for state and local governments or private mental health organizations to provide associated services or to train disaster workers[41]

Emergency declaration assistance, as introduced in Chapter 3, to state and local governments usually makes available fewer types of assistance and less funding than major disaster declarations do. The types of assistance autho-rized to be provided under an emergency decla-ration include the following:

- Activities to support state and local emergency assistance

- Coordination of disaster relief provided by federal and nonfederal organizations

- Technical and advisory assistance to state and local governments

- Emergency assistance through federal agencies

- Debris removal through grants to state and local governments

- Grants to individuals and households for temporary housing and uninsured personal needs

- Distribution of medicine, food, and consumables[42]

The declaration process for emergencies is similar to that used for major disasters, but the criteria (based on the definition of "emergency") are less specific.[43] Also, in some cases, the president may make Individual and Household Assistance available under an emergency decla-ration, as President Obama did for the state of Texas, city of West, after a massive agrochemical plant explosion in 2013 destroyed a major portion of that unfortunate municipality.

State or Indian Tribal Government Administration of FEMA's Other Needs Assistance

If a state or Indian tribal government applies and contracts with FEMA, it may obtain permission to implement FEMA's Other Needs Assistance (ONA) sub-program (part of the Individual and Households Program), in place of FEMA, when major disasters are declared for the respective jurisdiction. In these circumstances, state and Indian tribal governments operate in place of FEMA and its workers. They must, however, demon-strate that they have created an application process as rigorous as FEMA's. Interestingly, FEMA provides state and Indian tribal governments grant funds to undertake this plus reimbursement of their administrative costs when they work a federally declared major disaster.

According to FEMA, "the delivery of Other Needs Assistance by a State/Indian Tribal Government is contingent upon an approval of a State/Indian Tribal Government 'Administrative Plan,' which describes the partnership between FEMA and the State/Indian Tribal Government for the delivery of assistance under section 408 of the Stafford Act, 42 U.S.C. 5174. If a State/Indian Tribal Government requests a grant to admin-ister Other Needs Assistance, the State/Indian Tribal Government shall develop an Administrative Plan to describe the procedures the State/Indian Tribal Government will use to administer Other Needs Assistance. All implementation procedures must be in compliance with Federal requirements and State/Indian Tribal Government laws and procedures. The Administrative Plan provides a description of the State/Indian Tribal Government's procedures for implementing Other Needs Assistance. The [FEMA] Regional Administrator and the Governor/Tribal Chief or his/her designee will exe-cute the Administrative Plan annually."[44] Such contracts are worked out before declared disasters; states and Indian tribal governments must apply for this arrangement before November 30 of each year. If approved, the contract remains in effect for a year; however, renewal of the contract from year to year is common. State and Indian tribal governments may ask FEMA to approve amendments to the contract at any time.[45]

There are several good reasons why state and Indian tribal governments benefit from such contracts. First, the Other Needs Assistance program may be more sensitively run if the state or tribal government manages the work. Those governments are closer to disaster victims than is FEMA. They are also closer to the zone of damage and can more easily judge victim needs than can a more remote federal agency. On top of this, state, local, and tribal responsiveness in implementing the ONA program becomes evident in state and local news and social media reportage. When FEMA is over-taxed by management of many large and small disasters at one time, as it often is, it makes sense that this responsibility be delegated to state and tribal governments. It relieves some of the administrative burdens imposed on FEMA workers and contractors, and it may help people in the disaster zone get local help when they must deal with impersonal ONA rules and paperwork. Moreover, approved state and tribal administrative plans represent evidence of emergency management capacity-building in disaster victim assistance.

Memorandums of Understanding

Over its history, FEMA has worked out **memorandums of understanding (MOUs)** with each respective state emergency management agency. At the same time the agency has endeavored to reduce the administrative burden it imposed on state programs and officials. For example, the Clinton FEMA routinely dispatched a representative to the staff of any governor whose state faced imminent disaster or whose state had experienced a major disaster. This was an attempt to smooth out FEMA-state relations and to ensure coordination and cooperation in their intergovernmental activities. This practice continues today.

Officials of various government agencies usually negotiate and abide by MOUs. Unless approved through a formal rulemaking process as a regulation, they usually do not have the force of law behind them and stand as voluntary agreements. Nevertheless, given the immense number of government agencies involved in a disaster response and recovery, MOUs are a tool that can help prevent "road blocks" or "bureaucratic foot-dragging."

FEMA has used MOUs as a means of negotiating agreements with a variety of federal–state–local agencies. The Disaster-Specific Memorandum of Understanding (Disaster-Specific MOU) is an agreement to be used by federal, tribal, state, and local agencies to assist and define the relationship between and among Agencies during disaster recovery efforts. For example, FEMA advises, "The Disaster-Specific MOUs are crafted so as to consider the unique circumstances that parties may face while coordinating Environmental or Historic Preservation reviews. Additionally, General Counsel should review Disaster-Specific MOUs before execution."[46]

FEMA's standard MOU template addresses environmental and historic preservation matters. It first asks applicants to insert agency names that are entered into the Memorandum of Understanding. The template then allows applicants to combine environmental and historic preservation reviews for disaster recovery projects that are associated with a presidentially declared disaster. MOUs formalize the commitments among the listed agencies enabling them to work together to facilitate uniformity, consistency, and transparency. These agreements set forth "roles and responsibilities for Lead and Cooperating Agencies, establishing interagency communication protocols (or procedures), and identifying environmental and historic preservation priorities related to this disaster."[47] This MOU "hereby commit[s] [the parties], to the extent practicable, to early involvement and cooperation so as to ensure timely decisions are made and that the responsibilities of each Party are met. The Parties commit to working together and as appropriate with Indian tribes, multistate entities, state agencies, and other interested persons. In particular, the Parties agree to:

A. Timely Coordination: Cooperating Agencies will submit reviews in accordance with the timeline for each project established by the Lead Agency with the concurrence of Cooperating Agencies.

B. Project Meetings: Parties will meet every [insert time length] to share project developments, project status, and project reviews.

C. Interagency Communication: The Cooperating Agency will notify the Lead Agency when it determines it has no related action and further participation is no longer warranted.

D. Project Development: Lead Agency, in conjunction with Cooperating Agency(ies), will provide recommendations for avoidance, minimization, and mitigation at the earliest stage possible in project development.

E. Personnel and Expertise: Cooperating Agencies will provide appropriate personnel and/or expertise to the Lead Agency, as appropriate, and as resources allow.

F. Provide Data and Studies: Cooperating Agencies will be responsible for the provision of any information necessary to complete application reviews and authorizations in accordance with the target timeline established by the Lead Agency with the concurrence of Cooperating Agencies. Lead Agencies, where appropriate, will provide information to the Cooperating Agency(ies).[48]

Mutual Aid Agreements

Mutual aid agreements are usually mandated in law and negotiated as legal contracts. Mutual aid is a prearranged agreement to provide essential resources when local resources are inadequate to meet the needs of a disaster.[49] Mutual aid agreements may or may not have a financial component.

Agencies may draw up agreements for reciprocal assistance under certain conditions or may set out contingent acquisition agreements between providers, vendors, and contractors. For example, California and Florida have elaborate mutual aid agreements and systems among their respective state and local governments. The **Emergency Management Assistance Compact (EMAC)** (discussed ahead) also provides for state-to-state mutual aid.[50]

An example of a mutual aid agreement might be a local multiagency plan regarding how the residents of a nursing home are to be evacuated during an emergency. Consider this example:

To ensure coordination among nursing homes, the committee provided mutual aid agreements to evacuating and hosting nursing homes, to be completed and included in each nursing home's disaster plan. These agreements outlined understandings between facilities operators with respect to transfer of patients and medical information, transportation costs, and so on.[51]

An agreement, however expressed, identifies which agency controls certain resources in the field and how and when they may be reassigned. Agreements help create working relationships between agency and government officials and so may build trust among these people. Mutual aid agreements are common both in conventional emergency management and in homeland security matters.

According to Morton, "Statewide mutual aid agreements vary by state. Generally, they provide for a statewide mutual aid system that covers a variety of local government entities. In addition to counties and municipalities, the system may include school districts, emergency services districts, and so forth. Agreements have been generally fashioned by state emergency management agencies with local parties that include tribes and special districts. They may establish disaster district coordination committees with representatives from district stakeholders. The statewide mutual-aid agreement covers those jurisdictions that do not have any pre-existing mutual aid agreement but does not supersede the terms of those that do. Mutual-aid systems are generally not mandatory."[52]

State-to-State Relations and Interstate Assistance Compacts

Interstate compacts and state-to-state compacts are common in the United States. **Interstate compacts** are authorized in the U.S. Constitution, need the formal state legislative approval of each member state, signify that previous states laws affected by the compact are superseded, and require approval of the U.S. Congress in law.[53] Certain forms of state-to-state agreements do not necessarily require approval of the U.S. Congress. States often derive benefits from such agreements: helps to address a problem shared with adjacent states (river pollution), promotes a common agenda (coordinate mass transit), produces a collective good (e.g., clean air, response to natural disasters, law enforcement), harmonization of policies and advancement of societal experiments, etc.

On October 9, 1996, Congress approved the Emergency Management Assistance Compact (EMAC) initiated by the Southern Governor's Association. EMAC began an agreement between 14 states and territories made during 1995 and 1996 that committed them, through their respective governors, to cooperate in planning for state-to-state extension of emergency management help. The compact was open to any state or territory that chose to join, and today all the states belong to EMAC. FEMA officials testified in favor of EMAC before Congress and FEMA is a participant endorser of the compact. FEMA, however, decides funding of EMAC operations on a case-by-case basis.

The National Emergency Management Association (NEMA), an organization representing the interests of state emergency managers through its Emergency Management Assistance Committee, moved the compact forward. EMAC represents a strong collective effort of the states to facilitate state-to-state mutual aid when major disasters and emergencies take place. In general terms, a compact represents an important intergovernmental agreement and it also indicates how political authorities provide consent for, and lawfulness to, such arrangements. For more about EMAC, see the "Tell Me More" 6-4 box.

Pre-disaster Preparedness and Response Agreements

Emergency management in the United States has evolved into a complex and, since 9/11, federally dominated latticework of preparedness and response agreements. "The Federal Response Plan (FRP), created in 1992, explained how the Federal government would mobilize Federal resources and conduct activities to assist State and local

TELL ME MORE 6-4
HOW THE EMERGENCY MANAGEMENT ASSISTANCE COMPACT WORKS

EMAC is the nation's state-to-state mutual aid system. EMAC has been ratified by U.S. Congress (PL 104-321) and is law in all 50 states, the District of Columbia, Puerto Rico, Guam, and the U.S. Virgin Islands. All EMAC member states have enacted EMAC legislation and have agreed to use the EMAC process and procedures. EMAC is implemented through the State Emergency Management Agencies (State EMAs) of the member states on behalf and their respective governors.[54]

When an incident occurs and various local resources are exhausted, resource requests are sent to the State EMA. From here the state submits those resource requests to intrastate mutual aid parties, federal entities, private-sector organizations, volunteer groups, or EMAC. The state's governor declares an emergency or disaster, thus authorizing that state funds to be expended for response and recovery and for activating EMAC. The affected state's EMAC Authorized Representative or EMAC Designated Contact then opens an event in the online EMAC Operations System. This alerts both the National Coordinating State and the NEMA that a request for resources is likely. Note, only the impacted state needs to declare an emergency or disaster; that state does not need to have received a presidential disaster declaration.[55]

The impacted state then forwards resource requests to the EMAC A-Team whose people then contact EMAC member states to fulfill the request, beginning with the closest states (in terms of travel time/distance). Officials of the potential assisting states are expected to assess risk to their own state if they join in. If possible, the assisting state should activate its in-state EMAC protocols and contact resource providers to determine what is being made available. They should then collect the assistance or resources offered. For accepted offers of aid, the requesting state EMA and the assisting state EMA then complete the EMAC Request for Assistance Form (REQ-A). The completed REQ-A constitutes a legally binding agreement between the two states. The EMAC authorized representatives from the requesting and assisting states are helped by the EMAC A-Team in this negotiation.[56]

Once the requested assistance is received (REQ-A), responders "mobilize" (prepare for their mission), "deploy" (conduct the mission in the requesting state), and "ultimately demobilize" (return home). It is imperative that those who are about to deploy be given a pre-deployment briefing, an EMAC Mission Order Authorization Form, and instruction about EMAC. They must understand their duties in tracking mission expenses, in collecting documentation, and in maintaining contact with their home assisting state EMA during their deployment. Those who deploy need to be prepared for difficult living and working circumstances, limited communications and power, traumatized residents and co-workers, long hours, primitive field conditions, and more.[57]

Deployed personnel, resource providers, as well as assisting- and requesting-state officials, share responsibility for the timely processing of reimbursements. Reimbursement starts when deployed personnel and resource providers submit a reimbursement package to the assisting state. Assisting states audit reimbursement packages and then send them on to requesting states. The requesting state completes its own audit, resolves outstanding issues, and then issues payment back to the assisting state. The requesting state is obligated to pay EMAC reimbursements whether they have received federal disaster assistance funding or not. The EMAC REQ-A, the legally binding agreement completed for every EMAC mission, is based upon estimated costs. Reimbursements should approximate what the REQ-A originally called for.[58]

governments in responding to disasters. The Plan relied on the personnel, equipment, and technical expertise of 27 Federal agencies and departments, including the American Red Cross, in the delivery of supplemental assistance. FEMA was responsible for the Plan's overall coordination.[59] The (FRP) arrayed a set of **emergency support functions (ESFs)**; various federal agencies were expected either to lead the coordination of these functions or to serve within them.[60] The system of ESFs continues to apply today under the NRF.

ESFs and other components of the NRF and the suite of frameworks, as well as NIMS (both discussed more fully later in the chapter) constitute pre-disaster preparedness and response agreements. Figure 6-2 presents ESFs with each function's lead federal agency— in the NRF.[61] The original Federal Response Plan (FRP), as the title connotes, involved only federal agencies and the American Red Cross. Owing to the 9/11 terror attacks and ensuing federal laws and reorganizations, states and local governments are today integral participants in the NRF. By 2013, FEMA and its participating stakeholders set forth the National Disaster Recovery Plan, and in 2016, this was followed by the suites of frameworks developed as part of the National Preparedness System.

DHS-FEMA tells us, "The ESFs provide the structure for coordinating Federal interagency support for a Federal response to an incident. They are mechanisms for grouping functions most frequently used to provide Federal support to States and Federal-to-Federal support, both for declared disasters and emergencies under the Stafford Act and for non-Stafford Act incidents."[62]

THE FRAMEWORKS AND THE NATIONAL INCIDENT MANAGEMENT SYSTEM

It is one thing to study U.S. government layer by layer, although some question whether the layers are as distinct as they seem.[63] It is another matter to consider how governments function when they must interact. Intergovernmental relations have both vertical and horizontal features. As shown in this chapter, when states fashion disaster mutual aid agreements and interstate disaster assistance compacts (although interstate compacts require congressional approval in law), they operate on a horizontal line. When federal, state, and local disaster agency officials establish pre-disaster preparedness and response agreements to facilitate the coordination of their respective agencies during future disasters, they do so along a vertical line. The war on terror has implications on the domestic front that affect intergovernmental relations on both dimensions.

Homeland security policymakers have engaged in massive government planning efforts aimed fundamentally at a broad pool of federal, state, and local disaster responders. Since 9/11, it has largely been the president and federal agency officials who have steered homeland security policy. Congress has provided the president new authority and has made regular infusions of program funding for purposes set forth in law and policy. As said before, homeland security policy manifests itself as a colossal intergovernmental, multiagency, multimission enterprise facilitated by widely distributed and highly conditional federal grants to state and local governments. Planning in homeland security is more than simply reorganization or realignment of existing functions; it represents the federal government's official response to terrorism, with nonterror emergency management a companion concern. Key emergency support functions with lead federal agency appear in Figure 6-2.

Chapter 6 ■ Intergovernmental Relations in Disaster Policy

FIGURE 6-2 ■ Emergency Support Functions with Lead Federal Organization[64]

 1. **Transportation**
   Department of Transportation

 2. **Communications**
   National Communications System

 3. **Public Works and Engineering**
   U.S. Army Corps of Engineers

 4. **Firefighting**
   Department of
   Agriculture/Forest Service

 5. **Emergency Management**
   Federal Emergency Management
   Agency

 6. **Mass Care, Housing, Human Services**
   Department of Homeland Security
   American Red Cross

 7. **Resource Support**
   General Services Administration

 8. **Public Health and Medical Services**
   Department of Health and
   Human Services

 9. **Urban Search and Rescue**
   Federal Emergency Management Agency

 10. **Oil and Hazardous Materials Response**
   Environmental Protection Agency

 11. **Agriculture and Natural Resources**
   U.S. Department of Agriculture/
   Department of the Interior

 12. **Energy**
   Department of Energy

 13. **Public Safety and Security**
   Departments of Homeland
   Security/Justice

 14. **Community Recovery, Mitigation, and Economic Stabilization**
   U.S. Small Business Administration

 15. **External Communications**
   Federal Emergency Management Agency

Source: FEMA, https://www.fema.gov/media-library-data/20130726-1825-25045-0604/emergency_support_function_annexes_introduction_2008_.pdf

Development of an NRP was mandated in the Homeland Security Act of 2002 and Homeland Security Presidential Directive-5 (HSPD-5). The basis for the NRP flowed from the FRP that had preceded it; however, as mentioned, the NRP was a "national" plan that would now include "state and local government," rather than exclusively federal organizations. The NRP was to embody a single, comprehensive national approach; advance coordination of structures and administrative mechanisms; provide direction for incorporation of existing plans with emphasis on concurrent implementation of existing plans; and set forth a consistent approach to reporting incidents, providing assessments, and making recommendations to the president, the DHS secretary, and the Homeland Security Council.

The NRP (2004–2006) and the NRF set forth a national template that leaders may use to determine the appropriate level of federal involvement in response to domestic incidents. The goal of the plan was to harmonize intergovernmental and interagency incident management.

A basic premise of the NRF has been that incidents need to be handled at the lowest governmental level possible. Reflecting its antiterrorism mission, DHS becomes involved through the routine reporting and monitoring of threats and incidents, and when notified of an incident or potential incident. Based on the severity, magnitude, complexity, and threat

FIGURE 6-3 ■ Organization of the National Response Framework for a Domestic Emergency from a U.S. Department of Homeland Security Perspective

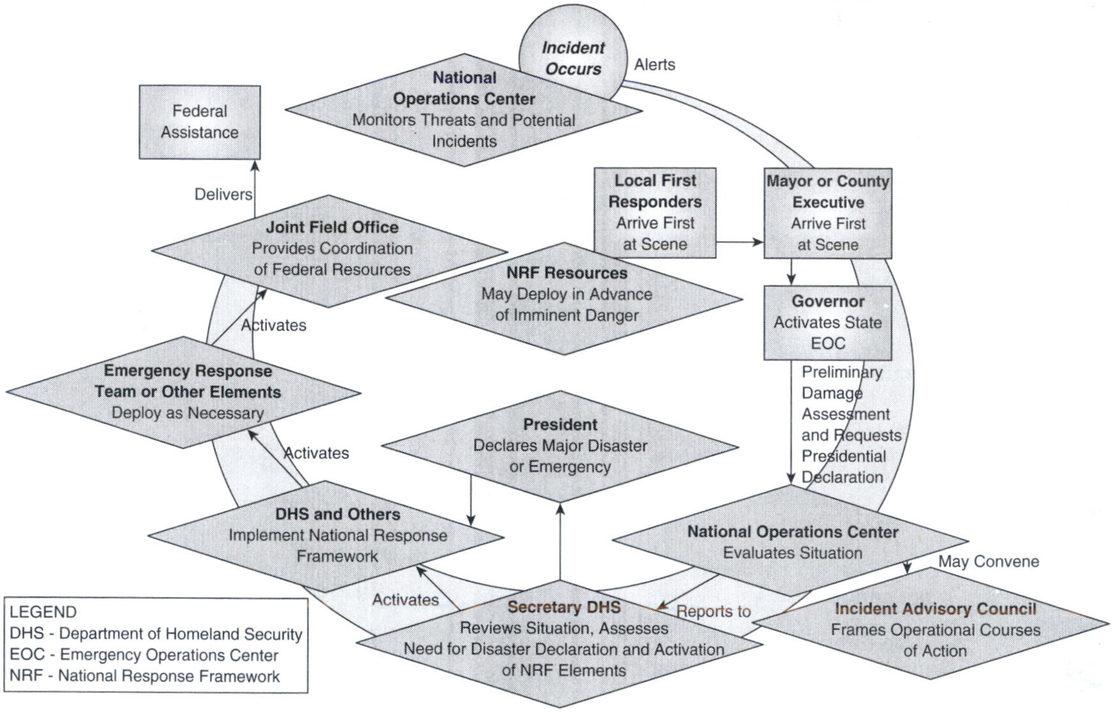

Source: Defense Procurement and Acquisition Policy, "Domestic Emergencies," https://www.acq.osd.mil/dpap/pacc/cc/domestic_emergencies.html (accessed May 28, 2018).

to homeland security posed by the incident, the president, the DHS secretary, and when appropriate the FEMA administrator, decide whether the incident warrants a response. DHS uses various organizations at its headquarters, region, and field levels to coordinate efforts and to provide support to responders on-scene, who themselves are using a system long used by local responders, the **Incident Command System (ICS)**. Other federal agencies carry out their incident management and emergency response authorities within this overarching framework.

The NRF is composed of several layers, depicted in Figure 6-3. Most noticeable is the absence of FEMA in Figure 6-3, but it resides within DHS. Also, this being so, the FEMA administrator and FEMA officials themselves would be participants in all of the locations where DHS is mentioned.

Implementation of the National Response Framework and the National Incident Management System

The NRP, and its successor, the NRF, was supposed to improve local capabilities and not diminish local ability to respond to more routine, localized emergencies. The federal, state, and local bonding element that emerged from HSPD-5 was NIMS. HSPD-5 states the following:

Beginning in Fiscal Year 2005, Federal departments and agencies shall make adoption of the NIMS a requirement, to the extent permitted by law, for providing Federal preparedness assistance through grants, contracts, or other activities. The secretary shall develop standards and guidelines for determining whether a State or local entity has adopted the NIMS.[65]

Under the directive, federal agencies were required to adopt, conform to, and apply the NIMS.

State and local governments were not "preemptively" compelled to adopt and use the NIMS but were "encouraged" to work within the NIMS concept of operations. However, state and local officials understood that their prospects of winning many types of homeland security federal grants would be much improved if they agreed to join in and comply with the requirements of the NRP and the NIMS.

The NIMS was a product of the collaboration of DHS with state and local government officials and representatives.[66] Many in the group were from public safety organizations. The NIMS incorporated many existing emergency management "best practices" into a comprehensive national approach to domestic incident management, applicable at all jurisdictional levels and across all responder occupational fields. The aim of the NIMS was to help responders at all jurisdictional levels and across all disciplines to work together more effectively and efficiently.

A core component of the NIMS was the ICS, a standard, on-scene, all-hazards incident management system already in use by many firefighters, hazardous materials teams, rescuers, and emergency medical teams. DHS officials declared that the ICS would henceforth be the standard method for addressing all incidents.

Local emergency managers were expected to learn the ICS, to participate in ICS exercises, and to acquire various certifications under NIMS, NRP, and later NRF protocols. Many local officials had to devise new, or modify existing, mutual aid agreements to suit NRP and NIMS requirements. Many state and local emergency management organizations were expected to modify their standard operating procedures as well. The NRP was to overlay existing response systems. DHS added three new ESFs and made some modifications to other ones. Three new structures were added to the NRP as well—the Homeland Security Operations Center, the Joint Field Office, and the Interagency Incident Management Group—all federal entities.

The NRP was issued as an unfunded mandate. States were expected to use a portion of the annual Emergency Management Performance Grant (EMPG) funds they received from FEMA to subsidize both state and local costs associated with meeting NRP and NIMS requirements. At the outset, the (now defunct) DHS Office of Domestic Preparedness and FEMA **Emergency Management Institute** (still in operation) were to provide training, educational materials, and practice exercise opportunities. The institute developed an online independent study course to help emergency managers and others gain familiarity with the NRP, and today its successor the NRF.

The NIMS has a core set of doctrines, principles, terminology, and organizational processes. It is supposed to be based on a balance between flexibility and standardization. The recommendations of the National Commission on Terrorist Attacks upon the United States further highlight the importance of the ICS.[67] The commission's report recommends national adoption of the ICS to enhance command, control, and communications capabilities.

Before the NIMS launch year, fire and police departments of some cities had already worked together using the ICS for years. In other municipalities, only the fire department used the ICS. Although law enforcement, public works, and public health officials were aware of the concept, many of these officials regarded the ICS as a fire service system. HSPD-5 required state and local adoption of the DHS-approved NIMS definition of the ICS as a condition for receiving federal preparedness funding. According to DHS officials, although the ICS was first pioneered by the fire service, it was and still is, at its heart, a management system designed to integrate resources so as to effectively attack a common problem.[68]

NIMS is regularly revised, but in 2008 it was said to provide the following:

> A consistent, nationwide template to enable federal, state, tribal, and local govern-ments; nongovernmental organizations (NGOs); and the private sector to work together to prevent, protect against, respond to, and recover from the effects of incidents, regardless of cause, size, location, or complexity.[69]

DHS officials attached great significance to the NIMS. They envisioned that the NIMS and the ICS would be necessary to address future terror attacks of 9/11 scale or worse. For them, it was imperative that all responding agencies be able to interact and work together. The ICS component of the NIMS was supposed to make this possible. Not only would every state and local government be expected to establish an ICS-based system of emergency or disaster response, but they were expected to stay up to date and in conformity with the DHS-approved version of the ICS.[70]

Figure 6-4 is a chart of the ICS structure. The ICS structure and response system has become standard in countless fire departments, police emergency operations, and emergency management systems across the nation. Many thousands of emergency responders in the United States not only know the ICS but use it to practice, exercise, and train frequently.

The NIMS contains a Joint Field Office component, depicted in Figure 6-5. Figure 6-6 graphically presents the federal incident planning structure under the NIMS. Also see the NIMS "Tell Me More" 6-5 box on page 249.

Figure 6-7 is a slide of the Multi-agency Coordination System that serves incident command when an incident must be managed over many locations or when there are multiple incidents covering a wide area. Figure 6-8 provides a graphic description of the links between the NFR, NIMS, and ICS.

More broadly, the push toward universal adoption of the NIMS and the ICS reflects the dubious assumption that once a consistent management structure is adopted, pre-paredness and response effectiveness will automatically improve. Such an assumption ignores many other factors that contribute to effective disaster management, such as ongoing contacts among crisis-relevant agencies during normal times, common under-standings of community vulnerability and the likely consequences of extreme events, realistic training and exercises, and sound public education programs.[71]

One highly experienced emergency manager puts it this way:

> While NIMS is based on the highly regarded Incident Command System, ICS is primarily a field operating system that is useful for hierarchical paramilitary organizations. In other words, it works for fire, police, and emergency medical services. NIMS fails to take into account, however, the qualitative differences that emerge as one approaches crises of increasing complexity that must be managed by non-hierarchical organizations.

FIGURE 6-4 ■ Incident Command General Structure and Duties/National Incident Management System Structure

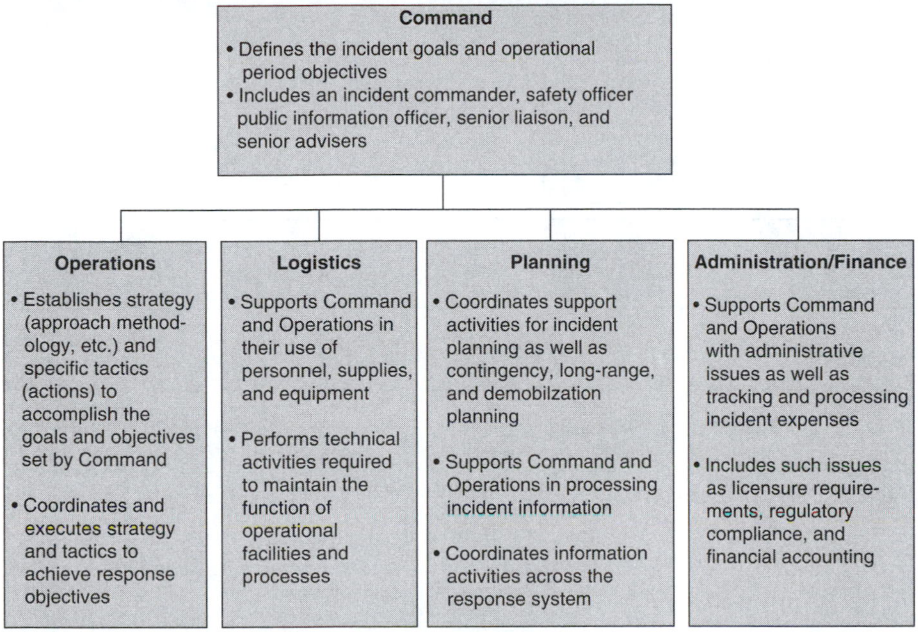

Command
• Defines the incident goals and operational period objectives
• Includes an incident commander, safety officer public information officer, senior liaison, and senior advisers
Operations
• Establishes strategy (approach methodology, etc.) and specific tactics (actions) to accomplish the goals and objectives set by Command
• Coordinates and executes strategy and tactics to achieve response objectives
Logistics
• Supports Command and Operations in their use of personnel, supplies, and equipment
• Performs technical activities required to maintain the function of operational facilities and processes
Planning
• Coordinates support activities for incident planning as well as contingency, long-range, and demobilzation planning
• Supports Command and Operations in processing incident information
• Coordinates information activities across the response system
Administration/Finance
• Supports Command and Operations with administrative issues as well as tracking and processing incident expenses
• Includes such issues as licensure requirements, regulatory compliance, and financial accounting

Source: U.S. Department of Health and Human Services, Office of the Assistant Secretary for Emergency and Preparedness, Public Health Emergency, "Emergency Management and the Incident Command System," February 14, 2012, https://www.phe.gov/Preparedness/planning/mscc/handbook/chapter1/Pages/emergencymanagement.aspx (accessed May 28, 2018).

FIGURE 6-5 ■ Joint Field Office

Joint Field Office
Operational Coordination: Who is doing what?
Operational Support: Novel or controversial strategies?
JFO CG
O
P
L
F
Planning Coordination: Unity of effort? Gaps and overlaps?
Logistical Support: What do they need?
Financial Support: How much funding do they need? How much is left?
Zone of Coordination
IC
O
P
L
F

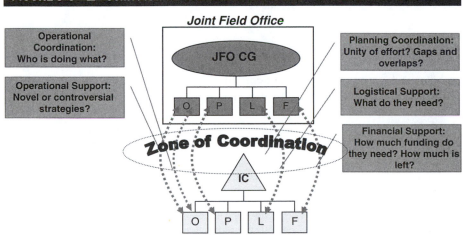

O = Operations, P = Planning, L = Logistics, F = Finance & Administration, and CG = Coordinating Group

Source: U.S. Department of Homeland Security, "Joint Field Office Activation and Operations: Interagency Integrated Standard Operating Procedure," *Appendixes and Annexes Version 8.3*, April 2006, p. 24. https://www.fema.gov/pdf/emergency/nrf/NRP_JFO_SOPAnnexes.pdf (accessed May 28, 2018).

FIGURE 6-6 ■ Incident Command System Structure

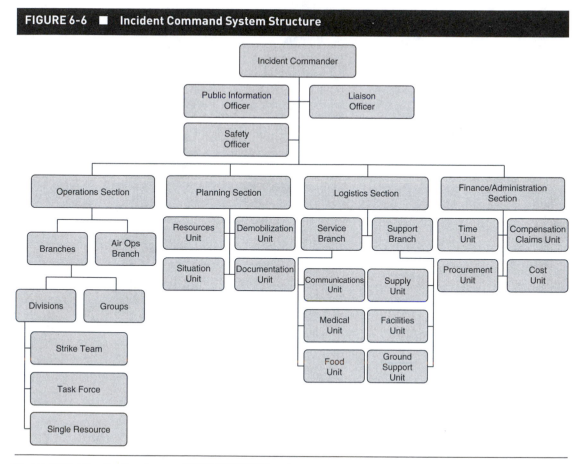

Source: FEMA, https://emilms.fema.gov/IS200b/ICS0102280text.htm.

The growing emphasis on terrorism readiness and ICS principles has led to a concomitant emphasis on "first responder" agencies and personnel. In current homeland security parlance, the term "first responder" refers to uniformed personnel (fire, police, and emergency services personnel) that arrive at the scene of a disaster. Missing from this discourse is a recognition that, as numerous studies reveal, ordinary citizens are the true "first responders" in all disasters. For example, in Homeland Security Presidential Directive-8 (HSPD-8), a mere two sentences are devoted to the topic of citizen participation in preparedness activities. These new policies and programs may leave vast reserves of emergent talent and capability untapped in future extreme events.[72]

Many post-9/11 investigations have highlighted problems associated with "stovepiping" or the tendency for organizations and agencies to closely guard information, carry out their own specialized activities in isolation from one another, and resist efforts to encourage cross-agency collaboration.[73] Indeed, DHS itself was created to overcome stovepipes, better integrate disparate agencies and programs, and improve information sharing and cooperation. However, many homeland security initiatives have created new stovepipes, owing to the effects of organizational turf wars and to the imposition of state secrecy requirements in realms that did not have them before.

An economics professor offers this illuminating observation:

One must remember that all disasters are local and few events ever rise to the level of national significance. Similarly, when communities respond to requests for help, they provide temporary excess capacity—that amount of help available at the time of the event for a specific time. Perhaps most significant is the fact that capacities in communities ebb and flow based on funding, conditions, preferences, and demographic changes. These capacities are not finite and fixed. Federal government officials would be well served to remember that most events are local, focused, and discrete, and any response builds from the bottom up to include support from other jurisdictions horizontally and from different levels of government vertically.[74]

TELL ME MORE 6-5
KEY CONCEPTS OF THE NATIONAL INCIDENT MANAGEMENT SYSTEM

The NIMS is not easy to summarize in brief. However, it contains some core ideas and assumptions, which its authors define as concepts. Below is a rudimentary list of some of those ideas and assumptions.

NIMS provides a core set of common concepts, principles, terminology, and technologies in the following areas:

- *ICS.* Much of NIMS is built upon the ICS, which was developed by the federal, state and local wildland fire agencies during the 1970s. ICS is normally structured to facilitate activities in five major functional areas: command, operations, planning, logistics, and finance/administration. In some circumstances, intelligence and investigations may be added as a sixth functional area.

- *Multiagency coordination systems.* Examples of **multiagency coordination systems (MACS)** include a county **emergency operations center (EOC),** a state intelligence fusion center, the DHS National Operations Center,

the DHS/FEMA National Response Coordination Center, the Department of Justice/Federal Bureau of Investigation (FBI) Strategic Information and Operations Center, and the National Counterterrorism Center.

- *Unified command.* Unified command provides the basis from which multiple agencies can work together with a common objective of effectively managing an incident. Unified command ensures that regardless of the number of agencies or jurisdictions involved, all decisions will be based on mutually specified objectives.

- *Training.* Leaders and staff require initial training on incident management and incident response principles, as well as ongoing training to provide updates on current concepts and procedures.

- *Identification and management of resources.* Classifying types of resources is essential to ensure that multiple agencies can effectively communicate and provide resources during a crisis.

(Continued)

(Continued)

- *Situational awareness.* **Situational awareness** is the provision of timely and accurate information during an incident. Situational awareness is the lifeblood of the incident management and effective response operations. Without it, decisions will not be informed by information on the ground and actions will be inefficient and ineffective. Situational awareness requires continuous monitoring, verification, and integration of key information needed to assess and respond effectively to threats, potential threats, disasters, or emergencies.

- *Qualifications and certification.* Competent staff is a requirement for any leader managing an incident. During a crisis there will not be time to determine staff qualifications if such information has not yet been compiled and available for review by leaders. To identify appropriate staff to support a leader during a crisis, qualifications based on training and expertise of staff should be pre-identified and evidenced by certification, if appropriate.

- *Collection, tracking and reporting of incident information.* Information today is transmitted instantly via the Internet and the 24/7 news channels. While timely information is valuable,

it also can be overwhelming. For an effective response, we must leverage expertise and experience to identify what information is needed to support decision makers and be able to rapidly summarize and prioritize this information. Information must be gathered accurately at the scene and effectively communicated to those who need it. To be successful, clear lines of information flow and a common operating picture are essential.

- *Crisis action planning.* Deliberative planning during non-incident periods should quickly transition to crisis action planning when an incident occurs. Crisis action planning is the process for rapidly adapting existing deliberative plan and procedures during an incident based on the actual circumstances of an event. Crisis action planning should also include the provision of decision tools for senior leaders to guide their decision making.

- *Exercises.* Consistent with the National Exercise Program, all stakeholders should regularly exercise their incident management and response capabilities and procedures to ensure that they are fully capable of executing their incident response responsibilities.

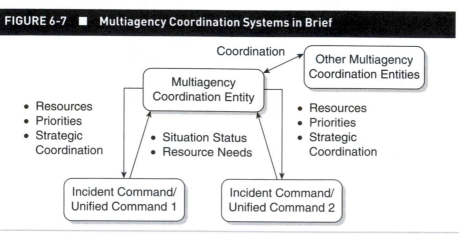

FIGURE 6-7 ■ Multiagency Coordination Systems in Brief

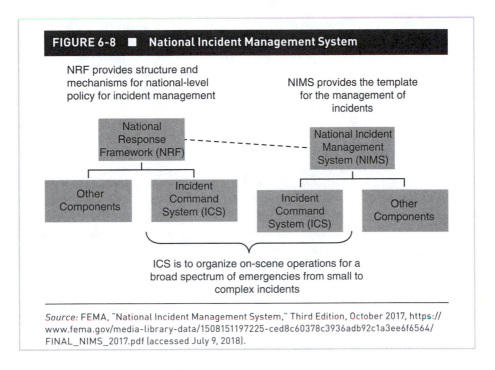

FIGURE 6-8 ■ National Incident Management System

NRF provides structure and mechanisms for national-level policy for incident management

NIMS provides the template for the management of incidents

National Response Framework (NRF) ---- National Incident Management System (NIMS)

Other Components

Incident Command System (ICS)

Incident Command System (ICS)

Other Components

ICS is to organize on-scene operations for a broad spectrum of emergencies from small to complex incidents

Source: FEMA, "National Incident Management System," Third Edition, October 2017, https://www.fema.gov/media-library-data/1508151197225-ced8c60378c3936adb92c1a3ee6f6564/FINAL_NIMS_2017.pdf (accessed July 9, 2018).

INTERGOVERNMENTAL DISASTER MANAGEMENT CHALLENGES

In any field of endeavor, the effectiveness of a human system depends upon how well those who are part of that system understand what must be carried out and what their own roles and responsibilities are. Certainly, this is true of emergency management. The potential for human suffering and devastation in a disaster makes it critical that emergency managers and related personnel understand fully the character of potential hazards, what can be done about these hazards through the application of emergency management principles and programs, and their role and responsibilities in the system of emergency management.

In the U.S. system of disaster management, a broad range of political and managerial transactions take place between and among governments of all levels. Each of the 50 states and each American commonwealth territory has an emergency management agency of some type. These agencies, like their local counterparts, are supposed to be well organized and to have emergency plans, facilities, and equipment. To become and remain eligible for federal emergency management financial assistance, each state must manage a state emergency management program that augments and facilitates local emergency management.

To make an intergovernmental system work, improvisation and flexibility must be part of the ethos of the system. Officials in this system must identify various emergency task domains, and they must reach a consensus about who is going to perform within each. Nevertheless, many disasters present unanticipated demands, so emergency managers must be able to improvise.

Intergovernmental relations in matters of disaster management are not always affable. For example, federal, state, and local officials are supposed to conduct a Preliminary Damage Assessment (PDA) after a disaster. These assessments help to determine whether the disaster is beyond the response and recovery capabilities of the state and local governments affected. A determination that the disaster has produced damage, or has created ongoing dangers, beyond the response and recovery capabilities of the affected governments serves to justify issuance of a presidential declaration of major disaster or emergency.[75] However, disputes sometimes arise over the matter of how extensive damage is and what is "clearly beyond" recovery capability and what is not. Sometimes these disputes must be resolved by the president himself through approval or rejection of a governor's request for a declaration of major disaster or emergency.

Some suspect that after many "disasters" intergovernmental interchanges embody a **crying poor syndrome**.[76] Local governments sustaining disaster losses and costs have every incentive to exaggerate their scales of damage to maximize outside state and federal post-disaster aid. If state governments shield their local governments from having to pay little or no money into the state–local matching share required in many federal disaster relief programs, these local governments have even greater incentive to detail every conceivable disaster loss eligible for state and federal assistance. Zero local matching share means that federal and state relief provide a 100 percent local recovery subsidy. So, repairs to city hall would impose no costs on local taxpayers.[77]

States also have an incentive to maximize, if not exaggerate, their magnitudes of disaster loss. Ordinarily, each presidential declaration of major disaster or emergency conveys federal–state matching aid of 75 to 25 (see the "Tell Me More" 6-6 box). In other words, $.75 of every dollar of state disaster loss is subsidized by federal assistance. When states share their matching burden with localities, the state government derives an even greater subsidy. Since the federal government carries the bulk of financial burden in paying for the public costs of presidentially declared emergencies and major disasters, it is no surprise that FEMA officials are often highly suspicious of state and local estimates of disaster loss.[78] They sometimes suspect state and local government officials of conspiring to maximize federal disaster dollars dispatched to their jurisdictions. Such behavior on the part of these officials exemplifies distributive politics, under which political actors seek resources in excess of their actual need.

TELL ME MORE 6-6
GOVERNORS, MAYORS, AND PRESIDENTIAL DECLARATIONS

For all major disasters, and for emergencies that do not primarily involve federal responsibility and authority, governors of the affected states requesting presidential declarations must first certify that necessary action has been taken under state law; damage estimates have been made; state and local resources have been committed; and cost-sharing requirements of the statute will be met.[79]

The collection of information on damages involves a collaborative effort involving FEMA staff, state officials, and personnel from affected local governments. Teams of assessors conduct a PDA to estimate the degree of damage and potential costs resulting from the disaster. The assessment is broken down into categories (such as the number of homes damaged or destroyed and the number of public facilities damaged or destroyed) that correspond to the broad categories of disaster relief and assistance that FEMA provides through the individual assistance or public assistance programs authorized by the Stafford Act. Information in the PDAs is used to determine whether a declaration will be issued and, if one is issued, whether individual and public assistance programs will be provided to the areas (generally, counties, parishes, and independent cities) included in the declaration.

It is in these interchanges that political and managerial factors often come into play. Mayors press governors for more state and federal aid. A governor, lamenting the high costs of a disaster and the state matching share obligations they produce, sometimes receives permission to borrow from the federal government the money his or her state needs to pay its own match. At least one U.S. Government Accountability Office (GAO)

report disclosed that states sometimes fail to repay all or most of the federal money they have borrowed to cover their matching share. In catastrophic disasters, governors sometimes succeed in securing from the president a higher federal match (100 percent for Florida after Hurricane Andrew in 1992; 90 percent for California after the Northridge earthquake in 1994; 90 percent for Louisiana, Mississippi, and Alabama after Hurricane Katrina in 2005). Such generous federal matching shares impel state and local loss estimators to identify every single dollar of eligible disaster cost.

FEMA sets forth criteria its own officials use to judge state and local eligibility for a declaration of major disaster, but as Chapter 4 documented, the decision to confer a declaration is the president's alone, and the president can freely use or disregard FEMA criteria.[81] Each year, FEMA issues a notice that identifies the threshold to be used as one factor to be considered in the determination of whether public assistance or individual assistance or both will be made available after a major disaster declaration has been issued.

Public Assistance is FEMA's largest grant program, at $4.7 billion per year, comprising 51 percent of all grant dollars.[80]

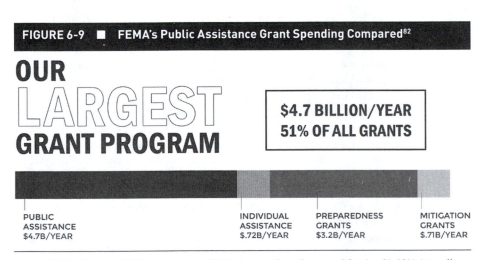

FIGURE 6-9 ■ FEMA's Public Assistance Grant Spending Compared[82]

OUR LARGEST GRANT PROGRAM

$4.7 BILLION/YEAR
51% OF ALL GRANTS

PUBLIC ASSISTANCE $4.7B/YEAR

INDIVIDUAL ASSISTANCE $.72B/YEAR

PREPAREDNESS GRANTS $3.2B/YEAR

MITIGATION GRANTS $.71B/YEAR

Source: FEMA, "Graphic: Public Assistance is FEMA's Largest Grant Program," October 21, 2016, https://www.fema.gov/media-library/assets/images/126480 (accessed July 9, 2018).

Nonprofit Organizations and Volunteers

A great many **nonprofit voluntary organizations** are involved in disaster mitigation, preparedness, response, and recovery efforts. Disasters trigger an outpouring of individual contributions of money or in-kind donations central to the operation and sustenance of many of these bodies. Some volunteer-based organizations are spawned by disasters themselves. Sociologists refer to these as **emergent organizations.** Government emergency management agencies often interact with these organizations and do so for a variety of reasons. The dynamics of that interchange, the interdependence of public and private disaster management organizations, and the political positives and negatives of relying upon nonprofit voluntary organizational help will be addressed here.

By definition, a nonprofit voluntary organization is one that provides service to a community free of charge or for the minimal cost that is required to defray the cost of the service(s) furnished. Financial support for voluntary agencies is generally through donations, contracts, and grants. Private nonprofit organizations are legally characterized by holding the special nonprofit federal tax-exempt status. Many such organizations provide educational, social services, emergency, medical, rehabilitation, and temporary or permanent custodial care facilities (including those for the aged and disabled), or other facilities that produce essential services for the general public.

Nonprofit voluntary organizations, community service groups, and religious organizations that provide assistance in the aftermath of a disaster or an emergency are often referred to as **voluntary agencies (VOLAGs).** VOLAG involvement in disaster response and recovery has a long history in America. For example, in 1905, the U.S. Congress mandated that the American Red Cross do the following:

> [Continue and] carry on a system of national and international relief in time of peace and apply the same in mitigating the sufferings caused by pestilence, famine, fire, floods, and other great national calamities, and to devise and carry on measures for preventing the same.[83]

Likewise, the Salvation Army, a recognized church, has been providing disaster relief assistance since 1899.

A great many not-for-profit and volunteer organizations in the United States actively engage in emergency management. **Secular nonprofit voluntary relief organizations** have historically provided considerable disaster assistance to victims, particularly by distributing food, medical supplies, and temporary shelter. Organized volunteer groups come in a great variety of forms. Besides the American Red Cross and the Salvation Army there are Volunteers of America, the Mennonite Disaster Service, the Southern Baptist Convention, Catholic Charities, Episcopal Relief and Development, United Jewish Communities, Islamic Relief USA, Friends Disaster Service, Church World Services, Save the Children, to name a few. **National Volunteer Organizations Active in Disaster (National VOAD)**, mentioned ahead, include many of these and a great many more. As Chapter 4 disclosed, in 2017, under the Trump administration, houses of worship, owing to their status as community centers, have become eligible to receive FEMA rebuilding or repair assistance under presidential declarations of major disaster.

States, localities, and NGOs respond to many disasters that do not involve federal assistance. These organizations also play a vital role when federal authorities are involved in disaster work under a presidential disaster declaration. However, government emergency managers and those in voluntary assistance organizations do not necessarily share the same definition of disaster or emergency. Even voluntary organizations themselves use different emergency management terminology, follow different methods of budgeting and management, and have different perceptions of government's role in disaster management.

VOLAGs assist in developing disaster plans and in training disaster responders; they provide facilities and resources as well as community disaster education; and they join in drills, exercises, and simulations. In the response phase, VOLAGs furnish resources such as trained personnel, masses of untrained but instrumental helpers, and various facilities. In cooperation with local, state, and federal authorities, VOLAGs often provide the bulk of **mass care** services, sheltering, feeding, and clothing individuals and families; assisting high-risk, **"gap group" clients**; and through an extended network of service organizations, helping to coordinate interests not generally involved in disaster response. Gap group clients are those who fall "between the cracks" of eligible government assistance; some are low income but not poor enough to qualify for government individual and household cash assistance, which is means tested. Some lack proper documentation, some cannot prove they live in the area of the disaster, others filled out their application for aid incorrectly, some cannot get through tele-registration to file a claim with FEMA, some have not been able to find local disaster service centers where they can make application, and so on. The point is that there are a host of reasons why people fall into unassisted gap groups. Government efforts to prevent fraudulent claims often have the effect of disqualifying people who are genuinely eligible but unable to factually document to FEMA satisfaction their request for help, often through no fault of their own (see the case of Herman Smallwood in Chapter 9).

In recovery operations, VOLAGs work in partnership with government and affected communities to identify and meet remaining long-term recovery needs of families and individuals. In mitigation, VOLAGs often press elected and appointed officials to adopt sound land-use planning and zoning as well as appropriate building codes and standards aimed at safeguarding people and property from disaster forces. They often lead or participate in community disaster education activity.

Years of previous experience have helped the people of established volunteer organizations learn that cooperation and coordination in disaster relief is essential. The National VOAD is a forum and assemblage of national, state, local, and umbrella organizations (see below) that have made preparation for all phases of the disaster cycle their collective priority. National VOAD grew out of the response to Hurricane Camille in 1969, when organizations that had been involved in providing resources and services to victims and communities affected by the disaster shared their mutual concern about their frequent duplication of services. Representatives of these organizations began to meet together on a regular basis. In those meetings, participants learned about their respective activities, concerns, and frustrations, and they labored to prevent duplication and inefficiencies in their responses to future disasters.

The National VOAD is a nonprofit, nonpartisan membership organization that serves as a forum in which organizations share knowledge and resources throughout the disaster cycle—preparation, response, recovery and mitigation—to help communities prepare for and recover from disasters. The National VOAD coalition includes over 50 national organizations, some **faith-based nonprofit voluntary organizations**, some community-based, and others secular NGOs. There are also 55 state/territory VOAD groups, which represent local/regional VOAD groups and hundreds of other member organizations throughout the country.[84]

Also, part of National VOAD are 61 umbrella groups working at the state, District of Columbia, or trust territory levels. These state-level VOAD groups help coordinate the work of many hundreds of smaller organizations. VOAD member organizations provide more effective disaster aid and less duplication in service by getting together before disasters strike. Once disasters occur, National VOAD or an affiliated state VOAD encourages members and other voluntary agencies to convene on site. This cooperative effort helps a wide variety of volunteers and organizations to work together in a crisis.

National VOAD serves member organizations in the following ways:

- *Communication:* disseminating information via electronic mechanisms, newsletters, directories, research and demonstration, case studies, and critiques

- *Cooperation:* creating a climate for cooperation at all levels (including grassroots)

- *Coordination:* coordinating policy among member organizations and serving as a liaison, advocate, and national voice

- *Education:* providing training and increasing awareness and preparedness in each organization

- *Leadership development:* giving volunteer leaders training and support so as to build effective state VOAD organizations

- *Convening mechanisms:* conducting seminars, special meetings, board meetings, regional conferences, training programs, and local conferences

- *Outreach:* encouraging the formation of, and furnishing guidance to, state and regional VOADs

National VOAD policy stipulates the following: "The role of a VOAD group is not to manage disaster response operations, but it is instead to coordinate planning and preparations in advance of disaster incidents and operations."

Volunteer Organizations in the Field

Most volunteer organizations are involved in immediate emergency response, such as mass care, which includes feeding, sheltering, clothing of victims, and the like. Some are involved in recovery activities, such as rebuilding, cleanup, and reconstituting community mental health. Many organizations provide the same or similar services. Problems of overlap or competition usually are avoided if the agencies coordinate and cooperate.

VOLAGs must collectively agree to share the work by coordinating their limited resources so that as many agencies as possible are able to take part in the response and recovery effort. By sharing and cooperating, VOLAGs may share credit for the recovery of their communities and for promoting the community healing process. Sometimes VOLAGs argue with each other at the expense of the people they are trying to serve.

However, VOLAGs, by nature, compete for the donated dollar. This is not necessarily a problem unless during relief operations various VOLAGs are not provided an opportunity to serve or be publicly recognized for the help they provide. VOLAGs need a chance to demonstrate their abilities to both their supporters and to the community at large. Sometimes government public information officers report on the efforts of just a few VOLAGs without acknowledging the legitimate contributions of all VOLAGs engaged in a response or recovery operation. Such omissions can create rancor and misunderstanding. VOLAGs themselves need to draft cooperative, or joint, press releases to illustrate their collaborative efforts.

VOLAGs are private organizations with their own missions and responsibilities. Local VOLAGs often report to a parent organization whose headquarters are located outside of the disaster area. Sometimes an agency's national headquarters will support their local agency by sending in national leadership or a response team to assist the disaster relief effort. Conflicts sometimes arise when the national teams and the local response element do not coordinate, collaborate, cooperate, or communicate. Occasionally problems and awkwardness result when the national team makes a decision on behalf of its local affiliate without thinking about the long-term ramifications that decision might have on the agency after the national team returns home. Sometimes a national team fails to understand cultural, economic, and political sensitivities of the local community and acts in a way that induces the community to look unfavorably upon the local affiliate. This may undermine years of trust and good faith built up under conditions of normalcy before the disaster. It is important that parent organizations not jeopardize the credibility or funding base of local affiliates during a disaster response or recovery effort. (See the "Tell Me More" 6-7 box on page 259.)

In addition to those nonprofit voluntary organizations outside of government, some voluntary organizations engaged in disaster response and emergency management are part of government. The **Citizen Corps,** which is an arm of U.S.A. Freedom Corps, invites people at the community level to volunteer. Citizen Corps councils working at the state and local level regularly receive federal funding used to promote training and education of community volunteers, in some ways helping them to respond to disasters or emergencies in their communities.[85] Moreover, the federal Corporation for National and Community Service administers and, through grants, funds AmeriCorps, Senior Corps, and Learn and Serve America. These three organizations engage in volunteer-based activity, a portion of which is directed to serving emergency management and homeland security purposes.[86]

FEMA reports that "a national network of over 1,200 state, local, and tribal Citizen Corps Councils bring together local government, business, and community leaders who work to prepare their communities for disaster and to make them more resilient. The Councils harness the power of individuals through education, training, and volunteer service with the aim to make their communities safer, stronger, and better prepared to respond to the hazards and threats.[87]

FEMA encourages development of **Community Emergency Response Teams (CERTs)**. CERTs have proliferated across the United States. DHS-FEMA tells us that there are over 2,700 local CERT programs nationwide, with more than 600,000 individuals trained since CERT became a national program.[88] CERTs members are unpaid, voluntary workers who are invited to earn qualifications for various type of post-disaster relief specialization, including elemental search and rescue, first aid, shelter management, and more. This type of volunteer coproduction activity augments the pool of people available to help in times of disaster or emergency, increases the likelihood that neighborhood responders will be more qualified to provide appropriate help after a disaster, and fosters popular support for local, state, and federal emergency management people and programs. The logic behind efforts like CERTs is to remind people that they themselves may be "first responder" helpers in disasters and their immediate aftermath. In the CERT training this author received, a major in the Delaware National Guard opened with a disturbing revelation. She said that in recent years, "more Americans are dying in terror attacks here inside the United States than are American military people posted in danger spots abroad." Whether the culprits are foreign terrorists or Americans with grievances or mental illnesses, mass murders inside the United States are becoming commonplace. She remarked that both civilian and military authorities have come to recognize that in some respects battlefield conditions are being mimicked in domestic attacks. In some ways, CERT groups and training are intended to help at the neighborhood level when disaster or attacks take place.

For many years, FEMA could mobilize small armies of Disaster Service Workers, or later Reservist (On-call) Disaster Assistance Employees. The agency declares that it "consistently seeks talented and hard-working people who are eager to assist disaster survivors and first responders on an on-call basis as a Reservist employee. They are the main FEMA workforce during an emergency or disaster."[89] Under the program, "Reservists travel, receive training, build professional networks and support those in need. The work is available intermittently. Applicants must commit to working on an on-call basis, be available to travel within 24-48 hours, be deployed for 30 or more days and possess a strong work ethic."[90] Under the system, FEMA Reservists are temporary, paid employees who "are hired under the Robert T. Stafford Act and are excluded from the provisions of title 5, United States Code, governing jobs in the competitive service. Appointments are for two years and can be renewed."[91]

FEMA adds, "Reservists are also hired to a position within a Cadre based on their skills and experience. Cadres are groups of personnel organized by operational function. Cadre specialty areas are: Cadre Options Acquisitions, Dispute Resolution, Disability Integration, Disaster Emergency Communications, Disaster Field Training Operations, Disaster Survivor Assistance, Environmental Historic Preservation, Equal Rights, External Affairs, Federal Coordinating Officer, Financial Management, Hazard Mitigation, Human Resources, Individual Assistance, Information Technology, Logistics, National Disaster Recovery Support, Office of Chief Counsel, Operations, Planning, Public Assistance, Safety, and Security."[92] These workers are, at this writing, referred to as the **Cadre of On-Call Response/Recovery Employees (CORE).** The agency strives to amass, train, and maintain a workforce that is ready to deploy and respond quickly to critical events when called upon.[93]

DHS-FEMA today has an Individual and Community Preparedness Division (ICPD). Here the assumption is that preparedness begins with the individual and ICPD is expected to serve as the main preparedness link to individuals and families. "The Division draws from science-based research to improve communications and community education so as to empower communities to prepare for, protect against, respond to, and recover from a disaster. FEMA's individual and community preparedness programming uses the National Household Survey (NHS) and protective actions guidance. The NHS, conducted annually since 2013, provides insight into people's preparedness attitudes, beliefs, behaviors, and actions. Findings from the NHS are helping to refine and improve the Agency's engagement and capacity building strategies for individuals and communities."[94] ICPD toils to provide current, research-validated guidance (e.g., hold on for earthquakes; run, hide, fight in active shooter confrontations; leave your car and get to high ground in canyons experiencing flash flood) for the public about how to protect themselves from threats and hazards, and ultimately save lives. This research enables FEMA to refine its preparedness actions to motivate the public to take appropriate actions.[95] FEMA is conducting new research to understand and improve how people of underserved communities receive critical preparedness information and what they do as a result. Much of this endeavor could be guided by decades of disaster sociology research and publication.[96]

TELL ME MORE 6-7
VOLUNTEER ORGANIZATIONS IN DISASTER

Government emergency management officials can never be sure how much post-disaster help voluntary organizations are able to provide. Often, voluntary organizations augment government assistance and do so admirably. However, sometimes voluntary organizations are overwhelmed by the scale of need they encounter. Clearly, many voluntary organizations were for weeks overwhelmed by the human needs created by Hurricane Andrew in south Florida in 1992 and by Hurricane Katrina in the Gulf Coast in 2005. Sometimes they are only modestly involved in offering assistance, and occasionally they choose not to respond to a disaster at all. Some organizations are reluctant to offer assistance if they have problems with those needing help. They may be reluctant to aid undocumented aliens, corrections parolees, victims suffering illness or disease, the severely mentally ill, or people of religious faiths or cultures drastically different from their own.

The disaster assistance process is based on an interagency referral system. Referrals are made between VOLAGs, between governments, and between VOLAGs and governments. Government assistance supplements individual and family resources, and VOLAG assistance augments these resources and helps address unmet needs. VOLAG people serve communities after disasters. However, they also know that government programs often provide more assistance, and in recent years, with greater speed than most nonprofit and private organizations do after a disaster.

Moreover, VOLAGs must take into account that if they provide certain forms of financial assistance, that assistance may make the client ineligible to receive certain types of government

(Continued)

(Continued)

disaster assistance. Ironically, by providing certain forms of aid too quickly, VOLAGs may decrease the total sum of government disaster assistance that might have flowed to the community. VOLAGs must reconcile their desire to respond and assist quickly in recovery efforts with the knowledge that more resources may be conserved if they wait for government to distribute its resources and only then offer help to meet the remaining needs of disaster clients. Perhaps most significant is how such organizations support and nurture disaster victims and their families. Yet, despite this historical and traditional role, it is not possible to measure accurately the amount of assistance provided through such voluntary efforts.

National Voluntary Organizations Active in Disaster

There are a great many volunteer organization members in the National Voluntary Organizations Active in Disaster (National VOAD); however, there are also some that work outside of NVOAD. NVOAD was selected here as an example of a major umbrella VOLAG group. Its website states, "National VOAD, an association of organizations that mitigate and alleviate the impact of disasters, provides a forum promoting cooperation, communication, coordination and collaboration; and fosters more effective delivery of services to communities affected by disaster."[97]

National VOAD is the forum through which "organizations share knowledge and resources throughout the disaster cycle—preparation, response and recovery—to help disaster survivors and their communities. Members of National VOAD form a coalition of nonprofit organizations that respond to disasters as part of their overall mission."[98]

Prior to the 1970 founding of National VOAD, numerous organizations served disaster victims independent of one another."[99] Government, private-sector, and nonprofit-sector aid flowed out as independent streams. "As a result, help came to the disaster victim haphazardly."[100] Often there was an unnecessary duplication of effort, with some needs over-met and others not met at all. Training for potential volunteers was insufficient. Victims were provided woefully inadequate information about available services and resources. Communication between and among voluntary disaster agency workers was very limited and so there was little coordination of services.[101]

The seven founding organizations came together and committed to fostering the four C's—communication, coordination, collaboration, and cooperation—to better serve people impacted by disasters. Today, National VOAD is a leader and voice for the nonprofit organizations and volunteers that work in all phases of disaster—preparedness, response, relief, recovery, and mitigation. National VOAD is the primary point of contact for voluntary organizations in the National Response Coordination Center (at FEMA headquarters) and is a signatory to the National Response Plan (and today Framework).[102]

National VOAD member organizations are diverse, highly competent organizations that provide a wide range of skills. All organizations have service-oriented missions and include volunteer engagement as a key component of their operations. Our state/territory VOAD members represent many local and regional VOADs, and hundreds of additional local organizations. All are dedicated to whole community engagement and recognize that the VOAD movement values and practices represent a proven way to build resilient communities. Our dynamic combination of faith-based, community-based, and other nonprofit, non-governmental organizations (NGOs) represents thousands of professional staff and volunteers with unique skills and a resourceful spirit.[103]

Another complicating factor is that disasters provide a major impetus for the solicitation of charitable contributions needed to administer these organizations and to fund their assistance programs. Many nonprofit assistance organizations derive income for their budgets from governments both before and after disasters. The federal government may provide reimbursement of some of the costs of relief provided by VOLAGs. However, law and policy dictate that FEMA cannot reimburse a VOLAG that proselytizes its religion in the course of dispensing relief assistance to disaster victims.

Voluntary organizations must generate positive publicity to reassure contributors that their donations are getting to where they are intended. However, voluntary organizations compete with each other for donors and donated dollars. Emergency managers must be aware of the possibility that competition among nonprofit organizations may complicate coordination of relief efforts. Certain organizations have strong political backing that they may bring to bear on disaster managers.

Nonprofit voluntary organizations enjoy a special tax status that exempts them from paying many federal, state, and local taxes and that provides their donors with a tax deduction for charitable dollar or in-kind donations. However, this special tax benefit limits these organizations from engaging in political activity, especially lobbying legislatures. Consequently, voluntary organizations appear not to be formally involved in public political issues.

However, they are very much involved informally in public and community issues that are part of the world of politics and policy. These organizations and their members are free to express their views and to publish recommendations on matters of public policy. They are less able to make campaign contributions or directly lobby the government for special benefits to their organizations.

On top of this, they often champion the causes of the general interests they represent: women, children, the elderly, the disabled, minorities (racial, ethnic, religious), the LGBTQ community, the poor and homeless, victims of crime or abuse, victims of disaster, the seriously ill or those needing hospice care, ex-convicts, people suffering drug addictions or mental illness, health or social welfare clients, and the like. Consequently, by advocating government benefits for the interests they represent, they may gain from government programs indirectly.

GOVERNMENT CONTRACTORS AND DISASTER MANAGEMENT

When the federal government hires private businesses to perform specific jobs, the government becomes the customer. Ingrained in the customer-to-supplier relationship is the supplier's obligation to satisfy the customer. If the contracted business is to satisfy the government, the contracted task(s) must be completed in an efficient, effective, and equitable manner. Ordinarily, contracts are awarded through a competitive bidding process, but in emergency circumstances the federal government may award a firm a contract if it is the only applicant, a form of sole source contracting. The federal government can also lump together many tasks into one, large contract and allow the winning contractor to subcontract distinct sections of the prime contract work to other businesses, again in the interest of speed. Because government agencies cannot fulfill every disaster management task, these agencies award contracts to businesses to handle specific tasks, to engage in certain types of activity, or to produce or supply some type of product or service.

The federal government is quite dependent on contractors, and this is especially so for DHS and FEMA. One argument in favor of using government contractors is that contractors have more flexibility and freedom to complete work, and often at less cost, than government does. A counter-argument is that government contractors, as profit-maximizing businesses, have an incentive to minimally meet the terms of the contract, nothing more. Some government contractors have been accused of being unresponsive to taxpayers or have been prosecuted for fraud and corruption. Contractors are often rapacious in their effort to win government funding.

Observations on Government Contractors and Contracting

There has been a very significant increase in federal government contracting since 9/11, and this includes the years of the George W. Bush, Barack Obama, and Donald Trump administrations. A great many of these contracts have been awarded by DHS and FEMA. Is government becoming too dependent on government contractors? Is the process under which contracts are bid and awarded fair, legal, and appropriately monitored? Has the system of bidding and application become so complex, so burdened by crosscutting legal requirements, so time consumptive, so hobbled by reporting and auditing rules, so labor intensive, and so capriciously affected by the whims of congressional funding that S-corporations and small companies cannot expect to be competitive in seeking and winning government contracts? Federal contract seeking in the disaster field has evolved into a giant casino-like system in which "high rollers" are overrepresented. Smaller firms increase their chances by combining with larger firms, often those possessing a strong lobbying presence in Washington, DC. More than this, big firms accumulate federal contract acquisition and fulfillment experience over time, and combined with their massive economies of scale, they can afford to run the full gamut of government grant application, grant approval, grant payments, and ultimately audit by government.[104] This is one reason why an assortment of huge corporations, several of them major defense contractors, have carved out a place for themselves in federal contracting for disaster work, products, construction, research, training, decision support, and so on.

Many major federal contractors seek out and recruit DHS-FEMA employees who are experienced in grants management, issuance, and supervision. If a federal worker resigns and two years later is hired by a firm he or she previously worked with as a federal employee, there is no conflict of interest under federal law. This so-called "swinging door rule" is extremely difficult to enforce because there are many ways to legally evade the rule.

What specific services and products have government agencies contracted out to businesses? These may range from speechwriting to development of drones to be used in post-disaster aerial damage surveys. Some contracted activities seem essential: removing massive debris; restocking public shelters; replacing totally destroyed public office buildings, repairing hospitals, highways, bridges, main railway corridors, major airports, under-river auto and train tunnels, high-tension power lines and electric substations, natural gas pipelines, fiber-optic or copper-based telecommunications infrastructure, and the like. Some contracted recovery spending appears questionable: fixing expensive public stadium scoreboards and public golf courses, repairing tourist railway lines, reimbursing some homeowner civic associations for snowplowing costs when these bodies set aside paltry sums for this purpose before the declared snow event, subsidization of local reconstruction that far exceeds the cost or market value of the original structure, and so on. There obviously are many tasks the government cannot perform alone, but clearly some tasks could be, and have in the past, been executed by the federal government. For many years, FEMA relied on its own force of disaster assistance employees, who are in fact paid volunteers with needed expertise, to handle many disaster recovery duties. However, FEMA has contracted out a considerable portion of these disaster service worker duties to private businesses.[105]

Positives and Negatives of Subcontracting

Most companies that win government contracts rarely do all the work on their own; instead, they subcontract work out to other companies. This has positive and negative consequences. A positive consequence is that smaller firms less capable of competing for prime federal contracts sometimes win business on the rebound via subcontracting. A negative consequence is that government oversight of contracted work becomes extremely difficult when layers of subcontractors are engaged. This practice makes it difficult to ensure accountability to the government issuing the contract, the U.S. Treasury, and the national taxpayer. The practice also sometimes adds substantial overhead charges such that the ultimate services and products provided are of less volume and of greater per unit cost than what the government expected when it awarded the contract. Waste and misuse become more difficult to ferret out.[106]

Another problem of government contracting is public transparency. It is extremely difficult if not impossible to find public records of FEMA awards to private contractors. There are many thousands of big, medium-sized, and small private contractors. They range from firms as large as Microsoft and Verizon to local roofers, plumbers, small university centers, and individual consultants. Moreover, the contractors themselves have little incentive to reveal publicly the nature and dollar amounts of the government contracts they have won. Some contractors are happy to disclose this information and others less so. In some cases, various private, for-profit government contractors have been taken to court for allegations of abuse and fraud.[107]

Summary

U.S. disaster policy and management are intergovernmental and immensely complex. Overlap and interdependence of American governmental jurisdictions abounds. Moreover, U.S. intergovernmental relations are ever changing. Often, as in this era, the federal government appears dominant in its relations with states or localities (consistent with the inclusive-authority model of intergovernmental relations theory). However, state and local governments sometimes successfully exercise "pushback." For the United States, homeland security priorities were triggered by acts of terrorism. The trauma of 9/11 for the United States produced massive repercussions in a great many domains of public policy. As in many European nations since formation of the European Union, the United States traded considerable individual rights and privacy protections for increased security from attacks by even lone wolf terrorists.

Counterterrorism efforts demanded colossal information collection, processing, and management aimed at preventing, or responding to, "incidents." These efforts required information sharing from bottom to top, although not necessarily the reverse. The job of coordination necessary under the much touted "Whole of Community" approach becomes laughably infeasible when so much authority is being centralized through DHS "soft glove" dictates. Build these capabilities and advance these missions, and "we will suggest to you" how to do it. The resulting homogenization and standardization under the "incident" management approach preempts and subsumes "conventional disaster management." The latter would henceforth become a sub-category of the former, regardless of incident cause. Approaching floods, hurricanes, tornadoes, and earthquake devastation as if they were variants of terrorist attack will neither make U.S. disaster management easier, nor make homeland security more popular with the public. A cascading torrent of security restrictions, federal credentialing rules, badging protocols, plus the hierarchy of command and control authority needed in homeland security, complicates intergovernmental relations, diminishes the role of civilian—and particularly private or voluntary—parties, and subsumes all-hazards emergency management under a new form of American civil defense.[108] A favorite refrain of former President Obama when he was asked to okay a proposed federal initiative impacting states, localities, and the public was, "You can do it, but no Bigfoot!" Under the suites frameworks of the emergency preparedness, "Bigfoot" lives, roams, and does not tread lightly. All is not lost. FEMA administrator Brock Long recently lamented before Congress that FEMA may have made its work overly complex, particularly for the public and stakeholders who regularly interact with it. Perhaps the Leviathan of Homeland Security rules and thinking permeating the multiple frameworks approach will loosen and vaporize as a bad symbolic politics dream. Or not.

A vital but under-appreciated aspect of disaster policy is how NGOs, such as VOADs, play a role in the making of disaster policy and in disaster management. These altruistic organizations do much more than "gap fill" by serving the unmet needs of disaster victims. They are often a human, largely unselfish, compassionate arm of disaster preparedness, response, and recovery. However, these organizations have their own agendas, work together with varying degrees of success, are not necessarily compelled to respond to a disaster, and depend on the donated dollar and on publicity for the good works they do. However, it is people from these organizations that are likely to help you and your family in the middle of the night when your home has been destroyed by a fire. Local firefighters may have rescued you and extinguished the fire. But in the absence of help from family and friends, it will likely be people from a charitable organization that will provide you and your family clothing, temporary shelter, food, and even short-term financial help. The loss of a home represents a "major disaster" for a family or household.

Finally, as national policy for the past 20 or more years, the federal government has engaged either in outright privatization of many functions previously handled by the government or in out-sourcing selective functions and activities to private-sector firms and NGOs. State and local governments have also engaged in privatization and outsourcing as well. On top of this, the federal government has retained private for-profit corpo-rations either to manage various short-term proj-ects and tasks or to produce and distribute certain products. Privatization and outsourcing have cor-responded with a freeze or growth deceleration in the size of the full-time federal workforce. The world of "government" programs has become a world heavily occupied by for-profit businesses co-existing with a hollowed out federal workforce. Many federal emergency management officials dedicate their workdays to managing and oversee-ing contracts issued to private firms, firms that today implement gigantic swathes of emergency management duties. Heavy disaster management contracting to private firms has reduced federal need for small armies of voluntary, although gov-ernment paid, temporary disaster workers. Those who seek to understand the modern intergovern-mental relations of disaster management need to understand the world of government contracting.

Key Terms

U.S. Coast Guard Petty Officer Second Class Kenneth Krowel drops a box of MREs from a helicopter near Utuado, Puerto Rico, on October 3, 2017.

Coast Guard photo by Petty Officer Third Class Eric D. Woodall

CIVIL-MILITARY RELATIONS AND NATIONAL SECURITY

The military is a major player in the nation's system of disaster response; however, the military's suitability to undertake some of this work, as well as disputes about the nature and duration of the military role in homeland disasters, have been matters of controversy. Nonetheless, disaster policy and emergency management in the United States has been, and continues to be, massively affected by military concerns. Moreover, homeland security is part of national security. The U.S. Department of Homeland Security's (DHS) chief mission is to prevent, prepare for, respond to, and recover from acts of terrorism inside the nation in its entirety. DHS has one of the largest federal departmental workforces, some 240,000 employees as of September 2017. DHS contains a wide assortment of agencies, among them: The Transportation Security Administration, U.S. Secret Service, U.S. Coast Guard, U.S. Citizen and Immigration Services, U.S. Customs and Border Protection, U.S. Immigration and Customs Enforcement, and FEMA.

This chapter examines military, intelligence, and law enforcement concerns that are now part of U.S. emergency management. Some of this involves the role of state National Guard forces and their relationships with the Pentagon's U.S. Armed Forces, particularly in the realm of response to domestic disasters and incidents. This introduces special federalism issues and the in-military implications of the Posse Comitatus Act of 1878. State National Guards, under state governor control in most cases, and the U.S. Armed Forces under commander-in-chief control, will get considerable play in this chapter. Included as well is a short analysis of Dual Status Commander Authority, something approved in 2004, applied thereafter in Hurricane Katrina in 2005 and in a succession of National Special Security Events. It was rigorously employed in New York State during the Superstorm Sandy response and recovery operations in late 2012. Dual Status Commanders are becoming the norm in mega-disasters. They were used in the major 2017 hurricanes, and in 2018's Hurricane Florence, several were used in North and South Carolina.

This chapter also paints a picture of the U.S. trend toward a security-focused[1] disaster policy. There is a short summary of DHS organizations—some military, some quasi-military, and some civilian—that through the years have become inter-linked with FEMA. Also covered is how modern homeland security overlaps domestic emergency management, law enforcement, and terrorism prevention, protection, and mitigation. Owing to their civil-military and national security relevance, this chapter surveys several major homeland security grant programs and how these influence state and local governments, particularly their respective state emergency management and homeland security people and organizations.

CIVIL DEFENSE TO HOMELAND SECURITY

For decades, U.S. civil defense and homeland security policy has been enmeshed in the nation's disaster policy. In the 1950s, civil defense against nuclear attack was the platform upon which American emergency management, at all levels, evolved. In the Carter administration of the late 1970s, when FEMA was established, President Carter chose to entrust the agency with several national security responsibilities, the most significant of which involved Continuity of Government, a multiagency program that involved communications, protection, surreptitious relocation, and sheltering of the president and other top U.S. leaders in periods of direct threat to the nation or the president himself. Consequently, FEMA's formative stages involved infusing it with both national security duties and a conventional all-hazards approach to emergency management. For FEMA workers, the "marriage" of emergency management and national security has been both uneasy and awkward. Separating offices run under strict national security rules from those offices expected to work openly with the full range of FEMA's stakeholders, including the general public, for many years did little to build *esprit de corps* within the agency. Disputes about national security and domestic disaster management took place, or are continuing, in at least three arenas:

- Defining what the administrative culture of FEMA should be

- Determining FEMA personnel policies concerning recruitment, qualification, hiring, and security clearances

- Devising FEMA's annual budget requests by program as well as re-programming received budget monies where permitted

Unsurprisingly, the dispute between FEMA's national security side and its emergency management side has been emulated in many states and localities, albeit with immense differences. Owing to the 9/11 attacks of 2001, ensuing laws and directives, and the *9/11 Commission Report,* U.S. state and municipal governments continue to shoulder a considerable portfolio of duties related to national security. This grew by orders of magnitude during and after 2002 owing to new federal laws and executive orders that, by 2003, created the massive U.S. Department of Homeland Security. Beyond this, new or reinvigorated federal grant programs targeting terrorism prevention, protection, and response, and immigration and border controls, ballooned federal homeland security spending. For example, the State Homeland Security Grant program and the Urban Area Security Initiative came with detailed conditions, requirements, and standards of performance that became a sizable share of what was before 2001 largely the domain of disaster policy and emergency management. The massively detailed requirements of these DHS grants promote centralization of authority at the federal level exactly at a time when DHS is promoting its suite of frameworks (for prevention, protection, mitigation, response, and recovery) as a "whole community," decentralized effort.

Disaster management in the United States has long been referred to as being "bottom-up"—that is, local emergency management organizations and governments address disasters and emergencies first, seeking help from their state government or from nearby local governments. Federal government help is perceived as "last resort" assistance when a state cannot respond to and recover from a disaster or emergency using its own resources. However, since the terrorist attacks on September 11, 2001, political pressures and national fears surrounding the threat of more spectacular and devastating attacks have created a disaster policy that has become very much centralized,[2] "top-down," president-dominated, and federal government-dominated, despite political rhetoric to the contrary. Before the 9/11 attacks, one would have been hard-pressed to identify instances of municipal involvement in national security affairs, but in the months and years following these attacks, many local governments have been expected and compensated to shoulder a variety of "homeland" security responsibilities embedded in national security.[3] Threaded through all of this as well are military and intelligence collection matters.

THE MILITARY'S ROLE IN DISASTER RESPONSE AND RECOVERY EFFORTS

The military is often a magnificent asset in humanitarian disaster response. The state National Guard and U.S. Armed Forces under Pentagon authority are trained to follow orders, to operate in the field, and to move into hazard zones with enough equipment to sustain themselves independently for considerable periods. Military people are willing, and sometimes ordered, to put their lives on the line.

Military people and certain highly trained emergency responders—firefighters, police officers, and pre-hospital medical care providers—are expected to take reasonable personal risks in disaster circumstances. Still, civil servants, often dedicated to their work in valiant ways, are not expected to enter danger zones that pose a significant risk to their health and welfare.[4] These civilian officials, including FEMA workers, are in fact prohibited by federal law from taking dangerous personal risks in disaster response.

There are an immense number of post-disaster tasks that military units are well-qualified to undertake. Certain types of military services and equipment may be used to augment the services and equipment deployed by civilian governments, the private sector, or nonprofit sector organizations. For example, military units may engage in the following:

- Search and rescue, including aerial and waterborne

- Emergency medical care

- Emergency transport of people

- Mass feeding

- In-kind distribution of food, clothing, and other necessary commodities

- Epidemiological work and disease control

- Decontamination (in hazardous materials or radiological circumstances)

- Temporary sheltering

- Firefighting

- Help in restoration of electric power and other utility services

- Debris removal to reopen roads

- Bridge repair or temporary bridge replacement

- Offer of security and property protection aid[5]

Arguably, ever since the Great San Francisco earthquake in 1906, American policymakers have, in dire circumstances, put the U.S. military to work on acute disaster response needs. Military capabilities and resources have served as laudable supplements to the aid provided by civilian public and private organizations. Regardless, the military must avoid undercutting state and local authority. For example, in very major disasters the military has been used to transport victims and medical supplies, provide shelter and mass feeding operations, direct traffic, reopen roads and highways clogged by disaster debris, provide presence patrols, and engage in emergency repair of infrastructure. However, when disasters occur and the military moves into damage zones to conduct quasi-law enforcement functions, whether inside or outside of Posse Comitatus restrictions, controversy sometimes results. News and social media sometimes spotlight military confrontations with alleged looters, soldier-citizen friction in the post-disaster enforcement of mandatory curfews, and disputes that arise when armed military people prevent homeowners and renters from returning to inspect their domiciles, and so on.

In 2005, the Pentagon responded to the Hurricane Katrina catastrophe around New Orleans, deploying some 20 ships, 360 helicopters, and 93 fixed-wing aircraft. It was allegedly the largest and fastest deployment of U.S. military forces in support of a natural disaster in the nation's history.[6] Almost 50,000 National Guard[7] people were deployed to support hurricane relief, and more than 17,000 U.S. Armed Forces active-duty troops from the 82nd Airborne and First Cavalry pitched in as well.[8] The nation's experience with Hurricane Katrina highlighted the importance of the military in disasters. In some respects, the military temporarily fulfilled needs ordinarily served by local police and fire services.

When local and state assets are overwhelmed during a disaster or emergency, military people and assets help to bridge the gap until civilian responders and officials can handle the incident. And that did indeed happen in the response to Hurricane Katrina.[9] However, military organizations are often ill-equipped to handle many short- and long-term disaster recovery needs: rebuilding homes, managing shelters, feeding the displaced, resettling people, helping businesses resume operation, providing disaster unemployment aid, servicing the long-term medical needs of disaster victims, replacing major public infrastructure, and bringing back public utilities, to name a few. See the "Tell Me More" 7-1 box on the following page, which pertains to the military response to Hurricane Maria devastation in Puerto Rico in 2017.

Owing to changes made after the 9/11 terrorist disaster, the U.S. military now has a greater presence in addressing domestic disaster, but the military is chiefly poised and prepared for various forms of war or terrorist-caused disasters.

THE MILITARY, HOMELAND SECURITY, AND DISASTER POLICY

Modern homeland security highlights the overlap of domestic emergency management and **terrorism consequence management** at home. Owing to the range of weapons and instruments potentially available to modern terrorists and the damage these might cause, antiterror emergency management and conventional disaster management may complement each other better today than civil defense (against nuclear attack) and conventional disaster management did during the Cold War of 1946–1990.

Many conventional disaster management duties and homeland security obligations are interwoven. Homeland security obligations have contributed to the militarization of more realms of disaster management. Preparation for hazardous materials incidents overlaps much of that for bioterrorism events. Preparedness and response planning for a major urban earthquake parallels some elements of preparedness and response planning in the event of the detonation of a low-yield nuclear weapon in a large metropolitan area. In some ways, hurricane civil evacuation planning dovetails with civil evacuation planning for threatened or actual dirty bomb incidents.

Under current arrangements, the military provides key support and partners with civilian emergency responders, but the overall tasks of assessing needs, interagency coordination, deployment of urban search and rescue teams, and overall management of "federal" disaster response have been entrusted to DHS and its FEMA. Many of the functions, tasks, and skills that are essential in all phases of emergency management fall outside the scope and mission of the military, whose primary functions are to deter war and provide security for the nation. In the United States, most emergency management responsibilities continue to be entrusted to civilian, not military, people, organizations and institutions.[10]

Sometimes in the wake of catastrophic disasters, lawmakers propose that the military become more intimately involved in response to major disasters. Proponents "for more military involvement" maintain that the military's command and control structure, plus its logistical systems, provide the kind of framework and efficiency that was missing in civilian agency responses to Hurricanes Katrina (2005) and Andrew (1992), for example. Others underscore the usefulness of military resources such as helicopters and watercraft for rescue, as well as tents and portable facilities to provide for human shelter. Just as the U.S. military responds to disasters abroad, it is able to do likewise at home. Still others argue that the military's most important role could be in providing security following the most catastrophic and destabilizing events. The most extreme arguments advocate transferring the responsibility for emergency response from civilian agencies like FEMA to the Department of Defense (DOD).[11]

However, use of the military in domestic disaster management has generated a sizable "against more military involvement" bloc. For many critics, it is not simply the matter of using the military in law enforcement. Surprisingly, even some senior military leaders are ambivalent or opposed to increasing the role and duties of the military in disaster or incident management. The American military role in Puerto Rico's devastating Hurricane Maria in 2017, according to the "Tell Me More" 7-1 box, reveals military leader trepidation about involvement in domestic disasters.

TELL ME MORE 7-1

THE MILITARY RESPONSE TO HURRICANE MARIA DEVASTATION IN PUERTO RICO

The Harvard Humanitarian Initiative studies the role of the armed forces in disaster relief and humanitarian emergencies worldwide. Under this initiative, researchers decided to examine the U.S. military's deployment to Puerto Rico after Hurricanes Irma and Maria.[12] What follows is an extract of findings about the military's Hurricane Maria response in Puerto Rico.

Hurricane Maria struck the Island of Puerto Rico on September 20, 2017. The first U.S. soldiers from the mainland[13] arrived in Puerto Rico eight days later and would stay until mid-November. "Eventually, 17,000 troops—including active duty, reserves, and National Guard—were deployed to both Puerto Rico and the U.S. Virgin Islands. Their missions were to conduct search and rescue, provide medical care, and restore power. Soldiers also delivered food and water to both residents and emergency responders there."

However, nine days after Maria struck, less than half of the PR National Guard had been mobilized. "Of the Puerto Rico Guard's 8,000 members, some 2,750 are activated, said Kurt Rauschenberg, a National Guard Bureau spokesman. That number is growing by the day, but it illustrates a crucial difference in how states and territories responded to hurricanes this year."[14] In contrast, Florida governor Rick Scott quickly activated all 7,000 members of Florida's National Guard before Hurricane Irma rolled through his state. In only two days, Texas governor Greg Abbott called up all 12,000 members of the Texas National Guard to confront Hurricane Harvey's massive flooding effects in his state. Yet, nine days after Hurricane Maria, less than half of Puerto Rico's National Guard were deployed. "Army Lt. Gen. Jeffrey Buchanan, the top U.S. officer overseeing military operations on the island, attributed this to a combination of factors. Many personnel are dealing with the devastation in their own lives, he said, and some are providing help in their full-time jobs as police, firefighters or other first responders rather than through the Guard."[15]

Why did it take the military from the mainland of the United States over a week to get to Puerto Rico? By comparison, U.S. troops were in Haiti two days after its 2010 earthquake. According to one source, the answer has to do in part with "an 1878 law called the Posse Comitatus Act, which prohibits American armed forces (operating under Title 10 authority and duty status) from performing domestic law enforcement duties. In other words, the U.S. military Title 10 forces do not respond to disasters on home soil unless ordered to do so by an act of Congress or as directed by the president (perhaps under the president's authority to declare a National Emergency) for a "humanitarian assistance mission."[16] (There will be a more detailed analysis of Title 10 and what it means later in this chapter.)

In late September 2017, "Sen. Marco Rubio, R-Fla., suggested that the military should take over aid distribution in Puerto Rico from the Federal Emergency Management Agency—which was clearly stretched thin by its simultaneous responses to hurricanes Harvey, Irma, and Maria. Lt. Gen. Jeffrey S. Buchanan, commander of the U.S. Army North, rejected the idea. His response invoked the limits imposed by the Posse Comitatus Act." Buchanan declared, "This is not a dictatorship. The military does not take charge of these kinds of operations in the homeland."[17]

The Department of Defense had sent several FEMA liaisons to the Caribbean before Maria. The Harvard study said, "But, by law, it could not mobilize troops until it was determined that civilian agencies were unable to manage the disaster response." For this reason, the (Title 10) U.S. military can respond more quickly to international emergencies than it can at home. By September 27 (2017), FEMA had requested help and the military was preparing to dispatch its first brigade of soldiers to Puerto Rico. Lt. Gen. Buchanan was named chief of the mission.[18]

State National Guard units, operating under Title 32 (also discussed ahead), are paid by their respective state government. As such, they may be deployed by their respective governor to address disasters or incidents that befall their home state, or under an EMAC agreement, they may be dispatched to help a nearby state that requests this help. However, according to the Harvard study, U.S. Armed Forces, always serving under Title 10, seldom engage in disaster relief at home, but they frequently respond to emergencies abroad. Between 1970 and 2000, American troops provided international humanitarian assistance and disaster relief 366 times, mostly in the Pacific. In the same period, they engaged in combat just 22 times.[19] See section ahead about the National Guard.

The Harvard University Initiative Examines the U.S. Military Response in Puerto Rico after Maria

Harvard Initiative researchers used these foreign deployments as a basis of comparison for evaluating the U.S. military's Puerto Rico mission.

(Continued)

(Continued)

They asserted, "Though some experts have recommended more training for these missions, our prior research has generally found that U.S. troops are quite good at international disaster response. The U.S. Armed Forces score well on what we've identified as critical indicators of military success in a relief mission. They typically deploy quickly, bring a specialized skill set, coordinate well with aid agencies on the ground and plan their arrival and exit appropriately."[20]

The Harvard team added, "We modified these indicators slightly to assess the military's humanitarian response in Puerto Rico, a domestic emergency. And, beyond the slow mobilization, we found the military performed about as well in the Caribbean as it has abroad. The deployment of 17,000 troops, 82 aircraft and three combat support hospitals were comparable in size to the U.S. military's mission in the Philippines after 2013's Typhoon Haiyan. There, 13,400 troops were deployed to some 450 disaster zones across the country. As critics have observed, that is far smaller than the Haiti earthquake response, when 22,000 troops and 33 U.S. military ships were sent to the island."[21]

Arguably, "This makes sense when given the death tolls of these various disasters. Some 230,000 people died in Haiti's earthquake. Roughly 12,000 died in the Philippines. When (authorities from) the U.S. (mainland) went to Puerto Rico, the government there maintained that just 16 people had died in the storm (although that would later turn out to be many orders of magnitude too low). Critically, however, fewer other organizations were working in post-hurricane Puerto Rico than were present in Haiti or Philippines."[22] On June 1, 2018, the *Chicago Tribune* published a *Washington Post* article that shed more light on the Maria death count in Puerto Rico: "The Puerto Rico Department of Health released data late Friday that shows there were at least 1,400 additional deaths on the island in the months after Hurricane Maria as compared to the prior year. It was the first time in months that the territorial government has released mortality data, and the numbers indicate that the death toll from the

hurricane was far greater than the official tally of 64. The data show that deaths were far higher in September and October than in the prior two years. According to the new data, 3,040 people died in Puerto Rico in October 2017—the first full month after the devastating storm hit on September 20 (2017)—an increase of 680 over the prior year."[23] A follow-up Harvard University research report employing a statistical extrapolation estimated that as many as 4,645 people in Puerto Rico may have perished during, or in the aftermath of, Hurricane Maria.[24] A more sophisticated analysis by George Washington University's Milken Institute School of Public Health and the University of Puerto Rico's Graduate School of Public Health conducted over the spring and summer of 2018 concluded, "Total excess mortality post-hurricane using the migration displacement scenario is estimated to be 2,975 (95% CI: 2,658-3,290) for the total study period of September 2017 through February 2018."[25] As that report discloses, "We estimate that in mid-September 2017 there were 3,327,917 inhabitants and in mid-February 2018 there were 3,048,173 inhabitants of Puerto Rico, representing a population reduction by approximately 8%. We factored this into the migration 'displacement scenario' and compared it with a 'census scenario,' which assumed no displacement from migration in the hurricane's aftermath. We found that, historically, mortality slowly decreased until August 2017, and that rates increased for the period of September 2017 through February 2018, with the most dramatic increase shown in the displacement scenario accounting for post-hurricane migration."[26] Migration displacement here refers to the number of people who left Puerto Rico, many emigrating to locations in the lower 48 states, shortly before and in the days and months after Hurricane Maria struck.

The Harvard study continues, "After Typhoon Haiyan [smashed major parts of the Philippines], 23 militaries jointly responded, including 23,000 Filipino troops, 13,400 U.S. troops and at least another 10,000 soldiers from other countries. Dozens of international organizations also typically rush in to help after a disaster in the developing world."[27] However, "International armies and charities do not (customarily) undertake humanitarian relief in the United States. As a result, just a handful of national aid groups—among them the American Red Cross, Caritas de Puerto Rico and Habitat for Humanity—deployed to Puerto Rico after Hurricane Maria. They were soon joined by the military. But, in the end, there simply was not enough manpower to get the job done."[28]

The Harvard Initiative findings insist "that the most critical factor in any humanitarian response—whether in a post-disaster scenario or in a conflict setting—is coordination. To succeed, military responders must work together with the civilian groups and government agencies on the ground. One big reason why the 2005 Hurricane Katrina response in New Orleans failed, for example, was lack of coordination between the Department of Defense—which oversees the U.S. military—and FEMA. That disaster spurred the DOD to create a liaison position integrated with FEMA."[29] It also encouraged development and use of the **Dual Status Commander** post (see ahead in the "National Guard" section), a military officer assigned to lead both state National Guard people (deployed by a governor under Title 32) and active-duty U.S. military people (deployed by the president under Title 10 duty status).

Harvard University researchers claimed, "The Puerto Rico response shows that this new system has in fact improved coordination. Our study determined that when military personnel arrived, they complemented—rather than duplicated—the efforts of the federal officials, local authorities and humanitarian organizations already on the ground. The military brought manpower to the island, including engineers, medical staff and airlift capabilities. This aided in the search and rescue, health care and power restoration work underway. The military also provided translators, mortuary affairs teams, and even tower climbers."[30]

"Coordination was not flawless. A recent report from the Center for Army Lessons Learned finds that FEMA and the military were not always 'aligned and synchronized.' Sometimes, for example, they competed to conduct airlifts. But, in our assessment, the DOD-FEMA liaisons effectively ensured the coordination necessary for the Puerto Rico mission. Even so, Puerto Rico's recovery has clearly lagged. At this writing, power has yet to be entirely restored and over a thousand people (perhaps 4000 to 5000 or more) died from storm-related causes in the weeks after Maria."[31]

What went wrong? Harvard Initiative "interviews with Department of Defense responders suggest that the biggest challenge was the sheer scale of the damage left by Hurricane Maria. Puerto Rico's government was completely overwhelmed, making it very difficult for FEMA and the U.S. military to get a clear picture of what was most urgently required—and where—in the first days after the storm. The island's total power outage, in particular, hobbled emergency aid. Troops and FEMA staff deployed across the island could not communicate with affected communities. The rundown condition of the power grid, already fragile before Maria, also made it massively harder to get the lights turned back on. No brigade of soldiers, no matter how well trained, can overhaul the energy infrastructure of a place as big as Puerto Rico in days."[32]

"Finally, because Puerto Rico is an island territory with no neighboring states, first responders like the National Guard units dispatched from the mainland struggled to arrive quickly. When parts of Texas were badly hit by Hurricane Harvey in September 2017, the National Guard was simply dispatched from elsewhere in Texas and from nearby states."[33]

"Overall, we believe that the U.S. military itself performed as well in Puerto Rico as it does in its international relief missions. But our assessment reveals real shortcomings in planning for disasters—especially considering that hurricanes occur regularly in the Caribbean. Puerto Rico in 2017 is not the first time the U.S. military has been called in to provide humanitarian assistance on domestic soil."[34] It certainly will be called on to do so again in the future.

THE NATIONAL GUARD, THE U.S. ARMED FORCES, AND POSSE COMITATUS

A State Government Perspective

Chapter 6 examined state homeland security and emergency management agencies and offices. Part of that analysis considered the role of state adjutants general and state military departments. There it was revealed that some state governments administratively position their state emergency management or homeland security agency so that it reports to the **state adjutant general**, a state military official, or an overhead state Military Department official. Chapter 6 showed that the state National Guard or a state military department serves as the overhead organization for emergency management or homeland security, or both, in some 14 states: Alaska, Arizona, Hawaii, Idaho, Kansas, Kentucky, Maine, Maryland, Montana, Oregon, South Carolina, Washington State, West Virginia, and Wisconsin (see gray shaded blocks of Chapter 6's Table 6-1 to see states with HS and/or EM embodied in a military department).[35]

States with emergency management organized on a military-dominant model usually assign emergency management work to a state military department or division (often headed by a state adjutant general). These departments or divisions employ a combination of military and civilian workers. Chapter 6 also made clear that National Guard- or military department-dominant states often encompass fully civilian emergency management offices such that the only military link is at the top through the head of the state National Guard and/or state adjutant general. In addition, there has been a trend in many states to move emergency management and homeland security out of military departments. Regardless of whether states organize their emergency management under the state adjutant general military model or not, every state's emergency management is influenced by its state military, owing to the prominent place the National Guard holds in disaster response in all states.

Presidents, the U.S. Military, and Posse Comitatus

The Posse Comitatus Act of 1878 has deep roots in American history. Most Americans of the original 13 colonies concluded that they were being subjected to tyrannical and repressive British control. The Boston Massacre of 1770 was a turning point for the American colonists. The British Army was sent to Boston to serve as a *de facto* police force. The now-infamous story of the confrontation between the British troops and colonists, who were rioting, ended with the British soldiers turning their weapons on the civilian population. These were the first recorded deaths of the American Revolutionary War. One significant result was written into the Declaration of Independence; the King "has kept among us, in times of peace, Standing Armies without the Consent of our legislatures." The King "has affected to render the Military independent of and superior to the Civil Power," and has without our assent quartered "large bodies of armed troops among us."[36]

Moreover, the founding fathers who drafted the U.S. Constitution detailed a citizen's right to due process as well as the manner in which an American army would interact with citizens. For example, the army was not to be quartered among the population and was required to be servile and accountable to civilian authority. This reasoning inheres in the Posse Comitatus Act, a measure also aimed at placating the post–Civil War concerns of many people living in former Confederate states. The law bars active-duty military from operating as a domestic police force.[37]

The **Posse Comitatus Act of 1878** was passed during Reconstruction following the Civil War to prohibit the military from enforcing civilian laws. The law sought to codify the long-standing aversion of Americans to a standing army that could become an instrument of governmental tyranny and control.[38] It established clear boundaries regarding the role the military could play in civil law enforcement. The aim was to ensure that the military would not assume police powers exempted from civilian control.[39]

Under the Posse Comitatus Act, the armed services are generally prohibited from engaging in law enforcement activities inside the United States, such as investigating, arresting, or incarcerating individuals, except as authorized by federal law. The **National Guard**, however, enjoys a unique legal status. Guard troops are frequently referred to as citizen soldiers, part of the military's substantial Reserve components. Reserve forces were traditionally called to active service only for limited periods, such as for annual training or for short overseas deployments. Since 2003, however, National Guard units of almost every state have been called up for short- or long-term deployments abroad in Iraq, Afghanistan, and elsewhere. When not on active duty, National Guard units remain on call to support the governors of their respective states. If a governor declares **martial law** in specific areas of his or her state, the National Guard, not the active-duty U.S. military, could assume law enforcement powers free of Posse Comitatus law restrictions. In this context, martial law means "the law administered by military forces that is invoked by a government in an emergency when the civilian law enforcement agencies are unable to maintain public order and safety."[40]

Under U.S. law, Posse Comitatus does not apply to National Guard forces when they are mobilized by governors. Nonetheless, when they are called up by the president or the national command authority as "federal" troops, they are not legally allowed to engage in criminal law enforcement.[41] As a result, unless federalized, the National Guard plays the primary role in augmenting state and local law enforcement under state control, whereas U.S. Department of Defense military forces, under Title 10 duty status, play a supporting role, providing soldiers (with no law enforcement powers), resources, and logistical support.[42]

However, the military's role in civil law enforcement has expanded. In the 1980s, specific laws were passed to allow the DOD a greater role in drug interdiction and border security. In the 1990s, following the first World Trade Center attack (by truck-bomb) in February 1993 (6 killed and over 1,000 injured) and the **Oklahoma City terrorist bomb attack** in April 1995, when 168 were killed, public pressure for more robust anti-terror security measures grew.[43] The American public became increasingly wary of global terrorism, much of it emanating from the Middle East. President Clinton and Congress gave the U.S. military an expanded role in responding to terrorist attacks, particularly those employing so-called weapons of mass destruction.[44] The 9/11 terrorist attacks gave further impetus to greater military involvement in terrorism prevention and response. In that event, 19 Middle-Eastern terrorists highjacked four commercial jetliners, which they then used to cause massive destruction and a great many deaths and injuries.

Under the homeland security regime established in the years after September 11, 2001, the military has been entrusted with invigorated authority to address vast homeland security concerns in matters of bioterrorism and terrorist use of other weapons of mass destruction. There are a small number of military officials involved in local disaster-related grant programs (e.g., in chemical weapons disposal transport and routing agreements with local governments, and military base impact programs aiding local governments), but most of these are for highly specific purposes and some are classified.

When is the military called in? State governors may call up their respective state National Guard in disaster or emergency circumstances. Sometimes, governors choose to deploy selected units of the National Guard that have the technical expertise needed to address certain problems that may have overwhelmed or exceeded the capabilities of civilian authorities. The president may ask the secretary of defense to deploy the military, and military leaders themselves possess authority to independently respond to disasters. For the president and the military, authority to do this resides in Article IV, section 4, of the U.S. Constitution, the Civil Defense Act of 1950, and the National Emergencies Act of 2002.

In 2005, President G. W. Bush publicly advocated amending the Posse Comitatus Act to allow the military to become involved immediately and automatically following natural disasters.[45] During his address to the nation on September 15, 2005, following Hurricane Katrina, President Bush stated that he believed the military should play a greater role in future disasters: "It is now clear that a challenge on this scale requires greater federal authority and a broader role for the armed forces—the institution of our government most capable of massive logistical operations on a moment's notice."[46] When the military is deployed to a disaster site, its people and resources sometimes dwarf those of civilian authorities.[47]

Thus, the government response to Hurricane Katrina renewed debate over the efficacy of the Posse Comitatus Act. Several scholars, among them James Jay Carafano, Gregory M. Huckabee, and James F. Miskel, believe that amending the law to grant federal troops greater authority in restoring order in the wake of a domestic emergency is not a good idea and changing Posse Comitatus would be a mistake.[48] One newspaper report disclosed, "Many Pentagon officials have expressed concern about broadening the military's responsibilities to include what would, in effect, be police work, along with its combat role. They argue that it would require very different training, equipment and force levels."[49] An assistant secretary of defense for homeland security said in an interview about the military's response to Hurricane Katrina, "What we ought not do is convert D.O.D. into a department of first responders."[50]

If policymakers granted the U.S. Armed Forces law enforcement authority such that all Posse Comitatus Act restrictions were removed, the U.S. military would simultaneously gain and lose. It would gain in the sense that those last vestiges of federal law that inhibit U.S. military law enforcement inside the nation would be removed. The military might be more freely deployed by the president to locations inside the nation when the president determined that the respective state National Guard, along with state and local law enforcement, were incapable or unwilling (perhaps owing to a governor's or a mayor's resistance) to meet a threat or incident of some type.

Conversely, the military would lose in the sense that its public image might suffer if its soldiers carried out law enforcement actions improperly and unjustly. The military might also suffer if domestic disaster management responsibilities undermined its primary national defense mission.[51]

Owing to past and present massive deployment of American military units to Afghanistan, Iraq, Africa (Mali, Niger, Somalia, Djibouti, etc.), the Philippines, South Korea, Okinawa, and of course in European NATO base locations, and elsewhere, there are those who worry that the military is being asked to do too many things as it is. Assigning the U.S. Armed Forces military law enforcement duties inside the United States for anything less than a condition of constitutionally authorized national emergency is arguably unreasonable.[52] Care must be taken in use of the term "active duty" because state National Guard soldiers may be placed on "active duty" for assignments inside or outside the United States. Moreover, people in parts of the U.S. Armed Forces under control of the president may not always be on "active duty" (see the "National Guard and the U.S. Armed Services" section ahead).

The Case of National Emergencies

As Chapter 4 disclosed, national emergency authority applies outside of the Stafford Act process of governor-requested presidential declarations of major disaster.[53] However, since the early 1900s, presidents have infrequently invoked national emergency authority. Military leaders are even more reluctant to exercise their disaster response authority independently except under the gravest circumstances, as when military people and bases directly experience a disaster. The military, outside the National Guard and other reserve units, ordinarily responds (only to) presidentially declared major disasters and under conditions set forth in the often-revised National Response Framework (NRF) and the National Preparedness System.[54]

Nevertheless, the president always has constitutionally protected authority to declare a national emergency, thus freeing the U.S. military to take part in criminal law enforcement or to support domestic operations. For example, federal forces helped to quell riots by miners in Idaho in 1899; protected James Meredith, the University of Mississippi's first Black student, in 1961; and assisted in quelling the 1992 Los Angeles riots.[55] During Hurricane Katrina, tens of thousands of active-duty military and National Guard troops (also on active duty) streamed into the damage zone, many of them assisting local law enforcement and operating under state law.[56] In fact, federal forces have been used to enforce laws over 175 times in the past 200 years under the authority of the U.S. Constitution and various enabling laws. In short, federal troops can be there when they are needed.[57] The deployment of active-duty military people to domestic zones of disaster is not unusual; however, as yet most presidents have been both reluctant and careful not to invest those forces with police powers. Still, there have been exceptions.

The National Guard and the U.S. Armed Forces

The National Guard is made up of the Army National Guard, the Air National Guard, and reservists called up to serve. Army National Guard personnel are commanded in each state by the state's governor unless that guard is mobilized for federal duty by the president. There are stages of involvement in the National Guard that include voluntary activation, involuntary activation, and deactivation. At any point in time, under Title 10 presidential authority, the National Guard may have more than 100,000 soldiers, air men and reservists activated and it may in times of great emergency mobilize as many as 600,000+ as it did in the period immediately after the 9/11 attacks and in the aftermath of Superstorm Sandy in 2012.[58] The Army and Air National Guard forces are hybrid state–federal militias whose roots reach back to before the American Revolution. Normally under the control of state governors, the state National Guard is heavily funded and equipped by the federal government,[59] and the troops are trained to approximately the same standard as federal active-duty military personnel (**Title 10 duty status**). With or without the governors' permission, the president can mobilize National Guard troops, thus federalizing them. The U.S. Department of Defense supports and works with state Nation Guard units in all circumstances.[60]

Guard troops can perform law enforcement functions (**Title 32 duty status**) under a state's laws but, as explained earlier, cannot enforce criminal law when they are federalized (Title 10)—when they are under the direct control of the president. The National Guard is a principal and major resource for governors who must respond to a disaster or incident. The National Guard provides well-trained people, "communications systems and equipment, air and road support, heavy construction and earth-moving equipment, and emergency supplies such as beds, blankets, and medical supplies."[61]

In 1992, the Florida National Guard was fully available in the aftermath of Hurricane Andrew. By contrast, in 2005, only about 60 percent of the Mississippi National Guard and 65 percent of the Louisiana National Guard were available to deploy to Hurricane Katrina's (much bigger) zone of devastation because so many were on overseas missions.[62] National Guard units were deployed in the states of New York and New Jersey to address Superstorm Sandy in 2012. In 2017, the Texas National Guard responded for Hurricane Harvey and the Florida Guard did likewise for Hurricane Irma. The "Tell Me More" 7-1 case study (page 272) disclosed that Puerto Rico's National Guard deployed as it could in the aftermath of Hurricane Maria. The issue here is whether or not civilian authorities need to reconsider their disaster management dependence on the National Guard given the guard's heavy obligations abroad and given concerns about its ability to recruit sufficient numbers of soldiers.

Relatedly, there are disputes over whether National Guard forces should be federalized by the president when the president judges that circumstances warrant doing so. When a president determines that it is necessary to federalize National Guard units, this sometimes signals that a breakdown in president-governor relations has occurred. However, what matters most is the proper use of the military, including the National Guard, in disasters and the realization that military help is highly temporary. The deployment of the National Guard and the federal military to a zone of disaster connotes failure of civilian government in that zone. The military would be expected to engage in search and rescue, protect property and life, and maintain civil order. However, martial law is a last resort act of desperation in the United States (see Posse Comitatus section).

Assigning Title 10 U.S. Armed Forces a lead role in domestic disaster response raises a host of other difficult questions. Should this force be entrusted with authority to exercise deadly force inside the nation? What happens when governors over-reach in their deployment of state National Guard units?[63] Will there be disputes about who is in charge when National Guard units operating under Title 32 and the U.S. Armed Forces, under Title 10, both respond to the same incident? At least this last question has been largely answered through creation of **Dual Status Command Authority**.

Dual Status Command Authority

According to Burke and McNeil, "The issue of federal control versus state sovereignty" is "a significant point of friction between the States and the Federal Government that continues to challenge the effective command and control of the military."[64] Much of this dispute is about the National Guard and its various duty statuses during domestic operations. National Guard forces, unlike the Active and Reserve components of the federal armed forces, can serve in three different duty statuses during a domestic operation.

First, the National Guard, when activated in **State Active Duty (SAD)** status, serves under the command of the state governor through the state adjutant general (TAG), receives state pay and benefits, and is not subjected to the restrictions of Posse Comitatus; that is, they can engage in law enforcement activities when directed.[65]

Second, when supporting operations undertaken at the request of the president or secretary of defense, the National Guard serves under the authority of 32 United States Code (U.S.C.) § 502f or in Title 32 status. Unlike SAD, a Title 32 designation must be requested by the governor and approved by the president. Once approved, Title 32 status entitles National Guard forces to receive federal pay and benefits *while they remain under command and control of the state governor.* This is advantageous for operations outside of home states, as it eliminates the disparity in state pay rates and ensures that state governors retain command of their National Guard forces.[66] Remember, that Title 32 status National Guard people, while paid by the federal government, are NOT federalized and may conduct law enforcement activity as directed, because they are NOT subject to Posse Comitatus prohibitions.

Third, Title 10 U.S.C. pertains to the laws regulating the Armed Forces. In accordance with the language of the U.S. Constitution, Title 10 provides the legal authority for the president to "call into actual service" elements of the National Guard for federal duty. This ability to "federalize" state National Guard forces sets the legal precedent for the president to assume full authority over the militia. While the National Guard can serve under Title 10 status, this authority is used almost exclusively in support of overseas operations. All Active and Reserve components of the Army, Navy, Air Force, and Marine Corps are considered federal military forces and serve under Title 10 authority. Title 10 forces, as they are referred to during civil support scenarios, receive federal pay and benefits, and are subjected to the restrictions of Posse Comitatus.[67]

These distinctions are important because the type of duty status under which the National Guard is deployed affects its relationship with U.S. Armed Forces (all of whom serve under Title 10 authority), which may be deployed to address the same disaster or incident. Please note that governor control applies both in state Active Duty status and under Title 32 status. What is different is that under SAD the state provides its soldiers pay and benefits; under Title 32, once the president approves the governor's request, the federal government provides soldiers pay and benefits. There are few internal National Guard command and control problems in managing soldiers under SAD or Title 32 status. However, problems have been encountered in the past when National Guard SAD and Title 32 soldiers must work in conjunction with, or cooperatively with, Title 10 forces. National Guard soldiers who are not federalized work under a different command structure than do Title 10 U.S. Armed Forces (in rare cases some of them could be federalized Guards people from other states).

One can envision the problems that might arise when two militaries are working a disaster together but each serves under a different set of commanders. Governor-directed forces and Pentagon-directed forces work under different leadership. A solution has emerged in the form of the dual status commander. Each dual status commander is specially trained and is assigned to work within a specific state. A dual status commander could be chosen from the National Guard (SAD or Title 32) or from the U.S. Armed Forces (Title 10).[68] Consequently, for a multistate disaster in which both SAD or Title 32 Guard's people and Title 10 federal military people are called up, it may be that there are several dual status commanders responsible for specific geographic zones; usually there is one for each state (yet conceivably there could be several working specific geographic zones in a single state, as was done for Hurricane Florence in 2018).

Burke and McNeil tell us, "State and Federal Government lawmakers adopted policy and law authorizing a single military commander, referred to as a dual status commander, to legally assume simultaneous but mutually exclusive command and control over both Title 32 and Title 10 forces during domestic operations."[69] They disclose, "The coordinated military response to Hurricane Sandy in the fall of 2012 was the first time in U.S. history dual status commanders assumed command of both Title 10 and Title 32 forces during a no-notice/limited-notice incident."[70]

Burke and McNeill give us several definitions of Dual Status Command Authority. "The dual status commander (DSC) concept offers a command arrangement legally authorizing one military officer to assume simultaneous but mutually exclusive command authority over both National Guard forces under State Active Duty (SAD) or Title 32 status and Title 10 federal military forces."[71] The Department of Defense offers this definition: "A military commander who may, in accordance with the law, serve in two statuses, Federal and State, simultaneously while performing the duties of those statuses separately and distinctly."[72] The U.S. Government Accountability Office (GAO) defines dual status commanders as, "Military officers who serve as an intermediate link between the separate chains of command for state and federal forces—have authority over both National Guard forces under state control and active duty forces under federal control during a civil support incident or special event."[73] Simply stated: a DSC is "responsible for performing two separate and distinct but related jobs with two separate and distinct teams for two separate and distinct bosses, all at the same time."[74]

Dual status commanders were used in the hurricanes of 2017, in Superstorm Sandy in 2012, and as mentioned for U.S.-landfalling major hurricanes in 2017 and 2018, as well as in National Special Security Event military management.

The U.S. Army Corps of Engineers

The **U.S. Army Corps of Engineers (USACE)** has for more than two centuries carried out work inside and outside the nation. Since it was formed in 1802, the USACE has built, owned, maintained, and managed an enormous amount and variety of public infrastructure inside the United States, much of it designed to provide structural and non-structural coastal and flood mitigation. The corps' role in responding to natural disasters emerged in its epic flood control endeavors after the Civil War. In the past, and even today, floods on large rivers such as the Mississippi impaired commerce, destroyed property, and took lives. Over the years, USACE was asked by the federal government to contribute to both military construction and works "of a civil nature," many of these related to water resources, maintenance of navigable waterways, and flood control. Throughout the 19th century, the corps supervised the construction of coastal fortifications, lighthouses, jetties, and piers for harbors. It also mapped navigational channels and much of the American West as well. In the 20th century, the corps became the lead federal flood control agency and significantly expanded its civil works activities, its projects becoming a major provider of hydroelectric energy and water impoundment recreation areas.

The corps' first formal disaster relief mission was during the Mississippi Flood of 1882, when it supported efforts to rescue people and property. Army engineers also played a critical role in responding to the Johnstown, Pennsylvania, flood of 1889 and the San Francisco earthquake of 1906. Under the Disaster Relief Act of 1950, USACE continued to be the lead federal agency during flood disasters.[75] Under the National Response Framework, the corps is the lead agency for one of the working groups of Emergency Support Function 3: Public Works and Engineering. After Hurricane Katrina in 2005, the corps "led the effort to repair the levees that flooded New Orleans and its environs."[76] The corps has also played a role in response and recovery from Superstorm Sandy, which struck coastal areas of New York and New Jersey in late 2012. It has taken on similar responsibilities in addressing the nation's 2017 hurricanes: Harvey, Irma, and Maria.

However, one critic of the corps alleged, "Shoddy Army Corps engineering crippled the Greater New Orleans flood-control system," thus contributing to the hurricane vulnerability of the levees in and around New Orleans.[77] The corps has also been criticized for overreliance on engineered structures to mitigate flood threat. Sometimes these structures provide a false sense of security to people in communities threatened by flood. Yet, to be fair, in the 1990s and beyond, the USACE has made significant commitments to nonstructural flood mitigation and environmental protection.

The U.S. Coast Guard

Since the 9/11 terrorist attacks, Hurricane Katrina in 2005, and the Harvey-Irma-Maria trilogy of hurricanes in 2017, the militarization of disaster management has advanced in some interesting ways. For example, the **U.S. Coast Guard**, a part of the DHS since 2003, has a much higher profile in disaster management today than in the past.[78]

The U.S. Coast Guard is a military organization highly praised for its Hurricane Katrina disaster response, in which its people carried out a great many rescues. The U.S. Coast Guard rescued more than 33,000 people during and after the storm, often under harrowing conditions.

President George W. Bush responded to dissatisfaction with civilian agency response to the needs of people in New Orleans and surrounding areas by assigning a Coast Guard admiral, Thad Allen, the lead DHS-FEMA role in managing disaster response operations in and around New Orleans.[79] Admiral Allen resigned from this post once he judged that his Katrina disaster response work was largely complete.

The U.S. Coast Guard has a long history of involvement in maritime safety and disaster response. For many years, the U.S. Coast Guard has served as a federal emergency management organization but one with an on-the-water focus. The U.S. Coast Guard has been highly active in matters of port and maritime disaster mitigation, planning, response, and recovery as well as drug interdiction, boater safety, facilitation of marine navigation, port security, border patrol, fisheries regulation, and environmental protection along coasts and waterways.

The North American Command

The 9/11 terrorist attacks dramatically opened the door to heavier military involvement in disaster policy. One domain of this advance has been continental defense. As the *9/11 Commission Report* vividly recounts, civilian and military air controllers and authorities encountered a series of major problems in their efforts to cope with hijacked commercial airliners being used as weapons of terror.

Authorized by President George W. Bush on April 17, 2002, the DOD established the **U.S. Northern Command (USNORTHCOM)** to consolidate under a single unified command existing homeland defense and civil support missions that were previously handled by other military organizations. The purpose of the USNORTHCOM is to provide command and control of DOD homeland defense efforts and to coordinate the defense support the military provides to civil authorities. USNORTHCOM considers its primary role as that of defending America's homeland. USNORTHCOM has a civil support mission that includes domestic disaster relief operations needed to address fires, hurricanes, floods, and earthquakes. Civil support also includes counter-drug operations and managing the consequences of a terrorist event involving a weapon of mass destruction. When asked by the DOD, USNORTHCOM provides assistance to each civilian-led agency in cases of natural or human-caused disaster or catastrophe and for national special security events. In compliance with the Posse Comitatus Act, USNORTHCOM military forces may provide civil support but cannot become directly involved in law enforcement.

The U.S. military has engaged in massive studies and preparations gearing up for homeland deployments in catastrophic disasters, most of those envisioned as the result of terrorism. Since 2002, USNORTHCOM has fulfilled many duties under the NRP (through 2007) and under the NRF (2008–). USNORTHCOM has the job of "orchestrating the operational aspects of defense support to civil authorities in all of its forms."[80]

The Pentagon has been included in federal emergency response planning for decades; however, USNORTHCOM itself was not created until 2002. The National Response Plan (NRP) was a product of the Homeland Security Strategy of 2002, the Homeland Security Act of 2002, and the November 2002 Reorganization Plan to create the DHS. It was also tailored to conform with Homeland Security Presidential Directives 5 and 8 (HSPD-5 and HSPD-8) issued by President George W. Bush. There has been a significant military thread in federal and national response plans for many years owing to protocols and agreements about military support to civil authorities in times of disaster. Also, there have been longstanding roles for the military in various emergency support functions (ESFs) under federal response plans dating back at least as far as 1992.

USNORTHCOM was established to better protect the homeland from attack. USNORTHCOM people have worked to find their place in national disaster management. However, military culture is rarely compatible with the culture of civilian emergency management.[81] The USNORTHCOM mission is to help prevent another terrorist attack on the homeland by militarily defeating attacks by foreigners, if possible, by protecting U.S. borders or airspace from encroachment or penetration by attackers, or by aiding in the response to an incident involving a weapon of mass destruction inside the United States.

USNORTHCOM has occasionally been a target of criticism. Critics of USNORTHCOM acknowledge the need to protect America from terrorist attack, but they also "argue that the delicate task of domestic intelligence gathering should be left to law enforcement."[82] However, domestic intelligence gathering continues apace through DHS protection and prevention frameworks, through fusion centers that dot the national landscape from coast to coast, and through federal intelligence organizations (see the "Patriot Act Reform" section ahead).

Owing to the national security features of homeland security evident in USNORTHCOM operations and the inclusive requirements of the NRF, the National Protection and National Prevention frameworks, and the National Incident Management System (NIMS), disaster policy today is shot through with military and national security functions. Much of what USNORTHCOM does is conducted under rules of state secrecy. **Security classification** now shrouds from public view a variety of emergency management activities, including those in place for facilities whose operation may pose a danger to surrounding communities. Homeland security law and policy, also suffused with security restrictions, have also directed major sums of federal money into state and local emergency management and homeland security. However, homeland security laws and policies have also made disaster management more closed, secretive, and dominated by the military and law enforcement. These are problems that continue to be flash points of controversy.

HOMELAND SECURITY SUPPLEMENTS NATIONAL SECURITY

State and local governments have been in the business of managing and budgeting for disasters and emergencies for a great many years, perhaps dating from about 1736 when Benjamin Franklin helped organize the nation's first volunteer fire department in Philadelphia.[83] Nearly every local government municipal charter obligates the jurisdiction to provide for public safety, which encompasses local emergency management and today homeland security. Owing to homeland security obligations and expanded emergency management duties, state and local governments are now important and active coparticipants in the suite of frameworks[84] and NIMS.[85]

In the aftermath of the 9/11 attacks, the 9/11 Commission and a great many policymakers, including President George W. Bush and Vice President Dick Cheney, labored to better integrate terrorism-related federal grants and programs. John Fass Morton claims:

> The 9/11 attacks provided greater urgency for the consolidation of grant policy and grant management into one federal office. Cheney and FEMA Director [Joseph] Allbaugh contemplated a transfer of the Justice's Office of Domestic Preparedness (ODP) with its Nunn-Lugar-Domenici grants to FEMA's newly established Office of Domestic Preparedness. The 9/11 and anthrax attacks focused attention on all of the new intergovernmental resourcing of the federal government's domestic preparedness support to the states.[86]

Consider several homeland security programs that have penetrated the world of state and local government since 9/11 (see the "Tell Me More" 7-2 box on page 310).

Homeland Security Grant Programs: A Trio

"The Homeland Security Grant Program (HSGP)" is comprised of three grant programs. They provide federal funding to states, territories, urban areas, and other local and tribal governments to prevent, protect against, mitigate, respond to, and recover from potential terrorist attacks and other hazards." This short quote is illuminating in two respects.

First, it shows that HSGP is a three-program collection devoted to addressing all matters terrorism:

- State Homeland Security Grants (SHSP)

- Urban Area Security Initiative Grants (UASI)

- Operation Stonegarden Grants (OPSG)

Second, concerns the phrase "potential terrorist attacks and other hazards." Non-terror emergency management seems relegated dismissively to the phrase "other hazards." The words "other hazards" connote emergency management's current predicament: attempting to survive while deep in the bowels of a terrorism-focused department of Leviathan proportions. Is it possible that emergency management has devolved into a "back-office" DHS concern? Emergency management may be ancillary to the prime mission of DHS: helping the nation address terrorism. DHS senior officials may believe that emergency management is merely a secondary function largely delegated to its small FEMA unit.

The main goal of national preparedness is to bring forth a secure and resilient nation. DHS claims that this trio of grants supports the building, perpetuation, and delivery of "core capabilities" essential to the fulfillment of one sub-goal of the main goal: strengthening national preparedness and resilience.

DHS-FEMA is required by law to make sure that "at least 25 percent of appropriated grant (HSGP) funding goes to law enforcement terrorism prevention activities under **Law Enforcement Terrorism Prevention Activities (LETPA)** funding" (see ahead for more about LETPA). DHS-FEMA meets this requirement, in part, "by requiring (that) all **State Homeland Security Program (SHSP)** and UASI recipients devote at least twenty five percent (25%) of the funds they are allocated under SHSP and UASI to law enforcement terrorism prevention activities.[87] To be clear, it is the grant recipients, not DHS, who direct a quarter of the SHSP and UASI funds they receive to law enforcement counterterrorism or terrorism prevention purposes.

The National "Prevention" Framework, one of the five suites of frameworks, describes the actions that should be taken when an imminent threat to the homeland is detected. Some of this may stem from state or local discovery or it may be the product of intelligence gathering or information collection. The detection of such a threat may help law enforcement thwart the attack or perhaps prevent a follow-on terrorist attack.[88] **Operation Stonegarden**, which will also be examined ahead, received an FY 2018 appropriation of only $55 million, and this sum is augmented by certain LETPA accounts. It is fully earmarked to go to states with an international border, states with an ocean coastline, and fractionally to states that are adjacent to states in one or both of the first two categories. Stonegarden supports state and local law enforcement activity that serves border and immigration control purposes.

The details of the protection and prevention frameworks are voluminous. Consequently, it makes sense to present several graphics that condense verbiage and demonstrate the aims of each framework, the relationship of the frameworks with each other, and the relationship of the frameworks and the three grant programs examined here. Table 7-1 outlines core capabilities by mission area under each of the five frameworks.

TABLE 7-1 ■ DHS Core Capabilities by Mission Area with Respective Framework				
Prevention	**Protection**	**Mitigation**	**Response**	**Recovery**
Planning				
Public Information and Warning				
Operational Coordination				
Intelligence and Information Sharing		Community Resilience	Infrastructure Systems	
Interdiction and Disruption		Long-term Vulnerability Reduction	Critical Transportation	Economic Recovery
Screening, Search, and Detection		Risk and Disaster Resilience Assessment	Environmental Response/Health and Safety	Health and Social Services
Forensics and Attribution	Access Control and Identity Verification	Threats and Hazards Identification	Fatality Management Services	Housing
	Cybersecurity		Fire Management and Suppression	Natural and Cultural Resources
	Physical Protective Measures		Logistics and Supply Chain Management	
	Risk Management for Protection Programs and Activities		Mass Care Services	
	Supply Chain Integrity and Security		Mass Search and Rescue Operations	
			On-scene Security, Protection, and Law Enforcement	
			Operational Communications	
			Public Health, Healthcare, and Emergency Medical Services	
			Situational Assessment	

Source: U.S. Department of Homeland Security, "National Preparedness Goal," Second Edition, September 2015, p. 3, https://www.fema.gov/media-library-data/1443799615171-2aae90be55041740f97e8532fc680d40/National_Preparedness_Goal_2nd_Edition.pdf (accessed July 9, 2018).

FIGURE 7-1 ■ Depiction of the Connections of Core Capabilities and Mission Frameworks

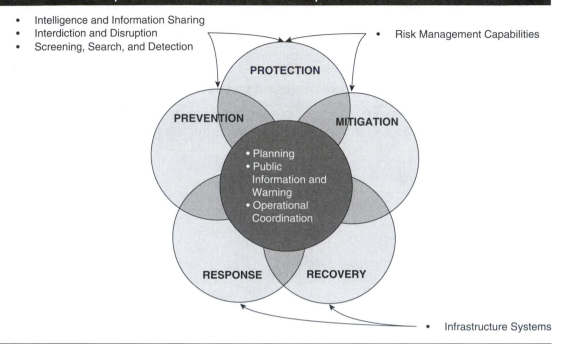

- Intelligence and Information Sharing
- Interdiction and Disruption
- Screening, Search, and Detection

- Risk Management Capabilities

- Infrastructure Systems

Source: U.S. Department of Homeland Security, "National Protection Framework," First Edition, July 2014, https://www .fema.gov/media-library-data/1406717583765-996837bf788e20e977eb5079f4174240/FINAL_National_Protection_ Framework_20140729.pdf (accessed July 9, 2018).

The five framework titles appear in the upper boxed line. Planning, Public Information & Warning, and Operational Coordination span all five frameworks. Intelligence and Information Sharing, Interdiction and Disruption, and Screening-Search-Detection all span Prevention and Protection. Infrastructure Systems are part of both Response and Recovery. Each single column under each framework also arrays duties and capabilities within each framework. Each of the five frameworks is a mission area.

Figure 7-1 conveys a wealth of information in a condensed graphic. As mentioned above, intelligence and information sharing, interdiction and disruption, and screening-search-detection are all part of the prevention and protection frameworks. Risk management is part of both the protection and mitigation frameworks. Oddly, Figure 7-1 shows infrastructure systems as core "capabilities" in the response and recovery frameworks and no other capability is charted. Response and recovery are two major components of emergency management, and in the figure emergency management goes unmentioned.

STATE HOMELAND SECURITY GRANTS

Tables 7-2a and 7-2b capture FY 2018 funding distribution in three major DHS grant programs, the Urban Area Security Initiative, the State Homeland Security Grant Program, and the Law Enforcement Terrorism Prevention Activity funding. These

TABLE 7-2a ■ DHS FY 2018 SHSP, UASI, and LEPTA Minimums (Alphabetically, Alabama to Montana) Including the District of Columbia and U.S. Territories (column totals in Table 7-2b)						
State/ Territory	Funded Urban Area(s)	UASI Allocation	Total UASI Allocation	SHSP Allocation	Total Allocation by State	LETPA
Alabama				$3,980,000	$3,980,000	$995,000
Alaska				$3,980,000	$3,980,000	$995,000
American Samoa				$1,000,000	$1,000,000	$250,000
Arizona	Phoenix Area	$4,000,000	$4,000,000	$3,980,000	$7,980,000	$1,995,000
Arkansas				$3,980,000	$3,980,000	$995,000
California	Anaheim/ Santa Ana Area	$5,000,000	$122,700,000	$59,235,000	$181,935,000	$45,483,750
	Bay Area	$27,500,000				
	Los Angeles/ Long Beach Area	$68,000,000				
	Riverside Area	$3,000,000				
	Sacramento Area	$2,500,000				
	San Diego Area	$16,700,000				
Colorado	Denver Area	$3,000,000	$3,000,000	$3,980,000	$6,980,000	$1,745,000
Connecticut				$3,980,000	$3,980,000	$995,000
Delaware				$3,980,000	$3,980,000	$995,000
District of Columbia	National Capital Region	$52,750,000	$52,750,000	$3,980,000	$56,730,000	$14,182,500
Florida	Miami/Fort Lauderdale Area	$6,000,000	$10,500,000	$10,566,000	$21,066,000	$5,266,500
	Orlando Area	$1,500,000				
	Tampa Area	$3,000,000				
Georgia	Atlanta Area	$6,000,000	$6,000,000	$6,508,000	$12,508,000	$3,127,000
Guam				$1,000,000	$1,000,000	$250,000
Hawaii	Honolulu Area	$1,500,000	$1,500,000	$3,980,000	$5,480,000	$1,370,000
Idaho				$3,980,000	$3,980,000	$995,000
Illinois	Chicago Area	$68,000,000	$68,000,000	$15,712,000	$83,712,000	$20,928,000
Indiana				$3,980,000	$3,980,000	$995,000

(Continued)

TABLE 7-2a ■ (Continued)

State/ Territory	Funded Urban Area(s)	UASI Allocation	Total UASI Allocation	SHSP Allocation	Total Allocation by State	LETPA
Iowa				$3,980,000	$3,980,000	$995,000
Kansas				$3,980,000	$3,980,000	$995,000
Kentucky				$3,980,000	$3,980,000	$995,000
Louisiana				$3,980,000	$3,980,000	$995,000
Maine				$3,980,000	$3,980,000	$995,000
Maryland	Baltimore Area	$4,000,000	$4,000,000	$5,882,000	$9,882,000	$2,470,500
Massachusetts	Boston Area	$17,500,000	$17,500,000	$5,395,000	$22,895,000	$5,723,750
Michigan	Detroit Area	$5,000,000	$5,000,000	$6,368,000	$11,368,000	$2,842,000
Minnesota	Twin Cities Area	$5,000,000	$5,000,000	$3,980,000	$8,980,000	$2,245,000
Mississippi				$3,980,000	$3,980,000	$995,000
Missouri	St. Louis Area	$3,000,000	$3,000,000	$3,980,000	$6,980,000	$1,745,000
Montana				$3,980,000	$3,980,000	$995,000

Source: U.S. Department of Homeland Security (DHS). Notice of Funding Opportunity (NOFO), Fiscal Year (FY) 2018 Homeland Security Grant Program (HSGP), May 21, 2018, pg 41. https://www.fema.gov/media-library-data/1526578809767-7f08f471f36d22 b2c0d8afb848048c96/FY_2018_HSGP_NOFO_FINAL_508.pdf (accessed June 4, 2018).

TABLE 7-2b ■ **DHS FY 2018 SHSP, UASI, and LEPTA Minimums (Alphabetically, Nebraska to Wyoming) Including U.S. Territories and Column Funding Totals**

State/ Territory	Funded Urban Area(s)	UASI Allocation	Total UASI Allocation	SHSP Allocation	Total Allocation by State	LETPA
Nebraska				$3,980,000	$3,980,000	$995,000
Nevada	Las Vegas Area	$5,000,000	$5,000,000	$3,980,000	$8,980,000	$2,245,000
New Hampshire				$3,980,000	$3,980,000	$995,000
New Jersey	Jersey City/ Newark Area	$22,750,000	$22,750,000	$7,993,000	$30,743,000	$7,685,750
New Mexico				$3,980,000	$3,980,000	$995,000
New York	New York City Area	$178,750,000	$178,750,000	$76,930,000	$255,680,000	$63,920,000
North Carolina	Charlotte Area	$2,500,000	$2,500,000	$5,246,000	$7,746,000	$1,936,500
North Dakota				$3,980,000	$3,980,000	$995,000

Northern Mariana Islands				$1,000,000	$1,000,000	$250,000
Ohio				$7,364,000	$7,364,000	$1,841,000
Oklahoma				$3,980,000	$3,980,000	$995,000
Oregon	Portland Area	$2,500,000	$2,500,000	$3,980,000	$6,480,000	$1,620,000
Pennsylvania	Philadelphia Area	$17,500,000	$20,000,000	$9,622,000	$29,622,000	$7,405,500
	Pittsburgh Area	$2,500,000				
Puerto Rico				$3,980,000	$3,980,000	$995,000
Rhode Island				$3,980,000	$3,980,000	$995,000
South Carolina				$3,980,000	$3,980,000	$995,000
South Dakota				$3,980,000	$3,980,000	$995,000
Tennessee				$3,980,000	$3,980,000	$995,000
Texas	Dallas/ Fort Worth/ Arlington Area	$14,800,000	$39,050,000	$20,591,000	$59,641,000	$14,910,250
	Houston Area	$22,750,000				
	San Antonio Area	$1,500,000				
U.S. Virgin Islands				$1,000,000	$1,000,000	$250,000
Utah				$3,980,000	$3,980,000	$995,000
Vermont				$3,980,000	$3,980,000	$995,000
Virginia	Hampton Roads Area	$1,500,000	$1,500,000	$7,120,000	$8,620,000	$2,155,000
Washington	Seattle Area	$5,000,000	$5,000,000	$6,208,000	$11,208,000	$2,802,000
West Virginia				$3,980,000	$3,980,000	$995,000
Wisconsin				$3,980,000	$3,980,000	$995,000
Wyoming				$3,980,000	$3,980,000	$995,000
Total		$580,000,000	$580,000,000	$402,000,000	$982,000,000	$245,500,000

Source: U.S. Department of Homeland Security (DHS). Notice of Funding Opportunity (NOFO), Fiscal Year (FY) 2018 Homeland Security Grant Program (HSGP), May 21, 2018, pg 42. https://www.fema.gov/media-library-data/1526578809767-7f08f471f36d22b2c0d8afb848048c96/FY_2018_HSGP_NOFO_FINAL_508.pdf (accessed June 4, 2018).

amounts are posted as "minimums," or floor amounts for state and local budgeting purposes. It is possible that allocated amounts may not be completely obligated and spent during the federal fiscal year. Conversely, minimum amounts do not necessarily mean that eligible applicants will receive more than the congressionally determined minimums. As Chapter 6 made evident, state, tribal, and territorial governments, and some 32 major urban areas (comprised of the local governments in each UASI eligible urban area), are participants in America's ongoing battle against terrorism. The UASI portion of Tables 7-2a and 7-2b is revisited in a more visually friendly format later in this chapter.

Building from the FY 2017 example, SHSP funds are allocated based on two factors: minimum amounts as legislatively mandated, and DHS's risk methodology. Each fiscal year states, territories, and tribal governments receive a minimum allocation under SHSP using the thresholds established in the Homeland Security Act of 2002, as amended. All 50 states, the District of Columbia, and Puerto Rico receive 0.35 percent of the total funds allocated for grants under Section 2003 and Section 2004 of the Homeland Security Act of 2002. Four territories (American Samoa, Guam, the Northern Mariana Islands, and the U.S. Virgin Islands) receive a minimum allocation of 0.08 percent of the total funds allocated for grants under Section 2003 and 2004 of the Homeland Security Act of 2002.

One major purpose of State Homeland Security Grants is to compensate state, territorial, and tribal governments for the expenses they incur in annually revising their respective emergency operation plans. Those approved to receive money to upgrade their Emergency Operation Plan (EOP) "must update their EOP at least once every two years to comply."[89] Another requirement is submission of a State Preparedness Report (SPR). The SPR is an annual capability assessment. The Post-Katrina Emergency Management Reform Act of 2006 (Pub. L. No. 109-295) has a provision that requires an SPR from any state or territory receiving federal preparedness assistance administered by DHS-FEMA. Each state submits an SPR to DHS-FEMA. Tribal government funding is not shown, however, in Tables 7-2a and 7-2b FEMA data.

Tables 7-2a and 7-2b show us that 35 states and the District of Columbia, by formula, are each provided State Homeland Security Program grants of $3.98 million over FY 2018. Inspection of the tables reveals that states receiving the largest minimum allocations are, largest on down: New York State, California, Texas, Illinois, Florida, Pennsylvania, New Jersey, Ohio, Virginia, Georgia, Michigan, Washington State, Maryland, Massachusetts, and North Carolina. Each one of these states received more than $3.98 million.

Under SHSP, **Threat and Hazard Identification and Risk Assessment (THIRA)** work must be conducted by states, territories, and urban areas. They should review and, if necessary, revise and update their respective THIRAs on an annual basis. A single THIRA submission will support multiple DHS grant awards received by a jurisdiction. The THIRA submission is valid for the entire period of performance of the individual grant award(s). THIRA is part of HSGP requirements. SHSP recipients are also expected to adopt and maintain use of the National Incident Management System (NIMS). Emergency management and incident response activities require carefully managed resources (personnel, teams, facilities, equipment, and/or supplies) to meet incident needs.

The Homeland Security Grant Programs have become interwoven with federal law enforcement and terrorism concerns; this has come to permeate almost every vestige of federal emergency management and national disaster policy. DHS and

DHS-FEMA impose direct federal regulation through grant rules, conditions, part-nerships, intergovernmental information exchange, and reporting and auditing requirements.

Before 9/11, when FEMA grants to states and localities were modestly funded and largely "soft-gloved" regulation, states and localities were free to determine their degree of commitment to the purposes of FEMA between-disaster grants. Most senior FEMA officials serving from 1979 to 2001 hoped that exhortation, best-practices learned in declared disasters and emergencies, and state and local employee commitment to the profession of emergency management would be enough to move slow-to-advance states and localities toward improved disaster mitigation, preparedness, and response. Over that period, most "recovery" lessons were learned in the days, weeks, and months after declared incidents. Today, under the homeland security regime dominating the federal government, many of America's states, cities, counties, and territories work terrorism like federal contractors.[90] Federal money is the primary inducement and the contract work itself is simply a means to that end.

Under the State Homeland Security Program, DHS sets aside 80 percent of its appro-priated funds for local governments. Both SHSP and UASI programs began in the years after the 9/11 attacks, along with smaller grant programs for public transit systems and ports. Among its purposes, the grants help city police departments cope with a terrorism reality that requires more than traditional crime fighting. After 9/11, police needed new expertise and equipment for terrorist attacks. Approaching two decades since the horrific attacks, thanks in part to the funding provided by SHSP and UASI, now police are in a much better position in terms of intelligence collection, analysis, and information shar-ing among police departments.

The Urban Area Security Initiative

Since no one knows, or at least very few know for sure, where terrorists will strike next, officials of nearly every state and local jurisdiction came to see that they had a vested interest in the lavishly funded, homeland security terrorism mission. The Urban Area Security Initiative became law in 2003 and initially included 50 major urban areas of the nation. Through the years, either owing to changes in the congressional or DHS risk formula or to the public administrative fatigue municipal officials suffered in meet-ing the vast and seemingly never-ending requirements of UASI, the pool of UASI areas have shrunk. By FY 2018, owing to fluctuations up and down, there were only 32 UASIs left.[91]

The **Urban Area Security Initiative (UASI)** is a major DHS program, and it involves emergency management. The program is highly complex and a challenge to administer on the federal, state, and, especially, local levels. UASI encapsulates many of the counterterrorism duties and problems that have been imposed on local law enforcement and local emergency management. One aim of UASI is to facili-tate rapid response to attacks from weapons of mass destruction. The urban areas that were selected have high international profiles and large populations.[92] UASI addresses planning, operations, equipment acquisition, training, and exercise needs. The program provides financial assistance to these areas based on a risk-and-needs approach. The amount given to each city is determined by a formula that combines current threat estimates, critical assets within the urban area, and population density. There is no state or local matching fund requirement for this program.

As time has passed, UASI has been used to prepare for "acts of terrorism" and WMDs. The UASI Program helps the designated urban areas "build and sustain the capabilities necessary to prevent, protect against, mitigate, respond to, and recover from both threats and acts of terrorism." The UASI furnishes financial assistance to qualifying urban area local governments that officials can use to address "planning, organization, equipment needs, training, and exercise practices." While UASI local governments are the major stakeholders and clients of the program, the full stakeholder pool is vast because it includes FEMA's much-vaunted "Whole Community Approach."[93]

When local governments align and apply for UASI grants, DHS and FEMA encourage them to consider national priority areas. These include:

- Cybersecurity
- Infrastructure systems
- Economic recovery
- Housing
- Supply chain integrity and security
- Natural and cultural resources
- Risk management for protection programs and activities[94]

"Core" capability activities carried out with UASI funds are expected to support terrorism preparedness across all five mission areas: prevention of, protection from, mitigation of, response to, and recovery from terrorism to be considered eligible. However, many capabilities that support terrorism preparedness simultaneously support preparedness for other hazards. However, grantees must demonstrate the dual-use quality for any activities they want funded. Dual-use activity must be explicitly focused on terrorism preparedness foremost.[95] It is ironic that over the 1970s and 1980s, dual use was a path by which state and local civilian emergency management could grow within the crucible of civil defense against nuclear attack. Under UASI today, planning and preparing for terrorism consequence management is arguably a nest for complementary major city emergency management activities.

The Urban Area Security Initiative in 2018–2019

According to a May 22, 2018, DHS announcement, for federal fiscal year (FY) 2018, the Urban Area Security Initiative (UASI) funds will be awarded directly to 32 high-threat, high-density urban areas for the purpose of improving regional preparedness and capabilities. The sum of funding devoted to the program represents congressional intent to limit FY 2018 UASI funding to those urban areas that represent up to 85 percent of the nationwide risk.[96]

Grant recipients are encouraged to use grant funding to maintain and sustain current critical core capabilities through investments in training and exercises, updates to current planning and procedures, and lifecycle replacement of equipment. New capabilities that win homeland security grant funding must be available to support regional and national efforts. All capabilities being built or sustained must have a clear linkage to the core capabilities articulated in the National Preparedness Goal.

Table 7-3 depicts FY 2018 (October 1, 2017 to September 30, 2018) congressionally determined allocations for UASI funding. Table 7-3 has columns for state, funded urban area, and amount of allocation. Note that the urban areas of 21 states and the District of Columbia are included, thus excluding 29 states and all U.S. territorial and tribal governments.[97]

Many of the urban areas making the list are not only highly populated and commercially important, but are located near critical military facilities, naval ports, air bases or air stations, army bases, and major defense industries. Nearly all of them have major international airports through which travelers enter and exit the United States.

Table 7-3 indicates that 21 states and the District of Columbia were allocated UASI funds. The in-state metropolitan area of New York City and its environs are understandably promised the largest amount: $178.75 million. The Los Angeles/Long Beach area of California comes in second with $68 million. However, California contains six UASI areas, including Los Angeles/Long Beach. If funds for all six California UASI areas are summed, the state as a whole received a $122.7 million allocation. Moving down the list, Florida and Texas each have three UASI areas. The Texas total is $16.32 million and Florida's total is about $10.5 million. Pennsylvania (Philadelphia and Pittsburgh) has two UASI areas and the UASI total going to these areas is $20 million.

Early in the life of the program DHS officials informed states of their cities' eligibility for the program. The state government must obligate at least 80 percent of all federal funding provided through the program to the designated urban area within 60 days after receipt of funds. The UASI program was part of the consolidated HSGP and operates on biennial (two-year) cycles, which means UASI recipients do not need to reapply to receive second-year funding.

Central to the UASI mission is helping state and local governments build and maintain the capability to prevent, protect against, respond to, and recover from threats or acts of terrorism. The range of expected terrorism (whether state-sponsored or non-state-actor-initiated) threats includes an array of attack weapons commonly referred to as **chemical, biological, radiological, or nuclear (CBRN)**. The radiological includes dirty bombs, and the nuclear involves atomic weapons.

In the aftermath of Hurricane Katrina in 2005, however, policymakers called for a change in UASI national planning priorities. They required that the program also address issues such as pandemic influenza and catastrophic disaster (as might be caused by a major hurricane or earthquake). Administrators of UASI were asked to accommodate catastrophic events like Hurricane Katrina, something most local emergency managers were happy to see. In effect, post-Katrina changes in the program reintroduced "dual-use" requirements of the type common in the Cold War civil defense era. UASI grants could fund nonterror disaster management but only on condition that these activities "also" enhanced the jurisdiction's ability to address terrorism: "dual use."

TABLE 7-3 ■ Federal Fiscal Year 2018 UASI Funding Allocations by State, Urban Area, and Amount of Allocation

State/Territory	Funded Urban Area	FY 2018 UASI Allocation
Arizona	Phoenix Area	$4,000,000
California	Anaheim/Santa Ana Area	$5,000,000
	Bay Area	$27,500,000
	Los Angeles/Long Beach Area	$68,000,000
	Riverside Area	$3,000,000
	Sacramento Area	$2,500,000
	San Diego Area	$16,700,000
Colorado	Denver Area	$3,000,000
District of Columbia	National Capital Region	$52,750,000
Florida	Miami/Fort Lauderdale Area	$6,000,000
	Orlando Area	$1,500,000
	Tampa Area	$3,000,000
Georgia	Atlanta Area	$6,000,000
Hawaii	Honolulu Area	$1,500,000
Illinois	Chicago Area	$68,000,000
Maryland	Baltimore Area	$4,000,000
Massachusetts	Boston Area	$17,500,000
Michigan	Detroit Area	$5,000,000
Minnesota	Twin Cities Area	$5,000,000
Missouri	St. Louis Area	$3,000,000
Nevada	Las Vegas Area	$5,000,000
New Jersey	Jersey City/Newark Area	$22,750,000
New York	New York City Area	$178,750,000
North Carolina	Charlotte Area	$2,500,000
Oregon	Portland Area	$2,500,000
Pennsylvania	Philadelphia Area	$17,500,000
	Pittsburgh Area	$2,500,000

	Dallas/Fort Worth/Arlington Area	$14,800,000
Texas	Houston Area	$22,750,000
	San Antonio Area	$1,500,000
Virginia	Hampton Roads Area	$1,500,000
Washington	Seattle Area	$5,000,000
Total		$580,000,000

Source: U.S. Department of Homeland Security (DHS). Notice of Funding Opportunity (NOFO), Fiscal Year (FY) 2018 Homeland Security Grant Program (HSGP), May 21, 2018, pg 40. https://www.fema.gov/media-library-data/1526578809767-7f08f471f36d22 b2c0d8afb848048c96/FY_2018_HSGP_NOFO_FINAL_508.pdf (accessed June 4, 2018).

Although the program dispensed the grants by formula, eligible governments had to apply for UASI funds and win DHS approval. Funds provided were to address the unique needs of large urban municipal government areas and mass transit authority special district governments. As mentioned previously, UASI funds could be used for equipment, training, exercises, and planning but could neither be used to hire new employees nor subsidize salaries of current workers. This program limitation produced considerable managerial and political controversy. Some state and local officials objected to the limited sets of purposes UASI funds could be used to address. The program was heavily biased toward the purchase of DHS-approved equipment. This may appear to be a minor problem, but because almost all of the DHS-approved equipment was geared for counterterrorism purposes and because UASI money came almost exclusively for the purchase of equipment (not for salaries to pay personnel), distortions resulted at the local level.

In some cases, state and local governments were accused of using UASI funds to purchase lavish, unnecessary, and exotic counterterrorism equipment. News investigations of such activity triggered claims of wasteful spending and pork barreling.[98] The counterargument might be that local officials, fearing that seemingly one-time federal UASI or other homeland security grant funds would be lost or would go to other jurisdictions and appreciating that they are rarely the beneficiaries of federal largess, may have felt justified in purchasing vehicles and equipment that were excessive or of questionable necessity. Where that equipment had dual-use application that worked to the benefit of local emergency management, such equipment acquisitions might have been judged acceptable by both the public and journalist investigators.

Federal UASI funding came with an immense number of "strings attached." For governments in eligible urban areas, UASI imposed prodigious paperwork and office computing demands. Applicant governments had to demonstrate that they had prepared an Urban Area Homeland Security Strategy and that their state government had in place a state program and Capability Enhancement Plan. Even then, applicant governments had to document that their request for UASI funding was consistent with the goals, objectives, and priorities of the national Urban Area Homeland Security Strategy and in conformity with UASI policies and conditions. Applicant local governments also had to prove that their Urban Area Homeland Security Strategy was consistent with their respective state's Homeland Security Plan. The state government itself was expected to have in place a program and Capability Enhancement Plan, under requirements of the DHS SHSP. Of late, UASI has sought to build greater regional capabilities across selected geographic areas.

All eligible applicants must submit an "investment justification." This identifies needs and outlines the intended security improvement plan to be addressed with the funding. That plan is expected to meet the target capabilities outlined in the National Preparedness Goal, itself a product of HSPD-8, issued in December 2005. **Target capability** is homeland security jargon that refers to the ability of a government jurisdiction to prevent, or respond to, a range of different types of terrorist attacks. Investment justifications are reviewed, scored, and prioritized (by DHS-FEMA officials) along with risk factors to determine which investments should be funded to best address need and minimize risk.

UASI is only one of several HSGPs directed to state and local government. Unfortunately, each of these programs is rife with federal "boilerplate" language that for many state and local officials (as well as professors, students, and others) makes them unclear and arbitrary. The complexity of these programs opens the door to considerable misunderstanding. UASI demands that local recipients of government grants collect a massive amount of information and use it to engage in elaborate planning work. More than this, the plans are tested against envisioned scenarios, most of them anticipating some type of terror attack with some type of terror weapon. The burden of UASI paperwork reportage represents a partially unfunded mandate imposed by the federal government on state and local governments. Moreover, several scholars who have researched UASI have concluded, "Without a clear definition of outcome measures to determine program effectiveness and empirical evaluations on counter-terrorism initiatives, it appears that the UASI program and other counterterrorism policies that espouse the elimination of terrorism in the United States seem a futile gesture and only appease the public's fear of terrorism rather than contributing to real-world outcomes. Even more problematic, without clear and defined definitions of terrorism, how are we to implement counter-terrorism initiatives that work? At the end of the day, we are left with the questions: Is it worth it? Are the billions of dollars being spent in efforts to curb terrorism offset by lives being saved? Does counter-terrorism policy match the threat of terrorism?"[99] Van Um and Pisoiu provide one possible answer: "It is not the policy-makers or those executing a specific law any longer who determine the effectiveness of a policy, but the reaction of the target of such a policy, the one that in the end makes a certain policy a success or failure."[100]

Law Enforcement Terrorism Prevention Activities

As indicated, DHS-FEMA is required by law to make sure that "at least 25 percent of appropriated grant (HSGP) funding goes to law enforcement terrorism prevention activities under Law Enforcement Terrorism Prevention Activities (LETPA) funding."

DHS/FEMA meets this requirement, in part, "by requiring (that) all SHSP and UASI recipients devote at least twenty five percent (25%) of the funds they are allocated under SHSP and UASI to law enforcement terrorism prevention activities.[101]

Tables 7-2a and 7-2b have a column for LETPA funding. That column reveals that New York State received the largest LETPA allocation for FY 2018: $63.92 million. California received the second largest LETPA allocation: $45.484 million. Illinois received $20.928 million followed by Texas with $14.91 million and the District of Columbia with $14.182 million. Twenty-nine states each collected $950,000 (about $1 million) in LETPA funding allocations for FY 2018.

The **Law Enforcement Terrorism Prevention Program (LETPP)**, whose name was changed to Law Enforcement Terrorism Prevention Activities program (LETPA) in 2016, supports law enforcement communities in their efforts to detect, deter, disrupt, and prevent acts of terrorism. Categories of aid include the following:

- Information sharing to preempt terrorist attacks

- Target hardening to reduce vulnerability of selected high-value targets

- Recognition and mapping of potential or developing threats

- Interoperable communications

- Interdiction of terrorists before they can execute a threat or intervention activities that prevent terrorists from executing a threat

- As in other Homeland Security program grants, federal funding is disbursed first to the state government. Local law enforcement agencies are then advised to work with and seek LETPP funding from the state's lead law enforcement agency.

The LETPA encourages its participating organizations to collaborate with private security organizations, government agencies outside law enforcement, and with the private sector in general. The LETPA has no matching grant provisions. Why mention the LETPA in a study of disaster management? The LETPA recruits local law enforcement into the counterterrorism business. The program's use of so-called Fusion Centers provides a nexus of local, state, and federal terrorism-focused law enforcement; and local emergency managers are part of this realm.

Fusion Centers

In the past 10 years, the federal government has given state and local governments more than $35 billion for planning, response, and recovery efforts related to natural disasters, terrorist attacks, and other events. As a result, there are now 78 information hubs—officially called **fusion centers**—that allow federal, state, and local public safety agencies to collaborate effectively in circumstances similar to those of the Boston Marathon bombing. The money covers a range of uses, including training exercises for mass shootings and the replacement of first-responder radios. But as Coburn's report points out, some of the projects that received funding have a less clear-cut role in combatting terrorism.[102] See Figure 7-2 for a list of federal participants in fusion centers, which includes DHS, DHS-FEMA, and others.

FIGURE 7-2 ■ Major Participants in Fusion Centers

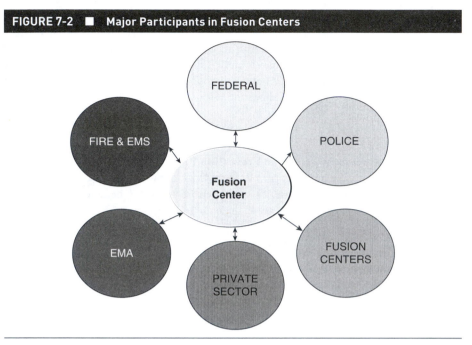

Source: Indiana Intelligence Fusion Center Communities of Interest, Liaison Outreach Program, https://www.in.gov/iifc/2364.htm (accessed June 5, 2018).

Private-sector members often include executives of major privately owned utilities or managers of critical infrastructure. EMA stands for state emergency management agency. Note that all fusion centers over the United States are linked with one another and share information.

The National "Prevention" Framework describes the actions that should be taken when an imminent threat to the homeland is detected. Some of this may stem from state or local discovery or it may be the product of intelligence gathering or information collection. The detection of such a threat may help law enforcement thwart the attack or perhaps prevent a follow-on terrorist attack.[103]

The National Prevention Framework offers guidance to authorities and the public that they can presumably use to prepare for, possibly prevent, avoid the effects of, or stop an act of terrorism. Some of the costs incurred in conducting the activities outlined in the National Prevention Framework may be covered by LETPA funds. In addition, LETPA funding may also be used to help achieve National "Protection" Framework capabilities. Other terrorism prevention activities proposed for funding under LETPA must be approved by the FEMA administrator. Determining if funding will go to a new law enforcement counterterrorism initiative is an interesting and different assignment for the FEMA administrator.[104]

DHS-FEMA uses risk calculations in its grant allocation decisions. DHS defines risk as "potential for an unwanted outcome resulting from an incident, event, or occurrence, as determined by its likelihood and the associated consequences."[105] Obviously, DHS means to apply this definition to incidents caused by terrorists, natural forces, or non-terror human causes.

DHS utilizes a **comprehensive risk methodology** focused on three principal elements:

- Threat

- Vulnerability

- Consequence[106]

The risk methodology calculates the relative risk of terrorism faced by a given area. It takes into account the potential risk of terrorism to people, critical infrastructure, and economic security. The threat analysis also considers threats from domestic violent extremists as well as international terrorist groups and those individuals inspired by terrorists abroad.[107]

OPERATION STONEGARDEN

Operation Stonegarden (OPSG) aims to improve "cooperation and coordination among Customs and Border Protection (CBP), United States Border Patrol (USBP), and local, Tribal, territorial, state, and Federal law enforcement agencies. The OPSG Program funds joint efforts to secure the United States borders along routes of ingress from international borders. Such routes include travel corridors in states bordering Mexico and Canada, as well as states and territories with international water borders."[108] OPSG supports border states and territories in accomplishing these objectives:

- Increase capability to prevent, protect against, and respond to border security issues

- Encourage local operational objectives and capabilities to enhance National and State Homeland Security Strategies (such as the Federal Secure Borders Initiative and United States CBP/BP strategies)

- Increase coordination and collaboration among federal, state, local, tribal, and territorial law enforcement agencies

- Continue the distinct capability enhancements required for border security and border protection

- Provide intelligence-based operations through CBP/BP Sector Level experts to ensure safety and operational oversight of federal, state, local, tribal, and territorial law enforcement agencies participating in OPSG operational activities

- Support a request to the governor to activate, deploy, or redeploy specialized National Guard Units/Packages and/or elements of State law enforcement to increase or augment specialized/technical law enforcement elements operational activities

- Continue to increase operational, material and technological readiness of state, local, tribal, and territorial law enforcement agencies[109]

OPSG funds must be used to improve federal, state, local, tribal, and territorial law enforcement capabilities. The aim is to create "a layered, coordinated approach to law enforcement within United States Border States and territories."[110]

The FY 2017 allocation to the Operation Stonegarden program was $55,000,000. For FY 2018, up to $85,000,000 is available. OPSG funds are allocated based on the risk to the security of the border. Cost sharing/matching is not required. Project periods will extend up to 36 months, starting September 1, 2018.

Subrecipients eligible to apply for funding from their State Administrative Agency (SAA) are divided into three tiers:

- Tier 1: are jurisdictions on a physical border in states bordering Canada, states bordering Mexico, and states and territories with international water borders.

- Tier 2: are jurisdictions not located on the physical border or international water but are contiguous to a Tier 1 county.

- Tier 3: are jurisdictions not located on the physical border or international water but are contiguous to a Tier 2 eligible subrecipient.[111]

This system of tiers instructs qualifying states to direct OPSG funds they receive to local jurisdictions directly on an International Border or with an ocean coastline to get priority funding. Tier 2 are jurisdictions adjacent to Tier 1 jurisdictions. Tier 3 are jurisdictions adjacent to Tier 2. Awards are made to SAAs of international border states. The state administering agency must pass through 100% of OPSG allocations to eligible jurisdictions. State agencies, local and tribal law enforcement agencies that are located along the border of the United States may then apply to states for sub-grants.

In 2018, administering state agencies were to apply to FEMA on behalf of local agencies by June 20. Local deadlines vary based on state administration. As disclosed previously, $85 million is available for OPSG funding for FY 2018. OPSG funds are allocated based on the risk to the security of the border. Project periods extend up to 36 months, starting September 1, 2018.[112] DHS justifies this arrangement by insisting, "Delivering core capabilities requires the combined effort of the whole community, rather than the exclusive effort of any single organization or level of government."

While Stonegarden looks impressive, its $85 million FY 2018 budget is to be allocated across every international border state and ocean coastal state (and territory) on the basis of a 100 percent pass-through to qualifying local governments inside those jurisdictions. When apportioned over the entire pool of potential applicants, Stonegarden money for any single recipient promises to be modest.

The OSGP is included in this study because it is evidence that through DHS, federal laws, and DHS funding, FEMA is now part of border security and immigration control. Recall that about a quarter of all State Homeland Security and Urban Area Security Initiative grant funds are funneled to LETPA with a share going to Stonegarden purposes. State and local governments receive these SHSG and UASI obligated funds but only on condition that within the approved set of state and local projects and initiatives approved, they make sure to devote a quarter of the funds each receives to LETPA, and indirectly to Stonegarden.

In plain language, if you are a local official applying for and receiving SHSG and UASI money for your agency, you must demonstrate that you have dedicated a quarter of these funds to LETPA purposes and for certain states, to meet Stonegarden objectives: border security and immigration control. Whereas, in the past American local government leaders did not see their jurisdictions as in the "business" of border security and immigration enforcement, today owing to interlocking homeland security grants, many are being federally paid (free of state–local match) to do exactly that. Controversially, the design of this system of federal funding subsidizes anti-terrorism state and local law enforcement broadly and border security and immigration control narrowly.

HOMELAND SECURITY GRANTS AND THEIR EFFECTS AT THE LOCAL LEVEL

Since the 1980s the all-hazards approach to civil defense and emergency management has developed into an intricate system of intergovernmental relations dominated by a panoply of homeland security missions and purposes. On September 11, 2001, the United States withstood its most catastrophic terrorist attack by non-state actors. Despite the tragic and heroic losses of a great many firefighters, police officers, and other emergency responders, as well as several thousand innocent victims, the existing broad-gauged intergovernmental system for disaster and recovery management worked well. The intergovernmental response to the terror attack on the Pentagon has been widely praised. However, the president and other policymakers concluded that prevention should be the focus in addressing future terror threats and attacks. Consequently, authorities introduced prevention as a phase in emergency management.[113]

Homeland Security Presidential Directive-1 (HSPD-1) of October 29, 2001, made terrorism a national security responsibility to be handled in a coordinated way by federal, state, and local officials. Natural and technological hazards were still judged to be the responsibility of the local and state governments, with federal assistance. Yet, HSPD-1 defined terrorism preparedness as "a critical national security function" requiring extensive coordination across all levels of government.[114] Other homeland security presidential directives, federal laws, and a battery of federal grant programs were enacted into law. Collectively, these measures prescribed to local governments the exact steps they were expected to take. These measures gave terrorism preparedness priority over preparedness for other types of disaster agents.

After enactment of the Homeland Security Act of 2002, it soon became apparent that the entire federal homeland security mechanism would be dominated by criminal justice and national security officials. Terrorism prevention again took precedence over all other types of mitigation and preparedness.[115] Policymakers used homeland security funding to induce state and local authorities to join a system of reinforcing cross-jurisdictional information sharing. Much of this involved building up data sets about "persons of interest." A great share of UASI work came at the expense of preparing for non-terrorism hazards, emergencies, and disasters. The presence of potential terrorists and their supporters, known as "persons of interest," was one of the few bases for rating a locality's vulnerability to terrorism, or "threat level," under the 2004 UASI.[116]

The SHSP, the UASI, Emergency Management Performance Grants (EMPGs), Community Emergency Response Teams (CERTs), and LEPTA were at first separate grant-issuing programs with individual purposes. However, in accord with evolving law and policy, DHS consolidated these programs under the SHSP to ensure that all would need to operate with state government as an intermediary between federal and local governments. At first, homeland security grants did not directly permit funding of conventional disaster mitigation and preparedness. Although the 2002 Homeland Security Act references "major disaster" as defined in the Stafford Act, the core mission of DHS is to prevent and prepare for terrorism. Other provisions of the act refer to the phases of the terrorism management cycle (prevention, response, and recovery) for which the department is responsible. Furthermore, the law declares that "the department shall also be responsible for carrying out other functions of the entities transferred to the department as provided by law." Because the law is vague, DHS has funneled its resources heavily toward its main priority: terrorism.

Mitigation has changed from public works activities to those related to criminal justice. Preparedness is defined in terms of surveillance capabilities. Owing to these reforms, local emergency planning has been subsumed within a nation-centered, president-dominated authority model [the inclusive-authority model].[117] For local emergency managers, compliance with homeland security requirements is both daunting and seemingly never ending.

The National Preparedness Goal aims to create "capability-based planning." This has three components: **national planning scenarios**, a Universal Task List, and a **target capabilities list**. About "target capabilities," granting it seems strange to attribute capabilities to inanimate objects, it is the military-like thinking and verbiage that is telling. Today's DHS and its FEMA have replaced emergency management disaster phases terminology with "capabilities and missions" terminology; these are part of "military-speak."

The DHS developed a set of 15 "planning scenarios" that encompass the range of "plausible" events that could pose the greatest risk to the nation.[118] These scenarios were intended to be used in evaluating the ability of a jurisdiction to manage a major disaster. Local officials were supposed to select those scenarios they thought most likely to occur in their areas and determine if their current capabilities would enable them to save lives, protect property, and revive their local economies.

The 15 scenarios encompass disasters caused by the following:

- Improvised nuclear device

- Aerosol anthrax

- Pandemic influenza

- Plague

- Blister agent

- Toxic industrial chemicals

- Nerve agent

- Chlorine tank explosion

- Major earthquake

- Major hurricane

- Radiological dispersal device

- Improvised explosive device

- Food contamination

- Foreign animal disease

- Cyberattack[119]

In practice, leaders are asked to count their jurisdiction's response resources and to engage in "tabletop" exercises playing each of these 15 scenarios.

The 2006 UASI grant guidance changed the exercise from an evaluation of performance to a commitment to using future grant money to correct the deficiencies.[120] The annual exercise cycle topic is dictated by the state, which may select only from the scenario list provided by the federal government. The type of disaster agent selected may not be important for a given location; in other words, the participating UASI local government officials may be asked to conduct an exercise to address what for them is an extremely rare and unlikely event.

The purpose of developing a set of scenarios was to prompt consideration of a wide range of potential disaster events, with a goal of identifying "the critical tasks and capabilities that would be required from all sources in a coordinated national effort to manage major events."[121]

The **Universal Task List** was developed to describe "what tasks need to be performed," "who needs to perform them," and "how to perform them."[122] Individual governments were to use the list to document their existing capabilities to respond to the 15 planning scenarios. They were expected to create a plan for the use of federal counterterrorism grant funds and locally available funds to address missing capabilities they discover in their planning. The Universal Task List contains an astounding 1,600 different tasks. Moreover, it is impossible for local government officials to maintain a correct list of all the resources needed and available to fulfill each task. Equipment breakdowns, personnel absenteeism, and shift-work schedules all prevent an accurate operational picture of the resources available in a community at any moment. Asking local officials to address 1,600 different tasks as part of the "All Hazards Taxonomy of National Preparedness Tasks," combined with associated planning and preparedness demands, is both daunting and unrealistic.[123]

Mitigation, a core phase of conventional emergency management, is located under "Protect" in the "All Hazards Taxonomy" and is stipulated as "Mitigate Risk to Public," but there is no provision for capital projects. The purpose of physical protection is subjugated under the criminal justice mind-set of "Prevent." The UASI program uses evocative imperatives such as "Detect Threats," "Control Access," and "Eliminate Threats," all of which are focused on human suspects and weapons. Little to nothing in the taxonomy addresses preventing loss of life and maintaining economic viability in anticipation of natural disasters through mitigation measures like construction of protective structures or the application of building codes.[124]

From 2006 onward, the principal scheme for allocating federal preparedness funds to local governments was based on a combination of threat analysis and population. The funding distribution scheme also penalizes local emergency response groups when hazards they must prepare for fall outside the accepted threat analysis. For local governments without a significant terrorism threat, there may be little or no funding available for emergency preparedness for disasters previously supported by federal funding assistance. Even those larger and more complex municipalities that have continued to receive homeland security funding have experienced some erosion in their nonterror emergency management capability.

In 2005, federal agencies undertook an evaluation of critical infrastructure based on the CARVER technique, developed by the DOD for "the military's target prioritization purposes."[125] Infrastructure was evaluated according to the following criteria:

Criticality. How important is the target? Importance is determined by the impact of its destruction on operations and whether or not substitutes or backups exist for the target.

Accessibility. How easily can a target be reached, either by infiltration or weapons?

Recoverability. How long will it take to replace or repair the target once it is damaged or destroyed?

Vulnerability. How susceptible is the target, and its construction, to an attack?

Effect. What impact will the target's destruction have on the public, including psychological, domestic, and international ramifications? For instance, will it shake the public's confidence in the enterprise's systems, policies, processes?

Recognizability. How readily can a target be identified and not confused with other structures?[126]

CARVER was part of the UASI and so local officials whose jurisdictions fell within or overlapped UASI eligible areas were, as a condition of the grant, put to work on this type of target identification, management, and hardening. These confidential site lists were developed by a committee within the executive branch of the federal government. The national list of critical sites was kept confidential but was used to estimate threat in the early days of the UASI program. Priority targets tended to be large stadiums and iconic structures (e.g., the Golden Gate Bridge, the Statue of Liberty, major sports stadiums, civic events); lower priority targets were high-tech and utility facilities. Each state was "assigned" a certain number of sites. The state could then contest the priority of the specific sites and substitute other locations the state deemed more critical, provided the number of sites assigned to the state remained the same.

THE EMERGENCY MANAGEMENT PERFORMANCE GRANT PROGRAM

Emergency Management Performance Grants (EMPGs) are allocated to states, which then use the money to bolster their intrastate emergency management programs and capabilities. EMPG funds are to "support comprehensive emergency management at the state and local levels and to encourage the improvement of mitigation, preparedness, response, and recovery capabilities for all-hazards."[127] DHS-FEMA wants states to use EMPG money to foster partnerships of government, business, volunteer, and community organizations. DHS-FEMA also suggests that the funds be used to pay for joint operations, mutual aid, local and regional support, and state-to-state cooperation. For many years, EMPGs were based on dual-use Cold War funding for local emergency preparedness programs that had evolved from civil defense against nuclear attack.[128]

States are free to decide on their own how much EMPG money they will pass on to their local jurisdictions.[129] EMPGs are designed to help state and local emergency managers develop, maintain, and improve their emergency management capabilities, providing assistance in emergency planning, training, exercising, and interdisciplinary coordination. Although only part of the DHS grants package, EMPG recipients are asked to concentrate on the most likely hazards of their respective local jurisdictions, such as earthquake, hurricane, and flood. Through this program, FEMA provides states the flexibility to allocate funds according to their respective risk and to address the most urgent state and local needs in disaster mitigation, preparedness, response, and recovery. Under the program, DHS-FEMA expects these governments to achieve measurable results in key functional areas of emergency management. All states are eligible.[130] Local governments must apply through their state governments to FEMA. Funding under this program is ultimately used by emergency management organizations.

Why is the EMPG program included in a civil-military and national security chapter? Perhaps the notice posted by DHS-FEMA for FY 2018, shown below, answers this question.

Over FY 2018, "FEMA regional administrators and state emergency management directors will negotiate an exercise program that addresses capability gaps in the priority areas of logistics, housing, and catastrophic planning. These exercises will be included in the EMPG work plan submitted for FEMA regional approval and the state's Training and Exercise Plan."[131] It adds in great bureaucratese, "EMPG recipients will report through the new THIRA/SPR methodology that will be implemented in 2018, with a revised THIRA methodology for response, recovery, and crosscutting core capabilities by December 31, 2018. Jurisdictions will need to complete the entire methodology for all 32 core capabilities by December 2019. Beginning in 2019, recipients will submit a THIRA only every three years. An annual capability assessment will still be required." Hence, EMPG has been yoked to serve the terrorism mission first and an emergency management mission second.[132]

EMPGs were funded at a national total of $332.5 million in fiscal year 2013, but since 2014 they have been funded each fiscal year (FY 2014–FY 2018) at $350.1 million nationwide. The EMPG program supports core capabilities across the five mission areas of Prevention, Protection, Mitigation, Response, and Recovery based on allowable costs.

Eligible applicants include all 50 states, the District of Columbia, tribal governments, plus commonwealth and trust territories, including the Republic of the Marshall Islands and the Federated States of Micronesia.[133]

REPLACEMENT OF THE USA PATRIOT ACT OF 2001

A few first principles: FEMA has been part of the Department of Homeland Security since 2003. DHS is in the business of domestic surveillance and data collection as a member of the nation's intelligence community. Presumably, DHS intelligence work serves a counterterrorism purpose and this work also furnishes information to many arms of the department: Transportation Security Administration, U.S. Secret Service, U.S. Coast Guard, U.S. Citizen and Immigration Services, U.S. Customs and Border Protection, U.S. Immigration and Customs Enforcement, and FEMA, to name a few. This information serves a terrorism prevention and preparedness purpose. Through its nearly two decades of operation in DHS, FEMA has been "read in" to this intelligence work. Recall, FEMA has long shouldered various forms of national security work. Consequently, FEMA's continued integration into the DHS community of agencies means it is doing much more intelligence-related work than it did as an independent agency (1979–2002). Hence, the subject of intelligence gathering interweaves modern federal disaster policy and management.

The **USA PATRIOT Act** (Uniting and Strengthening America by Providing Appropriate Tools Required to Intercept and Obstruct Terrorism) hurriedly enacted into law after the 9/11 attacks significantly changed public policy and expanded collaboration between the federal, state, and local governments and the U.S. military. Article 2 of the Patriot Act stated that information sharing could take place among government agencies (to enhance investigative efforts). This removed a long-established barrier that prevented law enforcement, intelligence, and defense agencies from exchanging information and cooperating in investigations.

In addition, Article 2 established new rules of collaboration between police and military that permitted the exchange of military tactics, organization, and hardware to support state and local law enforcement investigations and operations. Article 3 of the Patriot Act provided for the rapid updating of cybertechnology countermeasures to fight a more advanced digital-age battle with terrorists. The Patriot Act was subject to reauthorization and, in the absence of a renewal, sunsetting (termination).

Under the Patriot Act, outside of domestic intelligence gathering, militarization was carried out through the purchase of, or transfer of, large amounts of surplus military equipment to state and local law enforcement agencies. The Patriot Act provided the legal basis for the transfer of surplus military equipment while the Homeland Security Grant Program (HSGP) provided the financial resources.

By June 2013, revelations of global and comprehensive telecommunications and Internet spying by the National Security Agency divulged by disgruntled computer analyst Edward Snowden, a federal contractor employee who sought and secured temporary asylum in Russia, underscored the end of telephonic and Internet communication privacy for Americans and most of the rest of the world.[134]

Meanwhile, the American Civil Liberties Union (ACLU) maintained that the greatest threat to our civil rights is posed by the militarization of law.[135] The excessive militarization of law enforcement operations runs counter to the Fourteenth Amendment wherein it asserts the guaranteed privileges and immunities of citizenship, due process, and equal protection. A backlash to the Patriot Act grew during the Obama administration (2009–2017).

The USA PATRIOT Act Is Overhauled and Replaced

"When the National Security Agency's (NSA's) secret programs were made public in leaks by whistleblower Edward Snowden, it resulted in debates on the balance between liberty and security. Many argued that it isn't so much about what the government is allowed to know but what government, holding unique powers, is allowed to do with what it knows. The Fourth Amendment tacitly speaks of the extent of the government's authority and the right of the people to be protected from unwarranted spying. Without curtailment, such a scale of power could cripple civil liberties, and the surveillance of the public could be considered an overreach of the government's authority."[136]

By 2015, there was growing bipartisan support in Congress for revision and replacement of the Patriot Act. The response came in the form of a bill entitled the **USA Freedom Act**. The Patriot Act had been re-authorized at least twice since its original enactment, but it faced a June 1, 2015, expiration unless it was again reauthorized. After several unsuccessful attempts, the U.S. Senate ultimately passed, along with a more agreeable U.S. House, the Patriot Act's replacement, the USA Freedom Act. The new law would end the bulk collection of phone records by the National Security Agency (NSA) and restore the protection of people's rights by allowing a streamlined and transparent process of getting access to Americans' phone records by means of a specific "selector" such as customer names, or numbers.[137]

Generally, the Freedom Act's interventions were met with acclaim from privacy advocates, reformists, and the tech industry. While hailed as a "milestone" achievement, many insisted that it only addressed a "small slice" of the mass surveillance apparatus and that a bigger move beyond mere fixes was still needed.[138]

As mentioned, the Freedom Act, law since 2015, bans bulk collection of metadata on phone calls. A tech journal report comments that "the language of Section 215 of the Patriot Act allowed for confidential court orders to collect 'tangible things' with no restraint, which includes everything from driver's license information to Internet browsing patterns—anything that could be relevant to government investigations for the purpose of counter-terrorism. Following the 9/11 attacks, it seemed fairly prudent to widen the government's counterintelligence capabilities to 'connect the dots' of probable terrorist plans. The tension between individual freedom and national security accelerated when the single-minded focus on counterterrorism shifted toward an intensified concern over civil liberties. After the Snowden revelations . . . something that initially seemed okay simply didn't seem okay anymore."[139]

The article added, "With domestic clandestine programs like Prism and Xkeyscore, as well as global surveillance programs such as Tempora, Muscular, Stateroom, and others, it could be presumed that metadata—or Big Data—could be misused, especially considering that they are covertly run on innocent, unknowing people, and not just to catch a terrorist. What does it mean to you? Ultimately, transparency is crucial for trust. If someone enters a purchase, their information and credentials (i.e. debit card and pin data) are collected in order to complete the transaction, and the customer expects the bank to hold their information securely. This also applies to sensitive information and associated metadata used by the healthcare industry, schools, and government bodies where data is expected to be held anonymously. While the NSA moderately collects data for good purposes, it could also hypothetically be used to arbitrarily frame an innocent citizen, and it's a situation that no one should have to deal with."[140]

THE HOMELAND SECURITY ADVISORY SYSTEM

On March 12, 2002, DHS launched the highly problematic **Homeland Security Advisory System (HSAS)**. It was a threat-based, color-coded system used to inform the American public and its safety officials about the status of terrorist threat to the nation or to parts of the nation. Government authorities and the public could thereby exercise heightened vigilance that might thwart a terrorist attack, or, should an attack of some sort be imminent, they could take appropriate protective measures.

State and local criticism of, and resistance to, the threat-based, color-coded HSAS contributed to its elimination. The HSAS was replaced by the **National Terrorism Advisory System (NTAS)** in April 2011. Color coding was eliminated, and only two levels of alert were employed. See the "Tell Me More" 7-2 box.

TELL ME MORE 7-2
THE NATIONAL TERRORISM ADVISORY SYSTEM

The NTAS was launched to replace the highly controversial and unpopular HSAS. The HSAS color-ramped alert schema was poorly conceived and operated by DHS and, worse still, it alienated a great many state and local public officials, including emergency managers. The NTAS offered simplification; somewhat greater specificity about threat posed, possible target(s), and recommended response actions; time limits on how long advisories stand; and a two-tiered audience notification method.

NTAS alerts come through two categories:

Imminent Threat Alert: Warns of a credible, specific, and impending terrorist threat against the United States.

Elevated Threat Alert: Warns of a credible terrorist threat against the United States.

After reviewing the available information, the secretary of DHS will decide, in coordination with other federal entities, whether an NTAS alert should be issued.

NTAS alerts will only be issued when credible information is available.

These alerts will include a clear statement that there is an imminent threat or elevated threat. The alerts will provide a concise summary of the potential threat; information about actions being taken to ensure public safety; and recommended steps that individuals, communities, businesses, and governments can take to help prevent, mitigate, or respond to the threat.

The NTAS alerts will be based on the nature of the threat: in some cases, alerts will be sent directly to law enforcement or affected areas of the private sector, while in others, alerts will be issued more broadly to the American people through both official and media channels.

Sunset Provision

An individual threat alert is issued for a specific time period and then automatically expires. It may be extended if new informa-tion becomes available or the threat evolves. Thus, NTAS alerts contain a sunset provision indicating a specific date when the alert expires; there will not be a constant NTAS alert or blanket warning that there is an overarching threat. If threat information changes for an alert, the secretary of DHS may announce an updated NTAS alert. All changes, including the announcement that cancels an NTAS alert, will be distributed the same way as the original alert.[141]

Summary

Most disasters, including terrorist attacks, can be handled by civilian emergency responders. However, as mentioned, for some truly cata-strophic disasters in which civilian authorities and nongovernmental organizations (NGOs) are overwhelmed, a military role is necessary. It may be that catastrophic disasters—events that over-whelm the capacity of state and local govern-ments—require a large-scale military response. Use of the National Guard (Title 32) in domestic disaster response is not as contentious an issue as employing active-duty military (Title 10) per-sonnel in disaster response. The establishment of USNORTHCOM has opened the door to more fre-quent introduction of federal military people in U.S. disaster management. The federal military plays a major role in matters of bioterrorism and weapons of mass destruction attacks, as well as in federal catastrophic disaster planning; this means that the Pentagon's (Title 10) military is now integral in the national system of emergency management. The overlap of homeland security and catastrophic disaster management in the United States sug-gests that it would be both counterproductive and inefficient to wall off U.S. Armed Forces (Title 10) from assisting in domestic disaster management.

However, undermining or supplanting the authority of mayors and governors in a moment of national crisis would be a mistake. Rather than tinkering with constitutional relationships, Congress and presidential administrations should focus on creating mechanisms to get these offi-cials the forces they will need to get the job done. "The greatest obstacle to overcome is not the legal barriers, but the tyranny of time and dis-tance and the destroyed infrastructure, such as downed bridges and flooded roads, which might limit access."[142] Development of the Dual Status Commander post before Superstorm Sandy in 2012, and the subsequent use of the DSCA for the 2017 hurricanes that struck Texas, Florida, and Puerto Rico, is helpful in at least resolving in-military disputes about command and control of governor-deployed Guards people and president-deployed federal forces.

"All disasters are local" is an oft-repeated and re-validated assertion of emergency man-agers and students of disaster. Nevertheless, the United States is a large nation, operated through a massive and complex federal system. Emergency management capacity at the local level varies sig-nificantly across the nation. Large cities and many localities in major metropolitan areas have experienced disasters before and have considerable ability to work all phases of disaster. However, these jurisdictions may find the homeland security world of "missions and capabilities" (in part aimed at replacing the phases model of emergency management) and the labyrinth of five massive frameworks used to serve the National Preparedness System, overwhelming. Meeting the framework requirements, even if imposed with soft federal gloves, will be daunting for states and major cities. Add to this, state and local compliance with the rules, conditions, and performance expectations of UASI and the State Homeland Security Grant programs, and it is obvious that state and local homeland security and emergency management people will be consumed by federal paper and digital online work for much of their careers.

Not to be forgotten is also a vast array of counties, cities, towns, and villages; their homeland security and emergency response capacity differs, ranging from high quality to merely adequate. A great many localities rely on volunteer firefighters, most of whom are unpaid. The experience, education, and training of these firefighters vary from outstanding to satisfactory. Moreover, the emergency management capability of law enforcement officers also varies dramatically across the nation. As mentioned, emergency management includes emergency response, but so too prevention, protection, mitigation, response, and recovery. Local government must now cope with homeland security "missions and capabilities," especially if they desire continued federal homeland security and emergency management funding. The question is, when will federally imposed planning requirements and grant rules become so labor-intensive and costly for state and local officials that they find it necessary to forgo the federal money and "jump off" the DHS and FEMA "bandwagon"? Such an outcome is possible even if

state workers meeting the federal requirements and rules are federally salaried.

Many state and local officials appreciate the dramatically scaled-up grant funding they have received in this post-9/11 homeland security era, but many also lament the federal preoccupation with terrorism at the expense of established emergency management, the hierarchical system for dispensing funds, and the immense paper- and computer-work burdens they must now shoulder.

Many military officials are ambivalent about assuming what they see as civilian emergency management duties. Admittedly, the military has been willing to play a more active role in short-term emergency response to homeland disasters, particularly through the National Guard and the U.S. Armed Forces. Yet the understandable military preoccupation remains national defense against threats posed to the nation by other nations or by stateless terrorists. The military culture and the civilian emergency management culture are in many ways highly incompatible. Emergency management has paramilitary participants, but most emergency managers, even most of those in paramilitary occupations, appreciate the need to work consultatively, cooperatively, and consensually. The Incident Command System (ICS) discussed in Chapter 6 implies a military model of decision making, but ICS is fundamentally used as a nexus of cooperative decision making applied to emergency response. The multiagency coordination system employed in emergency management is vital. Clearly, ICS works satisfactorily for concentrated and localized disasters, but command and control regimentation of ICS becomes infeasible in catastrophic disasters covering large areas. It is then that the value of multiagency coordination and cooperation becomes apparent.[143]

The world of state and local homeland security is dramatically influenced by federal laws, rules, funding conditions, and administrative actions. U.S. public policy after the 9/11 terrorist attacks called for the nation to recruit, hire, and oversee state and local government homeland security and emergency management officials so they could better prevent and respond to acts of terrorism. One major result of this policy change was a profusion of federal homeland security programs and a dizzying array of grant programs with far-ranging and sometimes bizarre requirements.

Many of these programs dramatically affected state and local emergency management. Some were arms of homeland security and disaster policy implementation. Some enriched state and local emergency management and law enforcement with major infusions of federal funds. However, some undercut or distorted state and local emergency management and law enforcement in controversial ways. Some of these programs also imposed massive stress on state and local emergency management and law enforcement officials.

Some studies have demonstrated that substantial federal and state aid to local government in particular policy areas can undermine local control of local government agencies.[144] In state and local emergency management, heavy federal subsidization, combined with conditions attached to the money dispensed, may potentially undercut local control of local emergency management. In other words, the greater the share of federal and state funding in local emergency management budgets, the greater the probability that a condition of dependency will evolve such that local emergency management becomes more an arm of state and federal emergency management and homeland security and less a locally controlled municipal function. Recruiting state and local government to fight the war on terror has had, and will continue to have, major effects on how disaster policy and emergency management is carried out.

Key Terms

Chemical, biological, radiological, or nuclear (CBRN) 295

Comprehensive risk methodology 301

Dual Status Command Authority 280

Dual status commander 275

Emergency Management Performance Grants (EMPGs) 307

Fusion centers 299

Homeland Security Advisory System (HSAS) 310

Law Enforcement Terrorism Prevention Activities (LETPA) 286

Law Enforcement Terrorism Prevention Program (LETPP) 299

Martial law 277

National Guard 277

National planning scenarios 304

National Terrorism Advisory System (NTAS) 310

Oklahoma City terrorist bomb attack 277

Operation Stonegarden 286

Posse Comitatus Act of 1878 277

Security classification 285

State Active Duty (SAD) 281

State adjutant general 276

State Homeland Security Program (SHSP) 286

Target capabilities list 304

Target capability 298

Terrorism consequence management 271

Threat and Hazard Identification and Risk Assessment (THIRA) 292

Title 10 duty status 280

Premier Rachel Notley and Prime Minister Justin Trudeau visited Fort McMurray in Alberta, Canada, on May 13, 2016, to see for themselves the damage caused by a wildfire that prompted the evacuation of the city over a week ago.

Chris Schwarz/Government of Alberta

8

GLOBALIZATION OF DISASTERS[1]

American astrophysicist Neil deGrasse Tyson has remarked, "Even with all our technology and the inventions that make modern life so much easier than it once was, it takes just one big natural disaster to wipe that all away and remind us that, here on Earth, we're still at the mercy of nature."[2] Many experts anticipate that future disasters will be larger and more destructive owing to such factors as climate change and environmental degradation. Disaster vulnerability is also growing because the world population is increasing, accelerating the pace of urbanization. A massive share of the world's populace resides along coastlines vulnerable to a variety of weather- and waterborne hazards. The systems and infrastructure to sustain and nurture the world population are of uneven quality and durability. Many disasters befall developing nations that lack financial resources, infrastructure, adequate preparedness and response capability, and resilience.[3] Disaster forces and the

315

effects of disasters often spill over or straddle borders, and disasters may easily overwhelm individual states, so they are sometimes difficult for many nation-states to address independently.[4] Owing to the frequency and expansive effects of disasters and catastrophes, disaster management increasingly requires responses that are multinational or even global in scope. International disaster management involves not only the nations themselves but all relevant actors and loci of authority, be they multilateral and multilevel governmental, public, or private. Consequently, international disaster management, most particularly in post-disaster response and relief, constitutes a major domain of emergency management.[5]

The international community, development banks, and nongovernmental organizations (NGOs) must consider legal, ethical, and humanitarian criteria before they launch an intervention into disaster-stricken areas of other nations. Rising transnationalism and increased interdependency between developing and developed nations has given new urgency to matters of disaster management. The **globalizing forces** that have characterized the post–Cold War era—notably the massive movement of individuals, capital, goods, information, and technologies across borders—have resulted in ever-expanding relations between developing nations and more developed nations and multinational corporations. For many developing nations vulnerable to major disasters, this interdependence may produce negative, destabilizing effects.[6] Disaster damage often jeopardizes ongoing externally sponsored development projects. Developing nations lacking diversified economies or that are heavily dependent on export of single commodities or raw materials may discover that a disaster has not only undercut production but has seriously contracted the nation's gross domestic product. Many developing nations carry sizable debt burdens such that a major disaster imperils both their ability to repay and their creditworthiness.[7] Moreover, disasters in developing nations often trigger massive outflows of refugees who seek to escape zones of destruction and civil strife.[8] Disasters sometimes contribute to security threats from within or from forces in adjacent states. Disasters may contribute to conditions of state failure. Failed states often prove incapable of stanching the spread of radicalism, terrorism, and anti-democratic movements.[9]

Security and peace are linked to long-term, sustainable political and economic development. Therefore, the international community as a whole has a stake in preventing developing states from collapsing. By extension, this also entails helping developing nation governments cope with disasters both before and after they strike. Owing to interdependency and humanitarian altruism, the international community has a vested interest in assisting nations whose people and governments have experienced disaster.

In the international realm disasters are commonly categorized as natural disasters, technological disasters, or **complex humanitarian emergencies (CHEs)**. Among these three, CHEs are often the most difficult to address. CHEs signify that a country or region is at or near complete breakdown of civil authority. CHEs sometimes involve ethnic conflict, displacement of population groups, market collapse, and mass starvation.[10] In a CHE, the success or failure of a disaster relief operation often rests on the degree of coordination, the fairness and equality in relief distribution, and whether the relief effort connects with (or at least does not impede) the country's reconstruction and economic development.[11] CHEs often coincide with natural disasters. For example, Yemen on the Arabian Peninsula, a nation of immense human suffering in recent years, is not only riven by several years of warfare internally and with Saudi Arabia but is also experiencing extended drought and famine, which has added to the misery of several million people.

Territorial sovereignty—the internationally recognized principle that a government should be the ultimate authority within the boundaries of its jurisdiction and should be free of unwanted external interference—may in some cases constitute a powerful obstacle to extending humanitarian assistance.[12] Leaders of some nation-states, in times of disaster, choose to protect their national sovereignty even if this disadvantages many of their own citizens. Sometimes leaders of newly independent nations fear that post-disaster intervention by a rival state or a great power may bring about their recolonization or result in subjugation by a neighboring nation. Also, political strife owing to competing or warring groups or political parties within a nation make it unclear as to who is leading the country. Sometimes the leadership of a nation is challenged by one or more political figures to the point that state power becomes delegitimized. Furthermore, people in one or more regions of a nation may be seeking secession and independence from the central government. For these reasons, humanitarian assistance tends to be more successful when the leaders of recipient nations perceive it as offered by neutral parties or see it as undertaken by the international community collectively rather than by one or a few nations.

The international relief and humanitarian assistance mechanisms and tools of the United Nations are examined here along with the international disaster management system of the United States. America is a world superpower. The United Nations is an international organization of 193 member-states, at the time of this writing.[13] UN enforcement capacity and its resources flow from the permission and goodwill of its members. Both the United States and the UN are constrained in their freedom of action and response capability. Interestingly, the UN, a confederation of nation-states, and the United States, a federal system and representative democracy of 50 states (plus the District of Columbia and trust or commonwealth territories), must deal with a plethora of public and private actors, many having their own standards, procedures, and agendas.

The UN and U.S. agencies involved in international disaster relief are examined in this chapter, and the UN and U.S. disaster response and recovery mechanisms are compared, contrasted, and evaluated. This chapter also includes a Canada–U.S. case study that compares and contrasts Canadian and American emergency management. Both Canada and the United States are democracies operating with federal structures. Both nations have large and sophisticated national disaster management organizations, which also operate within national homeland security super-departments. Canadian provincial and American state governments have emergency management agencies geared to protect and maintain provincial–state interests. Provinces and states by law must be responsive to the disaster and emergency management needs of their local governments. Consequently, a portion of this chapter is dedicated to this topic and to the subject of U.S.–Canada near-international border or international border-spanning disasters.

THE U.S. RESPONSE SYSTEM FOR TERRITORIES AND FOREIGN STATES

America has a disaster policy and politics embedded in its international relations. First, the United States has committed itself to serving the disaster management needs of its trust and commonwealth territories. Many Americans may be unaware that U.S. trust and commonwealth territories are eligible to request and receive presidential declarations of major disaster and emergency just as are all of the 50 U.S. states and the District of Columbia. Puerto Rico is a commonwealth of the United States, and the U.S. Virgin Islands is a U.S. trust territory (see Chapters 4 and 6). Both are located in the Caribbean, and both have emergency management systems. Guam, American Samoa, the Marshall Islands, the Northern Marianas, and the Federated States of Micronesia also maintain an emergency management capability. In the Pacific, American Samoa has been an unincorporated territory of the United States since 1899 and is administered by the U.S. Department of the Interior.

Today, the Republic of the Marshall Islands, the Republic of Palau, the Northern Marianas, and the Federated States of Micronesia are fully independent nations and are no longer American trust territories. However, these four nations and the remaining American family of trust or commonwealth territories remain eligible to receive presidential declarations of major disaster or emergency and all of the federal relief assistance these declarations convey. Providing disaster relief and long-term recovery aid to present or former trust or commonwealth governments is often a daunting logistical challenge and an exceedingly expensive proposition for the federal government.

Highly destructive hurricanes sometimes sweep through Puerto Rico or the U.S. Virgin Islands, as happened in the fall of 2017. Both governments have received a share of presidential declarations of major disaster since 1953. In 2017–2018, FEMA disaster assistance to Puerto Rico in the aftermath of Hurricane Maria exceeds FEMA relief spending for both Hurricane Harvey and Hurricane Irma. In the Pacific, too, typhoons periodically devastate present and former U.S. trust and commonwealth states. Some of the most expensive "per capita" federal disaster declaration spending has flowed to U.S. trust and commonwealth states in the Pacific.

Sometimes hurricanes or typhoons destroy coastal infrastructure and jeopardize public water supplies. The U.S. military possesses air- and sea-lift capacity to ship food, water, clothing, building materials, and other commodities to these distant locations. Every eligible present or former trust or commonwealth territory of the United States is within either Federal Emergency Management Agency Region 2 headquartered in New York (includes Caribbean) or FEMA Region 9 headquartered in Oakland (includes Pacific). Thus FEMA, as well as each responding federal agency, sends both representatives and aid to these governments in times of emergency or disaster.

The United States also has treaty obligations to offer disaster help to a great many nations, which cannot be comprehensively reviewed here. Long-standing treaties, many of them predicated on defense pacts, obligate America to offer help to nations in Europe, Asia, South America, and Africa as well. The United States, then, is part of an international web of disaster response and emergency management. U.S. government organizations active in international disaster management, both in its own territories and abroad, are considered in more detail in the following section.

The U.S. Agency for International Development

The **U.S. Agency for International Development (USAID)**, for many years an independent agency, is now again part of the Department of State. The agency is officially obligated to further U.S. foreign policy interests in expanding democracy and free markets while improving the lives of the citizens in developing countries.[14] Receiving a budget of half of one percent of the total U.S. budget, USAID is the chief U.S. agency in charge of overseas development. USAID extends assistance to countries recovering from disasters. Rooted in the Marshall Plan, which was designed to reconstruct Europe after World War II, and in President Truman's Point Four Program, USAID was authorized in the Foreign Assistance Act of 1961 and launched under an executive order issued by President Kennedy.[15] USAID symbolized the American recommitment to long-term foreign development, and it clearly separated U.S. military and nonmilitary international assistance programs. However, since 1961 the USAID annual budget has been an object of political controversy almost every year.

USAID in 2018 declared, "Ultimately, our goal is to achieve a future in which foreign assistance is no longer needed and to support partners that are self-reliant and capable of leading their own development journeys. By reducing the reach of conflict, preventing the spread of pandemic disease, and counteracting the drivers of violence, instability, transnational crime and other security threats, this budget will help bring us closer to that day. It is designed to promote American prosperity through investments that expand markets for U.S. exports; help create a level playing field for U.S. businesses; support more stable, resilient and democratic societies; and address crises."[16] The State Department and USAID budget requested by the Trump administration for FY 2019 is "$39.3 billion, which includes $16.8 billion in assistance that USAID fully or partially manages through the Economic Support and Development Fund, Global Health Programs, Transition Initiatives, International Disaster Assistance, and USAID operational accounts."[17] The USAID states that "programs funded through these accounts will help developing countries make progress on their path to self-reliance and prosperity."[18]

USAID receives guidance from the U.S. secretary of state. USAID also works closely with more than 3,500 American companies (300 of these companies are domestically based) and the Overseas Private Investment Corporation (a federal corporation).[19] The agency addresses economic growth, agriculture, trade, global health, democracy, conflict prevention, and humanitarian assistance. It provides assistance in sub-Saharan Africa, Asia, the Near East, Latin America, the Caribbean, and Europe/Eurasia.[20] Within USAID, the Bureau for Democracy, Conflict, and Humanitarian Assistance coordinates the agency's response to emergencies in other nations. Within the bureau, a special office, the **Office of U.S. Foreign Disaster Assistance (OFDA)**, manages all nonfood assistance directed to disaster victims.[21]

The Office of U.S. Foreign Disaster Assistance

Within USAID, the OFDA facilitates and coordinates U.S. emergency response overseas. The OFDA is divided into four units. These are the Operations Support Division; the Program Support Division; the Disaster Response Division; and the Prevention, Mitigation, Preparedness, and Planning Division.

The OFDA is authorized to respond to all natural disasters (earthquakes, volcanic eruptions, cyclones, floods, droughts, fires, pest infestation, disease outbreaks) and manmade disasters (civil conflicts, acts of terrorism, industrial accidents). Besides furnishing immediate assistance, OFDA funds mitigation activities to lessen the effects of recurring disasters. It also makes available guidance and training intended to help those in other nations develop their own disaster management and response capacity.[22]

When disaster strikes, OFDA sends regional and technical experts to the affected country to identify and prioritize humanitarian needs. In the wake of a large-scale disaster, OFDA can deploy a **Disaster Assistance Response Team (DART)** to coordinate and manage an optimal U.S. government response, while working closely with local officials, the international community, and relief agencies. OFDA also maintains stocks of emergency relief supplies in warehouses worldwide and has the logistical and operational capabilities to deliver them quickly.[23]

U.S. Ambassadors Declare Disasters

When a U.S. ambassador judges that his or her posted nation's capability to address a disaster is overwhelmed, and if the nation's government requests international assistance, the ambassador or the chief of mission can issue a disaster declaration on behalf of the United States. This action initiates a set of U.S. emergency procedures and the ambassador can dispense $25,000 to $50,000 in immediate financial aid.[24] The USAID administrator then dispatches a team to the nation in question. Various response activities then transpire that are scaled to the severity of the crisis. Such responses evolve from the immediate allocation of discretionary money through the embassy and from the immediate dispatch of regional advisers. Those authorities provide shelter and medical aid supplies. DART assesses the scale of damage, proposes a strategy, and estimates how much assistance is required and what it will cost.[25] The response team often provides logistical support and coordinates the efforts of all actors and responders involved. These include the UN and other international organizations, NGOs, and governments. DARTs monitor and evaluate U.S. operations as well.[26]

In very great disasters, response management teams are formed in Washington and sent to the field to facilitate coordination between the various DARTs involved.[27] A special assistance team, or technical assistance group, composed of experts in fields as varied as agriculture and public health, often share their expertise with and assist DARTs and response management teams in their work.[28] The OFDA furnishes direct assistance and may follow this up by also offering a wide variety of project grants to public and private recipients. These are intended to help them develop and share best practices in disaster relief and mitigation.[29]

The Role of the Department of Defense and the U.S. Military

The U.S. Department of Defense (DOD) has crucial responsibilities in foreign disaster relief and response. A special office within the DOD, the **Office of Peacekeeping and Humanitarian Affairs**, has the job of leading or coordinating the U.S. military response to disasters beyond U.S. borders. Use of the U.S. military in disaster-stricken nations is sometimes controversial because for many the military's war-oriented missions do not comport well with the humanitarian aspirations of disaster relief. However, the military generally has excellent and necessary equipment, extensive training, and well-entrenched standards of procedure required to handle such operations. A request for military support by USAID/OFDA is usually transferred to the U.S. Department of State's **Bureau of Political-Military Affairs** before following the chain of command. International disaster relief by the military is designated as a Humanitarian Assistance Operation or Foreign Humanitarian Assistance, the latter being authorized by the DOD at the request of the OFDA.

Once on foreign soil, U.S. forces involved in a **humanitarian assistance** mission are limited by the principles of force protection and rules of engagement; in other words, they must ensure the security of their own military personnel as well as the security of civilians, facilities, and equipment, and they are restricted in their ability to engage in combat by certain rules ("no fire first," for instance). In conflict-ridden zones of intervention, the priority of the military often shifts from providing security and leadership to a strict mission of assistance through logistical, physical, and communications support, and the distribution of food and medical relief. During deployments, **Humanitarian Assistance Survey Teams** are often sent to evaluate the needs on the ground to ensure that the intervention is proceeding effectively.[30] A joint task force is usually set up on site in disaster zones to coordinate the activities of diverse military units and civilian agencies. The commander of this task force is in charge of creating a civil-military operations center. The center's job is to coordinate military-civilian activities, to serve as the connection with the overall response structure, and to provide the effective logistical support to other agencies and responders (e.g., the OFDA, the United Nations, and NGOs).

The DOD launched an extraordinary response to the December 26, 2004, tsunami in Southeast Asia, an event triggered by a 9.0 Richter magnitude earthquake. The catastrophic tsunami killed an estimated 225,000 people; fatalities occurred in 11 nations, most of them with coastlines on the Indian Ocean. The DOD supplied the logistic elements of the operation through the use of its airplanes, helicopters, military ships, and other equipment. USAID also coordinated the work of various civilian organizations.[31] In the Indian Ocean tsunami case, more than 15,000 military personnel contributed to the relief effort and were dispatched to the affected nations. More than 2.2 million pounds of supplies were sent by the U.S. military to the region, including 16,000 gallons of water, 113,000 pounds of food, and 140,000 pounds of relief supplies during the first 24 hours.[32]

EMERGENCY MANAGEMENT IN OTHER NATIONS

America is not the only nation engaged in emergency management. Virtually every developed nation has some system of disaster management. Many have disaster management agencies, and some of those predate FEMA.[33] Some have developed emergency management on a platform of civil defense, but a great many have advanced emergency management as a form of public safety or civil preparedness.

Many nations have had long experience with domestic or international terrorism and so have their own forms of homeland security.[34] It is also true that many developed nations support foreign aid programs and international disaster assistance activities.[35] Many nations belong to treaty organizations or regional alliances that also engage in international emergency management endeavors.

It is developing nations that often have limited capacity to engage in the full range of emergency management activity.[36] Poverty, dangerous patterns of human settlement, unsafe agricultural and infrastructure construction practices, low public awareness of disaster vulnerability, inadequate public warning and sheltering systems, poor transportation infrastructure, deficient power and communications systems, and other problems often confound emergency management in other nations. Many developing nations have little or no history of insurance use and so lack the ability to employ insurance as a disaster recovery and mitigation tool. Moreover, some governments of developing nations lack political legitimacy and the public support of their citizenry. Some governments do not consider emergency management a priority for their people and so lack the political will to respond to post-disaster needs. In many developing nations the chief governmental arm of disaster response is the military. In many nations with a history of military repression, the citizens react to their national military with suspicion and fear. When national military help is extended to disaster victims in such places, people fear that unfair arrest, exploitation, corruption, or even torture might ensue. Such problems have given rise to international disaster management activity based on humanitarianism. Much of this activity seeks to at least temporarily fill the gaps in developing nation emergency management capacity. In some respects, capable humanitarian assistance provided by other nations and international organizations in the post-disaster response and recovery work they do serves to highlight and diffuse emergency management principles and ideas to new places across the world.

A wide variety of **development banks** have taken a strong interest in emergency management, among them the World Bank, the Asian Development Bank, the International Monetary Fund, and the Inter-American Development Bank.[37] Moreover, a host of **emergency-management–oriented multinational organizations** have emerged. Among them are the Coordination Center for Natural Disaster Prevention in Central America, the Caribbean Disaster Emergency Response Agency, and the Pan American Health Organization. The North Atlantic Treaty Organization, the European Union, the Organization of American States, and the Southern African Development Community all have programs under way that promote emergency management internationally.[38]

THE UNITED NATIONS AND INTERNATIONAL DISASTER RELIEF

With 193 member states, the United Nations constitutes one of the most experienced international organizational actors in the management of international disaster response and mitigation. UN agencies are generally involved on the ground in disasters and catastrophes. In the 1990s the UN reformed its disaster response in a way that better addressed the increasing complexity of emergencies. In 1987 the UN declared the decade of the 1990s the International Decade for Natural Disaster Reduction. By 1989, the UN had set up an office in Geneva, Switzerland, tasked with coordinating the implementation of the decade's activities across all UN agencies. In 1994 UN member states met at the World Conference on Natural Disaster Reduction in Yokohama, Japan, and developed a strategy and plan of action that embodied a vast array of emergency management principles. In January 2005 the UN convened the World Conference on Disaster Reduction in Hyogo, Japan, a meeting that included representatives from 168 governments and 78 UN specialized agencies and observer organizations. Some 161

NGOs were also represented at the conference. The Hyogo meeting yielded a framework for action and a plan to substantially reduce disaster losses of communities and countries by the year 2015.[39]

Words matter. UN officials do not use the word *victim* in their international humanitarian operations. In their information releases, publicity, and advertising activities, UN people are taught to recognize disaster survivors as dignified human beings, not hopeless objects. They call them beneficiaries, recipients of aid, or disaster-affected people/communities/individuals. *Victim* infers that those impacted do not have sufficient capacity or resources to recover on their own, when in fact most are capable individuals who simply need temporary assistance.

The United Nations Office for the Coordination of Humanitarian Affairs

In 1998 the UN General Assembly established the **United Nations Office for the Coordination of Humanitarian Affairs (OCHA)** to be headed by the emergency relief coordinator. The OCHA coordinator acts as the primary adviser and strives to harmonize the work of the various relief organizations in humanitarian emergency responses. He or she does so through the Inter-Agency Standing Committee, itself composed of both UN and non-UN humanitarian leaders.[40] OCHA seeks to build consensus and share best practices among all UN partners. OCHA also identifies issues that arise in disaster management and response and which need to be addressed. OCHA also amasses information from its Disaster Response System, a unit that monitors ongoing disasters, conducts post-disaster assessments and evaluations, and manages a bank of data made available to the international community of responders.

OCHA coordinates the field missions of an assortment of UN agencies. These agencies assess needs, mobilize resources by launching interagency appeals, organize donations, monitor the contributions, and issue follow-up reports to update various actors on post-disaster developments.[41] OCHA advocates conformity to humanitarian norms and principles in its dealings with partners and world governments. Foremost among those norms and principles is respect for human rights. Regarding financial assistance, OCHA is in charge of the Central Emergency Revolving Fund. The fund operates as a cash reserve available to humanitarian agencies with cash-flow problems. OCHA is able to loan money, but reimbursement is expected within a year.[42]

When a disaster strikes, OCHA works in close cooperation with government groups and NGOs, including America's USAID/OFDA, to formulate a joint and coordinated course of action. It helps set priorities and prevents overlap in the work of various agencies.[43] OCHA dispatches some of its personnel to provide on-site support to UN agencies. When needed, OCHA can set up a **United Nations Disaster Assessment and Coordination (UNDAC) team**. The team aids in the coordination of the relief effort, in the assessment of damage, and in gauging the response required. UNDAC teams help to harmonize the relief assistance made available by many of the UN organizations presented next.

OCHA responsibility is particularly crucial in the immediate post-disaster phase. It helps restore damaged communications and helps first responders work in harmony.[44] OCHA New York and Geneva provide surge capacity for its own field offices or when establishing a new field presence.

The United Nations High Commissioner for Refugees

Founded in the aftermath of World War II, the **Office of the United Nations High Commissioner for Refugees (UNHCR)** protects and aids refugees and internally displaced persons (IDPs).[45] The most basic responsibility of UNHCR is to guarantee refugees' fundamental rights, including their ability to seek asylum. It strives to make sure that no person is involuntarily returned to a country if doing so would subject that person to persecution or otherwise put his or her life in danger.[46] The UNHCR facilitates the necessary movement of masses of people, often refugees, during emergencies. It promotes education, health, and shelter programs and is expected to provide for the well-being of refugees.

It manages the repatriation of people who freely wish to return to their home country and resettles those refugees seeking asylum to nations willing to accept them.[47] If refugees do return to their home countries, the UNHCR works closely with other agencies and organizations to prevent disrupting socioeconomic infrastructures of the home country and to facilitate refugee reintegration.

To be clear, only a person who crosses an international border can be considered a refugee and is protected under the provisions of the Geneva Conventions; the same protection does not apply to internally displaced people. These people have recognized rights under international humanitarian law, however.

The UNHCR has a long-term commitment to the cause of refugees. Its special mission, the United Nations Relief and Works Agency for Palestine Refugees in the Near East, has provided relief, health care, and education help to Palestine ever since the 1948 Arab-Israeli conflict.[48] The agency originally aided about 750,000 Palestinian refugees who had lost their homes or livelihoods or both. By the year 2000, it was working to help 3.7 million registered Palestinian refugees dispersed over areas of Lebanon, Jordan, Syria, and the combined West Bank and Gaza Strip. In 2018, the Trump administration discontinued all federal funding for this mission.[49]

Since the Bosnia conflict (1992–1995), UNHCR has experienced internal struggles about whether to also take on aid to IDPs. This has been a controversy both within UNHCR and for the UN system as a whole. IDPs sometimes fall into a mandate gap, as a result of the nation in question. Sometimes UNHCR decides not to get involved. So sometimes IDPs do not get UN help and sometimes this work falls to the UN International Office of Migration.

The United Nations Children's Fund

Formerly known as the United Nations International Children's Emergency Fund, the **United Nations Children's Fund (UNICEF)** was created after World War II to alleviate the suffering of European children. Since then its mandate has been expanded. UNICEF has an in-country permanent presence in many nations.[50] Thus, the agency may be able to respond rapidly to natural or man-made disasters from its offices in nations where it already has permission to operate.[51] The necessity of a swift response is highlighted by the especial vulnerability of new mothers and families with small children. Children and women caring for small children are often weaker members of their societies and are less capable of rebounding in disasters than others. During natural disasters or CHEs, UNICEF works with other relief agencies to restore basic services, such as food distribution, water, and sanitation. UNICEF officials also try to make available basic medical services and immunizations. UNICEF is empowered to advocate children's rights worldwide.[52] In conflict-prone areas, the agency has, with help, sometimes managed to negotiate cease-fires so as to provide humanitarian relief and to immunize children.[53]

UNICEF is well known for its excellent public relations. It has the best advocacy strategies in the UN system, but then many do not realize that it is a UN agency. UNICEF has become an iconic household name, worldwide.

The United Nations Development Programme

The **United Nations Development Programme (UNDP)**, created in 1965, has jurisdiction over many disaster-related activities. It has duties in all phases of emergency management, including reconstruction. The UNDP operating norm is that disaster vulnerability remains fundamentally connected to weak or absent infrastructures, the failure or inadequacy of environmental policies, and human settlement in high-hazard zones.[54] The mandate of UNDP is prevention, mitigation, preparedness, recovery, and reconstruction—not so much relief and response (i.e., a mandate of other UN entities).

UNDP is a development organization, with a different organizational structure and management than that required for a response operation.

However, the UNDP early recovery team works with the response partners so that strong links are established and maintained between response and recovery through to mitigation and preparedness.

Because disasters hold the potential to quickly reverse a nation's previous progress or set a nation's economic development back decades, UNDP officials consider disaster mitigation and risk reduction to be priorities. The UNDP ties its response and recovery efforts to long-term and sustainable development. In 1995 it reorganized itself and created an **Emergency Response Division**, which accelerated the capacity of UNDP to respond to disasters. A response team is now routinely deployed to help coordinate relief and recovery efforts of other UN agencies and NGOs with the efforts of disaster-stricken national governments. The response teams also prepare comprehensive redevelopment projects in disaster recovery operations.

The UNDP has programs adapted to virtually all existing emergency circumstances. In 1997 the Emergency Response Division was granted more extensive duties over disaster and mitigation through the creation of the **Disaster Reduction and Recovery Program**. Through this program, the UNDP makes sure that its long-term development work includes the demobilization of combatants, land mine clearance, the reintegration of refugees and IDPs, and a plan for restoration of governance in the affected country.[55] The close collaboration of the UNDP with national and local officials often yields positive results. The UNDP has stimulated grassroots initiatives, promoted long-term resuscitation, and sought to improve people's living standards. It also facilitates recovery through the use of financial tools, notably microcredit to the poor in Central America. The UNDP often leads interagency workshops that identify potential risks, develop early warning systems, or build states' disaster response capabilities and programs.[56] In addition, the UNDP runs the UN International Strategy for Disaster Reduction Working Group on Risk, Vulnerability, and Disaster Impact Assessment. The group advocates standardized guidelines aimed at increasing emergency responder sensitivity to the social impact of disasters. It also operates a Disaster Management Training Program.[57]

The World Food Programme

The **World Food Programme (WFP)** is responsible for providing rapid and self-sustaining nutritional relief to the millions of victims of man-made or natural disasters.[58] Most nations that receive WFP aid eventually return to agricultural self-sufficiency. However, those nations that regularly fall victim to civil wars or ethnic conflicts usually also suffer food shortages or famine.[59] In cases of emergency, the WFP attempts quick response, but always with permission of the host government. WFP duties cover transport, delivery, and distribution of food made available by other UN agencies, other national governments, or NGOs. When called upon, the WFP joins in reconstruction and rehabilitation activity.

The WFP works in close collaboration with the Food and Agriculture Organization (FAO). The FAO issues early warnings of potential food crises and assesses food supply problems. Both the WFP and the FAO are critical in meeting the needs of disaster victims living in rural areas and who may be farmers. The FAO works to reestablish a nation's or region's food production. Its Special Relief Operations serve farmers. Many WFP programs operate under strict conditions and are tied to projects demobilizing combatants or clearing land mines.

The World Health Organization

The **World Health Organization (WHO)** is the UN central agency assigned to manage health and sanitation concerns throughout the world. The WHO uses its people, authority, and expertise to assess and respond to health needs in regions and countries affected by natural and man-made disasters. The WHO operates programs designed to help the governments manage first-aid supplies, improve their medical capabilities, and maintain epidemiological surveillance of disease. All of these purposes are important in the aftermath of disasters. The WHO works to eradicate diseases and reduce the effects of epidemics through campaigns of information and immunization.

U.S. DOMESTIC DISASTER RELIEF VERSUS THE U.S. INTERNATIONAL RELIEF SYSTEM

Although there are many differences between the way the United States engages in domestic disasters and international disasters, there are also striking similarities in the mechanisms and procedures used by FEMA and its foreign disaster aid counterpart USAID/OFDA. Both agencies are involved in activities extending beyond the mission of disaster relief; their disaster management encompasses not only relief distribution but also preparedness, mitigation, and recovery work. In both domestic and international cases, the scope of the disaster must be judged significant enough to overwhelm the authorities presumably in charge of such activity. In other words, a government must be judged to have been overwhelmed or incapable of meeting the needs created by a catastrophe or disaster, such that help from outside is necessary. In America, state governments are generally expected to ask the federal government for help before the president declares a disaster or emergency, although exceptions are permitted. People of UN organizations, as well as officials of USAID and its OFDA, expect that their help will be officially requested by the established governments of the disaster-affected nations.

Once approached, both UN agencies and USAID/OFDA first assess the scope of the damages and the needs of the victims. Both UN and U.S. agencies operate inclusively as they try to compile resources and assemble those with needed skills. Both strive to coordinate the efforts of public and private relief organizations. Finally, both domestic and international relief systems often rely on the U.S. military to provide logistical, physical, and communications support. Chapter 7 reviewed how the U.S. military responded to Hurricane Maria in Puerto Rico in 2017. The U.S. military and the militaries of other nations were involved in the response to the Southeast Asia earthquake and tsunami in 2004. The U.S. military responded again after the Hurricane Katrina disaster in 2005, after the Great Northeast Japan earthquake and tsunami catastrophe in 2011,[60] and after the Haiyan Typhoon tragedy of the Philippines in 2013. Ironically, U.S. military disaster responses inside America are sometimes just as controversial as U.S. military responses to disasters internationally.

One area of significant difference is that of funding. The UN tends to rely on annual dues funding by member states and the altruism of its donors, who can be nations, public or private organizations, or individuals. U.S. disaster response organizations at home operate on all levels of government and derive budget support from those respective governments. Certainly, organized charities and service organizations active in disasters have their own funding sources: foundations, corporations, and individual donors. Moreover, in very great disasters the U.S. president can draw spending authority from the Disaster Relief Fund approved in law and funded by Congress.

When America deploys its military abroad, foreign leaders, fairly or unfairly, sometimes consider this evidence of superpower interference. On the domestic side, for many Americans there is a long-standing suspicion about the use of the military in civil affairs and the application of martial law to control protesting or rebellious people (examined in Chapter 7).

United Nations Blue Helmets

The United Nations as an organization has no military "combat" forces of its own; it relies on the goodwill of member states and sometimes its **"blue helmeted" peacekeeping soldiers**, a force comprising units contributed by certain member states. UN peacekeepers are defined as follows:

> Soldiers, police officers, and military observers from the United Nations' member countries. UN soldiers are paid volunteers from the armed services of various member states. All member states are invited to send volunteers, however, albeit with a few exceptions soldiers from the developing world do most of the volunteering.[61]

UN soldiers work alongside UN police and civilian colleagues to protect personnel and property; maintain close cooperation with other military entities in the mission area; and work to promote stability and security. The UN claims its soldiers work with local communities and local military personnel to bring about greater mutual understanding and lasting peace. Protecting civilians is very often at the heart of the UN mandate, and it is the Blue Helmets that are key to providing this security. All military personnel working under the blue helmet are first and foremost members of their own national armies and are then seconded to work with the UN. The UN has more than 97,000 UN uniformed personnel (military and police) coming from over 110 nations. They come from nations large and small, rich and poor. They bring different cultures and experience to the job, but they are united in their determination to foster peace.[62] UN military personnel can be called upon to do the following:

- Monitor a disputed border.

- Monitor and observe peace processes in post-conflict areas.

- Provide security across a conflict zone.

- Protect civilians.

- Assist in-country military personnel with training and support.

- Assist ex-combatants in implementing the peace agreements they may have signed.[63]

Troops typically are dispatched to peacekeeping missions for at least six months at a time, with the exact details of the deployment schedule left up to the country that sent them.[64] Blue helmet forces and related workers are counted on to provide the logistical and physical contributions necessary to carry out UN disaster relief and recovery missions.

The most common sort of UN peacekeeper is the infantry soldier. However, increasingly the UN needs specialized personnel who are referred to as "enablers." These skilled soldiers include engineers, who, for example, were able to help with the post-earthquake reconstruction in Haiti or who are building roads in the new nation of South Sudan. The UN also needs helicopters and their crews so as to extend their area of service and increase their visibility. Other specialist enablers include transport companies, communicators, and medical personnel. Modern peacekeeping operations are often very complex and place high demands on UN personnel. High levels of training are required before deployment, and the UN works closely with troop-contributing countries to provide help and advice. Troops must know what to do if they find themselves in an ambush, for example, and must be capable of responding appropriately, even robustly, if necessary.[65]

The UN can only deploy military personnel when there is a UN Security Council resolution authorizing them to do so. The Security Council will say how many military personnel are required, and then UN Headquarters will confer with officials of the member states to identify personnel and deploy them. This can take time—perhaps more than six months from the date of the resolution. As the late former UN secretary-general Kofi Annan said, the UN is "the only fire brigade in the world that has to wait for the fire to break out before it can acquire a fire engine." A standing reserve sounds logical, but it would be immensely costly to have a force of several thousand people on permanent standby. It would require training, accommodating, feeding, etc., and then might not even be used. Although it takes time, it is much more practical to generate the military personnel once the go-ahead has been given. This also ensures that recruited personnel have appropriate background, training, and language skills.[66]

FEMA VERSUS OFDA

Returning to the American context, there are some fundamental distinctions regarding the use of FEMA and USAID/OFDA. The U.S. government is ultimately accountable to its own citizens, and therefore is more likely to pay a political price for failing to provide an adequate response to a disaster occurring on American soil (the bungled federal response to Hurricanes Katrina or Maria as examples). As a result, the U.S. government tends to be more responsive to disasters occurring on domestic soil than to international disasters, as would be true in any nation.

The mission of FEMA is to protect and assist Americans in times of man-made and natural disaster; this is achieved through FEMA coordination of the work of federal departments and agencies working under the National Response Framework (NRF) and through the National Incident Management System. The mission of USAID/OFDA is subordinated to the pragmatic goals of American foreign policy and interests abroad. The U.S. federal government by law and custom has to consider the needs, powers, and wishes of the state and local governments. Nevertheless, since the 9/11 attacks of 2001, federal intervention in disaster response and recovery has been allowed to grow, particularly with respect to national concerns about the threat of attacks by terrorists inside the United States

At the international level, relations between nation-states remain profoundly affected by respect for national territorial sovereignty. The capacity and authority of USAID/OFDA abroad remains deeply limited by both presiding U.S. presidents and by the U.S. Congress. The UN-protected system of international relations is also sometimes a constraint. Often USAID/OFDA must work as simply one of many foreign relief agencies. The permission and goodwill of the host government are conditions that determine whether USAID/OFDA is welcomed or turned away.

As indicated, USAID/OFDA often becomes involved in a disaster response after it has received a request from the ambassador or chief of mission in the nation suffering a misfortune. Each request is evaluated according to precise criteria. As mentioned, an ambassador, often after consultation with the White House, makes available a sum of up to $50,000 for disaster work to be spent at his or her discretion. That sum appears small but it is intended to mobilize more responders and elicit funding from other sources. In turn, OFDA dispatches its Disaster Assessment Response Team to evaluate the magnitude of the disaster and the range of unmet needs. In domestic U.S. disasters the president has the authority to approve a state governor's request for a major disaster declaration. For disasters outside the United States and its trust or commonwealth territories, the president may provide help to nations that request it through USAID and through the DOD.

A CASE STUDY: BORDERLINE DISASTER: U.S. AND CANADIAN DISASTERS AND EMERGENCIES 1994–2013

Since the **North American Free Tree Agreement** took effect in 1994, the United States and Canada have established closer ties in the domain of emergency management. Owing to massive Canada–U.S. economic, social, and cultural ties, plus a shared concern for security and emergency management (EM), both nations share a vested interest in managing and mitigating disaster and terrorism events that span their respective borders or that transpire in their neighbor nation. Both nations embrace federalism but in different forms. This study reviews a variety of U.S.–Canada agreements that facilitate relief assistance when one, the other, or both nations experience disaster.

Canada and the United States have independently constructed their own systems for providing disaster assistance to their subnational governments. The aim here is to explore emergency management federal–provincial and federal–state relations, respectively, with consideration of near-border and border-spanning incidents. This study presents tables of natural disaster loss data plus ensuing U.S. and Canada post-event federal assistance. Wherever mention is made of Canadian loss figures, note that they are always in Canadian dollars. Likewise, all U.S. federal disaster assistance spending is in U.S. dollars. Inflation is not controlled for in this study. Among major conclusions, there are more U.S.–Canada "border-spanning" disasters and incidents than one would expect. There are also U.S.–Canada protocols in place to provide cross-border help for various types of disaster agents. The record of Canadian and U.S. declared disasters for provinces and states along the international border from 1994 to 2013 makes it obvious as to why Canada–U.S. cross-national, regional, state, provincial, and local emergency management collaboration is essential.

Map 8-1 shows Canada and the United States with province and state labels. Map 8-1 provides a visualization of where each of these U.S. northern international border states are and where each southern international border Canadian province is located. The U.S. data assembled for this study comes from the author's regular acquisition of FEMA declaration information year to year. The Canadian data comes from the Canadian Disaster Database (CDD), which was hosted and maintained by Public Safety Canada until 2015. This Canada–U.S. case study begins with NAFTA's start in 1994. Because the author's county-level data (a file of more than 36,000 lines of code) ends in late 2013, and because Canadian data ends in 2015, the interval of this analysis is 1994–2013 inclusive.

Canada's System of Government in Brief

Canada's system of government varies from that of the United States. Elizabeth II, queen of Canada, is Canada's formal head of state. The governor general represents Queen Elizabeth in Canada and carries out the duties of head of state. The House of Commons makes Canada's laws. Canadians elect representatives to the House of Commons. These representatives are called "members of parliament" (MPs), and they usually belong to a political party. The political party that has the largest number of MPs forms the government, and its leader becomes prime minister. The prime minister is the head of government in Canada. The prime minister chooses MPs to serve as ministers in the cabinet. There are ministers for citizenship and immigration, justice, public safety, and other subjects. The cabinet makes important decisions about government policy. Canada's Senate reviews laws that are proposed by the House of Commons. Senators come from across Canada. The prime minister chooses the senators.[67]

Relatedly, at the provincial level, the lieutenant governor represents Queen Elizabeth. The Legislative Assembly of each province makes provincial law. In Ontario, for example, elected representatives are called "members of provincial parliament" (MPPs). The political party that has the largest number of MPPs forms the government, and its leader becomes premier. The premier is the head of government in Ontario. There are 12 provincial premiers (Newfoundland and Labrador have the same premier). The provincial premier leads the government and chooses MPPs to serve as ministers in the cabinet. The cabinet sets government policy and introduces laws for the Legislative Assembly to consider. [68]

MAP 8-1 ■ Canada and the United States

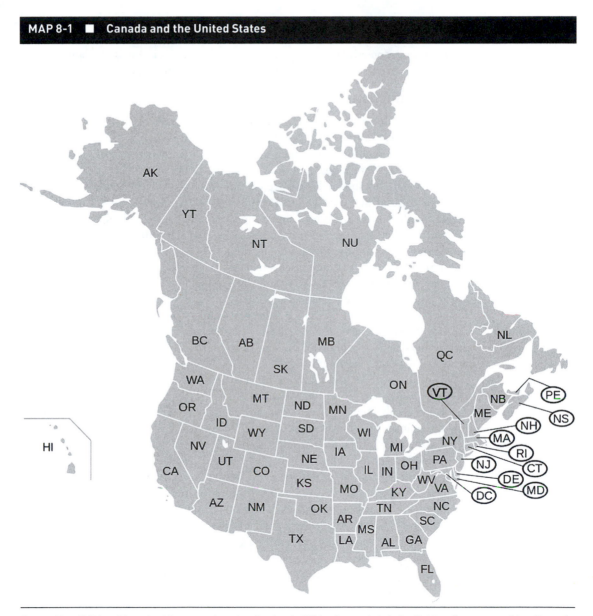

At the local level, each province defines the structure, finances, and management of the local governments of cities, towns, and villages. Residents of each municipality elect the mayor and council members to lead the local government. Committees of councillors discuss budget, service, and administrative issues that are then passed on to the council for debate. Citizens, business owners, and community groups can present their concerns to councillors at committee meetings. Municipalities may also be part of a larger county or regional government.[69] Few provinces have American-type county governments.

Case Introduction

Since ratification of the North American Free Trade Agreement (NAFTA) in 1993 by the United States, Canada, and Mexico, the United States and Canada have established closer ties in the realm of emergency management.[70] Both share a parallel, generally affable, and peaceful relationship despite the United States versus Canada trade dispute of 2018.[71] Owing to absolutely massive Canada–U.S. trade and economic exchange,[72] social and cultural ties, plus a shared concern for security and disaster management, Canada and the United States have a vested interest in managing and mitigating disasters and incidents that span their respective borders or that transpire domestically, but near their neighbor nation. An estimated $680 billion (USD) in trade exchanges between the United States and Canada take place annually.[73] Moreover, Canada is a constitutional monarchy within a parliamentary system, while the United States evolved as a constitutionally based democratic republic. Regardless, both nations embody federalism.

Since 1993, a variety of U.S.–Canada agreements have been approved in the realm of emergency management. Some facilitate cross-border mutual assistance when one, the other, or both nations experience disaster, in any form. Others are based on joint commissions or regional planning boards.[74]

Well before NAFTA and since, the national governments of Canada and the United States have independently set forth their own unique systems of providing disaster assistance to their subnational governments, as this analysis will explain. A purpose of the study was to investigate disaster experience (1994–2013 inclusive) along the border of the United States and Canada to reveal documented losses and where possible the respective federal aid that ensued. Another major goal was to inspect and display the record of Canadian and U.S. declared disasters and emergencies at the respective provincial and state levels, most particularly for counties or county equivalents situated on the international border of Canada and America. This may facilitate cross-national comparisons of Canadian and U.S. homeland security and emergency management.

A secondary purpose was to identify significant cross-national disaster events in which American border counties and their adjacent and neighboring Canadian counterparts experienced the same incident. How many U.S.–Canada "border-spanning," or transnational disasters, have occurred since NAFTA took effect in 1994? Relatedly, singling out incidents that, while not necessarily border-spanning, were co-synchronous and destructive for both Canada and the United States at a sub-state or sub-provincial level, is a secondary purpose. Are the two governments overlooking a need to better coordinate and address disasters that straddle the international dividing line? Does each nation overlook the consultation needed in addressing disasters or emergencies that either straddle the international border or that flow across that border? Are there shared Canada–U.S. natural disaster vulnerabilities? Does the recurrence of the same type of disaster along the border mean that disaster mitigation is inadequate by one or both nations? How often does one nation's emergency become a neighbor nation's disaster?

THE U.S. SYSTEM OF FEDERAL EMERGENCY MANAGEMENT

Chapter 4 provided a fairly comprehensive review of the disaster declaration process used in the United States. That chapter emphasized that since 1950 the U.S. president has been afforded the discretion and flexibility to decide what is and what is not a disaster or emergency. Each president makes declaration decisions on a case-by-case basis advised by the FEMA Administrator and Homeland Security Secretary.[75] As covered previously, presidents can declare major disasters or emergencies (usually by a governor's request) or they can turn down such requests. For major disasters, damage must be "of sufficient severity and magnitude to warrant major disaster assistance under [the Stafford Act (1988)] to supplement the efforts and available resources of the States, Local Governments [including Native American tribal governments and U.S. territorial governments] and disaster relief organizations in alleviating the damage, loss, hardship, or suffering thereby."[76]

Major disaster declarations tend to mobilize a sizable assortment of federal agencies under the National Response Framework (NRF). The NRF has a scalable National Incident Management System (NIMS) intended to promote so-called "seamless" coordination between each level of government (i.e., federal, state, and local) in times of disaster, crisis, or emergency.

Under a 1974 federal law an emergency was defined as "any occasion or instance for which, in the determination of the president, federal assistance is needed to supplement state and local efforts and capabilities to save lives and to protect property and public health and safety, or to lessen or avert the threat of catastrophe in any part of the United States."[77] An emergency is often of less magnitude and scope than a major disaster (DR). However, the president may issue an emergency declaration (EM) before a disaster or to address an ongoing event that may later be declared a major disaster.

At the risk of some repetition, a presidential declaration of major disaster or emergency has far-reaching consequences because it opens the door to federal assistance and aid by legitimizing the disaster for affected populations.[78] The declaration specifies the state and its eligible counties or county-equivalents, including tribal governments, and thereby delineates by location exactly who is eligible for federal relief. Presidential declarations may be issued to a state, the District of Columbia, or American trust territories or commonwealths. When a declaration identifies counties eligible to receive federal disaster assistance, unincorporated jurisdictions within the county will be eligible for assistance. Incorporated (often chartered) municipalities within a county may receive federal assistance passed through by the state or by the county, depending upon the procedures used in each state. Governors identify the counties they judge to have suffered disaster loss, regardless of cause, in their initial declaration request letter to the president (usually submitted through the respective FEMA regional office and headquarters).

U.S. FEMA public disaster assistance loss thresholds of qualification for major disaster declarations, unlike qualifying rules in Canadian government, are NOT law and whether they apply or not is the exclusive decision of the president. This is always the case whenever a governor asks the president for a declaration.

Presidential declarations of major disaster and emergency are intriguing because authority to make the essential decision rests with the president alone. By contrast, as this case will show, the Canadian government system for providing disaster financial assistance to provinces and territories relies much less on the discretion of the prime minister and much more on provincial and territorial eligibility under a Canadian federal system of pre-disaster provincial deductibles and graduated percentage cost-shares of financial support.

As an aside, American northern border counties are relevant in another respect. They are contiguous with the U.S.–Canada international border, in cooperation with their respective home state government, and are Tier 1 eligible entities for DHS Operation Stonegarden funding (which was examined in Chapter 7). Stonegarden involves directing modest federal funds to local law enforcement organizations in border (and ocean coastal) counties to help them fulfill various border control and immigration enforcement functions.

U.S. Presidential Disaster Declarations and How States Request Them[79]

The Stafford Act (§401) requires that "all requests for a declaration by the President that a major disaster exists shall be made by the Governor of the affected State." A state also includes the District of Columbia, Puerto Rico, the Virgin Islands, Guam, American Samoa, and the Commonwealth of the Northern Mariana Islands.[80]

Revisiting Chapter 4, the governor's request is made through the regional FEMA office. State and federal officials conduct a preliminary damage assessment (PDA) to estimate the extent of the disaster and its impact on individuals and public facilities. This information is included in the governor's request to show that the disaster is of such severity and magnitude that effective response is beyond the capabilities of his or her state and respective local governments and that federal assistance is necessary.[81] Normally, the PDA is completed before the governor makes his or her official federal declaration request. However, when an obviously severe or catastrophic event occurs, the governor's request may be submitted prior to the PDA. In FEMA parlance, this is an "expedited request." Nonetheless, the governor must still make the request.

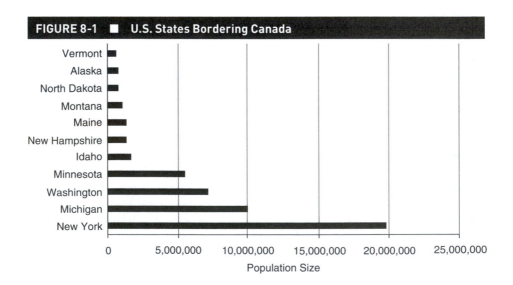

FIGURE 8-1 ■ U.S. States Bordering Canada

As part of the request, the governor must take appropriate action under state law and direct execution of the state's emergency plan.[82] In addition, the governor will need to certify that, for the current disaster, state and local government obligations and expenditures (of which state commitments must be a significant proportion) will comply with all applicable cost-sharing requirements.

Based on the governor's request, the president may declare that a major disaster or emergency exists.[83]

Some declarations will provide only individual assistance (IA) or only public assistance (PA), or both. Hazard mitigation projects and funding opportunities are assessed in most cases. Figure 8-1 arrays the U.S. northern border states with their 2010 populations. New York State, Michigan, Washington State, and Minnesota are first through fourth in population rank. Idaho, New Hampshire, Maine, Montana, and North Dakota range from 1.6 million to about 1 million in population.

CANADIAN GOVERNMENT SYSTEM OF FEDERAL EMERGENCY MANAGEMENT

In modern Canadian constitutional theory, the provinces are considered to be co-sovereign divisions and each province has its own "Crown" represented by the lieutenant governor. The territories are not sovereign, but simply part of the federal realm, and have a commissioner who represents the federal government. In the event of a large-scale natural disaster, the Government of Canada provides financial assistance to provincial and territorial governments through **Disaster Financial Assistance Arrangements (DFAA)**, administered by Public Safety Canada. When response and recovery costs exceed what individual provinces or territories could reasonably be expected to bear on their own, the DFAA provide the Government of Canada with a "fair and equitable" means of assisting provincial and territorial governments.

Through the DFAA, assistance is paid to the province or territory but not directly to affected individuals, small businesses, or communities. The U.S. system differs inasmuch as states and their localities receive federal assistance but so too do individuals, many of whom are compensated directly or offered SBA disaster loans. Businesses are also offered disaster loans. In Canada, a request for disaster cost reimbursement under the DFAA is processed immediately following receipt of the required documentation of provincial/territorial expenditures and a review by federal auditors. Thus, in Canada federal help to disaster victims is dispatched, if loss conditions are met, through provincial government.

In effect, provincial governments receive Canadian DFAA money as a form of block grant, which they are fully accountable for.[84] In America, DHS-FEMA disaster assistance flows through two channels. One is public assistance, which as explained is government to government aid usually for infrastructure repair or replacement. The other channel is for individual assistance, which is in some sub-program areas direct federal to individual or household interaction. Some individual assistance programs are administered by state,[85] tribal, or territorial governments under the declaration such that subnational government administrative costs are covered by DHS-FEMA and the actual aid dispensed through these entities are FEMA dollars to individuals or households.

On the one hand, Canada's collaborative federalism system relies heavily on provincial governments to devise the appropriate policies and mechanisms for distributing pre- and post-disaster aid.[86] The Canadian system also demands that each province requesting DFAA money must first agree to pay a **formula-derived deductible**. On the other hand, the U.S. FEMA system is highly intergovernmental. Pre- and post-disaster relief is highly conditional, employs categorical grants, imposes state–local matching costs, involves infrastructure project-by-project review and approval, and in a few areas relies on direct federal-to-victim interaction.[87] In FEMA Public Assistance to repair infrastructure, the federal government and county/municipal governments interact directly over nearly all phases of construction.

Since the inception of the DFAA program in 1970, the Government of Canada has paid out more than $4.8 billion (Cn) in post-disaster assistance to help provinces and territories. This funding has covered some or all of the costs of response and has subsidized repair or replacement of infrastructure and personal property.[88] Examples of payments include those for the 2005 Alberta floods, the 2003 British Columbia wildfires, and the 2006 flood in Newfoundland.[89] Canada's costliest disaster to date was the wildland fire that struck near Fort McMurray in the Province of Alberta in May 2016. According to the insurance industry, that fire generated losses exceeding $3.5 billion Canadian dollars. That loss is nearly three quarters of all Canadian DFAA spending devoted to provincial and territorial disasters over the life of that program to 2018. The fires reportedly forced nearly 90,000 people to flee their homes for weeks and destroyed roughly 2,400 houses and other buildings in Wood Buffalo.[90]

The provincial or territorial governments design, develop, and deliver disaster financial assistance, deciding the amounts and types of assistance that will be provided to those that have experienced losses. The DFAA places no restrictions on provincial or territorial governments in this regard—they are free to put in place the disaster financial assistance appropriate to the particular disaster and the circumstances, and the DFAA sets out what costs will be eligible for cost-sharing with the federal government.

Public Safety Canada works closely with the province or territory to review provincial/territorial requests for reimbursement of eligible response and recovery costs.

How a Province or Territory Requests Government of Canada Disaster Financial Assistance Arrangements Funding

The minister of **Public Safety Canada** is responsible for exercising leadership relating to emergency management in Canada by coordinating, among government institutions and in cooperation with the provinces and other entities, emergency management activities. Under Canada's Emergency Management Act of 2007, the minister of PSC has authority to

1. provide assistance other than financial assistance to a province if the province requests it;

2. provide financial assistance to a province if a provincial emergency in the province has been declared to be of concern to the federal government under section 7.[91]

The law has a provision enabling consultation with the United States. "In consultation with the Minister of Foreign Affairs, the Minister may develop joint emergency management plans with the relevant United States's authorities and, in accordance with those plans, coordinate Canada's response to emergencies in the United States and provide assistance in response to those emergencies."[92]

The law specifies that a government institution may not respond to a provincial emergency unless the government of the province requests assistance or there is an agreement with the province that requires or permits the assistance.[93]

"Any request for financial assistance under the DFAA must be made by the province within six months of the end of the event. The request takes the form of a letter from the Premier of the province to the Prime Minister or from the provincial Minister Responsible for Emergency Preparedness to the federal Minister."[94]

Rulings on the eligibility of specific individual cases will not be made. PSC Regional Directors (RDs) will continue to advise provinces on the interpretation and application of eligibility criteria. However, if unusual circumstances arise about which the guidelines are silent or ambiguous, Public Safety Canada may, on the advice of regional and headquarters staff, make "eligibility determinations" on issues raised by a province.[95] In other words, provincial eligibility is a function of the level of per capita provincial loss and the province's willingness to pay the deductible required, unless some type of anomalous or extreme condition not covered by the official guidelines emerges. In the latter case, PSC Regional Directors may move an otherwise ineligible provincial request for DFAA funding forward to approval.

The Emergency Management Act requires that a federal Order-in-Council be issued declaring that an emergency of concern to the Government of Canada has occurred in a province and that financial assistance has been authorized. Provinces are encouraged to submit requests for assistance as soon as possible after a disaster, emergency, or incident. If the eligible provincial expenditure threshold is not exceeded, the file is simply closed. In other words, the Canadian federal government does not confer DFAA funds. Provincial authorities are urged to quickly begin federal consultations on the eligibility of provincial expenditures for DFAA financial assistance.

The period of the disaster (including beginning and end dates) and the affected geographical area must be defined and accepted for the purposes of the DFAA by the province and the Government of Canada. Eligibility determinations will be based on the resulting dates and areas. Appropriate technical expertise will be consulted as needed for such determinations. In the United States, beginning and end dates apply to the incidents themselves; they also apply programmatically. Under a presidential declaration offering PA, start dates are determined by federal–state agreement dates and ended by program fulfillment (project completion or an aid application deadline). For Individual and Household Assistance, a start date is announced in the *Federal Register* and an end date is announced by FEMA in the same source when applications approach zero (no more individual or household requests for aid).

Just as in the United States, the Government of Canada calls for assessment and appraisal of damages. "The Regional Director (RD) of Public Safety Canada provides initial federal liaison with provincial officials responding to the immediate effects of a disaster. Subsequently, the RD co-ordinates the Government of Canada participation in damage assessment and review of provincial requests for assistance if requested. Federal departments with the appropriate expertise may be requested to provide the RD with advice and assistance in determining what constitutes reasonable costs for recovery and restoration. Alternatively, the RD and the affected province may agree to engage third parties for appraising damage and recovery costs.[96] Table 8-1a shows the cost share system employed by the Government of Canada over the years covered by this study.

A province or territory may request Government of Canada disaster financial assistance when eligible expenditures exceed an established initial threshold (based on provincial or territorial population).

Eligible expenses include, but are not limited to, evacuation operations, restoring public works and infrastructure to their pre-disaster condition, as well as replacing or repairing basic, essential personal property of individuals, small businesses, and farmsteads. The Government of Canada may provide advance and interim payments to provincial and territorial governments as funds are expended under the provincial/territorial disaster assistance program. All provincial or territorial requests for DFAA cost sharing are subject to federal audit to ensure that cost sharing is provided according to the DFAA guidelines. Canada's system of cost sharing was revised in 2015, but this study has been confined to the period 1994–2013.

Examples of provincial/territorial expenses that may be eligible for cost sharing under the DFAA include:

- Evacuation, transportation, emergency food, shelter, and clothing

- Emergency provision of essential community services

- Security measures including the removal of valuable assets and hazardous materials from a threatened area

- Repairs to public buildings and related equipment

- Repairs to public infrastructure such as roads and bridges

- Removal of damaged structures constituting a threat to public safety

- Restoration, replacement, or repairs to an individual's dwelling (principal residence only)

TABLE 8-1a ■ Canadian Cost-sharing Formula up to December 31, 2018 (Covers the 1994–2013 Period)	
Eligible Provincial Expense Thresholds (per Capita of Population)	**Government of Canada Share (Percentage)**
First $1	0
Next $2	50
Next $2	75
Remainder	90

Source: Public Safety Canada, "Disaster Financial Assistance Arrangements (DFAA)," Appendix A, Table 5, https://www.publicsafety.gc.ca/cnt/mrgnc-mngmnt/rcvr-dsstrs/dsstr-fnncl-ssstnc-rrngmnts/index-en.aspx#a01 (accessed July 9, 2018).

TABLE 8-1b ■ Example of a Disaster in a Province with a Population of 1 Million for 2018		
Eligible Expenditures	**Provincial or Territorial Government**	**Government of Canada**
First $3.12 per capita (100% provincial/territorial)	$3,120,000	Nil
Next $6.25 per capita (50%)	$3,125,000	$3,125,000
Next $6.25 per capita (75%)	$1,562,500	$4,687,500
Remainder (90%)	$438,000	$3,942,000
Total	$8,245,500	$11754,500

Source: Public Safety Canada, "Disaster Financial Assistance Arrangements (DFAA)," Appendix A, Formula effective January 1, 2018, https://www.publicsafety.gc.ca/cnt/mrgnc-mngmnt/rcvr-dsstrs/dsstr-fnncl-ssstnc-rrngmnts/index-en.aspx#a01 (accessed July 9, 2018).

- Restoration, replacement, or repairs to essential personal furnishings, appliances, and clothing

- Restoration of small businesses and farmsteads including buildings and equipment

- Costs of damage inspection, appraisal, and clean-up

Examples of expenses that would NOT be eligible for reimbursement include:

- Repairs to a non-primary dwelling (e.g., cottage or ski chalet)

- Repairs that are eligible for reimbursement through insurance

- Costs that are covered in whole or in part by another government program (e.g., production/crop insurance)

- Normal operating expenses of a government department or agency

- Assistance to large businesses and crown corporations

- Loss of income and economic recovery

- Forest fire fighting[97]

Figure 8-2 arrays provincial and territorial populations in Canada's 2016 Census with percentage change in respective population since 2011. Note that Ontario, Quebec, British Columbia, and Alberta rank first to fourth in population. Manitoba and Saskatchewan each exceed 1 million, while Nova Scotia, New Brunswick, and Newfoundland and Labrador range from slightly less than 1 million down to half a million. Alberta has a very high rate of growth, exceeded only by Nunavut, which is the lowest population Canadian territory.

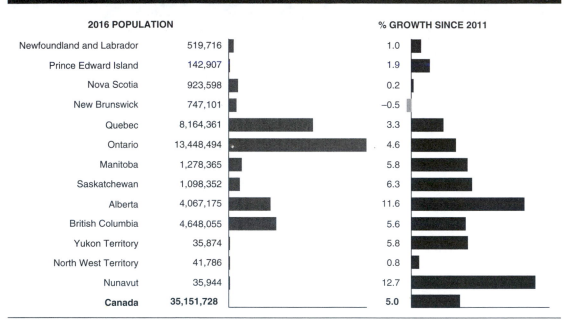

FIGURE 8-2 ■ Canada's Population Growth 2011–2016 (by Province/Territory)

	2016 POPULATION	% GROWTH SINCE 2011
Newfoundland and Labrador	519,716	1.0
Prince Edward Island	142,907	1.9
Nova Scotia	923,598	0.2
New Brunswick	747,101	–0.5
Quebec	8,164,361	3.3
Ontario	13,448,494	4.6
Manitoba	1,278,365	5.8
Saskatchewan	1,098,352	6.3
Alberta	4,067,175	11.6
British Columbia	4,648,055	5.6
Yukon Territory	35,874	5.8
North West Territory	41,786	0.8
Nunavut	35,944	12.7
Canada	**35,151,728**	5.0

Source: Statistics Canada.

U.S. FEMA

In review and for the purpose of contrast, the U.S. Federal Emergency Management Agency was established by President Jimmy Carter in 1979. It has progressed through several reorganizations and transformations, in part because it is a small federal agency and closely tethered to the White House and has only modest clientele group support. Presidential elections regularly trigger changes at FEMA, particularly in appointed leadership posts. In the aftermath of the 9/11 attacks in 2001, the agency took on greater importance both as an instrument of disaster preparedness, response and recovery and as a tool of homeland security's domestic side. "Billions of dollars of new funding were directed to FEMA to help communities face the threat of terrorism. Just a few years past its 20th anniversary, FEMA was actively directing its 'all-hazards' approach toward homeland security issues."[98]

On March 1, 2003, FEMA joined 22 other federal agencies, programs, and offices in becoming the Department of Homeland Security, with a workforce today of some 270,000.[99] The new department brought a coordinated approach to national security from emergencies and disasters—both natural and man-made. "On October 4, 2006, President George W. Bush signed into law the Post-Katrina Emergency Management Reform Act. The Act significantly reorganized FEMA, provided it substantial new authority to remedy gaps that became apparent in Hurricane Katrina in August 2005," returned FEMA's grants administration offices that had been pulled into DHS central administration, and included a more robust preparedness mission for FEMA.[100] FEMA has a Washington, DC, headquarters, 10 regional offices, the National Emergency Training Center, and the Center for Domestic Preparedness/Noble Training Center and other facilities.[101] President Barack Obama's FEMA administrator was Craig Fugate, a highly experienced emergency manager and firefighter, who has held the post through all of both Obama terms. President Trump was inaugurated president in January 2017. After nearly five months, the Trump administration was able to win Senate confirmation of his FEMA administrator nominee, W. Brock Long, in June 2017. Long is an experienced Alabama state emergency management director.

Public Safety Canada

Since its modern evolution in 2003, Public Safety Canada has experienced fairly high turnover in its Ministerial leadership even when one political party has held a governing majority for five or six continuous years (6 PSC leaders in 13 years).[102] Parliament began proposing legislation to create the PSC in 2001. The department was ultimately established in December 2003 during a reorganization of the federal government; the Department of Public Safety and Emergency Preparedness Act came into force on April 4, 2005. Emergency Preparedness Canada had existed under the auspices of Canada's Defence Department since enactment of the Emergency Preparedness Act of 1988; however, it was folded into Public Safety Canada.

The PSC was created to have a single entity with responsibility for ensuring public safety in Canada and is a direct result of lessons learned from the September 11 attacks on the United States in 2001. The department is in many ways similar to the U.S. Department of Homeland Security, granted that unlike DHS it does not cover the protection of maritime sovereignty (this is handled by the Canadian Forces, Transport Canada, and Fisheries and Oceans Canada). PSC has a current workforce of about 54,000.

Most of the department comprises organizations that were previously placed under the Department of Solicitor General of Canada; however, the reorganization of several federal departments and ministries added the Canada Border Services Agency to the portfolio, after the two streams of the former Canada Customs and Revenue Agency were split in 2003. In addition, the Office of Critical Infrastructure Protection and Emergency Preparedness (OCIPEP) from the Department of National Defence was also brought into the department.

In addition to the department there are five agencies and three review bodies within the Public Safety portfolio headed by the minister of Public Safety. PSC's associated agencies include Canada Border Services Agency, Royal Canadian Mounted Police, Canadian Security Intelligence Service, Correctional Service Canada, and the National Parole Board. The current minister of Public Safety Canada is Ralph Goodale, Liberal Party, appointed in November 2015 by Prime Minister Justin Trudeau. Goodale replaced Prime Minister Stephen Harper's appointed PSC minister, Steven Blaney, Conservative Party, who had served in this post since July 2013.

BILATERAL U.S.–CANADA EMERGENCY MANAGEMENT AGREEMENTS IN BRIEF

There are at least 10 emergency management relevant subjects of Canada–U.S. bilateral agreement. The subjects covered in brief below represent only a portion of all of those in these agreements.

Wildfire

Wildland fire mutual assistance applies between Canada and the United States. American coordinating authority resides in the National Interagency Coordinating Center (NICC) and the National Interagency Fire Center (NIFC). Canadian Coordinating Authority comes through the Canadian Interagency Forest Fire Centre (CIFFC). Requests for assistance under the operating plan are carried out through each nation's respective coordinating authorities, the NICC and CIFFC. Occasionally, when one nations' aerial firefighting tankers are over-taxed with fire suppression actions, the other may, if requested, send some of its fleet of water or retardant-carrying aircraft across the U.S.–Canada international border to help.

The operating plan addresses requests for assistance, designation of officials, information to supply to Customs & Immigration Points of Entry (POE), and information to include in situation reporting. The operating plan also includes a "Directory of Designated Officials," updated annually. The operating plan provides specific guidance on invoicing, payment, and reimbursement. The arrangement's diplomatic notes explicitly identify responsible parties for damages, losses, injury compensation, and death benefits. Sec. 3. (2)(B) of the U.S. Wildfire Suppression Assistance Act requires agreements "include waiver by each party to the agreement of all claims against every other party to the agreement for compensation for any loss, damage, personal injury, or death occurring in consequence of the performance of such agreement." Authority in the U.S. Pub. L. 101-11, the Wildfire Suppression Assistance Act, permanently authorized the U.S. secretary of agriculture and the U.S. secretary of the interior to enter into agreements with foreign fire organizations for assistance in wildfire protection.

Military and All-Hazards Emergency Management

Initially approved by each nation on February 14, 2008, and renewed January 26, 2012, the purpose of one provision "is to provide a framework for the military of one nation to provide support to the military of the other nation while in the performance of civil support operations to the primary agency (e.g., floods, forest fires, hurricanes, earthquakes, and effects of a terrorist attack)." Furthermore, "When approved, military forces from one nation augment the other nation's forces in civil support operations."

Lead organization(s) are (National Defence) Canada Command and U.S. Northern Command. The provision is activated and implemented on order of the Government of Canada and the U.S. president or U.S. secretary of defense. "The Canadian Department of Foreign Affairs and International Trade (DFAIT), acting on behalf of the Government of Canada, and the U.S. Department of State (DOS), acting on behalf of the United States Government, will, upon receipt of a formal request for, or offer of mutual assistance, coordinate an agreed upon bilateral response that may include military support."

One observation is necessary here. The United States has a long history of citizen soldiering through its use of Army and Air National Guard forces, which operate under state jurisdiction but which are part of the U.S. Department of Defense. In rare instances, the president can "federalize" state National Guards, thus removing them from state governor control. Canada has no equivalent counterpart to the National Guard system of the United States However, Canada, like the United States and its Department of Homeland Security, has consolidated at the federal level a pool of military or para-military organizations under Public Safety Canada (Coast Guard, Canada Border Services, the RCMP, Canadian Security Intelligence Services, etc.).

Cross-Border Response to Emergencies

One part of the bilateral agreement entrusts authority to the minister of public safety, in consultation with the minister of foreign affairs, to coordinate Canada's response to an emergency in the United States. Canada's 2007 Emergency Management Act defines emergency management as the prevention and mitigation of, preparedness for, response to, and recovery from emergencies. Under the Emergency Management Act, the minister of public safety is responsible for coordinating the Government of Canada's response to an emergency. The Federal Emergency Response Plan (FERP) is the Government of Canada's "all-hazards" response plan. Public Safety Canada developed FERP in consultation with other government departments. FERP outlines the processes and mechanisms to facilitate an integrated Government of Canada response to an emergency and to eliminate the need for departments to coordinate a wider Government of Canada response.

Conversely, the U.S. Foreign Assistance Act of 1961, as amended, involves international disaster assistance. Under this law, "The President is authorized to furnish assistance [for the relief and rehabilitation of people and countries affected by such disasters] to any foreign country, international organization, or private voluntary organization." It adds, "The President is authorized to appoint a Special Coordinator for International Disaster Assistance whose responsibility shall be to promote maximum effectiveness and coordination in responses to foreign disasters by United States agencies and between the United States and other donors." Sec. 607 authorizes an agency of the United States government to furnish services and commodities to foreign government international organizations and registered non-voluntary nonprofit relief agencies on a reimbursable basis. The statute requires a determination that the activity is in furtherance of the purposes outlined in Part I of the Foreign Assistance Act (FAA). The U.S. Department of State, and its United States Agency for International Development, Office of Foreign Disaster Assistance, are central in providing post-disaster foreign assistance, including to Canada.

Emergency Management

The U.S. National Response Framework's (NRF) International Coordination Support Annex (ICSA) was established in January 2008. The ICSA provides guidance on carrying out responsibilities for international coordination in support of the U.S. federal government's response to a domestic incident with international and diplomatic impacts and implications that call for coordination and consultations with foreign governments and international organizations. The coordinating agency is the Department of State. It responds to requests for information or support from foreign missions or other U.S. federal agencies when a U.S. domestic incident of any sort has major international implications or the potential for them. Department of State's Executive Secretariat and its Operations Center have established a DOS Task Force to communicate with the U.S. National Operations Center (NOC) and other U.S. government agencies, as appropriate.

The DOS Task Force also provides U.S. embassies/consulates with instruction on advising other governments and organizations on the domestic incident and furnishes support to foreign missions and foreign nationals in the United States. DOS also serves as an intermediary for foreign requests/offers of assistance through the International Assistance System/Concept of Operations Plans.

Under the Government of Canada and the Government of the United States of America Agreement on Emergency Management Cooperation (effective July 7, 2009) with precedents dating back to 1986 and 1967, respectively, the agreement establishes a consultative group on emergency cooperation between the two nations. This group is provided broad authority to work on emergency management topics affecting both the United States and Canada including those involving mutual aid. The agreement also identifies general principles of cooperation, subject to domestic laws, as a guide for civil emergency authorities. These principles include using best efforts to facilitate the movement of evacuees and emergency personnel and equipment, avoiding levying federal taxes on services, equipment, and supplies engaged in emergency activities in the territory of the other, and so on.

Critical Infrastructure

Under the Canada–United States Action Plan for Critical Infrastructure of 2010, an all-hazards plan specific to critical infrastructure was called for. Owing to the interconnectedness of American and Canadian critical infrastructure, a comprehensive cross-border approach to critical infrastructure resilience is essential. The plan identifies specific deliverables, sets out a framework for managing risks, and supports regional cross-border relations. The action plan is based on three objectives: building partnerships, improved information sharing, and risk management. A variety of specific actions are identified to support each. Communication and coordination actions include working together to improve sector-specific cross-border collaboration, establishing a virtual Canada–U.S. Infrastructure Risk Analysis Cell, developing compatible mechanisms and protocols to protect and share sensitive critical infrastructure information, collaborating to ensure effective information sharing during and following an incident, among others.

U.S.–CANADA CASE CONCLUSIONS

The American and Canadian international border separates two proud and sovereign nations, both of which regularly experience natural disasters, emergencies, and of late, terrorism. While most Canadian provincial and territorial lands are vast and lightly populated, humans and their settlements therein (whether small First Nation communities or major international cities) frequently experience disasters serious enough to meet and exceed conditions of eligibility for Government of Canada aid under Disaster Financial Assistance Arrangements. Even though it was not possible to show international border proximity for all Canadian emergencies, it is reasonable to assume that most of them occurred within 200 miles of that border.[103] This is in part owing to Canadian demographics: most of the population of Canada resides along the southern edge of Canada where winter weather conditions are considerably less severe than they are in areas more than 200 miles further north.

Conversely, American demographics are such that many fewer Americans reside along the northern border than in other regions of the nation. However, there are exceptions. The cities of Seattle and Tacoma (Washington State) are not far from the city of Vancouver, British Columbia. These big urban areas share a major earthquake vulnerability. Also, floods and severe storms often straddle or move across the U.S.–Canada border there. Detroit, Michigan, shares a bridge connection with Windsor, Canada. To the east, Buffalo and the city of Niagara Falls are close to Canada's Niagara Falls and the immensely large city of Toronto. Besides Toronto, other major Canadian cities like Montreal, Ottawa, and Quebec City also rely heavily on transportation corridors through upstate New York and northern New England. Electrical power generation, distribution, and transmission is, in the case of Canada and the United States, truly interdependent and cross-national. The Blackout of 2003, triggered in northeastern Ohio, produced calamity for the American northeast and for Canada's southeastern portions of Ontario Province.[104]

Disasters are sometimes a shared experience for the United States and Canada, even in areas spanning the vastly long international border. How Canadians and Americans officially define what a disaster is varies only slightly. Disaster laws in Canada and the United States are robust and the number of U.S.–Canadian emergency management agreements are large and ever-growing. Systems of Canada–U.S. mutual aid in time of emergency are maturing, but unfortunately systems of mutual disaster mitigation remain nascent. Moreover, finding hard evidence of U.S.–Canada cross-border cooperation in addressing any particular disaster, beyond diplomatic agreements between the two nations, is extremely difficult to ferret out.

How Canada and America compile, maintain, and make public records of federally compensated disaster losses to their sub-governments, and disaster victims, has many faults. The United States shortsightedly assembles for public disclosure disaster funding under declarations at only the state level, with no disaggregation of this information to the county or municipal level. FEMA data is difficult to obtain, although a White House agency data collection effort featuring FEMA declaration data (infrequently updated) is of some help, even though FEMA declaration spending itself is rarely disclosed. The United States, unlike Canada, does not furnish total estimated losses for any federally declared disaster. More unforgivable is that FEMA eschews tabulating disaster deaths, injuries, and number of evacuees for presidentially declared disasters—raising serious question about how it conducts emergency management concerning these subjects.

Worse, for the United States, FEMA spending data on disaster outlays to states and localities is not disclosed to the public on a regular basis. For most researchers, FEMA declaration data is nearly impossible to obtain. State and local governments are even more circumspect when it comes to publicly divulging how they spent FEMA, and their own, disaster dollars. Because so many declarations in the United States take years to close out in accounting terms, locating what little funding data that is made available is complicated because that data is a "moving target." It may change from day to day (until financial and auditing closeout). Researchers who rely on such FEMA data run the risk that their published work will be discredited by FEMA officials on grounds that the figures they used are no longer valid.

Canada, through its Canada Disaster Database (CDD), does provide information on fatalities, injuries, and number evacuated. CDD makes known the location, nature, and timing of incidents on the provincial level, and impacted areas are identified. This is generally so for U.S. federal disaster data as well.[105] Canada, to its credit, discloses estimated total losses.[106] However, Public Safety Canada (PSC) provides for each incident spending categories for DFAA funding, provincial matching totals paid to PSC under DFAA, and provincial department spending, and more. Moreover, the Canadian Disaster Database is loaded with small incidents in which losses were unknown or evidently outside of provincial DFAA qualification. Unfortunately, according to a study by the Parliament's budget office, the Canadian CDD site is not regularly updated.

Both America and Canada embrace and promote disaster mitigation, but both nations fail to make public all of their disaster data. If they did so this would enable others to more wisely advance disaster prevention and mitigation. Major natural disasters for both the United States and Canada, for a variety of reasons, are matters of national security. However, this is little justification for hiding from the North American public the costs of natural disaster and the ensuing federal compensation.

Most researchers of comparative emergency management tend to assume that U.S. federal disaster relief is both highly political and overgenerous. Comparative EM people who know something about Canadian federal disaster assistance tend to view the Canadian system as highly delegated and rationalized (i.e., the provinces are on their own until disaster losses exceed preset per capita deductibles, then almost mechanically, if requested, Public Safety Canada under DFAA pays out increasing sums of financial aid under graduated federal cost shares). Canada's disaster management system above the provincial level appears bureaucratized and largely apolitical. Exceptions come in the case of incidents receiving 100 percent DFAA help with no provincial cost share whatsoever. There may be more politics in the Canadian system than people are led to believe. It is a safe bet that most small and remote Canadian communities receive disproportionately less DFAA funding than do most well-populated, economically important, and politically influential urban and suburban Canadian localities. In some ways, in the case of Canada, who wins and who loses in securing government disaster assistance is much more a function of what each province is willing to do for its respective localities than it is a matter of what the Canada federal government is willing to do for its provinces. How well provincial emergency management is organized and run is crucial for Canadians. In the American case, who wins and who loses is a function of federal–state relations, somewhat softly applied FEMA criteria, and skill at loss documentation and public relations. It also matters how many congressional districts and states are impacted. As well, in America the FEMA administrator is a presidential appointee, and with some notable exceptions, since 1993, most have come from emergency management posts. In Canada, the head of the PSC is an MP of the prime minister's political party. The current minister of public safety and emergency preparedness is lawmaker Ralph Goodale, representing Regina-Wascana in Saskatchewan, who was appointed by Prime Minister Justin Trudeau in late 2015. The PSC has several other MPs who serve as ministers or deputy ministers in the organization. Presumably, the more districts of MPs and provincial MPs impacted by a disaster or emergency, the more that political pressure is applied to provincial governments affected.

The U.S. system is significantly political because since 1950, Congress has entrusted the president, as a single decision maker, to approve or deny state governor requests for declarations of disaster. This may account for why U.S. disaster spending is very high relative to most other developed nations, including Canada. However, most presidents have exhibited "tough love" in matters of small-loss and routine declaration requests; otherwise, governors would be tempted to completely abuse federal disaster aid by requesting federal money for every misfortune of any kind.

Canada's system has not gone unnoticed in the United States. For a period of years, FEMA, under Administrator Craig Fugate, President Barack Obama's FEMA head from 2009 to 2017, pressed (unsuccessfully) for use of state deductibles in considering governor requests for major disaster declarations. However, it is difficult to prove how much Fugate and his colleagues were influenced by the Canadian federal system of provincial disaster deductibles. Canadian provinces, on account of their co-sovereignty with the Government of Canada, are in relative terms more "self-reliant" than most (but not all) of America's state governments. While U.S. state-level emergency management has vastly improved in nearly all states since the 1960s, so too many state EM offices or their equivalents have worked to be proficient at requesting and winning federal disaster relief funds. There is a similar provincial and territorial press for federal funds in Canada, but front-end deductibles and the immense difficulties of damage assessment in Canada have slowed or discouraged provincial DFAA avarice.[107]

U.S. and Canadian emergency management have evolved in a largely independent manner, but each nation has noticed what its neighbor has done in the realm of disaster policy and process. The status of disaster-related insurance in each nation has been rife with problems. Too few people and organizations buy flood insurance, or earthquake insurance, and many masses of people are under-indemnified (under-protected) given the insurance they already own. Beyond this, if American governors can be accused of gaming the presidential declaration system to their advantage, so to a lesser extent can Canada's provincial premiers, who capitalize on how provincial per capita loss requirements advantage or disadvantage their residents when it comes to acquiring DFAA funding. Years ago, political scientists Gabriel Almond and Daniel Elazar posited that U.S. states manifest their own political cultures. These cultures were said to influence state willingness or unwillingness to work with the federal government on various problems. Some political cultures encourage their governors to almost always seek federal help. Conversely, others discourage this behavior and insist that their governors (and states) go it alone or seek help from adjacent states with similar cultures. This applies both for U.S. states and for Canadian provinces. So, for Canada, some provinces manifest federal dependency cultures and some do not. This may in part account for why DFAA help to some provinces seems minimal while in others it appears highly responsive and generous.

In closing, a dilemma that drew the interest of the U.S. Government Accountability Office not long ago was what to do about border-spanning disasters that wreak havoc in one state but only damages a neighborhood or a few homes in an adjacent state. Victims in the first state usually win federal disaster aid while victims in the adjacent state, through no fault of their own albeit an invisible state borderline, get no federal help. Is this fair? It was after all the same disaster force that struck each. Viewed at the household level this system of relief is unfair with discrimination by border. How soon will the families of households along the U.S.–Canada international border begin to sense the same inequity in their respective nation's system of disaster relief?

Summary

Both the UN and the United States play a crucial role in international disaster relief. Their competencies overlap and complement one another. For instance, sometimes the UN and the United States may not be directly involved on the ground in the same operation. The UN might address a nation's disaster through direct field operations, while the United States provides aid indirectly by funneling funds and in-kind assistance from U.S.-based NGOs to the affected nation or to UN agencies. Sometimes the United States and the UN do work together and are present at the site of devastation.

Comparing UN disaster assistance to U.S. foreign disaster assistance may seem inappropriate because the UN is an international alliance of (currently) 193 members and is a supranational body, whereas the United States is a territorial-based sovereign state and a superpower. The organizations and disaster response structure of the UN seem better able to deal with disasters in the international realm than are U.S. foreign disaster relief organizations. USAID/OFDA might respond faster if it limited the number of agencies involved in its response process, increased its flexibility in post-disaster activities, augmented and diversified its funding and the purposes to which it could be directed, and won government approval of major increases in its overall budget for international humanitarian assistance.

In some respects, U.S. strengths are UN weaknesses and vice versa. The U.S. government is primarily responsible and accountable to its own citizens and their elected representatives. When the American polity judges U.S. international disaster relief programs as a low priority, the U.S. system of relief suffers. U.S. government relief programs, and the missions of its specialized agencies, are supposed to assist people in other nations and at the same time promote U.S. interests abroad. The rationale underlying U.S. humanitarian assistance is that by encouraging democracy and building structures favorable to sustainable political and economic development, the U.S. government gains and keeps allies and promotes other U.S. interests, among them the security of the nation itself. Besides providing disaster aid to the people of other nations, an American secondary agenda is to prevent recipient nations from political or economic collapse, to forestall their subversion by enemies of the United States, and to prevent the spawning of failed states that may evolve into rogue states.

Owing to America's agenda and perceived motives, leaders of some nation-states elect to decline American offers of disaster relief. Some are wary of U.S. ambitions; many leaders fear the consequences of U.S. intervention and worry that American "help" might destabilize their governing regimes. For these and other reasons, they often judge UN help as less threatening because it is coming from an international body founded on humanitarian goals, such as alleviating human suffering and promoting human rights and peace around the globe. The UN often projects a more neutral and legitimate image than does the United States. This legitimacy is reinforced by long-standing relationships that the UN has with most of its member-states. To many in the international community, the collective and multilateral character of past UN interventions represents altruistic interests of a confederation of nations rather than the sometimes insincere help of an individual state.

The UN is not without flaws. The organization has had great difficulty protecting its own officials, sanctioning the behavior and practices of its own "blue helmet" military, and achieving coordination of its internal agencies and offices. For the most part, the UN is a capable overall coordinator of disaster relief and recovery programs, but it is also an organization poorly suited to separating combatants, forcefully protecting relief workers,[101] their aid stores, and their aid distribution networks. Moreover, the size of the UN budget (and therefore the UN capacity to intervene) depends on the benevolence of its member-states and private donors.

In contrast, the United States has its own international disaster relief system, usually has the workforce to implement its missions, and has the capacity to use its military people and capabilities when it so chooses. In addition, America is one of the largest contributors to the UN, although the United States has at times also resisted paying its full assessment.[102] The U.S. government and the American people also donate funds and in-kind resources to many international organizations capable of dispensing disaster relief. The UN is in many ways dependent on U.S. help and resources. A disagreement between UN and U.S. officials in a matter of international disaster relief has consequences for all parties. The United States remains a vital and fundamental player in the UN disaster response system.

Poor nations can rarely afford to engage in disaster preparedness and mitigation activities without outside help. Moreover, in some cases, the leaders of poor and developing nations adhere to political ideologies and conduct domestic and foreign policies disliked by other nations. Over the past 30-40 years, the need to curb terrorism and the dissemination of weapons of mass destruction coexist with the need to advance the moral imperatives of peace and development. Disasters must be addressed by a wide array of state and nonstate actors. Together, the United States and the UN do have important stakes in assisting such nations and their peoples. Both the UN and the United States are essential actors in a multilevel/multilateral disaster-relief global regime.

UN and U.S. agencies collaborate with many states, agencies, NGOs, private corporations, and international foundations. Each possesses various resources and capacities to intervene and provide relief in disaster-stricken areas. With so many actors involved in the response and recovery process, both the UN and America have a stake in maintaining and improving coordination and communication among themselves and with others. Each need to better allocate the funds of donors, avoiding redundancy and counterproductive outcomes. Effort and aid must be provided quickly, wisely, and efficiently so as to alleviate human suffering and advance healing, reconstruction, and economic welfare.

The extended review and comparison of American and Canadian emergency management, which included observations on cross-border incidents and an overview of provincial and state disaster management along the U.S.–Canada international border from 1994 to 2013, was aimed at exploring how two democratic nations, both with federal structures, operate their intergovernmental systems of emergency management. Sometimes one of the best ways to understand your own nation's disaster management system is to visit a neighboring nation and then compare and contrast it with the same system used your nation.

Key Terms

"Blue helmeted" peacekeeping
 soldiers 327
Bureau of Political-Military
 Affairs 320
Complex humanitarian
 emergencies (CHEs) 316
Development banks 322
Disaster Assistance Response
 Team (DART) 320
Disaster Financial Assistance
 Arrangements (DFAA) 335
Disaster Reduction and Recovery
 Program 325
Emergency-management–
 oriented multinational
 organizations 322
Emergency Response Division
 (of UNDP) 325

Formula-derived
 deductible 336
Globalizing forces 316
Humanitarian assistance 321
Humanitarian Assistance
 Survey Teams 321
North American Free Trade
 Agreement (NAFTA) 329
Office of Peacekeeping and
 Humanitarian Affairs 320
Office of the United
 Nations High
 Commissioner for
 Refugees (UNHCR) 324
Office of U.S. Foreign Disaster
 Assistance (OFDA) 319
Public Safety Canada 336
Territorial sovereignty 317

United Nations Children's Fund
 (UNICEF) 324
United Nations Development
 Programme (UNDP) 325
United Nations Disaster
 Assessment and
 Coordination (UNDAC)
 team 323
United Nations Office for
 the Coordination of
 Humanitarian Affairs
 (OCHA) 323
U.S. Agency for International
 Development (USAID) 318
World Food Programme
 (WFP) 326
World Health Organization
 (WHO) 326

People walk down a flooded street as they evacuate their homes after the area was inundated with flooding from Hurricane Harvey on August 28, 2017 in Houston, Texas.

Joe Raedle/Getty Images

9

HURRICANES HARVEY, IRMA, AND MARIA

U.S. Disaster Management Challenged

For the United States and its territories, 2017 was a record-breaking hurricane year. It brought 10 hurricanes, which collectively inflicted an estimated $265 billion in damage.[1] Hurricanes Harvey, Irma, and Maria of that year truly tested the capacities of federal, state, and local emergency management. During the responses to each, the U.S. Department of Homeland Security and its Federal Emergency Management Agency (FEMA) mobilized disaster assistance volunteers, a

"surge" workforce[2] of volunteering federal workers detailed from inside and outside of the department for up to 45-day assignments, plus an immense and largely corporate contractor force, and the altruistic nonprofit organizations so intrinsically part of disaster response and recovery. A host of other federal agencies, including the U.S. Army, Air Force, and Navy, worked the disasters as well. Impacted states and territories, along with their respective local governments, worked feverishly to address the escalating needs of their victims and communities, while they awaited much needed federal post-disaster assistance. The National Response Framework provided a schematic overlay about how the nation would respond, and the National Incident Management System guided the organization of the actual response in the field. However, all did not run flawlessly.

Hurricanes Harvey, Irma, and Maria struck one after the other, each about two weeks apart, lasting from mid-August to mid-September in 2017. On top of this, almost simultaneously, part of the nation also had to contend with record-breaking wildfires. Across the American West, particularly in California, several fires incinerated not just remote woodland homes but entire housing subdivisions. These disasters tested the new Trump administration, which had only been in office since mid-January of 2017. As Hurricane Harvey was about to strike, President Donald J. Trump had dutifully signed presidential declarations of emergency for the affected states and territories. He did this for each hurricane, and after each made landfall, he promptly issued major disaster declarations for the states and territories impacted by these disasters. He responded very much as preceding presidents had done for disasters of catastrophic proportions since the early 1950s. President Trump even reduced the state and local cost share that Puerto Rico, Texas, and Florida had been expected to pay under several FEMA sub-programs.[3] President Trump and Vice President Mike Pence eventually traveled together and separately to the scenes of the three major hurricane disasters. For each one, they offered support, encouragement, and small acts of kindness. Again, this was comparable to what presidents and vice presidents had done for decades whenever mega-disasters struck some part of the nation.

However, one thing turned out being uniquely different. President Trump, having learned that the mayor of San Juan, Puerto Rico, had overtly criticized both him and FEMA by claiming their response to Hurricane Maria devastation in Puerto Rico was too slow, retaliated in kind. In his reply, the president went so far as to seemingly threaten the commonwealth with an early federal departure. He intimated that the people of Puerto Rico needed to do more to help themselves, and he judged the mayor's remarks as a sign of ingratitude. No American chief executive, since presidential declaration authority was granted in 1950, had ever publicly issued such a threat, although a few presidents before Trump had had disputes with various governors in the aftermath of disaster. Even though the flap was short-lived national news, it shocked the emergency management community. A portion of this chapter will examine this dispute and its implications.

Chapter 9 of the second edition of this book was all about victim compensation after the 9/11 attacks of 2001. This edition's Chapter 9 looks into some aspects of post-hurricane victim compensation offered and conferred after Harvey, Irma, and Maria. In the Obama years, FEMA sought to become more "victim-centric." However, as previous chapters have made apparent, U.S. emergency management before 2014 is NOT the same as in 2016 and beyond. This chapter asks whether the dramatic changes that both FEMA and DHS have undergone in policy and management since 2014 have affected in meaningful ways post-disaster government assistance to victims in 2017 and beyond.

By one measure of activity called the ACE (**Accumulated Cyclone Energy**) index, which adds each tropical storm or hurricane's wind speed through its life cycle, the 2017 season is among the top 10 in cumulated full-cycle wind speed.[4] Through September 30, after the demise of former Hurricane Maria, 2017 was already the ninth most active Atlantic hurricane season of record, according to statistics compiled by Dr. Phil Klotzbach, a Colorado State University tropical meteorologist. Long-lived, intense hurricanes have a high ACE index, while short-lived, weak tropical storms have a low value. The ACE of a season is the sum of the ACE for each storm, and it takes into account the number, strength, and duration of all the tropical storms and hurricanes in the season.[5] According to a National Hurricane Center report, only 1933 and 2004 had a faster ACE pace through the end of September than 2017.[6]

IMPACT AND DECLARATIONS: HURRICANE HARVEY

Texas is the second largest U.S. state by land area, and it has an extraordinary 254 counties, some of which have histories dating back to Spanish rule. Texas is the second most populous state in the nation, with some 28.7 million residents. It has three cities that exceed 1 million in population: Houston with 2.2 million, San Antonio with 1.4 million, and Dallas with 1.3 million.[7]

Hurricane Harvey wreaked havoc on the Texas coast, dumping more than 50 inches of rain in parts of the Houston area, flooding thousands of homes and killing more than 80 people. Figure 9-1 shows Texas counties included in President Trump's major disaster declaration (DR 4332) as of October 17, 2017. It also shows the categories of assistance available to each county.[8] Figure 9-2 shows accumulated five-day point rainfall totals over eastern Texas, a small portion of southwestern Louisiana, and for many Gulf Coast counties.

Louisiana is home to some 4.5 million people. It has 64 parishes, which are comparable to counties in most other states. The *New York Post* reported that "Tropical Storm Harvey made an unwelcome return to a devastated region early Wednesday—this time hitting Louisiana, a state that was ravaged by 2005's Hurricane Katrina. The relentless storm made landfall just west of the town of Cameron, according to the National Hurricane Center, with 'flooding rains' drenching parts of southeastern Texas and neighboring southwestern Louisiana. Harvey is expected to produce as much as 10 more inches of rain over an area about 80 miles east of the paralyzed city of Houston as well as western Louisiana. Maximum sustained winds of about 45 mph also are in store."[9]

Louisiana suffered damage from Hurricane Harvey, and President Trump first granted the state an emergency declaration and later a major disaster declaration. Figure 9-3 shows the counties included in the declaration and, as in the Texas case, the types of disaster aid made available to each county. Under declaration DR-4345, according to Figure 9-3, nine parishes were eligible to receive FEMA's Public Assistance aid as well as FEMA's Individual Assistance program assistance. With the exception of St. Charles Parish near New Orleans, most of these counties were located in the southwestern portion of the state. Some 11 parishes along the Gulf and further inland received FEMA Public Assistance only.

FIGURE 9-1 ■ Texas Counties Included in Presidential Declaration of Major Disaster DR-4332 for Hurricane Harvey Damage and Its Effects with Types of Assistance Made Available

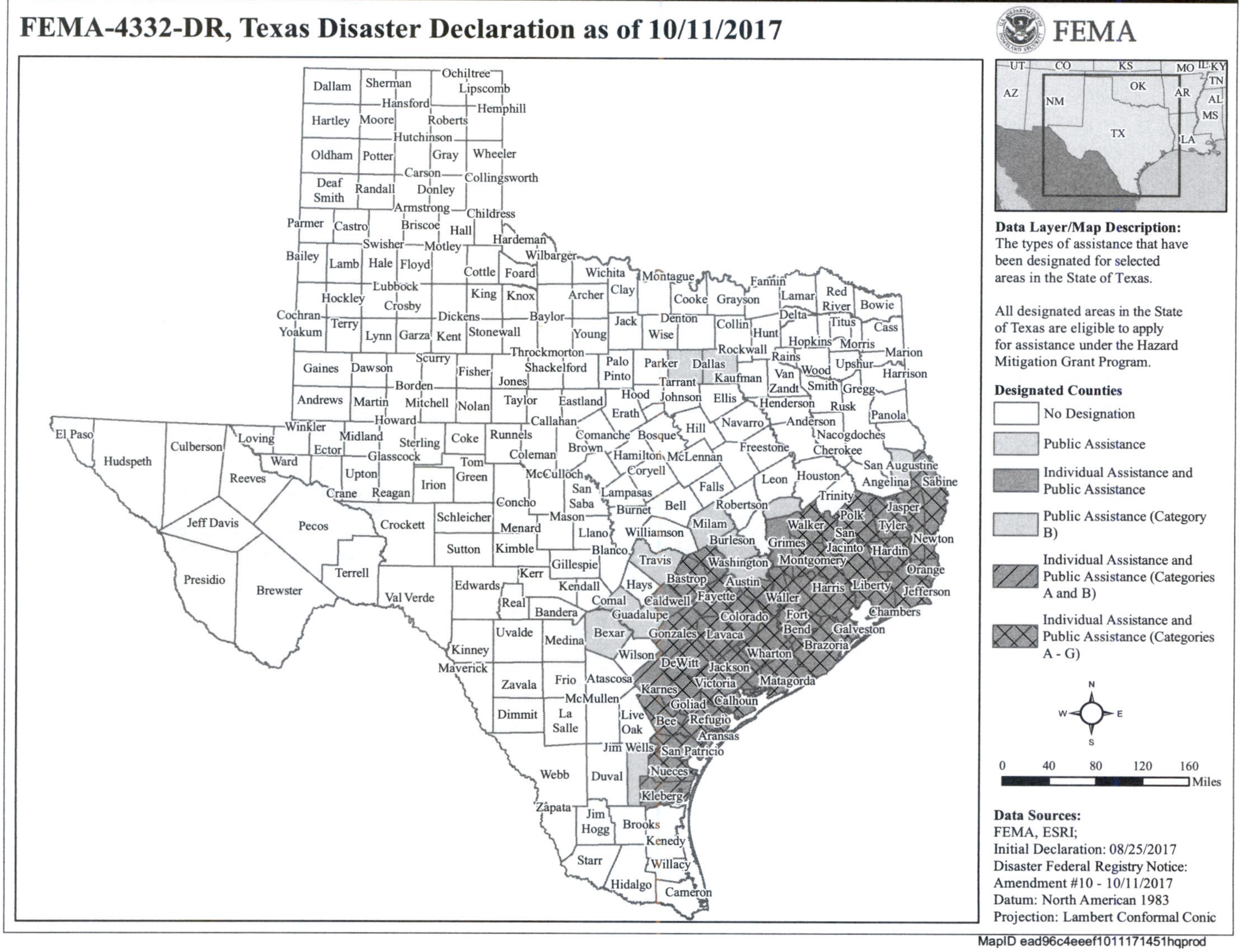

FEMA-4332-DR, Texas Disaster Declaration as of 10/11/2017

Data Layer/Map Description: The types of assistance that have been designated for selected areas in the State of Texas.

All designated areas in the State of Texas are eligible to apply for assistance under the Hazard Mitigation Grant Program.

Designated Counties

- No Designation
- Public Assistance
- Individual Assistance and Public Assistance
- Public Assistance (Category B)
- Individual Assistance and Public Assistance (Categories A and B)
- Individual Assistance and Public Assistance (Categories A - G)

Data Sources:
FEMA, ESRI;
Initial Declaration: 08/25/2017
Disaster Federal Registry Notice:
Amendment #10 - 10/11/2017
Datum: North American 1983
Projection: Lambert Conformal Conic

MapID ead96c4eeef101117145thqprod

Source: FEMA, "Texas Hurricane Harvey (DR-4332)," Incident Period: August 23, 2017 – September 15, 2017 with Major Disaster Declaration declared on August 25, 2017, https://www.fema.gov/disaster/4332 (accessed June 22, 2018).

FIGURE 9-2 ■ Five-day Point Rainfall Totals in Inches for Hurricane Harvey along East Texas Gulf Coast

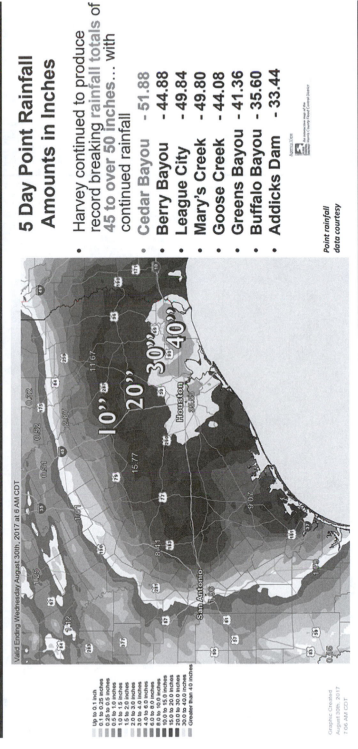

5 Day Point Rainfall Amounts in Inches

- Harvey continued to produce record breaking rainfall totals of 45 to over 50 inches... with continued rainfall

- Cedar Bayou - 51.88
- Berry Bayou - 44.88
- League City - 49.84
- Mary's Creek - 49.80
- Goose Creek - 44.08
- Greens Bayou - 41.36
- Buffalo Bayou - 35.60
- Addicks Dam - 33.44

Point rainfall data courtesy

Source: National Weather Service, courtesy of the West Gulf River Forecast Center, https://www.weather.gov/hgx/hurricaneharvey (accessed September 12, 2018).

FIGURE 9-3 ■ Louisiana Counties Included in Presidential Declaration of Major Disaster DR-4345 for Hurricane Harvey Damage and Its Effects with Types of Assistance Made Available

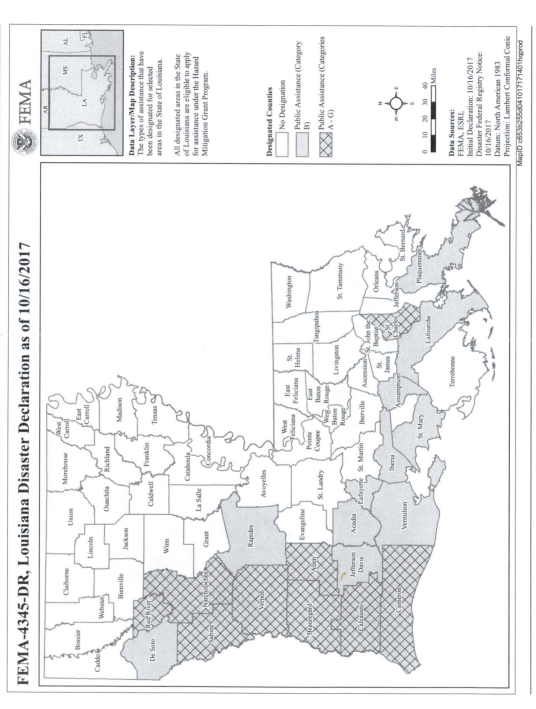

FEMA-4345-DR, Louisiana Disaster Declaration as of 10/16/2017

Data Layer/Map Description:
The types of assistance that have been designated for selected areas in the State of Louisiana.

All designated areas in the State of Louisiana are eligible to apply for assistance under the Hazard Mitigation Grant Program.

Designated Counties
- No Designation
- Public Assistance (Category B)
- Public Assistance (Categories A - G)

Data Sources:
FEMA, ESRI;
Initial Declaration: 10/16/2017
Disaster Federal Registry Notice: 10/16/2017
Datum: North American 1983
Projection: Lambert Conformal Conic

MapID c653b255d041071717401hqprod

Source: FEMA, "Louisiana Tropical Storm Harvey (DR-4345)," Incident Period: August 28, 2017 - September 10, 2017 with Major Disaster Declaration declared on October 16, 2017, https://www.fema.gov/disaster/4345 (accessed June 22, 2018).

IMPACT AND DECLARATIONS: HURRICANE IRMA

As of July 1, 2017, the U.S. Census Bureau estimated Florida's entire state population at just under 21 million. Florida has over 9.4 million housing units, of which 64.8 percent are owner occupied.[10] The state has a 1,350-mile-long coastline, second only to Alaska's in total length.[11] Florida's coastal areas are where most of its population resides. Of Florida's 67 counties, 5 have populations that exceed 1 million: Miami-Dade has 2,751,796; Broward 1,935,878; Palm Beach 1,471,150; Hillsborough 1,408,566; and Orange County 1,348,975.[12]

Hurricane Irma began its journey as a tropical storm on August 30, 2017, in the Atlantic just west of the Cape Verde Islands. Over the next 10 days, it grew into a Category 5 hurricane with a maximum sustained wind of 185 mph. The storm moved through parts of the Caribbean Islands, including Puerto Rico and between Cuba and Florida. Eventually the hurricane turned northwest and impacted the Florida Keys and areas near Naples, Florida; then it generally followed Interstate 75 north through the entire Florida peninsula. Hurricane Irma then moved into Georgia, Alabama, and Tennessee, prompting the first ever Tropical Storm warnings for Atlanta, Georgia. Both Georgia and Alabama applied for, and won, presidential declarations of major disaster.

Hurricane Irma hit Florida as a Category 4 storm the morning of September 10, 2017, ripping off roofs, flooding coastal cities, and knocking out power to more than 6.8 million people. By September 11, Irma weakened significantly to a tropical storm as it powered north. At 11 p.m. later that day, it weakened further to a tropical depression, and by September 13, it had dissipated over western Tennessee.[13] The storm and its aftermath killed at least 38 in the Caribbean, 34 in Florida, 3 in Georgia, 4 in South Carolina, and 1 in North Carolina. Irma is the fifth-costliest hurricane to hit the mainland United States, causing an estimated $50 billion in damage, according to the National Hurricane Center.[14]

Florida's landfalling Hurricane Irma impacted all the counties of the state, but most of the damage that occurred in the state's panhandle counties was light, relative to counties to the east. Irma's path was south to north, first blasting the Florida Keys, and then tracking northward almost through the center of the peninsular state. Figure 9-4 displays Florida counties impacted by Hurricane Irma and includes the types of federal assistance they were eligible to receive.[15]

Before moving on to consider the impact and declarations for Hurricane Maria and the Virgin Islands, remember that Irma had caused considerable damage in Puerto Rico over September 6, 2017, and in the Virgin Islands just before that. It reportedly left 1 million in that commonwealth without power as Irma brushed the northern coast of Puerto Rico.[16]

Florida has experienced many hurricanes in the past, and with the exception of various newcomers, many Floridians know how to heed hurricane warnings, how to prepare, how to effect evacuation or sheltering, and how to demobilize. Florida, like Texas, has a sophisticated state emergency management agency, and many of its localities employ capable emergency managers and responders. One of the success stories of the Irma experience in Florida was an "after-action-report" by the state health department chronicling how senior citizen, assisted living, health care, and special needs facilities carried out their emergency plans.[17]

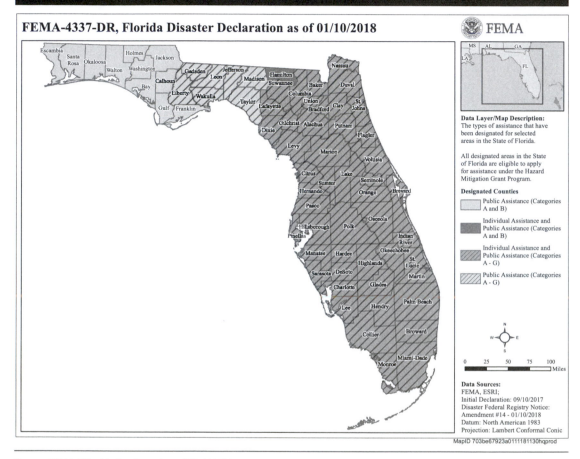

FIGURE 9-4 ■ Florida Counties Included in Presidential Declaration of Major Disaster DR-4337 for Hurricane Irma Damage and Its Effects with Types of Assistance Made Available

Source: FEMA, "Florida Hurricane Irma (DR-4337)," Incident Period: September 04, 2017–October 18, 2017 with Major Disaster Declaration declared on September 10, 2017, https://www.fema.gov/disaster/4337 (accessed June 22, 2018).

IMPACT AND DECLARATIONS: HURRICANE MARIA

Before Hurricanes Irma and Maria struck, Puerto Rico had an estimated July 1, 2017, population of 3.34 million, representing a 10.4 percent population loss since the 2010 U.S. Census.[18] The U.S. Census Bureau does not provide a 2017 housing total for Puerto Rico, but it does indicate that between 2012 and 2016, there were 1.24 million households and that owner-occupied housing was 68.6 percent of all housing.[19]

Recall that Hurricane Harvey struck the eastern coastal areas of Texas, most particularly areas in the Houston metroplex. Hurricane Irma ran a path of destruction up the entire peninsula of Florida but did less damage in its panhandle counties. In contrast,

FIGURE 9-5 ■ Puerto Rico Counties Included in Presidential Declaration of Major Disaster DR-4339 for Hurricane Maria Damage and Its Effects with Types of Assistance Made Available

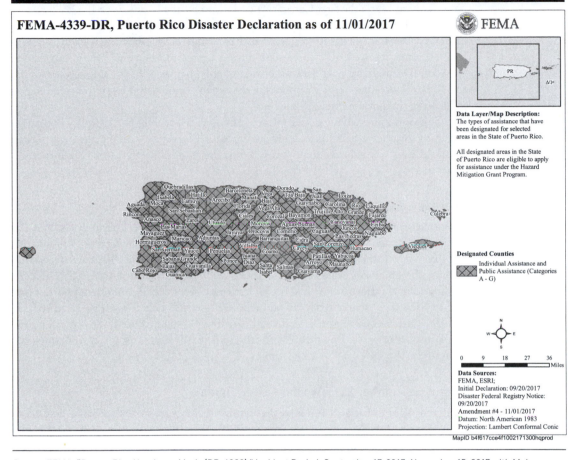

Source: FEMA, "Puerto Rico Hurricane Maria (DR-4339)," Incident Period: September 17, 2017–November 15, 2017 with Major Disaster Declaration declared on September 20, 2017, https://www.fema.gov/disaster/4339 (accessed June 22, 2018).

Hurricane Maria devastated every single county of Puerto Rico. Figure 9-5 confirms the impact of Hurricane Maria in terms of county-level political geography.[20]

The storm made landfall on September 20, wreaking havoc on the island and causing a level of widespread destruction and disorganization almost unparalleled in America's hurricane history. Two weeks after the storm abated, most of the island's residents still lacked access to electricity and clean water.[21]

From a meteorological standpoint, Maria was a worst-case scenario for the territory. The center of a huge, near Category 5 hurricane made a direct hit on Puerto Rico, lashing the island with wind and rain for more than 30 hours. "It was as if a 50- to 60-mile-wide tornado raged across Puerto Rico, like a buzz saw," Jeff Weber, a meteorologist at the National Center for Atmospheric Research, remarked. Here is a one-week timeline selectively quoted from *The Atlantic*:

Wednesday, September 20—Landfall

Hurricane Maria made landfall just south of Yabucoa Harbor in Puerto Rico at 6:15 a.m. The National Weather Service observed maximum sustained winds of 155 miles per hour, making Maria the first Category 4 cyclone to hit the island since 1932. The storm almost reached Category 5, defined as any tropical storm with winds 157 miles per hour or higher. Parts of Puerto Rico saw 30 inches of rain in one day, equal to the amount that Houston received over three days during Hurricane Harvey. The winds caused "tornado-like" damage over a swath of the island. They were strong enough to destroy the National Weather Service's observing sensors in the territory, forcing meteorologists to measure the storm entirely by satellite.[22]

The storm knocked out power to the entire island. Much of the island's population, including swaths of San Juan, could not access clean water without electrical power. Local officials warned that some towns would see 80 to 90 percent of their structures destroyed.[23]

Thursday, September 21—One day after landfall

In the morning, rain from the storm continued to deluge Puerto Rico, and the National Weather Service warned of "catastrophic" flooding in the territory's mountainous interior. Informal estimates put the storm's death toll on the island at 10. Ricardo Ramos, the chief executive of Puerto Rico's public power utility, told CNN that its entire electrical infrastructure had been "destroyed." President Trump told reporters that Puerto Rico was "obliterated." He said rebuilding would begin "with great gusto." He added, "Their electrical grid is destroyed." Trump also commented, "It wasn't in good shape to start off with. But their electrical grid is totally destroyed. And so many other things."[24]

Friday, September 22—Two days after landfall

Puerto Rican officials cautioned that restoring power to the island could take six to eight months. Luis Muñoz Marín International Airport in San Juan, its main airfield, reopened to military traffic, according to the U.S. Army Corps of Engineers. President Trump issued an emergency declaration for Puerto Rico. He called local officials on the island and pledged help.[25]

Friday, September 22—Two days after landfall

Puerto Rican officials advised that restoring power to the island could take six to eight months.[26]

Saturday, September 23—Three days after landfall

The main port in San Juan reopened. "1.6 million gallons of water, 23,000 cots, [and] dozens of generators" arrived on 11 ships. In news reports, it became clear that the island's entire communications infrastructure had been knocked out. Eighty-five percent of the island's 1,600 cell towers did not work, and neither did the vast majority of Internet cables and telephone lines. The Puerto Rican government forewarned that Guajataca

Dam, in the territory's northwest, could fail at any moment owing to heavy precipitation and the force of the storm. Authorities began evacuating the 70,000 people who live nearby. The 90-year-old dam had not been inspected since 2013.[27] [The U.S. Army Corps of Engineers inspected the dam and announced on September 26 that it needed reinforcement but was not expected to fail.]

Sunday, September 24—Four days after landfall

Vice President Mike Pence talked on the phone with Jenniffer González-Colón, Puerto Rico's non-voting representative in the House of Representatives. It is the only reported communication between a Puerto Rican leader and the president or vice president during the weekend.[28]

Monday, September 25—Five days after landfall

The first Trump administration officials visited Puerto Rico to survey the damage. They included Brock Long, the administrator of FEMA, and Tom Bossert, a Homeland Security adviser. Both returned to Washington that night. "We need to prevent a humanitarian crisis occurring in America. Puerto Rico is part of the United States. We need to take swift action," Puerto Rican governor Ricardo Rosselló told CNN.[29]

The Pentagon issued its first written update entirely about the effort in Puerto Rico. It reported that 2,600 Department of Defense employees were in the territory or the U.S. Virgin Islands. Eight members of the House of Representatives wrote to President Trump, asking him to waive the Jones Act for ports in Puerto Rico for one year. The Jones Act is a 1920 law that requires ships carrying goods between U.S. ports to fly the American flag, which means they must abide by U.S. laws. It also requires these ships to be built in the United States and owned and operated by American citizens. The government temporarily waived the Jones Act with little fanfare for ports along the Gulf Coast after Hurricanes Harvey and Irma struck.[30] [A few days later, President Trump waived the Jones Act for 10 days, allowing ships not flying the U.S. flag to access the island's ports.]

Tuesday, September 26—Six days after landfall

Forty-four percent of Puerto Rico's population, or 1.53 million people, lacked access to drinking water, the Pentagon declared. Power remained out across most of the island. Fifteen percent of the island's 69 hospitals, about 10, were open. Eight airports and eight seaports were re-opened across Puerto Rico, albeit some were only operating during daylight hours.[31]

President Trump held his first coordinating meeting in the Situation Room about the response in Puerto Rico. He talked to Governor Rosselló again and to Congresswoman González-Colón for the first time.[32]

The U.S. Navy announced the deployment of the **USNS *Comfort***, a hospital ship based in Norfolk, Virginia, to Puerto Rico. FEMA officials explained that the *Comfort* must take on emergency staff, and that it might take another week before the ship could leave port. The Pentagon also announced it would be tasking nine additional cargo aircraft with Puerto Rican relief and seven additional cargo planes with disaster response in the U.S. Virgin Islands.[33]

Wednesday, September 27—Seven days after landfall

The Puerto Rican government announced that 16 people had lost their lives in the storm. It did not update the official death toll for another six days. The Port of Mayagüez reopened for daylight operations, according to the Pentagon.[34]

Over the days thereafter, other problems arose. CNN revealed that more than 10,000 shipping containers full of food and supplies lay stranded in the Port of San Juan. They could not be shipped to the island's interior due to a lack of fuel, labor, and working roads. Governor Rosselló said that only about 20 percent of Puerto Rico's truckers have been able to work.[35]

Hector Pesquera, Puerto Rico's secretary of public safety, admitted to the Center for Investigative Journalism that death tolls were likely much higher than official estimates. He remarked, "I believe there are more dead, but I don't have reports telling me, [for example], eight died in Mayagüez because they lacked oxygen, that four died in San Pablo because they did not receive dialysis."[36]

The Pentagon revised downward its estimate of reopened gas stations, saying "more than 759" of 1,120 were selling gas again. It did not provide a reason for the change. It also announced that about 65 percent of grocery and big-box stores were open. The Federal Communications Commission disclosed that about 12 percent of cell towers on the island were operational again. Puerto Rican officials estimated that only about 40 percent of residents had any kind of Internet or cell service.[37] (Telephone or Internet service is necessary in filing for FEMA individual assistance programs via tele-registration or through online application. Recall that FEMA no longer accepts written applications for such assistance by mail.)

Thirteen days after landfall, President Trump visited Puerto Rico for the first time since Maria struck the island. During the visit, he tossed relief supplies, including paper towels and toilet paper, into a crowd of onlookers.[38] In fairness to the president, given the scale of damage in Puerto Rico and the high tempo of ongoing relief operations, visiting the island much earlier may have disrupted activities there.

The Virgin Islands and Maria

The Virgin Islands were also struck by Hurricane Maria on September 19, 2017, and its Island of St. Croix sustained major damage.[39] As another U.S. Trust Territory, the Virgin Islands, like the Commonwealth of Puerto Rico, was entitled to federal disaster assistance much like any disaster-stricken American state. Figure 9-6 is a map illustration of the Virgin Islands (VI). VI has only three county equivalents, and they are each an island: St. Croix, St. John, and St. Thomas. The Virgin Islands received a major disaster declaration that extended the full range of FEMA assistance to the island's governments as well as to disaster victims there.

Although there were no reports of casualties, the storm unleashed powerful winds and heavy rainfall, shearing off roofs, downing trees, and decimating the communications and power grid across the island, according to the U.S. Virgin Islands Emergency Operations Center. Two other main islands, St. John and St. Thomas, were pummeled by Hurricane Irma just 14 days earlier. The back-to-back storms delivered a one–two punch in the Caribbean territory, known for its white sand beaches.[40]

President Donald Trump declared a major disaster in the U.S. Virgin Islands one day after Maria hit. The move freed up federal funding for people on the island of St. Croix. FEMA began coordinating with the U.S. Virgin Islands to medically evacuate general

FIGURE 9-6 ■ Virgin Islands County Equivalents Included in Presidential Declaration of Major Disaster DR-4340 for Hurricane Maria Damage and Its Effects with Types of Assistance Made Available

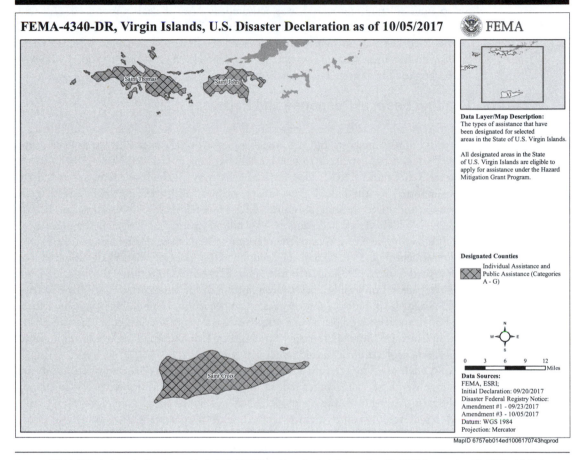

Source: FEMA, "Virgin Islands Hurricane Maria (DR-4340)," Incident Period: September 16, 2017–September 22, 2017 with Major Disaster Declaration declared on September 20, 2017, https://www.fema.gov/disaster/4340 (accessed June 22, 2018).

and dialysis patients. FEMA, along with its federal partners, provided millions of meals and millions of liters of water to the U.S. Virgin Islands and Puerto Rico. Additional meals and water continued to arrive in both territories "daily." The U.S. Virgin Islands established 17 sites for supplies distribution, according to FEMA.[41]

Over several weeks, the U.S. Virgin Islands' government labored to prioritize fuel distribution throughout the islands and to install generators for power restoration. The Henry E. Rohlsen Airport in St. Croix remained open to military aircraft, while Cyril E. King Airport in St. Thomas opened for limited commercial aircraft. FEMA said the U.S. Virgin Islands Water and Power Authority drinking water system was back online as of Thursday night, September 27, as well as the Concordia potable water pump station in St. Croix.[42] Each island of VI recovered at a different rate, but the Virgin Islands as a whole recovered much more rapidly than did Puerto Rico.

IMMEDIATE AND SHORT-TERM RESPONSE

For Harvey, Irma, and Maria, the Emergency Management Assistance Compact, a system of state-to-state mutual aid, was activated. EMAC officials announced, "All told, Massachusetts and other states sent more than 4,700 responders on 120 missions to Puerto Rico last year to help with disaster relief efforts. That came on top of nearly 5,300 who had been sent to Texas after Hurricane Harvey, and nearly 4,000 who were dispatched to Florida after Hurricane Irma."[43]

Funding Federal Response and Recovery

On September 8, 2017, the Congressional Research Service (CRS), aware of Hurricane Harvey's burgeoning costs and the probable impending damage Hurricane Irma would inflict, advised policymakers to pay special attention to the remaining balance of the Disaster Relief Fund (DRF). That fund pays for most of the immediate response activities supported by the federal government, primarily through emergency work grant assistance and direct federal assistance. CRS reported that "before Hurricane Harvey made landfall, the DRF had roughly $3.5 billion in total unobligated resources available." According to FEMA, as of the morning of September 5, eight days after Harvey began tormenting east Texas and the Louisiana Gulf, the DRF had $1.01 billion in total unobligated resources.[44] In other words, about $2.5 billion in funding from the DRF had been obligated in only eight days. Only a portion of this amount was spent by FEMA.

CRS added, "in order to conserve resources needed for response to Hurricane Harvey and Hurricane Irma, and other time-sensitive disaster assistance, since August 28, FEMA has implemented 'immediate needs funding restrictions,' which delays funding for all longer-term projects until additional resources are available."[45]

CRS advised, "Though the funding status of the DRF is perhaps most critical during the response phase, many other federal programs and accounts have provided support in the past. After Hurricane Sandy, P.L. 113-2 provided supplemental funding to over 66 different accounts and programs, including the Department of Housing and Urban Development (HUD)'s Community Development Block Grant (CDBG) program, the Department of Transportation's Emergency Relief Programs, and the civil works program of USACE (U.S. Army Corps of Engineers)."[46] Aware of the ongoing drawdown, on September 1, the Trump administration requested $7.85 billion in supplemental funding for FY 2018. To close out FY 2017 (which would end September 30, 2017), the administration requested $7.4 billion for the DRF and $450 million for the Small Business Administration (SBA) disaster loan program. This signaled support for faster-than-usual apportionment of DRF funds under a possible FY 2018 continuing resolution.[47]

This reaffirms that the DRF is often tapped by many federal agencies besides FEMA and other DHS organizations. Thus, DRF pays the bulk of FEMA's program costs including FEMA's mission assignment payments to other federal agencies, but it has been used by Congress and the president to pay other federal agencies for other purposes as well.

On September 6, 2017, the House passed the relief package requested by the Trump administration as an amendment to H.R. 601. On September 7, the Senate passed an amended version, which included the House-passed funding as well as an additional $7.4 billion for disaster relief through HUD's Community Development Fund, a short-term

FIGURE 9-7 ■ Obligations in the First 90 Days Post Landfall and as of December 31, 2017, for the Top Eight Hurricane Events by Contract Obligations (in Calendar Year 2017 Constant Dollars)

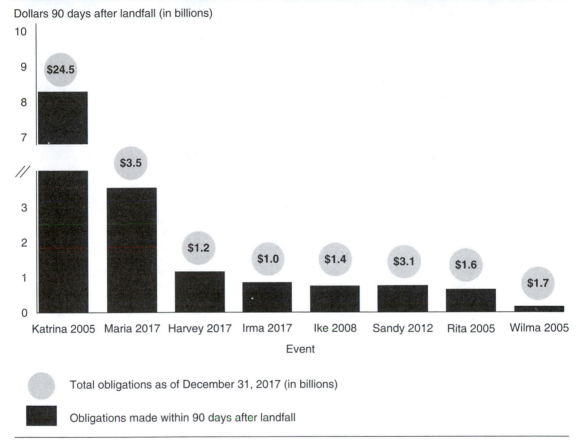

Dollars 90 days after landfall (in billions)

Total obligations as of December 31, 2017 (in billions)

Obligations made within 90 days after landfall

Source: U.S. Government Accountability Office, "2017 Disaster Contracting: Observations on Federal Contracting for Response and Recovery Efforts," February 2018, https://www.gao.gov/assets/700/690425.pdf (accessed July 9, 2018).

increase to the national debt limit, and a short-term continuing resolution that would fund government operations through December 8, 2017. The House passed the Senate-amended version of the bill on September 8, 2017.[48] Ironically, the funding emergency created by the 2017 hurricanes temporarily ended a heated congressional dispute about raising the national debt ceiling.

Figure 9-7 shows federal obligations in the first 90 days after hurricane landfall and as of December 31, 2017, covering the top eight hurricanes ranked by contract obligations. Amounts are shown in constant calendar year 2017 dollars. What is remarkable is that Hurricane Maria's 90-day post-landfall spending total stands at $3.5 billion, which is about half a billion less than Hurricane Katrina's 2005 first 90-day total. Hurricane Harvey's $1.2 billion and Hurricane Irma's $1 billion totals for the first 90-days after

FIGURE 9-8 ■ FEMA Allocations, Obligations, and Expenditures for Hurricanes Harvey, Irma, Maria, and California Wildfires 2017 (Cumulative) as of April 30, 2018

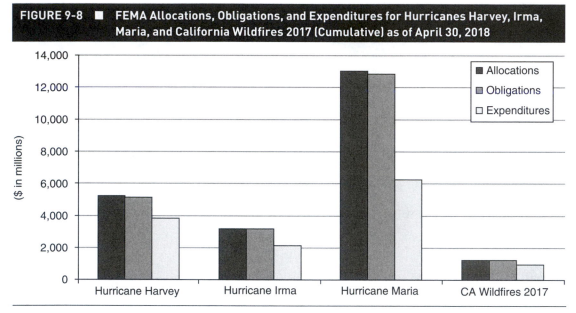

Source: FEMA, "Disaster Relief Fund: Monthly Report as of April 30, 2018," Fiscal Year 2018 Report to Congress," May 5, 2018, https://www.fema.gov/media-library-data/1526358994453-ab5a4d20c8e7136da5c6ed583286ff6a/May2018DisasterReliefFundReport.pdf (accessed June 7, 2018).

their respective landfalls places them sixth and seventh, respectively, as the most federally expensive U.S. hurricanes of this century for this category. Remember, federal spending on Maria, Harvey, and Irma could continue for 10 years or more. All three may eventually move beyond total federal spending for Ike, Sandy, Rita, and Wilma, respectively.

Figure 9-8 is a bar chart with vertical columns showing FEMA spending over the early period of Hurricanes Harvey, Irma, and Maria in 2017. Most of this federal spending was to cover the costs of disaster response and to underwrite federal assistance under FEMA's Individual and Households program and its Housing Program. Be aware that in Figure 9-8 a share of FEMA spending after Irma struck includes continued payments to Hurricane Harvey victims. Similarly, a sizable share of post-Maria FEMA spending is dedicated to meeting Harvey and Irma needs.

What is curious in Table 9-1 are the drops in spending. For example, the falloff in payments in the week Hurricane Irma struck Florida may reflect a FEMA and contractor retooling of some sort to accommodate the anticipated deluge of claims for assistance expected from Irma victims. It seems to have taken nearly three weeks for the same falloff to occur after Maria struck Puerto Rico. Some of the Maria spending delay may be attributable to cell tower and electric power loss across Puerto Rico in the aftermath of the hurricane that delayed applications for aid from the people there. The rebound in FEMA spending after all three disasters, plus payouts for other disasters declared in 2017 during the chart's three-month interval, is, by late September, astoundingly large.

RECOVERY

As of April 30, 2018, Hurricane Maria, at over $13.2 billion in allocations by FEMA, exceeded Hurricane Harvey's $5.2 billion and Hurricane Irma's $3.2 billion.[49] This is shown in Figure 9-8's left side vertical bars for each of the events drawing FEMA allocations as of April 30, 2018. Remember, obligations come out of allocations, and in turn, expenditures (outlays) come out of obligations. So, do not add the vertical bars of each hurricane and the wildfires.

Figure 9-8 includes FEMA's 2017 California wildfire spending, which was $1.4 billion. This sum includes Fire Management Assistance Grant spending. Figure 9-8 spending sums are by no means the final totals. Much of the California wildfire spending covered damage to homes, although FEMA housing aid covers emergency minimal repairs; if losses are more severe, FEMA may cover a portion of what homeowner's insurance policies do not cover. FEMA housing aid is also means-tested such that many homeowners whose annual incomes exceed FEMA's maximum level are denied FEMA housing aid and directed to the SBA disaster loan program.

The final amounts spent on these four disasters in the years ahead will most likely drive up spending totals shown here. Also, regarding the trio of hurricanes, these figures do not include FEMA payouts to cover claims filed by impacted National Flood Insurance policyholders.

Table 9-1 provides FEMA program spending for Hurricanes Sandy, Harvey, Irma, and Maria (Actual Obligations by Program) for FY 2017 with projections for FY 2018. Recall that Superstorm Sandy struck in the fall of 2012. Table 9-1 shows that FEMA spending on that disaster was still substantial some five years later. Cumulated FEMA spending on Sandy for Public Assistance (government-to-government spending that chiefly pays to repair, rebuild, or replace damaged infrastructure) was about $15.6 billion through FY 2017 and expected to rise to about $16.65 million by the end of FY 2018 (September 30, 2018). FEMA's Individual Assistance (IA) funding for Sandy is $1.6 billion, and that figure is fixed since the application period for funding was closed only a year or so after that disaster.[50]

What makes Table 9-1 extraordinary is that FEMA Individual Assistance funding was then the highest FY 2017 program spending category for the trio of 2017 hurricanes. Harvey shows cumulated obligations for IA in 2017 at $1.5 billion and actual first quarter FY 2018 IA spending at $1.15 billion. Irma has cumulated obligations for FY 2018 IA at $887 million and actual first quarter FY 2018 IA at $409 million. Maria's Individual Assistance spending starts low in FY 2017 and ramps up dramatically in FY 2018. Recall that Maria was the last of the three hurricanes and that people there had tremendous difficulty making application for FEMA IA, in part, due to the lack of electric power and cell tower availability. Maria IA spending begins at $371 million for the final month of FY 2017 and escalates to $1.795 billion by the end of the first quarter of FY 2018 (September 30, 2017–December 31, 2017).

Table 9-1's far right column shows estimated totals through FY 2018 (which ends September 30, 2018). Hurricane Sandy shows a Public Assistance (PA) total of about $16.65 billion and an Individual Assistance (IA) total of about $1.62 billion. Remember, these sums are cumulated from October 2012 through September 30, 2018.

TABLE 9-1 ◼ **Hurricanes Sandy, Harvey, Irma, and Maria (Actual Obligations by Program) for FY 2017 with Projections for FY 2018**

	Cumulative Obligations Thru FY 2017 [1]	Actual Obligations 1st Qtr	Actual Obligations 2nd Qtr	Actual Obligations/ Projections 3rd Qtr	Projections 4th Qtr	FY 2018 Totals	Totals Thru FY 2018
Sandy							
Public Assistance	$ 15,592	$ 330	$ 95	$ 305	$ 330	$ 1,060	$ 16,652
Individual Assistance	1,620	-	-	-	-	-	1,620
Mitigation	1,034	39	41	21	115	216	1,250
Operations	321	-	-	-	-	-	321
Administrative	1,456	16	10	17	11	54	1,510
Total [2]	$ 20,023	$ 385	$ 146	$ 343	$ 456	$ 1,330	$ 21,353
Harvey							
Public Assistance	$ 324	$ 180	$ 134	$ 308	$ 323	$ 945	$ 1,269
Individual Assistance	1,502	1,150	152	78	87	1,467	2,969
Mitigation	-	-	17	26	-	43	43
Operations	151	4	33	76	-	113	264
Administrative	894	446	137	183	146	912	1,806
Total [2]	$ 2,871	$ 1,780	$ 473	$ 671	$ 556	$ 3,480	$ 6,351

Irma

Public Assistance	$ 7	$ 19	$ 43	$ 347	$ 623	$ 1,032	$ 1,039
Individual Assistance	887	409	48	21	6	484	1,371
Mitigation	-	3	-	3	62	68	68
Operations	384	122	-	(1)	(2)	119	503
Administrative	574	489	127	68	84	768	1,342
Total [2]	$ 1,852	$ 1,042	$ 218	$ 438	$ 773	$ 2,471	$ 4,323

Maria

Public Assistance	$ 28	$ 582	$ 1,297	$ 2,312	$ 1,581	$ 5,772	$ 5,800
Individual Assistance	371	1,795	248	136	416	2,595	2,966
Mitigation	-	-	17	10	353	380	380
Operations	768	3,521	922	(32)	54	4,465	5,233
Administrative	355	1,368	441	597	279	2,685	3,040
Total [2]	$ 1,522	$ 7,266	$ 2,925	$ 3,023	$ 2,683	$ 15,897	$ 17,419

Source: FEMA, "Disaster Relief Fund: Monthly Report as of April 30, 2018," Fiscal Year 2018 Report to Congress," May 5, 2018, https://www.fema.gov/media-library-data/1526358994453-ab5a4d20c8e7136da5c6ed583286ff6a/May2018DisasterReliefFundReport.pdf (accessed June 7, 2018).

[1] Adjusted for recoveries that occur in FY 2018 against prior-year obligations.

[2] The totals also include obligations for both major declarations and emergencies.

Interestingly, Table 9-1 reveals, for Harvey and Irma FEMA spending on all declarations, that IA[51] totals exceed PA totals. Harvey shows an expected end-of-FY 2018 (September 30, 2018) total of $1.27 billion for infrastructure (PA) and $2.969 billion for individual assistance. Similarly, Irma end-of-FY 2018 FEMA infrastructure (PA) spending is about $1.04 billion and IA (for Individuals and Household Aid, which includes Housing and Other Needs assistance) is expected to exceed $1.37 billion.

Hurricane Maria findings track with Superstorm Sandy's. By this, infrastructure assistance FEMA spending far outpaces assistance to individual and household (IA) categories. Notice that Maria's FEMA infrastructure spending is expected to reach $5.8 billion and that Maria's FEMA individual assistance spending is projected to hit $2.97 billion. The deadline for people to apply for FEMA Individual Assistance was June 18, 2018, in Puerto Rico and was January 8, 2018, for Virgin Islanders.

As shown in Table 9-1, for Harvey, Irma, and Maria, individual assistance funding begins to taper off after the first year, particularly once the period for accepting victim assistance application is ended. However, infrastructure spending tends to start slowly and escalate significantly in years 2, 3, 4, and perhaps 5, until construction projects are completed and fully paid for. Obviously, infrastructure projects take time to plan, design, bid contracts on, win permits for, build, test, license or certify, audit, and eventually close the books on. Therefore, it may be possible that ultimately Harvey and Irma infrastructure spending grows beyond their respective individual assistance spending.

Table 9-1 is interesting in a few other respects. That table shows FEMA disaster mitigation funding paid out to states and territories for declarations received for these hurricanes. There appears to be a slow start for mitigation funding for Maria-impacted territories. Also, the administrative costs FEMA must pay are presented, and these are substantial. Finally, consider the cumulated expected totals in FEMA spending (all programs and categories) for each hurricane expected by September 30, 2018: Superstorm Sandy is $21.35 billion; Hurricane Harvey is $6.35 billion; Irma is $4.32 billion; and Maria is $17.42 billion. Be warned that figures for the 2017 hurricanes can be expected to rise in the months and years after September 30, 2018, particularly for infrastructure spending (PA).

National Flood Insurance Program (NFIP)

According to CRS, flood insurance claims made through the NFIP will be an important source of financial assistance to policyholders in the regions impacted by Harvey and Irma. CRS declared, "Given the potential severity of the hurricanes, the NFIP may need to borrow from the U.S. Treasury to pay future claims. As of August 27, 2017, FEMA reported that the NFIP had $1.799 billion in available funds to pay claims, which did not include additional resources that a recent reinsurance contract may provide. The NFIP currently owes $24.6 billion in debt to the U.S. Treasury, leaving $5.825 billion out of the total authorized $30.425 billion in borrowing authority. It is possible that this borrowing limit could be reached, in which case Congress may consider increasing it, as was done most recently following Hurricane Sandy (P.L. 113-1)."[52] In the Texas counties designated under the major disaster declaration, the NFIP has implemented temporary changes to the claims process to make it possible for policyholders to receive funds more quickly. Key provisions of the NFIP were extended from September 30, 2017, through December 8, 2017, when President Trump signed into law H.R. 601 as amended on September 8, 2017.[53]

PROBLEMS

According to *The Economist*, "America is much better prepared for hurricanes today than it was when Katrina struck in 2005. But the process for responding to such crises remains wasteful and inefficient. When a hurricane strikes, the Federal Emergency Management Agency (FEMA) uses its Disaster Relief Fund to pay for food, shelter and repairs to infrastructure. In the past eight months, FEMA has doled out over $17 billion from the fund [see Figure 9-9]. This pot of money, which pays for about half of all federal spending on hurricane relief and recovery, is often woefully close to empty: it held just $2.2 billion when Hurricane Harvey struck last August."[54] It is only after the roaring winds and rising waters have done their damage that Congress allocates new funds to top it up through "supplemental appropriations."

Figure 9-9 shows FEMA's monthly spending on disaster relief, flood insurance, and other items from 2004 to 2018 in billions. Hurricane Katrina in 2005 shows the tallest spike in monthly spending (nearly $10 billion). Superstorm Sandy in 2012 comes in third behind the cumulated hurricane FEMA spending of 2017 (nearly $6 billion). Several qualifications are in order. First, FEMA spending on Maria, Harvey, and Irma is likely to continue through 2018 and probably five or ten years beyond, just as Katrina and Sandy spending has run years beyond the respective time they struck. Second, the totals shown here are for FEMA and not for every federal agency that responded to the 2017 hurricanes. Third, these totals do not include money spent on the hurricanes by private insurance companies (non-National Flood

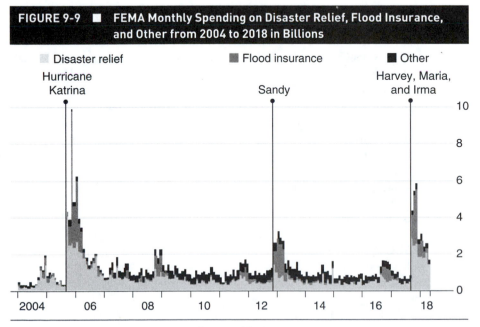

FIGURE 9-9 ■ FEMA Monthly Spending on Disaster Relief, Flood Insurance, and Other from 2004 to 2018 in Billions

Source: Data from the US Department of the Treasury; NOAA.

Insurance spending by insurers), money spent by private corporations, money spent by states and localities, money spent through capital construction fund borrowing by non-federal entities, and lest we forget, the money spent by the millions of victims of these disasters.

Hurricane Harvey and Housing Problems in Texas

According to reporter Brandon Formby of Austin's *The Texas Tribune*, "In the weeks immediately after Hurricane Harvey, thousands of Texans lingered in emergency shelters, small coastal communities scrambled to restore electricity and entire neighborhoods sat swamped with moldy mounds of housing innards. As more than half a million families sought disaster relief aid and damage estimates surpassed the $100 billion mark, the Federal Emergency Management Agency worried that it didn't have the capability to handle what was quickly becoming the largest housing recovery effort in American history, according to (Texas) Governor Greg Abbott's office."[55] In response, Governor Abbott "tasked the state's General Land Office (GLO) with a job that typically falls to FEMA: running short-term housing programs for Harvey victims. That undertaking includes everything from lining up contractors for minor repairs to securing trailers for displaced families. Abbott, Texas Land Commissioner George P. Bush, and FEMA officials touted the unprecedented arrangement as a way to rewrite the nation's disaster response playbook."[56]

Reporter Formby continues, "But six months after Harvey slammed the Texas coast as a Category 4 hurricane and dropped historic rainfall on large swaths of the state, that initial public optimism has crashed against the reality of trying to re-engineer an already-byzantine process of getting disaster aid to hurricane survivors. More than 890,000 families sought federal disaster aid in the three months after Harvey hit—including more than 40,000 who needed short-term housing help. Yet more than 100 days after Harvey's landfall, the General Land Office had provided short-term housing to fewer than 900 families."[57] And by the time the GLO contacted more than 33,000 families for the short-term housing help they sought, those Texans had made other arrangements. Many officials feared an untold number of people would end up living in moldy, unrepaired homes.[58]

The new process was delayed from the beginning. According to *The Texas Tribune*, Governor Abbott "didn't tell (George P.) Bush's (GLO) office about the plan until 19 days after the storm's Aug. 25 landfall—and one day before the governor and FEMA officials publicly unveiled it. Federal records suggest that state officials almost immediately had concerns that hiring and training the necessary personnel would require additional time."[59]

"The program probably didn't get started as quickly as any of us would have liked, but it is new,"[60] FEMA coordinating officer Kevin Hannes told *The Texas Tribune*. "The state-led plan was raising alarms from federal officials as well. The Department of Homeland Security's Office of Inspector General said in a Sept. 29 (2017) 'management alert' that because FEMA still hadn't developed policies and procedures for the disaster recovery efforts, officials in hard-hit communities had been forced to develop housing plans themselves on a 'disaster-by-disaster basis.'[61] Reportedly, "[t]he problem is no one really understands how FEMA works," Rockport mayor C. J. Wax said at a *Texas Tribune* event in October.[62] "When you don't understand how they work, then how can they understand what our needs are?"[63]

"Six months after Harvey caused an estimated $200 billion in damage, more than 8,000 Texans remained in hotel rooms and another 2,000 households had received temporary housing, such as mobile homes and trailers. About 5,000 families were getting basic emergency repairs done to their homes through the GLO, while 30,000 others await such work to be complete."[64]

In fairness to the Texas General Land Office, in an official 2018 report, that office "estimates the cost of damages from Hurricane Harvey at $160 billion," rivaling Louisiana's total damage from Hurricane Katrina in 2005. The GLO claimed, "The hurricane shut down ports, trade, tourism, oil and gas production, agricultural production, and general businesses across most of the Texas coast, including the fourth-largest city in the nation for almost a week and, in some cases, significantly longer. The impact of these interruptions is difficult to quantify at this time, but the effects of this disaster were felt across the nation, with commodities such as gas increasing in price by $0.33 a gallon in the weeks following Hurricane Harvey."[65] The GLO report disclosed that "Hurricane Harvey resulted in record rainfall totals of 34 trillion gallons of water. Combining this record rainfall together with the fact that Hurricane Harvey made landfall twice creates a three-event narrative: the initial landfall in Aransas County; the unprecedented rainfall in the Houston metroplex and surrounding areas; and Hurricane Harvey's second landfall which caused massive flooding in Southeast Texas. Following these three events, tens of thousands of homes that had never been flooded took on water, and evacuations continued for days after landfall."[66]

The GLO "continues its commitment to rebuilding while prioritizing resiliency. In assessing unmet needs, it is important to consider the additional costs of safeguarding housing and community infrastructure investments from future disasters. As such, Texas will not only assess projects and consider state-run programs that replace or repair lost property but will also seek to invest resources in efforts that promise to mitigate damage from a wide range of future types of disaster. Although this can increase costs initially, mitigating efforts can greatly reduce the cost of future damages. The success of this long-term recovery practice was seen firsthand during Hurricane Harvey. Resilient-enhanced projects from previous CDBG-DR (Community Development Block Grants and FEMA's assistance under a major disaster declaration [DR]) efforts suffered less damage from Hurricane Harvey: construction projects designed to prevent future flooding, mitigate further loss, and decrease evacuation times."[67]

While the Fornby article provides a strong critique of Texas GLO efforts, the scale of Harvey damage, the immensity of the housing challenges that office faced, plus the many demanding and expensive requirements of rebuilding to advance flood mitigation, resilience, relocations, housing elevation, buyouts, and a host of other purposes must be considered. It may have been that addressing the housing challenges posed by Harvey's colossal flood destructiveness to dozens of counties in east Texas, most particularly Harris County, was a task too great for Texas GLO, FEMA, and the U.S. Department of Housing and Urban Development. However, after Harvey, some of the poor who resided in flood damage zones suffered rejections by officials of FEMA's housing assistance program. See the "Tell Me More" 9-1 box.

TELL ME MORE 9-1

APPLICATION PROCESSING: THE PLIGHT OF HERMAN SMALLWOOD

According to *Houston Chronicle* reporter Mike Snyder, Herman Smallwood has lived in a humble wood-frame house in his East Aldine neighborhood for 48 years. Smallwood, who is 65 and disabled, rode out Hurricane Harvey's downpours in this house. "The water didn't reach the front door, he said, but it loosened the earth beneath his home's foundation of cinder blocks, causing them to shift and sink to different depths. As a result, there's hardly a level surface in the 830-square-foot house. Walls are cracked, floors tilted. Mold creeps up a bedroom wall after water poured through the roof, ruining his television and other belongings."[68]

Smallwood's request for money for repairs is 1 of more than 275,000 applications from Harvey survivors that FEMA has rejected so far. His case and others have fueled persistent concerns about the fairness and transparency of FEMA's process for determining who qualifies for help in the first, crucial months after a disaster. Research by the Houston-based Episcopal Health Foundation found that residents of low-income neighborhoods like Smallwood's were more likely to be deemed ineligible than were applicants from more affluent ZIP codes.[69]

Lawyers and community organizers who have worked with survivors of multiple disasters cite a range of reasons why deserving applicants may be turned down—unqualified or indifferent home inspectors, unclear rules, an assumption that many applicants have fraudulent intent. Some say applicants are being rejected because their homes were in poor condition before the storm. These issues have surfaced, to varying degrees, since Hurricane Katrina devastated New Orleans in 2005, advocates say. Despite signs of improvement, some are convinced that many people still aren't getting the help they deserve.[70]

"We've seen it getting better," said Saundra Brown, the disaster response manager for Lone Star Legal Aid, a service for the poor, "but FEMA is a giant bureaucracy, and they have to be sued periodically to change things." Texans began registering for FEMA assistance online, by phone, or in person within days after Harvey struck the coast in late August, dumping up to 51 inches of rain on parts of the Houston area and leading to massive flooding. Agency data provided to the *Houston Chronicle* show that 895,342 Texans had registered as of January 19, 2018. Forty-one percent had been approved, with 31 percent deemed ineligible. The remaining applications had been withdrawn, referred to the Small Business Administration for a possible loan, or were pending with FEMA or awaiting an insurance determination.[71]

To some extent, a high denial rate is built into FEMA's process. The agency encourages those affected by a disaster to register, and many people do so even though they have obvious disqualifications, such as insurance that covers damage. FEMA cannot duplicate insurance claim settlements. Such circumstances account for many of the "ineligible" determinations, federal officials say. "They might have registered to have access to an SBA low-interest disaster loan," spokesman Robert Howard wrote in an email. "They might have only suffered minor damage but registered because they heard a media report telling them they should."[72]

Smallwood's application was processed through the Individuals and Households program, which has assisted Americans affected by more than 800 hurricanes, earthquakes, tornadoes, and other natural disasters since 2002. So far, Harvey has triggered some $1.5 billion in assistance through this program. Nationally, FEMA spent $25.3 billion on individual assistance from 2005 through 2014, according to the Government Accountability Office.[73]

FEMA stopped taking applications from people affected by Harvey on November 30, 2017, but thousands of appeals are still being reviewed. New programs developed by federal agencies in partnership with the Texas General Land Office are providing a few comparable services as the focus of the recovery effort shifts to long-term needs. In addition to home-repair funds, FEMA's Individuals and Households program provides rental assistance, temporary housing such as mobile homes, and grants to replace damaged vehicles or other personal property. With the exception of the state cost share it pays when receiving FEMA public assistance grant funding and certain state tax relief provided to victims and businesses, the state of Texas has been reluctant to enact laws and programs that offer Texas disaster victims non-FEMA relief paid out from Texas state funds.

It is the process for approving home-repair grants, though, that has been most troublesome to advocates for disaster survivors—particularly poor and working-class people who are less likely to have other resources such as insurance or savings. Repairs funded through the Individuals and Households program are intended to be quick fixes—a make-do until the owner can pay for permanent renovations or replacement through long-term federal assistance or other sources. The current limit on assistance per household is $33,300.[74]

The law authorizing the program provides that it will pay only for repairs sufficient to make a disaster-damaged home "habitable." This was a basis for the first reason cited for denying Smallwood's application; the storm, in FEMA's judgment, had not made the house "unsafe to occupy." But what constitutes "habitable"? According to a 2016 lawsuit filed against FEMA on behalf of Texas disaster victims, lack of clarity on this point makes it impossible for applicants to understand what is required to qualify for help or to mount an effective appeal.[75]

Smallwood's house, like those of many people seeking help from FEMA, was in poor condition before Harvey. In cases like his, it can be difficult for inspectors to distinguish storm-caused damage from pre-existing problems, particularly since inspectors hired quickly in the rush to respond to a disaster may have limited experience or training. After Hurricanes Ike and Dolly struck Texas in 2008, FEMA denied help to many applicants after inspectors concluded that "deferred maintenance," rather than the storm, caused the poor condition of their homes. In response to litigation, FEMA agreed to stop using this standard in future disasters.[76]

But Brown, the Lone Star Legal Aid manager, said she suspects the agency is still denying claims based on deferred maintenance—without actually using the term. For example, she said, FEMA often denies requests based on damage from water that falls through the roof, as it did in Smallwood's house, but approves claims based on rising floodwaters. Inspectors assume the roof was already in poor condition due to deferred maintenance, Brown said. Smallwood, however, said his roof didn't leak before Harvey.

FEMA generally does not comment on individual applicants, citing privacy laws. Mary Lawler, executive director of Avenue Community Development Corp., a Houston nonprofit, made a similar point in testimony January 18 (2018) to the Texas House Urban Affairs Committee. "In our work, we're seeing that many of our low-income clients are being denied for FEMA assistance," Lawler said. "We're still trying to understand the reasons for those denials, but ... it appears that many of them are related to deferred maintenance on the homes, which of course disproportionately affects low-income households."[77]

The second reason for Smallwood's denial—lack of proof that he owned the house—has been common after Harvey, lawyers and advocates said. Brown said about half of the clients her agency is assisting have been denied on this basis. Smallwood said he inherited the house from his mother after her death some 30 years ago but never had the deed transferred to his name. However, he showed the inspector tax-payment receipts, and the Harris County Appraisal District website lists "Herman Smallwood et al." as the owner. FEMA's guidelines include "property tax receipt or property tax bill" as an "alternative certification document."[78]

Advocates say they understand that some errors are inevitable when government agencies have to mobilize quickly to help hundreds of thousands of people after a disaster. But they are concerned that attitudes within FEMA and its contractors may add to these problems.

"FEMA is on high **fraud alert**, which they should be, but I believe they're denying a lot of people, assuming (applications are) fraud when they're not," Brown said. The agency works

(Continued)

(Continued)

aggressively to prevent fraud. All applicants referred to the Individuals and Households program must sign a statement affirming that the information they are providing is true, that they are not submitting duplicate applications, and that they won't use federal benefits for unintended purposes. The document states that concealing information or making false statements can result in criminal and civil penalties. Herman Smallwood says he willingly signed FEMA's anti-fraud form. While he awaits a decision on his appeal, he is still living in his damaged house, looking down at the cracks in the floor that opened up when the foundation shifted.[79]

A San Juan Mayor versus a U.S. President: Suspending a Declaration?

A truly unusual and somewhat bizarre series of exchanges witnessed on television and posted in news media stories and in presidential tweets in late September 2017 concerned the mayor of San Juan and the president of the United States.

According to *The New York Times*, "President Trump lashed out at the mayor of San Juan on Saturday (September 30, 2017) for criticizing his administration's efforts to help Puerto Rico after Hurricane Maria, accusing her of 'poor leadership' and implying that the people of the devastated island were not doing enough to help themselves."[80] President Trump wrote on Twitter, "The Mayor of San Juan, who was very complimentary only a few days ago, has now been told by the Democrats that you must be nasty to Trump. Such poor leadership ability by the Mayor of San Juan, and others in Puerto Rico, who are not able to get their workers to help."[81] Mr. Trump said the people of Puerto Rico should not depend entirely on the federal government. "They want everything to be done for them when it should be a community effort," he wrote. "10,000 Federal workers now on Island doing a fantastic job. The military and first responders, despite no electric, roads, phones etc., have done an amazing job. Puerto Rico was totally destroyed."[82]

According to CNN, President Trump's declaration relevant tweet said, "We cannot keep FEMA, the Military & the First Responders, who have been amazing (under the most difficult circumstances) in P.R. forever!"[83]

"In the case of Ms. Cruz, President Trump took her outcry as a personal assault on him. While other presidents generally ignore most of the criticism they invariably attract,"[84] Mr. Trump is prone to rebutting criticism. Responding to Trump's tweets on Saturday, "Ms. Cruz said she would not be distracted by 'small comments' and denied that she was attacking the president at the behest of the Democrats. 'Actually, I was asking for help,' she told MSNBC. 'I wasn't saying anything nasty about the president.'[85] Ms. Cruz became a powerful voice of grievance on Friday when she went on television to plead for help and reject assertions by the Trump administration about how well it was responding. She was incensed by comments made by Elaine Duke, the acting secretary of Homeland Security, who had said on Thursday (September 28) that it was 'really a good news story in terms of our ability to reach people and the limited number of deaths' from the hurricane."[86]

CNN reported in February 2018 that "San Juan Mayor Carmen Yulín Cruz didn't mince her words Wednesday when asked about President Donald Trump's pledges of support to hurricane-ravaged Puerto Rico during his State of the Union speech, denouncing them as "hypocrisy."[87] In his speech to Congress, President Trump declared, "To everyone still recovering in Texas, Florida, Louisiana, Puerto Rico, the Virgin Islands, California and everywhere else—we are with you, we love you, and we will pull through together."[88]

But asked by CNN's Christiane Amanpour about Trump's comments, Yulín Cruz said, "The President has not been with the people of Puerto Rico," and that his words were an "utter statement of hypocrisy."[89] Mayor Cruz said, "Thirty-five percent of our people do not have electricity. Our children are going to school only part time. Half a million homes are totally disrupted, either need to be rebuilt completely or need to have their roof put back on," she said of the damage from both hurricanes Irma and Maria, which left more than 3 million Puerto Ricans in need of assistance.[90]

In September, Trump repeatedly criticized Cruz on Twitter after she accused the government of abandoning Puerto Rico. As far as Yulín Cruz is concerned, she told Amanpour, Trump "speaks out of both sides of his mouth." "On the one hand, he says he wants to help Puerto Rico. On the other hand, he imposed a 20% income tax on every good and service that comes from Puerto Rico into the United States.[91] On the one hand, he says we will be with you for the long run. And on the other hand, the [Food and Drug Administration] is trying to convince pharmaceutical companies to leave Puerto Rico," she told Amanpour.[92]

"He says he cares and he came here and threw paper towels at us," she continued, referring to Trump's visit to the city of Guaynabo in October. "And on the other hand, he doesn't provide his administration with a clear set of goals to help Puerto Rico."[93] Yulín Cruz also slammed FEMA, which announced plans to halt new shipments of food and water to the island by the end of January 2018. "FEMA said mission accomplished. I do not know what mission they have accomplished. Certainly, it wasn't the mission of doing what they were supposed to do," Yulín Cruz said.[94]

The disagreement between the president and the mayor of San Juan drew, for a short time, intense news media attention. See "Tell Me More" 9-2 box for a summary of the interchange between *Boston Globe* reporter Matthew Rocheleau and this author.

TELL ME MORE 9-2

THE AUTHOR'S OCTOBER 2017 INTERVIEW WITH A *BOSTON GLOBE* REPORTER

Boston Globe reporter Matthew Rocheleau asking questions. Dr. Richard Sylves (RTS) answering.

- What authority would the president have to do what he is suggesting he might do in terms of pulling back on some/all federal relief to Puerto Rico?

RTS: All U.S. presidents since 1950 have had authority to approve or turn down governor requests for declarations of major disaster (DR). All U.S. presidents since 1974 have possessed authority to approve or turn down governor requests for emergency declarations (EM).[95] In a nutshell, DRs ordinarily require documentation of economic loss. A scale of state per capita loss, and other criteria, has been used by FEMA (created in 1979) and its predecessor agencies in recommendations to the president

(Continued)

(Continued)

on whether to approve or reject a governor's request for a DR. Each president has discretion with regard to approving or rejecting a governor's DR request.

Since his inauguration, President Donald Trump has a DR approval rate that is numerically similar to President Obama's; however, I do not have access to his full turndown record so I do not know how his turndown record compares to that of other presidents. It is important to remember that once the president approves a major disaster declaration for a state, as he did for Puerto Rico, he cannot easily go back and restrict federal funding paid out on that disaster declaration, particularly if federally funded public infrastructure repair or replacement projects are under contract. Trump approved a major disaster declaration covering Puerto Rico's Hurricane Maria damage on October 2, 2017, in DR 4339, according to FEMA.

That said, to my knowledge, presidents from Truman to Obama have never threatened early termination of an in-force major disaster declaration; though in fairness, President Trump may not have meant actual cessation of the major disaster declaration he had previously approved for Puerto Rico.

I have asked researchers at the Congressional Research Service the same question you have asked me. Though no one offered attribution of their opinions, the consensus view among several lawyers there was that under the Stafford Act of 1988, a core federal emergency management law, the president (any president) can suspend or terminate an in-force presidential disaster declaration if he or she so desires. However, in my judgment, such an action may be subject to litigation, particularly once federal funds are obligated under a declaration to various state and local post-disaster purposes and once state and local governments begin paying their state/local cost shares on federally subsidized post-disaster projects. So, while the president may possess lawful authority to withdraw an approved, in-force disaster declaration, the implications of such an action could produce lawsuits on other grounds.

- Would he be able to make any such changes unilaterally or would it require approval from Congress and/or other agencies or would he perhaps have unilateral authority to pull back on just certain types of relief efforts while ending other relief efforts would require additional approval beyond the presidency?

RTS: President Trump cannot easily make unilateral changes in the implementation of an in-force presidential declaration of major disaster without legally defensible justification. Were he to do so in the case of Puerto Rico, the president would be subject to lawsuits by offended parties on a variety of grounds. Efforts by the president to single out Puerto Rico for funding penalties or disallowance (or disbarment) might require congressional assent and would need backing in law, perhaps under provisions of an amended Stafford Act.

Puerto Rico's pre-disaster fiscal problems cannot be conflated with federal disaster assistance spending. Should the state government of Illinois be denied federal funding under an in-force major disaster declaration because not long ago it was heavily in debt and lacked a necessary state budget law? The answer is NO—under the U.S. system of intergovernmental relations and under constitutional law.

President Trump, some nine months into his administration, may have still been learning about federal disaster law and policy. FEMA is an executive branch federal agency, not an arm of the White House and not the equivalent of a privately run corporation. A long series of federal laws and policies set forth FEMA's legal obligations and duties. Politically appointed administrators holding positions of authority in FEMA, or any other federal agency, are obligated to consider presidential instructions; however, to have effect those instructions need to come to them in a formal way (not merely through Tweets or presidential remarks). How FEMA distributes and manages its personnel and budgetary resources is not a direct determination of any sitting president, though as leaders of the executive branch, presidents can make some agency personnel changes, reorganize departments and agencies, re-program a share of congressionally budgeted funds within an agency, and propose agency budget requests to Congress.

- Are there any rules that say the federal government can't pull out of relief efforts if certain conditions still exist (for example, if a certain percentage or number of people are still without power or access to clean water)?

RTS: Here is how a major disaster declaration is closed out. In INDIVIDUAL ASSISTANCE, FEMA monitors the flow and volume of assistance requests being filed by individuals and families. When the volume of requests tapers to a low level or approaches zero for a period of days, FEMA administrators prepare an announcement for the *Federal Register*. That announcement declares that no more requests for individual assistance under the disaster declaration will be accepted after the stipulated date. Sometimes, lawmakers contest this proposal and demand that FEMA extend the deadline owing to late filers or other factors. FEMA sometimes obliges them. It is only after FEMA's published deadline has been passed that individual assistance is officially closed out under a major disaster declaration.

FEMA government-to-government assistance (PUBLIC ASSISTANCE) is more complex because state and local governments must prepare rebuilding or replacement plans for physical structures. State and local governments routinely face a federal/state–local cost share in this program. Usually, state and local governments have only 30 to 60 days to make application for FEMA Public Assistance. It may take months, years, or sometimes a decade, to complete all of the approved project work and spending on disaster-damaged infrastructure. Usually, FEMA does not keep eligibility for this program open for more than three to six months. Often after six months or slightly more, FEMA turns away state and local public assistance requests—this is especially so if the request is for damage NOT CAUSED by the disaster covered under the declaration or if it appears to FEMA officials that the request is to pay for routine maintenance.

- For the money that's already been allocated for Puerto Rico—could that be pulled back or would that money have to be spent?

RTS: Federal money for declared disasters is another matter which President Trump may not understand. There is a Disaster Relief Fund comprised of both an annual congressional infusion of spending authority and "carried over" unspent spending authority for other disasters in previous years. The amount of budget authority residing in the fund fluctuates over time as FEMA draws from it to pay out on its obligations for all presidentially declared disasters whose accounts remain open for spending. A massively expensive catastrophic disaster or series of catastrophes (as we have had with this year's hurricanes) tends to swallow up all of the budget authority in the fund. When this happens, Congress must recapitalize the fund through an appropriation (usually a supplemental [in budget-year] appropriation). This law requires a presidential signature.

If a presidential declaration of major disaster applies to a jurisdiction, let's say Puerto Rico, money FEMA (and other federal agencies with FEMA permission) draws from this fund goes out under the rules of the FEMA program through which it flows. In many respects, under a presidential disaster declaration, FEMA individual assistance is an **entitlement program** as long as recipients meet conditions of eligibility and are not committing fraud. No president can deny this aid or suspend funding once a major disaster declaration has been issued and people have applied for, and have begun receiving, federal aid. Do recall that there is a system for discontinuing individual assistance and no declaration offers permanent eligibility for federal funding.

It may be possible for a FEMA presidential appointee to shift some personnel resources were he or she to receive orders to do that from the president; however, as these officials take an oath to obey the law before they assume their duties, they would have to square this behavior with FEMA's mandated laws and policies as well as with their own conscience.

(Continued)

(Continued)

- Are the rules/policies around federal disaster relief for Puerto Rico different from rules/policies that exist for U.S. states?

RTS: Puerto Rico is a commonwealth and unincorporated territory of the United States; as such, in the realm of presidential disaster declarations, it holds the same status as an American state. It has only one non-voting observer elected every two years to a seat in the U.S. House of Representatives. This makes it very politically weak when compared to the size of the congressional delegations of Texas and Florida. Puerto Rico's governor is allowed to request presidential declarations of major disaster and emergency, just as governors of states do in the 50 states. Conversely, just as governor requests for declarations of major disaster or emergency are sometimes denied by the president (almost invariably on the basis of need), the PR governor's original request for such declarations may be lawfully denied by a president. Different U.S. Trust and Commonwealth Territories are linked to the United States under treaties and conventions that may vary based on what was agreed to originally and what changes may have been approved by both parties over time by U.S. Trust and Commonwealth Territories in the Caribbean and Pacific. However, if the operative convention or treaty holds that the jurisdiction in question can request and receive presidential declarations of major disaster and emergency, then that jurisdiction's governor or governor-equivalent is on par with every state governor in the United States.

- Can you think of any other cases in which a president or other federal leader has pulled back on federal disaster aid and/or threatened to do so?

RTS: No, I cannot. Some presidents have expressed dismay when they believed states and localities were gaming federal disaster relief at the expense of the national taxpayer (e.g., changing building codes to a much higher and expensive standard when federal assistance would cover most of this new cost. Or when governors seek to add more counties to a major disaster declaration when those counties in fact experienced barely qualifying levels of loss, etc.).

Presidents have had disagreements with governors and big-city mayors in times of disaster but a president publicly rebuking them through threats to diminish federal post-disaster assistance personnel or funding is something of a first. Sometimes what a president says is not manifested in what they do. Also, a presidential statement on its own is, as mentioned, not enough to compel federal officials to act on the intent of the statement: "policy through speech" so to speak.

President Trump may have been trying to spur Puerto Rico to reassume more of its rebuilding and recovery obligations. The major difference between Hurricanes Harvey & Irma versus Hurricane Maria is that the first two did not incapacitate state and local emergency management in Texas or Florida, respectively. However, Maria may well have incapacitated Puerto Rico's state and local emergency management. Moreover, Puerto Rico is a 100-mile-long, 35-mile-wide island located more than a thousand miles from Florida. Consequently, its recovery is doubly difficult and its dependency on FEMA and other federal recovery agencies for help might seem protracted, perhaps even to the president.

Before closing this "problems" section, students of the field of emergency management should read and review FEMA's July 12, 2018, "2017 Hurricane Season FEMA After-Action Report." In some respects, this report is lightly penitential for the agency, especially with respect to its response to Hurricane Maria in Puerto Rico. Some of its many findings are as follows:

- FEMA leaders at all levels made major adaptations to agency policy and programs to respond to significant operational challenges during the hurricane season. FEMA's plans guided response operations, but improvements to the planning process and format are needed to better usability during operations. FEMA could have better leveraged open-source information and preparedness data, such as capability assessments and exercise findings, for Puerto Rico and the U.S. Virgin Islands.[96]

- FEMA entered the hurricane season with a force strength less than its target, resulting in staffing shortages across the incidents. The agency has made progress on disaster workforce certification, but had not achieved its targets. Field leaders reported some resultant inefficiency in program delivery. FEMA strategically consolidated ongoing disaster operations facilities across the country to reallocate personnel to the hurricane-affected field operations, which increased capacity to deliver FEMA programs.[97]

- FEMA assumed a more active role in coordinating whole community logistics operations for Puerto Rico and the U.S. Virgin Islands due to the territories' preparedness challenges, geographic distance, and pre-existing, on-the-ground conditions. While FEMA mobilized billions of dollars in commodities, the agency experienced challenges in comprehensively tracking resources moving across multiple modes of transportation to Puerto Rico and the U.S. Virgin Islands due to staffing shortages and business process shortfalls. FEMA provided logistical coordination to move and distribute commodities from staging areas to survivors in Puerto Rico, supplementing a role that should largely be managed and coordinated at the state or territory level. In a three-month period, FEMA issued more contract actions than in an entire previous fiscal year to meet disaster requirements, which strained the Agency's contracting personnel.[98]

- To overcome limited situational awareness created by the loss of communications in Puerto Rico, FEMA found creative solutions to assess the situation and prioritize response activities, including emergency repairs to infrastructure. Also, challenged by an inoperable telecommunications environment in Puerto Rico, FEMA had to adapt field communications, program delivery, and command and control activities. FEMA and its federal partners installed a record number of generators to provide temporary power to critical infrastructure while facing significant challenges in identifying generator requirements and shortfalls in available generators.[99]

- As part of the federal government's response to three near-simultaneous incidents, FEMA deployed more than 17,000 personnel, including 4,063 non-FEMA and non-Department of Defense (DOD) federal employees through the federal Surge Capacity Force (SCF) and other methods. By comparison, FEMA deployed 9,971 staff for Hurricane Sandy response operations in 2012. In addition, DOD deployed nearly 14,000 personnel to affected areas across three different FEMA regions.[100]

- Between August 25 and October 16, President Trump issued a total of 20 disaster or emergency declarations for the three storms: Hurricane Harvey (3 declarations), Hurricane Irma (13 declarations), and Hurricane Maria

(4 declarations). Through its Incident Management Assistance Teams (IMATs), FEMA provided a forward federal presence of senior-level emergency managers to support the impacted states and territories in preparing for and responding to the storms. At the height of concurrent operations, all 28 of FEMA's National Urban Search and Rescue Task Forces rapidly deployed to support life-saving operations, searching more than 30,900 structures, and saving or assisting nearly 9,500 people. By the end of the hurricane season on November 30, more than 4.7 million households affected by hurricanes Harvey, Irma, and Maria had registered for federal assistance with FEMA, more than all who registered for hurricanes Katrina, Rita, Wilma, and Sandy combined.[101]

- Nearly simultaneously, the response to the historic wildfires across the Western United States, including 5 of the 20 most destructive wildfires in modern California history, required the deployment of additional FEMA personnel, commodities, and equipment. As of November 30, the fires had claimed 44 lives and damaged or destroyed nearly 10,000 structures. The response to the California Wildfires required a greater amount of DOD contracts and mission assignments than the hurricane response in support of Texas and Florida combined.[102]

COMPARISONS

CNN reported, "Almost a week since Hurricane Maria devastated Puerto Rico, the U.S. recovery efforts there have been markedly different from the recovery efforts after Hurricane Harvey in Texas and Irma in Florida. Fewer FEMA personnel are in place. Grassroots donations from fellow Americans are much smaller."[103] Furthermore, Puerto Rico remained without power, and President Donald Trump had yet to visit.

CNN added, "Those differences are partly because of issues unique to Puerto Rico, an island that already had a weakened infrastructure, a government struggling through bankruptcy—and that had only just been hit by Hurricane Irma. In addition, each hurricane posed different threats and caused different problems. Harvey brought massive flooding, Irma deadly storm surges, and Maria catastrophic high winds."[104] The total number of FEMA personnel, including surge workers, was another point of difference when comparing the hurricanes.

Hurricane Harvey: For Hurricane Harvey, FEMA had supplies and personnel positioned in Texas before the storm made landfall on August 25. Within days, the number of FEMA employees, other federal agencies, and the National Guard deployed topped 31,000.[105] In addition, FEMA supplied 3 million meals and 3 million liters of water to Texas to be distributed to survivors.

Hurricane Irma: "Even more federal personnel responded to Hurricane Irma when it made landfall in Florida on September 10. More than 40,000 federal personnel, including 2,650 FEMA staff, were in place by September 14. In addition, FEMA had transferred 6.6 million meals and 4.7 million liters of water to states in the Southeast after Irma as of the 14th."[106]

Hurricane Maria: By comparison, Puerto Rico and the Virgin Islands saw much fewer personnel after Hurricane Maria hit, according to FEMA. In a tweet on the Monday after the storm hit, FEMA said that more than 10,000 federal staff were on the ground in Puerto Rico and the Virgin Islands assisting search and rescue and recovery efforts. FEMA announced that "thousands" of federal staff, including 500 FEMA personnel, were on the ground in Puerto Rico and the U.S. Virgin Islands as of Tuesday morning.[107] White House press secretary Sarah Sanders defended the federal response to Hurricane Maria on Monday as "anything but slow."[108]

Speed of response and presidential visits are added issues for comparison.

Hurricane Harvey: Trump visited Texas twice after Hurricane Harvey. The first visit came on August 29, four days after the storm first made landfall. There, he met with local, state, and federal officials in Austin and Corpus Christi.

On September 2, Trump made a second visit to Texas, during which he visited a shelter and handed out boxed lunches with First Lady Melania Trump.

Hurricane Irma: After Hurricane Irma struck Florida, Trump visited the state on September 14, four days after the storm landed. He surveyed the damage, distributed meals in Naples in a hard-hit mobile home community, and thanked federal disaster relief officials in Fort Myers.

Hurricane Maria: Trump said that he would visit Puerto Rico the following Tuesday, which would be about two weeks after Hurricane Maria. That was the earliest date he could reach the island due to first responders' ongoing relief and recovery efforts, he said. He also said he would likely stop in the Virgin Islands as well.

"Some people say, I read it this morning, it's literally destroyed," Trump said, adding, "The infrastructure was in bad shape as you know in Puerto Rico before the storm, and now in many cases, it has no infrastructure, so it's—you're really starting from almost scratch."

At the time, President Trump said that the recovery was more difficult in Puerto Rico because of its geography. "It's very tough because it's an island," Trump said. "In Texas, we can ship the trucks right out there, you know, we've got A-pluses on Texas and Florida and we will also on Puerto Rico, but the difference is this is an island sitting in the middle of an ocean, and it's a big ocean."

FEMA administrator Brock Long also noted Tuesday that Puerto Rico's international airport[109] in San Juan was operating at a limited capacity, which made moving resources into the area more difficult.

Donations and the Hurricanes

Hurricane Harvey: The destruction in Houston from Hurricane Harvey prompted an outpouring of monetary donations. As of September 2, companies had pledged more than $157 million in relief efforts, and 69 companies had donated $1 million or more, according to the U.S. Chamber of Commerce.

Houston Texans defensive lineman J. J. Watt was the most prominent celebrity advocate of those donations, and he personally helped marshal $37 million before closing his fundraising effort on September 15. Separately, all five living former U.S. presidents joined together to raise money for storm relief under the One America Appeal site.

Hurricane Irma: Hurricane Irma's impact on Florida sparked a new wave of donations. Corporate donations for Harvey and Irma relief combined exceeded $222 million, according to the U.S. Chamber of Commerce.

Hurricane Maria: Donations for Hurricane Maria were much smaller by comparison. NBA star Carmelo Anthony, whose father is Puerto Rican, raised about $240,000 very quickly after the storm hit. Corporate donations were similarly limited, and four companies gave a collective $8.1 million, according to the U.S. Chamber of Commerce.

The federal spending response is another basis for comparison.

Hurricane Harvey: Trump signed a bill that included emergency funding for hurricane relief on September 8, about two weeks after Hurricane Harvey hit. The bill, part of a deal struck between Trump and Democratic leaders, included about $22 billion for FEMA's disaster relief fund, $15 billion of which was new funds.

In late August, FEMA had $5.03 billion available for disaster spending between then and the end of September 2017, a FEMA spokesperson told CNN. The disaster relief fund was replenished with another $6.7 billion in October when the new fiscal year (FY 2019) began.

Hurricane Maria: White House spokesperson Sarah Huckabee Sanders said shortly after the storm hit that it was too early to identify a spending amount to request from Congress. "Once we have a greater insight into the full assessment of damage then we'll be able to determine what additional funds are needed but we're still in that … fact-finding process on that piece of it," she said. House Speaker Paul Ryan and other congressional leaders said there was a "humanitarian crisis" in Puerto Rico because of the storm. "This is our country and these are our fellow citizens. They need our help and they're going to get our help," Ryan said. As examined previously in this chapter, in comparative terms, it took the federal government and Puerto Rico's government a considerable amount of time to conduct damage assessments and to ascertain individual and household needs. Such information is used in formulating post-Maria federal budget requests. Also unhelpful was that Hurricane Maria struck very close to the start of the new federal fiscal year, October 1, 2017. Congress has great difficulty formulating and enacting budgets for any new fiscal year, such that new funding requests to cover Maria's burgeoning costs short-circuited federal budgeting even more than the two preceding hurricanes.

LESSONS LEARNED

The Economist observes, "Whatever happens this hurricane season (2018), preparation will only become more important in the long run. According to the Congressional Budget Office, damage from hurricanes is expected to grow in the coming decades—in part because of climate change, which will cause sea levels to rise and increase the frequency of the most intense storms."[110]

The Economist adds, "America's policymakers would get better bang for their buck if they made greater efforts to prepare for disasters ahead of time. The National Institute of Building Sciences, a trade group, reckons that each dollar spent on disaster mitigation can save as much as six dollars in future losses. Yet such spending has been declining for over a decade. This year Donald Trump, who gave himself a grade of A+ for his responses to last year's hurricanes, proposed $61 million in cuts to FEMA's Pre-Disaster Mitigation grant programme—a 61% reduction."[111]

One of the thorniest issues plaguing Puerto Rico was restoring or replacing its electricity grid in the months after Maria struck. Most Americans consider it "disastrous" to lose power, Internet, and cell services for more than four or five hours. They have become so accustomed to continuous delivery of power, telephonic, and Internet services that they have watched their governments, at all levels, come to rely on such services to carry out their operations when big or small disasters and emergencies occur. Immensely grandiose national plans woven into nearly every program office of the U.S. Department of Homeland Security largely exist as sets of electrons in DHS computer hardware, software, and in the cloud. FEMA has four means of processing applications from individuals and households for post-disaster assistance, and they all rely on some combination of power availability, Internet service, or cell/telephone availability. FEMA invites applications but through registering for online help at DisasterAssistance.gov or by linking with FEMA via smartphone. Alternatively, victim survivors are also invited to call the toll-free registration number at 1-800-621-FEMA (3362). FEMA even touts the availability of its app, which can be uploaded to one's cell phone. The agency adds, "If **Disaster Recovery Centers [DRCs]** have been established in your area, they can assist you in the registration process."[112] However, if you are fortunate to be near one, these centers rely on power and emergency communications equipment, neither of which are continuously available in the days after a disaster as comprehensively destructive as Maria.

To compound this dependency on power, Internet, and cell technologies, shockingly, *FEMA does not take written applications for aid sent by mail.* Assuming one is able to file a complete application through one of the methods mentioned, FEMA then asks for a checking account number and a bank routing slip so they can dispatch your "direct deposit" money via email to your bank. If a person lived in Puerto Rico, and was lucky enough to file a claim in the weeks after Maria, even months later, there would have been no guarantee one's bank in Puerto Rico would have had power and/or Internet service enabling the processing of FEMA's emailed check.

Back to Puerto Rico's electric power plight: Electric utilities on the U.S. mainland, be they privately or publicly owned, generally work within regulated standards, own and maintain similar equipment, and operate with robust mutual aid agreements. Power generators and distributors work through intricate power pools that buy, sell, or trade electricity at rapid speed. "The system relies on interdependence and industry mutual aid. For example, in August and September of 2017, utility workers from Delaware, Pennsylvania, the Midwest, the Northeast, and elsewhere set off in convoys of trucks converging on Harvey and Irma power-loss zones in the South, and many were away for weeks. The same utilities did not show up in Puerto Rico for many weeks, and their workforces there were far less than for Harvey and Irma. When asked why they could not respond as they did to Texas and Florida, power crew officials complained, first, movement to an island more than a thousand miles from the tip of south Florida requires innumerable airline flights and massive water-freight shipments of both their equipment and personnel (in some cases, barging). Second, Puerto Rico's electric grid was so outmoded that mainland crews did not know how they could repair it short of completely replacing it. Third, they were uncertain that they would ever be paid for their work (usually double over-time rates), installed equipment, and living expenses. Remember, that Puerto Rico's major utility was verging on bankruptcy before Maria. Fourth, workers dispatched to Puerto Rico would be expected to know at least minimal Spanish, something important when working in teams with dangerous power equipment at or above ground." The landscape was often inhospitable for visiting utility workers as they were expected to trudge into steep terrain and thick jungles equipped with few accurate maps identifying the route of powerlines and towers.[113]

According to *E&E News*, Hurricane Irma was one of the strongest Atlantic hurricanes ever. It caused power blackouts that affected more than 6 million mainland customers in Florida, Georgia, and South Carolina. Ninety-five percent of those who lost electricity got it back in two weeks. However, Hurricane Maria, a Category 4 storm, collapsed the grid for all of Puerto Rico's 1.5 million electric customers. It took 15 weeks for the power company to regain the ability to even estimate how many customers were without power (45 percent). Service slowly returned and reached 96 percent, only to have the entire grid fail again in mid-April 2018.[114]

Shortly after Maria hit Puerto Rico, two thirds of electrical substations were flooded or heavily damaged. The same was true for the switchyards. Power plants, many on the coast, had been flooded by surging seas, and wind had battered cooling towers and turbines. However, most horrifying for utility experts was damage to "[t]he transmission system—I've never seen so much damage to a transmission system," Carlos Torres said, referring to the long-haul lines that deliver from power plant to customer.[115] Torres of Consolidated Edison (of New York) is vice president of emergency management for the utility. He was sent to assess the power problem in Puerto Rico. "A mainland hurricane of terrific force, like Katrina, might damage 20 percent of transmission towers. Maria was the reverse. Only 20 percent were functioning, and many of the 80 percent damaged had fallen from wind or foundered in mudslides."[116]

It was only on October 31, 2017, six weeks after the storm hit and after the Trump administration guaranteed that it would cover all grid-related expenses, that PREPA (Puerto Rico's electric utility) requested aid from the mainland. Unlike many mainland utilities, PREPA (Puerto Rico Electric Power Authority) had no command structure in place for recovering from an emergency. Torres needed to create one from scratch. With no other template, he organized the same way he had in New York and created regional incident-management teams to run the seven regions that make up PREPA's grid.[117]

On several occasions, Puerto Rico's governor has criticized the U.S. Army Corps of Engineers for a lack of urgency. On another, the Army Corps entered a PREPA warehouse and found supplies it was hoarding. Other tensions have existed behind the scenes. The Army Corps, several of its contractors, the U.S. Department of Energy, FEMA, and several mainland power utilities endeavored to work out the problem with Puerto Rico's utility workers. "They've taken it very well. Maybe in the beginning they weren't," Torres said of PREPA. The Puerto Rico disaster marks the first time that control of a recovery was taken out of the hands of the home utility. And the territory's status as a possession of the United States made the takeover even more grating to PREPA workers.[118] Moreover, as the mainland incident management teams arrived, miscommunication was common. Puerto Rico's utility workers think and speak in Spanish. And the island's removal from the mainland led to disconnects over technical jargon. Paul Vasquez, a supervisor for Austin Energy who ran logistics for a regional management team, said that calling things by different names led to some early delays. He said, "For the longest time, we didn't even think they had any maps or data that showed where their lines went. We would struggle to get some piece of information. Then we learned that they had it."[119]

A report has estimated that truly making Puerto Rico's grid hurricane-ready—including rerouting transmission lines off the mountaintops, hardening substations and towers, and moving to a more decentralized grid powered by more renewable energy—would cost $17.6 billion and take a decade.[120] Not to be overlooked is Maria's impact on the neighboring U.S. Virgin Islands and its 100,000 residents. Power there was only fully restored in March 2018.[121]

Summary

The federal response to all three hurricanes was immense but uneven. Had Harvey been the only catastrophic landfalling U.S. hurricane in 2017, FEMA, other responding federal agencies, and the White House would have probably earned generally high marks for their response and recovery actions. However, this was not to be. Soon after Harvey devastation, Hurricane Irma tracked through the eastern Caribbean, struck many populated islands there, including the Virgin Islands and Puerto Rico, and tore through the Florida Keys. It then nearly bisected the Florida peninsula from south to north. Irma rolled on into Georgia, eastern Alabama, and parts of South Carolina before eventually breaking up over Tennessee. In many ways, Irma complicated Harvey and Maria relief, although the damage Irma inflicted and the costs it imposed on victims was every bit as deserving of national attention as the two hurricanes that bookended it.

With all due respect to Sebastian Junger, Maria was "the Perfect Storm" of 2017. Maria, a powerful Category 4 hurricane that at times threatened to go to Category 5, almost razed the entire island of Puerto Rico. Whereas Harvey and Irma posed challenges for the states and territories they struck neither storm disabled state governments, nor most local government operations. Not so for Maria. Hurricane Maria destroyed homes, hospitals, roads, public buildings and infrastructure, businesses, and farms that were the livelihood of several million Puerto Rican citizens. Landslides blocked roads, countless trees of every type were damaged or destroyed, and belongings were strewn over the landscape. Many had to ride out the storm in basements or shelters as the roofs of their homes blew off. Puerto Rico's central and municipal governments were legitimately overwhelmed by Maria for several weeks. While major parts of east Texas, Louisiana, Florida, the Virgin Islands, and Puerto Rico lost electrical power and cell tower service from Harvey and Irma, Maria destroyed Puerto Rico's already outmoded and questionably run electric utility service.

The state and local response for each of the three hurricanes is more difficult to judge. Clearly, the Texas General Land Office was challenged by assuming FEMA's temporary housing duties. Search and rescue reports for Harvey in Texas were laudable. One might ask whether the temporal order of the hurricanes made a difference. Hurricane Harvey for the people of east Texas produced protracted rainfall amounts of seemingly biblical proportions. Thirty, 40, 50 inches of rain falling within a period of days challenges even the most farsighted flood-fighting and mitigation advocates.

Irma, as the intermediate hurricane, compounded the problems in managing Harvey recovery in Texas and hobbled mobilization in the wake of Hurricane Maria. While not the most devastating of the three, Irma was the most expansively troublesome of the three. Military resources were rapidly mobilized for Harvey and Irma, but Puerto Rico had trouble calling up even a third of its National

Guard soldiers. Worse still, assets of the U.S. Navy were not deployed to the island with alacrity.

This chapter opened with the following question: Have the dramatic changes that both FEMA and DHS have undergone in policy and management since 2014–2015 deleteriously affected post-disaster government assistance to states, localities, and disaster victims in 2017 or possibly beyond this time? Clearly, DHS and FEMA are "on the same page" more today than at the time of Hurricane Katrina. In some respects, FEMA is now better able to draw on the workforce and capabilities of greater DHS. However, FEMA's workload, particularly in grants management, has become ponderous. The culture of FEMA has changed in part because its workers now must work and build relationships with people of other DHS offices. Emergency management still has a central place in the work of the agency. FEMA people, however, are far more locked into the counter-terrorism mission of DHS and its many terrorism-focused organizations than has been the case in the past. Will the day come when FEMA people see themselves more as counter-terror authorities than as federal disaster management authorities? On a more positive note, FEMA's links to state and local emergency management remain strong, but as Chapter 6 made clear, homeland security has a growing presence in state and local law enforcement and military affairs. Under Administrator Long's leadership,

FEMA developed Integration Teams in July 2017. These are teams of highly trained and experienced FEMA workers, some of them technical experts, sent to work with state, local, territorial, and tribal government officials on a phased basis when needed. FEMA Integration Teams work through FEMA's respective regional administrators. FEMA's July 2018 After-Action Report on the 2017 Hurricane Season recommends that such teams be used to build state emergency management capacity.[122]

In conclusion, the story of the three hurricanes of 2017 is NOT one of FEMA incompetence or presidential indifference to the disaster plight of two U.S. territories in the Caribbean. The story flows more from the force and duration of the disaster agents themselves. On top of this, what seems to have made a difference in each hurricane is physical geography, differences in levels of disaster planning, economic health and demographics, donor fatigue, and the fact that Puerto Rico has only one non-voting observer in the U.S. House of Representatives (while Texas has two senators plus 36 Congress members and Florida has two senators and 27 Congress members). The recovery and build-back after these hurricanes, if conducted with reasonable disaster mitigation in mind, could go far in augmenting the resilience of the hardest hit states, including the Commonwealth of Puerto Rico.

Key Terms

Accumulated Cyclone Energy 353

Disaster recovery centers (DRCs) 385

Entitlement program 379

Fraud alert 376

Hurricane Harvey 353

Hurricane Irma 357

Hurricane Maria 359

"Surge" workforce 352

USNS *Comfort* 361

Empty pairs of shoes sit on display outside the Capitol Building in this aerial photograph taken during a protest against the government's reporting of the death toll from Hurricane Maria in San Juan, Puerto Rico, on June 1, 2018.

Xavier Garcia/Bloomberg via Getty Images

10

CONCLUSIONS AND THE FUTURE

The conclusion of the second edition of this book began with the declaration that emergency management is an evolving profession. In the four years since the second edition went to print, U.S. emergency management has indeed evolved as a profession, but today government employees working in that profession are much more deeply threaded into the fabric of homeland security. It is not enough to rationalize that terrorism is among many hazards that the U.S. Federal Emergency Management Agency's (FEMA's) all-hazards approach is expected to include. Thus, what else is an all-hazards-focused FEMA expected to do but address the Department of Homeland Security's primary mission? For many years, FEMA has helped define, shape, and advance the profession of emergency management in America and, by example, in other nations, However, at this writing of the third edition, it is obvious, even to people who now work or have worked at FEMA, that the agency is today fundamentally different than it was even four years ago.

The U.S. Department of Homeland Security (DHS) recently celebrated its 15th anniversary.[1] Over those 15 years, FEMA emergency management work has been refashioned such that it is tethered to DHS organizations that address border control, immigration enforcement, customs, terrorism-related law enforcement, apprehension of criminals, organized crime (especially that committed by gangs), money-laundering, protection of vital or iconic physical structures, drug-related crime, and transportation security. This chapter considers some of these changes and what they have meant to FEMA and its stakeholders. Management of natural, non-terror, human-caused, or hybrid disasters has become a sidebar or annex to what really matters in DHS—managing terrorism's prevention, protection, response, recovery, and mitigation.

Finally, this edition could not end without briefly examining the false alarm ICBM alert issued by Hawaii's Civil Defense (and emergency management) office on January 13, 2018. Many red flags were raised by this outrageous and disturbing incident. Resolving them will likely not bode well for state emergency management in Hawaii or for many other states nationwide.

WHAT HAS HAPPENED TO FEDERAL EMERGENCY MANAGEMENT?

The "phases (or cycles) of disaster management approach" (mitigation, preparedness, response, and recovery) has never been without critics. However, over the last 50 years, the phases/cycles approach has served many worthwhile purposes. Of course, teachers, students, and practitioners have understood that preparedness, response, and recovery overlap one another. And that it is admittedly difficult to identify where mitigation logically fits into the cycles or phases. The four-cycle approach, nevertheless, has evolved as predominant theory and practice (some in FEMA have labeled it "doctrine") in emergency management. DHS and FEMA today, though, have openly shelved the four-phase or -cycle approach and have replaced it with "**missions and capabilities**." Like a one-product industrial stamping plant, missions and capabilities are the department-wide basis for evaluation of all of DHS component offices. Too often the "missions" spring from the edicts or approvals of senior DHS officials rather than from the mythical grassroots local level of bygone years. Also alarming is that missions and capabilities have been suffused into the rules and conditions of DHS and FEMA grants to state and local governments.

DHS missions and capabilities indisputably give priority to counterterrorism, the paramount mission of DHS set forth in the Homeland Security Act of 2002. DHS began as a kind of "holding company" comprising some 22 so-called "legacy agencies," each doing separate jobs but in some semblance of cooperation with one another. Through the years, each agency has been gradually yoked into serving the department's terrorism mission foremost. Whatever missions or responsibilities these agencies had outside of terrorism prevention, protection, response, and apprehension became less important over time. Of course, DHS leaders realized that secondary (non-terror) duties performed with positive publicity helped enhance the image of DHS as a whole. What was not obvious when DHS began was that the department would morph into *de facto* appendages of the Pentagon, the national intelligence community, and federal law enforcement.

An old question used to be whether FEMA should remain inside the DHS or be returned to the independent agency status it enjoyed from 1979 to 2003. FEMA incorporation into DHS has had dramatic effects. The FEMA director, now called an "administrator," from 2003 through 2006 had no direct access to the president. Instead he had to go through an extra layer of DHS bureaucracy, and only then with the cooperation of the DHS secretary, could he get what was needed. Some claim "that even one extra layer has proved one too many in the critical moments."[2] Under the post–Hurricane Katrina Act of 2006, the FEMA administrator again has access to the president in times of disaster. However, the secretary of DHS also has direct access to the president. In formal terms, the DHS secretary is the FEMA administrator's supervisor.

Congress debated the FEMA "in or out" issue after Hurricane Katrina and elected to keep FEMA inside DHS. The George W. Bush, Barack Obama, and now Donald Trump administrations have supported, if not championed, this decision whenever the issue re-emerged. FEMA has been within DHS since 2003, so now there are considerable "sunk costs" that bind it to DHS. The National Response Framework (NRF) has interlaced homeland security with emergency management. Taking FEMA out of DHS might fracture administration of the NRF. DHS houses a massive set of expensive homeland security grant programs, and FEMA grant managers are involved in these programs. Most of this program funding is directed to terrorism, but dual-use components of these programs significantly benefit (but also distort) state and local emergency management. Over the past 15 years, FEMA has established linkages with other DHS offices. What will happen to these relationships if FEMA is moved out of DHS? At this writing, such a move seems highly unlikely. See the "Tell Me More" 10-1 box on this issue.

An even more speculative question might be what is the future of the DHS? Will Congress or a future president eventually pull DHS apart? Will DHS shrink under new laws or executive reorganizations? How will FEMA within DHS be affected by the downsizing of the department and the gradual conclusion of the U.S. "war on terrorism"? Only time will tell.

Credentials and Professionalization

The primacy of the DHS terrorism mission has had consequences for emergency management. For example, DHS, instead of widening the pool of professional emergency managers openly devoted to addressing hazards and disasters that befall all or parts of the nation, has put its emergency managers to work on things that narrow and divide the DHS-FEMA and state and local EM workforce. For example, DHS and FEMA have pressed for "**credentialing**" who can and who cannot respond to emergencies and disasters. Many DHS and FEMA workers today dedicate countless hours to creating training curricula, certification rules, and badging schemes.[3] Often even non-federal emergency responders must tolerate background checks, revalidation of their professional and education credentials, and field interviews of people who know

TELL ME MORE 10-1
PROS AND CONS OF IN OR OUT WORTH CONSIDERING

The U.S. Department of Homeland Security's Office of Inspector General prepared a report in February 2009 that examined the "pros and cons" of moving FEMA out of DHS and back to the independent federal agency status it had held from March 1979 until March 2003.[4] That report is well researched and written, but it is hardly objective. Unsurprisingly, the DHS OIG report basically argues the "con" position on the proposition that FEMA should be liberated from DHS and made independent once again. Many of the claims in the OIG report are well worth considering. Some of the strongest points of the report have been extracted and presented below. What follows is a pro and con debate aimed at provoking thought more than bias on the subject.

Pro-FEMA Out of DHS

Those who support the "pro" side of the argument, favoring pulling FEMA out of DHS, raise many worthwhile points.

Many of them lament the overwhelming effects DHS has had on the nature of the work FEMA is now tasked to do. FEMA has been reconstituted by the Post–Katrina Emergency Management Reform Act of 2006, but it still sits within a gigantic "security" agency composed of organizations that have little or nothing to do with emergency management. It is as if each hazard or disaster agent FEMA must address is a photograph arrayed in a scrapbook and DHS requires that the scrapbook reader remain fixed on only the "terrorism photographs." The International Association of Emergency Managers "formally adopted the position that FEMA's independent agency status should be restored, with the agency reporting directly to the president."[5]

It is ironic that the DHS OIG report quotes someone who claims that Clinton-era FEMA director James Lee Witt (see **Witt, James Lee, former FEMA director** in the Glossary) steered FEMA too much away from terrorism concerns.[6] Today that claim is completely reversed. That is, FEMA has been asked to address terrorism first and foremost,

with correspondingly less emphasis on non-terrorism disaster mitigation and preparedness.

Con-FEMA Out of DHS

Consider these claims from the "con" side. The DHS OIG report reminds us that "FEMA underwent several transformations between 2001 and 2005, but the most significant by far was the transfer of its functions, personnel, resources, and authorities to the Emergency Preparedness and Response Directorate of the newly-created Department of Homeland Security. Shortly after the transfer, members of the emergency management community began complaining that DHS was stripping FEMA of its authorities and resources, and that the department's overwhelming focus on terrorism, to the detriment of attention to natural disasters, was hurting morale. Critics argued that FEMA was beginning to suffer a 'brain drain,' losing experienced professionals in all aspects of emergency management. In late summer of 2005, when Hurricane Katrina hit the Gulf Coast, FEMA's division directors for preparedness, response, and recovery had left; FEMA had 500 vacancies; and 8 of its 10 regional offices were headed by 'acting' directors."[7]

Pro-FEMA Out of DHS

The preceding OIG paragraph will not be contested. In many ways, FEMA was transferred into DHS under conditions akin to a corporate hostile takeover. The clear intent was to terminate the agency. Not long after FEMA went into DHS, FEMA Administrator Michael Brown (see **Brown, Michael D., former FEMA administrator** in the Glossary) had to argue vociferously to save the agency's actual name. Roberts discloses that the George W. Bush White House had originally planned for FEMA to join DHS but at the same time the FEMA director would get cabinet-level appointee status. However, as it turned out, the president and Congress moved FEMA into DHS but as a much smaller unit headed by a "mid-level bureaucrat."[8] The FEMA director also lost authority to reorganize the agency.

Con-FEMA Out of DHS

The DHS OIG document continues, "In October 2006, the Post-Katrina Emergency Management Reform Act was signed into law. The Act contained provisions that directly addressed what were perceived as the major shortcomings of FEMA and its response to Hurricane Katrina. The Act made FEMA a distinct entity within DHS and placed restrictions on actions that the Secretary of DHS can take affecting FEMA, directed that the FEMA Administrator [sometimes referred to as FEMA Director] report directly to the (DHS) Secretary, created a direct line of communication between the FEMA Administrator and the President during times of emergency, and restored to FEMA many of the functions that had been transferred to other parts of the department."[9]

Pro-FEMA Out of DHS

What the DHS OIG report overlooks is that the 2005 pre-Katrina FEMA was a demoralized shell of what it had been before its incorporation into DHS. Moreover, many of the more egregious errors in the Katrina response can be attributed in part to DHS units (other than FEMA) that poorly mobilized, mired the federal response in security restrictions, failed to coordinate well with one another and with federal entities outside of DHS, and which bungled or "big-footed" their interactions with state and local governments impacted by the hurricane, storm surge, levee failures, and ensuing floods.

Moreover, a positive is return of FEMA administrator direct access to the president in 2006. However, no FEMA administrator would today attempt direct White House access without first notifying the DHS secretary. In at least one disaster of the post-Katrina George W. Bush administration, television viewers were able to watch real-time news video of the FEMA administrator sitting next to the president offering commentary on the event. While this visually confirmed or symbolized that the FEMA administrator again had direct White House access, it did not necessarily represent the best use of the FEMA administrator's time during the disaster response phase. Worse still, the DHS secretary was filmed in the field near the disaster zone engaged in supervisory work.

Con-FEMA Out of DHS

The DHS OIG may have made its strongest "con" arguments in these passages. The talk of removing FEMA from DHS generally focuses on the perceived benefits to FEMA—on which not all sides agree. What is not always included in the debate is consideration of the effect that FEMA's removal would have on the department. Since 2003, a number of support functions for the different components of DHS have been interwoven.[10] A reorganization would impact not only FEMA, which would have to reconstitute itself as a stand-alone agency, but also DHS as a whole, which would have to adjust to losing an important component. "A primary benefit to FEMA of being part of the 200,000-plus (270,000 by 2018) person Department of Homeland Security is the wealth of resources available to FEMA through other DHS components. These connections create synergies that were never available to FEMA as a stand-alone agency. In DHS, FEMA is coupled with components that have far-reaching responsibilities and capabilities, including search and rescue, communications, law enforcement, intelligence, and infrastructure protection."[11]

Pro-FEMA Out of DHS

Clearly, FEMA has been "interwoven" into the fabric of DHS; granted, it is unclear how much FEMA has merged with immensely larger DHS organizations such as the Transportation Security Administration, U.S. Customs and Border Protection, U.S. Citizenship and Immigration Services, and U.S. Immigration and Customs Enforcement. While FEMA interrelationships with the U.S. Coast Guard (also part of DHS) provide leveraged mutual benefits for each agency, less obvious benefits flow from FEMA relationships with the U.S. Secret Service, the former Federal Protective Service, and the National Protection and Programs Directorate. Even more bizarre is FEMA's engagement with organizations engaged in crime control, animal and plant health inspection, and infrastructure protection. It is also difficult to envision how much emergency management knowledge is being absorbed by those working in national security and law enforcement-focused DHS offices like these.[12]

(Continued)

(Continued)

However, in its absorption into DHS, FEMA was assigned a wider portfolio of national security duties. For example, FEMA picked up the former Justice Department's (DOJ) Office of Domestic Preparedness and DOJ's Domestic Emergency Support Teams, the Energy Department's Nuclear Incident Response Team, and the FBI's National Domestic Preparedness Office. This augments FEMA's already considerable duties in continuity of government, off-site nuclear power plant regulation, and emergency communications. Emergency management purists may be happy to have FEMA freed of these duties by departing DHS, but national security duties, in various degrees, have always been part of FEMA's portfolio of responsibilities. Some of those duties help draw the agency closer to the president, while others serve to compartmentalize the agency and invite internal office competition for personnel and budget funds.

Con-FEMA Out of DHS

The DHS OIG document states, "The Government Accountability Office (GAO) has cited areas of interconnectedness, including grants, through which Urban Area Security Initiative (UASI) and State Homeland Security Program (SHSP) funding can be used for mass evacuation planning; interoperable communications; **DHS Science & Technology** expertise for the Equipment Standards Program; and a huge surge capacity of personnel that can be tapped in case of a disaster."[13]

In responding to Hurricanes Gustav and Ike (both with landfalls in September 2008) the OIG writes, "FEMA was supported by all of the elements and all the powers of the Department of Homeland Security." CBP (Customs and Border Protection) provided security for the transit of life-sustaining goods and provided aerial assets that allowed surveying of damage. In the past, FEMA relied on DOD for aerial surveillance, which cost considerably more than using CBP. TSA (Transportation Security Administration) supported 20 FEMA commodity distribution locations, augmenting FEMA staff with 366 additional employees in the field. The Coast Guard performed land, maritime, and air search-and-rescue missions.

Pro-FEMA Out of DHS

Admittedly, local evacuation plans funded in part by UASI funds, or by a fraction of SHSP funds, could facilitate local evacuations made necessary by natural disaster threats and realities. The irony is that many national security focused UASI and SHSP plans are routinely kept out of the view of the public for, you guessed it, national security reasons. Too many of those plans are rarely seen beyond a small pool of security clearance–holding officials.

FEMA has since 1979 needed a larger, more sophisticated, and apolitical science and technology shop, even though FEMA's National Fire Administration engages in excellent fire-related S&T work. It is a mixed blessing that the DHS Science and Technology directorate is now a FEMA supporting office. Indisputably, a FEMA S&T capacity would benefit that agency in the realm of preventing cyber-security attacks that could cause disasters, for example. But what FEMA could truly benefit from is an in-house capacity to do open research of hazards on the scale done by the National Institute of Standards and Technology, the disaster research arm of the National Science Foundation, the U.S. EPA, the Commerce Department's National Weather Service, the National Hurricane Center, and the National Severe Storm Laboratory, plus the U.S. Geological Survey and the earth telemetry side of NASA satellite work, and more.

Con-FEMA Out of DHS

The DHS OIG study claims in a long passage that because FEMA's grants management office now handles funds appropriated for other DHS offices, FEMA should not be moved out of DHS owing to the disruption this would cause.[14]

Pro-FEMA Out of DHS

The claim above rests on reverse logic. When PKREMA ordered DHS to return to FEMA its grants office, few understood that it was coming back as a "Trojan horse." By running so many alien program funds through FEMA's grants office, powerful policymakers and DHS officials hoped to consolidate FEMA into its team of sundry security organizations. This may be an overstatement, but it is an argument worth considering. (See Figure 10-1 on page 398.)

them. The DHS system is rife with the issuance of many "waivers" that exempt various senior fire chiefs and chiefs of police, even though such waivers are issued less frequently for rank and file emergency responders. In-person and online "training" requirements are being used to purge out those who do not "buy-in" to the new DHS conception of "emergency management."

Today federal, state, and local government emergency managers are not "professionalized," as much as coached (as opposed to educated), vetted, programmed, and somewhat militarized. Understanding and mastering emergency management under a system of security restrictions and bureaucratic rules diminishes the role of higher education in their work. DHS and FEMA workers are today expected to understand a colossal and overly complex body of interlinked planning frameworks. Today federal emergency managers are thought to be appropriately educated if they can parrot back elements of the planning frameworks. Some expedient instructors and bodies of higher education are now issuing course credits for classes exclusively devoted to learning the details of national preparedness plans. These master documents are billed as serving a national preparedness goal. The prevention, protection, mitigation, response, and recovery frameworks, the so-called "suite of frameworks," are already elephantine. DHS and FEMA officials tinker with these frameworks almost daily always adding, but rarely removing, duties, obligations, and directions. Common passages in these plans are collections of "thou shalts" and "thou shall nots." Given the immense size and complexity of the suites frameworks, the plans risk becoming, in sociological language, "**fantasy documents**."[15]

Some may think these claims are exaggerated. Consider a small segment of the DHS National Protection Framework. The audience for this is DHS's "whole community" but most particularly for a subset of officials responsible for protecting vital interests, operations, and structures. Here are some "critical tasks":

- Deter movement and operation of terrorists into or within the United States and its territories

- Ensure the capacity to detect CBRNE devices or resolve CBRNE threats

- Interdict conveyances, cargo, and persons associated with a potential threat or act

- Implement public health measures to mitigate the spread of disease threats abroad and prevent disease threats from crossing national borders

- Disrupt terrorist financing or conduct counter-acquisition activities to prevent weapons, precursors, related technology, or other material support from reaching its target

- Enhance the visible presence of law enforcement to deter or disrupt threats from reaching potential target(s)

- Intervene to protect against the spread of violent extremism within U.S. communities

- Employ wide-area search and detection assets in targeted areas in concert with local, regional/metropolitan, state, tribal, territorial, insular area, and federal personnel or other federal agencies (depending on the threat)[16]

These "critical tasks" are wildly infeasible for people working or serving outside of law enforcement. In some respects, these shibboleths seem to shift responsibility for terrorism prevention from DHS to parties who are ill-equipped, unqualified, and unauthorized to fulfill the tasks. In many ways, these tasks are even beyond the mission and capacity of local law enforcement.

The transformation of DHS and FEMA into what it is today cannot be blamed on any single past or current president. In June 2009, Dr. Janet Napolitano, President Obama's DHS secretary, explained, "Yet, nearly five months into my tenure, the purpose of our Department is unambiguous: we must guard against terrorism; we must secure our borders; we must enforce our immigration laws; we must improve our readiness for, response to, and recovery from disasters; and we must unify the Department so that we can even more effectively carry out our mission."[17] She also said, "Finally, we must unify and mature our Department. *Our goal is simple: one DHS, one enterprise, a shared vision, with integrated results-based operations.* Through a consolidated headquarters, we are bringing 35 locations together. We have launched an expansive efficiency initiative that is leveraging the economies of scale in our Department in order to recover hundreds of millions of dollars and create a culture of responsibility and fiscal discipline. . . . [W]e are applying a series of cross-cutting approaches. We are bolstering cooperation with our partners at the local, tribal, state, federal and international levels; we are expanding our capabilities through the deployment of science and technology while developing and maturing new technologies for tomorrow; and we are maximizing efficiency to ensure every security dollar is spent in the most effective way."[18]

Follow the Money

Asked how they were able to break the Watergate case against President Nixon in the 1970s, *Washington Post* reporters Robert Woodward and Carl Bernstein replied in three words, "follow the money." One reason why FEMA is today tethered into serving so many purposes unrelated to emergency management is because of the implications of a money-related provision of the Post–Katrina Emergency Management Reform Act of 2006 (PKREMA). In the months after the 2001 attacks on 9/11, President George W. Bush reluctantly agreed under heavy congressional pressure to create through law the U.S. Department of Homeland Security. Former Bush FEMA director, Joseph Allbaugh (see **Allbaugh, Joseph, former FEMA directo**r in the Glossary), a critic of what he considered FEMA's profligate spending on disaster victims, prepared to step down once FEMA was officially embedded within DHS. Those who charted how and where FEMA would fit within DHS got the idea that FEMA's Grants Office should be moved up and out of the agency and into a higher, more central place within DHS. This move was enshrined in law. However, it came to impair FEMA's operations in a variety of ways. FEMA's role in managing and issuing between-disaster grants and post-disaster grants to state and local governments was confounded and undermined by this change. Ever since April 1979 when FEMA opened its doors, the agency has used the terms of grant conditions to advance disaster management and policy. Shifting management of FEMA's grants programs to a DHS-wide core office outside of FEMA weakened the agency's ability to guide state and local government emergency management work.

However, when Hurricane Katrina struck in 2005, DHS and FEMA were roundly criticized for poor situational awareness, a slow response, and poor preparation.[19] When DHS was formed, FEMA was one of its few agencies to have long-established relationships with state and local government. U.S. Citizenship and Immigration Services, U.S. Customs and Border Protection, U.S. Immigration and Customs Enforcement, the Transportation Security Administration, National Protection and Programs Directorate, the Federal Protective Service, the U.S. Secret Service, and other DHS offices, with the possible exception of the U.S. Coast Guard, could not match FEMA's network of inter-relationships with states and local government.

In their 2006 effort to correct mistakes that had been made in designing DHS and FEMA's place therein, lawmakers may have overcompensated. As mentioned, in PKREMA of 2006, Congress moved the Grants Office back to FEMA. When it was returned, that office now had a panoply of grants management duties in service of other DHS components. While FEMA officials may have celebrated the return of their old grants office, many may not have appreciated what managing this office now meant.

Figure 10-1 is a graphic timeline showing the organizational history of homeland security assistance programs from 1996 through 2008. DOD is the Department of Defense; NLD is the Nunn-Lugar-Domenici program approved under the Defense Against Weapons of Mass Destruction Act of 1996. TPG stands for Terrorism Preparedness Grants, and AHG is short for All-Hazards Grants. The graphic shows that when DHS was formed in 2003, it embodied a FEMA that still had management control of its all-hazard grant programs. However, by 2004, responsibility for AHG programs was moved up to the Office of Secretary of Homeland Security. Note, as well, the DHS Border and Transportation Security Directorate was relieved of its control of Terrorism Preparedness Grants when TPG was moved to the Office of the Secretary.

As CRS researcher Shawn Reese indicates, "ODP was transferred to DHS with enactment of the Homeland Security Act of 2002. Initially, ODP and its terrorism preparedness programs were administered by the Border and Transportation Security Directorate, and all-hazard preparedness programs were in the Federal Emergency Management Agency (FEMA). ODP and all preparedness assistance programs were transferred to the Office of the Secretary in DHS in 2004. After investigations into the problematic response to Hurricane Katrina, the programs were transferred to the National Preparedness Directorate. Currently all programs and activities are administered by the Grants Program Directorate (GPD) within FEMA."[20]

The point of these observations about federal organizational history is that it followed this track:

- 1996 to 2002—FEMA administered its own grant programs.

- 2003—FEMA saw its grant program management shifted upward to the Office of the Secretary.

- 2005—Hurricane Katrina reveals the flaws in separating FEMA from its grant programs.

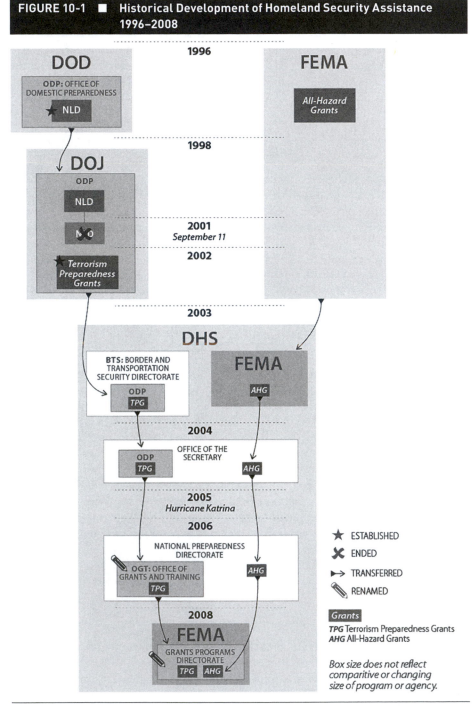

FIGURE 10-1 ■ Historical Development of Homeland Security Assistance 1996–2008

Source: Shawn Reese, "Department of Homeland Security Preparedness Grants: A Summary and Issues," *Congressional Research Service*, October 28, 2016, p. 3, https://fas.org/sgp/crs/homesec/R44669.pdf (accessed July 2, 2018).

- 2006—The DHS National Preparedness Directorate wins control of all-hazards grants management as well as control of the Office of Grants & Training, which manages terrorism preparedness grants.

- 2008—owing largely to provisions of the Post–Katrina Emergency Management Reform Act of 2006, FEMA regains control of its all-hazards grant program located in FEMA's Grants Program Directorate. This same directorate was also assigned management of terrorism preparedness grants.

The FEMA Grants Program Directorate now manages both all-hazard grants and terrorism preparedness grants. Had FEMA merely won back its AHG authority, it may have been able to concentrate on its mainstream duties in emergency management. However, by also entrusting a FEMA directorate with terrorism preparedness grant management, FEMA has been recast as a multitasking homeland security grants management agency.

Chapters 6 and 7 examined the State Homeland Security program, the Urban Area Security Initiative, and the Law Enforcement Terrorism Prevention Activities program. These mammoth grant programs now flow through the offices of FEMA. This has to have had a profound impact on how FEMA officials and workers now see themselves. Figure 10-2 provides a visual of the relative funding size of DHS grant programs directed to state and local governments from federal FY 2002 through FY 2016. One cannot help but notice that the Homeland Security Grant Program (HSGP), which combines HSGP, UASI, Operation Stonegarden, and by FY 2008, LETPA funding, FEMA's traditional Emergency Management Program Grants (EMPG in the bottom row) pales in comparison, even though its funding remains either level or tracks slightly upward. Other DHS grant programs of note in Figure 10-2 are the Port Security Grant program (PSGP), the Transportation Security Grant program (TSGP), and the Tribal Homeland Security Grant program (THSGP). Some of the smaller grant programs of Figure 10-2 ending in 2011 may have been shifted to other federal departments, folded into larger grant programs, or terminated.

Political Upheaval and DHS

Recently, throughout 2018, there has been news of protestors and certain elected government officials publicly demonstrating and advocating for the shutdown of the Immigration and Customs Enforcement (ICE) agency owing to its role in implementing President Trump's "zero tolerance" immigration policy. For a time, part of that policy involved separating parents from children as undocumented families struggled to prove they deserved asylum in the United States. Some ICE program funding today passes through FEMA and its grant office. Beyond this, through the Law Enforcement Terrorism Prevention Activities Act and initiatives like Operation Stonegarden, FEMA is intrinsically part of border control, immigration enforcement, crime prevention, fusion center operations, infrastructure counterterrorism protection, and much more. At minimum, FEMA's mission has been, as former DHS secretary Napolitano remarked, "integrated" into DHS's greater nexus of operations. Perhaps Clinton FEMA director James Lee Witt had great foresight when he warned against implanting FEMA within DHS, thus ending FEMA's independent agency life and arguably distorting and diminishing its emergency management mission.

FIGURE 10-2 ■   Individual DHS Assistance for States and Localities, FY 2002–FY 2016

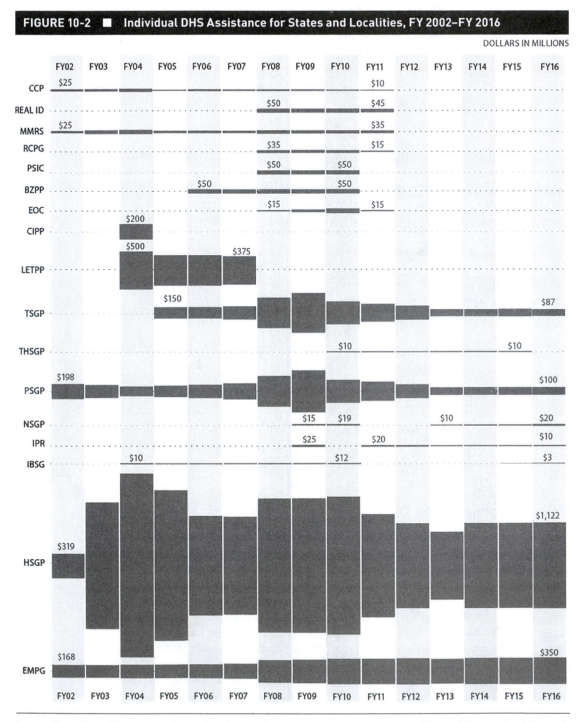

Source: Shawn Reese, "Department of Homeland Security Preparedness Grants: A Summary and Issues," Congressional Research Service, October 28, 2016, p. 15, https://fas.org/sgp/crs/homesec/R44669.pdf (accessed July 2, 2018).

American disaster policy rests on laws, regulations, rules, public–private contracts, intergovernmental relations, insurance, civil–military relations, science and technology, altruistic organizations, and countless volunteers. People do not have to become emergency managers or emergency responders to understand and appreciate the policy and politics of disaster, but they would be wise to have an open-minded grasp of what emergency management entails.

There is great need for full-time professional emergency managers in government who are able to direct an emergency management program, able in times of crisis to advise the elected or appointed executives they work under or with, and able to lead or coordinate the efforts of those working in their own and other organizations. The nation is fortunate to have many officials with these abilities. They can be found working at all levels of government, and they often work closely with public executives, governors, mayors, city managers, county executives, and the like.[21]

Disasters are episodic, but at the same time, they are increasingly predictable and, in some respects, inevitable. Tolerated vulnerabilities to known natural hazards often allow natural forces to inflict upon people and their property disastrous effects. When this happens, it may be better to refer to them as "unnatural" disasters. In 2010, the UN and the World Bank published a book titled *Natural Hazards and Unnatural Disasters*,[22] a work that implored senior officials of all governments to advance disaster mitigation and limit vulnerabilities to natural hazards.

Do Americans Expect Too Much?

Early in 2001, President George W. Bush's FEMA director, Joseph Allbaugh, testified before Congress that federal disaster assistance was "an oversized entitlement program and a disincentive to effective state and local risk management."[23] It was an overstatement to be sure, but many Americans expect the federal government to be the insurer of last resort for the disaster misfortunes they experience. This expectation is justifiable, especially in periods of crisis and economic anxiety. The expectation is subject to challenge when Americans fail to buy available insurance to help protect themselves against known risks to their life and property, particularly when they were aware of the risks and had the means to purchase the insurance.

For example, the National Flood Insurance Program (NFIP), discussed earlier in this book, has some worthwhile features that serve to help those whose homes and businesses are vulnerable to flood. Yet, too few Americans have purchased National Flood Insurance policies. And although many local governments across the United States participate in the NFIP, many of those governments have not gone far enough to discourage development in their floodplains or along their coasts and have not done enough to relocate structures from floodplains and from coastal storm surges and tidal flooding.

According to an article in *Forbes* magazine, "Recognizing that households do not (cannot) buy private flood insurance, the Federal government has long offered, under the National Flood Insurance Program administered by FEMA, subsidized flood policies. In some parts of the country, homeowners are buying these, but not in Texas. In Houston's Harris County, one of the hardest hit Texas counties in Hurricane Harvey), only 15% of homes have flood insurance. And in the coastal Corpus Christi vicinity, only 20% are covered. Simply put, many people . . . affected by Hurricane Harvey who were not required by mortgage lenders to buy flood insurance chose not to, despite the subsidies."[24] In effect, "Homeowners will have to bear their own losses because the great majority of them did not buy flood insurance. Despite living in the projected path of storms, most Houston area residents failed to add flood coverage to their property insurance policies. How could property owners be so careless? Private flood insurance is not cheap. Standard insurance policies cover losses from fire, theft, and even high winds, but these are relatively inexpensive. In contrast, flood coverage in coastal areas would be very costly and could easily raise an annual premium by $5000 on a typical policy that otherwise costs less than $1000."[25]

Homeowner's insurance policies in many U.S. coastal areas are becoming prohibitively expensive. Many homeowners have not adequately insured their homes against the hazards they reasonably face. Residential earthquake insurance in documented seismically active zones is often woefully inadequate. Wind, fire, property, casualty, business continuity, accident, and workers' compensation insurance coverage are often insufficient in many states and localities. Insufficiency is often two pronged. Private insurers choose not to market high-risk policies for disaster coverage, fearing that when the worst transpires, claims will be filed in overwhelming numbers in too short a time interval. Correspondingly, those who need to buy the insurance often elect not to purchase policies owing to high premiums, high deductibles, difficulty in collecting on claims, low confidence in the viability of the insurer, or for other reasons. Insurance is an important tool of both disaster preparedness and disaster mitigation, but it is often a tool only selectively used.

Public and private insurance is assuming a much larger role in people's relationships with disasters and emergencies. Creative applications of insurance instruments and in-force policies, both in the United States and in other nations, help unburden governments and their people from absorbing both great risk and great disaster costs. Americans may expect too much help when disaster strikes, yet they are gaining more awareness of the risks and vulnerabilities they face. Government regulation of private insurers in the United States remains an unevenly handled state-level responsibility. Yet oddly it is the federal government and the national taxpayer who are expected to fill the breach when insurance and charity cannot shoulder post-disaster demands.

Winners and Losers in Disaster Policy

Hurricane Katrina in 2005, Superstorm Sandy in 2012, and Hurricanes Harvey, Irma, and Maria of 2017 have reminded Americans that disasters often have profound effects on people who are poor or who are struggling to make ends meet. Disaster relief, especially long-term recovery relief to assist in rebuilding, relocation, and economic revival, is also a matter of **antipoverty social policy** for the nation. As Jim Wallis once said, "Sometimes it takes a natural disaster to reveal a social disaster."[26]

Many sociological studies have analyzed and described the problems of poverty, ethnic and racial discrimination, ageism, gender bias, and gay and lesbian discrimination associated with all phases of disaster.[27] In the United States, disaster policy is "conservative" in the sense that the aim of disaster relief is to return damaged areas, and disaster victims themselves, to the condition they were in before the disaster, albeit with some provision for mitigation against the possible repeat of the same type of disaster in the future.

Accounting for Disaster Deaths

Furthermore, FEMA has long resisted compiling information about the number of fatalities attributable directly or indirectly to declared major disasters and emergencies. They refer those who ask for this information to the American Red Cross, which unfortunately does not collect and publicly present such information on a county-by-county or state-by-state basis. Given the controversy about how many people actually perished in Puerto Rico as a direct or indirect result of Hurricane Maria, Congress and the president may compel FEMA to compile such information during and after future declared incidents.

Why would FEMA resist compiling information on disaster fatalities? There are many reasons. Agency officials may worry that disaster response and recovery spending will be statistically associated with fatality figures. The agency may worry about what victim profiles have to say about the effectiveness of government disaster response and mitigation efforts. The U.S. and state public health and medical communities conduct exceptionally good recordkeeping about cause of death. However, few U.S. trust or commonwealth territories can make the same claim.

Examining the forensics about how disaster victims perished, although necessary and important, carries a tremendously controversial downside for FEMA. It is fair to say that FEMA officials, past and present, do not relish being held accountable for changes in death rates from one major disaster or emergency to the next. While the agency promotes disaster mitigation assiduously, FEMA people do not want to be judged for how well, or for how poorly, they "reduce fatality counts" in future disasters. Congress and the president may need to enact a new federal law that compels FEMA to compile disaster fatality figures. Another fear is that disaster death counts may be factored into cost–benefit analyses regarding where federal mitigation and preparedness dollars should go: a valuation of life matter.

Addressing Disaster Survivor Needs

Victims of disaster usually expect and often demand full replacement of their damaged private property. Several chapters of this edition explored government programs regarding disaster victim compensation. Lawyer James L. Jaffe's 2015 book, *Financial Preparation and Recovery: Disaster Dollars*, is a remarkable manual of information regarding federal disaster assistance made available to state and local governments, businesses, farms, and individuals.[28] Nonetheless, what happens when victims do not receive all they think they deserve?

People sometimes die in disasters. Why should families of those who perished in certain spectacular high-fatality terror disasters get so much government and charitable help when families who lost loved ones in other disasters, including some less deadly terror disasters, rarely receive as much government and charitable assistance? Clearly, the horror and uniqueness of the 9/11 attack and the loss of nearly 3,000 people may account for the distinction Congress chose to make between that disaster and others since.[29]

Receiving more or receiving less after a disaster embodies other issues. Individual preparedness and "individual responsibility" are two mantras of emergency management. How is someone to gauge his or her vulnerability? Do individuals consciously engage in disaster risk-taking behavior, or is this a myth propounded by critics of heavy government disaster spending? Who is responsible for natural hazard risk assessment, and what is done about its results? Are people who work or live in high-rise buildings engaging in behavior that puts them at high risk of terrorism? Are people who live or work in or near national monuments or other symbols of U.S. power engaging in high-risk behavior?

In times of disaster, it is only natural for the survivors of those events to ask for and expect help. That help often comes in many forms. Federal, state, and local law and policy is to provide assistance and relief for some, but not all, types of individual and family losses. Government disaster managers tend to talk in terms of meeting the after-disaster needs of victims. State and local governments, with substantial federal subsidization, will repair, replace, and restore disaster-damaged infrastructure; FEMA even pays to replace or repair equipment and facilities owned and operated by privately owned utilities. However, U.S. disaster law and policy are neither designed nor intended to make disaster victims "whole" after a disaster. Those working for charitable organizations recognize this, and so they often seek to fill gaps or unmet needs of disaster survivors through their own aid programs.

Moreover, American social and political cultural norms maintain that people need to make provision for possible disaster losses by purchasing insurance as a hedge. Overly generous government disaster relief would undercut the private market as well as the market for National Flood Insurance. In addition, the American political culture manifests an aversion to government-promoted "moral hazard" behavior. Moral hazard applies when overly generous government disaster relief provided to victims encourages them to engage in hazard risk-taking behavior (e.g., building homes in high-risk locations vulnerable to failure during earthquakes, heavy rains, or floods; constructing homes and other structures in coastal high-hazard "V zones" subject to hurricanes and storm surges; erecting shopping malls and other businesses in known floodplains).

Nevertheless, the American government has tried to discourage moral hazard behavior and tolerance of risks that produce social inequities and injustices. Policymakers are forced to revisit this issue after many disasters, as was the case when the September 11 Victim's Compensation Fund was established. A long-standing issue likely to reemerge in the future is the wisdom of creating a national "all-hazards" insurance program through which Americans could reasonably insure themselves against the full range of disaster hazards they face. Private insurers and reinsurance firms would have to be satisfied that government was not "nationalizing" their casualty and property insurance lines, state government insurance regulation might have to be preempted by the federal government, and the government would have to deny government disaster relief to those who could have purchased all-hazards insurance and did not.[30]

In the United States, just as in most nations that espouse democracy, disaster policy is a product of law, public management, and political decision making. For America, disaster policy is distributive politics (introduced in Chapter 4) in the sense that costs of disaster recovery are shouldered nationally (with significant payouts by state and local governments experiencing the disaster), whereas benefits (aid dispensed) are concentrated at the sub-state and local levels. U.S. disaster policy is modestly redistributive politics (also introduced in Chapter 4) in that taxpayers living in areas with few presidentially declared disasters tend to subsidize taxpayers living in areas with many presidentially declared disasters.

Some disasters transfer resources from low-income taxpayers to high-income taxpayers. Disaster federal and state relief to high- and middle-income victims suffering loss of their coastal homes and properties, or loss of their properties in other high-hazard zones (floodplains, mountainsides, wildland areas vulnerable to fire, and the like), often eclipses relief payouts to low-income disaster victims. Wealthy people obviously stand to lose more because they have more to lose. But, also, wealthy people often freely choose to take greater risks in where they buy property and build, and they often purchase insurance to cushion any losses they may sustain from anticipated disaster forces. Certain losses sustained by the wealthy, and which were not covered by their insurance policies, may be eligible for federal disaster assistance if their property is located in a county included in a presidential declaration of major disaster. However, many categories of the FEMA Individuals and Households Program (IHP) require applicants to qualify through means-testing rules. Those whose incomes or total assets exceed a certain inflation controlled annual threshold are not allowed to receive certain forms of FEMA assistance, and those people are steered to the U.S. Small Business Administration (SBA) or other agencies to apply for disaster loans.

Volunteers in Disasters

When do volunteers and volunteer organizations make important contributions to disaster relief and recovery, and when do they complicate or impede emergency response and recovery? These questions will likely come up again in the near future.

Volunteers, especially through nonprofit organizations active in disasters, are hugely important in disasters. They are often the first on the scene, they frequently aid responders, they are there in varying degrees to help victims during the response and recovery, and their accounts of events are often presented by news organizations.

The rise of social media has made it immensely easy for emergency managers and others to mobilize small armies of volunteers of all ages on very short notice. There is a national proliferation of government-sponsored or -encouraged volunteer organizations, such as FEMA's Citizen's Corps and Community Emergency Response Teams. They are dedicated to educating and training unpaid volunteers for disaster management work. In public administrative parlance, this is known as *co-production* in provision of service delivery. Voluntarism helps public agencies meet goals and objectives at lower cost. Skilled volunteers are hugely beneficial to the advancement of emergency management and to the political support of improved disaster policy. In disaster policy and politics, volunteers, particularly those serving formal organizations, are a political force to be reckoned with.

FOR-PROFIT CONTRACTORS, SLAPP LAWSUITS, WHISTLEBLOWING, AND SCIENCE INTEGRITY

Many chapters of this edition have spotlighted the billions that federal, state, and local governments have obligated or spent on disaster response and recovery since 2014. What was not made apparent was that a growing share of this funding has gone, and is going, to for-profit contractors retained by federal, state, and local governments. Moreover, under FEMA mission assignment, many federal agencies outside DHS have been provided spending authority that, under competitive and/or sole source bidding, has been awarded to various businesses. Two things most Americans seldom realize: (1) For-profit federal contractors are allowed to build in a 20 percent profit when they are hired by "Uncle Sam"; and (2) politically appointed top tier officials in the contract issuing government agency often have a say, or influence, with regard to which firm wins or loses a contract.

Researching federal contractors is difficult and sometimes dangerous. Like almost all private companies, for-profit contractors enjoy proprietary protection of their trade secrets. What they choose to tell the public about themselves is largely up to them. If they compete for and win government contracts from federal, state, or local public agencies, they are legally obligated to comply with the many conditions of those contracts. Therefore, the government contract-related work that they do requires that they make reports, often quarterly, to the government that has issued them the contract. These firms must submit to government audits of the contract money they have received. In many respects, tens of thousands of big and small contractors and subcontractors are paid to act in place of direct government provision of products and services. Holding these businesses accountable to taxpayers, whose money they expend, is difficult in the extreme. Many provide value-for-dollar and perform admirable work; some do not. Some firms have found business opportunities in facilitating application for FEMA assistance.

Here is an example. "Veoci is the future of collaboration, operations, and response software. Through rapid development, depth of knowledge, innovative thinking, and commitment to diversity, we help people whose job is to save time, money, and lives. The innovative Veoci cloud platform is used in a wide range of industries spanning governments, airports, hospitals, universities and finance, providing solutions for Emergency Management, Social Services, Daily Operations, Business Continuity and Special Event Management. All FEMA reimbursements are completed seamlessly as all of your important information regarding completed projects, equipment/resources used, and people involved are in one central location. These details are documented during the emergency rather than after. Printable FEMA forms are available for quick and efficient completion, with all information accurate and centralized. In the case of a federally declared emergency, the cost of the many teams, equipment, vehicles and other resources used can be reimbursed by FEMA. This requires careful tracking and documentation of all work done and resources utilized."[31]

Researching disaster service or contractor businesses can be risky for individual researchers and investigative reporters. Many of the largest firms have in-house legal counsel or retain major private law firms who are adept at squelching investigations they do not like. Consider "strategic lawsuits against public participation" (SLAPP) as an example of a legal weapon sometimes used by government contractors.

SLAPPs have become an all-too-common tool for intimidating and silencing critics of businesses. "When a plaintiff brings a SLAPP lawsuit against someone attempting to exercise their right of free speech, it is usually under the guise of a defamation claim. The goal of plaintiffs in these cases is not necessarily to actually win the lawsuit, but to drag their critics to court and bury them under a pile of attorney's fees and embarrassment until they cry 'uncle!' and agree to be quiet. SLAPPs aren't just random meritless lawsuits, they are lawsuits that directly attack First Amendment rights."[32] Several giant energy companies have used SLAPP lawsuits to fend off public criticism and silence climate change activists and their groups. A few federal lawmakers are considering anti-SLAPP bills, but there is little chance such measures will become law anytime soon.

Also worrisome for emergency managers is that those who identify corporate or government wrongdoing and attempt to act on this through "whistleblowing" are discovering serious erosion in protections that they used to have. Add to this an article in *Science*, which warns, "With the new Donald J. Trump Administration comes uncertainty in the role that science will play in the U.S. federal government. Early indications that the Administration plans to distort or disregard science and evidence, coupled with the chaos and confusion occurring within federal agencies, now imperil the effectiveness of our government. Evidence from the past 20 years demonstrates that, when faced with such threats, supporters of science can take steps to protect the integrity of science in the federal policy-making process. The scientific community will need to connect science-informed policy to positive outcomes and staunchly defend scientific freedom. It must also spotlight political interference in science-based policy development and be prepared to protect scientists—both within and outside the government—against executive or legislative overreach. A range of scientific integrity and transparency policies across federal agencies provides critical tools but must be enforced and protected."[33]

The Rise of Resilience

The concept of resilience has found many advocates in the emergency management community. **Disaster resilience** is at the heart of the National Disaster Recovery Framework (NDRF). Resilience has many meanings, but it is well suited to the sociotechnical world of emergency management. *Designing Resilience for Communities at Risk: Sociotechnical Approaches* is an excellent and far-ranging treatment of the subject.[34]

The National Academies published *Disaster Resilience: A National Imperative*, which aims to promote the values of resilience at the individual, household, community, and national levels.[35] The report seeks to develop a scorecard and set of metrics by which disaster resilience may be measured over time. More of the world of emergency management will most definitely include greater efforts to advance disaster resilience. With the increasing frequency of natural and human-induced disasters and the increasing magnitude of their consequences, a clear need exists for governments and communities to become more resilient. The report also addressed the importance of resilience, the challenges in advancing it, and approaches for building resilience in addition to outlining steps for implementing resilience efforts in communities and within government. Financial resilience after disasters has also been a worthy subject of research.[36] Today FEMA has a Resilience Directorate.[37]

THE HAWAII NUCLEAR ATTACK ALERT SNAFU AND ITS IMPLICATIONS

Reporter Jim McKay wrote that the **Hawaii false ballistic missile alert** that terrified the islands' residents and visitors for 38 minutes prompted some self-evaluation among state officials of emergency management on the mainland. The alert, issued by the Hawaii Emergency Management Agency on January 13, 2018, warned of an inbound missile and wasn't corrected until 38 minutes later. It happened because a staffer had simply clicked on a wrong link.[38]

FIGURE 10-3 ■ The Hawaii Nuclear Attack False Warning

Source: Emergency Alert System.

An early-morning emergency alert (see Figure 10-3) mistakenly warning of an incoming ballistic missile attack was dispatched to smartphones across Hawaii on Saturday, January 13, setting off widespread fear in a state that was already on edge because of escalating tensions between the United States and North Korea. The alert, sent by the Hawaii Emergency Management Agency, was revoked 38 minutes after it was issued, prompting confusion over why it was released—and why it took so long to rescind. State officials and residents of a normally tranquil part of the Pacific, as well as tourists, all of whom were briefly terrified by the prospect of a thermonuclear bomb attack, immediately expressed outrage.[39]

"What happened today was totally unacceptable," said Hawaii governor David Y. Ige. "Many in our community were deeply affected by this. I am sorry for that pain and confusion that anyone might have experienced." Officials said the alert was the result of human error and not the work of hackers or a foreign government. The mistake occurred during a shift-change drill that takes place three times a day at the emergency command post, according to Richard Rapoza, a spokesman for the agency.[40]

Reporter McKay wrote, "Could it happen here?" This was a common refrain after the blunder, and the most common response was that human error does happen, but protocols and redundancies are in place to prevent that. Emergency managers in other states were impelled to recheck their own attack warning systems. "In Massachusetts, the procedures and protocols have enough built-in redundancy to virtually guarantee that it wouldn't happen there. The Massachusetts Emergency Management Agency has a platform for a live alert and another platform for tests. To send out a test alert, the live platform would first have to be turned off, then the test would go out and would be labeled as such."[41]

"Further, the test couldn't go out until three people—two managers and a dispatcher—signed off on it. For a live message, again, three people would have to sign off on it. 'Our platforms are different and when we do tests we have a pre-scripted message that says 'test, test, test, this is a drill,'" said Kurt Schwartz, emergency management director. Sending out a live message can be authorized only by Schwartz, his deputy or the chief of response and field services, and all three must be either on a conference call or in a room at the time."[42] The article said, "The only way I can see doing anything like what happened in Hawaii would be intentional misconduct by someone who has access to the system and intends to do it and that's a very hard thing to prevent," said Schwartz, "although our dispatch center is always staffed by a minimum of two people, so one person attempting misconduct would be immediately detected by the second person." Schwartz said he and his staff met to review protocols after the Hawaii incident and feel confident that no changes are necessary.[43]

In Hawaii on the day of the incident, "[t]he alert went out at about 8:10 a.m., lighting up phones of people still in bed, having coffee by the beach at a Waikiki resort, or up for early surfing. "BALLISTIC MISSILE THREAT INBOUND TO HAWAII. SEEK IMMEDIATE SHELTER. THIS IS NOT A DRILL," it read.[44] Hawaii had already been on high emotional alert—it began staging monthly air-raid drills, complete with sirens, in December 2017—since President Trump and Kim Jong-un, the supreme leader of North Korea, began exchanging nuclear threats. Estimates vary, but it would take a little more than half an hour for a missile launched from North Korea to reach Hawaii, traversing an arc of roughly 5,700 miles. State officials said that Hawaii residents would have as little as 12 minutes to find shelter once an alert was issued. Within moments of the first announcement, people flocked to shelters and crowded highways in scenes of terror and helplessness. Emergency sirens wailed in parts of the state, adding to the pandemonium.[45]

In an email, Cory Grogan, a spokesperson from the Oregon Office of Emergency Management, wrote, "We will be reviewing Oregon Emergency Response System protocols for sending messages with built-in authorities for certain types of messages and issuing corrections in the unlikely event that it is needed." Grogan added that there is always the risk of human error, but thousands of these test messages are sent annually without issue.[46]

Karina Shagren, communications director for the Washington [state] Military Department, said in an email that what happened in Hawaii is a teachable moment. "We look forward to reviewing and analyzing the lessons learned to see if there are any changes that we should implement to strengthen our own alert system. At the same time, we're working with our federal partners to review processes, develop possible improvements, etc."[47]

Jim Judge, the Volusia County, Florida, emergency management director, knows firsthand about false alerts. While in a conference call after Hurricane Irma, Judge kept getting alerts over his phone. At first he thought it was an Amber Alert but soon realized it was a notice advising residents to boil their water before using it. The message was a mistake.[48]

"The city managers were yelling at me and I didn't know anything about it," he said. The mistake came from the state, which finally corrected the error, but damage control had to be done. "We had to go to the media, we were already in recovery mode [from the hurricane] and going in a hundred different directions. It really threw a wrench into what we were doing."[49]

Vern T. Miyagi, the administrator of the Hawaii Emergency Management Agency, said that during the drill, an employee—whom he did not identify—mistakenly pushed a button on a computer screen to send out the alert, rather than one marked to test it. He said the employee answered "yes" when asked by the system if he was sure he wanted to send the message. The Hawaii Emergency Management Agency has been holding "are you ready" drills. As a chain of islands, Hawaii is subject to all kinds of threats—hurricanes, volcanoes, earthquakes, and tsunamis—but officials have made it clear that none is more urgent now than the threat of an attack by North Korea, given how little time there would be between an alert and the detonation of a bomb.[50]

The United States faces an especially difficult problem, not just because of uncertain relations with North Korea but also because of growing fears inside the military about the cyber vulnerability of the nuclear warning system and nuclear control systems. Because of its location, Hawaii—more than any other part of the United States—has been threatened by escalating tensions and the risks of war, and preparations have already begun there.[51]

Senator Brian Schatz of Hawaii said the mistake was "totally inexcusable. The whole state was terrified," he said. "There needs to be tough and quick accountability and a fixed process." While the cell phone alerting system is in state authorities' hands, the detection of missile launches is the responsibility of the U.S. Strategic Command and Northern Command. It was the military, not Hawaiian officials, that was the first to declare there was no evidence of a missile launch.[52]

CHAPTER TAKEAWAYS

Chapter 1 examined some of the essentials of emergency management and disaster policy. It pondered the status of emergency management as a profession. It explored stakeholder groups, furnished a brief overview of disaster as a field of scientific research, emphasized the low issue salience of disaster as a public and political phenomenon, and described the federalization of government responsibility for disaster management. Also introduced were the difficulties local governments face in addressing emergency management, the political aspects of disaster, the multifaceted problem of disaster insurance, and the challenge of training and educating emergency managers for a field that is technically complex and highly multidisciplinary.

Chapter 2 took on theory and methods. It averred that theories hold out the potential to continually advance emergency management as a profession. People new to the field can draw from this chapter's theories and concepts to independently analyze disaster policy as a domain of public policy analysis or policy studies. The chapter presented three simple normative theories: Jeffersonian, Hamiltonian, and Jacksonian. Arguably, Hamiltonian theory and assumptions were adduced to be the best of the three for professionalizing the work of emergency management.

However, Jacksonian theory, first added in the second edition, is consistent with much of the current polarized and politicized environment. Those who embrace or exhibit Jacksonian principles tend to emphasize state and local participation, and they demand highly loyal political responsiveness in their emergency management and homeland security leadership. Jacksonians have a dark side. As champions of populism, they often advocate particularistic values. Many of these values do not promote diversity in the public workforce, are suspicious of newly arrived immigrants, and advance strident nationalism as a counter to globalization in its many forms. Jacksonians spotlight the plight of the undereducated workers, men and women, who have very few champions of their causes in positions of political power. In the extreme, Jacksonians can be nativists rather than globalists, exclusive rather than inclusive, and highly suspicious of various institutions of central government.

Chapter 2 also covered principal-agent theory, network theory, and theories of federalism holding each as tools for both analyzing and conducting emergency management. The chapter also included topics ranging from customer satisfaction to a commentary about how emergency management knowledge is produced and how it is learned by others. Included as well was a section about methods: specifically, the emerging role of "big data analytics" in the field of disaster study and management.

Chapter 3 covered history but in terms of 13 common threads or issues, each addressed in order. The chapter also explored almost 70 years of disaster policy history. We were reminded that FEMA's portfolio has always included civil defense against nuclear attack. After the terror attacks of 2001, FEMA was also expected to serve the homeland security mission in a variety of ways. While FEMA has a unique ability to expand and contract its workforce to cope with multiple disaster management demands, plus a massive funding backstop in the form of the Disaster Relief Fund, it continues to remain dependent on sitting presidents, on an understanding Congress, and since 2003, on a tolerant and supportive DHS hierarchy. Moreover, FEMA must work cooperatively with governors and locally elected or appointed executives, satisfy a wide assortment of hard-to-please stakeholders, meet the needs of new disaster victims, and all the while protect the national taxpayer's dollar.

The Chapter 3 history reminded us that presidents from Truman to Carter conducted disaster policy implementation through an assemblage of federal organizations. Some of these organizations resided in the White House, some operated as major and minor arms of federal departments, and some labored in obscurity as back offices of independent agencies. It was not until year three of the Carter administration (1979) that U.S. disaster policy was granted a formal organizational and functionally integrated home. It came in the form of FEMA, a small independent agency whose workforce for many years was unrealistically capped at about 3,000. FEMA's top officials have always understood that they survived and succeeded politically largely as a result of how the agency was perceived and used by the president.

Chapter 4 was dedicated to presidential declarations of major disaster and emergency in terms of policies, process, programs, decisional power, politics, and payment of public money. Over time the U.S. Congress both granted and tolerated widening presidential discretion in deciding what constituted a declarable major disaster or emergency; thus, the system has become somewhat more politicized than lawmakers in 1950 ever expected. Also, in presidential judgments about the deservedness of governors' requests, the system tolerates a degree of subjectivity and sometimes political bias. Owing to this freedom to decide, some presidents have created new categories of emergency, thus setting precedents governors have been able to exploit in their quest for declarations and federal help. On top of this, the availability of the Disaster Relief Fund furnishes presidents a convenient pool of spending authority to pay the federal costs of major disasters and emergencies they choose to declare.

Chapter 4 demonstrated that homeland security law and policy has augmented presidential authority and responsibility. These laws and policies have expanded the range of presidential declarations to include terrorism or even terrorist threats (see NSSEs). They threaten to bond conventional Stafford Act declaration issuance for non-terror disasters with a president-led declaration system preoccupied with terrorism and terrorism threat in its many forms. Regardless, the U.S. disaster declaration process is the "Main Street" of American emergency management. This is made necessary by American federalism, a complex marriage of federal, state, and local interdependencies, as well as by a quest for endurance, resilience, burden sharing, and human compassion.

Chapter 5 pointed out that "big science" applications of disaster research require subtle forms of political lobbying of lawmakers. It is clear that disaster study informs but also transcends emergency management. The chapter also posited that different types of disaster agents are of interest to different types of scientific and engineering clientele groups. Furthermore, communities of practice (CoPs) sometimes conflict with one another when they seek to secure government support and funding of their respective scientific endeavors. However, these groups also have a great deal in common. They often form alliances, or at least tolerate their differences, in the interest of showing a united front to policymakers.

Chapter 5 conceded that an unfortunate feature of U.S. disaster management is that most of the government scientific and engineering agencies, offices, and programs important to emergency managers are neither in FEMA nor in the DHS. Some of these organizations are capable of making predictions of disaster frequency and magnitude, some design various countermeasures or advance disaster mitigation research and engineering, some work to improve government disaster preparedness and response, and some are capable of facilitating disaster recovery. In addition, the public works engineering side of emergency management is critical in disaster policy's intergovernmental relations. In many homeland security realms, research involves sizable pools of government contractors and universities working on security-related technologies. This has moved emergency management deeper into the world of national security and defense-related contracting.

Chapter 6 covered the intergovernmental relations of disaster management. Those relations are extremely complex. Since the 9/11 terror attacks of 2001, those relationships have become much more centralized at the federal level, much more security-focused, and much more obsessed with colossal framework building to advance national preparedness and to yoke every component of DHS into the planning factory. Chapter 6 examined state and local government, particularly with respect to how the matters of federal homeland security and emergency management have shaped both kinds of work organizationally at the state level and, secondarily, at the local level.

Chapter 6 also considered the importance of nonprofit organizations active in disaster and the impact of privatization of more services previously provided by government. Among major concerns are ensuring that homeland security–induced transformation of FEMA does not alienate or drive away the universe of nonprofit altruistic organizations and volunteering individuals; that for-profit contractors are not overused; and that the tremendous burden of cross-cutting federal grant requirements does not reduce the pool of FEMA contract bidders to a handful of gigantic corporations.

Chapter 7 was the civil–military chapter. Of particular concern was the role of the U.S. military in disaster management domestically. Within this crucible was an analysis of the federal active duty forces and the state National Guard forces. Moreover,

Posse Comitatus was defined and explained. This edition's discussion of the military better explained the duty status of each of these military forces. It also introduced the dual status commander, which has proven so far to be a useful and constructive solution to military coordination of state National Guard (governor-directed forces) and federal military forces (directed by the president and under Pentagon control) in response to domestic disasters.

Chapter 7 also looked into major homeland security grant programs geared to aligning state and local counterpart organizations into a more unified and more easily coordinated whole. Many of these programs have imposed tremendous planning and information management burdens on state and local governments, despite heavy DHS and FEMA subsidization.

Chapter 8 was the globalization chapter. As in the second edition, the U.S. system of international disaster assistance was compared and contrasted with the UN system of disaster aid. In the second edition, great attention was given to how the United States handled offers of help from other nations in the wake of Hurricane Katrina. That material was replaced in this edition with a study of U.S.–Canada disaster management relations. It encompassed as well the 1994–2013 disaster experience of provinces and states, and their subunits, located along the U.S.–Canada international border. In the course of this work, Canadian emergency management was compared and contrasted with U.S. emergency management. A few judgments were made about how Canadian intergovernmental relations differ from U.S. intergovernmental relations in matters of disaster management.

Chapter 9 covered the 2017 hurricane trio of Harvey, Irma, and Maria. Many issues were raised. In Texas, search and rescue, flood control, and property loss were priority concerns. In Florida, evacuation, sheltering, storm surge and wind damage, and reconstruction were paramount issues. While flaws and perceived errors in hurricane disaster response and recovery garner news and social media attention, it is also true that for Harvey and Irma, there were many success stories. Conversely, Puerto Rico had the misfortune of having been partially struck by Hurricane Irma only a week or so before it was ravaged by Hurricane Maria. Puerto Rico and the U.S. Virgin Islands suffered epic damage. The vast assortment of responding federal agencies, including FEMA and the U.S. military, could not easily cope with the sea of needs they encountered. The failure of Puerto Rico's entire electrical grid, requiring many months to repair and replace, confounded relief efforts there in every way possible. Puerto Rico had little electrical power and even less political power, particularly when compared with the mega-states of Texas and Florida, each suffering its own hurricane woes. Multiple catastrophes posed a tremendous disaster management challenge for American emergency managers of all stripes in 2017.

The Future

It is no surprise that many scholars today conclude that the definition of disaster is socially constructed.[53] It is also fair to say that the definition of disaster is "politically constructed" by the media portrayals of an event, how the president chooses to define and comprehend the event, and how people among the general public, including those on social media, perceive and judge the event.[54]

In another sense, the political definition of disaster flows from law; judgments of previous presidents; a sitting president's previous actions modulated by the political circumstances of the time when his or her judgments were made; the strategic behavior of governors seeking federal assistance; and the pressure imposed by elected representatives at the federal, state, and local level. Understanding disaster policy and politics is worthwhile, although it demands work, focus, and objectivity. Disaster policy and emergency management have made and will continue to make a difference both inside and outside the United States.

Today, a cardinal concern of the U.S. emergency management community must be whether the field will be supplanted and marginalized by homeland security leaders, agencies, and political forces or whether it can sustain itself by preserving its identity, professional norms, and values. Has the current DHS become an extreme overreaction to the tragedy of 9/11? Has anyone truly reasoned out what it meant to amalgamate some 22 federal agencies, each operating under different laws with different purposes, into a mega-department resolutely fixated on terrorism in all of its real and imagined manifestations? It is not that FEMA people resist joining the DHS team, as much as FEMA has been asked to compete in the wrong "sport." The openness, humanitarian values, and public-mindedness of emergency management does not comport well with the secrecy, national security/military values, and the people-targeting surveillance of homeland security. FEMA is being tarnished by its increasing association with DHS offices ostensibly fighting terrorism by tormenting political asylum seekers and undocumented aliens, some of them children. FEMA's reputation suffers, as does that of DHS, by paying local law enforcement to track suspicious people and share information about them through a vast network of fusion centers. Can homeland security itself be changed such that it accommodates emergency management on its own terms? Homeland security as a department is based on the cohesiveness that it must achieve and maintain among its many component organizations. The real test of the value of homeland security will come in the next weapon of mass destruction incident. The real test of emergency management's value will come when a string of mega-disasters occurs weeks apart wreaking havoc on parts of the nation, as happened in 2017. Can preparations and response for terrorism confound preparations and response for natural and non-terror human-caused disasters? What should our policymakers and public managers do when one undermines the other?

Key Terms

Allbaugh, Joseph, former FEMA director 396

Antipoverty social policy 402

Brown, Michael D., former FEMA administrator 392

Credentialing 391

DHS Science & Technology 394

Disaster resilience 407

Fantasy documents 395

Hawaii false ballistic missile alert 407

Missions and capabilities 390

Witt, James Lee, former FEMA director 392

GLOSSARY

Abstract reasoning (Ch. 2) Helps produce testable knowledge and propositions that are generalizable and applicable in many contexts. Helpful in mathematical computation, in logic, and in making comparisons and identifying various associations among different types or sets of data and information.

Accumulated Cyclone Energy (ACE) (Ch. 9) An index that records each tropical storm or hurricane's wind speed through its life cycle. Long-lived, intense hurricanes have a high ACE index, while short-lived, weak tropical storms have a low value. The ACE of a season is the sum of the ACE for each storm and takes into account the number, strength, and duration of all the tropical storms and hurricanes in the season. The National Weather Center phrase "total overall seasonal activity" refers to the combined intensity and duration of Atlantic named storms and hurricanes occurring during the season. The measure of total seasonal activity used by NOAA is the Accumulated Cyclone Energy (ACE) index. The ACE index is a wind energy index, defined as the sum of the squares of the maximum sustained surface wind speed (knots) measured every six hours for all named storms while they are at least tropical storm strength. "NOAA uses the ACE index, combined with the seasonal total number of named storms, hurricanes, and major hurricanes, to categorize North Atlantic hurricane seasons as being above normal, near normal, or below normal."[1]

Algorithm (Ch. 2) In mathematics and computer science, an algorithm is a step-by-step procedure for calculations and it is a procedure or formula for solving a problem, based on conducting a sequence of specified actions. Algorithms are used for calculation, data processing, and automated reasoning. Actually, operations performed on one's personal computer consist of algorithms. Furthermore, an algorithm is a well-defined procedure that allows a computer to solve a problem.[2] Another way to describe an algorithm is a sequence of unambiguous instructions.

Allbaugh, Joseph, former FEMA director (Ch. 10) Appointed by President George W. Bush and began his service as FEMA director in early 2001 until stepping down in March 2003 when FEMA was transferred into the new U.S. Department of Homeland Security. Allbaugh had been a G. W. Bush campaign manager in 2000 and had no emergency management experience before joining FEMA. Allbaugh was FEMA director at the time of the September 11, 2001, terror attacks.

All-hazards emergency management (Ch. 1) Assumes common sets of emergency preparedness and response procedures and practices are applicable in any locality and that an economy of scale is achieved by planning and preparing for disaster in generic terms rather than for each unique type.

Analytical approaches (Ch. 2) Approaches and models that allow for experimentation, trial, and error. They were the early basis of public policy analysis.

Antipoverty social policy (Ch. 10) Disasters often push many disaster victims over an economic brink they may not be able to climb back to. Disaster often highlights the existing problems of poverty, ethnic and racial discrimination, ageism, antifeminism, disability, and LGBTQ discrimination. Social policies, laws, and programs sometimes may not be enough to protect people in marginalized groups from increased discrimination in times of disaster. In the United States, disaster policy tends to be "conservative" in the sense that the aim of disaster relief is only to return damaged areas, and disaster victims themselves, to the condition they were in before the disaster, albeit with some provision for mitigation against the possible repeat of the same type of disaster in the future.

Applied heuristics approach (Ch. 2) Based on heuristics, verbal explanatory sketches, or conceptual frameworks that help public managers produce adequate explanations for puzzling things. Heuristics embody propositions subject to confirmation or disconfirmation; that is, their usefulness can be tested.

Assistance to Firefighters Grant Program (AFG) (Ch. 5) Promotes mitigation and preparedness in fire departments across the United States. Provides assistance to fire companies at state or local levels, enabling them to identify and obtain the necessary public safety resources. These one-year grants go directly to fire departments.

Best-practices approach (Ch. 2) Wisdom gained from practice, learning from prior mistakes, sharing knowledge about innovative practices, and making improvements through analysis of after-action reports. If followed in accord with the social scientific approach, this approach may help produce scholarship that is a basis for practice.

Big science (Ch. 5) A term used to refer to fields of disaster study that require substantial outside funding and expensive technical equipment for scientists to pursue their research and experimentation, putting many disaster researchers in the world of government lobbying. One assumption of big science is that the growing dependence of researchers on government funding and participation means that more and more research must to be conducted under terms acceptable to the government.

"Blue helmeted" peacekeeping soldiers (Ch. 8) Contributed by various member states, UN peacekeepers are "soldiers, police officers, and military observers" from the UN member countries. UN blue helmeted soldiers are paid volunteers, counted on to provide the logistical and physical contributions necessary to carry out UN disaster relief and recovery missions.

Boston Marathon bombing (Ch. 1) Two foreign terrorists built, planted, and detonated two pressure cooker bombs near the finish line of the marathon in April 2013 to retaliate against the United States for its military action in Muslim countries. The twin blasts killed 3 people and wounded more than 260 others.[3]

Bottom-up approach (Ch. 6) In U.S. intergovernmental relations, the assumption that primary responsibility for emergency management lies with local political subdivisions (towns, cities, and counties) and with the local officials and emergency managers or responders within those respective jurisdictions.

Brown, Michael D., former FEMA administrator (Ch. 10) A President George W. Bush appointee assigned to head FEMA in January 2003; he held the title Undersecretary for Emergency Response and Preparedness when FEMA was relegated to division status within the new U.S. Department of Homeland Security. Brown had no prior experience in emergency management before he came to FEMA. To his credit, he managed to help FEMA retain its "brand-like" title when it was threatened with renaming. Brown is infamous for his poor handling of the FEMA response to Hurricane Katrina in September 2005, and he resigned his post following a storm of public controversy.

Bureau of Political-Military Affairs (Ch. 8) An agency within the U.S. Department of State that bridges with the U.S. Department of Defense (DOD). It provides policy in the areas of international security, security assistance, military operations, defense strategy and policy, military use of space, and defense trade. It is headed by the assistant secretary of state for Political-Military Affairs.[4]

Bureaucratic politics model (Ch. 2) A set of theories that strives to explain the motives of public executives and managers as they make decisions. This model suggests that the desire of these public officials to protect or promote their own and their agency's special interests, as they compete with other agencies, forms a major motivating factor in shaping the timing and the content of their decisions.

Bureaucratic "turf wars" (Ch. 6) An expression that denotes heavy competition for jurisdiction and budget funding among government bureaus, agencies, and program offices—even those within the same department of the executive branch.

Buyout program (Ch. 4) A program, usually noncompulsory, involving the direct government purchase of houses or other structures from owners, at fair market value, on account of extremely high disaster risk or repeated damage to the structures by the same disaster agent. Federal emergency managers sometimes use buyouts to help stanch the problem of recurring national flood insurance loss claims and to reduce government post-disaster relief spending.

Cadre of On-Call Response/Recovery Employees (CORE) (Ch. 6) Two-year, full-time, exempted service appointments. According to the agency, "These CORE positions establish a new opportunity within the disaster workforce and successful candidates will be afforded the opportunity to be deployed for up to 300 days per year.

The incumbents will serve as mid-level emergency managers at Joint Field Offices in support of disaster and emergency operations."[5] CORE workers help FEMA maintain a regular state of readiness, for response to major events. Though CORE people could be assigned anywhere across the United States, general management and oversight will be maintained geographically by each Federal Emergency Management Agency (FEMA) region.

Catastrophic incidents (Ch. 4) Any natural or man-made incident, including terrorism, which results in extraordinary levels of mass casualties, damage, or disruption severely affecting the population, infrastructure, environment, economy, and national morale or government functions.

Celebrity-branded post-disaster online fund raising for survivors (Ch. 1) The actions of one or more celebrities who lend their name(s) to formal post-disaster fundraising campaigns intended to solicit donated money for those with post-disaster needs. These campaigns have been facilitated by the evolution of organizations such as GoFundMe, and others, which provide online platforms and administrative support. The logic is that celebrity endorsement of such campaigns will provide an additional inducement for fans and others to make contributions for worthy post-disaster causes.[6]

Chemical, biological, radiological, or nuclear (CBRN) (Ch. 7) Types of weapons of mass destruction that terrorists may seek to acquire and use. A core mission of U.S. Department of Homeland Security (DHS) policy is to prevent terrorists from obtaining, transporting, and detonating such weapons; denying them the opportunity to develop CBRN weapons on their own; and developing countermeasures and recovery strategies in the event a CBRN weapon is detonated or released.

Citizen Corps (Ch. 6) An arm of U.S.A. Freedom Corps that invites people at the community level to volunteer. Citizen Corps councils working at the state and local level regularly receive federal funding used to promote training and education of community volunteers, in some ways helping them to respond to disasters or emergencies in their communities.

Civil defense (Ch. 1) A U.S. national policy since World War I aimed at preparing the nation for possible attack by enemy nations. After 1949, civil defense policy transitioned to preparation for nuclear attack but became defunct after the end of the Cold War.

Civil defense preparedness (Ch. 3) During the Cold War, from about 1949 to 1990, various civil defense measures were taken against the possibility of nuclear attack. Tools of civil defense preparedness have included mass evacuation planning, public shelter programs, and home fallout shelters.

Cloud (Ch. 2) Software storage and service run on the Internet.

Codified knowledge (Ch. 2) Impersonal knowledge that is learned through thinking and reasoning, not through social relationships. Such knowledge is often conveyed through scholarly publications. Much technocratic knowledge is produced from data analysis, repeated experimentation, scientific study, and ultimately published research products. If such knowledge is widely diffused and open to the public, people have an opportunity to study, learn, and perhaps master such information. If it is not diffused, only those with permission and opportunity to see it may learn from it.

Command and control strategies (Ch. 6) The hierarchical relations in which those in subordinate positions working in a bureaucratic organization are expected to strictly comply with the orders or instructions of their immediate supervisor, thus creating a chain of command.

Communities of practice (CoPs) (Ch. 2) Groups of people who share a concern or a passion for something they do, and they learn how to do it better as they interact regularly. A CoP is composed of practitioners or researchers who have specialized their work to address the concern they share.

Community of interest (COI) (Ch. 2) A gathering of people assembled around a topic of common interest. Its members take part in the community to exchange information, to obtain answers to personal questions or problems, to improve their understanding of a subject, to share common passions, or to play.[7]

Community Emergency Response Teams (CERTs) (Ch. 6) A Federal Emergency Management Agency (FEMA)-backed effort pursued on the local level in participating communities. CERTs members are unpaid, voluntary workers who are invited to earn qualifications for various types of post-disaster specializations, including elemental search and rescue, first aid, shelter management, and more.

Complex humanitarian emergencies (CHEs) (Ch. 8) The designation of a CHE signifies that a country or region is at or near complete breakdown of civil authority, something occasionally resulting from a major natural disaster. CHEs sometimes involve ethnic conflict, displacement of population groups, market collapse, and mass starvation. In a CHE, the success or failure of a disaster relief operation often rests on the degree of coordination, the fairness and equality in relief distribution, and whether the relief effort connects with (or at least does not impede) the country's reconstruction and economic development.

Compound disaster (Ch. 5) A disaster that triggers a secondary hazard. Compound disasters can occur simultaneously or sequentially.

Comprehensive risk methodology (Ch. 7) DHS utilizes a comprehensive risk methodology focused on three principal elements: threat, vulnerability, and consequence.[8] The risk methodology calculates the relative risk of terrorism faced by a given area. It takes into account the potential risk of terrorism to people, critical infrastructure, and economic security. The threat analysis also considers threats from domestic violent extremists as well as from international terrorist groups and those individuals inspired by terrorists abroad.[9]

Computational social science (Ch. 2) An approach to social inquiry defined by the use of large, complex datasets, often—although not always—measured in terabytes or petabytes; the frequent involvement of "naturally occurring" social and digital media sources and other electronic databases; the use of computational or algorithmic solutions to generate patterns and inferences from these data; and, the applicability of social theory in a variety of domains from the study of mass opinion to public health, from examinations of political events to social movements.[10] It is a sub-category of data analytics and helpful in social inquiry.

Computer program (Ch. 2) A sequence of instructions that apply the rules of a specific programming language and is written to perform a specified task with a computer. Algorithms are general and so have to be translated into a specific programming language.[11]

Congressional dominance model (Ch. 4) Postulates that the political geography of presidential disaster declaration issuance over time demonstrates the Federal Emergency Management Agency (FEMA) effort to reward congressional lawmakers on its authorizations and appropriations oversight committees.

Contractors (for-profit) (Ch. 6) Private-sector businesses that contract with the government to deliver a product (a deliverable) or a service and that are allowed to charge a profit of some amount or percentage assuming the conditions of the contract are met. Government contractors range from individuals, to small businesses, to large businesses. Contractors respond to government requests for proposals and submit bids in what is usually a competitive process. For-profit contractors sometimes save government considerable sums of money owing to expertise government does not have in-house because contractors work from project to project under time limits and so do not generate permanent costs for government; also, by choosing lower cost competitive bids, government has potentially reduced the costs of the work the contractor has committed to do.

Contractors (nonprofit) (Ch. 6) Nonprofit government contractors, often 501(c)(3) IRS tax entities, may compete for and win government contracts just as "for profit" contractors do. However, nonprofits are not allowed to make a profit in the same sense private contractors are. FEMA, as well as state and local government agencies, often contract with nonprofits to maintain supplies and materials needed before disasters and emergencies, to respond to the needs of victims when disasters or emergencies do occur, and to rebuild the nonprofits' own disaster damaged facilities. Nonprofits are not allowed to proselytize their religions or religious views in the course of the work they do under contract with FEMA. Nonprofit voluntary organizations, community service groups, and religious organizations that provide assistance in the aftermath of a disaster or an emergency are often referred to as voluntary agencies (VOLAGs).

Coordinate-authority model (Ch. 2) A theory of intergovernmental relations that assumes a sharp and distinct boundary between separate national and state governments. National and state governments appear to operate independently and autonomously, and they are linked only tangentially. In the model, local governments are abjectly dependent on their respective state governments.

Counterterrorism (Ch. 1) Offensive measures taken to prevent, deter, and respond to terrorism and terrorist attacks. Along with antiterrorism, it is the core mission of U.S. Department of Homeland Security (DHS) policy and involves threat detection, prevention, mitigation, target hardening, policing, and other preparedness and response activities.

Credentialing (Ch. 10) DHS and FEMA engage heavily in "credentialing" who can and who cannot respond to emergencies and disasters. Many DHS and FEMA workers today create training curricula, certification rules, and badging schemes. Often even non-federal emergency responders must tolerate background checks, re-validation of their professional and education credentials, and field interviews of people who know them.

Crisis leadership (Ch. 1) Examines how presidents and prime ministers have performed during crises and in the aftermath of crises.

Crisis Relocation Plan (CRP) (Ch. 3) Part of civil defense planning against nuclear attack in the Cold War era (1947–1989). Done at the state level with federal funds, common CRP activity included provision for population relocation, food distribution, and medical care.[12]

Crying poor syndrome (Ch. 6) An expression sometimes voiced by federal officials to characterize the behavior of governors, mayors, or other government leaders seeking presidential declarations of major disaster. They allege that these leaders "cry poor" after relatively small-scale disasters by insisting that their respective jurisdictions are unable to respond to or recover from the "disaster" without the federal help a disaster declaration would provide. Sometimes, governors and other state officials accuse local government officials of engaging in the same behavior in order to secure undeserved state disaster relief.

Cybersecurity (Ch. 5) Computer hackers who disrupt Internet usage recognized as potential "terrorists" and purveyors of disaster. By the 1990s, cyberattack disasters and emergencies that damaged or threatened to damage critical infrastructure systems and facilities became a new core area of responsibility for the Federal Emergency Management Agency (FEMA). The vulnerability of these systems and facilities to both terrorism and natural disaster forces encouraged policymakers to fund scientific and engineering endeavors aimed at advancing the fortification and resilience of these systems and structures.

Debris flow (Ch. 1) Massive quantities of rocks, boulders, trees, and mud are launched downhill. They are typically triggered after wildfires on steep mountainsides when heavy rains wash away the soil. In more technical terms, they are "movements of fluidized soil and rock fragments acting as a viscous mass. They occur when loose materials become saturated and start to behave as a fluid rather than a solid."[13]

Decentralization (Ch. 1) Refers to the decentralized nature of the U.S. government and its functions; it is necessary due to the great size and population of the nation, the thousands of subnational governments, and the U.S. system of federalism. It is also part of a national policy of devolution of certain federal powers back to the state and local levels.

Development banks (Ch. 8) Institutions, called *multilateral development banks* and *multilateral financial institutions*, which provide financial support and professional advice for economic and social development activities in developing countries. The World Bank and International Monetary Fund are two examples. Many have taken considerable interest in disaster management.

DHS Science & Technology (Ch. 10) The research and development (R&D) arm of the Department of Homeland Security (DHS). The Science and Technology Directorate (S&T) focuses on providing the tools, technologies, and knowledge products serving the nation's homeland security needs. DHS S&T works with industry and end-user communities across the nation. S&T's R&D uses a network of industry, national laboratory, and other partners to seek solutions to fill capability gaps and to define topics for future research.[14] DHS S&T was established in 2003 under provisions of the Homeland Security Act of 2002.

Disaster Assistance Response Team (DART) (Ch. 8) Dispatched by the Office of U.S. Foreign Disaster Assistance (OFDA), a DART assesses the scope of damage, proposes a strategy, and estimates how much assistance is required and what it will cost.[15] The response team often provides logistical support to and coordinates the efforts of all actors and responders involved. These include the UN and other international organizations, nongovernmental organizations (NGOs), and governments. DARTs monitor and evaluate U.S. operations as well.

Disaster Financial Assistance Arrangements (DFAA) (Ch. 8) In the event of a large-scale natural disaster, the Government of Canada provides financial assistance to provincial and territorial governments through DFAA, administered by Public Safety Canada. When response and recovery costs exceed what individual provinces or territories could reasonably be expected to bear on their own, DFAA funding may be requested. Through the DFAA, assistance is paid to the province or territory—but not directly to affected individuals, small businesses or communities. In Canada, a request for disaster cost reimbursement under the DFAA is processed immediately following receipt of the required documentation of provincial/territorial expenditures and a review by federal auditors. Thus, in Canada federal help to disaster victims is dispatched, if loss conditions are met, through provincial government. In effect, provincial governments receive Canadian DFAA money as a form of block grant, which they are fully accountable for.[16]

Disaster Insurance (Ch. 1) Many forms of private insurance cover losses or damage from various hazard agents, some of which may be produced by disaster forces or causes. Homeowner's insurance and insurance on other forms of private property (cars, boats, out-buildings, etc.) may provide "disaster insurance coverage." However, private insurers are reluctant to cover certain disaster agents or causes likely to produce a deluge of claims in a short period of time. Also, private insurance is profit driven and relies on a much larger pool of paying policyholders than claims filers. Certain forms of disaster prove to be uneconomic when regulated insurance rates are too low and the sums paid out to claimants is high. The National Flood Insurance Program was established to offer low-cost insurance coverage and to discourage local development in flood hazard zones. Insurance is a perennial problem for both government and private insurers in matters of earthquake, terrorism, and nuclear power plant accidents with offsite consequences, among others.

Disaster management (Ch. 1) The tactical and operational implementation of an emergency planning strategy at the time of a crisis. In presidentially declared emergencies and disasters, emergency managers are also disaster managers in both strategic and tactical terms. The terms *disaster management* and *emergency management* are often used interchangeably in this book.

Disaster Mitigation Act of 2000 (DMA 2000) (Ch. 3) Amended the 1988 Stafford Act and gave the Federal Emergency Management Agency (FEMA) authority to establish a program of technical and financial assistance for improved pre-disaster mitigation directed to state and local governments. FEMA was to help state and local governments develop and carry out pre-disaster hazard mitigation measures that were cost effective and designed to reduce injuries, loss of life, and damage to and destruction of property, including damage to critical services and facilities under the jurisdiction of the states or local governments. Mandated that states prepare a comprehensive state program for pre-disaster emergency and disaster mitigation before they could receive post-disaster declaration mitigation funds from FEMA. It also required local governments to identify "potential mitigation measures that could be incorporated into the repair of damaged facilities" before being eligible for pre- and post-disaster funding. The aim of this policy was to encourage local governments to engage in mitigation activities such as "hazard mapping, planning, and development of hazard-sensitive building codes."

Disaster recovery (Ch. 2) Often the most expensive and most protracted phase of the disaster cycle. The term has different meanings in different contexts. It involves restoration, rebuilding, and return to normalcy. The pool of players involved in recovery is often huge and far exceeds the number of players usually involved in disaster response. Late stages of disaster recovery may involve only small numbers of emergency managers. Decisions regarding disaster recovery are fundamentally made at the local level of government.[17]

Disaster recovery centers (DRCs) (Ch. 9) Established in affected communities where individuals can obtain information, discuss their disaster-related needs, learn how to apply for various types of assistance or check on the status of their applications, and find out more about mitigation measures they might use to reduce future risk. Federal and state agencies staff DRCs with knowledgeable officials who provide recovery program information, advice, counseling, and technical assistance.

Disaster Reduction and Recovery Program (Ch. 8) A UN program focused on the demobilization of combatants, land mine clearance, the reintegration of refugees and internally displaced persons (IDPs), and a plan for restoration of governance in a disaster-affected country.[18]

Disaster Relief Act of 1974 (Ch. 3) Public Law 93-288 created a program that provided direct assistance to individuals and families following a disaster. Although preceding laws had provided temporary housing aid and other modest forms of individual assistance, the new Individual and Family Grant (IFG) program—later renamed the Individual and Households Program (IHP)—finally bridged the gap that had existed between public and individual assistance. It also brought state and local governments into all-hazards preparedness activities and provided matching funds for their emergency management programs. In addition, the act authorized in law the emergency declaration category of presidential declaration. Granting the president authority to issue emergency declarations opened the door to governor-requested, president-approved proactive federal mobilization for disasters that had not yet transpired but appeared imminent.

Disaster Relief Fund (Ch. 3) The main repository of federal disaster spending authority available to the president. Funded from an annual congressional appropriation and from residual, accumulated spending authority on previous disasters, it is often replenished and expanded to pay for extremely costly disasters by congressionally approved disaster supplemental appropriations.

Disaster research (Ch. 5) Conducted by a broad array of experts in the physical sciences and engineering, the geosciences, the atmospheric sciences, biomedicine, physical geography, and the information sciences. Researchers also include disaster sociologists, political scientists, economists, social geographers, demographers, urban planners, and public administration specialists.

Disaster resilience (Ch. 10) The concept of resilience has found many advocates in the emergency management community. One way to reduce the impacts of disasters on the nation and its communities is to invest in enhancing resilience. Resilience is *the ability to prepare and plan for, absorb, recover from, and more successfully adapt to adverse events*. Increased resilience allows better anticipation of disasters and better planning to reduce disaster losses—rather than waiting for an event to occur and paying for it afterward.[19]

Disaster Unemployment Assistance (DUA) Program (Ch. 1) Administered by the state and supported by the Federal Emergency Management Agency (FEMA) and the U.S. Department of Labor. Benefits and reemployment services are available to individuals who become unemployed due to a major disaster, beginning with the date the individual was unemployed and extending as long as 26 weeks after the major disaster declaration.

Distributive politics (Ch. 4) A theory of political science that holds that political actors, most particularly elected legislators, have great incentive to ensure that government programs and their administrators work to the benefit or over-benefit of the constituencies they respectively represent. Often in distributive politics government resources are allocated in excess of genuine need. Distributive politics is tolerated in part because it provides lawmakers with electoral advantages and because lawmakers themselves devise allocation rules and sometimes influence discrete public spending decisions. Also, benefit receivers are narrowly localized and payers are broadly national. In other words, those who benefit receive their gain at seemingly no cost to themselves, and those who do not benefit are so numerous, dispersed so broadly, and pay individually only pennies of the cost that they are indifferent about what the distributive expenditure costs them: benefits targeted, funding base broad. Inefficient public budgeting but highly popular, rational behavior for elected officials.

Domestic incidents (Ch. 3) Acts of terrorism and disasters in the homeland stemming from natural or other human causes. Their management was addressed by the secretary of homeland security in the National Response Plan (NRP) and the National Incident Management System (NIMS). In official terms, domestic incidents came to represent a marriage of conventional disaster management and terrorism consequence management.

Doppler radar (Ch. 5) A type of detection technology used by the National Weather Service (NWS) at facilities across the country. The early detection of tornadoes that Doppler radar makes possible allows authorities to issue lifesaving watches or warnings before a tornado forms or in advance of its impact.

Dual federalism (Ch. 2) A government system in which sovereignty is constitutionally split between at least two territorial levels so that units at each level have final authority and can act independently of the other in some areas. Citizens thus have political obligations to two authorities. In U.S. history, the period from 1789 to 1901 has been termed the era of "dual" federalism because there was little collaboration between the national and state governments.

Dual Status Command Authority (Ch. 7) "The dual status commander (DSC) concept offers a command arrangement legally authorizing one military officer to assume simultaneous but mutually exclusive command authority over both National Guard forces under State Active Duty (SAD) or Title 32 status and Title 10 federal military forces."[20]

Dual status commander (Ch. 7) The Department of Defense offers this definition: "A military commander who may, in accordance with the law, serve in two statuses, Federal and State, simultaneously while performing the duties of those statuses separately and distinctly."[21] The U.S. Government Accountability Office (GAO) defines dual status commanders as, "Military officers who serve as an intermediate link between the separate chains of command for state and federal forces—have authority over both National Guard forces under state control and active duty forces under federal control during a civil support incident or special event."[22]

Dual-use approach (Ch. 3) Approved in law in 1973, an approach in which civil defense activities could also be used conjointly to prepare for natural disasters; the merging of civil defense and natural disaster management.

Earthquake retrofitting (Ch. 5) Structural improvements made to existing buildings or infrastructure that enable these structures to retain their integrity and protect their occupants against seismic forces greater than those they were originally designed to withstand.

EMAP Standard (Ch. 1) The Emergency Management Accreditation Program (EMAP), a joint project of the Federal Emergency Management Agency (FEMA), the International Association of Emergency Managers (IAEM), and the National Emergency Management Association (NEMA), sets forth an appropriate level of emergency management capacity. State and local governments, through a series of steps, are peer reviewed and ultimately judged worthy or unworthy of EMAP Standard accreditation. It is also an internationally recognized standard of emergency management based on the National Fire Protection Association (NFPA) 1600 standards (also acknowledged as the national preparedness standard for the private sector) that were developed by state, local, and federal emergency management practitioners.

Emergency (Ch. 4) A condition of disaster or of extreme peril to the safety of persons and property caused by such conditions as air pollution, fire, flood, hazardous material incident, storm, epidemic, riot, drought, sudden and severe energy shortage, plant or animal infestations or disease, warning of an earthquake or volcanic eruption, or other conditions.

Emergency Alert System (EAS) (Ch. 5) A national public warning system that requires TV and radio broadcasters, cable television systems, wireless cable systems, satellite digital audio radio service providers, direct broadcast satellite service providers, and wireline video service providers to offer to the president the communications capability to address the American public during a national emergency. The system also may be used by state and local authorities to deliver important emergency information such as Amber (missing children) Alerts and emergency weather information targeted to a specific area.[23]

Emergency declaration (Ch. 3) A category of presidential declaration authorized in law in the Disaster Relief Act of 1974 and issued as a matter of life and safety before an event or when a disaster is still transpiring. Unlike major disaster declarations, emergency declarations can be issued by the president with or without a governor's request, and governors are not required to document need or estimate losses as a condition of their request. Emergency declarations ordinarily include FEMA's Public Assistance (PA) but only for Categories A (debris removal) and B (emergency protective measures). Categories C–G (permanent work) are not available under an emergency declaration. This PA is generally provided on a 75% federal, 25% non-federal cost sharing basis. Emergency declarations seldom include FEMA's Individual Assistance (IA)—the Individuals and Households Program (IHP)—the only form of IA that may be authorized under an emergency declaration. Under IHP, Housing Assistance is made available by FEMA under a 100% federal share. Other Needs Assistance under IHP requires a 25% non-federal cost share.[24]

Emergency management (Ch. 1) The discipline and profession of applying science, technology, planning, and management to deal with extreme events that can injure or kill great numbers of people, do extensive property damage, and disrupt community life. Efforts are made to limit losses and costs through the implementation of strategies and tactics reflecting the full life cycle of disaster: preparedness, response, recovery, and mitigation.

Emergency Management Accreditation Program (EMAP) (Ch. 1) Organization that maintains a voluntary assessment and accreditation process for state or territorial, tribal, and local government emergency management programs. EMAP conducts baseline assessments of all state and territorial emergency management programs. EMAP combines self-assessment in accord with accepted national standards; documentation of compliance; independent evaluation by trained assessors; and for accreditation, committee and commission review.

Emergency Management Assistance Compact (EMAC) (Ch. 6) Originally an agreement between 14 states and territories made during 1995 and 1996 that committed them, through their respective governors, to cooperate in planning for state-to-state extension of emergency management help. Today, all the states belong to EMAC.

Emergency Management Institute (FEMA) (Ch. 6) Part of the U.S. Department of Homeland Security (DHS) Federal Emergency Management Agency (FEMA). The Emergency Management Institute provides national leadership in developing and delivering training to ensure that individuals and groups having key emergency management responsibilities, including FEMA employees, possess the requisite skills to effectively perform their jobs.[25] It is part of DHS-FEMA's National Emergency Training Center in Emmitsburg, MD.

Emergency-management–oriented multinational organizations (Ch. 8) Organizations working independently or through multiple nation-state arrangements that promote emergency management work and capabilities in developing nations.

Emergency Management Performance Grants (EMPGs) (Ch. 7) Allocated by the Federal Emergency Management Agency (FEMA) to state and local governments to improve their intrastate emergency management programs and their mitigation, preparedness, prevention, response, and recovery capabilities for disasters of any type.

Emergency manager (Ch. 1) A person who manages a comprehensive program for hazards and disasters and who is responsible in whole or in part for disaster mitigation, preparedness, prevention, response, and recovery within his or her government jurisdiction or organization.

Emergency operations center (EOC) (Ch. 6) An organizing concept as well as a central management and coordination facility responsible for carrying out emergency management or disaster management functions at a strategic level in an emergency situation. EOCs, when activated at the municipal level, provide a site in which leaders and representatives of government agencies (all levels), nonprofit disaster assistance organizations, critical corporations (particularly public utility companies), and others meet, confer, render decisions, and communicate with one another and externally to others. EOCs are usually preestablished, and they endeavor to support disaster managers in the field, including incident commanders.

Emergency Response Division (of UNDP) (Ch. 8) A division of the United Nations Development Programme (UNDP) created in 1995. It deploys response teams to disaster sites to help coordinate relief and recovery efforts of other UN agencies and nongovernmental organizations (NGOs) with the efforts of disaster-stricken national governments. The teams also prepare comprehensive redevelopment projects in disaster recovery operations.

Emergency supplementals (Ch. 4) Congressional appropriations often used to pay for mega-disasters or catastrophes that have swallowed up all or most available spending authority in the president's Disaster Relief Fund. Legislators sometimes use this almost veto-proof legislation to add non-germane spending riders (special amendments) that would not win majority votes or enactment any other way. This sometimes results in wasteful spending. Most emergency supplementals are funded by federal borrowing rather than by new revenue schemes or budget reprogramming of funds dedicated to certain discretionary spending purposes.

Emergency support functions (ESFs) (Ch. 6) They consolidate government and certain private-sector capabilities into an organizational structure to provide support, resources, program implementation, and services that are needed to save lives, protect property and the environment; restore essential services and critical infrastructure; and help victims and communities return to normal following domestic incidents.[26] There are 15 ESFs: ESF1 Transportation; ESF2 Communications; ESF3 Public Works and Engineering; ESF4 Firefighting; ESF5 Emergency Management; ESF6 Mass Care, Housing, and Human Services; ESF7 Resources Support; ESF8 Public Health and Medical Services; ESF9 Urban Search and Rescue; ESF10 Oil and Hazardous Materials Response; ESF11 Agriculture and Natural Resources;

ESF12 Energy; ESF13 Public Safety and Security; ESF14 Long-term Community Recovery and Mitigation; and ESF15 External Affairs.[27]

Emergent organizations (Ch. 6) Organizations that form spontaneously after a disaster, often from the efforts of volunteers. Some emergent organizations become long-standing established bodies, some take on new problems, while others fade away once their purpose is served or when their volunteers leave and their donor funding ends.

Enhanced Fujita Scale (EF Scale) (Ch. 5) Operational on February 1, 2007, and is used to assign a tornado a "rating" based on estimated wind speeds and related damage. When tornado-related damage is surveyed, it is compared to a list of Damage Indicators (DIs) and Degrees of Damage (DoD) that help estimate better the range of wind speeds the tornado likely produced. From that, a rating (from EF0 to EF5) is assigned. The EF Scale was revised from the original Fujita Scale to reflect better examinations of tornado damage surveys so as to align wind speeds more closely with associated storm damage. The new scale has to do with how most structures are designed.[28]

FIGURE G-1 ■ The Enhanced Fujita Scale (EF) of Tornado Wind Speed	
EF Rating	**3 Second Gust (mph)**
0	65–85
1	86–110
2	111–135
3	136–165
4	166–200
5	Over 200

Source: National Weather Service, "Enhanced Fujita Scale," undated, https://www.weather.gov/oun/efscale (accessed July 24, 2018).

Entitlement program (Ch. 9) A type of government program that provides individuals, and sometimes corporations or state or local governments, with financial benefits or special government-provided goods or ser-

vices under terms in which beneficiaries have a legal right (enforceable in court, if necessary) to the benefits whenever they meet eligibility conditions that are specified by the law that authorizes the program. Spending control over entitlements only comes through changes in the legal rules of the program, not as a result of exhausting budget authority allotted to the program. In other words, entitlement funding each budget year is a function of the number of claimants, ultimate payouts, and the rules of the program—so-called "mandatory spending." Budgeting funds in advance for entitlement programs is extremely difficult, and many entitlement programs exceed their budgets each year because the number of claimants and payouts are often underestimated and difficult to predict when the budget is prepared.

Ethical code (Ch. 2) Expresses principles and practices of behavior. Often adopted by a profession and promulgated by a government agency responsible for licensing a profession. Violations of these codes may be subject to remedies that are administrative (e.g., loss of license), civil, or criminal.

Event driven (Ch. 4) Decisions on policy and politics influenced by the latest memorable incident, disaster, or catastrophe. The flaws of event-driven policymaking include a preoccupation or fixation with the type of major disaster that most recently occurred; a failure to maintain a coherent, balanced, all-hazards emergency management capability; and a tendency to be underprepared for disasters that do not mimic or parallel the last major disaster or catastrophe.

Executive privilege (Ch. 4) President Dwight Eisenhower was the first president to coin the phrase "executive privilege" but not the first to invoke its principle: namely, that a president has the right to withhold certain information from Congress, the courts, or anyone else—even when faced with a subpoena. Presidents have argued that executive privilege is a principle implied in the constitutionally mandated separation of powers. To do their job, presidents contend, they need candid advice from their aides—and aides simply won't be willing to give such advice if they know they might be called to testify, under oath, before a congressional committee or in some other forum.[29]

Faith-based nonprofit voluntary organizations (Ch. 6) Organizations established by recognized and organized religions. Those that accept federal disaster relief funding are prohibited from engaging in unlawful forms of discrimination and from proselytizing their religion or distributing religious materials in the course of dispensing government-furnished disaster relief.

Fantasy documents (Ch. 10) A term coined by sociologist Lee Clarke in his book about how organizations fantasize (in writing!) about their ability to cope with disaster. In his view, organizations whose activities are prone to large-scale disaster have to engage in planning even when it is apparent to everyone involved that "planning" for such occurrences is an improbable task. Hence, Clarke argues that planning becomes a rhetoric directed at outside audiences that need to be reassured about safety concerns.[30]

Federal Disaster Relief Act of 1950 (FDRA) (Ch. 3) Public Law 81-875 provided an orderly and continuing means of assistance by the federal government to states and local governments in carrying out their responsibilities to alleviate suffering and damage resulting from major disasters, including floods. It created the first permanent system for disaster relief without the need for congressional post-disaster action. It also clearly stated for the first time that federal resources could and should be used to supplement the efforts of others in the event of a disaster. The law made federal disaster assistance more immediately accessible because it no longer required specific congressional legislation to address each new disaster but instead simply allowed the president to decide when federal disaster assistance was justified and necessary.

Federal Response Plan (FRP) (Ch. 3) A plan that established a process and structure that was more systematic, coordinated, and effective in delivery of federal assistance, all to address the consequences of any major disaster or emergency. The FRP also directly stated that sometimes a major disaster or emergency may affect the national security of the United States. Devised over the late 1980s and formally emplaced in 1992, the FRP was based on a template of emergency support functions (ESFs) that drew on the personnel and resources of a wide range of federal agencies, some with lead authority for certain support functions. It was revamped to include terrorism response after the 9/11 attacks, and it remained federal policy until it was replaced by the National Response Plan (NRP) in 2003.

Federal–state agreements (Ch. 6) Usually negotiated agreements between specific federal agencies and their state government agency counterparts. From about 1979 through 2003, the Federal Emergency Management Agency (FEMA) relationship with states and localities was primarily through agreements with state offices of emergency management and then, by extension, with local emergency management offices.

Federal zoning (Ch. 3) Zoning by the authority of the federal government. It is fiercely contested by protectors of local land-use authority, who perceive it as federal encroachment into matters of local land-use, zoning, and building regulation. This perception has sometimes impeded federal efforts to promote disaster mitigation at the local level, such as National Flood Insurance Program (NFIP) risk mapping of local governments.

Federalism (Ch. 2) The theory or advocacy of federal political orders, where final authority is divided between subunits and a center. Unlike a unitary state system, in a federal system, sovereignty is constitutionally split between at least two territorial levels so that units at each level have final authority and can act independently of the others in some area or domain of policy.

Federalized government responsibility (Ch. 1) The tendency of the federal government, often at the behest of Congress and the president, to gradually co-opt or preempt state and/or local governments with respect to specific public duties or functions. This is sometimes accomplished through new federal laws tailored to override or evade restrictions of the Tenth Amendment (powers reserved to the states). It may also be done more subtly under conditions and rules that accompany federal grants or subsidies to state and local governments.

FEMA standard federal regions (Ch. 6) Since its inception, FEMA has worked from a Washington, DC, headquarters and through 10 region offices geographically distributed in accord with the 10 standard federal region format used by most federal departments and agencies. Each FEMA region office is directed by a politically appointed (or acting) regional director. Each regional office is located in a major city of the respective region.

FEMA temporary housing assistance (Ch. 4) Money to rent a different place to live or a temporary housing unit (when rental properties are not available). Money for homeowners to repair damage from the disaster that is not covered by insurance. The goal is to repair the home to a safe and sanitary living or functioning condition. The Federal Emergency Management Agency (FEMA) may provide up to the Individuals and Households Program (IHP) maximum for home replacement. Direct assistance or money for the construction of a home occurs only in very unusual circumstances, in locations specified by FEMA, where no other type of housing assistance is possible.

Fire Investment and Response Enhancement (FIRE) grants (Ch. 5) Awarded to local fire departments for equipment, protective gear, training, and prevention programs. FIRE grants may be used to hire or train personnel, buy more equipment, or develop prevention plans, all aimed at improving response. They allow underfunded fire departments to purchase equipment and receive training they could not otherwise afford.

Formula-derived deductible (Ch. 8) The Canadian system of disaster assistance demands that each province requesting DFAA money must first agree to pay a formula-derived deductible. A province or territory may request Government of Canada disaster financial assistance when eligible expenditures exceed an established initial threshold (based on provincial or territorial population). Effective January 1, 2018, the initial threshold for all new events is defined as $3.12 (CnD) per capita of the provincial population (as estimated by Statistics Canada to exist on July 1 in the calendar year of the disaster). Once the threshold is exceeded, the federal share of eligible expenses is determined by the formula. The formula is graduated such that the loss total for the province is divided by the province's population. If a province has a million people it must have sustained $3.12 (CnD) million in damage, at which point losses beyond that total are shared 50/50 between the Government of Canada and the respective province. Using the same example, if disaster losses for the province exceeded $6.25 (CnD) million, losses above that amount would be covered on a 75/25 basis. There are two more threshold levels based on provincial disaster losses above $6.25 (CnD) million. The highest level of Government of Canada assistance under the formula is 90/10.[31] Remember, the first $3.12 (CnD) million in provincial disaster loss is fully absorbed by the province as a deductible that must be paid "before" DFAA funding is made available.

Fraud alert (Ch. 9) FEMA instituted additional verification and controls in cases where there was suspicious activity to ensure that only eligible applicants receive assistance. DHS Office of Inspector General (OIG) continues to aggressively investigate allegations of disaster fraud after every federally declared disaster and works with other law enforcement agencies to identify and prosecute individuals who take advantage of programs meant to help those in need.[32]

Fraudulent claims (Ch. 6) False documentation or other forms of deceit in people's applications for government assistance. Government efforts to prevent and ferret out fraudulent claims often have the unintended consequence of delaying or complicating delivery of program assistance to claimants who legitimately deserve the aid they apply for.

Fukushima Daiichi nuclear power plant disaster (Ch. 5) After a major earthquake, a 15-meter-high tsunami disabled the power supply and cooling of three Fukushima Daiichi reactors, causing a nuclear accident on March 11, 2011. Three reactor cores largely melted in the first three days. High radioactive releases occurred over four to six days. Over 100,000 people had to be evacuated from their homes in the vicinity of the plant. Owned by Japan's Tokyo Electric Power Company (TEPCO), plant managers and operators struggled for years to prevent radiation leaks to the air, ground, and sea.

Fusion centers (Ch. 7) The Law Enforcement Terrorism Prevention Program (LETPP) uses so-called "fusion centers," which provide a nexus of local, state, and federal terrorism-focused law enforcement interchange, and local emergency managers are part of this nexus.

"Gap group" clients (Ch. 6) Those who fall between the cracks and are denied, or unable to qualify for, government post-disaster assistance; some are low income but not poor enough to qualify for government individual and household cash assistance, which is means tested. Some lack proper documentation, some cannot prove they live in the area of the disaster, others filled out their application for aid incorrectly, some cannot complete tele-registration to file a claim with the Federal Emergency Management Agency (FEMA), some have not been able to find local disaster service centers where they can make application, etc. The point is that there are a host of reasons why people fall into unassisted gap groups.

Generalists (Ch. 2) Broadly educated people who in public management are likely to be highly politically responsive and able to fulfill government executive obligations of public responsiveness. It is assumed that generalists are better able than specialists to address humanitarian aspects of disaster assistance and are better able to work compatibly with others in the intergovernmental world of domestic disaster management.

Generalized knowledge (Ch. 2) Furnishes reasoning tools or conceptual lenses that hold explanatory power applicable within or across a wide variety of cases and circumstances.

Globalizing forces (Ch. 8) The massive movement of individuals, capital, goods, information, and technologies across borders, which bonds developing nations to new and old industrialized nations. Disasters and this interdependence combine to produce negative, destabilizing effects in many developing nations.

Hamiltonian approach (Ch. 2) Officials as managers expect others, especially strong elected executives, to judge them by whether their efforts produce the desired results. They work under after-the-fact accountability, and their concerns are performance and evaluation under public law. Requires education, professionalism, knowledge, skills, and abilities. One makes independent judgments and decisions drawing on one's authority of expertise.

Hamiltonian public managers (Ch. 2) A normative theory of public management in which public managers must learn and apply a growing body of knowledge, some of it practical knowledge and some of it academic knowledge. Hamiltonian public managers embody an authority of expertise, have mastered a specialized field of theoretical and applied knowledge, and are considered technocratic officials.

Hawaii false ballistic missile alert (Ch. 10) Issued by the Hawaii Emergency Management Agency on January 13, 2018, the alert warned of an inbound missile. The alert terrified the islands' residents and visitors and was not corrected until 38 minutes later. It happened because a staffer had simply clicked on a wrong link.[33]

Hazards (Ch. 1) A potential threat to humans and their welfare arising from a dangerous phenomenon or substances that may cause loss of life, injury, property damage, and other community losses or damage.

Hazards U.S. (HAZUS) (Ch. 2) See the definition for Hazards U.S.-Multi-Hazard (HAZUS-MH).

Hazards U.S.-Multi-Hazard (HAZUS-MH) (Ch. 2) An earthquake computer simulation applicable and adaptable to most of the nation developed by the Federal Emergency Management Agency (FEMA) in the 1990s; it is a powerful risk assessment software program for analyzing potential losses from earthquakes. HAZUS-MH, a newer generation of HAZUS, models potential losses from hurricanes, winds, and floods as well as earthquakes for specific locations across the nation.

Home rule (Ch. 6) In some states, local governments are accorded certain powers under home rule provisions of their respective state constitution, or through enabling statutes.[34] It is the right to local self-government, including the powers to regulate for the protection of the public health, safety, morals, and welfare; to license; to tax; and to incur debt. Home rule involves the authority of a local government to prevent state government intervention with its operations. The extent of its power, however, is subject to limitations prescribed by state constitutions and statutes.[35]

Homeland Security Act of 2002 (Ch. 3) Public Law 107-296 enacted November 25, 2002. It authorized creation of U.S. Department of Homeland Security (DHS), a super department opened in 2003 and today has some 270,000 employees. It was formed by transferring some 22 federal agencies or offices into the new department. The DHS secretary, holding cabinet rank, and deputy secretary are managerial supervisors of the Federal Emergency Management Agency (FEMA) administrator. The law also recruited state and local government into the nation's war on terror.[36] Title 1 of the law stated, "The primary mission of the Department is to—(A) prevent terrorist attacks within the United States; (B) reduce the vulnerability of the United States to terrorism; (C) minimize the damage, and assist in the recovery, from terrorist attacks that do occur within the United States; (D) carry out all functions of entities transferred to the Department, including by acting as a focal point regarding natural and manmade crises and emergency planning; (E) ensure that the functions of the agencies and subdivisions within the Department that are not related directly to securing the homeland are not diminished or neglected except by a specific explicit Act of Congress; (F) ensure that the overall economic security of the United States is not diminished by efforts, activities, and programs aimed at securing the homeland; and (G) monitor connections between illegal drug trafficking and terrorism, coordinate efforts to sever such connections, and otherwise contribute to efforts to interdict illegal drug trafficking. (2) Responsibility for Investigating and Prosecuting Terrorism—Except as specifically provided by law with respect to entities transferred to the Department under this Act, primary responsibility for investigating and prosecuting acts of terrorism shall be vested not in the Department, but rather in Federal, State, and local law enforcement agencies with jurisdiction over the acts in question."[37]

Homeland Security Advisory System (HSAS)   (Ch. 7) A threat-based, color-coded, five-tiered system used to communicate to the American public and safety officials the status of terrorist threat to the nation or to parts of the nation. Replaced by the National Terrorism Advisory System (NTAS) in April 2011.

Horizontal fragmentation (Ch. 1) Sometimes occurs when a disaster or emergency must be addressed by many different and competing government agencies, all working at the same level of government but with different duties and functions and sometimes overlapping jurisdictions. Common when officials of these agencies fail to coordinate their responsibilities with one another, act too independently of one another, duplicate their efforts, or work at cross-purposes with one another.

Humanitarian assistance (Ch. 8) Involves concern for human welfare and social reforms. Within the realm of disaster humanitarian assistance, acute post-disaster concerns involve providing emergency food, water, shelter, medical services and supplies, clothing, and other items to disaster victims to ensure their immediate survival. From a U.S. government perspective, it also means humanitarian assistance is used to encourage democracy and building structures favorable to sustainable political and economic development. In this way, the U.S. government gains and keeps allies and promotes other U.S. interests, among them the security of the United States itself. In providing disaster aid to the people of other nations, an American secondary agenda is to prevent recipient nations from political or economic collapse, to forestall their subversion by enemies of the United States, and to prevent the spawning of failed states that may evolve into rogue states.

Humanitarian Assistance Survey Teams (Ch. 8) Are often sent to evaluate the needs on the ground to ensure that the intervention is proceeding effectively. An instrument of the U.S. Department of Defense (DOD) used in circumstances of foreign disaster relief aid.

Hurricane Harvey (Ch. 9) A mid-August 2017 Category 4 hurricane that struck the eastern coast of Texas, most particularly areas in the Houston metroplex, as well as southwestern Louisiana. It wreaked havoc on the Texas Coast, dumping more than 50 inches of rain in parts of the Houston area, flooding thousands of homes. Harvey formed August 17 and dissipated about September 1. According to the National Hurricane Center, "Harvey rapidly intensified into a category 4 hurricane (on the Saffir-Simpson Hurricane Wind Scale) before making landfall along the middle Texas coast. The storm then stalled, with its center over or near the Texas coast for four days, dropping historic amounts of rainfall of more than 60 inches over southeastern Texas. These rains caused catastrophic flooding, and Harvey is the second-most costly hurricane in U.S. history, after accounting for inflation, behind only Katrina (2005). At least 68 people died from the direct effects of the storm in Texas, the largest number of direct deaths from a tropical cyclone in that state since 1919."[38] As of May 9, 2018, the NOAA damage estimate from Harvey is $125 billion, with the 90% confidence interval ranging from $90 to $160 billion. The mid-point of the estimate would tie Katrina (2005) as the costliest U.S. tropical cyclone, which was also $125 billion.[39] Harvey damaged some 300,000 structures and a half-million automobiles; it may exceed Katrina damage once more insurance and assistance payouts for Harvey are compiled and adjusted for inflation since Katrina struck in 2005.

Hurricane Irma (Ch. 9) Began as a tropical storm on August 30, 2017, in the Atlantic just west of the Cape Verde Islands; over the next 10 days, it grew into a Category 5 hurricane with a maximum sustained wind of 185 mph. The storm moved through parts of the Caribbean Islands, including Puerto Rico and between Cuba and Florida. Eventually the hurricane turned northwest and impacted the Florida Keys and areas near Naples, Florida; then it generally followed Interstate 75 north through the entire Florida peninsula. Hurricane Irma then moved into Georgia, Alabama, and Tennessee. It hit Florida as a Category 4 storm the morning of September 10, 2017, ripping off roofs, flooding coastal cities, and knocking out power to more than 6.8 million people. By September 11, Irma weakened significantly to a tropical storm as it powered north. At 11 p.m. later that day, it weakened further to a tropical depression, and by September 13, it had dissipated over western Tennessee. Irma is the fifth-costliest hurricane to hit the mainland United States, causing an estimated $50 billion in damage, according to the National Hurricane Center.[40] In the United States, 10 direct deaths were reported, and an additional 82 indirect deaths occurred, 77 of which were in Florida. Hundreds more were injured before, during, or after the hurricane. About 6 million residents in Florida were evacuated from coastal areas.[41] Irma produced heavy rain across much of the state of Florida, and rainfall totals of 10 to 15 inches were common across the peninsula and the Keys. The maximum reported storm-total rainfall was near Ft. Pierce, Florida, in St. Lucie County, where 21.66 inches of rain was measured between September 9 and 12.[42]

Hurricane Maria (Ch. 9) Made landfall just south of Yabucoa Harbor in Puerto Rico at 6:15 a.m., September 20, 2017. The National Weather Service observed maximum sustained winds of 155 miles per hour, making Maria the first Category 4 hurricane to hit the island since 1932. The storm almost reached Category 5, defined as any tropical storm with winds 157 miles per hour or higher. Parts of Puerto Rico saw 30 inches of rain in one day, equal to the amount that Houston received over three days during Hurricane Harvey. The storm knocked out power to the entire island. Much of the island's population, including swaths of San Juan, could not access clean water without electrical power.[43] Hurricane Maria devasted every county of Puerto Rico. The island was ravaged by winds and floods. The death toll produced by Maria is still under investigation, although some estimates are that direct and indirect deaths attributable to Maria could exceed 4,600.[44] The NOAA estimate of damage in Puerto Rico and the U.S. Virgin Islands due to Maria is $90 billion, with a 90% confidence range of +/−$25.0 billion, or $65.0 to $115.0 billion, which makes Maria the third costliest hurricane in U.S. history, behind Katrina (2005) and Harvey (2017). Maria is by far the most destructive hurricane to hit Puerto Rico in modern times, as the previous costliest hurricane on record for the island was Georges in 1998, which in 2017 dollars "only" caused about $5 billion of damage. The combined destructive power of storm surge and wave action from Maria produced extensive damage to buildings, homes, and roads along the east and southeast coast of Puerto Rico as well as the south coasts of Vieques and St. Croix.[45] Maria knocked down 80 percent of Puerto Rico's utility poles and all transmission lines, resulting in the loss of power to essentially all of the island's 3.4 million residents. Practically all cell phone service was lost and municipal water supplies were knocked out. At of the end of 2017, nearly half of Puerto Rico's residents were still without power.[46]

Hyper-partisanship (Ch. 1) A sharply polarized situation in which political parties are in fierce disagreement with each other.[47] In the United States, it also denotes stark ideological, social, and cultural divisions based on partisan affiliation.

Incident Command System (ICS) (Ch. 6) A standardized on-scene, all-hazards incident management system required by the U.S. Department of Homeland Security (DHS). It had been used by many firefighters, hazardous materials teams, rescuers, and emergency medical teams before its adoption as a key component of the National Incident Management System (NIMS) under Homeland Security Presidential Directive (HSPD-5) in 2005. It is a management system designed to integrate resources so as to effectively attack a common problem.

Incidents of national significance (Ch. 3) High-impact events that under the former National Response Plan (NRP) require an extensive and well-coordinated multiagency response to save lives, minimize damage, and provide the basis for long-term community and economic recovery. The president or the secretary of homeland security had authority to declare incidents of national significance, which may be acts of terrorism or major disasters or emergencies. The term *incident of national significance* was discontinued in 2008 when the National Response Framework (NRF) replaced the NRP. The term was judged to be confusing, duplicative, and a questionable grant of authority to the secretary of the U.S. Department of Homeland Security (DHS).

Inclusive-authority model (Ch. 2) A model of intergovernmental relations in which each level of government has a diminishing proportion of responsibilities, from the national to the state to the local government level. The federal government coordinates and shares power and responsibility; however, the authority is essentially hierarchical (top-down control).

Individual and Family Grant (IFG) program (Ch. 3) Former Federal Emergency Management Agency (FEMA)-funded, state-administered program that under a presidential declaration of major disaster provided disaster victims cash help for essential needs. Established by the Disaster Relief Act of 1974, IFG operated as a means-tested grant program for victims of presidentially declared disasters. The grant could be used for home repair; for vehicle repair or replacement; as well as for medical, dental, funeral, transportation, and other disaster-related costs. As long as insurance claim payouts for these needs was counted first, IFG could cover eligible remaining uninsured losses. A grant may help pay to fix or replace furniture, appliances, and other essential property. The grants may also help victims pay for moving and storage expenses, sandbagging, and mobile home towing,[48] IFG required 75 percent/25 percent federal/state dollar matching. IFG was renamed the Individuals and Households Program (IHP) in mid-2002, and it was merged with another FEMA housing program.

Individual and Household Assistance (Ch. 6) The Federal Emergency Management Agency (FEMA) financial grants to rent alternative housing; direct assistance through temporary housing units (mobile homes); limited financial assistance for housing repairs and replacement; and financial assistance for uninsured medical, dental, funeral, personal property, transportation, and other expenses. It is delivered through a variety of FEMA program and subprogram offices.

Individuals and Households Program (IHP) (Ch. 4) Launched in 2003 and called the Individual and Family Grant (IFG) program from 1974 to 2002, the IHP encompasses a set of federal post-disaster assistance programs available to individuals, families, or household groups under terms of a presidential declaration of major disaster or emergency. Among types of aid are financial grants to rent alternative housing; direct assistance through temporary housing units (mobile homes); limited financial assistance for housing repairs and replacement; and financial assistance for uninsured medical, dental, funeral, personal property, and transportation expenses. Some are federal-funded but state-administered programs that under a presidential declaration of major disaster provide disaster victims cash help for essential needs. Authorized by the Disaster Relief Act of 1974, IFG and later IHP. Note, IHP is 100 percent federally funded with the exception of a 75 percent/25 percent federal/state matching requirement for its Other Needs Assistance program. IHP is a major human services program managed by the Federal Emergency Management Agency (FEMA).

Insufficient technical expertise (Ch. 1) A common criticism of many emergency managers owing to confusion about the kind of expertise one needs to be an effective emergency manager. Controversy about the technical expertise needed to identify and assess hazards adequately, predict the occurrence of disasters, and provide the requisite technical information for the design and implementation of effective programs in emergency management. Even when hazards have been identified, it is often unclear just how much risk is involved and how this risk is to be measured. Emergency management as a field is highly dynamic, so the education and skills required to do it are ever changing.

Intergovernmental relations (Ch. 1) The interaction and exchanges of public and private organizations across all layers of government. Intergovernmental relations reflect the growth of societal interdependence, in economic and technological terms, and have created a webbed and networked system of governance.

International Association of Emergency Managers (IAEM) (Ch. 1) A nonprofit educational organization dedicated to promoting the goals of saving lives and protecting property during emergencies and disasters. IAEM is primarily composed of local emergency managers. It operates a Certified Emergency Manager (CEM) program.

Interstate compacts (Ch. 6) An agreement between two or more states of the United States. Article I, Section 10, of the U.S. Constitution provides that "no state shall enter into an agreement or compact with another state" without the consent of Congress.

Issue-attention cycle (Ch. 1) A pattern of public perception of certain domestic problems. The cycle has five stages and concerns the way major communications media interact with the public.

Issue salience (Ch. 1) The importance of an issue to the public and to elected leaders.

Jacksonian approach (Ch. 2) Highly populist, advocates decentralization, which grants local governments greater autonomy with direct governance, concentrates authority in elected executives, minimizes legislative interference in public management, and allows elected executives to appoint their political partisans and allies to many government jobs.

Jacksonian public managers (Ch. 2) Self-reliant, courageous, individualistic, and entrepreneurial public managers who construct their own destiny despite once working within the patronage system of placing political supporters into appointed government offices. Jacksonian public managers present themselves as bold, prominent figures and assert their personality with zeal while adhering unconditionally to their beliefs.[49] They articulate public desires sometimes in defiance of political elites, particularly legislators, whom they tend to view with profound suspicion. Individualistic and entrepreneurial, the Jacksonian public manager will take the initiative and pursue new directions in light of government perversion or inefficiency.[50]

Japan Meteorological Agency (JMA) (Ch. 5) Leads Japan's mitigation and prevention of natural hazards, particularly those capable of catastrophic consequences. The office is within the Ministry of Land, Infrastructure, and Transport and part of the Courts branch of government. Responsible for tracking all weather-related phenomena as well as for monitoring, predicting, identifying, and measuring seismic events associated with tsunamis, earthquakes, and volcanoes. The agency is charged with both detecting earthquakes and formulating earthquake warning messages communicated to appropriate audiences.

Jeffersonian approach (Ch. 2) Calls for administrators to maintain community support and support from senior-elected and appointed officials, the news media, and the public as much as possible. Requires that one possess not only skill in consultation, negotiation, and communication but also deftness in probing for public understanding and consent.

Jeffersonian public managers (Ch. 2) A normative theory of public management in which public managers possess skill in consultation, negotiation, and communication and deftness in probing for public understanding and consent. Jeffersonian public managers are broadly educated generalists who are strictly accountable to the public and to elected overseers.

Law Enforcement Terrorism Prevention Activities (LETPA) (Ch. 7) DHS-FEMA is required by law to make sure that "at least 25 percent of appropriated grant

(HSGP) funding goes to law enforcement terrorism prevention activities under Law Enforcement Terrorism Prevention Activities (LETPA)" grants. DHS/FEMA meets this requirement, in part, by requiring (that) all State Homeland Security Program (SHSP) and UASI recipients devote at least twenty five percent (25%) of the funds they are allocated under SHSP and UASI to law enforcement terrorism prevention activities.[51] It is the grant recipients, not DHS, who direct a quarter of the SHSG and UASI funds they receive to law enforcement counter terrorism or terrorism prevention purposes.

Law Enforcement Terrorism Prevention Program (LETPP) (Ch. 7) Supports law enforcement communities in their efforts to detect, deter, disrupt, and prevent acts of terrorism. Categories of aid include information sharing to preempt terrorist attacks; target hardening to reduce vulnerability of selected high-value targets; recognition and mapping of potential or developing threats; interoperable communications; and interdiction of terrorists before they can execute a threat or intervention activities that prevent terrorists from executing a threat. Employs fusion centers.

Local emergency management committees (LEMCs) (Ch. 2) A disaster-planning network used by local emergency managers that increases coordination among local agencies.[52] LEMCs succeed when they effectively receive and respond to community information requests, when they establish and maintain good working relationships with people of the news media, when they earn and maintain local support, and when they retain the confidence and backing of local officials.[53]

Long-term recovery (Ch. 1) "Addresses the basic dimensions of a community's existence: permanent housing, economic conditions, the environment, the infrastructure (e.g., roads, bridges), and lifelines (e.g., water, power, telephone service)."[54]

Love Canal, in Niagara Falls, New York, hazardous waste incident (Ch. 5) In 1978, Love Canal, located near Niagara Falls in upstate New York, was a modest working-class enclave with hundreds of houses and a school. Unfortunately, by the early to mid-1970s, it was found to sit atop 21,000 tons of toxic industrial waste that had been buried underground in the 1940s and 1950s by a local company. Over the years, the waste began to bubble up into backyards and cellars. By 1978, the problem was unavoidable, and hundreds of families sold their houses to the federal government and evacuated the area. The disaster led to the formation in 1980 of the Superfund program, which helps pay for the cleanup of toxic sites.[55]

Major disaster (Ch. 4) "Natural catastrophe (including any hurricane, tornado, storm, high water, wind-driven water, tidal wave, tsunami, earthquake, volcanic eruption, landslide, mudslide, snowstorm, or drought) or, regardless of cause, any fire, flood, or explosion, in any part of the United States, which, in the determination of the President, causes damage of sufficient severity and magnitude to warrant major disaster assistance under federal law to supplement the efforts and available resources of States, local governments, and disaster relief organizations in alleviating the damage, loss, hardship, or suffering caused thereby."[56]

Major disaster assistance (Ch. 4) Post-disaster federal assistance made available to disaster victims, as well as to state and local governments, under the terms of a presidential declaration of major disaster.

Major disaster declaration (Ch. 1) A category of presidential declaration established initially by the Federal Disaster Act of 1950 and revised and augmented by the Stafford Act of 1988. It opens the door to federal disaster assistance, mobilizes federal agencies to respond in accord with a national response plan or framework, specifies one or more political jurisdictions (a state and eligible counties), delineates who is eligible for relief, and contains an initial statement about the kinds of assistance people or subnational governments may request. Acting on a governor's request for such a declaration, the president has authority to approve it or turn it down. Incorporated municipalities in a county are eligible to receive federal assistance under a major disaster declaration through county government and often under conditions set in place by the respective state government.

Marginal disaster request approvals (Ch. 4) Governor requests for presidential disaster declarations that are arguably not major destructive events but that the president has nonetheless approved as a major disaster or emergency under his authority to declare disasters. Event judged to be at or barely over the threshold required for administrative approvability. It is also possible that the event did not meet Federal Emergency Management Agency (FEMA) minimum conditions of qualification but fell below its per capita damage approval threshold, and the president chose to approve the request regardless.

Marginal disaster request denials (Ch. 4) Governor requests for presidential disaster declarations that are arguably "not" major destructive or threatening events and that the president has asked the Federal Emergency Management Agency (FEMA) administrator to turn down. Event judged to be at or under the FEMA threshold required for administrative approvability. President assents to the FEMA turndown recommendation. To this author's knowledge, no one has been able to factually prove that any president rejected a governor request for a declaration of major disaster or emergency despite a FEMA recommendation to approve that request.

Marginal disasters (Ch. 4) Those events that are far less than catastrophic, that are not matters of national security, and that are near or within the response and recovery capacity of the state or states in which they occur.[57] Low-damage, marginal incidents involve small federal payouts, usually a small portion of a local area, and few-to-no fatalities and injuries. The smaller the federal payouts are for various declarations, the greater the probability that political considerations at the presidential level played a role in a president's approval of a declaration.

Martial law (Ch. 7) Temporary rule by military authority imposed upon a civilian population in time of war or when civil authority is unable to maintain public safety. In the United States, both the president and state governors hold authority to declare martial law. Presidents are likely to apply it only under extreme conditions of war, national emergency, or crisis. Governors sometimes declare martial law in state emergencies and disasters, using the state National Guard to carry it out.

Mass care (Ch. 6) Services such as sheltering, feeding operations, emergency first aid, bulk distribution of emergency items, and collecting and providing information on victims to family members. Mass care is part of Emergency Support Function #6.[58]

Memorandums of understanding (MOUs) (Ch. 6) Administrative agreements, usually voluntary and usually negotiated by officials of various government agencies, which in emergency management establish commitments regarding how each agency will cooperate with the others and what specific duties will be performed in future disasters or emergencies.

Mission assignment by (FEMA) (Ch. 3) A work order issued by FEMA, with or without reimbursement, that directs another federal agency to use its authorities and the resources granted to it under federal law in support of state, local, tribal, and territorial government assistance. The mission assignment (MA) program is authorized by the Robert T. Stafford Disaster Relief and Emergency Assistance Act (Stafford Act). Often FEMA provides reimbursement to the requesting federal agency under mission assignment. MA can be "pre-scripted" before an imminent disaster or emergency, but mission assignment spending authority follows issuance of a presidential declaration of major disaster or emergency. FEMA cannot provide mission assignment funding to subsidize what is already the mission or responsibility of the requesting federal agency. Mission assignment for DHS-FEMA is a type of force multiplier that furnishes federal funds to other federal agencies, including DHS agencies, to cover the extraordinary needs and purposes sometimes produced by disasters and emergencies. DHS-FEMA has a process for requesting, reviewing, issuing, implementing, and closing out or terminating mission assignments.[59]

Missions and capabilities (Ch. 10) DHS and FEMA have since 2016 de-emphasized the "four phases or cycles" approach to disaster management and have supplanted it with "missions and capabilities." In so doing, "missions and capabilities" are now the department-wide basis for evaluation of all of DHS offices and programs. Many "missions" are more products of DHS edicts than they are original products of "grass-roots" local and state government officials. Also, "missions and capabilities" have been suffused into the rules and conditions of DHS and FEMA grants to state and local governments.

Mitigation (Ch. 1) Activities, laws, or policies that attempt to prevent disasters or reduce potential losses from disasters. Mitigation is often between-disaster activity. Mitigation may be structural (engineered) or nonstructural (behavior changes, zoning laws, land-use restrictions, and the like).

Modified Mercalli scale (Ch. 5) One way to measure the strength of an earthquake is to use the Mercalli scale. Invented by Giuseppe Mercalli in 1902, this scale uses the observations of the people who experienced the earthquake to estimate its intensity. The Mercalli scale isn't considered as scientific as the Richter scale. "The effect of an earthquake on the Earth's surface is called the intensity. The intensity scale consists of a series of certain key responses such as people awakening, movement of furni-

ture, damage to chimneys, and finally—total destruction. Although numerous *intensity scales* have been developed over the last several hundred years to evaluate the effects of earthquakes, the one currently used in the United States is the Modified Mercalli (MM) Intensity Scale. It was developed in 1931 by the American seismologists Harry Wood and Frank Neumann. This scale, composed of increasing levels of intensity that range from imperceptible shaking to catastrophic destruction, is designated by Roman numerals. It does not have a mathematical basis; instead it is an arbitrary ranking based on observed effects."[60] The Modified Mercalli Intensity value assigned to a specific site after an earthquake has a more meaningful measure of severity to the nonscientist than the magnitude because intensity refers to the effects actually experienced at that place. See Glossary Figure 2.

Moment magnitude scale (Ch. 5) Many scales, such as the Richter scale, do not provide accurate estimates for large magnitude earthquakes. Today the moment magnitude scale is preferred because it works over a wider range of earthquake sizes and is applicable globally. The moment magnitude scale is based on the total moment release of the earthquake. Moment is a product of the distance a fault moved and the force required to move it. It is derived from modeling recordings of the earthquake at multiple stations. Moment magnitude estimates are about the same as Richter magnitudes for small-to-large earthquakes. But only the moment magnitude scale is capable of measuring M8 (read "magnitude 8") and greater events accurately.[61]

Moral hazard (Ch. 1) An increase in the probability of loss caused by the behavior of a holder of insurance. In the realm of the insurance market, those whose homes are insured behave carelessly or dishonestly by failing to take reasonable measures to protect their homes from a known disaster threat because they expect that insurance will cover their losses if a disaster transpires. In the realm of government, this applies when lower level governments forgo reasonable disaster mitigation measures because their leaders expect post-disaster assistance from upper level government to cover their losses and so they believe they have realized a savings by not spending money on pre-disaster mitigation.

Multiagency coordination systems (MACS) (Ch. 6) Primary function of MACS is to coordinate activities above the field level and to prioritize the incident demands for

FIGURE G-2 ■ Abbreviated Description of the Levels of Modified Mercalli Intensity

Intensity	Shaking	Description/Damage
I	Not felt	Not felt except by a very few under especially favorable conditions.
II	Weak	Felt only by a few persons at rest, especially on upper floors of buildings.
III	Weak	Felt quite noticeably by persons indoors, especially on upper floors of buildings. Many people do not recognize it as an earthquake. Standing motor cars may rock slightly. Vibrations similar to the passing of a truck. Duration estimated.
IV	Light	Felt indoors by many, outdoors by few during the day. At night, some awakened. Dishes, windows, doors disturbed; walls make cracking sound. Sensation like heavy truck striking building. Standing motor cars rocked noticeably.
V	Moderate	Felt by nearly everyone; many awakened. Some dishes, windows broken. Unstable objects overturned. Pendulum clocks may stop.
VI	Strong	Felt by all, many frightened. Some heavy furniture moved; a few instances of fallen plaster. Damage slight.
VII	Very strong	Damage negligible in buildings of good design and construction; slight to moderate in well-built ordinary structures; considerable damage in poorly built or badly designed structures; some chimneys broken.
VIII	Severe	Damage slight in specially designed structures; considerable damage in ordinary substantial buildings with partial collapse. Damage great in poorly built structures. Fall of chimneys, factory stacks, columns, monuments, walls. Heavy furniture overturned.
IX	Violent	Damage considerable in specially designed structures; well-designed frame structures thrown out of plumb. Damage great in substantial buildings, with partial collapse. Buildings shifted off foundations.
X	Extreme	Some well-built wooden structures destroyed; most masonry and frame structures destroyed with foundations. Rails bent.

Source: Abridged from *The Severity of an Earthquake*, USGS General Interest Publication 1989-288-913.

critical or competing resources, thereby assisting the coordination of the operations in the field. MACS consist of a combination of elements: personnel, procedures, protocols, business practices, and communications integrated into a common system. Emergency operations centers (EOCs) are one of several system elements included within the MACS. Integral elements of MACS are dispatch procedures and protocols, the incident command structure, and the coordination and support activities taking place within an activated EOC. Fundamentally, MACS provide support, coordination, and assistance with policy-level decisions to the Incident Command System (ICS) structure managing an incident.

Multi-hazard approach (Ch. 3) An approach in which the government would manage all kinds of hazards, rather than maintaining unique and separated capacities to deal with different types of disaster agents. To the extent possible, methods and tools used to address one type of disaster would be applied to a variety of types.

Mutual aid agreements (Ch. 6) Written agreements, often formal and matters of law, between agencies or government jurisdictions to assist one another on request by making available personnel, equipment, and expertise in a specified manner. The Emergency Management Assistance Compact (EMAC), which now includes nearly all state governments, facilitates state-to-state mutual aid agreements to be used in emergencies and disasters. Such agreements commonly set forth terms of reimbursement, conditions of liability if responders are hurt or somehow cause harm, and contingent acquisition agreements between providers, vendors, and contractors.[62]

Na-tech disasters (Ch. 5) Disasters that occur when natural hazards result in dangerous technological spills or releases.[63] Na-tech events involve a combination of natural and technological interactions. Many na-tech disasters begin from lightning strikes and floods.

National Academies, The (Ch. 5) Composed of the National Academy of Sciences, the National Academy of Engineering, and the Institute of Medicine, facilitated by their National Research Council, the National Academies conduct numerous disaster-related research studies for various sponsors, among them federal agencies that contract with them to form panels and conduct studies.[64] The research reports of the National Academies have been known to greatly influence makers of public policy who are struggling to find solutions or policy approaches to the complex problems they must address.

National Disaster Recovery Framework (NDRF) (Ch. 2) Promotes management and consultation schemes by which the Federal Emergency Management Agency and its stakeholders can plan disaster recovery long before disasters occur. It is a FEMA-led initiative encouraged at the grassroots level.

National Earthquake Hazards Reduction Program (NEHRP) (Ch. 5) Under Public Law 92-124 enacted in 1977, the measure supports federal, state, local, and private research and planning to attenuate earthquake losses in seismic risk areas. It provides the framework for a national earthquake policy. The Federal Emergency Management Agency was designated the lead agency charged with coordinating that program from 1979 to 2002. However, the National Institute of Standards and Technology (NIST) was assigned lead agency responsibility for the NEHRP in 2003. The program has been reauthorized by Congress several times (2004 and 2017).

FEMA today works collaboratively with partnering federal agencies to advance the goals of the program. "Focusing on building code standards, technical guidance, and education, NEHRP is a collaborative effort among the Federal Emergency Management Agency (FEMA); the National Institute of Standards and Technology (NIST), the NEHRP lead agency; the National Science Foundation (NSF); and the United States Geological Survey (USGS). These agencies work in close coordination to improve the understanding of earthquake hazards and to reduce the Nation's vulnerability to earthquakes. The agencies research the causes and effects of earthquakes to produce technical guidance; develop earthquake-resistant design, construction standards, and techniques; and educate the public about earthquake hazards and mitigation."[65]

National Emergency Management Association (NEMA) (Ch. 1) The professional association of and for emergency management directors from all 50 states, eight territories, and the District of Columbia. It provides national leadership and expertise in comprehensive emergency management; serves as a vital emergency management information and assistance resource; and advances continuous improvement in emergency management through strategic partnerships, innovative programs, and collaborative policy positions.

National Fire Academy (Ch. 5) Promotes the professional development of the fire and the emergency response community and its allied professionals. The National Fire Academy supports state and local training organizations to fulfill their obligation to the career and volunteer fire and emergency services. The National Fire Academy also develops, delivers, and manages educational and training programs having a national focus that is outside state and local training mission or exceeds state and local capabilities because of cost or audience. The programs are designed to support the U.S. Department of Homeland Security (DHS) and the Federal Emergency Management Agency (FEMA) goals to help state and local response agencies prevent; mitigate; prepare for; and respond to local, regional, and national emergencies.[66]

National Flood Insurance Program (NFIP) (Ch. 5) A national insurance program operated by the Federal Insurance & Mitigation Administration of FEMA that invites localities to join if they promise to meet federal standards aimed at limiting development in floodplains and promoting flood-proof construction. People living in the communities that joined the NFIP would then be eligible to buy low-cost flood insurance from the federal government. In effect, the federal government would use insurance as a key form of disaster assistance and as a tool of flood mitigation. Flood insurance is only available to Americans through the NFIP.

National Guard (Ch. 7) Composed of the Army National Guard, the Air National Guard, and reservists called up to serve. National Guard personnel are commanded in each state by the state's governor unless the Guard is mobilized for federal duty by the president. The U.S. Army and Air National Guard forces are hybrid state–federal militias whose roots reach back before the Revolution. Normally under the control of state governors, the National Guard is almost entirely funded and equipped by the federal government, and the troops are trained to the same standard as active-duty personnel. National Guard troops can perform law enforcement functions under a state's laws but cannot enforce criminal law when they are federalized—that is when they are under the direct control of the president.

National Incident Management System (NIMS) (Ch. 1) The elaborate tactical arm of the National Response Framework (NRF), designed to help federal, state, and local governments address domestic incidents, whether acts of terrorism or disasters stemming from natural or other human causes. All federal agencies were required to adopt NIMS, and state and local governments were required to use it as a condition of federal assistance. The NIMS incorporated many existing emergency management "best practices" into a comprehensive national approach to domestic incident management, applicable at all jurisdictional levels and across all responder occupational fields. Its purpose was to help responders at all jurisdictional levels and across all disciplines to work together more effectively and efficiently. A core component of the NIMS was the Incident Command System (ICS). The NIMS has a core set of doctrines, principles, terminology, and organizational processes. It is supposed to be based on a balance between flexibility and standardization. It seeks a consistent, nationwide template for incident management.

National Planning Frameworks (Ch. 3) The National Planning Frameworks, one for each preparedness mission area, describe how the "whole community"

is expected to work together to achieve the National Preparedness Goal. The goal is "[a] secure and resilient nation with the capabilities required across the whole community to prevent, protect against, mitigate, respond to, and recover from the threats and hazards that pose the greatest risk."[67] The goal is the cornerstone for the implementation of the National Preparedness System. The National Planning Frameworks are part of the National Preparedness System. There is one Framework for each of the five preparedness mission areas: National Prevention Framework, National Protection Framework, National Mitigation Framework, National Response Framework, National Disaster Recovery Framework.[68]

National planning scenarios (Ch. 7) Fifteen "planning scenarios" developed by the U.S. Department of Homeland Security (DHS), intended to be used in evaluating the ability of a jurisdiction to manage a major disaster. They encompass the range of "plausible" events, most of them stemming from terror attacks involving weapons of mass destruction, that are assumed to pose the greatest risk to the nation.

National preparedness (Ch. 3) A set of goals established by the secretary of homeland security under Homeland Security Presidential Directive-8 (HSPD-8), primarily focused on preparedness for terrorism-related events, especially the training and equipping of emergency response agencies.

National Response Framework (NRF) (Ch. 1) A comprehensive all-hazards approach and master plan intended to strengthen and improve the ability of the United States to manage domestic incidents. In 2008, the federal government officially replaced the National Response Plan (NRP), with changes, as the NRF. The NRF provides a template for federal, state, and local governmental cooperation and coordination in disaster response. In December 2013, the second edition of the NRF was launched. It is based on the version released in 2008. The new NRF incorporates a focus on whole community and core capabilities. For example, the framework now describes the important roles of individuals, families, and households in response activities. Also, the frameworks are intended to be strategic documents, with tactical planning and concept of operations content reserved for the new Federal Interagency Operational Plans (FIOPs). As a result, the revised NRF is shorter and more strategic than its predecessor.[69]

National Response Plan (NRP) (Ch. 1) The National Commission on Terrorist Attacks Upon the United States, commonly referred to as the 9/11 Commission, called on the George W. Bush administration to prepare a comprehensive national response plan that would replace the Federal Response Plan (FRP) and give greater attention to terrorism prevention, preparedness, and consequence management. The NRP, launched in 2003, included state and local government as well as nonprofit and for-profit corporation stakeholders. It retained the FRP template of emergency support functions (ESFs) that called on a variety of federal agencies and their resources when needed. Under the NRP, primary responsibility for managing domestic crises was now to rest with the secretary of homeland security. The plan contained language strongly suggesting that the federal government would in the future assume more responsibility for directly managing some crises. The NRP, in place but lacking complete mastery by many state and local emergency managers, was carried out with great criticism and controversy in the intergovernmental response to Hurricane Katrina in 2005. The NRP was replaced by the National Response Framework (NRF) in 2008.

National Science Foundation (NSF) (Ch. 5) An independent federal agency created by Congress in 1950 "to promote the progress of science; to advance the national health, prosperity, and welfare; to secure the national defense." With an annual budget of $7.5 billion (FY 2017), NSF funds approximately 24 percent of all federally supported basic research conducted by America's colleges and universities. In many fields such as mathematics, computer science, and the social sciences, NSF is the major source of federal backing.[70] A fraction of NSF awards support research pertinent in disaster research and engineering.[71]

National Special Security Events (NSSEs) (Ch. 4) An "incident of national significance" category. NSSEs are designated by the president and/or the secretary of the Department of Homeland Security (DHS) and usually encompass any high-profile, large-scale event believed vulnerable to terror attack. The U.S. Secret Service, part of the DHS since 2003, is the lead agency in preparing for and responding to NSSEs. The Secret Service is authorized to participate "in the planning, coordination and implementation of security operations at special events of national significance." When an event is designated by the secretary of DHS an NSSE, the Secret Service assumes

its mandated role as the lead agency for the design and implementation of the operational security plan. The Secret Service has developed a core strategy to carry out its security operations, which relies heavily on its established partnerships with law enforcement and public safety officials at the local, state, and federal levels (often including the Federal Emergency Management Agency (FEMA). The goal of the cooperating agencies is to provide a safe and secure environment for Secret Service protectees, other dignitaries, the event participants, and the general public. There is a tremendous amount of advance planning and coordination in preparation for NSSEs, particularly in regard to venue and motorcade route security, communications, credentialing, and training.[72]

National Terrorism Advisory System (NTAS) (Ch. 7) Replaced the controversial color-coded Homeland Security Advisory System (HSAS) in April 2011. NTAS alerts now are reduced to two categories: (1) imminent threat alert, which warns of a credible, specific, and impending terrorist threat against the United States and (2) elevated threat alert, which warns of a credible terrorist threat against the United States. The secretary of the U.S. Department of Homeland Security (DHS) decides, based on available information and in coordination with other federal entities, whether an NTAS alert should be issued. NTAS has a provision for declaring the end of a posted alert.

National Volunteer Organizations Active in Disaster (National VOAD) (Ch. 6) A nonprofit, nonpartisan membership organization that serves as a forum in which organizations share knowledge and resources throughout the disaster cycle—preparation, response, recovery and mitigation—to help communities prepare for and recover from disasters and to avoid volunteer organization duplication of effort. The National VOAD coalition includes over 50 national organizations, some faith-based, some community-based, and others secular nongovernmental organizations (NGOs). There are also 55 state/territory VOAD groups, which represent local/regional VOAD groups and hundreds of other member organizations throughout the country. The group includes the American Red Cross and the Salvation Army.[73]

National Weather Service (NWS) (Ch. 5) A part of the National Oceanic and Atmospheric Administration (NOAA) within the U.S. Department of Commerce, its mission is to provide weather, water, and climate data;

forecasts; and warnings for the protection of life and property and for benefitting the national economy. Has some 5,000 employees in 122 weather forecast offices, 13 river forecast centers, 9 national centers, and other support offices. NWS provides a national infrastructure to gather and process data worldwide.[74]

Need-based, means-tested model (Ch. 4) Explains declaration decision-making in terms of rules and proven qualification, often in the interest of federal deficit control. The need-based, means-tested model applies in emergency management if local government pursues sustainability in its emergency management. In the model, disaster response and recovery funds are largely self-generated and applicants have no designs on exploiting national taxpayer money beyond the minimum needed to reestablish themselves after a disaster or emergency.

NEHRP Reauthorization Act of 2004 (Ch. 5) Public Law 108-360 was signed into law on October 24, 2004. This measure authorized funding for the National Earthquake Hazard Reduction Program (NEHRP) from fiscal year 2005 through fiscal year 2009. In addition, it made several reforms to the program, including designating National Institute of Standards and Technology (NIST) as the program's lead agency. It also established an Interagency Coordinating Committee and an Advisory Committee on Earthquake Hazards Reduction to improve the program's coordination and implementation.[75]

Network theory (Ch. 2) A field of computer science and network sciences and a part of graph theory (the study of graphs and mathematical structures). It is often deployed to examine the method of characterizing and modeling complex networks. Many complex networks share some common features. Network theory is also applied to logistic networks, gene regularity networks, metabolic networks, the World Wide Web, ecological networks, epistemological networks, and social networks. It is applied in multiple disciplines, including biology, computer science, business, economics, particle physics, operations research, and, most commonly, in sociology.[76]

New Federalism (Ch. 3) A component of President Ronald R. Reagan's political ideology. It maintained that states too often relied on the federal government for help in matters they could easily address on their own. Reagan insisted that the federal government needed to be less intrusive in matters traditionally left to state and local

government. A catchword of the Reagan era was "devolution" of certain federal responsibilities back to the states and localities.

New normal (Ch. 4) A new view of normalcy in the national psyche and in the domain of disaster policy and homeland security brought about by certain disasters, often catastrophes, that stress the nation's disaster management system and force massive policy reforms.[77]

NOAA National Severe Storms Laboratory (NSSL) (Ch. 5) Part of the scientific laboratory system of the National Oceanic and Atmospheric Administration's (NOAA), Office of Oceanic and Atmospheric Research. The mission of NSSL is to improve NOAA's capabilities to provide accurate and timely forecasts and warnings of hazardous weather events. "NSSL accomplishes this mission through research to advance the understanding of weather processes, research to improve forecasting and warning techniques, and development of operational applications. NSSL transfers new scientific understanding, techniques, and applications to the National Weather Service (NWS)."[78] NSSL is also NOAA's primary radar laboratory and a world leader in ingenuity and creativity, pushing radar technology to the edge. From the original WSR-57 research project to Doppler radar, NEXRAD, and follow-on dual-polarized and phased array radars, and of late the Advanced Technology Demonstrator, NSSL research has made radar one of the most valuable tools available to a forecaster. NSSL researchers want to better understand when and where severe weather will occur, by studying thunderstorms through direct observation in the field or by making computer simulations. They apply this knowledge as they develop and perfect weather prediction models and techniques to support the NWS mission to provide weather and water forecasts for the U.S. NSSL researchers work to develop new weather and water related applications and water resource management tools help NWS forecasters produce more accurate and timely warnings of flood events. NSSL resides in the National Weather Center (NWC) located in Norman, Oklahoma. The NWC houses a University of Oklahoma complex plus various NOAA and state organizations that work together to improve understanding of weather.[79]

Nonprofit voluntary organizations (Ch. 6) Organizations composed largely, but not exclusively, of volunteers. Faith-based or not, they are often part of both the official and the unofficial response to a disaster or emergency, and all enjoy a nontaxable federal income tax status, as well as exemption from various state and local income and property taxes. Those who make cash and in-kind donations to these organizations often enjoy a federal income tax deduction that effectively subsidizes their contributions. Some of these organizations operate internationally as well as inside the United States.

Nonstructural hazard mitigation (Ch. 3) The use of "soft" engineering and other approaches, such as zoning laws, building codes, land-use regulations, and education of the public, to buffer wetlands against flooding, protect coastlines and barrier islands from erosion and development, encourage the use of landscaping that protects structures from flooding or wildfires, and otherwise protect hazard-prone, high-risk areas.

Nonterrorism missions (Ch. 6) The original missions of the Federal Emergency Management Agency (FEMA) and many other agencies, unrelated to terrorism, that became part of the U.S. Department of Homeland Security (DHS) in 2003. Many of these agencies, including FEMA, are still struggling to fulfill both their terrorism-related duties and their original nonterrorism missions.

North American Free Trade Agreement (NAFTA) (Ch. 8) A Canadian–U.S. free-trade agreement was concluded in 1988, and NAFTA basically extended that agreement's provisions to Mexico. NAFTA was negotiated by the administrations of U.S. President George H. W. Bush, Canadian Prime Minister Brian Mulroney, and Mexican President Carlos Salinas de Gortari. Preliminary agreement on the pact was reached in August 1992, and it was signed by the three leaders on December 17. NAFTA was ratified by the three countries' national legislatures in 1993 and went into effect on January 1, 1994. NAFTA's main provisions called for the gradual reduction of tariffs, customs duties, and other trade barriers between the three members, with some tariffs being removed immediately and others over periods of as long as 15 years. The agreement ensured eventual duty-free access for a vast range of manufactured goods and commodities traded between the signatories. "National goods" status was provided to products imported from other NAFTA countries, banning any state, local, or provincial government from imposing taxes or tariffs on such goods.[80] President Trump had the United States renegotiate the trade terms of NAFTA in 2018, reaching agreements first with Mexico and then with Canada. Trump advocates renaming NAFTA as MCUSA, for Mexico, Canada, and the United States of America.

Occupations (Ch. 2) Categories of jobs, livelihoods, or vocations. People in certain occupations may be represented by labor unions or trade unions, but the occupations themselves may not necessarily conform to the definition of a "profession."

Office of Peacekeeping and Humanitarian Affairs (Ch. 8) Has the job of leading or coordinating the U.S. military response to disasters beyond U.S. borders and resides in the U.S. Department of Defense (DOD).

Office of the United Nations High Commissioner for Refugees (UNHCR) (Ch. 8) Protects and aids refugees and internally displaced persons (IDPs).[81] The most basic responsibility of the UNHCR is to guarantee refugees' fundamental rights, including their ability to seek asylum. It strives to make sure that no person is involuntarily returned to a country if doing so would subject that person to persecution or otherwise put his or her life in danger.[82] The UNHCR facilitates the necessary movement of masses of people, often refugees, during emergencies. It promotes education, health, and shelter programs and is expected to provide for the well-being of refugees. It manages the repatriation of people who freely wish to return to their home country and resettles those refugees seeking asylum to nations willing to accept them.[83]

Office of U.S. Foreign Disaster Assistance (OFDA) (Ch. 8) Facilitates and coordinates U.S. emergency response overseas. Part of the U.S. Agency for International Development (USAID), OFDA is divided into four units. OFDA is authorized to respond to natural disasters (earthquakes, volcanic eruptions, cyclones, floods, droughts, fires, pest infestation, disease outbreaks) and man-made disasters (civil conflicts, acts of terrorism, industrial accidents). Besides furnishing immediate assistance, it funds mitigation activities to lessen the effects of recurring disasters. OFDA also makes available guidance and training intended to help those in other nations develop their own disaster management and response capacity.

Oklahoma City terrorist bomb attack (Ch. 7) On the morning of April 19, 1995, an ex–U.S. Army soldier and security guard named Timothy McVeigh parked a rented truck in front of the Alfred P. Murrah Federal Building in downtown Oklahoma City. It contained a homemade bomb. At precisely 9:02 a.m., the bomb exploded. Within moments, the surrounding area looked like a war zone. A third of the building had been reduced to rubble, with many floors flattened like pancakes. Dozens of cars were incinerated, and more than 300 nearby buildings were damaged or destroyed. The human toll was still more devastating: 168 people lost, including 19 children, with several hundred more injured. It was the worst act of homegrown terrorism in the nation's history.[84]

Operation Stonegarden (Ch. 7) supports state and local law enforcement activity that serves border and immigration control purposes. Operation Stonegarden (OPSG) aims to improve "cooperation and coordination among Customs and Border Protection (CBP), United States Border Patrol (USBP), and local, Tribal, territorial, state, and Federal law enforcement agencies. The OPSG Program funds joint efforts to secure the United States borders along routes of ingress from international borders. Such routes include travel corridors in states bordering Mexico and Canada, as well as states and territories with international water borders."[85] OPSG funds must be used to improve federal, state, local, tribal, and territorial law enforcement capabilities. The aim is to create "a layered, coordinated approach to law enforcement within United States Border States and territories."[86] The FY 2017 allocation to the Operation Stonegarden program was $55,000,000. For FY 2018, up to $85,000,000 is available. OPSG funds are allocated based on the risk to the security of the border. Cost sharing/matching is not required. Project periods will extend up to 36 months, starting September 1, 2018.

Opinion mining (Ch. 2) Synonymous with "sentiment analysis"; it involves deriving the opinion or attitude of a speaker. A common purpose in using this technology is to discover how people feel about a particular topic. "In essence, it is the process of determining the emotional tone behind a series of words, used to gain an understanding of the attitudes, opinions and emotions expressed within an online mention."[87] Big data analytics makes possible opinion mining of people regarding many disaster or emergency management relevant subjects.

Organizational process model (Ch. 2) Model developed by political scientist Graham Allison, which posits that presidential decisions are essentially a routine administrative determination handled by a stovepipe-connected assortment of lower level government officials. In this model, the president or executive has either largely delegated decision authority to someone else or rubber-stamps the official recommendation of his or her functionaries.

Other Needs Assistance (FEMA) (Ch. 4) A FEMA program that provides grants for uninsured, disaster-related necessary expenses and serious needs. Items covered include funeral and burial costs; repair, cleaning, or replacement of clothing and household items (room furnishings, appliances); specialized tools or protective clothing and equipment required for one's job; necessary educational materials (computers, school books, supplies); cleanup items (wet/dry vacuum, air purifier, dehumidifier), fuel for primary heat source (heating oil, gas; repairing or replacing vehicles damaged by the disaster, or providing for public transportation or other transportation costs; moving and storage expenses related to the disaster (including storage or the return of property to a pre-disaster home); other necessary expenses or serious needs (e.g., towing or setup or connecting essential utilities for a housing unit not provided by the Federal Emergency Management Agency (FEMA). Unlike the FEMA Public Assistance Program, there are no set thresholds that counties must meet to be deemed eligible for the Individuals and Households Program (IHP). States, territories, and tribal governments may be approved by FEMA to directly administer the ONA program in their jurisdiction.

Overlapping-authority model (Ch. 2) A model of intergovernmental relations in which substantial areas of governmental operations involve national, state, and local governments simultaneously. Areas of autonomy or single-jurisdiction independence and full discretion are small. Power and influence for any one jurisdiction is substantially limited, and authority patterns involve heavy bargaining.

Performance Partnerships (Ch. 6) A type of negotiated agreement, which for many years the Federal Emergency Management Agency (FEMA) used in its administrative transactions with state emergency management organizations and, through these state organizations, local emergency management organizations. Performance partnerships were based on collaborative schemes through which various federal funds were disbursed by FEMA to state and local emergency management agencies under prearranged levels and terms of agency performance.

Posse Comitatus Act of 1878 (Ch. 7) Established clear boundaries regarding the role the military could play in civil law enforcement. The aim was to ensure that the military would not assume police powers exempted from civilian control. Passed during Reconstruction after the Civil War to prohibit the military from enforcing civilian laws, it sought to codify the long-standing aversion of Americans to a standing army that could become an instrument of governmental tyranny.

Post-Katrina Emergency Management Reform Act (PKEMRA) of 2006 (Ch. 3) Public Law 109-295, 120 State. 1394 enacted October 4, 2006, PKEMRA gives the Federal Emergency Management Agency (FEMA) more organizational autonomy than it has had since becoming part of the U.S. Department of Homeland Security (DHS). Like the U.S. Coast Guard and the U.S. Secret Service, FEMA is now classified as a distinct entity within DHS. In addition, the agency is no longer subject to the DHS secretary's broad reorganization authority under the 2002 Homeland Security Act. The act authorizes the FEMA administrator, as of March 31, 2007, to provide emergency-management–related recommendations directly to Congress after informing the secretary. The act also explicitly prohibits substantial or significant reductions, by the secretary, of the authorities, responsibilities, or functions of FEMA, or FEMA capability to perform them. Furthermore, the PKEMRA prohibits most transfers of FEMA assets, functions, or missions to other parts of DHS. PKEMRA has additional important provisions, which cumulatively and significantly boosted the powers and duties of FEMA and its administrator.

Preliminary Damage Assessment (PDA) (Ch. 4) Teams of assessors conduct an initial assessment to estimate the degree of damage and potential costs resulting from a disaster. The assessment is broken down into categories (such as the number of homes damaged or destroyed and the number of public facilities damaged or destroyed) that correspond to the broad categories of disaster relief and assistance that the Federal Emergency Management Agency (FEMA) provides through the individual assistance or public assistance programs. The information a PDA generates is used by FEMA and the president to determine whether a declaration will be issued and, if one is issued, whether individual and public assistance programs will be provided to the areas (generally, counties, parishes, and independent cities) included in the declaration.

Preparedness (Ch. 1) Activities, laws, or policies designed to increase readiness or improve capabilities for disaster response and recovery operations. A pre-disaster activity aimed at helping the public survive and cope with the effects of possible future disasters.

Primary waves (P-waves) (Ch. 5) Emanate from an epicenter and are the initial indicators an earthquake has been triggered. Although these waves are almost imperceptible to humans, sensor detection of primary waves may be used to calculate the epicenter of a seismic event and its magnitude. They are capable of traveling through solids, liquids (including oceans), and even the earth's core.[88]

Principal-agent theory (Ch. 2) Assumes that managers (the principals) function in an environment in which they cannot observe whether their agents (subordinate workers and contractors) in fact carried out the instructions they issued. The theory, from economics and used extensively in performance-based government contracting studies, also assumes that agents hide information from principals and may use the information to act in ways contrary to what principals intended.

Private, for-profit contractors (Ch. 6) For-profit contractors, often corporations and other business entities, many of whom are retained by the government to perform work, produce a product, accomplish a task, provide a service, build or repair a structure, and the like. They are used by the federal government, as well as by subnational governments, as part of the official response to a disaster and to carry out certain tasks or to produce certain products for short- or long-term disaster recovery and for disaster mitigation. Although government contractors usually have to go through a public bidding process, sometimes the slowness of that process has prompted the issuance of "no-bid" contracts, which have often become subjects of political controversy.

Profession (Ch. 2) A vocation that is esoteric, complex, and discretionary and embodies self-directing work. It requires theoretical and applied knowledge, skill, and judgment that others may not possess or cannot easily comprehend. Theory-grounded knowledge, acquired through higher education, is the basis of most professions.

Professional body (Ch. 2) Sets examinations of competence for a profession, acts as licensing authority for practitioners of the profession, and enforces adherence to an ethical code of conduct adopted by the professional association it serves. Most professions are regulated by respective professional bodies or organizations of some type.

Programming algorithm (Ch. 2) A computer procedure that is much like a recipe (called a *procedure*) and tells your computer precisely what steps to take to solve a problem or reach a goal. The ingredients are called *inputs*, while the results are called *outputs*. The characteristics of a good algorithm are as follows: Precision—the steps are precisely stated (defined); Uniqueness—the results of each step are uniquely defined and only depend on the input and the result of the preceding steps; and Finiteness—the algorithm stops after a finite number of instructions are executed.[89] Algorithms describe the solution to a problem in terms of the data needed to represent the problem instance and the set of steps necessary to produce the intended result. Programming languages must provide a notational way to represent both the process and the data. To this end, languages provide control constructs and data types.[90] Programming is the process of taking an algorithm and encoding it into a notation, a programming language, so that it can be executed by a computer. Although many programming languages and many different types of computers exist, the important first step is the need to have the solution. Without an algorithm there can be no program.[91]

Project Impact (Ch. 3) In October 1997, the Clinton–Witt Federal Emergency Management Agency (FEMA) launched an effort that sought to build disaster-resistant communities through public–private partnerships. It included a national public awareness campaign, the designation of pilot communities, and an outreach effort to community and business leaders. Under Project Impact, FEMA encouraged communities to assess the risks they faced, identify their vulnerabilities, and take steps to prevent disasters. Lawmakers so much liked the project that they wrote many Project Impact features into the Disaster Mitigation Act of 2000.

Public Assistance Program (FEMA) (Ch. 4) Provides grants to state and local governments and certain nonprofit entities to assist them with the response to and recovery from disasters. Specifically, the program provides assistance for debris removal, emergency protective measures, and permanent restoration of infrastructure. One of three major post-disaster assistance programs of the Federal Emergency Management Agency (FEMA).

Public Safety Canada (Ch. 8) The minister of Public Safety Canada is responsible for exercising leadership relating to emergency management in Canada by coordinating, among government institutions and in cooperation with the provinces and other entities, emergency management activities. Under Canada's Emergency Management Act of 2007, the minister of PSC has authority to (1) provide assistance other than financial assistance to a province if the province requests it; and, (2) provide financial assistance to a province if a provincial emergency in the province has been declared to be of concern to the federal government under section 7.[92] The law has a provision enabling consultation with the United States. "In consultation with the Minister of Foreign Affairs, the Minister may develop joint emergency management plans with the relevant United States' authorities and, in accordance with those plans, coordinate Canada's response to emergencies in the United States and provide assistance in response to those emergencies."[93] The law specifies that a government institution may not respond to a provincial emergency unless the government of the province requests assistance or there is an agreement with the province that requires or permits the assistance.[94]

Public works (Ch. 5) A constructed internal improvement that augments a government's economic infrastructure. The term is often used interchangeably with *municipal infrastructure* or *urban infrastructure*. Highways, bridges, water ports, seaports, railways, mass transit systems, water supply and sewage treatment systems, government office buildings, electricity and natural gas distribution systems, communications systems, public stadiums, and other physical structures, often funded through capital borrowing, are examples of public works.

Rational actor model (Ch. 2) Emanating from rational choice theory, the model has been widely applied in international relations (realist theory) and in organizational theory. It posits in the ideal that a person (sometimes assumed to be the president or a leader of some type) makes decisions largely on his or her own, with the information available or which others have provided. It assumes the decision maker has rationally ordered preferences and motivations, as a unitary or single actor. It holds that the decision maker knows and understands the problem requiring a decision and that he or she has considered all reasonable alternatives or courses of action before making the decision. Under assumptions of the model, the president is assumed to be making rational decisions on behalf of the entire national government and that these decisions are definitive at the time they are made. It also assumes that individual rationality inheres in that decision making. There are many criticisms and critics of the rational actor model, and there are alternative models and theories used to understand how leaders make decisions. Scholars who analyze the decisions of leaders using this model find it helpful in that factors and forces judged to be extraneous or irrelevant are ignored as a matter of simplification.

Recovery (Ch. 1) Begins as a disaster is ending or at the close of the disaster response phase. Involving activities, laws, or policies that return disaster-affected governments, communities, and people to their pre-disaster conditions, it may take months or years to complete and is usually the most expensive phase in the disaster cycle.

Redistributive politics (Ch. 4) is a type of zero-sum game, in which one part of the nation gains at the expense of another part of the nation. Redistribution of income and redistribution of wealth are, respectively, the transfer of income and of wealth (including physical property) from some individuals to others by means of a social mechanism such as taxation, charity, welfare, public services, land reform, monetary policies, confiscation, and others.[95]

Regional administrators (FEMA) (Ch. 6) Presidentially appointed, subject to U.S. Senate confirmation, regional administrators (directors) contribute mightily to emergency management work in their regions, particularly when they work well with federal coordinating officers (FCOs) assigned by the president to the disaster or emergency. It is also important that they maintain good working relationships with governors and state emergency management directors in their respective region.

Reinventing government movement (Ch. 2) An extension of the New Public Management movement of the 1990s, a movement that offered low-level administrators more power and, informed by modern management consultants, concluded that organizations need to redis-

cover the importance of customer satisfaction. It also advocated broader governance, under which public- and private-sector organizations might work together under more cooperative or blended arrangements. The movement was embraced by the Clinton administration as a tool for improving federal public management.

Resilience in disaster management (Ch. 2) Resilience in economic terms involves pre-disaster surpluses and shortages. Resilience also relates to actions taken during recovery. "Disaster resilience is the ability of individuals, communities, organizations and states to adapt to and recover from hazards, shocks or stresses without compromising long-term prospects for development. According to the Hyogo Framework for Action, disaster resilience is determined by the degree to which individuals, communities and public and private organizations are capable of organizing themselves to learn from past disasters and reduce their risks to future ones, at international, regional, national and local levels."[96]

Response (Ch. 1) Begins when a disaster event occurs or is imminent. It is also activities, laws, or policies applied in the immediate aftermath of a disaster to protect life and property, prevent secondary disaster effects, and reconstitute government operation.

Richter scale (Ch. 5) One way to measure the magnitude of an earthquake, and the first widely used method, was the Richter scale, developed by Charles F. Richter in 1934. It used a formula based on amplitude of the largest wave recorded on a specific type of seismometer and the distance between the earthquake and the seismometer. That scale was specific to California earthquakes; other scales, based on wave amplitudes and total earthquake duration, were developed for use in other situations and they were designed to be consistent with Richter's scale."[97] "Unfortunately, many scales, such as the Richter scale, do not provide accurate estimates for large magnitude earthquakes.

Risk (in the context of hazards) (Ch. 1) Is the likely consequence of a hazard, and so is "the combination of the probability of a hazardous event and its negative consequences."[98] To some degree, risk can be measured in objective, probabilistic, mathematical terms. Risk analysis is at the core of hazard identification and hazard vulnerability assessment. The study of risk is also a central part of insurance underwriting.

Samaritan's dilemma (Ch. 1) "When providing assistance after a disaster reduces the economic incentives of potential victims to invest in protective measures, such as buying appropriate insurance and taking reasonable mitigation measures, prior to a disaster. If the expectation of disaster assistance reduces the demand for insurance, the political pressure on the government to provide assistance after a disaster is reinforced or amplified."[99]

Sandy Recovery Improvement Act of 2013 (Ch. 4) Public Law 113-2 enacted January 29, 2013, as a Disaster Relief Appropriations law. Destructive Superstorm Sandy in November 2012 generated major disaster declarations for 13 Mid-Atlantic and Northeast states and property losses rivaling those of Hurricane Katrina in 2005. Congress devoted $50.7 billion to Sandy relief and recovery and approved a nearly $10 billion increase in national flood insurance borrowing authority to help cover National Flood Insurance Program (NFIP) claims from the disaster and to recapitalize the NFIP fund. The law revised and streamlined many provisions of the Federal Emergency Management Agency (FEMA) Public Assistance and Individual and Households programs (IHP). It also authorized the chief executive of federally recognized tribal governments to directly request disaster or emergency declarations from the president, much as a governor can do for a state.[100]

Sarin nerve gas (Ch. 5) "Sarin is a nerve agent. Once inside a body, nerve agents affect the signaling mechanism that nerve cells use to communicate with one another. Sarin is a cholinesterase inhibitor—it gums up the cholinesterase enzyme, which nerve cells use to clear themselves of acetylcholine. When a nerve cell needs to send a message to another nerve cell (for example, to cause a muscle to contract), it sends the message with the acetylcholine. Without cholinesterase to clear the acetylcholine, muscles start to contract uncontrollably—this eventually causes death by suffocation since the diaphragm is a muscle. It acts in five to 12 hours."[101]

Secondary waves (S-waves) (Ch. 5) Seismic force that moves through the earth at about half the speed of primary waves. Waves move at right angles to direction of travel much like wave travel along a flexed rope held between two people. S-waves cannot travel through water. They are responsible for much of the damage caused by an earthquake.[102] They are more damaging than P-waves. Secondary waves travel about three kilo-

meters [1.86 miles] per second.[103] According to the U.S. Geological Survey, an S-wave, or shear wave, is a seismic body wave that shakes the ground back and forth perpendicular to the direction the wave is moving.[104]

Secular nonprofit voluntary relief organizations (Ch. 6) A nongovernmental organization (NGO) is an organization that is not part of a government and was not founded by states. NGOs are therefore typically independent of governments. Although the definition can technically include for-profit corporations, the term is generally restricted to social, cultural, legal, and environmental advocacy groups having goals that are primarily noncommercial, including providing disaster relief and assisting disaster victims. NGOs are usually nonprofit organizations that gain at least a portion of their funding from private sources. Nongovernmental organizations (NGOs) vary in a great many ways. Secular nonprofit voluntary organizations are those not predicated on an organized religion.

Securitization (Ch. 5) Involves extension of national security concerns into other domains of public policy, including emergency management. Securitization also involves development of new types of security-related research and technologies. It also connotes a trend toward increased security classification of many documents that were previously open and publicly available.

Security classification (Ch. 7) A means of government protection of sensitive information from unauthorized disclosure. The federal government maintains a tiered system of security classification, and individuals may be granted security clearances following background checks, their taking of legal oaths that they will not divulge secret information, and other requirements, including drug testing. Many aspects of federal emergency management are today subject to security restriction. This means that only those with appropriate security clearances may read, use, act on, or alter this information, thus narrowing the pool of people responsible for conducting work or duties called for in the documents.

Seismic building codes (Ch. 5) Intended to protect people inside or near buildings by preventing collapse and allowing for safe evacuation. Structures built according to code are earthquake resistant, not earthquake proof. They should be able to resist minor earthquakes undamaged, moderate earthquakes without significant structural damage, and severe earthquakes without collapse.

Seismic mapping (Ch. 5) Serves as the basis for seismic provisions used in building codes and influences how and where new construction or seismic retrofitting takes place every year.

Self-help (Ch. 3) A government policy of encouraging individual responsibility for disaster preparedness and, conversely, less public dependence on government for the same purpose.

Sentiment analysis (Ch. 2) See also "opinion mining." Sentiment analysis refers to the use of natural language processing, text analysis, and computational linguistics to identify and extract subjective information in source materials. It is also the process of determining whether a piece of writing is positive, negative, or neutral.[105]

Short-term recovery (Ch. 1) May overlap some of the disaster response phase. It routinely includes "search and rescue, damage assessments, public information, temporary housing, utility restoration, and debris clearance."[106]

Situational awareness (Ch. 6) The provision of timely and accurate information during an incident. It is critical in incident management and effective response operations. Without it, decisions will not be informed by what is going on at the disaster site and actions will be inefficient and ineffective. Situational awareness requires continuous monitoring, verification, and integration of key information needed to assess and respond effectively to disasters or emergencies, as well as to threats or potential threats.

Social constructivism (Ch. 2) Explains problems and policy issues by focusing on people's behavior and beliefs rather than on the putative "conditions" that are the object of those actions. Social constructivists maintain that it is the actions and persuasiveness of people, perhaps amplified through mass communications, which define what a phenomenon is or is not. Maintains that all cognitive functions originate in and must therefore be explained as products of social interactions and that learning is not simply the assimilation and accommodation of new knowledge by learners but is the process by which learners are integrated into a knowledge community. Language and culture play essential roles both in human intellectual development and in how humans perceive the world. Humans' linguistic abilities enable them to overcome the natural limitations of their perceptual field by imposing culturally defined sense and meaning on the world. Language and culture are the frameworks through which humans experience, communicate, and understand reality.[107]

Social disaster (Ch. 5) Sometimes caused by social vulnerability, meaning the inability of people, organizations, and societies to withstand adverse impacts from multiple stressors to which they are exposed. These impacts are due in part to characteristics inherent in social interactions, institutions, and systems of cultural values.

Social media (Ch. 1) Internet communications systems, software, and platforms that facilitate social networking, including blogging, microblogging, photo sharing, video sharing, video streaming, wiki sourcing, virtual worlds, online radio, and aggregators (collective real-time monitoring tools of selected types of user exchanges).[108]

Staffing for Adequate Fire and Emergency Response (SAFER) (Ch. 5) A federal grant program that took effect in late 2003 and that advances local disaster preparedness. SAFER grants are crucial to helping fire departments hire sufficient firefighters to meet safe staffing levels.

Stafford Disaster Relief and Emergency Assistance Act of 1988 (Ch. 3) Public Law 93-288, signed November 23, 1988, reauthorizes presidential authority to issue major disaster and emergency declarations, specifies the type of assistance the president may authorize, and amends the Disaster Relief Act of 1974. Refines the definition of *emergency* clearly affording the president more latitude in determining what is or is not an emergency. The Stafford Act came to demarcate the beginning of modern-era national disaster management. In general terms, "It is the intent of the Congress, by this Act, to provide an orderly and continuing means of assistance by the Federal Government to State and local governments in carrying out their responsibilities to alleviate the suffering and damage which result from such disasters by (1) revising and broadening the scope of existing disaster relief programs; (2) encouraging the development of comprehensive disaster preparedness and assistance plans, programs, capabilities, and organizations by the States and by local governments; (3) achieving greater coordination and responsiveness of disaster preparedness and relief programs; (4) encouraging individuals, States, and local governments to protect themselves by obtaining insurance coverage to supplement or replace governmental assistance; (5) encouraging hazard mitigation measures to reduce losses from disasters, including development of land use and construction regulations; and (6) providing Federal assistance programs for both public and private losses sustained in disasters."[109]

Stakeholders (Ch. 1) Persons, individually or in a group, who have, or think they have, something to gain or lose. In emergency management, they are people and organized interests of people affected by the decisions of policymakers and emergency managers. Some stakeholders unselfishly seek benefits or protections for the people or groups whose interests they champion.

State Active Duty (SAD) (Ch. 7) The National Guard, when activated in State Active Duty (SAD) status, serves under the command of the state governor through the state adjutant general (TAG), receives state pay and benefits, and is not subjected to the restrictions of Posse Comitatus; that is, it can engage in law enforcement activities when directed.[110]

State adjutant general (Ch. 7) A military officer who is de facto commander of the National Guard and other military forces in one of the U.S. states. This person usually works cooperatively with his or her respective state governor, although he or she may not be directly accountable to, nor appointable by, that governor. Every U.S. state has an adjutant general.

State Homeland Security Program (SHSP) (Ch. 7) A U.S. Department of Homeland Security (DHS) program that provides funds to state and local governments for help in planning, equipping, and training, as well as exercise activities intended to improve their ability to prepare for, prevent, and respond to terrorist attacks and other disasters. The program also supports the implementation of state homeland security strategies and key elements of the national preparedness architecture, including the National Preparedness Goal, the National Incident Management System (NIMS), and the National Response Framework (NRF).

Structural hazard mitigation (Ch. 3) Efforts to contain a hazard, such as building dams and other flood abatement works and coastal infrastructure or strengthening buildings and other structures to withstand disaster stresses. Often entails use of "hard" engineered structures.

"Surge" workforce (Ch. 9) "The Post-Katrina Emergency Management Reform Act of 2006 (Public Law 109-295) established the Surge Capacity Force to deploy volunteering Federal employees in the aftermath of a catastrophic event to help support response and recovery efforts. The Department of Homeland Security (DHS) activated the Surge Capacity Force for the first time in 2012 in support of Hurricane Sandy. More than 1,100 (non-FEMA) DHS employees deployed to New York and New Jersey to supplement FEMA's substantial disaster workforce. In the aftermath of Hurricanes Harvey and Irma in September 2017, Acting DHS Secretary Duke activated the Surge Capacity Force for the second time; this time expanding the program to the entirety of the Federal Government. Over 2,000 Federal employees have already deployed as of September 21, 2017."[111] Under the program federal employees in agencies outside of FEMA volunteer and are detailed to work in short-term capacities (never longer than 45 days). They continue to receive their full pay and benefits, and they are also paid for their overtime and reimbursed for their travel expenses.

Tacit knowledge (Ch. 2) Vague and ambiguous knowledge that depends on sharing expectations and values through social relationships. Neither easily conveyed nor learned from the outside, this form of knowledge is often acquired through observation, internships, apprenticeships, mentoring, or on-the-job socialization experiences.

Target capabilities list (Ch. 7) Among the National Preparedness Goals aimed at establishing "capability-based planning" for various types of terrorist attack and a small subset of nonterror disasters and emergencies is a requirement that major municipalities prepare a target capabilities list. Based on the targets municipal officials believe are vulnerable, they then need to demonstrate to the U.S. Department of Homeland Security (DHS) how their current capabilities would enable them to save lives, protect property, and revive their local economies.

Target capability (Ch. 7) A term that refers to the ability of a government jurisdiction to prevent, or respond to, a range of different types of terrorist attacks on specific likely targets within a jurisdiction.

Technocrat (Ch. 2) Official of a public bureaucracy who possesses special knowledge and expertise most average citizens do not have and who works under norms of objectivity and political neutrality.

Territorial sovereignty (Ch. 8) The internationally recognized principle that a government should be the ultimate authority within the boundaries of its jurisdiction and should be free of unwanted external interference. A principle embedded in the original Charter of the United Nations that promises each member nation that the UN will respect each member state's national territorial sovereignty.

Terrorism consequence management (Ch. 7) All government activities undertaken to address the effects or aftermath of a terrorist-caused disaster or emergency. These include not only emergency responder functions but also law enforcement, intelligence work, and the like.

Threat and Hazard Identification and Risk Assessment (THIRA) (Ch. 7) A three-step risk assessment process that helps communities answer the following questions: What threats and hazards can affect our community? If they occurred, what impacts would those threats and hazards have on our community? Based on those impacts, what capabilities should our community have? The THIRA helps community officials understand their community's risks and helps them determine the level of capability they need to address those risks. The products of this work help community leaders identify gaps in their jurisdiction's ability to address the threats and hazards. Such work is a necessary part of the Stakeholder Preparedness Review.[112]

Thresher (Ch. 2) A technique to discover the right keywords for what you want to find in net searches. It suggests keywords to you as you advance.[113]

Tightly coupled interdependence[114] (Ch. 1) A concept employed by Charles Perrow in his seminal book *Normal Accidents*. It is a theory of organization that holds that high-risk systems of many modern complex and technology-dependent organizations are vulnerable to failure, sometimes with catastrophic consequences, because the sociotechnical operations on which they function manifest tight interdependencies or linkages. Owing to their complexity and interlocking operations, they tend to fail quickly, unexpectedly, often with little or no warning (or misread warnings), and they defy correction by operators, who themselves sometimes compound rather than resolve problems. Owing to tight coupling and interdependence of operations, failures or errors, whether human or technological, tend to produce effects and consequences that spread rapidly, uncontrollably, and often in unanticipated ways.

Title 10 duty status (Ch. 7) U.S. Department of Defense military forces ordinarily operate under Title 10 duty status, play a supporting role in domestic deployments, providing soldiers (with no law enforcement powers) resources, and logistical support.[115] National Guard forces may be federalized by order of the president, and when they are, they operate under Title 10 duty status.

Title 32 duty status (Ch. 7) National Guard troops can perform law enforcement functions in Title 32 duty status under a state's laws but cannot enforce criminal law when they are federalized (Title 10 duty status)—when they are under the direct control of the president. The National Guard is a principal and major resource for governors who must respond to disasters or incidents. The National Guard provides well-trained people, "communications systems and equipment, air and road support, heavy construction and earth-moving equipment, and emergency supplies such as beds, blankets, and medical supplies."[116] In Title 32 duty status, the governor of the state deploying his or her National Guard has direct control (often aided by the state's adjutant general) of these forces and the state is in the position of paying and supporting its National Guard troops and units.

Tolerated disaster vulnerabilities (Ch. 5) Unintentionally overlooked, discounted, or deliberately ignored or discounted hazard and disaster risk vulnerabilities, which are thus tolerated. Human settlement patterns, commercial and government building decisions and infrastructure construction, and known geophysical and meteorological phenomena often combine to create a realm of tolerated disaster vulnerabilities.

Top-down command and control system (Ch. 6) A form of command and control under which federal officials get to assume top-down leadership positions, and state and local authorities are expected to submit to their direction.

Turndown (Ch. 4) A turndown is the action authorized by the president and signed by the director of the Federal Emergency Management Agency (FEMA) that denies a governor's request for a major disaster or emergency declaration.

Twitter sentiment analysis (Ch. 2) A method by which one can learn why people think something is good or bad, often by extracting the exact words that indicate why people did or didn't like some particular thing.[117]

United Nations Children's Fund (UNICEF) (Ch. 8) Created after World War II to alleviate the suffering of European children, UNICEF is able to respond rapidly to natural or man-made disasters from its offices in nations where it already has permission to operate. It works to help and reduce the vulnerability of new mothers and families with small children. Children and women caring for small children are often weaker members of their societies and are less capable of rebounding in disasters than others. During natural disasters or complex humanitarian emergencies, UNICEF works with other relief agencies to restore basic services, such as food distribution, water, and sanitation. UNICEF officials also try to make available basic medical services and immunizations. UNICEF is empowered to advocate children's rights worldwide.

United Nations Development Programme (UNDP) (Ch. 8) Has duties in disaster mitigation, prevention, preparedness, recovery, and reconstruction. The UNDP operating norm is that disaster vulnerability remains fundamentally connected to weak or absent infrastructures, the failure or inadequacy of environmental policies, and human settlement in high-hazard zones. As a development agency, it strongly seeks to advance disaster mitigation and sustainability. UNDP early recovery teams work with the response partners, so that strong links are established and maintained between response and recovery through to mitigation and preparedness.

United Nations Disaster Assessment and Coordination (UNDAC) team (Ch. 8) Helps to harmonize the disaster relief assistance made available by many of the UN organizations.

United Nations Office for the Coordination of Humanitarian Affairs (OCHA) (Ch. 8) Headed by an Undersecretary General, the Emergency Relief Coordinator harmonizes the work of the various UN relief organizations in humanitarian emergency responses. She or he does so through an Inter-Agency Standing Committee, itself composed of both UN and non-UN humanitarian leaders.[118] OCHA seeks to build consensus and share best practices among all UN partners, and it identifies issues arising from disaster management and response that need to be addressed. OCHA also amasses

information from its Disaster Response System, a unit that monitors ongoing disasters, conducts post-disaster assessments and evaluations, and manages a bank of data made available to the international community of responders. OCHA operates to advance respect for human rights. It is also in charge of a Central Emergency Revolving Fund, which operates as a cash reserve available to humanitarian agencies with cash-flow problems. OCHA is able to loan money, but reimbursement is expected.

Universal Task List (Ch. 7) Developed by the U.S. Department of Homeland Security (DHS) to describe what tasks need to be performed, who needs to perform them, and how to perform them in the event of terrorist attack disaster or natural or human-caused (non-terror) disaster. The Universal Task List contains some 1,600 different tasks, and local government officials are expected to maintain a correct list of all the resources needed and available to fulfill each task.

Urban Area Security Initiative (UASI) (Ch. 7) Authorized by federal law in 2005 to facilitate rapid response in the nation's 50 largest cities [32 as of December 2018] to attacks from weapons of mass destruction. UASI addresses planning, operations, equipment acquisition, training, and exercise needs and provides financial assistance based on a risk-and-needs approach. Funding allotments are determined by a formula that combines threat estimates, critical assets within the urban area, and population density.

U.S. Agency for International Development (USAID) (Ch. 8) For many years an independent agency, it is now again part of the U.S. Department of State. The agency is officially obligated to further U.S. foreign policy interests in expanding democracy and free markets while improving the lives of the citizens in developing countries. USAID extends assistance to countries recovering from disasters. The agency addresses issue areas as broad as economic growth, agriculture, trade, global health, democracy, conflict prevention, and humanitarian assistance. It provides assistance in sub-Saharan Africa, Asia, the Near East, Latin America, the Caribbean, and Europe/Eurasia.

U.S. Army Corps of Engineers (USACE) (Ch. 7) Formed in 1802, the USACE has built, owned, maintained, and managed an enormous amount and variety of public infrastructure inside the United States. The corps' role in responding to natural disasters emerged in matters of flood control after the Civil War. In the 20th century, the corps became the lead federal flood control agency and significantly expanded its civil works activities, becoming a major provider of hydroelectric energy and water impoundment recreation areas.

U.S. Coast Guard (Ch. 7) A military organization that since 2003 has been part of the U.S. Department of Homeland Security (DHS). It has a long history of involvement in maritime safety and disaster response. For many years, the U.S. Coast Guard has behaved as a federal emergency management organization but one with an on-the-water focus. The U.S. Coast Guard has been highly active in matters of port and maritime disaster mitigation; planning, response, and recovery; as well as drug interdiction, boater safety, facilitation of marine navigation, port security, border patrol, fisheries regulation, and environmental protection along coasts and waterways.

U.S. Fire Administration (USFA) (Ch. 5) Provides training to fire service personnel on a national level. By augmenting existing state and local fire service training programs, it works to improve and maintain high fire company standards of capacity and performance across the nation. The USFA helps develop the technology that fire services must obtain to help them promote fire prevention and to improve response. The USFA assists state and local groups in collecting and interpreting data on fires in their respective areas.

U.S. Northern Command (USNORTHCOM) (Ch. 7) Refers to the North American Command, which provides command and control of U.S. Department of Defense (DOD) homeland defense efforts and coordinates the defense support the military provides to civil authorities. The USNORTHCOM mission is to help prevent terrorist attacks on the homeland by militarily defeating attacks by foreigners if possible, protecting U.S. borders or airspace from encroachment or penetration by attackers, and aiding in the response to an incident involving a weapon of mass destruction inside the United States.

USNS *Comfort* (Ch. 9) U.S. Navy hospital ship based in Norfolk, Virginia,[119] that provides afloat, mobile, acute surgical medical facilities for the U.S. military, and offers hospital services to support U.S. disaster relief and humanitarian operations worldwide and domestically.

It deployed to Puerto Rico to aid in Hurricane Maria disaster relief.

U.S. Small Business Administration (SBA) (Ch. 3) Within the U.S. Department of Commerce. Offers three types of federally subsidized disaster loans to help qualified homeowners and businesses—home disaster loans, business physical disaster loans, and economic injury loans. A major source of funding help for those who do not qualify for federal disaster assistance because their incomes are too high under Federal Emergency Management Agency (FEMA) means-tested relief programs.

USA Freedom Act (Ch. 7) Enacted in 2015, this law replaced the Patriot Act of 2001. The USA Freedom Act called for an end to the bulk collection of phone records by the National Security Agency (NSA) and the restoration and protection of people's rights by establishing a streamlined and transparent process for gaining access to Americans' phone records by means of a specific "selector," such as customer names, or numbers.[120]

USA PATRIOT Act (Ch. 7) Enacted into law after the 9/11 attacks significantly changed public policy and expanded collaboration between the federal, state, and local governments and the U.S. military. Article 2 of the act stated that information sharing could take place among government agencies to augment investigative efforts. This removed a long-established barrier that prevented law enforcement, intelligence, and defense agencies from exchanging information and cooperating in investigations. The same article established new rules of collaboration between police and military that permitted the exchange of military tactics, organization, and hardware to support state and local law enforcement investigations and operations. Article 3 of the measure provided for the rapid updating of cybertechnology countermeasures to fight a more advanced digital-age battle with terrorists. Most controversial in this law was authorization of the government to conduct warrantless searches and seizures unbeknownst to the target of such actions.

Vertical fragmentation (Ch. 1) Occurs in disaster management when officials of these levels of government—federal, state, and local—fail to coordinate their responsibilities, act too independently of one another, duplicate their efforts, or work at cross-purposes, or when one level of government fails to carry out its obligations in an intergovernmentally organized system.

Video journalism (Ch. 3) The ability of both news media and social media people to record, edit, and share video of major and minor disasters or incidents before, during, and after the time they occur. Some of this video is recorded by personal mobile phones or other devices. Since the early 1980s, video journalism has been fueled by the ability of television broadcast news to cover breaking stories almost anywhere in the world via remote linkups aided by orbiting communications satellites, and other technology. Since the mid-1980s, the rise in Internet and World Wide Web connectivity and storage capacity has made possible video uploading, sharing, and streaming to sites like YouTube, Veoh, Dailymotion, Vimeo, Flickr, and others. News commentators and reporters as well as political officials and pundits use video material to help create a "politics of a disaster" and so are customarily parts of the phenomenon. The public's massive use of smartphones with video and Internet connectivity in recent years has increased the video journalism phenomena by many orders of magnitude.

Volition (Ch. 5) Refers to a conscious choice or decision made by an individual or group. In the realm of disaster risk, individuals use volition when they are aware of the degree of risk or the extent of vulnerability and intentionally decide to assume that risk or accept that vulnerability in some action they take.

Volkmer Amendment (Ch. 3) Contained within the Hazard Mitigation and Relocation Assistance Act of 1993, it amended some parts of the 1988 Stafford Act. It increased Federal Emergency Management Agency (FEMA) funds dedicated to community assistance disaster funding for relocation or hazard mitigation activities from a subsidy of 10 percent (in the original Stafford Act of 1988) to 15 percent. Once FEMA has paid out a sum total of federal disaster relief to a state under a presidential declaration of major disaster, the state is then entitled to receive additional federal money equivalent to 15 percent of the total funds the state received from the federal government under the declaration. The state may use this additional federal money to subsidize state and FEMA-preapproved disaster mitigation projects. The Volkmer Amendment also increased from 50 percent to 75 percent the federal share of the cost of specific pre-disaster mitigation activities or projects. This increase greatly benefited states and localities that put forward worthy mitigation projects and that were willing to come up with the remaining matching costs.

Voluntary agencies (VOLAGs) (Ch. 6) Defined as voluntary nonprofit organizations, community service groups, and religious organizations that provide assistance in the aftermath of a disaster or emergency.

Voluntary risk (Ch. 5) A risk accepted on one's own initiative or from one's own free will. The reverse, involuntary risk, implies that a risk is imposed on someone without that person's agreement, permission, or perhaps even knowledge.

War on terror (Ch. 3) A policy authorized by the U.S. Congress under the Authorization for Use of Military Force against Terrorists resolution enacted into law following the 9/11 attacks on the United States. Both the phrase *war on terror* and the policies it denotes have been a source of ongoing controversy, as critics argue they have been used to justify unilateral preemptive war, perpetual war, human rights abuses, and other violations of international law. The Obama administration sought to discontinue official use of the expression "war on terrorism."[121]

Weather Channel, The (Ch. 5) An American basic cable and satellite television channel begun in 1982 that by 2008 became a jointly owned venture between NBCUniversal and investment firms the Blackstone Group and Bain Capital. The channel broadcasts weather forecasts and weather-related news, domestically and internationally, along with documentaries and entertainment programming related to weather.[122]

White House package (Ch. 4) Contains documents prepared for the president's action on a governor's request. It includes the governor's request and the Federal Emergency Management Agency (FEMA) director's memorandum, made up of a summary of significant aspects of the event, statistics relative to damage and losses; outlines of the contributions made by federal, state, local, and private agencies; a list of the unmet needs for which the governor seeks federal assistance; and a recommended course of action for the president. It also contains appropriate letters and announcements related to the action, including the FEMA director's recommendation to the president regarding whether to approve or deny the governor's request.

Witt, James Lee, former FEMA director (Ch. 10) Headed FEMA through both terms of the Clinton administration (1993–2001). Made significant reforms and advances in federal emergency management, de-emphasized nuclear attack preparedness and terrorism, but promoted mitigation, preparedness response, and recovery for natural and non-terror human-caused disasters. Is generally credited with improving the morale of FEMA employees, and he advanced Vice President Gore's reinventing government initiative within FEMA. Witt had previous experience as an emergency manager in the state of Arkansas before his FEMA directorship.

"Wind" versus "water" dispute (Ch. 1) A problem of claims adjustment and contested insurance coverage often encountered after disasters that cause both wind and water damage to a private structure. Private insurers cover wind damage (but not that caused by floodwater) in their homeowner insurance policies. The National Flood Insurance Program (NFIP) covers floodwater damage but not wind-caused damage. Consequently, sometimes after hurricanes or severe storms, many homeowners have fallen into insurance "limbo" as their private insurer's claims adjuster denies claims for damage they believe is caused by flooding (not wind) and the NFIP claims adjuster rejects claims for damage they conclude was caused by wind (not floodwater). A vast number of NFIP and private homeowner insurance policyholders in Katrina-damaged zones ended up having their claims denied by both the NFIP and their private insurer on these grounds.

World Food Programme (WFP) (Ch. 8) Responsible for providing rapid and self-sustaining nutritional relief to the millions of victims of man-made or natural disasters. In cases of emergency, the WFP attempts quick response but always with permission of the host government. WFP duties cover transport, delivery, and distribution of food made available by other UN agencies, other national governments, or nongovernmental organizations (NGOs). When called upon, the WFP joins in reconstruction and rehabilitation activity.

World Health Organization (WHO) (Ch. 8) UN central agency assigned to manage health and sanitation concerns throughout the world. The WHO uses its people, authority, and expertise to assess and respond to health needs in regions and countries affected by natural and man-made disasters. The WHO operates programs designed to help the governments manage first aid supplies, improve their medical capabilities, and maintain epidemiological surveillance of disease, all important in the aftermath of disasters. The WHO works to eradicate diseases and reduce the effects of epidemics through campaigns of information and immunization.

NOTES

Preface

1. David Alexander, *Natural Disasters* (New York: Chapman & Hall, 1993), 3.

2. Ibid.

3. Dennis S. Mileti, *Disasters by Design: A Reassessment of Natural Hazards in the United States* (Washington, DC: Joseph Henry Press, 1999), 3.

4. See David Butler, "Focusing Events in the Early Twentieth Century: A Hurricane, Two Earthquakes, and a Pandemic," in *Emergency Management: The American Experience 1900-2010*, 2nd ed., Ed. Claire B. Rubin. (Boca Raton, FL: CRC Press of Taylor & Francis Group, 2012), 13–50.

5. The current era as characterized by the discovery, technological applications, and sociopolitical consequences of nuclear energy. See *American Heritage Dictionary of the English Language*, 5th ed. Copyright © 2016 by Houghton Mifflin Harcourt Publishing Company. Published by Houghton Mifflin Harcourt Publishing Company, https://www.thefreedictionary.com/Atomic+Era (accessed July 18, 2018).

6. See Patrick S. Roberts, *Disasters and the American State: How Politicians, Bureaucrats, and the Public Prepare for the Unexpected* (New York: Cambridge University Press, 2013).

7. See John Hannigan, *Disasters without Borders: The International Politics of Natural Disasters* (Malden, MA: Polity Press, 2012) and Peter D. Ward, *The Flooded Earth: Our Future in a World without Ice Caps* (New York: Basic Books, 2010). Public Safety Canada considers solar radiation storms to be an agent of disaster, owing to their potential impact on communications across that vast nation. The Pentagon and the U.S. Department of Homeland Security, among other federal organizations, consider cyberterrorism a tremendous threat to the nation, considered capable of generating widespread disastrous effects.

8. See John Fass Morton, *Next-Generation Homeland Security: Network Federalism and National Preparedness* (Annapolis, MD: Naval Institute Press, 2012).

9. For a defense of policy study and new ways policy science is advancing, see Kevin B. Smith and Christopher W. Larimer, *The Public Policy Theory Primer*, 2nd ed. (Boulder, CO: Westview Press, 2013).

10. See Thomas A. Birkland, *An Introduction to the Policy Process*, 4th ed. (New York: Routledge, 2016). Public policy theory work continues; see Kevin B. Smith and Christopher W. Larimer, *The Public Policy Theory Primer*, 2nd, cited previously, and Christopher M. Weible and Paul A. Sabatier, *Theories of the Policy Process*, 4th ed. (Boulder, CO: Westview Press, 2018).

11. Jonathan Haidt and Sam Abrams, "The Top 10 Reasons American Politics Are so Broken," *The Washington Post*, January 7, 2015, https://www.washingtonpost.com/news/wonk/wp/2015/01/07/the-top-10-reasons-american-politics-are-worse-than-ever/?utm_term=.0e5275bb7d91 (accessed July 22, 2018).

12. Ibid.

13. See Saundra K. Schneider, *Dealing with Disaster: Public Management in Crisis Situations*, 2nd ed. (Armonk, NY: M.E. Sharpe, 2011), 9–30.

14. Lucien G. Canton, *Emergency Management: Concepts and Strategies for Effective Programs* (Hoboken, NJ: Wiley-Interscience, John Wiley & Sons, Inc., 2007).

15. Arjen Boin, Paul t'Hart, Eric Stern, and Bengt Sundelius, *The Politics of Crisis Management: Public Leadership under Pressure,* 2nd ed. (New York: Cambridge University Press, 2017).

16. See Patrick Roberts, Robert Ward, and Gary Wamsley, "The Evolving Federal Role in Emergency Management," in *Emergency Management: The American Experience 1900–2010,* 2nd ed., ed. Claire B. Rubin (Boca Raton, FL: CRC Press, 2012), 247–276.

17. Thomas A. Birkland, *Lessons of Disaster: Policy Change after Catastrophic Events* (Washington, DC: Georgetown University Press, 2007), 2.

18. Wonderful books have been available on the public administration of disaster management, on the political geography of disasters, on the sociology of disaster, and on law and disaster, but few have been produced as a core text for political science, public policy, and public administration courses.

19. See Robert Sibley, "Veteran Journalism Teacher Joe Scanlon Dies at 82," *Ottawa Citizen*, May 3, 2015, https://ottawacitizen.com/news/local-news/veteran-journalism-teacher-joe-scanlon-dies-at-82 (accessed July 17, 2018).

20. Professor Rundquist was my mentor and professor of political science in his years at University of Illinois at Urbana–Champaign; later he relocated to the U. of I. Chicago campus.

21. See their book, Frances L. Edwards and Daniel C. Goodrich, *Introduction to Transportation Security* (Boca Raton, FL: CRC Press, 2013).

Chapter 1

1. Thomas Fullerjan, "A Rush to Find Survivors Amid the Mud of Southern California Enclave," *The New York Times*, January 10, 2018, https://www.nytimes.com/2018/01/10/us/montecito-mudslides-california.html (accessed April 27, 2018).

2. Ibid.

3. Ibid.

4. James Queally and Louis Sahagun, "Death Toll from Montecito Mudslide Rises to 18," *Los Angeles Times*, January 12, 2018, https://www.latimes.com/la-lb-771-39548-la-me-montecito-mudsides-101-htmlstory.html (accessed April 27, 2018).

5. Ibid.

6. Ibid.

7. Melinda Burns, "When It Rains Again: Science of a Disaster," *Newsmakers with Jerry Roberts*, January 16, 2018, https://www.newsmakerswithjr.com/single-post/2018/01/16/When-It-Rains-Again-Science-of-a-Disaster (accessed April 27, 2018).

8. Fullerjan, *The New York Times*, January 10, 2018.

9. Ibid.

10. Ibid.

11. Ibid.

12. Giana Magnoli, "Disaster Relief Available for Santa Barbara County Victims of Thomas Fire, Montecito Floods," *NoozHawk* (Santa Barbara, CA) Local News, January 17, 2018, https://www.noozhawk.com/article/disaster_relief_and_recovery_resources_for_thomas_fire_montecito_floods (accessed May 17, 2018).

13. Ibid.

14. Ibid.

15. Ibid.

16. Fullerjan, *The New York Times*, January 10, 2018.

17. Queally and Sahagun, *Los Angeles Times*, January 12, 2018.

18. Burns, *Newsmakers with Jerry Roberts*, January 16, 2018.

19. Ibid.

20. Ibid.

21. Ibid.

22. Cal Fire, "Top 20 Largest California Wildfires," https://www.fire.ca.gov/communications/downloads/fact_sheets/Top20_Acres.pdf (last modified January 15, 2019).

23. Ibid.

24. Ibid.

25. Ibid.

26. Ibid.

27. Lindsey Holden, "FEMA Approves Federal Disaster Relief Money for Montecito Mudslides," *The Tribune* (San Luis Obispo, CA), January 12, 2018, http://www.sanluisobispo.com/news/state/california/

article194416414.html (accessed May 18, 2018). Insert is by this author. No events can be added to an in-force major disaster declaration without the approval of the president. However, any county not included in an original approved declaration may be, if it meets FEMA damage cost criteria, added by FEMA to a major disaster declaration without seeking presidential pre-approval.

28. Major disasters begin from DR-1 in May 1953 and continue serially to DR-1999 in 2011. In 2011, numbering restarts with DR-4000 and continues to the present in the 4000 series. The 2000 series is for fire management assistance, and the 3000 series is dedicated to emergency declarations. Hence, major disaster declarations run from DR-1 to DR-1999 and immediately thereafter from DR-4000 upward.

29. Holden, *The Tribune* (San Luis Obispo, CA), January 12, 2018.

30. Ibid.

31. Ibid.

32. Ibid.

33. Giana Magnoli, *NoozHawk* (Santa Barbara, CA), Local News, January 17, 2018.

34. Ibid.

35. Ibid.

36. Peter J. May, *Recovering from Catastrophes: Federal Disaster Relief and Politics* (Westport, CT: Greenwood Press, 1985), 18. See also David Butler, "Focusing Events in the Early Twentieth Century: A Hurricane, Two Earthquakes, and a Pandemic," in *Emergency Management: The American Experience 1900-2010*, 2nd ed., ed. Claire B. Rubin (Boca Raton, FL: CRC Press, 2012), 13–50.

37. Ted Steinberg, *Acts of God: The Unnatural History of Natural Disaster* (New York: Oxford University Press, 2000).

38. David Alexander, *Natural Disasters* (New York: Chapman and Hall, 1993), 327.

39. See Howard Kunreuther and Michael Useem, eds., *Learning from Catastrophes: Strategies for Reaction and Response* (Upper Saddle River, NJ: Pearson Education, 2010). See also Keith Smith, *Environmental Hazards: Assessing Risk and Reducing Disaster*, 6th ed. (New York: Routledge, 2013), 114–118.

40. See U.S. Department of the Treasury, Resource Center, *Terrorism Risk Insurance Program*, *Overview*, August 19, 2013, http://www.treasury.gov/resource-center/fin-mkts/Pages/program.aspx (accessed September 4, 2018).

41. See Martin Dockrill, Nick Ford, and Andrew Dlugolecki, *Climate Change Research Report 2009*, Chapter 5, Market Failure and Climate Change, Coping with Climate Change Risks and Opportunities for Insurers (London: The Chartered Insurance Institute, 2009), 1–29 for chapter and 2 for page of citation.

42. Deborah Stone, *The Samaritan's Dilemma: Should Government Help Your Neighbor?* (New York: Nation Books, 2008), 111.

43. *Around the NFL*, "J.J. Watt Reveals Plans for Hurricane Harvey Funds," October 26, 2017. See http://www.nfl.com/news/story/0ap3000000867498/article/jj-watt-reveals-plans-for-hurricane-harvey-funds (accessed June 7, 2018). After initially setting a goal to raise $200,000 in Hurricane Harvey relief, J. J. Watt ended up raising more than $37 million from more than 200,000 donors. The Houston Texans linebacker announced plans as to how the funds will be distributed to those in need. A total of $31.5 million will be distributed among four partners—Americares, Feeding America, SBP, and Save the Children—over the next 18–24 months. The funds will be used to rebuild homes, restore child-care centers, provide food, and address health needs of those affected most by Hurricane Harvey in Houston and the surrounding areas. The remaining $7 million will be set aside for distribution in 2018 as the Justin J. Watt Foundation continues to assess and analyze the evolving relief efforts. Ibid.

44. See Mariana Budjeryn, Simon Saradzhyan, and William Tobey, "25 Years of Nuclear Security Cooperation by the US, Russia and Other Newly Independent States: A Timeline," Russia Matters, June 16, 2017, https://www.russiamatters.org/analysis/25-years-nuclear-security-cooperation-us-russia-and-other-newly-independent-states (accessed June 7, 2018).

45. This book will use the terms *disaster management* and *emergency management* interchangeably.

Some scholars of the field may object to this interchangeable use because emergency managers are usually defined as those "who possess the knowledge, skills, and abilities to effectively manage a comprehensive [emergency] management program." Michael K. Lindell, Carla Prater, and Ronald W. Perry, *Introduction to Emergency Management* (Hoboken, NJ: Wiley, 2007), 445. Canton calls disaster management "the tactical and operational implementation of that [planning] strategy at the time of the crisis." Lucien G. Canton, *Emergency Management: Concepts and Strategies for Effective Programs* (Hoboken, NJ: Wiley, 2007), 60. Much of this book addresses president-declared emergencies and disasters. It is fair to say that emergency managers in those circumstances are also disaster managers in both strategic and tactical terms. Also, within emergency management are emergency responders, who act directly on disaster. Emergency responder occupational specialties include firefighters, police officers, and emergency medical technicians (Lindell et al., *Introduction to Emergency Management,* 445). Much of this study does not draw distinctions between emergency managers and emergency responders. However, it is important to recognize that emergency managers, broadly construed, and emergency responders, many qualified as emergency managers in accord with the definition above, are in the field of disaster management. Disaster management, as used in this book, includes emergency management and those organizations and individuals outside government—nonprofit organizations active in disasters, disaster insurers, corporate emergency managers, and business continuity managers.

46. See James F. Miskel, *Disaster Response and Homeland Security: What Works, What Doesn't* (Westport, CT: Praeger Security International, 2006), 23–38. Miskel makes a distinction between hazards involving life and safety and hazards calling for the protection, preservation, or restoration of agricultural resources, the environment, and certain forms of property not immediately essential to humans. He devotes an entire chapter to why the disaster management system regularly fails in catastrophic events. See also Steinberg, *Acts of*

God, 128. In a "tongue-in-cheek" fashion, Steinberg recounts bizarre proposals of the U.S. Air Force to terminate threatening tornadoes using atomic bombs. For Steinberg the story is about how humans have come to use their modern scientific and technological expertise to cope with natural forces still well beyond their control, even as people have dramatically increased their vulnerability to the same forces.

47. Damon P. Coppola, *Introduction to International Disaster Management*, 2nd ed. (Burlington, MA: Butterworth-Heinemann, 2011). 6.

48. Ibid.

49. The World Bank, *Natural Hazards, Unnatural Disasters* (Washington, DC: The World Bank, 2010).

50. William L. Waugh Jr., *Living with Hazards, Dealing with Disasters: An Introduction to Emergency Management* (Armonk, NY: M.E. Sharpe, 2000).

51. Alex Wellerstein, The Hawaii Alert Was an Accident. The Dread It Inspired Wasn't. *The Washington Post*, January 16, 2018. See https://www.washingtonpost.com/news/posteverything/wp/2018/01/16/the-hawaii-alert-was-an-accident-the-dread-it-inspired-wasnt/? utm_term=.3a2789320c2b (accessed June 7, 2018).

52. Waugh, *Living with Hazards*, 11–12.

53. George D. Haddow, Jane A. Bullock, and Damon P. Coppola. *Introduction to Emergency Management,* 6th ed. (Boston: Butterworth-Heinemann, 2017), 2.

54. Ibid.

55. For an excellent synopsis of emergency management's professionalization and its advancement within FEMA, see Patrick S. Roberts, *Disasters and the American State: How Politicians, Bureaucrats, and the Public Prepare for the Unexpected* (New York: Cambridge University Press, 2013), 92–96.

56. FEMA's National Continuity Programs (NCP) established the Continuity Excellence Series (CES)—Level I, Professional Continuity Practitioner and Level II, Master Continuity Practitioner on April 16, 2008. The Series is designed for continuity professionals throughout the federal government

and among our state, local, tribal, and territorial governmental partners, private-sector owners of critical infrastructure/key resources, and nongovernmental organization (NGO) disaster response entities. CES addresses the full spectrum of requirements to support a viable continuity capability. Courses are available for students at all levels, from individuals new to continuity to program managers with many years of experience. Training classes enable personnel to develop and enhance their continuity knowledge and expertise. Some courses are offered in a web-based independent study (IS) setting to allow students an opportunity to expand their knowledge of continuity. See U.S. FEMA at https://www.fema.gov/faq-details/Professional-Development-Series-PDS.

57. Ibid., 4.

58. For more information about the IAEM's Certified Emergency Manager program, visit http://www.iaem.com/page.cfm? p=certification/getting-started (accessed June 7, 2018). FEMA's Professional Development Series (PDS) includes seven Emergency Management Institute Independent Study courses that provide a broad set of fundamentals for those in the emergency management profession. Students who complete all the courses receive a PDS Certificate of Completion. See U.S. FEMA at https://www.fema.gov/faq-details/Professional-Development-Series-PDS.

59. Glen Karpovich, "Professional Certification in Emergency Management," April 17, 2007, http://www.officer.com/article/10249956/professional-certification-in-emergency-management (accessed September 4, 2018).

60. The International Association of Emergency Managers (IAEM), which has more than 6,000 members worldwide, is a nonprofit educational organization dedicated to promoting the "Principles of Emergency Management" and representing those professionals whose goals are saving lives and protecting property and the environment during emergencies and disasters. The mission of IAEM is to advance the profession by promoting the principles of emergency management; to serve its members by providing information, networking, and professional development opportunities. See

About IAEM, http://iaem.com/page.cfm?p=about/intro (accessed June 7, 2018).

61. The National Emergency Management Association (NEMA) is a nonpartisan, nonprofit 501(c)(3) association dedicated to advancing public safety by improving the nation's ability to prepare for, respond to, and recover from all emergencies, disasters, and threats to our nation's security. NEMA is the professional association of and for emergency management directors from all 50 states, eight U.S. territories, and the District of Columbia. NEMA provides national leadership and expertise in comprehensive emergency management; serves as a vital emergency management information and assistance resource; and advances continuous improvement in emergency management through strategic partnerships, innovative programs, and collaborative policy positions. NEMA began in 1974 when state directors of emergency services first united to exchange information on common emergency management issues that threatened their constituencies. The state directors of emergency management are the core membership of NEMA. Membership categories also exist for key state staff, homeland security advisors, federal agencies, nonprofit organizations, private-sector companies, and concerned individuals. NEMA, "What is NEMA?" https://www.nemaweb.org/index.php/about/what-is-nema (accessed June 7, 2018).

62. The Emergency Management Committee's mission is to provide APWA members with resources and a forum for exchanging and developing ideas, knowledge, and technologies for minimizing the impact and consequences of disasters. It also intends to foster recognition of public works' important role(s) in emergency management, including its strong involvement in mitigation and recovery, as well as to influence public policies that will strengthen the ability of government at all levels to better address disaster management. Collaboration between APWA and FEMA/EMI led to the creation of four public works-centric online courses, available as independent study programs. Courses are offered free of charge. Compliance with National Incident Management System (NIMS) requires that all agency responders complete IS-100, IS-200, IS-700, and IS-800 online

courses. Included as well are IS-552 The Public Works Role in Emergency Management; IS-554 Emergency Planning for Public Works; IS-556 Damage Assessment for Public Works; and IS-558 Public Works and Disaster Recovery. See American Public Works Association, Emergency Management at http://www3.apwa.net/technical_committees/Emergency-Management.

63. For more about the International Sociological Association (ISA), Research Committee, Sociology of Disasters, see https://www.isa-sociology.org/en/about-isa/history-of-isa/.

64. Roberts, *Disasters and the American State,* 15.

65. The International Association for Disaster Preparedness and Response, which is also known as DERA, is a professional member association that was created in 1962 with the purpose of giving professionals, volunteers, and organizations the platform that they need to stay connected and to network. This is one of the few associations that includes global members and not just members in the United States. The association provides support, gives a platform for members to share their resources, and gives members a place where they can stay actively involved. Emergency Management Degree Program Guide, "What Emergency Management Associations Should I Join?" 2015, https://www.emergency-management-degree.org/faq/what-emergency-management-associations-should-i-join/ (accessed June 7, 2018).

66. See Katarzyna Fertala, "EMAP Proves Invaluable as Method of Standardization for Emergency Management Programs," The University of Maryland, Center for Health & Homeland Security, July 26, 2013, https://www.mdchhs.com/emap-proves-invaluable-as-method-of-standardization-for-emergency-management-programs/.

67. Emergency Management Accreditation Program, *The EMAP Standard* refers to *ANSI/EMAP 4-2016, which is an Emergency Management Standard,* composed of 64 standards, by which programs that apply for EMAP accreditation are evaluated. The *Emergency Management Standard* is intended to serve as a tool for continuous improvement.

It is part of the voluntary accreditation process for local, state, federal, higher education, and tribal emergency management programs. The *Emergency Management Standard* covers Program Management, Administration and Finance, and Laws and Authorities; Hazard Identification, Risk Assessment and Consequence Analysis; Hazard Mitigation; Prevention; Operational Planning and Procedures; Incident Management; Resource Management, Mutual Aid and Logistics; Communications and Warning; Facilities; Training; Exercises, Evaluations and Corrective Action; and Emergency Public Education and Information. See EMAP, "What is EMAP?" 2018, https://emap.org/index.php/what-is-emap/the-emergency-management-standard (accessed June 7, 2018).

68. Keith Smith, *Environmental Hazards: Assessing Risk and Reducing Disaster*, 6th ed. (New York: Routledge, 2013), 11.

69. Ibid., 21.

70. CNN launched its 24-hour television news organization in 1982 in Atlanta, Georgia. Cable News Network is an American basic cable and satellite television news channel owned by the Turner Broadcasting System, a division of Time Warner. CNN was founded in 1980 by American media proprietor Ted Turner as a 24-hour cable news channel. See https://www.cnn.com/2014/01/17/cnn-info/about/index.html (accessed June 7, 2018).

71. See Louise K. Comfort, ed., *Managing Disaster: Strategies and Policy Perspectives* (Durham, NC: Duke University Press, 1988). See also Richard T. Sylves and Zoltan I. Buzas, "Presidential Disaster Declaration Decisions, 1953–2003: What Influences Odds of Approval." *State & Local Government Review* 39, no. 1 (2007): 3–15; Thomas A. Garrett and Russell S. Sobel, "The Political Economy of FEMA Disaster Payments," *Economic Inquiry* 41, no. 3 (2003): 496–509; Rutherford H. Platt, "Shouldering the Burden: Federal Assumption of Disaster Costs," in *Disasters and Democracy: The Politics of Extreme Natural Events*, ed. Rutherford H. Platt (Washington, DC: Island Press, 1999), 11–46.

72. Richard T. Sylves, "The Politics and Budgeting of Federal Emergency Management" in *Disaster Management in the U.S. and Canada*, eds. Richard T. Sylves and William L. Waugh Jr. (Springfield, IL: Charles C Thomas, 1996).

73. See Platt, "Shouldering the Burden," 11–46. See also Miskel, *Disaster Response and Homeland Security.*

74. Charles R. Wise, "Organizing for Homeland Security," *Public Administration Review* 62 (September 2002): 131–144. William L. Waugh Jr. and Richard T. Sylves, "Organizing the War on Terrorism," special issue, *Public Administration Review* 62 (September 2002): 145–153.

75. The author would like to acknowledge the contributions of William L. Waugh Jr. on these points. See William L. Waugh Jr., "Emergency Management and State and Local Government Capacity," in *Cities and Disaster: North American Studies in Emergency Management*, eds. Richard T. Sylves and William L. Waugh Jr. (Springfield, IL: Charles C Thomas, 1990), 229–233.

76. John W. Kingdon, *Agendas, Alternatives, and Public Policies,* 2nd ed. (New York: Longman, 1995), 166.

77. Donald F. Kettl, *System under Stress: Homeland Security and American Politics,* 2nd ed. (Washington, DC: CQ Press, 2007), 126.

78. See John W. Kingdon, "Agendas, Alternatives, and Public Policies," in *Classics of Public Policy*, eds. Jay M. Shafritz, Karen S. Layne, and Christopher P. Borick (New York: Pearson, 2005), 148–159.

79. H.R. 4667—115th Congress, "Making Further Supplemental Appropriations for the Fiscal Year ending September 30, 2018, for Disaster Assistance...," from www.GovTrack.us. 2017, https://www.govtrack.us/congress/bills/115/hr4667 (accessed March 29, 2018).

80. See Thomas A. Birkland, *Lessons of Disaster: Change after Catastrophic Events* (Washington, DC: Georgetown University Press, 2006).

81. Anthony Downs, "Up and Down with Ecology: The 'Issue-Attention Cycle,'" *Public Interest* 28 (Summer 1972): 38–50.

82. Ibid., 39.

83. See California Earthquake Authority, "An Earthquake Could Happen Today," webpage at https://www.earthquakeauthority.com/ (accessed April 2, 2018).

84. Andrew Blankstein and Monica Alba, "Why Do So Few California Homeowners Have Earthquake Insurance?" NBC News, Oct. 17, 2014 at https://www.nbcnews.com/news/investigations/why-do-so-few-california-homeowners-have-earthquake-insurance-n227711 (accessed April 2, 2018). The report lists seven reasons, many of which stem from public denial, confidence a great quake will not occur, trust that the federal government will bail everyone out, the false belief that one's standard homeowner's insurance covers earthquake losses, the high cost of quake insurance policies and their deductibles, and fear that even if they own quake policies, their quake damage claims might still be rejected.

85. See CNN, "Mass shootings in America are a serious problem -- and these 9 charts show just why," A.J. Willingham and Saeed Ahmed, at https://www.cnn.com/2016/06/13/health/mass-shootings-in-america-in-charts-and-graphs-trnd/index.html (accessed April 2, 2018).

86. Although Downs, in "Up and Down with Ecology," is not discussing disaster specifically, his arguments are quite appropriate within the realm of disaster policy and politics.

87. See U.S. Federal Emergency Management Agency, *National Flood Insurance Program and the Consolidated Appropriations Act of 2014*, https://www.fema.gov/media-library/assets/documents/90829 (accessed April 2, 2018). The Homeowner Flood Insurance Affordability Act of 2014, at the same source, shielded homeowners residing in high-flood risk from rate hikes likely to have been imposed under Biggert-Waters. Ironically, Representative Maxine Waters (D-CA) was one of the leaders of the effort to weaken the 2012 law co-named for her.

88. See *Sun Sentinel*, "Florida School Shooting at Stoneman Douglas High School," April 2, 2018, http://www.sun-sentinel.com/local/broward/parkland/florida-school-shooting/ (accessed April 2, 2018).

89. Downs, 40.

90. Note that Hurricane Irma is not mentioned in this example because most Floridians have for a long period been required to pay for costly hurricane insurance policies on their homes, apart from their standard homeowner's insurance policies. Florida state law requires that insurers offer residential property owners hurricane insurance for windstorm and driven-water damage. Many banks require their home mortgage holders buy and maintain homeowner policies on their property sufficient to cover hurricane windstorm and rain damage. Homeowners are advised to also buy National Flood Insurance policies for flood losses attributable to hurricanes or riverine and coastal flooding.

91. Douglas Brinkley, *The Great Deluge: Hurricane Katrina, New Orleans, and the Mississippi Gulf Coast* (New York: Morrow, 2006).

92. Downs, "Up and Down with Ecology."

93. Liz Pulliam Weston, "Rethinking Your Stance on Earthquake Coverage," *The Los Angeles Times*, December 18, 2017 at http://www.latimes.com/la-homeauto-story1-story.html (accessed April 2, 2018).

94. Downs, 40–41.

95. U.S. Centers for Disease Control and Prevention, "2014-2016 Ebola Outbreak in West Africa," Ebola (Ebola Virus Disease), at https://www.cdc.gov/vhf/ebola/outbreaks/2014-west-africa/index.html (accessed March 28, 2018).

96. Downs, "Up and Down with Ecology," 41.

97. Miskel, *Disaster Response and Homeland Security,* 76.

98. Canton, *Emergency Management,* 28.

99. Charles Perrow, *Normal Accidents* (New York: Basic Books, 1984). See also Charles Perrow, *The Next Catastrophe: Reducing Our Vulnerabilities to Natural, Industrial, and Terrorist Disasters* (Princeton, NJ: Princeton University Press, 2011).

100. Jurgen R. Winkler, "Political Culture: Political Science," *Encyclopedia Britannica*, May 4, 2018 at https://www.britannica.com/topic/political-culture (accessed September 13, 2018).

101. Daniel Sutter and Kevin M. Simmons, "The Socioeconomic Impact of Tornadoes," in *The Economics of Unnatural Disasters*, ed. William Kern (Kalamazoo, MI: W.E. Upjohn Institute for Employment Research, 2010), 103–130. See also Ibid., 6.

102. Thomas A. Birkland, *After Disaster: Agenda Setting, Public Policy, and Focusing Events* (Washington, DC: Georgetown University Press, 1997), 128. See Birkland's, *Lessons of Disaster: Change after Catastrophic Events* (Washington, DC: Georgetown University Press, 2006).

103. See May, *Recovering from Catastrophes,* and Peter J. May and Walter W. Williams, *Disaster Policy Implementation: Managing Programs under Shared Governance* (New York: Plenum Press, 1986).

104. As of 2016, the United States had 3,007 counties, 64 parishes (Louisiana), 18 organized boroughs (parts of Alaska), 11 census areas (parts of Alaska), 41 independent cities (Virginia, Maryland, Missouri, and Nevada, where these cities are county equivalents), and the District of Columbia for a total of 3,142 counties and county-equivalents in the United States. See Google.com at https://www.google.com/search?q=How+many+counties+does+the+U.S.+have%3F&rlz=1C1CHWA_enUS634US641&oq=How+many+counties+does+the+U.S.+have%3F&aqs=chrome.69i57j0.13418j1j7&sourceid=chrome&ie=UTF-8 (accessed April 4, 2018).

105. For an explanation of the "policy window" concept in disaster policy see Elliott Mittler, "Nonstructural Hazard Mitigation," in *Managing Disaster: Strategies and Policy Perspectives*, ed. Louise K. Comfort (Durham, NC: Duke University Press, 1988), 89.

106. See Ira Helsloot, Arjen Boin, Brian Jacobs, and Louise K. Comfort, eds., *Mega-Crises: Understanding the Prospects, Nature, Characteristics, and the Effects of Cataclysmic Events* (Springfield, IL: Charles C Thomas Publishers, 2012). This is a superb collection of 25 scholarly articles, a share of which are about natural disasters or terrorism. Also included in the book are chapters about the "Sub-Prime Crisis," "Corporate Meltdowns," "Mega-Cities," "Food Security," "The H1N1 Pandemic," and "Energy Vulnerability."

107. Arjen Boin, Paul 't Hart, Eric Stern, and Bengt Sundelius, *The Politics of Crisis Management: Public Leadership under Pressure*, 2nd ed. (Cambridge, U.K.: Cambridge University Press, University Printing House, 2017), 5. Hereafter "Boin et al., 2017."

108. Ibid.

109. For an excellent study of the political, campaign, and electoral consequences of Hurricane Andrew, read David K. Twigg, *The Politics of Disaster: Tracking the Impact of Hurricane Andrew* (Gainesville: University of Florida Press, 2012).

110. Richard T. Sylves, "President Bush and Hurricane Katrina: A Presidential Leadership Study," in *Annals of the American Academy of Political and Social Science* 604 (March 2006): 26–56.

111. Steinberg, *Acts of God,* 103.

112. Gilbert F. White passed away in 2006. For a thoughtful biography see Robert E. Hinshaw, *Living with Nature's Extremes: The Life of Gilbert Fowler White* (Boulder, CO: Johnson Books, 2006).

113. Gilbert F. White et al., "Changes in Urban Occupancy of Flood Plains in the United States" (Research Paper 57, Department of Geography, University of Chicago, 1958).

114. Howard Kunreuther, "Insurability Conditions and the Supply of Coverage," in *Paying the Price: The Status and Role of Insurance against Natural Disasters in the United States*, eds. Howard Kunreuther and Richard J. Roth Sr. (Washington, DC: Joseph Henry Press, 1998), 36.

115. Howard Kunreuther, "Has the Time Come for Comprehensive National Disaster Insurance?" in *On Risk and Disaster*, eds. Ronald J. Daniels, Donald E. Kettl, and Howard Kunreuther (Philadelphia: University of Pennsylvania Press, 2006), 188.

116. Howard Kunreuther, "Disaster Mitigation: Lessons from Katrina," *Annals of the American Academy of Political and Social Science* 604 (March 2006): 216.

117. Omri Ben-Shahar, contributor, "Lessons from Hurricane Harvey: Federal Flood Insurance is the Problem, Not the Solution" *Forbes Magazine*, https://www.forbes.com/sites/omribenshahar /2017/08/30/lessons-from-hurricane-harvey-federal-flood-insurance-is-the-problem-not-the-solution/2/#70a8ae59614d (accessed April 4, 2018).

118. Ibid.

119. See U.S. FEMA, "Flood Insurance Reform—The Law." Homeowner Flood Insurance Affordability Act of 2014 at https://www.fema.gov/flood-insurance-reform-law (accessed April 4, 2018).

120. See U.S. Department of Homeland Security, James A. Sadler, W-13058, "FEMA's Participation in State-Sponsored Non-Binding Wind versus Flood Disaster Claims Mediation Program" (Washington, DC: U.S. DHS-FEMA, FIMA, September 26, 2013). This information is issued as a FEMA policy to facilitate implementation of the provision of BW-12 requiring FEMA to participate in state-sponsored, nonbinding mediation of wind versus water disputes, when appropriate. A FEMA policy is an appropriate medium to articulate FEMA's interpretation of the BW-12 provision and will enable our state partners, Write Your Own (WYO) companies, and NFIP insureds to understand the role of FEMA, WYO companies, and other stakeholders in wind-versus-water mediation. This policy is necessitated by the importance of the subject, the statutory requirements, limited available federal resources, and limitation to the Claims and Appeals Branch participation. See https://bsa.nfipstat.fema.gov/wyobull/2013/w-13058.txt (accessed April 4, 2018).

121. See Adam Crowe, *Disasters 2.0: The Application of Social Media Systems for Modern Emergency Management* (Boca Raton, FL: CRC Press, 2012).

122. See U.S. Department of Homeland Security, Federal Emergency Management Agency website, http://training.fema.gov/emiweb/edu, for an excellent compendium of information about FEMA higher education and training programs. Dr. B. Wayne Blanchard and Barbara Moore of FEMA deserve credit for their years in building and cultivating the FEMA higher education program.

123. EMAP website.

124. Federal Emergency Management Agency, "The College List: Colleges, Universities and Institutions Offering Emergency Management Courses," http://

www.training.fema.gov/emiweb/edu/collegelist (accessed September 4, 2018). The College List displays the colleges and universities offering bachelor's, master's, and doctoral level courses in emergency management and homeland security. The list is regularly updated.

125. Brenda D. Phillips and David M. Neal, "Recovery," in *Emergency Management: Principles and Practice for Local Government,* 2nd ed., eds. William L. Waugh Jr. and Kathleen Tierney (Washington, DC: ICMA Press, 2007), 208.

126. Ibid., 208.

127. George D. Haddow and Jane A. Bullock, *Introduction to Emergency Management,* 2nd ed. (Boston: Butterworth-Heinemann, 2006), 58–59.

128. Miskel, *Disaster Response and Homeland Security,* 12.

128. See Alessandra Jerolleman and John J. Kiefer, eds., *Natural Hazard Mitigation* (Boca Raton, FL: CRC Press, 2013).

130. Roberts maintains that Clinton FEMA director James Lee Witt not only championed disaster mitigation as a core purpose of FEMA but also shifted the agency away from national security work and more toward response to natural disasters, while cleverly convincing federal lawmakers that capable FEMA coordinated disaster management could advance their re-election goals. Roberts, *Disasters and the American State,* 97–103.

131. Haddow and Bullock, *Introduction to Emergency Management,* 2nd ed., 58–63. See also Jerolleman and Kiefer, *Natural Hazard Mitigation.*

132. See Brenda D. Phillips, David M. Neal, and Gary R Webb, *Introduction to Emergency Management* (Boca Raton, FL: CRC Press, 2012), 178–181.

133. EMAP website.

134. Canton, *Emergency Management,* 66.

135. David A. McEntire, *Disaster Response and Recovery* (Hoboken, NJ: Wiley, 2007), 24.

136. William J. Petak, "Emergency Management: A Challenge to Public Administration," special issue, *Public Administration Review* 45 (January 1985): 3.

137. Haddow and Bullock, *Introduction to Emergency Management,* 2nd ed., 131–132.

138. Alethia H. Cook, "Towards an Emergency Response Report Card: Evaluating the Response to the I-35W Bridge Collapse," *Journal of Homeland Security and Emergency Management* 6, no. 1 (2009), Article 39.

139. Boin et al., p. 13.

Chapter 2

1. See Thomas A. Birkland, *After Disaster: Agenda Setting, Public Policy, and Focusing Events* (Washington, DC: Georgetown University Press, 1997). See also Peter J. May, *Recovering from Catastrophes: Federal Disaster Relief Policy and Politics* (Westport, CT: Greenwood Press, 1985); Peter J. May and Walter W. Williams, *Disaster Policy Implementation: Managing Programs under Shared Governance* (New York: Plenum Press, 1986); and Louise K. Comfort, Arjen Boin, and Chris C. Demchak, eds., *Designing Resilience: Preparing for Extreme Events* (Pittsburgh, PA: University of Pittsburgh Press, 2010).

2. The Jeffersonian and Hamiltonian models discussed here stem from work on public management by Laurence E. Lynn Jr., *Public Management as Art, Science, and Profession* (Chatham, NJ: Chatham House, 1996). See also Richard T. Sylves, "A Précis on Political Theory and Emergency Management," *Journal of Emergency Management* 2, no. 3 (Summer 2004). This author added the Jacksonian model in the second edition of *Disaster Policy and Politics* (Thousand Oaks, CA: Sage/CQ Press, 2015).

3. David A. McEntire, *Disaster Response and Recovery* (Hoboken, NJ: Wiley, 2007), 35.

4. Ainsley Harris, "How GoFundMe Is Redefining the Business of Disaster Relief," in *Fast Company Newsletter,* December 8, 2017 at https://www .fastcompany.com/40490985/how-gofundme-is-redefining-the-business-of-disaster-relief (accessed April 5, 2018).

5. Ibid.

6. Ibid.

7. McEntire, 2007, 282–283.

8. Ibid., 49.

9. Ibid., 55.

10. Ibid., 66.

11. See Federal Emergency Management Institute (EMI), FEMA Training, *Chapter 3, Building an Effective Emergency Management Organization* (Emmitsburg, MD: FEMA EMI, 2014), 2. At https://training.fema.gov/hiedu/docs/fem/chapter%20 3%20-%20building%20an%20effective%20em%20 org.doc (accessed March 30, 2018).

12. Biography.com website, *Alexander Hamilton Biography: Military Leader, Economist, Journalist, Political Scientist, Lawyer, Government Official (c. 1755–1804)* at https://www.biography.com/people/ alexander-hamilton-9326481 (accessed March 30, 2018). See also Ron Chernow, *Alexander Hamilton* (New York: The Penguin Group, 2004).

13. See Google, Hamilton: What is the Play About?, at https://www.google.com/search?rlz=1C1CHWA_ enUS634US641&ei=iIS-WsCEJ-Gigge2v4ToDA& q=Alexander+Hamilton+play&oq=Alexander+ Hamilton+play&gs_l=psy-ab.3..0l10.10884.11967 .0.28311.5.5.0.0.0.0.99.353.5.5.0....0...1.1.64.psy-ab ..0.5.352...0i131k1j0i67k1.0.RmMg9i20gp4 (accessed March 30, 2018). See also Lin-Manuel Miranda and Jeremy McCarter, *Alexander Hamilton: The Revolution* (New York: Grand Central Publishing, a Division of Hachette Book Group, 2016).

14. See Britannica.com, *Pendleton Civil Service Act*, at https://www.britannica.com/topic/Pendleton-Civil- Service-Act (accessed March 30, 2018).

15. See Lynn, Jr., *Public Management as Art, Science, and Profession*, 1996, 29.

16. John C. Pine, *Technology in Emergency Management* (Hoboken, NJ: John Wiley and Sons, 2007). See also John C. Pine, *Technology in Emergency Management*, 2nd ed. (Hoboken, NJ: John Wiley and Sons, 2018).

17. See works by geographers Susan L. Cutter, the late David Godschalk, David Alexander, James M. Kendra, James K. Mitchell, Rutherford H. Platt, and the late Gilbert White, to name a few.

18. Adam Crowe, *Disasters 2.0: The Application of Social Media Systems for Modern Emergency Management* (Boca Raton, FL: CRC Press, 2012).

19. See Dennis S. Mileti, *Disasters by Design* (Washington, DC: Joseph Henry Press, 2001). See also National Research Council's Committee on Geotargeted Disaster Alerts and Warnings: Current Knowledge and Research Gaps, *Geotargeted Alerts and Warnings* (Washington, DC: National Academies Press, 2013) at https://www.nap.edu/ read/18414/chapter/2 (accessed April 9, 2018).

20. See works by William L. Waugh, Jr., Gary L. Wamsley, Frances E. Edwards, Beverly A. Cigler, Louise K. Comfort, Naim Kapucu, Michael K. Lindell, Peter J. May, William J. Petak, John Kiefer, and Saundra K. Schneider, who are scholars of political science, public administration, or both. This is a partial list.

21. There are many scholarly works on the economics of disaster. Among them are the following: Howard Kunreuther and Michael Useem, eds., *Learning from Catastrophes: Strategies for Reaction and Response* (Upper Saddle River, NJ: Pearson Education, Inc., publishing as Wharton School Publishing, 2010); Willian Kern, *The Economics of Natural and Unnatural Disaster* (Kalamazoo, MI: W.E. Upjohn Institute for Employment Research, 2010); and Stéphane Halligatte, *Natural Disasters and Climate Change: An Economic Perspective* (New York: Springer International Publishing, 2014).

22. See Christine Wamsler, *Cities, Disaster Risk, and Adaptation* (New York: Routledge, 2014).

23. National Research Council, Committee on Disaster Research in the Social Sciences, *Facing Hazards and Disasters: Understanding Human Dimensions* (Washington, DC: National Academies Press, 2006) is an excellent edited compilation of disaster- related social scientific research.

24. Federal Emergency Management Agency, "HAZUS: The Federal Emergency Management Agency's Methodology for Estimating Potential Losses from Disasters," November 12, 2013, http://www .fema.gov/hazus (accessed September 4, 2018). HAZUS-MH is a powerful risk assessment software

program for analyzing potential losses from floods, hurricane winds, and earthquakes. HAZUS-MH, current scientific and engineering knowledge, is coupled with the latest GIS technology to produce estimates of hazard-related damage before, or after, a disaster occurs. Federal, state, and local government agencies and the private sector can order HAZUS-MH free of charge from the FEMA Publication Warehouse.

25. Dwight Waldo, *The Administrative State* (New York: Ronald Press, 1948).

26. See also H. George Frederickson and Kevin B. Smith, *The Public Administration Theory Primer* (Boulder, CO: Westview Press, 2003), 43. Hereafter, "Frederickson and Smith, *Theory Primer.*"

27. Portions of this section were drawn from Jeffrey H. Rubini, "Use of Volunteers During the Deepwater Horizon Oil Spill in the Gulf of Mexico in 2010" (unpublished paper written for the author's EMSE 6305 Introduction to Crisis and Emergency Management course, George Washington University, Washington, DC, Fall 2011).

28. Bio. *True Story, Andrew Jackson* www.biography .com/people/andrew-jackson-9350991?page=1 (accessed April 13, 2018).

29. Walter R. Mead, "The Jacksonian Tradition," *The National Interest* 58 (Winter 1999/2000). http:// denbeste.nu/external/Mead01.html (accessed April 13, 2018).

30. Ibid.

31. Ibid.

32. Ibid.

33. Rubini, "Use of Volunteers during the Deepwater Horizon Oil Spill."

34. Crowe, *Disasters 2.0*, 5, 9, 12.

35. Lynn, *Public Management as Art, Science, and Profession*, 147.

36. Much of the reasoning in this section's paragraphs about professions and professionalism flow from Lynn, Jr., *Public Management as Art, Science, and Profession*, 145–166.

37. See Robert McCreight, "Educational Challenges in Homeland Security and Emergency Management," *Journal of Homeland Security and Emergency Management*, 2009, 6(1), 34. Available at http:// www.bepress.com/jhsem/vol6/iss1/34/ (accessed April 13, 2018).

38. See Thomas E. Drabek, John Evans Professor, Emeritus, Department of Sociology and Criminology, University of Denver, Denver, CO, "Emergency Management and Homeland Security Curricula: Contexts, Cultures, and Constraints," A paper presented at the annual meeting of the Western Social Science Association, Calgary, Alberta, Canada, April 2007. The Drabek article discusses the friction between emergency management and homeland security higher education.

39. See John Barry's *The Rising Tide: The Great Mississippi Flood of 1927 and How It Changed America* (New York: Touchstone, 1998). See also Douglas Brinkley, *The Great Deluge: Hurricane Katrina, New Orleans, and the Mississippi Gulf Coast* (New York, William Morrow, an imprint of HarperCollins, 2006). There are a vast number of disaster case study books: these two are offered as examples.

40. Kathleen J. Tierney, Michael K. Lindell, and Ronald W. Perry, *Facing the Unexpected: Disaster Preparedness and Response in the United States* (Washington, DC: Joseph Henry Press, 2001), 233–240.

41. Richard T. Sylves, "Political Theory and Emergency Management" (paper presented at the FEMA Emergency Management Higher Education Conference, FEMA Emergency Management Institute, Emmitsburg, Maryland, June 8, 2004), 7.

42. Something addressed in Gary L. Wamsley, "Escalating in a Quagmire: The Changing Dynamics of the Emergency Management Policy Subsystem," *Public Administration Review* 56 (May/June 1996): 235–244, and in Richard T. Sylves, "Ferment at FEMA: Reforming Emergency Management," *Public Administration Review* 54 (May/June 1994): 303–307.

43. Graham T. Allison, *Essence of Decision: Explaining the Cuban Missile Crisis* (Boston: Little, Brown, 1971). Hereafter, "Allison, *Essence of Decision.*"

44. Graham T. Allison, *Destined for War: Can America and China Escape Thucydides's Trap?* (Boston, MA: Houghton, Mifflin, Harcourt, 2017).

45. Realism is an approach to the study and practice of international politics. It emphasizes the role of the nation-state and makes a broad assumption that all nation-states are motivated by national interests, or, at best, national interests disguised as moral concerns. In political realism, presidents, prime ministers, or other types of national chief executives are assumed to be the embodiment of the nation-state they lead. In other words, a form of reification (projecting human or material characteristics onto something that is immaterial, or vice versa) applies such that nation-states are assumed manifest human-like characteristics, such as the ability to behave rationally and to make rational decisions. The rational actor model invites people to think that the behavior of a government's chief executive is the behavior of the nation-state itself. The rational actor model allows for great simplification when trying to explain why or how a government rendered a decision of some type. For very short definitions of political realism and realism, see Google at https://www.google.com/search?q=realism+in+international+politics&rlz=1C1CHWA_enUS634US641&oq=realism+in+in&aqs=chrome.2.0j69i57j0l4.17779j1j7&sourceid=chrome&ie=UTF-8 (accessed April 12, 2018).

46. Lynn, *Public Management as Art, Science, and Profession*, 91.

47. Ibid. 91.

48. Ibid.

49. Please note that the list of points presented is an adaptation of Frederickson and Smith's discussion of public management theory. See Frederickson and Smith, *Theory Primer*, 113.

50. Lynn, *Public Management as Art, Science and Profession*, 97, quotes Chester I. Barnard, *Functions of the Executive*, 30th anniversary ed. (Cambridge, MA: Harvard University Press, 1968).

51. *The New York Times*, "Pick as Acting FEMA Leader Has Disaster Relief Experience," September 13, 2005, https://www.nytimes.com/2005/09/13/us/nationalspecial/pick-as-acting-fema-leader-has-disaster-relief.html (accessed September 4, 2018).

52. See Federal Emergency Management Agency, "FEMA Leadership, William Craig Fugate," https://www.fema.gov/profile/william-craig-fugate (accessed September 4, 2018).

53. James L. Witt and J. Morgan, *Stronger in the Broken Places: Ten Lessons for Turning Crisis into Triumph* (New York: Times Books, 2002).

54. See Len Elisha Clark, *Implementation of the National Incident Management System in New Jersey*, a doctoral dissertation, University of Baltimore, 2010, University of Baltimore Libraries at http://ubalt.worldcat.org/title/implementation-of-the-national-incident-management-system-in-new-jersey/oclc/636022706&referer=brief_results (accessed April 12, 2018).

55. See Lynn, *Public Management as Art, Science, and Profession*, 15.

56. See U.S. Department of Homeland Security, Science and Technology, *Best Practices for Incorporating Social Media into Exercises*, Social Media Working Group for Emergency Services and Disaster Management and DHS S&T First Responders Group March, 2017. At https://www.dhs.gov/sites/default/files/publications/Best-Practices-Incorporating-Social-Media-Into-Exercises-508%20.pdf (accessed April 12, 2018).

57. See Sergeant Johnny Jines of the Jackson, TN, Police Department, for Hendon Media Group, *Best Practices for Disaster Preparedness* (undated) at http://www.hendonpub.com/resources/article_archive/results/details?id=1602 (accessed April 12, 2018).

58. See Federal Aviation Administration, Notices to Airmen at https://www.faa.gov/air_traffic/publications/notices/ (accessed April 15, 2018).

59. See Richard T. Sylves and William L. Waugh Jr., *Disaster Management in the U.S. and Canada* (Springfield, IL: Charles C Thomas, 1996), and William L. Waugh Jr., *Living with Hazards, Dealing with Disasters: An Introduction to Emergency Management* (Armonk, NY: M.E. Sharpe, 2000).

60. Sylves, "Political Theory and Emergency Management," 10.

61. Tierney et al., *Facing the Unexpected*, 17.

62. See Robert A. Stallings, *Promoting Risk: Constructing the Earthquake Threat* (New York: Aldine de Gruyter, 1995). See also T. Jean Blocker, E. Burke Rochford Jr., and Darren E. Sherkat, "Political Responses to Natural Hazards: Social Movement Participation Following a Flood," *International Journal of Mass Emergencies and Disasters* 9 (1991): 367–382.

63. Stallings, *Promoting Risk*, 13–14.

64. Elizabeth A. Shanahan, Michael D. Jones, Mark K. McBeth, and Claudio M. Radaelli, "The Narrative Policy Framework," in *Theories of the Policy Process*, eds. Christopher M. Weible and Paul A. Sabatier (New York: Westview Press, 2018), 174. Hereafter "Shanahan et al., 2018."

65. See Havidan Rodriguez, Enrico L. Quarantelli, and Russell R. Dynes, eds. *Handbook of Disaster Research* (New York: Springer, 2007).

66. See Tierney et al., *Facing the Unexpected*, 194–195. See also Saundra K. Schneider, *Dealing with Disaster: Public Management in Crisis Situations*, 2nd ed. (Armonk, NY: M.E. Sharpe, 2011).

67. An excellent social constructivist work on humanitarian behavior by a political scientist is Deborah Stone, *The Samaritan's Dilemma* (New York: Nation Books, 2008).

68. See Arjen Boin, Paul 't Hart, Eric Stern, and Bengt Sundelius, *The Politics of Crisis Management: Public Leadership under Pressure*, 2nd ed. (Cambridge, U.K.: Cambridge University Press, University Printing House, 2017). Hereafter "Boin et al., 2017."

69. Ibid., 1.

70. Shanahan et al., 2018, 202.

71. Ibid., 176.

72. Ibid., 202.

73. Ibid., 173.

74. See Birkland, 2006.

75. Rationalism extends from reasoning. Rationalism in science is pursued through systematic analysis, experimentation, verification, and questioning of the nature of reality. Scientific rationalism is grounded in the scientific method, but generally, it posits that nothing should be accepted as knowledge until it is proven as true and is consistently verified to be so. See *Encyclopaedia Britannica*, s.v. "rationalism," www.britannica.com/EBchecked/topic/492034/rationalism (accessed April 13, 2018).

76. An epistemic community is a transnational network of knowledge-based experts who help decision-makers to define the problems they face, identify various policy solutions, and assess the policy outcomes. See Peter M. Haas, "Introduction: Epistemic Communities and International Policy Coordination," *International Organization* (Volume 46, Issue 1 Winter 1992, pp. 1–35.

77. See Cory Janssen, "Network Theory," Techopedia, www.techopedia.com/definition/25064/network-theory (accessed April 13, 2018).

78. Gareth Morgan, *Images of Organization*, updated ed. (Thousand Oaks, CA: Sage, 2006), 100.

79. Ibid., 76.

80. Source of quote is Tara Blume, News Channel 4, KFOR-TV Oklahoma City, "Disaster Assistance from FEMA," May 25, 2013, https://kfor.com/2013/05/25/disaster-assitance-from-fema/ (accessed September 28, 2018).

81. See "10 Ways Purpose-Built Rugged Tablets Smooth the Way for Emergency Managers," posted on November 7, 2017 at http://www.dtresearch.com/blog/10-ways-purpose-built-rugged-tablets-smooth-the-way-for-emergency-managers/ (accessed April 13, 2018).

82. Ibid.

83. Lynn, *Public Management as Art, Science, and Profession*, 116.

84. For more about principal-agent theory, see Kenneth J. Arrow, "The Economics of Agency," in *Principals and Agents: The Structure of Business*, eds. John W. Pratt and Richard J. Zeckhauser (Boston: Harvard Business School Press, 1988), 37–51.

85. See Amisha M. Mehta, Axel Bruns, and Judith Newton, "Trust, but Verify: Social Media Models for Disaster Management," in *Disasters*, Wiley Online Library (Volume 41, Issue 3, July 2017), 549–565. At https://onlinelibrary.wiley.com/doi/full/10.1111/disa.12218 (accessed April 13, 2018).

86. Richard F. Elmore, "Backward Mapping: Implementation Research and Policy Decisions," *Political Science Quarterly* 94, no. 4 (1979/1980): 69–83.

87. Deil S. Wright, "Models of National/State/Local Relations," in *American Intergovernmental Relations*, ed. Laurence J. O'Toole Jr. (Washington, DC: Congressional Quarterly, 1985), 59. Many scholars besides Wright have developed theories of federalism, among them Martha Derthick, Daniel Elazar, Richard H. Leach, Vincent Ostrom, and David B. Walker. Wright's intergovernmental relations theory was used here because it provides a good fit of theory to the reality of U.S. disaster policy.

88. Deil Wright, *Understanding Intergovernmental Relations*, 3rd ed. (Pacific Grove, CA: Brooks/Cole, 1988), 58.

89. *Stanford Encyclopedia of Philosophy*, s.v. "federalism," http://plato.stanford.edu/entries/federalism (accessed August 31, 2018).

90. Eugene Boyd, "Summary" and "Dual Federalism: Part II 1865 to 1901," *American Federalism, 1776 to 1997: Significant Events*, January 6, 1997, https://usa.usembassy.de/etexts/gov/federal.htm (accessed August 31, 2018).

91. Frances Edwards, "Federal Intervention in Local Emergency Planning: Nightmare on Main Street," *State and Local Government Review* 39, no. 1 (2007): 31–43.

92. Wright, *Understanding Intergovernmental Relations*, 64.

93. Wright, "Models of National/State/Local Relations," 60.

94. See David B. Walker, *The Rebirth of Federalism*, 2nd ed. (New York: Chatham House, 2000), 314.

95. Edwards, "Federal Intervention in Local Emergency Planning."

96. Portions of this section were developed by the author and others as a working group unpublished document for an interdisciplinary Disaster Recovery Workshop held at the University of North Carolina under sponsorship of the Public Entity Risk Institute in November 2010. See Center for the Study of Natural Hazards and Disasters, University of North Carolina at Chapel Hill, https://www.google.com/search?rlz=1C1CHWA_enUS634US641&ei=-6quW5bzBIP8zgLvsbyYCg&q=Disaster+Recovery+Workshop+held+at+the+University+of+North+Carolina+in+2009&oq=Disaster+Recovery+Workshop+held+at+the+University+of+North+Carolina+in+2009&gs_l=psy-ab.12...2135.13358..15926...0.0..1.428.6397.29j20j4j0j1......0....1j2..gws-wiz.....0..0j0i67j0i131.wcw6cdMRFdw (accessed September 28, 2018). Clicking on this site opens a PowerPoint presentation, "Teaching Recovery: A Report for the Theory of Recovery Workshop," by Ryan Alaniz, Jessica Hubbard (The Public Entity Risk Institute), Claire Rubin, Richard T. Sylves, and William L. Waugh, Jr.

97. Brenda D. Phillips, David M. Neal, and Gary R Webb, *Introduction to Emergency Management* (Boca Raton, FL: CRC Press, 2012), 308.

98. F. Henri and B. Pudelko, "Understanding and Analysing Activity and Learning in Virtual Communities," *Journal of Computer Assisted Learning* 19, no. 4 (2003): 478.

99. Federal Emergency Management Agency, "National Disaster Recovery Framework," http://www.fema.gov/national-disaster-recovery-framework (accessed August 31, 2018).

100. Ibid.

101. Ibid.

102. Ibid.

103. Gili Merin, "AD Classics: The Dymaxion House/Buckminster Fuller," in Architecture Daily, 01:00 - 12 July, 2013, https://www.archdaily.com/401528/ad-classics-the-dymaxion-house-buckminster-fuller (accessed September 28, 2018).

104. Thomas A. Birkland, *Lessons of Disaster: Policy Change after Catastrophic Events* (Washington, DC: Georgetown University Press, 2007).

105. Health Knowledge, "Social Networks and Comm-unitiesofInterest,"http://www.healthknowledge.org .uk/public-health-textbook/organisation-mana gement/5b-understanding-ofs/social-networks (accessed August 31, 2018).

106. Evie Blad, "Issues A-Z: School Shootings: Five Critical Questions," *Education Week* (February 16, 2108). Retrieved April 15, 2108 from http://www .edweek.org/ew/issues/school-shootings/

107. Vivian Yee and Alan Blindermarch, "National School Walkout: Thousands Protest Against Gun Violence Across the U.S., *The New York Times*, March 14, 2018 at https://www.nytimes.com/2018/03/14/us/ school-walkout.html (accessed April 15, 2018).

108. See selected chapters of Christopher M. Weible and Paul A. Sabatier, eds., *Theories of the Policy Process* (New York: Westview Press, 2018).

109. See Richard T. Sylves, "Budgeting for Emergency Management," in *Emergency Management: Principles and Practice for Local Government*, 2nd ed., eds. William L. Waugh Jr. and Kathleen Tierney (Washington, DC: ICMA Publications, 2007), 299–318.

110. See Committee on Increasing National Resilience to Hazards and Disasters (Susan L. Cutter, chair), for the Committee on Science, Engineering, and Public Policy, *Disaster Resilience: A National Imperative* (Washington, DC: The National Academies Press, 2012. See also Comfort et al., *Designing Resilience*, 2010, cited above.

111. Michael Barzelay, *Breaking through Bureaucracy: A New Vision for Management in Government* (Berkeley: University of California Press, 1992).

112. Lynn, *Public Management as Art, Science, and Profession*, 145.

113. This author's claim may be overly optimistic. FEMA may be reluctant to share information with a history office located outside of its administrative home. Moreover, in times of heavy partisanship or when certain selfish administrators exploit their history offices as instruments of self-promotion, history offices may be misused, exploited, heavily censored, or marginalized. It is not uncommon for federal history offices to be purged of information about previous presidential administration(s) when a new one replaces it.

114. See *U.S. Code of Federal Regulations*, Title 44 and Title 6. Government Printing Office, Electronic Code of Federal Regulations Title 44, Part 208.11, http://www.ecfr.gov/cgi-bin/text-idx?SID=42961 c3bc038b5a165752bc530d8628e&node=44:1.0.1 .4.59&rgn=div5 (accessed August 31, 2018). For U.S. Department of Homeland Security (DHS) rules, see Government Printing Office, Electronic Code of Federal Regulations Title 6, http://www .ecfr.gov/cgi-bin/text-idx?SID=76dfb460b5b808 305c4eb20404290ce9&c=ecfr&tpl=/ecfrbrowse/ Title06/6cfrv1_02.tpl (accessed August 31, 2018).

115. William R. Cumming, FEMA Office of General Counsel, retired, e-mail exchange with the author, March 15, 2003.

116. Or through transnational organizations such as the United Nations and the World Bank.

117. Gary King, the Albert J. Weatherhead, III, University Professor, Director: Institute for Quantitative Social Science, Harvard University, Public Lecture transcribed from personal notes by Richard Sylves, "The Big Deal about Big Data: Improving National Security and Public Policy" (Senate Dirksen 106, Washington, DC, May 11, 2016; 4-5:30 p.m.). Hereafter "G. King lecture, 2016."

118. Ibid.

119. Ibid.

120. See Recode at https://www.recode.net/2015/ 4/30/11562024/too-embarrassed-to-ask-what-is-the-cloud-and-how-does-it-work Most cloud services can be accessed through a Web browser like Firefox, Internet Explorer, Bing, Google, Google Chrome, Safari, and many more. Some companies offer dedicated mobile apps. Some cloud services are offered by Google Drive, Apple iCloud, Netflix, Yahoo Mail, Dropbox, and Microsoft OneDrive. Because the cloud's remote servers handle much of the computing and storage, people do not necessarily need an expensive, high-end machine to get their work done. In fact, some companies are making cloud-based computers as a low-cost option for consumers and the education market, the most notable example of this being Google's Chromebooks.

121. Ibid.

122. Shahriar Akter and Samuel Fosso Wamba, "Big Data and Disaster Management: A Systematic Review and Agenda for Future Research," *Annals of Operations Research*, Springer Science+Business Media, LLC 2017, published online 21 August 2017. See https://link.springer.com/article/10.1007/s10479-017-2584-2 Cited hereafter as "Akter and Wamba, 2017."

123. Ibid.

124. Ibid.

125. Ibid.

126. Ibid.

127. G. King lecture, 2016.

128. Google at https://www.google.com/search?q=an +algorithm+is+a+well-defined+procedure+that+al lows+a+computer+to+solve+a+problem.&rlz=1C1 CHWA_enUS634US641&oq=an+algorithm+is+a+w ell-defined+procedure+that+allows+a+computer+ to+solve+a+problem.&aqs=chrome..69i57.2681j0j7 &sourceid=chrome&ie=UTF-8

129. G. King lecture, 2016.

130. Ibid.

131. Ibid.

132. Ibid.

133. Dhavan V. Shah, Joseph N. Cappella, and W. Russell Neuman, "Big Data, Digital Media, and Computational Social Science: Possibilities and Perils," *The Annals of the Academy of Political and Social Science*, Vol. 659, No. 1, (May 2015), 6–13. Hereafter "Shah et al., 2015."

134. G. King lecture, 2016.

135. Ibid.

136. Ibid.

137. Ibid.

138. Ibid.

139. See Brandwatch at https://www.brandwatch.com/ blog/understanding-sentiment-analysis/

140. See Connie M. White, *Social Media, Crisis Communication, and Emergency Management*, (Boca Raton, FL: CRC Press of Taylor & Francis Group, 2012). White's book offers many examples of Twitter's use and benefits in emergency management.

141. From Lexalytics at https://www.lexalytics.com/ technology/sentiment (accessed August 31, 2018).

142. George D. Haddow, Jane A. Bullock, and Damon P. Coppola, *Introduction to Emergency Management*, 4th ed. (Burlington, MA: Butterworth-Heinemann, and imprint of Elsevier, 2011), 135.

143. G. King lecture, 2016.

144. Ibid.

145. See Matt Weinberger, "Why Amazon's Echo is Totally Dominating—and What Google, Microsoft, and Apple Have to Do to Catch Up," *Business Insider*, January 14, 2017 at http://www.businessinsider .com/amazon-echo-google-home-microsoft-cortana-apple-siri-2017-1

146. Shah et al., 2015, 7.

147. Ibid.

148. Ibid., 6–7.

149. See *The Guardian*, U.S. Edition, "Cambridge Analytica Scandal: The Biggest Revelations So Far," March 22, 2018 at https://www .theguardian.com/uk-news/2018/mar/22/ cambridge-analytica-scandal-the-biggest-revelations-so-far

150. Shah et al., 2015, 9.

151. Ibid., 11.

152. Ibid.

Chapter 3

1. James E. Anderson, "Policy Implementation," in *Public Policymaking: An Introduction*, 3rd ed. (Boston: Houghton Mifflin, 1997). See also Saundra K. Schneider. *Dealing with Disaster: Public Management in Crisis Situations*, 2nd ed. (Armonk, NY: M.E. Sharpe, 2011).

2. Homeland Security National Preparedness Task Force, *Civil Defense and Homeland Security: A Short History of National Preparedness Efforts* (Washington, DC: U.S. Department of Homeland Security, 2006), 7.

3. Keith Bea, "The Formative Years: 1950–1978," in *Emergency Management: The American Experience: 1900-2010*, 2nd ed., ed. Claire B. Rubin (Boca Raton, FL: CRC Press, 2012), 91.

4. [USC 10] 42 USC 5121: Congressional Findings and Declarations, (b), This chapter, referred to in subsec. (b), was in the original "this Act," meaning Pub. L. 93 -288, May 22, 1974, 88 Stat. 143. see http://uscode.house.gov/view.xhtml?req=(title:42%20section:5121%20edition:prelim)

5 See Lucien G. Canton, *Emergency Management: Concepts and Strategies for Effective Programs* (Hoboken, NJ: John Wiley & Sons, 2007), 20.

6. For a history of the era of U.S. nuclear research and nuclear advances in the military and civilian domain, see Richard T. Sylves, *The Nuclear Oracles: A Political History of the General Advisory Committee of the U.S. Atomic Energy Commission, 1947–1977* (Ames: Iowa State University Press, 1986).

7. Standard presidential administrations usually begin and end on or about January 21. Republican Dwight David Eisenhower was inaugurated in January 1953 and left office at the end of his second term in January 1961.

8. President Kennedy, a Democrat, was inaugurated in January 1961 and was assassinated in November 1963. His vice president, Lyndon Johnson (LBJ), was then sworn in as president.

9. President Johnson, as mentioned in note 7, was sworn in as president in November 1963 soon after President Kennedy was assassinated. LBJ won the 1964 presidential election and served until January 1969. He opted not to run for reelection in 1968.

10. Homeland Security National Preparedness Task Force, *Civil Defense and Homeland Security*, 13.

11. President Richard M. Nixon, a Republican, was elected in November 1968 and inaugurated in January 1969. He won reelection in 1972 but resigned from office prematurely owing to the Watergate scandal in August 1974.

12. Keith Bea, "The Formative Years: 1950–1978," in *Emergency Management: The American Experience, 1900–2005*, ed. Claire B. Rubin (Fairfax, VA: Public Entity Risk Institute, 2007), 92. For an updated version, see Keith Bea, "The Formative Years: 1950-

1978," in *Emergency Management: The American Experience: 1900-2010*, 2nd ed. (Boca Raton, FL: CRC Press, Taylor & Francis Group, 2012), 83–113.

13. Bea, 2nd ed., 101.

14. Former Speaker of the House Gerald R. Ford, a Republican, and President Nixon's appointed vice president chosen under the Constitution's Twenty-Fifth Amendment regarding presidential succession, took the presidential oath of office in August 1974. This immediately followed President Nixon's resignation. Nixon's first vice president, Spiro Agnew, having held the office five years, resigned in October 1973 under a plea agreement involving failure to report income. Ford hoped to win a full term in the White House in 1976 but lost to former Georgia governor Jimmy Carter, a Democrat. Ford left office in January 1977 when President Carter was inaugurated.

15. In formal terms, to rescind spending authority means, "The cancellation of budget authority previously provided by Congress. The Impoundment Control Act of 1974 specifies that the president may propose to Congress that funds be rescinded. If both Houses have not approved a rescission proposal (by passing legislation) within 45 days of continuous session, any funds being withheld must be made available for obligation." See U.S. Senate, "Glossary Term: Rescission" at https://www.senate.gov/reference/glossary_term/rescission.htm (accessed April 19, 2018).

16. Homeland Security National Preparedness Task Force, *Civil Defense and Homeland Security*, 16.

17. Ibid., 16.

18. Bea, 2nd ed., 106. Bea adds that Congress "amended the CDA to allow the use of the civil defense 'structure' for disasters other than those caused by enemy attack" (Ibid., 106).

19. Homeland Security National Preparedness Task Force, *Civil Defense and Homeland Security*, 14.

20. Ibid., 17.

21. Jack Corbett, "Nuclear War and Crisis Relocation Planning: A View from the Grassroots," *Impact Assessment*, 1983, 2:4, 23-33, DOI: 10.1080/07349165.1983.9725997. To link to this article: https://doi.org/10.1080/07349165.1983.9725997 (accessed April 19, 2018).

22. Ibid.

23. Thomas E. Baldwin, *Revised Historical Chronology of FEMA's Terrorism Consequences Management Role as Assigned by Section 2-103 of E.O. 12148* (Argonne, IL: Argonne National Laboratory, 2006), 1. Supplied as e-file to the author March 18, 2007, by William R. Cumming, FEMA General Counsel's Office, retired.

24. Ibid., 14.

25. Keith Smith, *Environmental Hazards: Assessing Risk and Reducing Disaster*, 6th ed. (New York: Routledge, 2013), 100–101.

26. Ibid.

27. Jerry V. Graves Jr., "Intergovernmental Relations and Hazard Mitigation," in *Natural Hazard Mitigation*, eds. Alessandra Jerolleman and John J. Kiefer (Boca Raton, FL: CRC Press, 2013), 51.

28. Smith, 6th ed., 101, 103.

29. Ibid., 103–105.

30. U.S. Small Business Administration, "About the Office of Disaster Assistance." Undated. At https://www.sba.gov/offices/headquarters/oda/about-us (accessed May 6, 2018).

31. See Benefits.gov, The U.S. Small Business Administration (SBA), "Home and Property Disaster Loans," undated. At https://www.benefits.gov/benefits/benefit-details/1503 (accessed May 6, 2018).

32. Ibid.

33. Ibid.

34. Ibid.

35. Ibid.

36. In addition to replacement of the Office of Civil Defense with the DCPA, Nixon Reorganization Plans No. 1 (1970) and No. 2 (1973) abolished the Office of Emergency Planning, an agency established in 1961. The Office of Emergency Planning had managed programs, functions, and activities previously housed in the Office of Emergency Preparedness, Executive Office of the White House. Nixon Reorganization Plan No. 1 reassigned preparedness tasks, doling them out to HUD (which created the Federal Disaster Assistance Administration to assume this jurisdiction), the General Services Administration (GSA), and to the departments of the Treasury and Commerce.

37. Homeland Security National Preparedness Task Force, *Civil Defense and Homeland Security*, 16.

38. James F. Miskel, *Disaster Response and Homeland Security: What Works, What Doesn't* (Westport, CT: Praeger Security International, 2006), 69.

39. William L. Painter. Congressional Research Service, R45084. *2017 Disaster Supplemental Appropriations: Overview*. March 20, 2018. At https://fas.org/sgp/crs/homesec/R45084.pdf (accessed May 6, 2018).

40. Claire B. Rubin and Irmak R. Tanali, *Disaster Time Line: Selected Milestone Events and U.S. Outcomes, 1965–2001* (Arlington, VA: Claire B. Rubin and Associates, 2001). Hurricane Agnes produced widespread damage. Seven states won presidential declarations of major disaster: Florida, Maryland, New York, Ohio, Pennsylvania, Virginia, and West Virginia. New York and Pennsylvania sustained damage. See also Bea, 2nd ed., 100.

41. Code of Federal Regulations 1949-1984, Section 205–405, Column 1, below Hazard Mitigation Clause Added to Federal-State Agreement, see https://tinyurl.com/y852n66f.

42. Richard Sylves, "The Political and Policy Basis of Emergency Management," FEMA Training, session no. 7, page 9. Available for download at https://training.fema.gov/hiedu/docs/polpolbasis/political%20and%20policy%20basis%20-%20session%207%20-%20disaster%20law.doc.

43. See H. Crane Miller, "Defense Production Act of 1950 and Homeland Security," in *A Legal Guide to Homeland Security and Emergency Management for State and Local Governments*, eds. Ernest B. Abbott and Otto J. Hertzel (Lanham, MD: National Book Network, 2006), 237.

44. Democrat Jimmy Carter beat the incumbent, although unelected, Republican president Gerald R. Ford in the 1976 general election. Carter was defeated by Reagan in the 1980 general election and so left office in January 1981.

45. Henry B. Hogue and Keith Bea, *Federal Emergency Management and Homeland Security Organization: Historical Developments and Legislative Options*,

CRS Report RL33369 (Washington, DC: U.S. Congressional Research Service, 2006).

46. See Richard T. Sylves, "Federal Emergency Management Comes of Age: 1979–2001," in *Emergency Management: The American Experience: 1900-2010*, 2nd ed., ed. Claire B. Rubin (Boca Raton, FL: CRC Press, 2012), 115–166.

47. William C. Nicholson, *Emergency Response and Emergency Management Law: Cases and Materials* (Springfield, IL: Charles C Thomas, 2003), 236.

48. William L. Waugh Jr., *Living with Hazards, Dealing with Disasters: An Introduction to Emergency Management* (Armonk, NY: M.E. Sharpe, 2000), 28–29.

49. Baldwin, *Revised Historical Chronology*, 2.

50. Ibid., 2.

51. Ibid.

52. See William G. Blair, "John W. Macy, Jr., 69, Ex-Leader of the Civil Service Commission Dies." *The New York Times*, Archives 1986 at https://www.nytimes.com/1986/12/25/obituaries/john-w-macy-jr-69-ex-leader-of-civil-service-commission-dies.html (accessed April 21, 2018).

53. See Marc Ambinder, "America's Doomsday Secrets," *The Week*, November 2, 2012, http:// http://theweek.com/articles/470754/americas-doomsday-secrets (accessed September 4, 2018). Most of Ambinder's article is about his journalistic study of the classified history of the Continuity of Government program of which FEMA is a major part.

54. Homeland Security National Preparedness Task Force, *Civil Defense and Homeland Security,* 18.

55. Ibid., 19.

56. Rutherford H. Platt, "Shouldering the Burden: Federal Assumption of Disaster Costs," in *Disasters and Democracy: The Politics of Extreme Natural Events,* ed. Rutherford H. Platt (Washington, DC: Island Press, 1999), 23–26. See also Ruth McCambridge, "Study Reveals Shocking Rise in Federal Disaster Relief Costs," *Nonprofit Quarterly*, May 23, 2013, http://www.nonprofitquarterly.org/policysocial-context/22344-study-reveals-shocking-rise-in-federal-disaster-relief-costs.html (accessed September 4, 2018).

57. Allen K. Settle, "Disaster Assistance: Securing Presidential Declarations," in *Cities and Disaster:*

North American Studies in Emergency Management, eds. Richard T. Sylves and William L. Waugh Jr. (Springfield, IL: Charles C Thomas, 1990).

58. Ibid., 51–52.

59. In effect, at the state level, the total estimated disaster cost to be paid out by the state is divided by the total state population in the last decennial U.S. Census. This figure is then compared to FEMA's annually determined pre-set per capita loss threshold for the respective state. Counties not included in an original presidential declaration, but that seek to be added to a declaration, also face a qualifying threshold: Total estimated disaster cost to be paid out by the county is divided by total county population in the last U.S. Census. This resulting amount is then compared to FEMA's annually determined pre-set per capita loss threshold for the respective county. Remember, FEMA has authority to add or reject the addition of a county to an in-force presidential declaration of major disaster without the need to seek the president's approval. See Chapter 4.

60. Settle, 1990, 6–14.

61. See Canton, 2007. Canton, a former FEMA Region 9 official, is the epitome of the reflexive practitioner—someone who has worked in the field of emergency management but who has gone beyond that experience by advancing academic and practice knowledge in the discipline.

62. President Ronald Reagan, a Republican, beat incumbent President Jimmy Carter in the 1980 presidential election and was inaugurated in January 1981. Reagan won a second term in 1984 and ultimately completed his presidency in January 1989, turning that post over to his newly elected former vice president, George H. W. Bush.

63. *New Georgia Encyclopedia,* s.v. "CNN," http://www.georgiaencyclopedia.org/articles/arts-culture/cnn (accessed September 4, 2018).

64. U.S. Central Intelligence Agency, Library, "Field Listing: Broadcast Media," *World Fact Book*, Broadcast Media by County, at https://www.cia.gov/library/publications/the-world-factbook/fields/2213.html (accessed September 28, 2018). This site includes information about news broadcast organizations (TV and radio) in every nation from Afghanistan to Zimbabwe.

65. See selection from Robert Scheer, *With Enough Shovels: Reagan, Bush and Nuclear War* (New York: Vintage Books, 1983), 18–26. History 1302, at http://www.austincc.edu/haney/Scheer.html (accessed April 26, 2018).

66. President George H. W. Bush, a Republican, was elected in 1988 and inaugurated in January 1989. He served only one term, being defeated in the 1992 presidential election by Democrat William Jefferson Clinton. G. H. W. Bush was Reagan's vice president for two full terms before he came to the presidency.

67. CNN Library, "Beirut Marine Barracks Bombing Fast Facts," June 13, 2013, http://www.cnn.com/2013/06/13/world/meast/beirut-marine-barracks-bombing-fast-facts (accessed September 4, 2018). The suicide truck bomb attack was traced to Hezbollah, a militant and political group originating in Lebanon, and killed 220 Marines and 21 other service personnel.

68. Besides FCOs, there are also principal federal officials also appointed by the president who coordinate domestic incidents that require multi-agency response. To avoid confusion, PFOs often assume the lead role in incidents not considered as Stafford Act–type incidents. These may include terrorist incidents not declared major disasters, pandemic outbreaks, and other types of events. George D. Haddow, Jane A. Bullock, and Damon P. Coppola, *Introduction to Emergency Management*, 4th ed. (Burlington, MA: Butterworth-Heinemann, 2011), 203–204.

69. Ibid., 204.

70. Federal coordinating officers should be free to write and publish accounts of their experience about incidents they are deployed to, with the exception of incidents directly involving national security and defense matters. If more FCOs wrote about their experiences, this would be a major benefit to all who study, conduct research, or work in the field of emergency management.

71. Keith Bea, *Federal Stafford Act Disaster Assistance: Presidential Declarations, Eligible Activities, and Funding*, CRS Report RL33053 (Washington, DC: U.S. Congressional Research Service, 2006), 3.

72. See Smith, 6th ed., 381–383.

73. Ibid., 389–390.

74. Bea, *Federal Stafford Act Disaster Assistance*, 1, 4.

75. Mission assignment works in the following way: When other federal agencies besides FEMA are doing emergency management work under a presidential declaration of major disaster or emergency and the spending authority of those agencies is insufficient for them to carry out their disaster-related work, officials of those agencies may ask FEMA permission to draw funding from the president's Disaster Relief Fund under a category called *mission assignment*. A sizable share of spending in many presidentially declared major disasters stems from mission assignment.

76. U.S. FEMA, FP 104-010-2, Mission Assignment Policy, as of November 6, 2015, https://www.fema.gov/media-library-data/1450099364660-fd855ba68f3189d974966ea259a2641a/Mission_Assignment_Policy.pdf (accessed April 23, 2018).

77. Hogue and Bea, "Federal Stafford Act Disaster Assistance," 14. See also John Fass Morton, *Next-Generation Homeland Security: Network Federalism and the Course to National Preparedness* (Annapolis, MD: Naval Institute Press, 2012), 22.

78. When FEMA was rejuvenated by the PKEMRA in 2006, it was granted permission to hire additional staff. This has allowed it to exceed its previous and usual upper limit of 3,000 full-time federal workers.

79. U.S. Department of Homeland Security, Federal Emergency Management Agency Disaster Relief Fund, "Table I. Changes in Full-Time Employment," 28, http://www.fema.gov/pdf/about/budget/11f_fema_disaster_relief_fund_dhs_fy13_cj.pdf (accessed September 4, 2018).

80. See U.S. Census Compendium, "Table 472: Federal Budget Outlays by Agency: 1990 to 2011," https://www.census.gov/library/publications/2011/compendia/statab/131ed/federal-govt-finances-employment.html (accessed September 28, 2018). Source: U.S. Office of Management and Budget, Government, Historical Tables, 9/30/2011, at http://www.whitehouse.gov/omb/budget (accessed September 28, 2018).

81. U.S. Government Accountability Office, *Federal Emergency Management Agency: Additional Planning and Data Collection Could Help Improve Workforce Management Efforts*, GAO 15-437

(Washington, DC: GAO, July 2015), 1. See https://www.gao.gov/assets/680/671276.pdf (accessed April 23, 2018).

82. U.S. Department of Homeland Security, Federal Emergency Management Agency, *Budget Overview, Fiscal Year 2018 Congressional Justification* (Washington, DC: DHS, 2017).

83. A qualification is necessary here. As part of the PKEMRA law, Congress stipulated that only well-qualified emergency managers should be appointed to head FEMA. President G. W. Bush contested this requirement on grounds that it improperly interfered with the president's authority to make executive branch appointments. The matter has been left unresolved as a legal dispute between the president and Congress. Regardless, after Katrina, G. W. Bush and succeeding presidents Obama and Trump have to date proposed only qualified emergency managers for appointment to FEMA administrator. Also, the U.S. Senate has the power to review, and approve or reject, nominees the president proposes to head FEMA.

84. Aaron Schroeder and Gary Wamsley, "The Evolution of Emergency Management in America: From a Painful Past to a Promising but Uncertain Future," in *Handbook of Crisis and Emergency Management,* ed. Ali Farazmand (New York: Marcel Dekker, 2002).

85. According to the Center for Responsive Politics, in 2013, insurances companies have lobbied congressional bills calling for the National Flood Insurance Program (NFIP) to advance floodplain management practices in rural and agricultural areas, bills amending the Terrorism Risk Insurance Act (TRIA) of 2002 (which backstops private insurers against a portion of their losses after costly terrorism attacks inside the United States), and changes in Coastal Act of 2011, Flood Insurance Reform issues. See Center for Responsive Politics, "Insurance Lobbying," https://www.opensecrets.org/industries/lobbying.php?cycle=2018&ind=F09 (accessed September 4, 2018). The total number of clients lobbying on insurance in 2012 exceeded 200. In 2018, it now exceeds 800.

86. See FEMA Emergency Management Institute, emiweb, PowerPoint presentation, slide #1, undated at https://training.fema.gov/emiweb/downloads/hdr/session%204%20powerpoint.pdf (accessed April 23, 2018).

87. Dianne Rahm, *United States Public Policy: A Budgetary Approach* (Belmont, CA: Wadsworth, 2004), 97–113.

88. See John T. Gasper and Andrew Reeves, "Make It Rain: Retrospection and the Attentive Electorate in the Context of Natural Disasters," *American Journal of Political Science* 55, no. 2 (April 2011): 340–355.

89. Kevin Arceneaux and Robert M. Stein, "Who Is Held Responsible When Disaster Strikes? The Attribution of Responsibility for a Natural Disaster in an Urban Election," *Journal of Urban Affairs* 28 (January 2006): 43.

90. See Patrick S. Roberts, *Disasters and the American State: How Politicians, Bureaucrats, and the Public Prepare for the Unexpected* (New York: Cambridge University Press, 2013), 122–126. Roberts discusses the politicization of FEMA, particularly from the Clinton–Witt era, through the 9/11 attack, and since it has joined DHS. He laments that FEMA is now yoked to a giant terrorism prevention department in which its operational mission is to protect the public against the new hazard of terrorism. He states, "Perceptions of the agency's power outstripped its actual capacity, and the ability of the agency to shape its own mission." Ibid., 126.

91. Morton, *Next-Generation Homeland Security*, 2. One study alleges that the Clinton FEMA largely ignored terrorism despite its mention in the FRP owing in part to FEMA director Witt's agenda. See also Roberts, 2013, 11–117.

92. Haddow et al., 2011, 183.

93. See FEMA, *National Response Framework (Third Edition)*, Information Sheet, June 16, 2016. At https://www.fema.gov/media-library-data/1466014891281-6e7f60ceaf0be5a937ab2ed0eae0672d/InformationSheet_Response_Framework.pdf (accessed May 6, 2018). See also FEMA, *National Response Framework (Third Edition)*, full report, June 2016. At https://www.fema.gov/media-library-data/1466014682982-9bcf8245ba4c60c120aa915abe74e15d/National_Response_Framework3rd.pdf (accessed May 6, 2018).

94. FEMA, *National Response Framework (Third Edition)*, Information Sheet, June 16, 2016, cited previously.

95. See National Archives, Executive Orders: Executive Order 12656—Assignment of Emergency Preparedness Responsibilities, *Federal Register* (Washington, DC: National Archives, November 18, 1988) at https://www.archives.gov/federal-register/codification/executive-order/12656.html (accessed April 23, 2018).

96. Homeland Security National Preparedness Task Force, *Civil Defense and Homeland Security*.

97. See Morton, *Next-Generation Homeland Security*, 13.

98. Ibid., 14.

99. President William J. Clinton, a Democrat, was elected in 1992, inaugurated in January 1993, re-elected in 1996, and left office at the end of his second term in January 2001.

100. Daniel Victor, "Hurricane Andrew: How The Times Reported the Destruction of 1992," *The New York Times*, September 6, 2017, at https://www.nytimes.com/2017/09/06/us/hurricane-andrew-florida.html (accessed April 23, 2018).

101. Hawaii News Now, "Hurricane Iniki: Quick Facts about Hawaii's Most Powerful Storm," Sept. 17, 2017, at http://www.hawaiinewsnow.com/story/36315106/hurricane-iniki-quick-facts-about-hawaiis-most-powerful-storm (accessed April 23, 2018). The article also disclosed that the hurricane disrupted final filming of the motion picture *Jurassic Park*. Producer Steven Spielberg and his staff rode out Iniki in a Kauai hotel and filmed some of the hurricane's impact, which Spielberg later used in the movie.

102. James F. Miskel, *Disaster Response and Homeland Security: What Works, What Doesn't* (Westport, CT: Praeger, 2006), 89. See also Sylves, "Federal Emergency Management Comes of Age," 116.

103. Homeland Security National Preparedness Task Force, *Civil Defense and Homeland Security*, 23.

104. Ibid., 23.

105. Morton, *Next-Generation Homeland Security*, 97.

106. Homeland Security National Preparedness Task Force, *Civil Defense and Homeland Security*, 23.

107. Patrick S. Roberts, "FEMA and the Prospects for Reputational Authority," *Studies in American Political Development* 20 (Spring 2006): 16.

108. U.S. FEMA, Manual 8600.7, Foreword signed by James Lee Witt, November 18, 1999. At https://www.fema.gov/pdf/library/8600_7.pdf (accessed April 26, 2018).

109. Eve E. Hinman and David J. Hammond, *Lessons for the Oklahoma City Bombing: Defensive Design Techniques* (Reston, VA: American Society of Civil Engineers, 1997), x. Corrected death and injury figures appear in CNN Library, "Oklahoma City Bombing Fast Facts," Updated 6:53 p.m. ET, Sun March 25, 2018. At https://www.cnn.com/2013/09/18/us/oklahoma-city-bombing-fast-facts/index.html (accessed April 26, 2018).

110. William R. Cumming and Richard T. Sylves, "FEMA's Place in Policy, Law, and Management: A Hazardous Materials Perspective 1979–2003," in *Homeland Security Law and Policy*, ed. William C. Nicholson (Springfield, IL: Charles C Thomas, 2004), 23–55.

111. President Carter spectacularly issued one as he flew in *Air Force One* over the Mt. St. Helen's volcanic eruption in Washington State on May 21, 1980, three days after the eruption began. Reportedly, then Washington State governor Dixie Lee Ray submitted her request only shortly before Carter's trip. The request was given highest priority and documents were faxed only hours after the eruption began. The declaration covered affected counties in both Washington State and Idaho. American Presidency Project, Jimmy Carter, "Portland, Oregon Remarks and a Question-and-Answer Session With Reporters Following an Inspection Tour of Areas Damaged by the Mount St. Helens Eruption," May 22, 1980 at http://www.presidency.ucsb.edu/ws/index.php?pid=45455 (accessed April 26, 2018).

112. Homeland Security National Preparedness Task Force, *Civil Defense and Homeland Security*.

113. Frances L. Edwards, "Homeland Security from the Local Perspective," in *Homeland Security Law and Policy*, ed. William C. Nicholson (Springfield, IL: Charles C Thomas, 2005), 114.

114. The National Defense Authorization Act of 1995 amended the Robert T. Stafford Disaster Relief and Emergency Assistance Act (Public Law 93-288).

115. Ibid.

116. U.S. House of Representatives, House Committee on Public Works and Transportation, Subcommittee on Water Resources and the Environment, *Midwest Floods of 1993: Flood Control and Floodplain Policy and Proposals,* hearing statement of Harold L. Volkmer, 103rd Cong., 1st sess., 1993, serial number 103-57, 241.

117. Alan Taylor, "The Northridge Earthquake: 20 Years Ago Today," *The Atlantic*, January 17, 2014. At https://www.theatlantic.com/photo/2014/01/the-northridge-earthquake-20-years-ago-today/100664/ (accessed April 26, 2018).

118. Richard Lee Colvin, "FEMA Answers Earthquake Disaster with a Blizzard of Aid Checks," *Los Angeles Times*, April 2, 1994. At http://articles.latimes.com/1994-04-02/news/mn-41370_1_fema-aid (accessed April 26, 2018).

118. Haddow et al., *Introduction to Emergency Management,* 4th ed., 10–11.

120. George D. Haddow and Jane A. Bullock, *Introduction to Emergency Management,* 2nd ed. (Burlington, MA: Butterworth-Heinemann, 2011), 63.

121. Ibid., 12.

122. Robert Anderson and Ines Pearce, "Public Private Partnerships in Mitigation Initiatives," in *Natural Hazard Mitigation*, eds. Alessandra Jerolleman and John J. Kiefer (Boca Raton, FL: CRC Press, 2013), 68.

123. Michael K. Lindell, Carla Prater, and Ronald W. Perry, *Introduction to Emergency Management* (Hoboken, NJ: Wiley, 2007), 361–362.

124. Ibid., 66.

125. Edwards, "Homeland Security from the Local Perspective," 120.

126. President George W. Bush was inaugurated in January 2001, was reelected to a second term in 2004, and left office with the inauguration of President Barack H. Obama in January 2009.

127. Kathleen J. Tierney, "Recent Developments in U.S. Homeland Security Policies and Their Implications for the Management of Extreme Events," in *Handbook of Disaster Research*, eds. Havidan Rodriguez, Enrico L. Quarantelli, and Russell R. Dynes (New York: Springer, 2007), 406.

128. Ibid.

129. David B. Truman, *The Governmental Process* (New York: Knopf, 1951).

130. Haddow and Bullock, *Introduction to Emergency Management,* 2nd ed., 299.

131. For the full text of HSPD-5, see Homeland Security Presidential Directive-5/HSPD-5, http://www.michigan.gov/documents/deq/deq-wb-wws-HSPD-5_268188_7.pdf (accessed September 4, 2018).

132. Tierney, *Recent Developments in U.S. Homeland Security Policies*, 408–409. See also William C. Nicholson, "The Shape of Emergency Response and Emergency Management in the Aftermath of the Homeland Security Act of 2002: Adopting the National Response Plan (NRP) and the National Incident Management System," in *Homeland Security Law and Policy*, ed. William C. Nicholson (Springfield, IL: Charles C Thomas, 2005), 68–106. See also Donald W. Walsh et al., *National Incident Management System: Principles and Practice*, 2nd ed. (Sudbury, MA: Jones and Bartlett, 2012).

133. Homeland Security Presidential Directive-5 February 28, 2003. Subject: Management of Domestic Incidents, Section 3 at https://www.dhs.gov/sites/default/files/publications/Homeland%20Security%20Presidential%20Directive%205.pdf (accessed April 26, 2018).

134. Ibid., section 4.

135. U.S. Department of Homeland Security, "FEMA Leadership Organizational Structure," *FEMA Organizational Chart in March 2018* (Washington, DC: U.S. FEMA, 2018) at .pdf file available at https://www.fema.gov/media-library/assets/documents/28183 (accessed April 23, 2018).

136. Tierney, *Recent Developments in U.S. Homeland Security Policies*, 408.

137. The NRF eliminated the Incident of National Significance declaration. In the past, the secretary of DHS could issue such declarations, but the NRF makes it clear that the secretary of DHS retains authorities "to coordinate large-scale national responses," but no longer issues incident of national significance declarations. See U.S. Department of Homeland Security, "National Response Framework," January 2008, 8, http://www.fema.gov/pdf/emergency/nrf/nrf-core.pdf (accessed August 31, 2018).

138. U.S. Department of Homeland Security, "National Response Plan," December 2006, 7, http://www.au.af.mil/au/awc/awcgate/nrp/index.htm (accessed August 31, 2018). The NRF eliminated the Incident of National Significance instrument in March 2008.

139. For the full text of HSPD-8, see U.S. Department of Homeland Security, "Presidential Policy Directive/PPD-8: National Preparedness," March 30, 2011, http://www.dhs.gov/presidential-policy-directive-8-national-preparedness (accessed August 31, 2018).

140. Tierney, *Recent Developments in U.S. Homeland Security Policies,* 408.

141. Debarshi Chaudhuri, "Government: Response to Katrina," *Mission 2010: New Orleans,* based on a class exercise at the Massachusetts Institute of Technology (Boston, MA: MIT, 2010) at http://web.mit.edu/12.000/www/m2010/finalwebsite/katrina/government/government-response.html (accessed April 26, 2018).

142. See Kevin Robillard, "10 Facts about the Katrina Response," *Politico,* October 3, 2012 at https://www.politico.com/story/2012/10/10-facts-about-the-katrina-response-081957 (accessed April 26, 2018).

143. U.S. FEMA, Emergency Management Institute, "Post-Katrina Emergency Management Reform Act," undated. At https://emilms.fema.gov/is230c/fem0101200.htm (accessed April 26, 2018).

144. Ibid.

145. U.S. House of Representatives, House Subcommittee on National Security, Emerging Threats, and International Relations and the Subcommittee on Energy Policy, Natural Resources and Regulatory Affairs, *Statement of James L. Witt,* 108th Cong., 2nd sess., March 24, 2004.

146. "A Big Storm Requires Big Government," *The New York Times,* October 29, 2012, http://www.nytimes.com/2012/10/30/opinion/a-big-storm-requires-big-government.html?_r=0 (accessed September 4, 2018). *The New York Times* editorial on October 29, 2012, alleged that former governor Mitt Romney during a Republican primary debate in 2011 was asked whether emergency management was a function that should be returned to the states. According to the editorial, he not only agreed but went further. "Absolutely," he said. "Every time you have an occasion to take something from the federal government and send it back to the states, that's the right direction. And if you can go even further and send it back to the private sector, that's even better." The editorial added, "Mr. Romney not only believes that states acting independently can handle the response" to expansive Superstorm Sandy "better than Washington, but that profit-making companies can do an even better job. He said it was 'immoral' for the federal government to do all these things if it means increasing the debt." The editorial also indicated that after the debate, Romney's campaign staff announced that the governor "does not want to abolish FEMA but that he still believes states should be in charge of emergency management." Ibid.

147. See the White House, Office of the Press Secretary, "Ongoing Response to Hurricane Sandy," November 15, 2012, http://www.whitehouse.gov/the-press-office/2012/11/15/ongoing-response-hurricane-sandy (accessed September 4, 2018). "Today, the President announced that he has asked Housing and Urban Development Secretary Shaun Donovan to continue to work closely with Governors, mayors and local officials of New Jersey and New York as they begin the process of identifying redevelopment plans for affected communities. While the DHS and FEMA continue to provide all available federal resources to support the immediate response and recovery efforts, Secretary Donovan will coordinate the federal support as states design their redevelopment plans, identify priorities, and

over time begin implementation of their plans. This structure will streamline this process for Governors as they seek assistance for longer term projects they identify as priorities for community redevelopment." Ibid.

148. Nicholas Schmidle, "Getting Bin Laden: What Happened that Night in Abbottabad," *The New Yorker*, August 8, 2011, at https://www.newyorker .com/magazine/2011/08/08/getting-bin-laden (accessed 23 September 2018).

149. James Barrett, "A Complete List of Radical Islamic Terror Attacks on U.S. Soil Under Obama," *Dailywire*, December 7, 2016 at https://www.dailywire.com/ news/11410/complete-list-radical-islamic-terror-attacks-us-james-barrett (accessed 23 September 2018).

150. *U.S. News & World Report*, "Senate Confirms Trump's Nominee to Head FEMA," June 20, 2017, at https://www.usnews.com/news/politics/ articles/2017-06-20/senate-confirms-trumps-nominee-to-head-fema (accessed April 23, 2018).

151. Michael Kaczmarek, "U.S. Counter-terrorism since 9/11: Trends under the Trump Administration," *European Parliament Think Tank*, May 25, 2018, at http://www.europarl.europa.eu/thinktank/en/ document.html?reference=EPRS_BRI(2018)621898 (accessed 23 September 2018).

Chapter 4

1. Personal email correspondence from Bruce R. Lindsay to this author, May 9, 2018. Dr. Lindsay observed that governor requests for emergency declarations are today routinely submitted along with preliminary damage assessment information.

2. Advances in computer modeling, plus geographical information system mapping of state and local infrastructure, housing, and business properties, have all made post-disaster damage assessment somewhat easier and faster than it had been in the past. Satellite telemetry showing spatial damage, social media feeds, news media coverage, aerial photographs of damage zones, and even drive-by "windshield surveys" have improved damage assessment for requesting governors.

3. See Naim Kapucu, Montgomery Van Wart, Richard Sylves, and Farhod Yuldashev, "U.S. Presidents and Their Roles in Emergency Management and Disaster Policy 1950–2009," *Risk, Hazards, & Crisis in Public Policy*, Vol. 2, Issue 3, October 2011, 1–34 at https://onlinelibrary.wiley.com/doi/ pdf/10.2202/1944-4079.1065 (accessed September 28, 2018; institutional or customer ID required for access to the full article).

4. Jack C. Plano and Milton Greenberg, *The American Political Dictionary*, 7th ed. (New York: Holt, Rinehart and Winston, 1985).

5. Thomas E. Cronin, "The Swelling of the Presidency," in *Classic Readings in American Politics*, eds. Pietro S. Nivola and David H. Rosenbloom (New York: St. Martin's, 1986), 413–426.

6. Harold Koh, "What War Powers Does the President Have?" *Slate*, September 13, 2001. At http:// www.slate.com/articles/news_and_politics/ explainer/2001/09/what_war_powers_does_the_ president_have.html (accessed April 28, 2018).

7. See U.S. Department of Homeland Security, "Weapons of Mass Destruction," December 7, 2017. At https:// www.dhs.gov/topic/weapons-mass-destruction (accessed April 29, 2018).

8. Koh, 2001.

9. Ibid.

10. Ibid.

11. Cornell Law School, *WEX*, "Commander in Chief Powers," undated. At https://www.law.cornell.edu/ wex/commander_in_chief_powers (accessed May 3, 2018).

12. Bob Drogin and David S. Cloud, "U.S. and Allies Fire Missiles at Syria in Retaliation for Suspected Poison Gas Attack," *Los Angeles Times*, April 13, 2018. At http://www.latimes.com/nation/la-na-pol-trump-syria-attack-20180411-story.html (accessed May 3, 2018).

13. See Benjamin A. Kleinerman, *The Discretionary President: The Promise and Peril of Executive Power* (Lawrence, KS: University Press of Kansas, 2009).

14. Eric A. Posner, "Executive Decision," *The New Republic*, March 29, 2010. At https://newrepublic.com/article/74041/executive-decision (accessed April 28, 2018).

15. Rutherford H. Platt, "Shouldering the Burden: Federal Assumption of Disaster Costs," in *Disasters and Democracy: The Politics of Extreme Natural Events,* ed. Rutherford H. Platt, 11–46 (Washington, DC: Island Press, 1999).

16. See Peter J. May, *Recovering from Catastrophes: Federal Disaster Relief Policy and Politics* (Westport, CT: Greenwood Press, 1985). See also Platt, "Shouldering the Burden." See also Keith Bea, "The Formative Years: 1950-1978," in *Emergency Management: The American Experience 1900-2010*, 2nd ed., ed. Claire B. Rubin (Boca Raton, FL: CRC Press, 2012).

17. Richard T. Sylves and William L. Waugh Jr., eds., *Disaster Management in the U.S. and Canada* (Springfield, IL.: Charles C Thomas, 1996).

18. See Bruce R. Lindsay, *Stafford Act Assistance and Acts of Terrorism*, U.S. Congressional Research Service report R44801 (Washington, DC: U.S. CRS, June 2, 2017), Summary. At https://fas.org/sgp/crs/homesec/R44801.pdf (accessed April 30, 2018). Lindsay painstakingly compares pre-Stafford declaration provisions with Stafford Act declarations provisions. His findings suggest that the Stafford Act did not specifically broaden what presidents could declare as disasters or emergencies. Rather, owing to a few minor wording changes, Congress limited the president's freedom to declare certain types of events as disasters or emergencies (i.e., immigration crises) but in other language opened the door to presidential declarations involving explosions, which later was applied in terror bombings inside the United States.

19. Richard T. Sylves, "Presidential Declaration of Disaster Decisions: The Case of Turndowns," Case 1.2, in *Critical Issues in Homeland Security: A Casebook*, eds. James D. Ramsay and Linda Kiltz (Boulder, CO: Westview Press, 2014), 60.

20. See Bruce R. Lindsay, *Stafford Act Declarations 1953-2016: Trends, Analysis, and Implications for Congress,* R42702 (Washington, DC: Congressional Research Service, August 28, 2017). This document features excellent tabular graphics that show presidential approvals and turndowns from 1953 to 2014 year by year, as well as approval and turndown percentage records of presidents from Eisenhower to Obama. The Lindsay CRS data and findings should be considered definitive.

21. U.S. Senate, Senate Committee on Governmental Affairs, *Hearing on Rebuilding FEMA: Preparing for the Next Disaster*, 103rd Cong., 1st sess., May 18, 1993, 151.

22. Saundra K. Schneider, *Flirting with Disaster: Public Management in Crisis Situations* (Armonk, NY: M.E. Sharpe, 1995). See also Saundra K. Schneider, *Dealing with Disaster: Public Management in Crisis Situations*, 2nd ed. Armonk, NY: M.E. Sharpe, 2011. There is a standard 4-page template form governors, tribal leaders, or their respective staffs are expected to complete when making a request for a presidential declaration of major disaster or emergency. Available at U.S. Department of Homeland Security, FEMA, "Request for Presidential Declaration of Major Disaster or Emergency," at https://www.fema.gov/media-library-data/1512409550714-752b7004a7c74c67a485a36551d7c889/FEMAForm010-0-13PresidentialDeclarationRequest.pdf (accessed October 1, 2018).

23. Presidents and FEMA are loath to obligate states to pay a state–local match when their respective governors have not first officially agreed to pay the state–local match.

24. James E. Anderson, "Policy Implementation," in *Public Policymaking: An Introduction,* 3rd ed. (Boston: Houghton-Mifflin, 1997), 213–270.

25. Peter J. May and Walter Williams, *Disaster Policy Implementation: Managing Programs under Shared Governance* (New York: Plenum Press, 1986). See also Richard T. Sylves, "President Bush and Hurricane Katrina: A Presidential Leadership Study," *Annals of the American Academy of Political and Social Science* 604 (March 2006): 26–56.

26. Before 1947, the federal government, if it responded at all, usually responded to disasters congressionally and on a case-by-case basis. Congress would enact

laws in a reactive manner. These measures were time-limited and conferred various types of relief directly through federal agencies (e.g., over its long history, the U.S. Army Corps of Engineers was regularly put to work on targeted post-disaster rebuilding for specific disasters) or through assistance to states, local governments, or major charities.

27. *U.S. Code of Federal Regulations*, Title 44-Emergency Management and Assistance, § 200.3 Policy, 314. http://books.google.com/books?id=pT07AAAAIAAJ&pg=PA314 (accessed September 5, 2018).

28. *U.S. Code of Federal Regulations*, Title 44-Emergency Management and Assistance, § 208.2 Definitions and Terms, 505. http://books.google.com/books?id=OgWjZvEaR0C&pg=PA505 (accessed September 5, 2018).

29. *U.S. Code of Federal Regulations*, Title 44-Emergency Management and Assistance, § 206.35 Requests for emergency declarations. http://www.ecfr.gov/cgi-bin/text-idx?SID=f588519a610591d690201d48c037060c&node=44:1.0.1.4.57&rgn=div5#44:1.0.1.4.57.2.18.5 (accessed September 5, 2018).

30. National Low Income Housing Coalition, "40 Years Ago: The Disaster Relief Act of 1974" Resource Library, September 29, 2014. At http://nlihc.org/article/40-years-ago-disaster-relief-act-1974 (accessed April 28, 2018).

31. See Bruce R. Lindsay, *Stafford Act Assistance and Acts of Terrorism*, U.S. Congressional Research Service report R44801 (Washington, DC: U.S. CRS, June 2, 2017), cited previously.

32. Federal Emergency Management Agency, *Robert T. Stafford Disaster Relief and Emergency Assistance Act, as amended, and Related Authorities*, "Title I—Findings, Declarations and Definitions," sec. 101 (2007), 1, https://www.fema.gov/media-library-data/1519395888776-af5f95a1a9237302af7e3fd5b0d07d71/StaffordAct.pdf (accessed September 5, 2018).

33. Jared T. Brown, Francis X. McCarthy, and Edwin C. Liu, *Analysis of the Sandy Recovery Improvement Act of 2013*, U.S. Congressional Research Service, 7-5700, R42991, March 11, 2013, ii, Summary.

34. Ibid., 2–3.

35. Ibid., 3–4.

36. Federal Emergency Management Agency, "The Disaster Declaration Process," update of January 8, 2018, https://www.fema.gov/disaster-declaration-process (accessed September 28, 2018). The "Declaration Types" pull down menu, when opened, provides details about the FEMA programs that are available to furnish aid under each respective type of disaster declaration.

37. Obviously, if the governor is somehow incapacitated or unavailable, federal law allows lieutenant governors to ask, and if that official cannot, the next highest-ranking state executive may make such requests.

38. U.S. Department of Homeland Security, Office of Inspector General, Opportunities to Improve FEMA's Public Assistance Preliminary Damage Assessment Process, OIG-12-79, May 2012, 9.

39. FEMA, "The Declaration Process," March 1, 2018. At https://www.fema.gov/declaration-process (accessed May 6, 2018).

40. Ibid.

41. Texas Department of Public Safety, Division of Emergency Management, "TCEQ Regional Workshop: Emergency Response Preparing for Disasters and Emergency Incidents," *SlidePlayer*, June 2, 2015. At http://slideplayer.com/slide/6083987/ (accessed May 3, 2018).

42. U.S. Government Accountability Office, "Disaster Assistance: Improvement Needed in Disaster Declaration Criteria and Eligibility Assurance Procedures, GAO-01-837" (Washington, DC: Government Printing Office, 2001), 5.

43. FEMA, "The Federal Emergency Management Agency," Publication 1, November 2010. At https://www.fema.gov/media-library-data/20130726-1823-25045-8164/pub_1_final.pdf (accessed May 1, 2018), 8.

44. *Federal Register* 64, no. 169 (September 1, 1999): 47697–47699. See also Francis X. McCarthy, *FEMA's Disaster Declaration Process: A Primer*, CRS Report RL34146 (Washington, DC: U.S. Congressional Research Service, 2007).

45. For a more complete explanation of why governor requests for declarations have been turned down, see Richard T. Sylves, "Presidential Declaration of Disaster Decisions: The Case of Turndowns," 45-47, cited previously.

46. Alethia H. Cook, "Towards an Emergency Response Report Card: Evaluating the Response to the I-35W Bridge Collapse," *Journal of Homeland Security and Emergency Management,* 6, no. 1 (August 2009).

47. See Sylves, "Presidential Declaration of Disaster Decisions," 35–72.

48. Richard T. Sylves, "The Politics and Budgeting of Federal Emergency Management," in *Disaster Management in the U.S. and Canada*, 33, 43. See also James F. Miskel, *Disaster Response and Homeland Security: What Works, What Doesn't* (Westport, CT: Praeger, 2006).

49. There is about a four-month turndown gap in the data for Obama years, and for Trump, turndown data were only available for his first seven months in office—and this was for major disaster turndowns only. No information about possible Trump turndowns of emergency requests has been made available to this author.

50. FEMA, "Public Assistance Per Capita Impact Indicator and Project Thresholds," October 11, 2017 (Washington, DC: FEMA), https://www.fema .gov/public-assistance-indicator-and-project-thresholds (accessed June 7, 2018). Note, FY 2018 figures are for all disasters declared from Oct. 1, 2017 through Sept. 30, 2018. Also, this release displays nationwide Public Assistance per capita damage thresholds from fiscal years 2008 to 2018.

51. U.S. Department of Homeland Security, Office of Inspector General, "Opportunities to Improve FEMA's Public Assistance."

52. See FEMA, "FEMA Hazard Mitigation Grants: 404 and 406," FS 001, May 3, 2017. At https://www .fema.gov/news-release/2017/05/03/4309/fema-hazard-mitigation-grants-404-and-406 (accessed May 6, 2018).

53. Executive Office of the President (Donald J. Trump), Annual Report to Congress on the White House Office Personnel, White House Office, June 29, 2018, at https://www.whitehouse.gov/wp-content/ uploads/2018/06/07012018-report-final.pdf (accessed September 28, 2018). This site provides name, status, salary, pay basis, position, and title of each White House employee.

54. Joseph A. Pika and John Anthony Maltese, *The Politics of the Presidency,* 6th ed. (Washington, DC: CQ Press, 2004), 149–153.

55. Charles S. Clark, "The Obama Way: Assessing the President's Management Approach," *National Journal*, August 3, 2012, https://www.yahoo. com/news/obama-way-assessing-presidents-management-approach-155437265.html (accessed September 5, 2018).

56. National Public Radio, *NPR*, "What Is Executive Privilege, Anyway?," June 28, 2007. At https://www.npr.org/templates/story/story .php?storyId=11527747 (accessed May 4, 2018). This source observes that use of executive privilege dates back as far as President George Washington and that presidents of all major political parties have invoked the privilege.

57. Although his book says nothing about how the Trump White House processes FEMA-prepared White House packages containing governor or tribal leader disaster declaration requests, Bob Woodward's, *FEAR: Trump in the White House*, describes life in the Trump White House and the president's mode of decision making in a variety of issue areas. See Bob Woodward, *FEAR: Trump in the White House* (New York: Simon & Schuster, 2018). As mentioned, owing to executive privilege, it is almost impossible to unearth internal White House procedures used in facilitating any president's handling of disaster declaration requests. However, some information is available about Trump White House offices on the domestic side. See The White House, "White House Internship Program Presidential Departments," undated but recent, at https://www.whitehouse.gov/get-involved/internships/presidential-departments/ (accessed October 1, 2018). This site provides one-paragraph descriptions of what various White House departments and offices do.

58. Federal Emergency Management Agency, *Public Assistance Program and Policy Guide*, FP 104-009-2, April 2018, at https://www.fema.gov/media-library-data/1525468328389-4a038bbef9081cd7dfe7538e7751aa9c/PAPPG_3.1_508_FINAL_5-4-2018.pdf (accessed October 1, 2018).

59. FEMA, "IS-634 Introduction to FEMA's Public Assistance Program, Lesson 2: Steps in the PA Process," undated. At https://emilms.fema.gov/IS634/PA0102summary.htm (accessed May 3, 2018).

60. Ibid.

61. FEMA, "Public Assistance: Private Non-Profit Houses of Worship," *Fact Sheet*, January 26, 2018. At https://www.fema.gov/media-library-data/1518794956930-8c2ade230f1a98b484895cacf63c1940/PublicAssistancePrivateNonprofitHousesofWorshipFAQ1.pdf (accessed April 30, 2018).

62. Ibid.

63. Ibid.

64. See FEMA," Public Assistance Per Capita Impact Indicator and Project Thresholds," October 11, 2017. At https://www.fema.gov/public-assistance-indicator-and-project-thresholds (accessed April 30, 2018).

65. Cost estimation requirements must be adhered to, but the president may approve costs that exceed the regulatory limitations. "Associated costs," such as the employment of National Guard forces, use of prison labor, and base and overtime wages for employees and "extra hires," may be reimbursed. The president must notify congressional committees with jurisdiction before providing more than $20 million to repair, restore, or replace facilities. See Keith Bea, *Federal Stafford Act Disaster Assistance: Presidential Declarations, Eligible Activities, and Funding*, CRS Report RL33053 (Washington, DC: U.S. Congressional Research Service, 2006), 10–11.

66. Federal Emergency Management Agency, "Fact Sheet: Individuals and Households Program," updated May 2018, at https://www.fema.gov/media-library-data/1528984381358-6f256cab09bfcbe6747510c215445560/IndividualsHouseholdsPrograms.pdf (accessed October 1, 2018).

67. See *Federal Register*, "A Notice by the Federal Emergency Management Agency on 10/12/2017," *A Notice by the Federal Emergency Management Agencyon 10/12/2017.* At https://www.federalregister.gov/documents/2017/10/12/2017-22032/notice-of-maximum-amount-of-assistance-under-the-individuals-and-households-program (accessed April 30, 2018). "Section 408 of the Robert T. Stafford Disaster Relief and Emergency Assistance Act (the Stafford Act), 42 U.S.C. 5174, prescribes that FEMA must annually adjust the maximum amount for assistance provided under the Individuals and Households Program (IHP). FEMA gives notice that the maximum amount of IHP financial assistance provided to an individual or household under section 408 of the Stafford Act with respect to any single emergency or major disaster is $34,000. The increase in award amount as stated is for any single emergency or major disaster declared on or after October 1, 2016," Ibid.

68. FEMA, "Assistance to Individuals and Households Fact Sheet," October 3, 2013.

69. FEMA, "Understanding Individual Assistance and Public Assistance," January 15, 2018. At https://www.fema.gov/news-release/2018/01/15/understanding-individual-assistance-and-public-assistance (accessed April 30, 2018).

70. FEMA, "What is FEMA's Individual Assistance Program?" *Fact Sheet*, undated. At https://www.fema.gov/media-library-data/1461689021638-cfcfd7f6c263635802fa7a76a19e00ea/FS001_What_is_Individual_Assistance_508.pdf (accessed April 30, 2018).

71. FEMA, "Understanding Individual Assistance and Public Assistance," January 15, 2018.

72. FEMA, "What is FEMA's Individual Assistance Program?" *Fact Sheet*, undated.

73. LGBTQ refers to those who are lesbian, gay, bisexual, transgender, questioning, or queer. The "Q" can stand for "questioning" or "queer," and sometimes the acronym is written as "LGBTQQ." When the Q is used as a stand-in for questioning, it means the individual is uncertain of his or her orientation. See Steven Petrow, "Civilities: What Does the Acronym 'LGBTQ' Stand For?" *The Washington Post*, May 23, 2014.

74. FEMA, "What is FEMA's Individual Assistance Program?" *Fact Sheet*, undated.

75. See Human Rights Campaign, "Working with the Lesbian, Gay, Bisexual, and Transgender Community," 2013. At https://nationalmasscarestrategy.files.wordpress.com/2013/01/emergencyresponders_-_lgbt_competency.pdf (accessed April 30, 2018). Also crucial is that a U.S. Supreme Court 2015 ruling declares that states cannot keep same-sex couples from marrying and must recognize their unions.

76. Patrick S. Roberts, *Disasters and the American State: How Politicians, Bureaucrats, and the Public Prepare for the Unexpected* (New York: Cambridge University Press, 2013), 146–173.

77. FEMA, "What is FEMA's Individual Assistance Program?" *Fact Sheet*, undated.

78. Ibid.

79. Ibid.

80. Ibid.

81. Ibid.

82. Ibid.

83. Ibid.

84. Ibid.

85. Ibid.

86. The author has several friends and colleagues who live in highly disaster-prone states and counties. Some have assumed that in the event of back-to-back disaster declarations, they can carry the damage costs from their first declared event combining them with damage costs from their second declared event. This appears to save on the document and paperwork burden of filing for FEMA aid, but it most assuredly will pose problems in qualifying for FEMA help. Clearly, it is a challenge to isolate damage in the first disaster from new damage sustained in a rapid follow-on second disaster transpiring a few weeks, or a month or so, later. In a few rare cases, lawmakers representing double hit districts or states have successfully convinced FEMA to allow their aggrieved constituents to combine damage from two declared disasters into one when they make FEMA IA application. When this occurs, FEMA simply treats the two back-to-back disasters as one.

87. Centralized authority: Donald F. Kettl, *System under Stress: Homeland Security and American Politics*, 2nd ed. (Washington, DC: CQ Press, 2004), 46, 113. Range of authority: Jane A. Bullock et al., *Introduction to Homeland Security*, 2nd ed. (Boston: Butterworth-Heinemann, 2006).

88. *9/11 Commission Report: Final Report of the National Commission on Terrorist Attacks upon the United States* (New York: Norton, 2004).

89. John Fass Morton, *Next-Generation Homeland Security: Network Federalism and the Course to National Preparedness* (Annapolis, MD: Naval Institute Press, 2012), 185–186. Ibid.

90. Ohio Emergency Management Agency, "Final Draft: National Response Plan," 2004, 8–9, quotation, 9, http://ema.ohio.gov/Documents/NRP_Final_Draft.pdf (accessed September 5, 2018). Under the NRF, which replaced the NRP and went into effect in early 2008, the Incident of National Significance designation and process was discontinued.

91. Long ago in a personal discussion with this author, George D. Haddow, a friend and former Clinton administration FEMA official, disclosed that he feared that presidents might use DRF money to cover terrorism incidents that were not disasters under the Stafford Act. Haddow was prescient, and his fears were justified. For example, several NSSEs have garnered presidential declarations of emergency that siphoned away some DRF monies. The Secret Service's congressionally approved budget is often grossly underfunded to pay state and local government reimbursements stemming from their work and costs under NSSEs.

92. Bruce R. Lindsay, *Stafford Act Assistance and Acts of Terrorism*, 2017.

93. Ibid.

94. See Joby Warrick, "FBI Investigation of 2001 Anthrax Attacks Concluded; U.S. Releases Details," Washington Post, February 20, 2010. At http://

www.washingtonpost.com/wp-dyn/content/article/2010/02/19/AR2010021902369.html (accessed May 1, 2018).

95. Ohio Emergency Management Agency, "Final Draft: National Response Plan," 2004, x.

96. U.S. Department of the Treasury, Resource Center, *Terrorism Risk Insurance Program*, March 29, 2018. At https://www.treasury.gov/resource-center/fin-mkts/Pages/program.aspx (accessed May 2, 2018). TRIA was enacted as a temporary measure but was extended in 2005, reauthorized in 2007 and again in 2015, and is not scheduled to expire until 2020, when it may again be reauthorized. Much of the concern about TRIA involved how federal Treasury officials should define a catastrophic terrorism disaster that would activate the TRIA program. This is still being worked out, although a certification process achieved Final Rule stage in December 2016.

97. Shawn Reese, National Special Security Events: Fact Sheet, U.S. Congressional Research Service, January 25, 2017. At https://fas.org/sgp/crs/homesec/R43522.pdf (accessed May 2, 2018). https://www.treasury.gov/resource-center/fin-mkts/Pages/program.aspx

98. Ibid.

99. Before 2003, presidents had authority to declare NSSEs through mobilizing the U.S. Secret Service. Since 2003, the Secret Service has been part of the DHS. Now NSSEs are interlaced with presidential authority to issue disaster declarations and to declare major disasters and emergencies. See EveryCRSReport.com, U.S. Congressional Research Service, "National Special Security Events: Fact Sheet," R43522, April 24, 2014–January 25, 2017, at https://www.everycrsreport.com/reports/R43522.html (accessed October 1, 2018). This source explains what NSSEs are, how they operate, and how much funding Congress has appropriated to this program from FY 2006 through FY 2017.

100. Single Audit Resource Center, "97.126 National Special Security Event," 2017, at https://singleaudit.org/program/?id=97.126 (accessed October 1, 2018). For a concise description of how NSSEs work, see Christopher T. Geldart, "Anatomy of a National Special Security Event," *Domestic Preparedness*, June 7, 2017, at https://www.domesticpreparedness.com/preparedness/anatomy-of-a-national-special-security-event/ (accessed October 1, 2018).

101. Reese, "National Special Security Events: Fact Sheet," January 25, 2017.

102. See William C. Nicholson, ed., *Homeland Security Law and Policy* (Springfield, IL: Charles C Thomas, 2005), and Bullock et al., *Introduction to Homeland Security,* 2nd ed.

103. Ted Steinberg, *Acts of God: The Unnatural History of Natural Disaster in America* (New York: Oxford University Press, 2000), 181.

104. George D. Haddow, Jane A. Bullock, and Damon P. Coppola, *Introduction to Emergency Management,* 4th ed. (Boston: Butterworth-Heinemann, 2011).

105. See William L. Waugh Jr. and Richard T. Sylves, "Organizing the War on Terrorism," *Public Administration Review* 62 (September 2002): 145–153. See also William L. Waugh Jr., "Terrorism, Homeland Security, and the National Emergency Management Network," *Public Organization Review* 3 (December 2003): 373–385.

106. House Select Bipartisan Committee to Investigate Preparation for and Response to Hurricane Katrina, *A Failure of Initiative,* 109th Cong., 2nd sess., February 16, 2006. This was emphasized in the testimony provided by Michael Brown, the former FEMA director forced to resign in the weeks after Hurricane Katrina struck in 2005, before the Select Bipartisan Committee to Investigate Preparation for and Response to Hurricane Katrina cited here.

107. David Porter, "Hurricane Sandy Was Second-Costliest in U.S. History, Report Shows," *Huffington Post,* https://www.cbsnews.com/news/report-sandy-second-costliest-hurricane-in-us-history/ (accessed September 6, 2018).

108. Anahad O'Connor and Timothy Williams, "Scores Die in Storms across South; Tornado Ravages City," *New York Times,* April 27, 2011, http://www.nytimes.com/2011/04/28/us/28storm.html?_r=0 (accessed September 6, 2018).

109. Thomas A. Birkland, *Lessons of Disaster: Policy Change after Catastrophic Events* (Washington, DC: Georgetown University Press, 2007).

110. Donald F. Kettl, *System under Stress: The Challenge to 21st Century Governance,* 3rd ed. (Washington, DC: CQ Press, 2014).

111. Miskel, *Disaster Response and Homeland Security*, 23.

112. Ibid., 76.

113. National Academy of Public Administration, *Coping with Catastrophe: Building an Emergency Management System to Meet People's Needs in Natural and Manmade Disasters* (Washington, DC: National Academy of Public Administration, 1993).

114. KABC-TV Los Angeles, CA, "Oklahoma Tornado: President Barack Obama Visits Moore, Vows Unwavering Support," http://www.abclocal.go.com/kabc/story?section=news/national_world&id=9116779 (accessed September 6, 2018).

115. See Heidi M. Przybyla, "Trump: Hurricane Harvey Recovery Response 'a Wonderful Thing,'" USA TODAY Published September 2, 2017. At https://www.usatoday.com/story/news/politics/2017/09/02/trump-houston-survey-hurricane-harvey-damage/628259001/ (accessed April 30, 2018).

116. Sylves, "President Bush and Hurricane Katrina," 33.

117. Sylves and Waugh, *Disaster Management in the U.S. and Canada*, 27.

118. Kettl, *System under Stress,* 2nd ed., 15.

119. Ibid.

120. As of September 17, 2017, DHS reports that it has 240,000 employees. See U.S. DHS, "About DHS," September 17, 2017. At https://www.dhs.gov/about-dhs (accessed May 3, 2018).

121. Bea, *Federal Stafford Act Disaster Assistance*.

122. DHS, "Surge Capacity Force," undated. At https://www.dhs.gov/topic/surge-capacity-force (accessed May 3, 2018).

123. R. Steven Daniels and Carolyn L. Clark-Daniels, *Transforming Government: The Renewal and Revitalization of the Federal Emergency Management Agency,* 2000 Presidential Transition Series (Arlington, VA: Pricewaterhouse Coopers Endowment for the Business of Government, 2000).

124. Jason D. Mycoff, "Congress and Katrina: A Failure of Oversight," special issue, *State and Local Government Review* 39, no. 1 (2007): 16–30.

125. Thomas A. Garrett and Russell S. Sobel, "The Political Economy of FEMA Disaster Payments," *Economic Inquiry* 41, no. 3 (2003): 496–509. See also John T. Gasper and Andrew Reeves, "Make It Rain? Retrospection and the Attentive Electorate in the Context of Natural Disasters, *American Journal of Political Science* 55, no. 2 (2011): 340–355, and Andrew Healy and Neal Malhotra, "Myopic Votes and Natural Disaster Policy," in *American Political Science Review* 103, no. 3 (2009): 387–406.

126. Garrett and Sobel, 2003, i.

127. Ibid., 2.

128. Ibid., 1. See also Andrew Reeves, "Political Disaster: Unilateral Powers, Electoral Incentives, and Presidential Disaster Declarations," *The Journal of Politics* 1, no. 1 (2009): 1–10.

129. See Richard T. Sylves and Zoltan I. Buzas, "Presidential Disaster Declaration Decisions, 1953–2003: What Influences Odds of Approval," *State & Local Government Review* 39, no. 1 (2007): 3–15.

130. Lindsay, "Stafford Act Declarations 1953-2016: Trends, Analysis, and Implications for Congress," 22, cited previously.

131. Sylves and Buzas, "Presidential Disaster Declaration Decisions, 1953–2003: What Influences Odds of Approval," cited previously.

132. Garrett and Sobel, "The Political Economy of FEMA Disaster Payments," 4.

133. Those who are fixated on approvals and turndowns as a function of FEMA's Public Assistance per capita threshold criterion tend to overlook the fact that presidents may make judgments of deservedness based largely on their perception of the amount of human suffering (the number of deaths and injuries, no-notice or high speed of onset, characteristics of victims, intensity of news coverage, etc.) caused by the disaster or emergency.

134. Miskel, *Disaster Response and Homeland Security*, 114–115.

135. Ibid., 114–117.

136. Other examples are the declaration that went to the state of Virginia and its Arlington County when the 9/11 terrorists flew one of the hijacked airliners into a side of the Pentagon.

137. In this book, the word *county* will be used to mean an official county or a state's equivalent of a county. Some states and U.S. territories or commonwealths do not have actual county governments (i.e., Alaska) but may employ political geographic designators used to represent county equivalents. The District of Columbia is treated as a state in its entirety. Native American tribal governments or associations have, since 2013, been given the right to directly request presidential declarations of major disaster or emergency, without having to file through any state government adjacent to their reservation lands (as they had to do before 2013).

138. Schneider, *Flirting with Disaster*, 32.

139. For a more thorough description and explanation of the fund, and for a table of Disaster Relief Fund spending from fiscal year 1974 to fiscal year 2006, see Bea, *Federal Stafford Act Disaster Assistance*, 28–33.

140. Personal email correspondence from Bruce R. Lindsay to this author, May 9, 2018, previously cited.

141. Daniel J. Weiss and Jackie Weidman, "Disastrous Spending: Federal Disaster-Relief Expenditures Rise Amid More Extreme Weather," April 29, 2013, http://www.americanprogress.org/issues/green/report/2013/04/29/61633/disastrous-spending-federal-disaster-relief-expenditures-rise-amid-more-extreme-weather (accessed September 6, 2018).

142. Ibid.

143. Allen K. Settle, "Disaster Assistance: Securing Presidential Declarations," in *Cities and Disaster: North American Studies in Emergency Management*, eds. Richard T. Sylves and William L. Waugh Jr. (Springfield, IL: Charles C Thomas, 1990).

144. Ibid., 50. See also U.S. Government Accountability Office, "Disaster Assistance."

145. James L. Witt and J. Morgan, *Stronger in the Broken Places: Nine Lessons for Turning Crisis into Triumph* (New York: Times Books, 2002). See also Platt, "Shouldering the Burden," and Daniels and Clark-Daniels, *Transforming Government.*

146. Roberts, 2013, 16.

147. Miskel, *Disaster Response and Homeland* Security, 118. See also Thomas A. Birkland, *After Disaster: Agenda Setting, Public Policy, and Focusing Events* (Washington, DC: Georgetown University Press, 1997).

148. William L. Waugh Jr. and Ronald John Hy, *Handbook of Emergency Management* (Westport, CT: Greenwood Press, 1990). See also Gary L. Wamsley, Aaron D. Schroeder, and Larry M. Lane, "To Politicize Is NOT to Control: The Pathologies of Control in Federal Emergency Management," *American Review of Public Administration* 26, no. 3 (1996): 263–285, and Platt, "Shouldering the Burden," 20–21.

149. The period 1989 to 2013 encompasses the presidencies of George H. W. Bush, Bill Clinton, George W. Bush, and Barack Obama.

150. Brian Tarcey, "Flooding the Ballot Box: The Politics of Disaster," *Harvard Magazine*, March–April 2004.

151. *American Heritage Dictionary*, 2nd collegiate ed., s.v. "overwhelm."

152. Andrew Reeves, "Political Disaster? Presidential Disaster Declarations and Electoral Politics," *The Journal of Politics* 73, no. 4 (October 2011): 1142–1151. See supporting material and data tables and charts at http://andrewreeves.org/sites/default/files/fema_supp.pdf (accessed September 6, 2018).

153. Ibid., 1144.

154. Ibid.

155. Sylves and Buzas, "Presidential Disaster Declaration Decisions," 13.

156. Reeves, "Political Disaster? Presidential Disaster Declarations," 5–6.

157. Tarcey, "Flooding the Ballot Box," 1.

158. Reeves, "Political Disaster? Presidential Disaster Declarations," 3.

159. Ibid., 11.

160. Ude J. Dymon and Rutherford H. Platt, "U.S. Federal Disaster Declarations: A Geographical Analysis," in *Disasters and Democracy: The Politics of Extreme Natural Events,* ed. Rutherford H. Platt (Washington, DC: Island Press, 1999).

161. Miskel, *Disaster Response and Homeland Security*, 118–120.

162. Ibid., 13–14.

163. Ibid., 14.

164. Ibid.

165. Sylves, "The Politics and Budgeting of Federal Emergency Management," 32; U.S. Government Accountability Office, "Disaster Assistance," 9–15.

166. Manny Fernandez, "FEMA Denied Texas Request for Full Disaster Aid, Rankling Stricken Town," *The New York Times*, June 22, 2013, http://www.nytimes.com/2013/06/23/us/fema-denies-texas-request-for-full-disaster-aid-rankling-stricken-town.html?pagewanted=all&_r=0 (accessed September 6, 2018). Governor Perry appealed the turndown and won his case. Texas was issued a major disaster declaration for the City of West explosion.

167. FEMA, "DR and EM Turndowns 12/6/2017," Excel table. Made available to this author in April 2018.

168. Among possible reasons why President Obama turned down the Michigan governor's request for a major disaster declaration are that other federal programs were already providing assistance and a major disaster declaration was not needed; the incident did not meet the definition of a major disaster (although President Reagan issued a major disaster declaration to protect public drinking water from contamination in Louisville, KY, in February 1981 after a sewer line explosion damaged 13 city blocks, not long after his first inauguration); the Flint event was already covered under an emergency declaration he had issued (see EM 3375); and as sometimes happens, pending litigation regarding claims to be paid out by responsible parties for the contamination would have been complicated if the president had the U.S. government preemptively assume control, clean-up responsibilities, and restitution duties.

169. James MacPherson, Associated Press, "Trump Denies Disaster Declaration for Dakota Access Pipeline," *U.S. News and World Report*, July 13, 2017. At https://www.usnews.com/news/best-states/north-dakota/articles/2017-07-13/trump-denies-disaster-declaration-for-dakota-access-pipeline (accessed May 3, 2018). "The Trump administration rejected North Dakota Gov. Doug Burgum's request for a 'major disaster declaration' to help cover some of the estimated $38 million cost to police protests of the Dakota Access pipeline, a spokesman for the Republican governor said Thursday. Burgum publicly announced in April his letter to President Donald Trump seeking the disaster declaration to pave the way for federal aid. The governor was notified in May that the request was denied by the Federal Emergency Management Agency [signifying it was denied by the president], Burgum spokesman Mike Nowatzki said. The governor's office didn't announce the denial until reporters asked about it this week. The denial was not unexpected because such declarations typically involve natural disasters, not 'civil-unrest-related disasters,' Nowatzki said.' Ibid.

170. James David Barber, "Presidential Character," in *American Government: Readings and Cases,* ed. Karen O'Connor (Boston: Allyn & Bacon, 1995), 204.

171. W. Brock Long, U.S. Department of Homeland Security, "Written testimony of FEMA Administrator Brock Long for a Senate Committee on Homeland Security and Governmental Affairs hearing titled 'FEMA: Prioritizing a Culture of Preparedness'," April 11, 2018. At https://www.dhs.gov/news/2018/04/11/written-testimony-fema-administrator-senate-committee-homeland-security-and (accessed May 3, 2018).

172. Miskel, *Disaster Response and Homeland Security*, 119–120.

Chapter 5

1. See National Action Council for Minorities in Engineering, "Types of Engineering: Discover the

Different Types of Engineering Careers," undated, at http://www.nacme.org/types-of-engineering (accessed May 9, 2018).

2. See Roger A. Pielke Jr., *The Honest Broker: Making Sense of Science in Policy and Politics* (New York: Cambridge University Press, 2007). See also Sylvia Kraemer, *Science and Technology Policy* (Piscataway, NJ: Rutgers University Press, 2006), and Kaye Husbands Fealing et al., eds., *The Science of Science Policy* (Palo Alto, CA: Stanford University Press, 2011).

3. The late Professor Stephen H. Schneider, someone this author was honored to know and work with for a short time at an Aspen Global Change Institute workshop, was an extraordinary and prolific researcher and public educator on climate change. He advised every president from Nixon to Obama on the subject, and for his work on the UN International Panel on Climate Change, he was awarded a Nobel Prize in 2007. Dr. Schneider understood the potential for more frequent and intense disasters owing to global climate change and its effects. He held a doctorate in mathematical engineering and plasma physics, worked 20 years at the National Center for Atmospheric Research, and joined the Stanford faculty in the mid-1990s. Douglas Martin, "Stephen H. Schneider, Climatologist, Is Dead at 65," *New York Times*, July 20, 2010, http://www.nytimes.com/2010/07/20/science/earth/20schneider.html?_r=0 (accessed September 6, 2018). See Stephen H. Schneider et al., *Climate Change Science and Policy* (Washington, DC: Island Press, 2010).

4. Edward A. Thomas, "Natural Hazards and the Law," in *Natural Hazard Mitigation*, eds. Alessandra Jerolleman and John J. Kiefer (Boca Raton, FL: CRC Press, 2013), 146–148.

5. See Jiah-Shin Teh and Harvey Rubin, "Dealing with Pandemics: Global Security, Risk Analysis, and Science Policy," in *Learning from Catastrophes*, eds. Howard Kunreuther and Michael Useem (Upper Saddle River, NJ: Pearson Education, 2010), 211–234.

6. See Adam Crowe, *Disasters 2.0: The Application of Social Media Systems for Modern Emergency Management* (Boca Raton, FL: CRC Press, 2012). See also Amanda L. Hughes, Leysia Palen, and Steve Peterson, "Chapter 11: Social Media and Emergency Management," Joseph E. Trainor and Tony Subbio, eds., *Critical Issues in Disaster Science and Management: A Dialogue Between Researchers and Practitioners*, for the FEMI Higher Education Project (Newark, DE: University of Delaware Library, Museums, and Press, 2014), 349–392. At http://udspace.udel.edu/handle/19716/13418 (accessed May 10, 2018).

7. Richard T. Sylves, "Federal Emergency Management Comes of Age: 1979–2001," in *Emergency Management: The American Experience, 1900–2010*, 2nd ed., ed. Claire B. Rubin (Boca Raton, FL: CRC Press, 2012), 136–137. See also John C. Pine, *Technology in Emergency Management* (Hoboken, NJ: Wiley, 2007).

8. See Louise K. Comfort, Arjin Boin, and Chris C. Demchak, eds., *Designing Resilience: Preparing for Extreme Events* (Pittsburgh: University of Pittsburgh Press, 2010). See also Susan L. Cutter, ed., *American Hazardscapes: The Regionalization of Hazards and Disasters* (Washington, DC: Joseph Henry Press, 2001). See David R. Godschalk, David J. Brower, and Timothy Beatley, *Catastrophic Coastal Storms: Hazard Mitigation and Development Management* (Durham, NC: Duke University Press, 1989).

9. See National Research Council, *Disaster Resilience: A National Imperative* (Washington, DC: National Academies Press, 2012). More examples include National Research Council, *Launching a National Conversation on Disaster Resilience in America: Workshop Summary* (Washington, DC: National Academies Press, 2013); National Research Council, *Building Community Disaster Resilience through Private-Public Collaboration* (Washington, DC: National Academies Press, 2011); and National Research Council, *Increasing National Resilience to Hazards and Disasters: The Perspective from the Gulf Coast of Louisiana and Mississippi: Summary of a Workshop* (Washington, DC: National Academies Press, 2011).

10. National Research Council, *Making the Nation Safer: The Role of Science and Technology in Countering Terrorism* (Washington, DC: National Academies Press, 2002).

11. Committee on Increasing National Resilience to Hazards & Disasters and Committee on Science, Engineering, and Public Policy, *Disaster Resilience: A National Imperative* (Washington, DC: The National Academies Press, 2012. At https://www.nap.edu/read/13457/chapter/1 (accessed May 9, 2018).

12. The National Laboratories system includes the Argonne, Brookhaven, Fermi, Idaho, Lawrence-Berkeley, Lawrence-Livermore, Los Alamos, Oak Ridge, Pacific Northwest, and Sandia National Laboratories, as well as the National Renewable Energy Laboratory.

13. Lauren Thomas, "Here's What It's Like to Be a Home Improvement Retailer in the Midst of a Hurricane," *CNBC*, September 14, 2017. At https://www.cnbc.com/2017/09/14/what-its-like-to-be-a-home-improvement-retailer-during-a-hurricane.html (accessed May 10, 2018). The article discloses that, "Home Depot and Lowe's began shipping emergency supplies to Florida in anticipation of Irma in the days leading up to the storm, while they continued cleaning up from Hurricane Harvey, which came ashore in Texas just days before. It's a costly process, but analysts have said that investments in logistics and the supply chain by home improvement retailers during a weather-related disaster typically bring in around 10 to 15 times more in sales. Illinois-based Ace Hardware, which operates 70 stores in Texas and about 200 in Florida, was not so much scrambling on news of when the damage would be done but reacted by pushing extra shipments to its stores in the hurricanes' paths." Quoting Richard Howells, an executive with SAP, Thomas adds, "This is something that can be practiced throughout the year, so when natural disasters or other obstacles surface, the communication necessary to handle these issues is already in place," he added. "Further, it's often to best to have a designated individual responsible for disaster relief programs, who can ensure that all parties are on the same page." Home Depot and Lowe's both activated similar command centers of their own, in adherence to the precedence set during prior storms. Ibid.

14. Sam Levin, "Questions for TSA after Reports of Laptop and Phone Searches on Domestic Flights," *The Guardian*, March 12, 2018. At https://www.theguardian.com/world/2018/mar/12/tsa-surveillance-laptops-cellphones-domestic-flights (accessed May 10, 2018).

15. See Rens van Munster, "Securitization," in Oxford Bibliographies, at http://www.oxfordbibliographies.com/view/document/obo-9780199743292/obo-9780199743292-0091.xml (accessed September 6, 2018). In international relations, "A securitizing speech act needs to follow a specific rhetorical structure, derived from war and its historical connotations of survival, urgency, threat, and defense. This leads the Copenhagen school [of international relations study] to define securitization as a speech act that has to fulfill three rhetorical criteria. It is a discursive process by means of which an actor (1) claims that a referent object is existentially threatened, (2) demands the right to take extraordinary countermeasures to deal with that threat, and (3) convinces an audience that rule-breaking behavior to counter the threat is justified. In short, by labeling something as 'security,' an issue is dramatized as an issue of supreme priority. One can therefore think of securitization as the process through which non-politicized (issues are not talked about) or politicized (issues are publicly debated) issues are elevated to security issues that need to be dealt with urgently, and that legitimate the bypassing of public debate and democratic procedures." Ibid.

16. Martin Giles, "Six Cyber Threats to Really Worry About in 2018," MIT *Technology Review*, January 2, 2018. At https://www.technologyreview.com/s/609641/six-cyber-threats-to-really-worry-about-in-2018/ (accessed May 10, 2018).

17. *The Economist*, "Sailing the Wired Seas," March 10, 2018. At https://www.economist.com/news/technology-quarterly/21738088-internet-infrastructure-being-built-span-oceans-sailing-wired-seas (accessed May 10, 2018).

18. For more than 30 years, scholars of many stripes have discussed "big science." The terms of this discussion were framed by the popular writings of the physicist Alvin Weinberg and the physicist-historian Derek de Solla Price in the 1960s. Both authors focused on the rapidly increasing size

and expense of scientific projects, both identified this increase in scale as a distinctive feature of science in the post–World War II era, and both worried about the consequences of the "disease" of "big science." Catherine Westfall, "Rethinking Big Science: Modest, Mezzo, Grand Science and the Development of the Bevalac, 1971–1993," *Isis* 94 (March 2003): 32.

19. Michael Aaron Dennis, "Big Science," *Encyclopedia Britannica*, November 3, 1988 original article. Added to Web site: Academia - Big Science, Thinley Kalsang Bhutia, May 19, 2017. At https://www .britannica.com/science/Big-Science-science (accessed May 10, 2018).

20. See also Alexander J. Morin, *Science Policy and Politics* (Englewood Cliffs, NJ: Prentice Hall, 1993), 142.

21. W. Henry Lambright, *Governing Science and Technology* (New York: Oxford University Press, 1993).

22. See National Science Foundation, "Interdisciplinary Research in Hazards and Disasters (Hazards SEES)," http://www.nsf.gov/pubs/2012/nsf12610/nsf12610. htm (accessed September 6, 2018). NSF officials write, "The overarching goal of Hazards SEES is to catalyze well-integrated interdisciplinary research efforts in hazards-related science and engineering in order to improve the understanding of natural hazards and technological hazards linked to natural phenomena, mitigate their effects, and to better prepare for, respond to, and recover from disasters. The goal is to effectively prevent hazards from becoming disasters. Hazards SEES aims to make investments in strongly interdisciplinary research that will reduce the impact of such hazards, enhance the safety of society, and contribute to sustainability. The Hazards SEES program is a multi-directorate program that seeks to: (1) advance understanding of the fundamental processes associated with specific natural hazards and technological hazards linked to natural phenomena, and their interactions; (2) better understand the causes, interdependences, impacts and cumulative effects of these hazards on individuals, the natural and built environment, and society as a whole; and (3) improve capabilities for forecasting or predicting hazards, mitigating their

effects, and enhancing the capacity to respond to and recover from resultant disasters." Ibid.

23. Becky Ham, "AAAS Seeks to Uphold Science's Role in Policy-making," *Science*, 31 Mar 2017: Vol. 355, Issue 6332, pp. 1383–1384. At http:// science.sciencemag.org/content/355/6332/1383. full (accessed May 10, 2018). One AAAS report done in partnership with the Gordon and Betty Moore Foundation called for better recognition of the civic contribution of scientists and engineers who engage with policymakers, and better institutional support, "to engage and nurture a new generation of scientists around the world to meet current and future demand," for scientists capable of navigating between science and policy. "Scientists must think more strategically about policy, especially in the face of potentially severe cuts to government R&D funding," said speakers discussing science budgets. Ibid.

24. The Bill and Melinda Gates Foundation, "What We Do: Emergency Response, Strategy Overview," undated. At https://www.gatesfoundation.org/ What-We-Do/Global-Development/Emergency-Response (accessed May 10, 2018).

25. John Twigg, *Corporate Social Responsibility and Disaster Reduction* (London: Benfield Greig Hazard Research Centre at University College London, 2001), http://drr.upeace.org/english/docu ments/References/Topic%207-Preparedness-%20 Early%20Warning,%20Planning,%20Monitoring %20and%20Evaluation/Twigg%202001%20CSR% 20and%20disaster%20management.pdf (accessed September 6, 2018).

26. National Research Council, *Facing Hazards and Disasters: Understanding Human Dimensions* (Washington, DC: National Academies Press, 2006).

27. William L. Waugh Jr., *Living with Hazards, Dealing with Disasters: An Introduction to Disaster Management* (Armonk, NY: M.E. Sharpe, 2000).

28. E. L. Quarantelli, "Disaster Planning, Emergency Management, and Civil Protection: The Historical Development of Organized Efforts to Plan for and to Respond to Disasters," DRC Preliminary Paper no. 301 (Newark: University of Delaware, Disaster

Research Center, 2000), http://udspace.udel.edu/handle/19716/673 (accessed September 6, 2018).

29. See David A. McEntire, *Disaster Response and Recovery* (Hoboken, NJ: Wiley, 2007), 65–69. For a general overview by an assortment of scholars regarding commonly held myths people have about disaster, see the National Research Council, *Facing Hazards and Disasters*.

30. See Dennis S. Mileti, *Disasters by Design: A Reassessment of Natural Hazards in the United States* (Washington, DC: Joseph Henry Press, 1999).

31. See Amanda Ripley, *The Unthinkable: Who Survives When Disaster Strikes—and Why* (New York: Three Rivers Press, 2009).

32. Dennis S. Mileti, "Opening Plenary Welcoming Speech" (speech presented at the University of Colorado Hazards Center Annual Workshop, Boulder, July 2004).

33. See also Institute for Crisis, Disaster and Risk Management of the George Washington University, University of Mississippi's Clinical Disaster Research Center, Center for Natural Hazards Research of East Carolina University, Hazards and Vulnerability Research Institute of University of South Carolina, Center for Hazards Research and Policy Development at the University of Louisville, Center for Hazards and Risk Research at Columbia University, Cascadia Hazards Institute of Central Washington University, International Hurricane Center at Florida International University, University of Wisconsin Disaster Management Center, Louisiana State University Hurricane Center, California State University's Chico Center for Hazards Research, Florida Catastrophic Storm Risk Management Center, Millersville University of Pennsylvania Center for Disaster Research and Education, Texas A&M University Hazards Reduction and Recovery Center, Texas State University's James and Marilyn Lovell Center for Environmental Geography and Hazards Research, University of California at Los Angeles Center for Public Health and Disasters, University of New Orleans Center for Hazards Assessment Response and Technology, University of North Texas Emergency Administration

and Planning, University of Pennsylvania Wharton Risk Management and Decision Processes Center, and University of South Florida Center for Disaster Management and Humanitarian Assistance. Most of these organizations are listed at University of Colorado Hazards Center, "Resources," https://hazards.colorado.edu/resources/research-centers (accessed September 6, 2018).

34. National Research Council, *Facing Hazards and Disasters*, 29.

35. Ibid., 30.

36. Chester Hartman and Gregory D. Squires, eds., *There Is No Such Thing as a Natural Disaster* (New York: Routledge, 2006).

37. The World Bank, *Natural Hazards and Unnatural Disasters: The Economics of Effective Prevention* (Washington, DC: The International Bank for Reconstruction and Development, 2010), and from a historian's perspective, see Ted Steinberg, *Acts of God: The Unnatural History of Natural Disaster in America* (New York: Oxford University Press, 2000).

38. See Arjen Boin, Paul 't Hart, Eric Stern, and Bengt Sundelius, *The Politics of Crisis Management: Public Leadership under Pressure*, 2nd ed. (Cambridge, U.K.: Cambridge University Press, University Printing House, 2017).

39. Dan Frosch and Cameron McWhirter, "Five Reasons Houston Is Especially Vulnerable to Flooding," *The Wall Street Journal*, Aug. 25, 2017. At https://www.wsj.com/articles/five-reasons-houston-is-especially-vulnerable-to-flooding-1503676480 (accessed May 10, 2018). The authors point to the following reasons: Houston's topography makes rising waters particularly dangerous; a recent construction boom has impeded drainage; flood protections have had trouble keeping pace with development; building regulations have not considered historic flooding levels; and drainage systems are largely obsolete. Ibid.

40. National Research Council, *Facing Hazards and Disasters*, 38.

41. George D. Haddow and Jane A. Bullock, *Introduction to Emergency Management*, 2nd ed. (Boston: Butterworth-Heinemann, 2006).

42. National Research Council, *The Impacts of Natural Disasters: A Framework for Loss Estimation* (Washington, DC: National Academies Press, 1999).

43. Ibid., 62. See also Howard Kunreuther, "Insurability Conditions and the Supply of Coverage," in *Paying the Price: The Status and Role of Insurance against Natural Disasters in the United States*, eds. Howard Kunreuther and Richard J. Roth Sr. (Washington, DC: Joseph Henry Press, 1998). See also Howard Kunreuther and Michael Useem, eds., *Learning from Catastrophes: Strategies for Reaction and Response* (Upper Saddle River, NJ: Pearson Education, 2010).

44. There were limited homeowner buyouts in 1973 under the program—NFIP—to reduce repetitive flood loss claims; on the Love Canal: Ted Steinberg, *Acts of God*, 181; on Times Beach: Kathleen J. Tierney, Michael K. Lindell, and Ronald W. Perry, *Facing the Unexpected: Disaster Preparedness and Response in the United States* (Washington, DC: Joseph Henry Press, 2001), 146.

45. McEntire, *Disaster Response and Recovery*, 414.

46. Lucien G. Canton, *Emergency Management: Concepts and Strategies for Effective Programs* (Hoboken, NJ: Wiley, 2007), 184.

47. Ibid., 184–185.

48. McEntire, *Disaster Response and Recovery*, 414.

49. Keith Smith, *Environmental Hazards: Assessing Risk and Reducing Disaster*, 6th ed. (New York: Routledge, 2013), 330.

50. Ibid., 330.

51. Lucien G. Canton, *Emergency Management,* 196. Canton advises, "Written plans do serve a purpose within the (local) program. They document the measures that a community has put in place to deal with risk and can provide continuity in organizations where turnover is high." Ibid., 196. He emphasizes that plans represent an organizational consensus, must be kept current, and must be used as the basis for training and exercises.

52. Smith, *Environmental Hazards,* 6th ed., 80.

53. C. V. Anderson, *The Federal Emergency Management Agency (FEMA)* (New York: Nova Science Publishers, 2003), 49.

54. William R. Cumming and Richard T. Sylves, "FEMA's Place in Policy, Law, and Management: A Hazardous Materials Perspective, 1979–2003," in *Homeland Security Law and Policy,* ed. William C. Nicholson (Springfield, IL: Charles C Thomas, 2005), 34.

55. Haddow and Bullock, *Introduction to Emergency Management,* 2nd ed., 169.

56. Ibid., 170.

57. Cumming and Sylves, "FEMA's Place in Policy, Law, and Management," 34, 36.

58. Anderson, *The Federal Emergency Management Agency,* 52.

59. Haddow and Bullock, *Introduction to Emergency Management,* 2nd ed., 285.

60. Anderson, *The Federal Emergency Management Agency,* 162–163.

61. In 2013, the International Association of Fire Fighters noted, "The SAFER and FIRE grant programs were created by Congress to help address the significant staffing, equipment, training and health and safety needs of fire departments. SAFER provides funding to help pay the costs associated with hiring personnel to maintain safe staffing levels, while FIRE grants fund equipment, training and other fire department needs." International Association of Fire Fighters, "IAFF Legislative Fact Sheet, SAFER and FIRE Grants," February 28, 2014, http://www.iaff .org/politics/legislative/SAFERFIREfactsheet.htm (accessed September 6, 2018).

62. Haddow and Bullock, *Introduction to Emergency Management,* 2nd ed., 68.

63. Federal Emergency Management Agency, "Welcome to the Assistance to Firefighters Grant Program," February 18, 2014, http://www.fema .gov/welcome-assistance-firefighters-grant- program (accessed September 6, 2018).

64. Haddow and Bullock, *Introduction to Emergency Management,* 2nd ed., 285.

65. Lennard G. Kruger, *Assistance to Firefighters Program: Distribution of Fire Grant Funding*, May 26, 2017. See Cornell University IRL School at https://digitalcommons.ilr.cornell.edu/cgi/view content.cgi?article=2932&context=key_workplace

(accessed May 12, 2018). Hereafter Kruger, *Assistance to Firefighters Program: Distribution of Fire Grant Funding.*

66. The first reauthorization was Title XXXVI of the FY2005 Ronald W. Reagan National Defense Authorization Act (P.L. 108-375), which authorized the program through FY2009. The second reauthorization is Title XVIII, Subtitle A of the FY2013 National Defense Authorization Act (P.L. 112-239), which authorizes the program through FY2017 and modifies program rules for disbursing grant money. It has since been reauthorized to 2023.

67. Kruger, *Assistance to Firefighters Program: Distribution of Fire Grant Funding.*

68. Ibid.

69. Ibid.

70. Ibid.

71. EveryCRSReport.com, *Staffing for Adequate Fire and Emergency Response: The SAFER Grant Program*, February 8, 2008–March 27, 2018 RL33375. At https://www.everycrsreport.com/reports/RL33375.html (accessed May 12, 2018).

72. Ibid.

73. See Avi Issacharoff, "Why Did Assad Use Chemical Weapons? Because He Can," *Times of Israel*, April 8, 2018. At https://www.timesofisrael.com/why-did-assad-use-chemical-weapons-because-he-can/ (accessed May 10, 2018).

74. Sam Klein, "Assessing the United States' Bioterrorism Preparation," *CIMSEC*, International Center for International Maritime Security, April 23, 2017, at http://cimsec.org/assessing-united-states-bioterrorism-preparation/32137 (accessed September 30, 2018). Klein adds, "While biological weapons research is a subset of all biological research, the downward [funding] trend in the greater field is not promising; the field must be considered holistically as epidemiology, immunology, and related subfields that can inform biological attack response even if they are not all classified as biological weapons defense research. Because the United States' biological WMD preparedness is inadequate, the United States government should substantially increase its investment in biological weapons response, including private- and public-sector biomedical research, treatment coordination infrastructure, and intelligence-driven threat mitigation." Ibid.

75. This author is proud to be among the certified non-medical shelter worker ranks of the Delaware Medical Reserve Corps (DMRC). Part of that training included FEMA Community Emergency Response Team training. The DMRC is sponsored by Delaware Health and Social Services, Division of Public Health, Emergency Medical Services and Preparedness Section, which has contracted with the University of Delaware School of Nursing to coordinate the three county units. The DMRC is sponsored by the Delaware Health and Social Services, Division of Public Health, Emergency Medical Services and Preparedness Section, which has contracted with the University of Delaware School of Nursing to coordinate the three county units. See Delaware Medical Reserve Corps, home page, at https://sites.udel.edu/delawaremrc/ (accessed May 12, 2018).

76. U.S. Nuclear Regulatory Commission, "The Near-Term Task Force Review of Insights from the Fukushima Dai-ichi Accident, Recommendations for Enhancing Reactor Safety in the 21st Century," 1–82, July 12, 2011.

77. Rutgers University, *Advancing Integration of Health and Community Engagement in Pre-Disaster Recovery and Resilience Planning: Opportunities for Health Impact Assessment*, July 2016. At http://phci.rutgers.edu/wp-content/uploads/2016/07/PHCI-report-Summary-Revised.pdf (accessed May 10, 2018).

78. Ibid.

79. Ibid.

80. Ibid.

81. U.S. Department of Homeland Security, Homeland Security National Preparedness Task Force, *Civil Defense and Homeland Security: A Short History of National Preparedness Efforts* (Washington, DC: U.S. Department of Homeland Security, 2006), 16.

82. Beverly A. Cigler, "Coping with Floods, Lessons from the 1990s," in *Disaster Management in the U.S. and Canada*, eds. Richard T. Sylves and William L. Waugh Jr. (Springfield, IL: Charles C Thomas, 1996), 196–198.

83. Keith Schneider, "The Midwest Flooding; In this Emergency, Agency Wins Praise for Its Response,"

New York Times, July 20, 1993, http://www.nytimes.com/1993/07/20/us/the-midwest-flooding-in-this-emergency-agency-wins-praise-for-its-response.html (accessed September 6, 2018).

84. The author would like to acknowledge that most of this boxed insert is adapted from part of an unpublished paper written by Alex Greer, "Earthquake Preparedness and Response: A Comparison of the United States and Japan" (paper written for POSC/UAPP 656 Politics and Disaster, graduate level, University of Delaware, Newark, May 2010).

85. Japan Meteorological Agency. "The National Meteorological Service of Japan," http://www.jma.go.jp/jma/indexe.html (accessed September 6, 2018).

86. Lucy Birmingham, "Japan's Earthquake Warning System Explained," *Time,* March 18, 2011. http://www.time.com/time/world/article/0,8599,2059780,00.html (accessed September 6, 2018).

87. Ibid. For a concise and humanistic account of the Great East Japan earthquake of March 11, 2011, written by a world-renowned seismologist for the U.S. Geological Survey, see Dr. Lucy Jones, *The Big Ones: How Natural Disasters Have Shaped Us*, Chapter 11, "The Island of Ill Fortune" (New York: Doubleday, a division of Penguin, Random House, LLC, 2018), 187–207.

88. Smith, *Environmental Hazards*, 6th ed., 376–378.

89. Ibid., 377. Note that lightning strikes often knock out electric power facilities and portions of the power grid. Floods often damage industrial and municipal facilities causing hazardous substance or oil discharges into water bodies threatening both humans and the natural environment.

90. Damon P. Coppola, *Introduction to International Disaster Management* (Burlington, MA: Butterworth-Heinemann, 2007), 26.

91. World Nuclear Association, "Fukushima Accident," December 2013, http://www.world-nuclear.org/info/Safety-and-Security/Safety-of-Plants/Fukushima-Accident (accessed September 6, 2018).

92. Tom Zeller, "U.S. Nuclear Plants Have Same Risks, and Backups, as Japan Counterparts," *New York Times*, March 13, 2011, http://www.nytimes.com/2011/03/14/world/asia/14industry.html?ref=global-home&_r=0 (accessed September 6, 2018).

93. Masaharu Kitamura, "Extraction of Lessons from the Fukushima Daiichi Accident Based on a Resilience Engineering Perspective" (proceedings of the Fourth Resilience Engineering Symposium, June 8–10, 2011, Sophia Antipolis, France, 142–174), http://books.openedition.org/pressesmines/1031 (accessed September 6, 2018). Kitamura adds, "Combinatorial events caused by a 'common cause.' This is well-known terminology in the area of PRA (probabilistic risk assessment). Typical examples of an event in this category are earthquakes, floods, fires, etc. At Fukushima, the combined earthquake and tsunami disaster, which had a low probability, actually happened. Note that Units 1 to 4 of the Fukushima NPP would have survived either the earthquake or tsunami alone. Based on the lessons, we can expand our scope to cover a wider class of common causes that may lead to the simultaneous occurrence of severe events. The failure to prevent the Fukushima disaster was caused by incorrectly estimating the probability of the combined occurrence of an earthquake and tsunami. In hindsight, it is clear that the two events are not independent at all." Ibid.

94. Ibid., 14.

95. William J. Petak and Arthur A. Atkisson, *Natural Hazard Risk Assessment and Public Policy* (New York: Springer-Verlag, 1982).

96. Ibid., 76–79.

97. Haddow and Bullock, *Introduction to Emergency Management,* 2nd ed., 66.

98. Richard T. Sylves, "Earthquakes," in *Handbook of Emergency Management*, eds. William L. Waugh Jr. and Ronald W. Hy (Westport, CT: Greenwood Press, 1991), 33–34.

99. UPSeis, Michigan Tech, "How Are Earthquake Magnitudes Measured?" undated. At http://www.geo.mtu.edu/UPSeis/intensity.html (accessed May 12, 2018).

100. Ibid.

101. Ibid.

102. Ibid.

103. Brett Israel, "How Are Earthquakes Measured?" LiveScience, August 20, 2010. At https://www

.livescience.com/32779-measuring-earthquake-magnitude-richter-scale.html (accessed May 12, 2018).

104. Ibid.

105. Ibid.

106. Federal Emergency Management Agency, "HAZUS, FEMA's Software Program for Estimating Potential Losses from Disasters," February 28, 2014, http://www.fema.gov/hazus (accessed September 6, 2018).

107. HAZUS News, HAZUS 4.2 Now Available: On January 29, 2018. This HAZUS version is available on the MSC Download page of the site. This release is a full-versioned software release with several key highlights: HAZUS 4.2 is compatible with ArcGIS 10.5.1; major processing time reductions for hydrology and hydraulics within level 1 flood; additional supported formats for level 2 flood depth grid import; high resolution ShakeMaps now compatible, with faster import times; restoration of the Fire Following Earthquake (FFE) module; and improvements to the Comprehensive Data Management System (CDMS) for easier import of user data. HAZUS 4.2 also includes an update from North American Datum 1983 (NAD83) to the World Geodetic System 1984 (WGS84) to better support U.S. territories and long-term goals for international hazard modeling. See FEMA, HAZUS News, last updated: April 24, 2018. At https://www.fema.gov/hazus (accessed May 10, 2018).

108. The U.S. Geological Survey, Earthquake Hazards Program, "Earthquake Notification Service," undated. At https://earthquake.usgs.gov/ens/ (accessed May 10, 2018).

109. MCEER is not the only NSF-supported earthquake engineering research center. There is also the Mid-America Earthquake Center, run by the University of Illinois at Urbana-Champaign, and the Pacific Earthquake Engineering Research Center, administered by the University of California at Berkeley. See National Research Council, *Facing Hazards and Disasters*, 30.

110. Haddow and Bullock, *Introduction to Emergency Management*, 2nd ed., 67.

111. See Keith Smith, *Environmental Hazards*, 6th ed., 247–250, 258, 260–261. Smith examines tornadoes as physical phenomena, reviews issues of life loss and damage from tornadoes, and takes up the political and social issues of local tornado preparedness.

112. Loran B. Smith and David T. Jervis, "Tornadoes," in Waugh and Hy, *Handbook of Emergency Management*, 106–128.

113. U.S. National Weather Service, National Oceanic and Atmospheric Administration, "The Enhanced Fujita Scale (EF Scale)," undated. Norman, OK. At https://www.weather.gov/oun/efscale (accessed May 12, 2018).

114. Ibid.

115. Ibid.

116. Ibid.

117. See Richard T. Sylves, *Disaster Policy and Politics*, 1st ed. (Washington, DC: CQ Press, 2008), 126.

118. U.S. Federal Communications Commission, "Guide, Emergency Alert System," http://www.fcc.gov/guides/emergency-alert-system-eas (accessed September 6, 2018).

119. NOAA National Severe Storms Laboratory, "About NSSL," http://www.nssl.noaa.gov/about (accessed September 6, 2018).

120. NOAA National Severe Storm Laboratory, "Tornado Research: Basic Convective and Mesoscale Research," http://www.nssl.noaa.gov/research/tornadoes (accessed September 6, 2018).

121. Ibid.

122. Portions of this section were adapted from Sylves, *Disaster Policy and Politics*, 1st ed., 128.

123 U.S. Army Corps of Engineers, Office of History, *The History of the U.S. Army Corps of Engineers* (Stockton, CA: University Press of the Pacific, 2004).

124. See Orrin H. Pilkey and Katherine L. Dixon, *The Corps and the Shore* (Washington, DC: Island Press, 1996).

125. U.S. Department of Homeland Security, "Homeland Security Presidential Directive 7: Critical Infrastructure Identification, Prioritization, and

Protection," December 17, 2003, http://www.dhs.gov/homeland-security-presidential-directive-7 (accessed September 6, 2018).

126. See Gary C. Kessler, "The Impact of Cyber-Security on Critical Infrastructure Protection," *in Critical Issues in Homeland Security*, eds. James D. Ramsay and Linda Kiltz (Boulder, CO: Westview Press, 2014), 237–238, and Sylves, *Disaster Policy and Politics*, 1st ed., 129.

127. The Disaster Relief Act of 1974 was one of the first laws to advance disaster mitigation through augmented federal post-disaster funding to states and localities.

128. Robert Bolin and Lois Stanford, *The Northridge Earthquake: Vulnerability and Disaster* (London: Routledge, 1999).

129. Thomas A. Birkland, *After Disaster: Agenda Setting, Public Policy, and Focusing Events* (Washington, DC: Georgetown University Press, 1997). See also Thomas A. Birkland, *Lessons of Disaster: Policy Change after Catastrophic Events* (Washington, DC: Georgetown University Press, 2006).

130. President Barack Obama, "Remarks by the President on Climate Change," at Georgetown University, Washington, DC, June 25, 2013, http://www.whitehouse.gov/the-press-office/2013/06/25/remarks-president-climate-change (accessed September 6, 2018).

131. Emily Holden, "Climate Change Skeptics Run the Trump Administration," *POLITICO*, March 7, 2018. At https://www.politico.com/story/2018/03/07/trump-climate-change-deniers-443533 (accessed May 10, 2018).

132. Ibid.

Chapter 6

1. The late Deil Wright deserves credit for advancing and researching American Intergovernmental Relations. His fine work has been carried on in Laurence K. O'Toole, Jr., and Robert K. Christensen, *American Intergovernmental Relations*, 5th ed. (Thousand Oaks, CA: CQ Press, an imprint of Sage, 2013).

2. David R. Morgan and Robert E. England, *Managing Urban America*, 4th ed. (Chatham, NJ: Chatham House, 1996), 41.

3. As of 2016, there were 3,007 counties, 64 parishes, 18 organized boroughs, 11 census areas, 41 independent cities, and the District of Columbia for a total of 3,142 counties and county-equivalents in the United States, https://www.google.com/search?rlz=1C1CHWA_enUS634US641&ei=d8L4Wo7RF8Kb5gLwvqKwDg&q=how+many+counties+are+there+in+the+united+states&oq=How+many+counties+are+there+&gs_l=psy-ab.1.1.0l10.3197.16987.0.18984.122.57.0.0.0.0.250.4888.20j22j3.46.0....0...1.1.64.psy-ab..93.26.2710.0..33i160k1j0i131k1j0i67k1.55.5ETcirAVOZ4 (accessed May 13, 2018).

4. Release Information, CB12-161, Thursday, August 30, 2012. "Census Bureau Reports There Are 89,004 Local Governments in the United States," https://www.census.gov/newsroom/releases/archives/governments/cb12-161.html (accessed May 13, 2018). In 2012, 89,004 local governments existed in the United States, down from 89,476 in the last census of governments conducted in 2007. Local governments included 3,031 counties (down from 3,033 in 2007), 19,522 municipalities (up from 19,492 in 2007), 16,364 townships (down from 16,519 in 2007), 37,203 special districts (down from 37,381 in 2007), and 12,884 independent school districts (down from 13,051 in 2007). Ibid.

5. Under the U.S. and Marshall Islands Compact of Free Association, an instrument approved in 1983 and amended in 2003, taking effect in 2004, "the U.S. established a Disaster Assistance Emergency Fund. Of the total grant assistance made available under subsection (a) of this section, an amount of $200,000 shall be provided annually, with an equal contribution from the Government of the Republic of the Marshall Islands, as a contribution to a Disaster Assistance Emergency Fund ("DAEF"). Any funds from the DAEF may be used only for assistance and rehabilitation resulting from disasters and emergencies. The funds will be accessed upon declaration of a State of Emergency by the Government of the Republic of the Marshall Islands, with the concurrence of the United States Chief of Mission to the Republic of the Marshall Islands. Administration of the DAEF shall be governed by the Fiscal Procedures Agreement." See U.S. Department of State, "Compact of Free Association Agreement between the United States of America

and the Marshall Islands Amending the Agreement of June 25, 1983, concerning the Compact of Free Association, As Amended Signed at Majuro April 30, 2003." (Effective May 1, 2004), 19, https://www.state.gov/documents/organization/173999.pdf (accessed May 13, 2018). The Republic of the Marshall Islands receives a yearly U.S. contribution to its disaster assistance emergency fund, and that nation retains the right to seek presidential declarations of major disaster and emergency. For example, President Obama issued that nation a major disaster for drought in 2016.

6   "Everything You Need to Know About the Territories of the United States," June 27, 2013, https://everything-everywhere.com/everything-you-need-to-know-about-the-territories-of-the-united-states/https://everything-everywhere.com/everything-you-need-to-know-about-the-territories-of-the-united-states/ (accessed May 13, 2018).

7. *Encyclopaedia Britannica*, "Trust Territory of the Pacific Islands," December 28, 2015, https://www.britannica.com/place/Trust-Territory-of-the-Pacific-Islands (accessed May 13, 2018).

8. In early 2008, the DHS updated, revised, and renamed the National Response Plan (NRP). The NRP was to be referred to as the National Response Framework (NRF). In June 2016, DHS and FEMA released the National Planning Frameworks: Prevention, Protection, Mitigation, Response and Recovery. These frameworks were to be developed for the National Preparedness System.

9. Thomas J. Anton, *American Federalism and Public Policy* (New York: Random House, 1989). See also David B. Walker, *The Rebirth of Federalism: Slouching toward Washington* (Chatham, NJ: Chatham House, 1995).

10. Peter J. May, *Recovering from Catastrophes: Federal Disaster Relief Policy and Politics* (Westport, CT: Greenwood Press, 1985). See also Peter J. May and Walter W. Williams, *Disaster Policy Implementation: Managing Programs under Shared Governance* (New York: Plenum Press, 1986).

11. FEMA, Fact Sheet, "National Urban Search & Rescue Response System," July 2015., https://www.documentcloud.org/documents/3988843-FEMA-Urban-Search-and-Rescue-task-force-fact-sheet.html (accessed May 13, 2018).

12. Ibid.

13. Ibid.

14. See DHS-FEMA, *Typed Resource Definitions Search and Rescue Resources*, November 2005, https://www.fema.gov/pdf/emergency/nims/508-8_search_and_rescue_resources.pdf (accessed May 13, 2018).

15. Lt. Wayne Cooke, Memphis Fire Department, for *Firehouse.Com* News, "Sixteen USAR Task Forces have been dispatched to help with myriad of duties following Hurricane Harvey," August 27, 2017, https://www.firehouse.com/rescue/news/12363165/rescue-teams-from-across-the-county-respond-to-tx (accessed May 13, 2018).

16. Ibid.

17. Ibid.

18. Ibid.

19. Ibid.

20. There are exceptions. For example, in cases of bioterror attack, federal law provides for federal agencies to direct state and local governments in a command and control fashion. In cases of national emergency, as might be expected after a weapon of mass destruction attack on the nation, federal authority is paramount. Some authorities contend that the NRF and NIMS embody command and control procedures, which they in fact do. However, it should not then be assumed that the federal government or federal agency officials are therefore in command and control relationships with state and local officials under either the NRF or the NIMS.

21. Charles R. Wise and Rania Nader, "Organizing the Federal System for Homeland Security: Problems, Issues, and Dilemmas," *Public Administration Review* 62 (September 2002): 44–57.

22. James Lee Witt and J. Morgan, *Stronger in the Broken Places: Nine Lessons for Turning Crisis into Triumph* (New York: Times Books, 2002).

23. DHS-FEMA, "Unit Three Overview of Federal Disaster Assistance," *A Citizen's Guide to Disaster Assistance*, 3–11, https://training.fema.gov/emiweb/downloads/is7unit_3.pdf (accessed May 24, 2018).

24. FEMA, "Fire Management Assistance Grant Program," October 26, 2015, https://www.fema.gov/fire-management-assistance-grant-program (accessed May 21, 2018).

25. Ibid.

26. Ibid.

27. FEMA, "FEMA-State Agreement–2017 Fire Management Assistance Grant Program, State of New Mexico," signed by New Mexico's Governor on July 19, 2017, https://www.fema.gov/media-library-data/1502899392296-beca921e0be140fd72cade474fbf46b3/2017NewMexicoSignedFSA.pdf (accessed May 15, 2018).

28. George D. Haddow and Jane A. Bullock, *Introduction to Emergency Management,* 2nd ed. (Boston: Butterworth-Heinemann, 2006), 5.

29. U.S. Department of Homeland Security, "About DHS," September 17, 2017, https://www.dhs.gov/about-dhs (accessed May 15, 2018).

30. To date, FEMA permanent staff has never exceeded 5 percent of the total DHS permanent staff.

31. *Recruited* may be too strong a word because it may well be that state and local officials were anxious to join the federal effort and do what they could to prevent future 9/11-scale attacks on the nation.

32. U.S. Fire Administration, "National Fire Department Registry Quick Facts," May 15, 2018, https://apps.usfa.fema.gov/registry/summary/ (accessed May 21, 2018).

33. National Law Enforcement Officers Memorial Fund, "Law Enforcement Facts," 2018, http://www.nleomf.org/facts/enforcement/?mfc_popup=t (accessed May 21, 2018). For a more detailed breakdown of police personnel information, see U.S. Department of Justice, Office of Justice Programs, Bureau of Justice Statistics, "National Sources of Law Enforcement Employment Data," Revised October 4, 2016, https://www.bjs.gov/content/pub/pdf/nsleed.pdf (accessed May 21, 2018).

34. For a classic work on federal reorganization politics, see Harold Seidman, *Politics, Position and Power: The Dynamics of Federal Organization,* 5th ed. (New York: Oxford University Press, 1998).

35. U.S. Department of Homeland Security, "State Homeland Security and Emergency Services," as of March 21, 2017, https://www.dhs.gov/state-homeland-security-and-emergency-services (accessed May 15, 2018).

36. Alice R. Buchalter and Patrick Miller, *A Guide to Directors of Homeland Security, Emergency Management, and Military Departments in the States and Territories of the United States,* Federal Research Division, Library of Congress under an Interagency Agreement with the Commission on the National Guard and Reserves, (December 2007), 3–4, https://www.loc.gov/rr/frd/pdf-files/CNGR_Guide-State-Directors-Rev.pdf (accessed May 15, 2018).

37. Ibid.

38. Keith Bea, *Federal Stafford Act Disaster Assistance: Presidential Declarations, Eligible Activities, and Funding,* CRS Report RL33053 (Washington, DC: Congressional Research Service, 2006), 10.

39. Because FEMA recommendations to the president are protected by executive privilege, it is not yet possible to know how many times, if ever, a president has denied a governor a FEMA-recommended category of disaster assistance. That said, a study issued by GAO examined approvals and turndowns of governor requests for FEMA Individual Assistance from 2008 to 2016. See U.S. Government Accountability Office, "Federal Disaster Assistance: Individual Assistance Requests Often Granted but FEMA Could Better Document Factors Considered," GAO-18-366, May 31, 2018 (Washington, DC: GAO, 2018), 1–62, https://www.gao.gov/products/GAO-18-366 (accessed May 31, 2018).

40. David A. McEntire, *Disaster Response and Recovery* (Hoboken, NJ: Wiley, 2007), 252–257.

41. Keith Bea, *Federal Stafford Act Disaster Assistance,* 7–8.

42. Ibid., 9.

43. Haddow and Bullock, *Introduction to Emergency Management,* 2nd ed., 5. Remember, almost all major disaster declarations first require a gubernatorial request and accompanying findings

and certifications. Emergency declaration documentation requirements are less rigorous. The president may even issue an emergency declaration without a gubernatorial request if there is a significant federal interest in the disaster or if the federal government is in some manner liable for the disaster itself. Also, specific thresholds or calculations of past averages are not considered for emergency declarations, but FEMA officials do assess whether all other resources and authorities available to meet the crisis are inadequate before recommending that the president issue an emergency declaration.

44. FEMA, "State/Indian Tribal Government Administrative Plan, Individual and Households Program (OtherNeedsAssistance)," July 16, 2014, https://www.fema.gov/media-library/assets/documents/31206 (accessed May 16, 2018).

45. Ibid.

46. FEMA, "Disaster-Specific Memorandum of Understanding," 2013, https://www.fema.gov/media-library-data/1416583062704-86cb8bebe23906b594ce14860d86f8af/Disaster-Specific_MOU_updated_weblinks.pdf (accessed May 16, 2018).

47. Ibid.

48. Ibid.

49. Lucien G. Canton, *Emergency Management: Concepts and Strategies for Effective Programs* (Hoboken, NJ: Wiley, 2007), 296.

50. Ibid., 297.

51. Guy E. Daines, "Planning, Training, and Exercising," in *Emergency Management: Principles and Practice*, eds. Thomas E. Drabek and Gerard J. Hoetmer (Washington, DC: International City Management Association, 1991), 164–165.

52. John Fass Morton, *Next-Generation Homeland Security: Network Federalism and the Course to National Preparedness* (Annapolis, MD: Naval Institute Press, 2012), 243.

53. Heather Perkins, Council of State Governments, "Why States Join Interstate Compacts," September 6, 2017, http://knowledgecenter.csg.org/kc/content/why-states-join-interstate-compacts (May 30, 2018).

54. EMAC, Emergency Management Assistance Compact, "How EMAC Works," National Emergency Management Association, 2018, https://www.emacweb.org/index.php/learn-about-emac/how-emac-works (accessed May 22, 2018).

55. Ibid.

56. Ibid.

57. Ibid.

58. Ibid.

59. DHS-FEMA, "Unit Three Overview of Federal Disaster Assistance," *A Citizen's Guide to Disaster Assistance*, 3–4, undated, https://training.fema.gov/emiweb/downloads/is7unit_3.pdf (accessed May 24, 2018).

60. See William L. Waugh Jr. and Ronald John Hy, "The Utility of All-Hazards Programs," in *Handbook of Emergency Management*, eds. William L. Waugh Jr. and Ronald John Hy (Westport, CT: Greenwood Press, 1991).

61. One of the best ways to get a sense of the immense array of ESF role assignments, crosswalks, and agency coordination schemes in place in 2018 is to visit FEMA, "Emergency Support Function Annexes," July 8, 2016, https://www.fema.gov/media-library/assets/documents/25512 (accessed May 26, 2018). Use the home page to visit pages describing what is to be done and who has responsibility in each of the 15 ESFs. Each Annex runs to 3–4 pages, so it was impossible to reproduce each of these annexes for this chapter or for an appendix. A key takeaway in reviewing these ESFs is that a great many DHS offices and organizations outside of FEMA now have a much greater role in national response than they did under the pre-2016 National Response Framework. This raises decision costs, imposes new coordination demands, requires more information sharing with many more DHS organizational partners, and potentially slows the federal response to incidents and disasters.

62. See FEMA, "Emergency Support Functions (ESF) (5)," July 8, 2016, https://www.fema.gov/media-library/resources-documents/collections/533 (accessed May 26, 2018).

63. See Walker, *The Rebirth of Federalism*, 23.

64. David A. Ishida, "Federal Role and Response to Disaster,",http://slideplayer.com/slide/5752941/and https://www.google.com/search?rlz=1C1CHWA_enUS634US641&tbm=isch&q=Emergency+Support+Function+Teams&chips=q:emergency+support+function+teams,online_chips:stafford+act&sa=X&ved=0ahUKEwjWoOXKjIvbAhXSk1kKHVD2CSMQ4lYIMSgK&biw=1600&bih=794&dpr=1#imgrc=9yEfqViAM3-CdM (both accessed May 16, 2018).

65. The NIMS document is available at http://www.fema.gov/nims.

66. At least one early draft of the NIMS produced by the DHS and others was criticized for failing to consult enough state and local emergency management officials.

67. *9/11 Commission Report: Final Report of the National Commission on Terrorist Attacks upon the United States* (New York: Norton, 2004).

68. Holly Harrington, "A Message from Michael D. Brown," *Transitioning Newsletter* (a weekly electronic newsletter with DHS transition information for FEMA employees), March 5, 2003.

69. Donald W. Walsh et al., *National Incident Management System: Principles and Practice*, 2nd ed. (Sudbury, MA: Jones & Bartlett, 2012), xxv.

70. Ibid., 24.

71. Kathleen J. Tierney, "Recent Developments in U.S. Homeland Security Policies and Their Implications for the Management of Extreme Events," in *Handbook of Disaster Research*, eds. Havidan Rodriguez, Enrico L. Quarantelli, and Russell R. Dynes (New York: Springer, 2007).

72. Canton, *Emergency Management*, 28.

73. *9/11 Commission Report* and the Gilmore Commission, Fifth Annual Report to the President and the Congress of the Advisory Panel to Assess Domestic Response Capabilities for Terrorism Involving Weapons of Mass Destruction (the so-called Gilmore Commission), in *Forging America's New Normalcy: Securing Our Homeland, Preserving Our Liberty* (Arlington, VA: RAND, 2003).

74. Samuel Clovis Jr., "Promises Unfulfilled: The Suboptimization of Homeland Security National Preparedness," *Homeland Security Affairs* IV, no. 3 (October 2008): 14–15, http://www.hsaj.org/?fullarticle=4.3.3 (accessed September 7, 2018).

75. Richard T. Sylves, "The Politics and Budgeting of Federal Emergency Management," in *Disaster Management in the U.S. and Canada*, 2nd ed., eds. Richard T. Sylves and William L. Waugh Jr. (Springfield, IL: Charles C. Thomas, 1996), 26–45.

76. See Rutherford H. Platt, "Federalizing Disasters: From Compassion to Entitlement," in *Disasters and Democracy: The Politics of Extreme Natural Events*, ed. Rutherford B. Platt (Washington, DC: Island Press, 1999).

77. Local governments in most states are obligated to pay some share of the state–local match. Some state governments require their local governments to pay the entire state–local match. However, most states have some type of arrangement for splitting payment of the state–local match between localities and the state government. When the president decides to significantly reduce the state–local match for a specific major disaster, perhaps approving a 90 percent/10 percent federal/state–local match as was done for Hurricane Katrina, states may have a further incentive to shoulder most of the match to maximize federal assistance. However, the incidence of the state-matching subsidy needs to be considered. In other words, sometimes states replace revenue dedicated to a generous state–local match by asking counties receiving disaster funds to increase their respective local sales tax by some percentage with the resulting revenue stream directed back to the state government.

78. See James F. Miskel, *Disaster Response and Homeland Security: What Works, What Doesn't* (Westport, CT: Praeger, 2006).

79. Bea, *Federal Stafford Act Disaster Assistance*, 3. See Cornell University Law School. Legal Information Institute. 42 U.S. Code § 5121 - Congressional findings and declarations. *Robert T. Stafford Disaster Assistance and Emergency Relief Act of 1988*, as Amended, 42 *U.S. Code*, title 42, chap. 68, sec. 5121, para. B, http://www.law.cornell.edu/uscode/text/42/5121 (accessed September 7, 2018). "All requests for a declaration by the President that a major disaster exists shall be made by the Governor of the affected State. Such a request shall

be based on a finding that the disaster is of such severity and magnitude that effective response is beyond the capabilities of the State and the affected local governments and that Federal assistance is necessary." *United States Code*, V. 26, Title 42, The Public Health and Welfare, (2), "Major Disaster" (Washington, DC: Government Printing Office, 2006).

80. FEMA, "New Public Assistance Delivery Model," FEMA Graphic, October 21, 2016, https://www .fema.gov/new-public-assistance-delivery-model (accessed May 16, 2018).

81. Bea, *Federal Stafford Act Disaster Assistance,* 4.

82. See Google, DHS-FEMA, Public Assistance Our Largest Grant Program graphic, https://www.google .com/search?rlz=1C1CHWA_enUS634US641&biw= 1600&bih=794&tbs=qdr%3Ay&tbm=isch&sa=1&ei= bfMOW52SBI6O8APZ_ZbYDQ&q=Public+Assis tance+Our+Largest+Grant+Program&oq=Public+ Assistance+Our+Largest+Grant+Program&gs_l= img.12...10308.11312.0.14107.5.5.0.0.0.0.146.656 .0j5.5.0....0...1c.1.64.img..0.0.0....0 .aRkdnierF9Q#imgrc=OOK8bxTC_lJvHM (accessed May 30, 2018)

83. American Red Cross, "Disaster Relief," https:// www.redcross.org/about-us/our-work/disaster-relief.html (accessed September 7, 2018).

84. National Voluntary Organizations Active in Disaster, "Who We Are," https://www.nvoad.org/about-us/ (accessed September 7, 2018).

85. Jane A. Bullock et al., *Introduction to Homeland Security,* 2nd ed. (Boston: Butterworth-Heinemann, 2006), 117.

86. Ibid., 116–117.

87. FEMA, Individual and Community Preparedness Division, March 12, 2018, https://www.fema.gov/ individual-and-community-preparedness-division (accessed May 30, 2018).

88. Ibid.

89. FEMA, "FEMA Careers: Reservists (On-call)," undated, https://careers.fema.gov/oncall (accessed May 28, 2018).

90. Ibid.

91. Ibid.

92. Ibid.

93. One of FEMA's outstanding reservists is Robert Klebs, a licensed California general building contractor who has for more than 25 years worked for FEMA in this capacity. He has deployed to several Pacific territorial island disasters for FEMA, once sleeping overnight in a bathtub on the beach owing to typhoon devastation. He spent several months living in a rural flood-ravaged Pennsylvania town. There from his desk in a local fire hall, he answered questions about individual assistance application. After the 1994 Northridge earthquake, Klebs served as a FEMA inspector visiting victims in the field for the housing arm of FEMA's Individual and Family Grant program (today the Individual and Households program). With this author, Klebs wrote about his experiences working the Northridge disaster. See, Robert W. Klebs and Richard T. Sylves, "The Northridge Earthquake: Memoir of a FEMA Inspector," in *Disaster Management in the U.S. and Canada*, 2nd ed., Richard T. Sylves and William L. Waugh, Jr., eds. (Springfield, IL: Charles C. Thomas, Publishers, 1996), 126–160. Recently, Klebs worked for FEMA in addressing damage from the Coffee Fire in California.

94. FEMA, Individual and Community Preparedness Division, March 12, 2018, https://www.fema.gov/ individual-and-community-preparedness-division (accessed May 30, 2018).

95. Ibid.

96. See Dennis Mileti, *Disasters by Design: A Reassessment of Natural Hazards in the United States* (Washington, DC: National Academies Press, 1999) and Kathleen Tierney, *The Social Roots of Risk* (Stanford, CA: Stanford University Press, 2014).

97. National Voluntary Organizations Active in Disaster (NVOAD),

98. U.S. Department of Homeland Security, Ready.gov, "Plan Ahead for Disasters," undated, https://www .ready.gov/voluntary-organizations-active-disaster (accessed May 28, 2018).

99. Ibid.

100. Ibid.

101. Ibid.

102. Ibid.

103. NVOAD, "VOAD Members," copyright 2014, https://www.nvoad.org/voad-members/ (accessed May 28, 2018).

104. There are many studies of federal contracting. Common challenges involve meeting cross-cutting federal requirements of laws having little or nothing to do with homeland security or emergency management, amassing and completing the documentation required in the application process, answering questions posed by federal officials who at various points read and evaluate the application, meeting federal tax reporting rules and requirements, proving the corporation applying is in good standing with the federal government in its other government grant transactions, divulging information about ownership of the company and its subsidiaries domestically and internationally, complying with frequent government reporting requirements, facilitating record keeping, and cooperating with government audits of funds received under the grant, etc. See U.S. Government Accountability Office, "2017 Disaster Contracting: Observations on Federal Contracting for Response and Recovery Efforts," February 2018, GAO-18-335 (Washington, DC: GAO, 2018), 1–23.

105. In 2012, FEMA discontinued its Disaster Assistance Employee (DAE) program and rehired many of the released DAEs under a new employment title. There are two sides to the matter of DAEs. Some DAEs complained that they were not appreciated by FEMA, got little or no health or injury insurance protection when FEMA-deployed, were poorly matched in terms of their respective skill sets to tasks assigned, and often were awkwardly demobilized by FEMA. Conversely, FEMA officials complained that the cost and labor of recruiting, selecting, and maintaining lists of qualified DAEs, many of whom had high turnover rates or who incurred some incapacity or aged out of safe deployment, was substantial. DAE travel and deployment expenses were also significant for a cash-strapped FEMA. There may have also been a better economy of scale in hiring contractors to directly do DAE work or compile and manage local and region lists of qualified DAE-type volunteers situated closer to disaster sites.

106. The DHS Office of the Inspector General maintains a website that displays the investigations and reports it has conducted, a share of which involve problems or misconduct of government contractors, as well as mismanagement of contracts by state and local emergency management agencies. U.S. Department of Homeland Security, Office of Inspector General, "Component: Federal Emergency Management Agency (FEMA)," http://www.oig.dhs.gov/index.php?option=com_content&view=article&id=25&Itemid=38 (accessed September 7, 2018).

107. Project on Government Oversight, "Federal Contractor Misconduct Database," http://www.contractormisconduct.org (accessed September 7, 2018).

108. William L. Waugh Jr. and Richard T. Sylves, "Organizing the War on Terrorism," special issue, *Public Administration Review* 62 (September 2002): 81–89.

Chapter 7

1. "Security-focused" refers to imbuing emergency management with national security and state secrecy duties and obligations.

2. Patrick S. Roberts, *Disasters and the American State: How Politicians, Bureaucrats, and the Public Prepare for the Unexpected* (New York: Cambridge University Press, 2013), 9 and 11.

3. An exception might be the case of municipal emergency plans for protecting foreign embassies and legations within their jurisdictions. Others might be aviation security at a municipal airport, special municipal functions that fall to cities situated on national borders, cooperation in local law enforcement relevant to addressing international narcotic or drug interdiction, and certain port security functions.

4. Civil servants are not trained or compensated to enter danger zones that pose a significant risk to their health and welfare. According to William Cumming, "It is an Occupational Safety and Health criminal law violation to send untrained, unprotected workers into harm's way." William R. Cumming (FEMA, Office of General Counsel, retired) e-mail to the author, June 2, 2007.

5. For an excellent exposition on what the military offers in the way of post-disaster support, see Gregory M. Huckabee, "Partnering with the Department of Defense for Improved Homeland Security," in *Homeland Security Law and Policy*, ed. William C. Nicholson (Springfield, IL: Charles C Thomas, 2005), 164.

6. Ibid.

7. The National Guard is composed of the Army National Guard, the Air National Guard, and reserve military people.

8. Ibid.

9. The White House, President George W. Bush, "Chapter Four: A Week of Crisis (August 29–September 5)," http://georgewbush-whitehouse.archives.gov/reports/katrina-lessons-learned/chapter4.html (accessed September 10, 2018). Active-duty military and National Guard personnel provided critical emergency response and security support to the Gulf Coast during the height of the crisis. State active duty and Title 32 National Guard forces that deployed to Louisiana and Mississippi operated under the command of their respective governors. Title 10 active-duty forces, on the other hand, fell under the command of the president and had more limited civil response authority. On August 30, Deputy Secretary of Defense Gordon England authorized U.S. Northern Command (USNORTHCOM) and the joint chiefs of staff to take all appropriate measures to plan and conduct disaster relief operations in support of FEMA. USNORTHCOM established Joint Task Force Katrina (JTF-Katrina) at Camp Shelby to coordinate the growing military response to the disaster. By September 1, JTF-Katrina, commanded by LTG Honoré, included approximately 3,000 active-duty personnel in the disaster area; within four days, that number climbed to 14,232 active-duty personnel. LTG Honoré's leadership, combined with DOD resources, manpower, and advanced planning, contributed to the military's success in the federal response, especially in areas such as search and rescue, security, and logistical support. Ibid.

10. Ibid.

11. James Lee Witt, "Military Role in Natural Disaster Response," *Disaster Preparedness* 1, no. 1 (Summer 2006).

12. WTOP, Washington's Top News, posting *The Associated Press*, "Military Mission in Puerto Rico after Hurricane Was Better than Critics Say but Suffered Flaws," March 30, 2018, https://wtop.com/national/2018/03/military-mission-in-puerto-rico-after-hurricane-was-better-than-critics-say-but-suffered-flaws/ (accessed June 2, 2018). Hereafter, WTOP, AP, "Military Mission in Puerto Rico after Hurricane Was Better than Critics Say but Suffered Flaws."

13. Puerto Rico has its own National Guard, and soldiers in that body responded to the disaster on orders from the PR governor. Consequently, there were in fact American soldiers on scene in the immediate aftermath of Hurricane Maria's impact.

14. Dan Lamothe, "Maria Hit 9 Days Ago. Less than Half of the Puerto Rico National Guard is on Duty." *The Washington Post*, September 29, 2017, https://www.washingtonpost.com/news/checkpoint/wp/2017/09/29/maria-hit-9-days-ago-less-than-half-of-the-puerto-rico-national-guard-is-on-duty/?utm_term=.2858d2e18bb3 (accessed June 2, 2018).

15. Ibid.

16. WTOP, AP, "Military Mission in Puerto Rico after Hurricane Was Better than Critics Say but Suffered Flaws." The Title 10 parenthetical insert was added by the author of this textbook.

17. Ibid.

18. Ibid. Title 10 inserted by this author.

19. Ibid.

20. Ibid.

21. Ibid.

22. Ibid.

23. Arelis R. Hernandez, "New Puerto Rico Data Shows Deaths Increased by 1,400 after Hurricane Maria," *Washington Post*, reprinted by the *Chicago Tribune*, June 1, 2018, http://www.chicagotribune.com/news/nationworld/ct-puerto-rico-hurricane

-maria-death-toll-20180601-story.html (accessed June 5, 2018).

24. David Emery, Snopes, "What Was the Actual Death Toll from Hurricane Maria in Puerto Rico?" June 4, 2018, https://www.snopes.com/news/2018/06/04/death-toll-hurricane-maria-puerto-rico/ (accessed June 5, 2018).

25. George Washington University, Milken Institute School of Public Health and University of Puerto Rico Graduate School of Public Health, iii, "Ascertainment of the Estimated Excess Mortality from Hurricane Maria in Puerto Rico," August 29, 2018, iii, at https://publichealth.gwu.edu/sites/default/files/downloads/projects/PRstudy/Acertainment (accessed October 2, 2018).

26. Ibid., ii.

27. WTOP, AP, "Military Mission in Puerto Rico after Hurricane Was Better than Critics Say but Suffered Flaws."

28. Ibid.

29. Ibid.

30. Ibid.

31. Ibid.

32. Ibid.

33. Ibid.

34. Ibid.

35. Please note that this research stemmed from online searches of official state HS & EM agency websites of all 50 states and the District of Columbia. Several of these websites were incomplete, poorly maintained, and irregularly updated. This tended to be the case when the state HS or EM office was imbedded in a much larger department handling multiple missions and purposes. Care should be taken in interpreting the data of Table 6-1. Also, newer and better state agency websites may replace outmoded old ones, particularly after reorganizations or gubernatorial elections.

36. See U.S. history.org, "The Declaration of Independence," http://www.ushistory.org/declaration/document/ (accessed June 8, 2018).

37. Kurt A. Heppard and Steve G. Green, "Department of Defense Capabilities in Homeland and Transportation Security," United States Air Force Academy (paper presented at the Annual Conference of the American Society for Public Administration, Denver, March/April 2006).

38. Ibid. See also M. C. Hammond, "The *Posse Comitatus* Act: A Principle in Need of Renewal," *Washington University Law Quarterly* 75, no. 20 (1997).

39. See James C. Holloway, "Are State & Local Emergency Response Agencies Exceedingly Militarized?" (unpublished paper for the author's EMSE 6305, Introduction to Crisis and Emergency Management, Fall 2012). See also Patrick S. Roberts, Robert Ward, and Gary Wamsley, "The Evolving Federal Role in Emergency Management: Policies and Processes," in *Emergency Management: The American Experience 1900–2010*, 2nd ed., ed. Claire B. Rubin (Boca Raton, FL: CRC Press, 2012), 270.

40. Merriam-Webster Dictionary, "martial law," 2018, https://www.merriam-webster.com/dictionary/martial%20law (accessed June 10, 2018).

41. There are certain special exceptions, but these relate to primarily military purposes as might apply under the Uniform Code of Military Justice, or which involve the authority of a commander on a military base, or that involve protection of state secrets or protection of military people and Defense Department property. See Huckabee, "Partnering with the Department of Defense for Improved Homeland Security," 171.

42. James Jay Carafano, "Catastrophic Disaster and the Future of the Military Response," *Disaster Preparedness* 1, no. 1 (Summer 2006).

43. George D. Haddow, Jane A. Bullock, and Damon P. Coppola, *Introduction to Emergency Management*, 4th ed. (Boston: Butterworth-Heinemann, 2011), 11 and 180.

44. Hammond, "The *Posse Comitatus* Act," 953. Weapons of mass destruction (WMD) are, in military terms, actually chemical, biological, nuclear, and radiological weapons (CBNR). However, the Department of Homeland Security defines a WMD as a "weapon capable of a high order of destruction and/or being used in such a manner as to destroy large numbers of people or an amount of property." See Bruce Oliver Newsome and Jack A. Jarmon, *A Practical Guide to Homeland Security and Emergency Management* (Thousand Oaks, CA: Sage CQ Press, 2016), 168.

Newsome and Jarmon add that in popular culture and judicial prosecutions, explosive weapons that rely on blast effects "have been conflated or are confused with weapons of mass destruction." Ibid.

45. Heppard and Green, "Department of Defense Capabilities."

46. Katherine M. Peters and Jason Vest, "Calling in the Cavalry," *Government Executive,* October 1, 2005, http://www.govexec.com/features/1005-01/1005-01s1.htm (accessed September 10, 2018). See also Heppard and Green, "Department of Defense Capabilities."

47. Miskel, *Disaster Response and Homeland Security,* 55.

48. See Jeffrey Spears, Brian Robinson, and Ben Gullo, eds. *Domestic Operational Law: 2011 Handbook for Judge Advocates* (Charlottesville, VA: Center for Law and Military Operations, September 1, 2011), 49–50.

49. David E. Sanger, "Bush Wants to Consider Broadening of Military's Powers during Natural Disasters," *New York Times,* September 27, 2005, http://www.nytimes.com/2005/09/27/national/nationalspecial/27military.html (accessed September 10, 2018).

50. Ibid.

51. L. M. Colarusso, "Air Force Told to Pick Up Noble Eagle Costs," *Air Force Times,* February 7, 2005, 1. See also Heppard and Green, "Department of Defense Capabilities."

52. Brookings Institution, *Protecting the American Homeland: A Second Look at How We're Meeting the Challenge, A Brookings Briefing* (Washington, DC: Brookings Institution, 2003), http://www.brookings.edu/events/2003/01/23defense (accessed September 10, 2018).

53. Ibid., 164.

54. James F. Miskel documents that the military was often called out by the president to address disasters in the 19th century. He explains that institutionalized disaster relief in the United States had its origins in the War Department during World War I. Miskel, *Disaster Response and Homeland Security: What Works, What Doesn't,* 41. Cited previously.

55. The president issued the declaration to California on the basis of the fires set by rioters. However, it may well have been that President George H. W. Bush did not want to set the precedent of issuing a presidential declaration of major disaster for a civil disturbance. The Los Angeles riots were triggered by a jury decision of innocence for Los Angeles police officers who had been videotaped beating Rodney King during his arrest.

56. Tom Bowman and Siobhan Gorman, "Increasing Military's Role Raises Questions," *Baltimore Sun,* September 20, 2005.

57. Brookings Institution, *Protecting the American Homeland.*

58. David Wood, "National Guard Increases Sandy Response, Sends Reinforcements to NY, NJ," *Huffington Post,* November 1, 2012, http://www.huffingtonpost.com/2012/11/01/national-guard-sandy-ny-nj_n_2060249.html (accessed September 10, 2018). Remember that some dozen mid-Atlantic and Northeast states were impacted by Superstorm Sandy, and many of those deployed all or some of their state National Guard units.

59. Recall that each state National Guard receives pay and benefits from its respective state government under "State Active Duty" status.

60. Wood, "National Guard Increases Sandy Response, Sends Reinforcements to NY, NJ," cited previously.

61. George D. Haddow and Jane A. Bullock, *Introduction to Emergency Management,* 2nd ed. (Boston: Butterworth-Heinemann, 2006), 85.

62. Bowman and Gorman, "Increasing Military's Role Raises Questions."

63. Ibid.

64. Ryan Burke and Sue McNeil, *Toward a Unified Military Response: Hurricane Sandy and the Dual Status Commander* (Carlisle, PA: Strategic Studies Institute and the U.S. Army War College Press, 2015), 10.

65. Ibid.

66. Ibid.

67. Ibid.

68. National Guard Association of the United States, "Understanding the Guard's Duty Status," NGAUS Fact Sheet, https://www.ngaus.org/sites/default/files/Guard%20Statues.pdf (accessed June 4,

2018). This Fact Sheet goes into considerable detail over two pages to explain concisely each category of National Guard duty status.

69. Burke and McNeil, "Toward a Unified Military Response," p. xii.

70. Ibid.

71. Ibid., p. 6.

72. Ibid.

73. Ibid.

74. Ibid., 6–7.

75. U.S. Army Corps of Engineers, *U.S. Army Corps of Engineers: A Brief History*, http://www.usace.army.mil/About/History/BriefHistoryoftheCorps/Introduction.aspx (accessed September 10, 2018).

76. Miskel, *Disaster Response and Homeland Security*, 54.

77. Douglas Brinkley, *The Great Deluge: Hurricane Katrina, New Orleans, and the Mississippi Gulf Coast* (New York: Morrow, 2006), 196.

78. For a history of the U.S. Coast Guard, see Thomas P. Ostrom, *The United States Coast Guard and National Defense: A History from World War I to the Present* (McFarland & Company, Inc., Jefferson, NC, 2012).

79. For a time after Hurricane Katrina, Admiral Thad Allen of the U.S. Coast Guard was the FEMA deputy director for Gulf Recovery.

80. Miskel, *Disaster Response and Homeland Security*, 53.

81. National Research Council, *Facing Hazards and Disasters: Understanding Human Dimensions* (Washington, DC: National Academies Press, 2006).

82. Ibid.

83. See www.FireServiceInfo.com, "A Little Fire Service History," June 28, 2016, http://www.fireserviceinfo.com/history.html#amfiredept (accessed June 5, 2018).

84. Recall, there are five: Prevention, Protection, Mitigation, Response, and Recovery.

85. Federal Emergency Management Agency, *National Emergency Management System: The NIMS Homepage*, http://www.fema.gov/national-incident-management-system (accessed September 10, 2018). See also U.S. Department of Homeland Security, "National Response Plan," December 2004, at Federation of American Scientists, https://fas.org/irp/agency/dhs/nrp.pdf (accessed September 25, 2018).

86. John Fass Morton, *Next-Generation Homeland Security: Network Federalism and National Preparedness* (Annapolis, MD: Naval Institute Press, 2012), 78–79.

87. This is required under section 2006 of the Homeland Security Act of 2002, as amended (6 U.S.C. § 607). Also, law enforcement is linked to one or more core capabilities within the goal.

88. U.S. Department of Homeland Security, "Fiscal Year 2017 Homeland Security Grant Program," 2016, Hereafter, "DHS FY 2017 Homeland Security Grant Program, 2016." https://www.fema.gov/media-library-data/1496327128641-40d3a338eaaa2ba7679f020410ce9847/FY_2017_HSGP_Fact_Sheet_FINAL_508.pdf (accessed June 6, 2018).

89. U.S. Department of Homeland Security, "Fiscal Year 2017 Homeland Security Grant Program," undated, p. 4, https://www.fema.gov/media-library-data/1496327128641-40d3a338eaaa2ba7679f020410ce9847/FY_2017_HSGP_Fact_Sheet_FINAL_508.pdf (accessed October 9, 2018).

90. The author elected to omit tribal governments from this sentence because tribal governments have for years received a disproportionally small amount of State Homeland Security Grant funding. See National Congress of American Indians (NCAI), "Homeland Security and Emergency Management," 2017, http://www.ncai.org/5_FY2018-NCAI-Budget-Request2-Homeland_Security.pdf (accessed June 9, 2018). This quote is illustrative. "Funding to tribal governments and tribal communities for critical homeland security needs has remained stagnant for over a decade. Without necessary resources dedicated to Indian Country, federal efforts to create a cohesive and coordinated homeland security strategy will create a significant and potentially dangerous gap in security. Congress and the Administration have a trust obligation to assist tribal governments to protect all citizens, Native and non-Native within their jurisdictions. The Department of Homeland Security recently issued infographics showing that it provides $17.6 million in federal assistance and

$4.4 million in homeland security grants daily. Tribal governments receive less than half of this daily allocation in an entire year. While the Department of Homeland Security provides this $22 million every day to states, it provides roughly $10 million to the Indian tribes in an entire year. On average states are allocated $26.24 of federal funding for each resident annually and Native Alaskans and American Indian tribes are allocated roughly $3.41 for each of their citizens. Additionally, state governors have access to federally funded state-centric programs like the Emergency Management Assistance Program that exclude tribes." Ibid. According to NCAI, there are 567 federally recognized tribes in the United States. Ibid.

91. As the second edition of this book disclosed, there were only 31 UASI locations in 2012.

92. Frances L. Edwards, "Federal Intervention in Local Emergency Planning: Nightmare on Main Street," *State and Local Government Review* 39, no. 1 (2007): 34.

93. Homeland Security Grants.info, "Urban Areas Security Initiative: Summary," 2017, https://www.homelandsecuritygrants.info/GrantDetails.aspx?gid=17162 (accessed June 2, 2018).

94. Ibid.

95. Ibid.

96. An "Explanatory Statement" accompanying the Department of Homeland Security Appropriations Act, 2018 (Pub. L. No. 115-141) is the source of this intent.

97. With the possible exception of tribal governments located, in whole or in part, in the urban areas listed.

98. Veronica de Rugy and Nick Gillespie, "The War on Hype: America's Fleecing in the Name of Security," *San Francisco Chronicle,* February 19, 2006, http://www.sfgate.com/cgi-bin/article.cgi?f=/c/a/2006/02/19/INGDDH8E311.DTL (accessed September 10, 2018).

99. Rebecca M. Nash, "Predicting the Impact of Urban Area Security Initiative Funding on Terrorist Incidents in the United States," *Criminology, Criminal Justice, Law & Society*, Vol. 18, Issue 2, (2017), 13, at https://ccjls.scholasticahq.com/article/1989.pdf (accessed October 2, 2018).

100. E. Van Um and D. Pisoiu, "Effective counterterrorism: What have we learned so far? Economics of Security," Working Paper 55. Retrieved from German Institute of Economic Research website: https://www.diw.de/documents/publikationen/73/diw_01.c.386651.de/diw_econsec0055.pdf (accessed October 2, 2018).

101. This is required under section 2006 of the Homeland Security Act of 2002, as amended (6 U.S.C. § 607). Also, law enforcement is linked to one or more core capabilities within the goal.

102. Ibid.

103. DHS FY 2017 Homeland Security Grant Program, 2016.

104. Ibid.

105. Ibid.

106. Ibid.

107. Ibid.

108. Homeland Security Grants. Info, "Operation Stonegarden (OPSG) Program," 2018, https://www.homelandsecuritygrants.info/GrantDetails.aspx?gid=21875 (accessed June 10, 2018).

109. Ibid.

110. Ibid.

111. Ibid.

112. Ibid.

113. Edwards, "Federal Intervention in Local Emergency Planning," 32–33.

114. President George W. Bush, "Homeland Security Presidential Directive-1," Federation of American Scientists, October 29. 2001, http://www.fas.org/irp/offdocs/nspd/hspd-1.htm (accessed September 10, 2018).

115. Edwards, "Federal Intervention in Local Emergency Planning," 34.

116. U.S. Department of Homeland Security, Office of Domestic Preparedness, *2005 Homeland Security Grant Guidance*, and Edwards, "Federal Intervention in Local Emergency Planning," 34.

117. Edwards, "Federal Intervention in Local Emergency Planning," 42.

118. U.S. Department of Homeland Security, "Strengthening National Preparedness: Capabilities-Based Planning" (fact sheet dated April 13, 2005, distributed at Regional Planning Conference, San Francisco, August 2005). See also Edwards, "Federal Intervention in Local Emergency Planning," 40.

119. See Federal Emergency Management Agency, "The 15 U.S. National Planning Scenarios," Version 20.2 draft, 2005. See Patrick Hardy, "The 15 U.S. National Planning Scenarios," April 28, 2012, http://hytropy .blogspot.com/2012/04/15-us-national-planning-scenarios.html (accessed September 25, 2018).

120. U.S. Department of Homeland Security, *FY 2006 Homeland Security Grant Program: Program Guidance and Application Kit* (Washington, DC: U.S. Department of Homeland Security, 2005), http://link.library.in.gov/portal/Department-of-Homeland-Security-DHS-fiscal-year/ mDv0NJrUiY4/ (accessed September 10, 2018).

121. U.S. Department of Homeland Security, "Strengthening National Preparedness," 205. See also Edwards, "Federal Intervention in Local Emergency Planning."

122. U.S. Department of Homeland Security, "Strengthening National Preparedness," 205.

123. Ibid.

124. See Edwards, "Federal Intervention in Local Emergency Planning."

125. Andrew J. Jackson, "The CARVER Method for Preppers," *Prepography: The Study of Self-Reliance,* http://prepography.com/carver-method-preppers (accessed September 10, 2018). See also Edwards, "Federal Intervention in Local Emergency Planning."

126. Ibid.

127. Bullock et al., *Introduction to Homeland Security,* 2nd ed., 324.

128. Edwards, "Federal Intervention in Local Emergency Planning," 34.

129. See Maria Medrano, Grants Department, Nueces County, Texas, Commissioners Court—Regular, AI4980 4. B. 2. Meeting January 8, 2014, http:// ncagenda.co.nueces.tx.us:8080/agenda_ publish.cfm?id=&mt=ALL&get_month=1&get_ year=2014&dsp=agm&seq=4980&rev=0&ag =248&ln=9810&nseq=&nrev=&pseq=4978&prev =0#ReturnTo9810 (accessed September 10, 2018). Medrano discloses, "States receive EMPG funding from DHS and, in turn, pass through EMPG funding to local governments to reimburse them for emergency management program expenses." Ibid. Please note that different states use different rules and procedures for passing EMPG funds to their respective local governments. Texas is given as a general example here.

130. This includes the District of Columbia and territories and possessions of the United States.

131. DHS-FEMA, "Fiscal Year 2018 Emergency Management Performance Grant (EMPG) Program Notice of Funding Opportunity–Key Changes," 2017, https://www.fema.gov/media-library-data/15265 78708333-010b3bbbeb00201b3b133a0366913696/ FY_2018_EMPG_Key_Changes_FINAL_508.pdf (accessed June 9, 2018).

132. Ibid.

133. The Fiscal Year 2013 EMPG Program funds were allocated in compliance with Section 662 of the Post-Katrina Emergency Management Reform Act (PKEMRA) of 2006 (6 U.S.C. 762). All 50 states, the District of Columbia, and Puerto Rico received a base amount of 0.75 percent of the total available grant funding. Four territories (American Samoa, Guam, Northern Mariana Islands, and the U.S. Virgin Islands) received a base amount of 0.25 percent of the total available grant funding. The balance of EMPG Program funds was distributed on a population-share basis. Pursuant to Title II of the Compact of Free Association Amendments Act of 2003 (Public Law 108-188), funds were also available for the Federated States of Micronesia and for the Republic of the Marshall Islands. See DHS-FEMA, "Department of Homeland Security (DHS) Notice of Funding Opportunity (NOFO) Fiscal Year 2016 Emergency Management Performance Grant Program (EMPG)," 2016, at https://www.fema.gov/ media-library-data/1455571902574-a84f5a1b2f4507 95a70cce1f5ee7b967/FY_2016_EMPG_NOFO_FINAL .pdf (accessed October 2, 2018). For federal fiscal years 2014-2018, the EMPG funding was budgeted at $350,100,000 each fiscal year. See FEMA, "Emergency Management Performance Grants (EMPG) Program." Last Updated June 7, 2018, at https://www.fema

.gov/emergency-management-performance-grant-program (accessed October 2, 2018).

134. Vivienne Walt, "Greenwald on Snowden Leaks: The Worst Is Yet to Come," *Time World,* http://world.time.com/2013/10/14/greenwald-on-snowden-leaks-the-worst-is-yet-to-come/#ixzz2i24YfwWd (accessed September 10, 2018).

135. American Civil Liberties Union, "The Militarization of Policing in America," http://www.aclu.org/militarization (accessed September 10, 2018).

136. Trend Micro Inc., "The Patriot Act Revision: What Does It Mean to You? [updated]," June 5, 2015, https://www.trendmicro.com/vinfo/us/security/news/online-privacy/patriot-act-revision-underway-what-does-it-mean-to-you (accessed June 2, 2018).

137. Ibid.

138. Ibid.

139. Ibid.

140. Ibid.

141. U.S. Department of Homeland Security, "National Terrorism Advisory System," https://www.dhs.gov/national-terrorism-advisory-system (accessed September 25, 2018). This site explains the origins and operation of the NTAS and posts alerts and bulletins as well as current and expired advisories.

142. Bowman and Gorman, "Increasing Military's Role Raises Questions."

143. Lucien G. Canton, *Emergency Management: Concepts and Strategies for Effective Programs* (Hoboken, NJ: Wiley, 2007), 275.

144. Allen K. Settle, "Disaster Assistance: Securing Presidential Declarations," in *Cities and Disaster: North American Studies in Emergency Management*, eds. Richard T. Sylves and William L. Waugh Jr. (Springfield, IL: Charles C Thomas, 1990), 33–57.

Chapter 8

1. The author wishes to thank doctoral student Cédric S. Sage, coauthor of this chapter in the first edition, for permission to draw from his paper, "International Disaster Relief from a Comparative Analysis: The Case of the UN and U.S. Apparatuses" (unpublished paper for the author's POSC 656 Politics and Disaster graduate course, University of Delaware, Newark, 2006). For the second and third editions, the author would also like to acknowledge the suggestions and advice of Dr. Yvonne Rademacher, a former UN official and former doctoral student at the University of Delaware (UD), School of Urban Affairs and Public Policy.

2. BrainyQuote, Disaster Quotes," 2018, https://www.brainyquote.com/quotes/neil_degrasse_tyson_531162?src=t_disaster (accessed June 11, 2018).

3. George D. Haddow and Jane A. Bullock, *Introduction to Emergency Management,* 2nd ed. (Boston: Butterworth-Heinemann, 2006). Haddow and Bullock mention UNICEF figures. They report that 90 percent of related injuries and deaths are sustained in countries that have per-capita income levels under $760 per year. Ibid., 219. See also The World Bank, *Natural Hazards and Unnatural Disasters: The Economics of Effective Prevention* (Washington, DC: International Bank for Reconstruction and Development, 2010), 23–32, 41–63.

4. See John Hannigan, *Disasters without Borders: The International Politics of Natural Disasters* (Malden, MA: Polity Press, 2012). See also J. M. Albala-Bertrand, "Globalization and Localization: An Economic Approach," in *Handbook of Disaster Research*, eds. Havidan Rodriguez, Enrico L. Quarantelli, and Russell R. Dynes (New York: Springer, 2007), 147–167.

5. See Adrian Wood, Raymond Apthorpe, and John Borton, eds., *Evaluating International Humanitarian Action* (London: Zed Books, 2001). See also Alejandro López-Carresi et al., eds. *Disaster Management: International Lessons in Risk Reduction, Response and Recovery* (New York: Springer, 2014).

6. For a thorough analysis of the security threat posed by developing nations to the industrialized world, see Robert Cooper, *The Breaking of Nations: Order and Chaos in the Twenty-First Century* (New York: Atlantic Monthly Press, 2003), 180. See also Charles Perrow, *The Next Catastrophe: Reducing Our Vulnerabilities to Natural, Industrial, and Terrorist Disasters* (Princeton, NJ: Princeton University Press, 2007), and Christine Wamsler,

Cities, Disaster Risk, and Adaptation (New York: Routledge, 2014).

7. Mark Schuller, *Killing with Kindness: Haiti, International Aid, and NGOs* (New Brunswick, NJ: Rutgers University Press, 2012), 23, 109. For an informative study of transnational disaster, see Thomas W. Haase, "International Disaster Resilience: Preparing for Transnational Disaster," in *Designing Resilience: Preparing for Extreme Events*, eds. Louise K. Comfort, Arjin Boin, and Chris C. Demchak (Pittsburgh: University of Pittsburgh Press, 2010), 220–243.

8. For an excellent examination of how natural disasters relate to complex humanitarian emergencies in developing nations, see Ed Tsui, "Initial Response to Complex Emergencies and Natural Disasters," in *Emergency Relief Operation,* ed. Kevin M. Cahill (New York: Fordham University Press, 2003), 32–54. See also David Keen, *Complex Humanitarian Emergencies* (Cambridge, MA: Polity Press, 2008).

9. See Department of State and U.S. Agency for International Development, *Security, Democracy, Prosperity—USAID-State Strategic Plan, Fiscal Year 2004–2009* (Washington, DC: U.S. Department of State, 2003). See also U.S. Department of State and U.S. Agency for International Development. *FY 2007–2012 Department of State and USAID Strategic Plan. Transformational Diplomacy* (Washington, DC: U.S. Department of State, 2007), http://www.state.gov/s/d/rm/rls/dosstrat/2007 (accessed September 11, 2018).

10. See Haddow and Bullock, *Introduction to Emergency Management,* 2nd ed., 220–221.

11. Ibid., 221–222.

12. Ibid.

13. Infoplease, "Members of the United Nations," 2018, https://www.infoplease.com/world/international-relations/members-united-nations (accessed September 11, 2018). See also World Bank, *Natural Hazards and Unnatural Disasters,* 41–63.

14. See U.S. Agency for International Development, *Policy Framework for Bilateral Aid, Implementing Transformational Diplomacy through Development* (Washington, DC: U.S. Agency for International Development, 2006). See also U.S. Department of State and U.S. Agency for International Development, *Security, Democracy, Prosperity.*

15. U.S. Agency for International Development, *At Freedom's Frontiers: A Democracy and Governance Strategic Framework* (Washington, DC: U.S. Agency for International Development, 2005).

16. U.S. Agency for International Development, "Home-Reports and Data-Budget," March 21, 2018, https://www.usaid.gov/results-and-data/budget-spending (accessed June 11, 2018).

17. Ibid.

18. Ibid.

19. U.S. Agency for International Development, *At Freedom's Frontiers*, 2005. Cited previously.

20. U.S. Agency for International Development, *Fragile States Strategy* (Washington, DC: U.S. Agency for International Development, 2005).

21. Other offices under the Bureau for Democracy, Conflict, and Humanitarian Response provide humanitarian assistance: among others, the Office of Food for Peace and the Office of Transition Initiatives and the Office for Civil-Military Cooperation. See U.S. Agency for International Development, "Bureau for Democracy, Conflict and Humanitarian Assistance," http://www.usaid.gov/who-we-are/organization/bureaus/bureau-democracy-conflict-and-humanitarian-assistance (accessed September 11, 2018).

22. See Haddow and Bullock, *Introduction to Emergency Management,* 2nd ed., 235.

23. U.S. Agency for International Development, Office of U.S. Foreign Disaster Assistance, "Organization Chart," http://www.usaid.gov/who-we-are/organization/bureaus/bureau-democracy-conflict-and-humanitarian-assistance/office-us (accessed September 11, 2018).

24. See Damon P. Coppola, *Introduction to International Disaster Management* (Boston: Butterworth-Heinemann, 2007), 309.

25. Haddow and Bullock, *Introduction to Emergency Management,* 2nd ed., 237.

26. Ibid.

27. Ibid.

28. Ibid.

29. Ibid.

30. Haddow and Bullock, *Introduction to Emergency Management,* 2nd ed., 239. They argue that Humanitarian Assistance Survey Teams remain focused on technical military matters rather than on the purely humanitarian-based issues of the nonmilitary organizations and agencies.

31. See U.S. Department of State, "Going the Distance: The U.S. Tsunami Relief Effort 2005: Americans Respond to Tragedy," 2005, for full .pdf, https://www .hsdl.org/?view&did=773838 (accessed September 25, 2018). The operation involved 25 ships and 94 cargo planes.

32. Ibid.

33. See Brian Toft and Simon Reynolds, *Learning from Disasters* (Boston: Butterworth-Heinemann, 1994).

34. See Edward P. Borodzicz, *Risk, Crisis, and Security Management* (Hoboken, NJ: Wiley, 2005). To examine emergency management in the United Kingdom, see this excellent case study: David Alexander, "Rapid Adaptation to Threat: The London Bombings," in *Designing Resilience: Preparing for Extreme Events*, eds. Louise K. Comfort, Arjin Boin, and Chris C. Demchak (Pittsburgh: University of Pittsburgh Press, 2010), 143–157.

35. See Uriel Rosenthal, R. A. Boin, and Louise Comfort, *From Crises to Contingencies: A Global Perspective* (Springfield, IL: Charles C Thomas, 2002).

36. See E. L. Quarantelli, *Future Disaster Trends and Policy Implications for Developing Countries* (Newark: Disaster Research Center, University of Delaware, 1994).

37. Coppola, *Introduction to International Disaster Management,* 507–516.

38. Ibid., 500–507.

39. Ibid., 5–10.

40. See Haddow and Bullock, *Introduction to Emergency Management,* 2nd ed., 228.

41. The Office for the Coordination of Humanitarian Assistance (OCHA) launches an average of 27 appeals each year and has raised $12 billion since 1992. In 2000 alone, OCHA launched 16 interagency appeals, which eventually raised $1.4 billion to assist 35 million individuals in 16 countries. United Nations, Office for the Coordination of Humanitarian Affairs, "ReliefWeb," http://reliefweb.int/disasters (accessed September 11, 2018). Ibid.

42. The fund has lent $127 million in more than 50 transactions since 1992. United Nations, Office for the Coordination of Humanitarian Affairs, "ReliefWeb." To research disasters from 1981 to 2014, use filter by date (year) at this location.

43. See Haddow and Bullock, *Introduction to Emergency Management,* 2nd ed., 228.

44. Ibid.

45. The UNHCR spends an average of $22 million per deployment. Haddow and Bullock, *Introduction to Emergency Management,* 2nd ed., 228.

46. Refugees are those who have fled their home countries due to their fears of persecution or for their lives and when fears are connected to issues of race, religion, nationality, or political or social group membership and who do not wish to return home. Their legal status, rights, and obligations are defined by the 1951 Convention Relating to the Status of Refugees and by its 1967 protocol. Kate Jastram and Marilyn Achiron, Office of the United Nations High Commissioner for Refugees. *Refugee Protection: A Guide to International Refugee Law* (Geneva, Switzerland: Inter-Parliamentary Union, 2001), http:// www.unhcr.org/publ/PUBL/3d4aba564.pdf (accessed September 11, 2018). By November 1, 2007, there were 147 states that had signed either the treaty or protocol or both. For information regarding treaty or protocol signatories, see United Nations High Commissioner for Refugees, "States Parties to the 1951 Convention Relating to the Status of Refugees and the 1967 Protocol," http://www.unhcr.org/protect/ PROTECTION/3b73b0d63.pdf (accessed September 11, 2018). See also ReliefWeb International at http:// reliefweb.int (accessed September 11, 2018).

47. Ibid.

48. Ibid.

49. Ibid.

50. See UNICEF, "UNICEF in Emergencies," http:// www.unicef.org/emergencies (accessed September 11, 2018).

51. See Haddow and Bullock, *Introduction to Emergency Management,* 2nd ed., 228.

52. These rights include minimum requirements for survival as well as an increase of children's opportunities for a successful future. Women are included under the mandate of UNICEF as they are considered to be vital to the care of children. See Haddow and Bullock, *Introduction to Emergency Management,* 2nd ed., 228–229.

53. UNICEF has sometimes successfully managed to impose "days of tranquility" and "corridors of peace" in war zones. Also, UNICEF has special programs that assist traumatized children and help reunite children with their families. In 1999, UNICEF provided humanitarian aid in 39 countries. See UNICEF, "Putting Children First All Over the World," https://www.unicefusa.org/mission (accessed September 11, 2018).

54. See Haddow and Bullock, *Introduction to Emergency Management,* 2nd ed., 225.

55. Here are the types of emergency programs Haddow and Bullock emphasize: emergency interventions; programming for peace and recovery; area rehabilitation to resettle uprooted populations; the reintegration of demobilized soldiers; de-mining programs; rebuilding institutions and government improvement; the organization of national elections; and the management of aid delivery. See Ibid., 226–227.

56. See Ibid., 227.

57. Coppola, *Introduction to International Disaster Management,* 9.

58. In 1999, the WFP provided food to 29 million refugees, IDPs, and returnees, as well as to 41 million natural disaster victims. In emergencies, WFP gets food to where it is needed, saving the lives of victims of war, civil conflict, and natural disasters. After the cause of an emergency has passed, WFP uses food to help communities rebuild their shattered lives. WFP is part of the UN system and is voluntarily funded. Born in 1961, WFP pursues a vision of the world in which every man, woman, and child has access at all times to the food needed for an active and healthy life. WFP works toward that vision with its sister UN agencies in Rome—Food and Agriculture Organization of the United Nations (FAO) and the International Fund for Agricultural Development (IFAD)—as well as other government, UN, and NGO partners. On average, WFP reaches more than 90 million people with food assistance in 80 countries each year. About 13,500 people work for the organization, most of them in remote areas, directly serving the hungry poor. See World Food Programme, "Overview," http://www1.wfp.org/overview (accessed September 11, 2018).

59. Ibid.

60. See Prof. Asaho Mizushima, Waseda University Faculty of Law, "The Japan-US 'Military' Response to the Earthquake, and the Strengthening of the Military Alliance as a Result," *Fukushima on the Globe,* December 10, 2012, http://fukushimaontheglobe.com/the-earthquake-and-the-nuclear-accident/whats-happened/the-japan-us-military-response (accessed June 11, 2018). According to Mizushima, the disaster response of the U.S. military, which deployed with Japan's Special Defense Forces (SDF), was fast. John Roos, the U.S. ambassador to Japan, woke up President Barack Obama, and the initial American response [to the disaster] was decided. (Yomiuri newspaper. May 13th, 2011.) The U.S. military deployed a carrier group off the coast of Miyagi Prefecture, with the U.S.S. *Ronald Reagan* (CVN 76), a nuclear-powered aircraft carrier of the U.S. Seventh Fleet, as its core: 19 naval vessels, 18,000 personnel, plus 140 aircraft were assembled, and the so-called "Operation Tomodachi [Friends]," was launched. The relief efforts of the U.S. military were centered mainly in Iwate prefecture and Miyagi prefecture. The "Fukushima" incident had an effect on Operation Tomodachi. Some 7,500 family members of U.S. military personnel who were living in Japan were sent back to the States. The nuclear-powered aircraft carrier, U.S.S. *George Washington* (CVN 73), whose homeport is Yokosuka, was kept on standby in the Sea of Japan. Plus, 145 members of special units called the *Chemical Biological Incident Response Force (CBIRF)* were dispatched to Japan, but their activities were restricted from getting within an 80-km radius of the Fukushima nuclear power plant. See Mizushima, "The Japan-US 'Military' Response to the Earthquake."

61. United Nations Peacekeeping, Home Page, https://peacekeeping.un.org/en (accessed September 25, 2018).

62. Ibid.

63. Ibid.

64. Ibid.

65. United Nations, "Military."

66. Ibid.

67. Settlement.Org (Ontario), "What Is Canada's Political System?" last updated July 13, 2016, at https://settlement.org/ontario/immigration-citizen ship/canadian-government/canadian-political-sys tem/what-is-canada-s-political-system/ (accessed October 4, 2018).

68. Ibid.

69. Ibid.

70. See "Agreement between the Government of Canada and the Government of the United States of America on Emergency Management Cooperation," E105173, 12 December 2008. *Source:* http://www.state.gov/documents/organization /142916.pdf (accessed September 11, 2018). A much more detailed elaboration of U.S.–Canada bilateral agreements regarding aspects of emergency management comes in the Compendium of U.S.–Canada Emergency Management Assistance Mechanisms: National-level acts, agreements, frameworks, guidance, plans, and procedures for response operations, communication and coordination, preparedness, and recovery, June 2012. See https://www.dhs.gov/xlibrary/assets/policy/btb -compendium-of-us-canada-emergency-manage ment-assistance-mechanisms.pdf (accessed June 11, 2018).

71. According to a CNN report, "The United States, Canada and Mexico came to a last minute agreement on a revised trade deal that could replace NAFTA. It's called the USMCA. President Donald Trump and his Mexican and Canadian counterparts are expected to sign the deal by the end of November. It will then be up to Congress to approve the deal, which is likely to come up for a vote next year. Negotiations between Canada and the United States pushed right up to a deadline imposed by the Trump administration." See Katie Lobosco, Donna Borak, and Tami Luhby, "What's New in the US, Canada and Mexico Trade Deal?" *CNN Politics*, October 1, 2018, at https://www.cnn. com/2018/10/01/politics/nafta-usmca-differences/ index.html (accessed October 4, 2018).

72. United States Trade Representative, Executive Office of the President, "Canada: U.S.-Canada Trade Facts," May 14, 2018, https://ustr.gov/countries- regions/americas/canada (accessed June 11, 2018). U.S. goods and services trade with Canada totaled an estimated $673.9 billion in 2017. Exports were $341.2 billion; imports were $332.8 billion. The U.S. goods and services trade surplus with Canada was $8.4 billion in 2017. However, the international shipment of non-U.S. goods through the United States can make standard measures of bilateral trade balances potentially misleading. For example, it is common for goods to be shipped through regional trade hubs without further processing before final shipment to their ultimate destination. This can be seen in data reported by America's two largest trading partners, Canada and Mexico. The U.S. data report a $17.5 billion goods deficit with Canada in 2017, and a $71.1 billion goods deficit with Mexico. Both countries, however, reported substantially larger U.S. goods surpluses in the same relationship. In 2017, Canada reported a $97.7 billion surplus, and Mexico a $132.4 billion surplus.

73. Brian Oliver Newsome and Jack A. Jarmon, *A Practical Introduction to Homeland Security and Emergency Management: From Home to Abroad* (Thousand Oaks, Calif.: Sage Publications, Inc., 2016), p. 57. Newsome and Jarmon state that 80% of Canada's global trade is with the U.S. while 20% of U.S. global trade is with Canada.

74. Tricia Wachtendorf, "When Disasters Defy Borders: What We Can Learn from the Red River Flood about Transnational Disasters," *Australian Journal of Emergency Management*, Volume 15 Issue 3, 2000. *Source:* https://ajem.infoservices.com.au/items/ AJEM-15-03-09 (accessed September 11, 2018).

75. Senate Committee on Governmental Affairs, *Hearing on Rebuilding FEMA: Preparing for the Next Disaster*, 103rd Cong., 1st sess., May 18, 1993, 151.

76. 42 U.S. Code § 5122 - Definitions, https://www.law .cornell.edu/uscode/text/42/5122.

77. See FEMA, "The Disaster Declaration Process," August 1, 2018, https://www.fema.gov/es/node/33733 (accessed October 4, 2018).

78. Saundra K. Schneider, *Flirting with Disaster: Public Management in Crisis Situations* (Armonk, N.Y.: M.E. Sharpe, 1995). See also Saundra K. Schneider, *Dealing with Disaster: Public Management in Crisis Situations*, 2nd ed. (Armonk, NY: M.E. Sharpe, 2011).

79. U.S. Federal Emergency Management Agency, Disaster Declaration Process, January 8, 2018, https://www.fema.gov/disaster-declaration-process (accessed June 11, 2018).

80. The Marshall Islands and the Federated States of Micronesia are also eligible to request a declaration and receive assistance.

81. Department of Homeland Security, Office of Inspector General, Opportunities to Improve FEMA's Public Assistance Preliminary Damage Assessment Process, OIG-12-79, May 2012, p. 9.

82. The governor shall furnish information on the nature and amount of state and local resources that have been or will be committed to alleviating the results of the disaster, provide an estimate of the amount and severity of damage including the disaster impact on the private and public sector, and provide an estimate of the type and amount of assistance needed under the Stafford Act.

83. This activates an array of federal programs to assist in the response and recovery effort. Not all programs, however, are activated for every disaster. The determination of which programs are activated is based on the needs found during damage assessment and on any subsequent information that may be discovered.

84. Provinces receiving DFAA funds must document what those monies were spent on, vow to return unspent or excess funds, and DFAA dollars are fully subject to Government of Canada audit.

85. Recall that FEMA's "Other Needs Assistance," reviewed in Chapter 6, may be delegated to applicant state, territorial, or tribal governments.

86. David Cameron and Richard Simeon, "Intergovernmental Relations in Canada: The Emergence of Collaborative Federalism," *Publius: The Journal of Federalism*, 2002, Volume 32, Issue 2, 49–72. http://publius.oxfordjournals.org/content/32/2/49.short (accessed September 11, 2018).

87. Care should be taken to understand that FEMA has a small federal full-time workforce of between 5,000 and 7,000 full-time employees. The agency frequently hires private contractors and paid volunteers to implement various victim assistance programs, including tele-registration and online aid request handling.

88. Public Safety Canada, "Disaster Financial Assistance Arrangements (DFAA)," May 15, 2018, https://www.publicsafety.gc.ca/cnt/mrgnc-mngmnt/rcvr-dsstrs/dsstr-fnncl-ssstnc-rrngmnts/index-en.aspx#a01 (accessed June 12, 2018).

89. See Damon P. Coppola, *Introduction to International Disaster Management*, 3rd ed. (Waltham, MA: Butterworth-Heinemann of Elsevier, 2015), 467.

90. Peter Harris, "The Worst Natural Disasters in Canadian History," *Yankler Magazine*, July 8, 2016, http://yackler.ca/blog/2016/07/08/worst-natural-disasters-in-canadian-history/ (accessed June 12, 2018).

91. Emergency Management Act, S.C. 2007, c. 15, Assented to 2007-06-22. An Act to provide for emergency management and to amend and repeal certain Acts. Her Majesty, by and with the advice and consent of the Senate and House of Commons of Canada, enacts.

92. Ibid.

93. Ibid.

94. Guidelines for the "Disaster Financial Assistance Arrangements," for events on or subsequent to January 1, 2008. Source: http://www.publicsafety.gc.ca/cnt/mrgnc-mngmnt/rcvr-dsstrs/gdlns-dsstr-ssstnc/index-eng.aspx (accessed June 11, 2018).

95. Ibid.

96. Ibid.

97. Public Safety Canada, "Disaster Financial Assistance Arrangements (DFAA)," May 15, 2018, cited previously.

98. See "About the Agency," at https://www.fema.gov/about-agency (accessed June 11, 2018).

99. When FEMA was absorbed into the U.S. Department of Homeland Security, it lost its name.

It was renamed the Emergency Preparedness and Response Directorate. On March 31, 2007, through the efforts of Administrator Michael Brown and others, the organization regained its original moniker, the Federal Emergency Management Agency. Brown and others understood that FEMA was a household name for most Americans and that FEMA had brand value as a federal entity.

100. See "About the Agency," cited previously.

101. Ibid.

102. Over its first three years under Liberal Party control, PSC had one continuous serving minister. Over the era of Conservative Party control, from 2006 to 2015, PSC had four different ministerial leaders, with turnover every 2 to 3 years.

103. The Canadian Disaster Database website has a geospatial feature that demarcates on provincial maps the locations of events included in its user-generated tables. However, incorporating geospatial data proved to be infeasible for this study owing to problems in producing that information visually.

104. See James Barron, "The Blackout of 2003: The Overview; Power Surge Blacks Out Northeast Hitting Cities in 8 states and Canada; Midday Shutdowns Disrupt Millions," *The New York Times*, August 15, 2003.

105. Over the last four or five years, FEMA authorities have begun publishing original governor disaster request letters (for president-approved declarations only). They have also intermittently posted Preliminary Damage Estimates for recent declarations. Both of these sources convey rudimentary and estimated costs of physical disaster losses by state.

106. Nonetheless, CDD does not make it clear how estimated total cost was measured.

107. Not to be overlooked is that Canadian provinces have a vast and complex assortment of sub-provincial governments. How these local entities interact with one another and with their respective provincial government is exceedingly important in disaster or emergency circumstances. Like the United States, Canada's provinces and local governments possess varying political cultures. Some prize self-reliance and resist seeking post-disaster aid from their province. Some are not adequately staffed to take advantage of provincial or federal disaster aid. Others are highly sophisticated in documenting disaster losses and well versed in local -provincial and local -provincial -federal modicums of disaster policy. Some of these are skilled in applying for and obtaining provincial and federal disaster assistance.

108. See P. W. Singer, "Strange Brew: Private Military Contractors and Humanitarians," in *Disaster and the Politics of Intervention*, ed. Andrew Lakoff (New York: Columbia University Press, 2010), 70–99.

109. Since about 1997, the United States has tried to negotiate reforms it seeks at the UN by withholding payment of a portion of its full national UN assessment. For an example, see Jon Greenberg, "How Much does the United States Contribute to the UN?" *Polifact*, February 21, 2017, https://www.politifact.com/global-news/statements/2017/feb/01/rob-portman/us-contribution-un-22-percent/# (accessed October 4, 2018). See also UN General Assembly GA/AB/3800, "Under-Secretary-General for Management Briefs Fifth Committee on Financial Situation; Says Regular Budget Position Weaker Now Compared to Last Year," May 18, 2007, http://www.un.org/News/Press/docs/2007/gaab3800.doc.htm (accessed September 11, 2018).

Chapter 9

1. *The Economist*, "America Is Good at Dealing with Hurricanes on the Mainland—After They Strike," June 1, 2018, https://www.economist.com/graphic-detail/2018/06/01/america-is-good-at-dealing-with-hurricanes-on-the-mainland-after-they-strike (accessed June 17, 2018).

2. U.S. Department of Homeland Security, "Surge Capacity Force," September 25, 2017, https://www.dhs.gov/topic/surge-capacity-force (accessed June 28, 2018). The Surge Capacity Force is only activated when an incident is catastrophic. Living conditions are often austere during deployments and may include, but are not limited to, no running water, no electricity, sleeping in tents or other non-conventional forms of housing (e.g., ships), and weather extremes. In the aftermath of a disaster,

housing is often in low supply, and limited hotel space is needed for disaster survivors. Conditions can be challenging. Deployments last no more than 45 days, although they can be shorter if the mission is completed. Surge Capacity Force volunteers continue to be paid by their home department/agency while they are deployed in support of FEMA. FEMA will reimburse the surge worker's department/agency for all eligible travel and overtime. As a federal employee, both health care coverage and worker's compensation will remain in effect during one's deployment.

3. Texas and Puerto Rico saw their post-hurricane debris removal and emergency minimal repair's cost share fall from 25% to only 10%. Florida communities were benefited by a reduction in their debris removal cost share from 25% to 10%. For Irma, see Stephen Hudak, "Trump Orders Feds to Pay More to Help Florida Cities, Counties Pay for Hurricane Irma Debris," *Orlando Sentinel*, October 4, 2017, http://www.orlandosentinel.com/news/orange/os-feds-to-pay-more-for-florida-storm-debris-20171003-story.html (accessed June 22, 2018). For Harvey, see FEMA, "Cost Share Adjustment for Public Assistance–Hurricane Harvey in Texas," *FEMA Fact Sheet*, September 3, 2017, https://www.fema.gov/media-library-data/1506702623604-b9738beff09d4126ba0cac2b77944ae2/FEMA_Cost_Share_Adjustment_Fact_Sheet_508_FINAL.pdf (accessed June 23, 2018). For Maria, see FEMA News Release 184, "President Donald J. Trump Amends Puerto Rico Disaster Declaration," May 24, 2018, https://www.fema.gov/news-release/2018/05/24/president-donald-j-trump-amends-puerto-rico-disaster-declaration (accessed June 23, 2018).

4. Jonathan Erdman, "2017 Atlantic Hurricane Season Among Top 10 Most Active in History," *The Weather Channel*, October 2, 2017, https://weather.com/storms/hurricane/news/2017-atlantic-hurricane-season-one-of-busiest-september (accessed June 27, 2018).

5. Ibid.

6. Ibid.

7. *World Population Review*, "Population of Cities in Texas (2018)," January 19, 2018, http://world

populationreview.com/states/texas-population/cities/ (accessed June 23, 2018).

8. Referring to Figure 9-1, the Texas counties included in DR 4332 receiving individual assistance are Aransas, Austin, Bastrop, Bee, Brazoria, Caldwell, Calhoun, Chambers, Colorado, DeWitt, Fayette, Fort Bend, Galveston, Goliad, Gonzales, Grimes, Hardin, Harris, Jackson, Jasper, Jefferson, Karnes, Kleberg, Lavaca, Lee, Liberty, Matagorda, Montgomery, Newton, Nueces, Orange, Polk, Refugio, Sabine, San Jacinto, San Patricio, Tyler, Victoria, Walker, Waller, and Wharton. More counties may have been added after the date FEMA posted the figure: October 17, 2017.

9. Yaron Steinbuch, "Tropical Storm Harvey Makes Landfall in Louisiana," August 30, 2017, https://nypost.com/2017/08/30/tropical-storm-harvey-makes-landfall-in-louisiana/ (accessed June 25, 2018).

10. U.S. Census Bureau, "Quick Facts: Florida," July 1, 2017, https://www.census.gov/quickfacts/fact/table/fl/PST045217 (accessed June 25, 2018).

11. *InfoPlease*, "The Top Ten: States with Longest Coastlines," December 10, 2017, https://www.infoplease.com/top-ten-states-longest-coastlines (accessed June 27, 2018)

12. Florida Demographics by Cubit, "Florida Counties by Population," July 1, 2017, Web March 2018, https://www.florida-demographics.com/counties_by_population (accessed June 25, 2018).

13. World Vision, "Hurricane Irma: Facts, FAQs, and How to Help," February 14, 2018, https://www.worldvision.org/disaster-relief-news-stories/hurricane-irma-facts (accessed June 23, 2018).

14. Ibid.

15. Florida counties eligible under DR-4337 for individual assistance include Alachua, Baker, Bradford, Brevard, Broward, Charlotte, Citrus, Clay, Collier, Columbia, DeSoto, Dixie, Duval, Flagler, Gilchrist, Glades, Hamilton, Hardee, Hendry, Hernando, Highlands, Hillsborough, Indian River, Lafayette, Lake, Lee, Levy, Manatee, Marion, Martin, Miami-Dade, Monroe, Nassau, Okeechobee, Orange, Osceola, Palm Beach, Pasco, Pinellas,

Polk, Putnam, Sarasota, Seminole, St. Johns, St. Lucie, Sumter, Suwannee, Union, and Volusia. Note that all counties in Florida were eligible to receive some form of FEMA assistance. The list provided here excludes mostly Florida panhandle counties eligible for only various forms of FEMA public assistance.

16. Alex Johnson, Daniel Arkin, Jason Cumming, and Bill Karins, NBC News, "Hurricane Irma Skirts Puerto Rico, Leaves 1 Million Without Power," September 6, 2017 / 10:34 PM ET / Updated September 7, 2017, https://www.nbcnews.com/storyline/hurricane-irma/hurricane-irma-skirts-puerto-rico-lashing-it-powerful-winds-flooding-n799086 (accessed June 25, 2018).

17. Florida Department of Health, Regional Health & Medical staff on behalf of the Tampa Bay Health & Medical Preparedness Coalition, "Hurricane Irma After Action Report for the Tampa Bay Area," November 7, 2017, http://www.tampabayhmpc.org/wp-content/uploads/2017/11/AAR-Hurr-Irma-9-5-thru-9-22-FINAL.pdf (accessed June 28, 2018).

18. U.S. Census Bureau, "Quick Facts: Puerto Rico," July 1, 2017, https://www.census.gov/quickfacts/fact/table/pr/PST045217 (accessed June 25, 2018).

19. Ibid.

20. Because DR-4339 information in Figure 9-5 is difficult to read, the names of every county in Puerto Rico are listed here: Adjuntas, Aguada, Aguadilla, Aguas Buenas, Aibonito, Anasco, Arecibo, Arroyo, Barceloneta, Barranquitas, Bayamon, Cabo Rojo, Caguas, Camuy, Canovanas, Carolina, Catano, Cayey, Ceiba, Ciales, Cidra, Coamo, Comerio, Corozal, Culebra, Dorado, Fajardo, Florida, Guanica, Guayama, Guayanilla, Guaynabo, Gurabo, Hatillo, Hormigueros, Humacao, Isabela, Jayuya, Juana Diaz, Juncos, Lajas, Lares, Las Marias, Las Piedras, Loiza, Luquillo, Manati, Maricao, Maunabo, Mayaguez, Moca, Morovis, Naguabo, Naranjito, Orocovis, Patillas, Penuelas, Ponce, Quebradillas, Rincon, Rio Grande, Sabana Grande, Salinas, San German, San Juan, San Lorenzo, San Sebastian, Santa Isabel, Toa Alta, Toa Baja, Trujillo Alto, Utuado, Vega Alta, Vega Baja, Vieques, Villalba, Yabucoa, and Yauco.

21. Robinson Meyer, "What's Happening with the Relief Effort in Puerto Rico? A Timeline of the Unprecedented Catastrophe of Hurricane Maria," *The Atlantic*, October 4, 2017, https://www.theatlantic.com/science/archive/2017/10/what-happened-in-puerto-rico-a-timeline-of-hurricane-maria/541956/ (accessed June 25, 2018).

22. Ibid.

23. Ibid.

24. Ibid.

25. Ibid.

26. Ibid.

27. Ibid.

28. Ibid.

29. Ibid.

30. Ibid.

31. Ibid.

32. Ibid.

33. Ibid.

34. Ibid.

35. Ibid.

36. Ibid.

37. Ibid.

38. Ibid.

39. On September 6, 2017, Hurricane Irma hit St. Thomas, St. John, and Water Island, leaving the islands devastated. St. Croix had received minor damage from Irma, offering hope to the USVI during the recovery period ahead. Less than 2 weeks later, however, on September 19, 2017, Hurricane Maria hit St. Croix, leaving it devastated and adding further damage to its sister islands. Both hurricanes were Category 5. See VI Now, "Hurricanes Irma & Maria," undated, http://www.vinow.com/gallery/hurricanes-irma-maria/ (accessed June 27, 2018).

40. Morgan Winsor, "US Virgin Islands in Ruins from Hurricane Maria," ABC News, September 29, 2017,

https://abcnews.go.com/International/us-virgin-islands-ruins-hurricane-maria/story?id=50178300 (accessed June 27, 2018).

41. Ibid.

42. Ibid.

43. Daniel C. Vock, "The Pact Changing How Governments Respond to Disaster," *Governing*, March, 2018, http://www.governing.com/gov-emergency-management-local-federal-fema-states.html (accessed June 22, 2018).

44. Jared T. Brown et al., "Congressional Considerations Related to Hurricanes Harvey and Irma," *CRS Insight*, IN10763, September 8, 2017, https://fas.org/sgp/crs/homesec/IN10763.pdf (accessed June 17, 2018).

45. Ibid.

46. Ibid.

47. Ibid.

48. Ibid.

49. FEMA, "Disaster Relief Fund: Monthly Report as of April 30, 2018," Fiscal Year 2018 Report to Congress," May 5, 2018, https://www.fema.gov/media-library-data/1526358994453-ab5a4d20c8e7136da5c6ed583286ff6a/May2018DisasterReliefFundReport.pdf (accessed June 7, 2018).

50. FEMA extended the deadline for New York State individual assistance applicants to March 29, 2013, for example. See FEMA, "FEMA Registration Deadline Extended for Hurricane Sandy Survivors in N.Y.," February 26, 2013, https://www.fema.gov/news-release/2013/02/26/fema-registration-deadline-extended-hurricane-sandy-survivors-ny (accessed June 28, 2018).

51. Remember, IA is Individual Assistance, which is FEMA's Individual and Households Program, which includes its Housing Assistance Program and its Other Needs Assistance Program. See FEMA, "Fact Sheet: What is FEMA's Individual Assistance Program?" February 2, 2017, https://www.fema.gov/disaster/4294-4297/updates/fact-sheet-what-femas-individual-assistance-program (accessed June 28, 2018).

52. Jared T. Brown et al., "Congressional Considerations Related to Hurricanes Harvey and Irma," *CRS Insight*, cited previously.

53. Ibid. The date President Trump signed H.R. 601 into law is from Leigh Ann Caldwell and Alex Moe, "Trump Signs Disaster Aid, and His Deal with Dems, Into Law," *NBC News Politics*, September 8, 2017, https://www.nbcnews.com/politics/congress/house-passes-disaster-relief-sending-trump-sign-n799796 (accessed October 6, 2018).

54. *The Economist*, "America Is Good at Dealing with Hurricanes on the Mainland—After They Strike," June 1, 2018, cited previously.

55. Brandon Formby, "Abbott and FEMA are Using Harvey to Reinvent Disaster Response. Some Say that Makes Displaced Texans 'Guinea Pigs,'" *The Texas Tribune*, February 27, 2018, https://www.texastribune.org/series/in-harveys-wake/ (accessed June 23, 2018).

56. Ibid.

57. Ibid.

58. Ibid.

59. Ibid.

60. Ibid.

61. Ibid.

62. Ibid.

63. Ibid.

64. Ibid.

65. Texas General Land Office Community Development and Revitalization Program, "State of Texas Plan for Disaster Recovery: Hurricane Harvey," January 18, 2018, http://www.glo.texas.gov/the-glo/public-information/notices/files/action-plan-final-draft-1-18-18.pdf (accessed June 23, 2018).

66. Ibid.

67. Ibid.

68. Mike Snyder, "Disaster Victim Activists Concerned about FEMA's Fairness, Transparency," *Houston Chronicle*, January 25, 2018, https://www.houstonchronicle.com/news/houston-texas/houston/article/FEMA-grants-Harvey-victims-fairness-equity-12526374.php (accessed June 28, 2018).

69. Ibid.

70. Ibid.

71. Ibid.

72. Ibid.

73. Ibid.

74. Ibid.

75. Ibid.

76. Ibid.

77. Ibid.

78. Ibid.

79. Ibid.

80. Peter Baker, "Trump Lashes Out at Puerto Rico Mayor Who Criticized Storm Response," *The New York Times*, September 30, 2017, https://www.nytimes.com/2017/09/30/us/politics/trump-puerto-rico-mayor.html (accessed June 25, 2018).

81. Ibid.

82. Ibid.

83. Jim Acosta and Sophie Tatum, "Source: Trump's Puerto Rico Tweets were Response to San Juan Mayor," *CNN Politics*, updated October 13, 2017, https://www.cnn.com/2017/10/12/politics/donald-trump-puerto-rico-twitter/index.html (accessed June 25, 2018).

84. Peter Baker, "Trump Lashes Out at Puerto Rico Mayor Who Criticized Storm Response," *The New York Times*, cited previously.

85. Ibid.

86. Ibid.

87. Alexandra King, "San Juan Mayor: Trump's Words on Puerto Rico Are 'Utter Hypocrisy,'" *CNN Politics*, February 1, 2018, https://www.cnn.com/2018/01/31/politics/san-juan-mayor-trump-hypocrisy-cnntv/index.html (accessed June 23, 2018).

88. Ibid.

89. Ibid.

90. Ibid.

91. Ibid.

92. Ibid.

93. Ibid.

94. Ibid.

95. CRS Analyst Dr. Bruce R. Lindsay insists that presidential power to declare emergencies was narrowly defined from 1974 until the 1988 enactment of the Robert T. Stafford Act. Stafford significantly broadened presidential authority in defining and declaring emergencies. Phone conversation with the author June 2, 2018.

96. FEMA, "2017 Hurricane Season After-Action Report," July 12, 2018, vi, https://www.fema.gov/media-library-data/1533643262195-6d1398339449ca85942538a1249d2ae9/2017FEMAHurricaneAARv20180730.pdf (accessed October 5, 2018).

97. Ibid., vii.

98. Ibid., viii.

99. Ibid.

100. Ibid., 3.

101. Ibid.

102. Ibid., 4.

103. Eric Levenson, "3 storms, 3 responses: Comparing Harvey, Irma and Maria," *CNN*, September 27, 2017, http://www.cnn.com/2017/09/26/us/response-harvey-irma-maria/index.html (accessed June 17, 2018).

104. Ibid.

105. FEMA, "Historic Disaster Response to Hurricane Harvey in Texas," Release date: September 22, 2017, Release Number: HQ-17-133, https://www.fema.gov/news-release/2017/09/22/historic-disaster-response-hurricane-harvey-texas (accessed June 17, 2018).

106. Eric Levenson, "3 storms, 3 responses: Comparing Harvey, Irma and Maria," CNN, cited previously.

107. FEMA, "Hurricane Maria" June 12, 2018, https://www.fema.gov/hurricane-maria (accessed June 17, 2018).

108. Eric Levenson, "3 storms, 3 responses: Comparing Harvey, Irma and Maria," CNN, cited previously.

109. Chris Isidore, "Puerto Rico's Main Airport is Barely Functioning," *CNN Money*, September 26, 2017, http://money.cnn.com/2017/09/26/news/puerto-rico-flights/index.html (accessed June 17, 2018).

110. *The Economist*, "America Is Good at Dealing with Hurricanes on the Mainland—After They Strike," June 1, 2018, cited previously.

111. Ibid.

112. FEMA, "Registering for Individual Assistance," September 10, 2017, https://www.fema.gov/faq -details/Registering-for-Individual-Assistance- 1370032115514 (accessed June 28, 2018).

113. David Ferris, "How Puerto Rico became the Worst Grid Disaster," *E&E News*, Energywire, April 19, 2018, https://www.eenews.net/stories/ 1060079499 (accessed June 28, 2018). How did one storm, sweeping across an island only 35 miles wide, cause the second-worst blackout in world history? How could it cut power longer than Hurricane Katrina, which killed more than 1,800 people and flooded a major American city? How did it exceed the complexity of Superstorm Sandy, which knocked out electricity in 21 states? Hurricane Maria became the perfect storm to destroy an electric grid and to make its resurrection drag on for almost seven months, with no end in sight.

114. Ibid.

115. Ibid.

116. Ibid.

117. Ibid.

118. Ibid.

119. Ibid.

120. Ibid.

121. Ibid.

122. FEMA, "2017 Hurricane Season After-Action Report," vii, cited previously.

Chapter 10

1. U.S. Customs and Border Protection, "CBP Hosts DHS' 15th Anniversary Event," news release March 1, 2018 with March 12, 2018 update, https://www .cbp.gov/newsroom/spotlights/cbp-hosts-dhs- 15th-anniversary-event (accessed July 2, 2018).

2. James Lee Witt, "Military Role in Natural Disaster Response," *Disaster Preparedness* 1, no. 1 (Summer 2006). See Richard T. Sylves, *Disaster Policy and Politics,* 1st ed. (Washington, DC: CQ Press, 2008), 250 fn.

3. FEMA, "National Qualification System," June 26, 2018, https://www.fema.gov/national-qualification- system (accessed July 4, 2018). The NIMS Resource Management Supplemental Guidance and Tools include (1) the National Incident Management System (NIMS) Guideline for the National Qualification System (NQS), which describes the components of a qualification and certification system, defines a process for certifying the qualifications of incident personnel, describes how to stand up and implement a peer review process, and provides an introduction to the process of credentialing personnel; (2) a set of NQS Job Titles/ Position Qualifications, which define minimum qualifications criteria for personnel serving in defined incident management and support positions (these documents can also be found on the Resource Typing Library Tool); (3) a set of NQS Position Task Books (PTBs), which identify the competencies, behaviors, and tasks that personnel should demonstrate to become qualified for a defined incident management and support position; and (4) the NIMS Guideline for Mutual Aid, which provides an overview of common mutual aid practices, defines common terminology and processes, and describes an approach for creating legal agreements and operational plans. Ibid.

4. U.S. Department of Homeland Security, Office of Inspector General, "FEMA: In or Out?" February 2009, https://www.oig.dhs.gov/assets/Mgmt/OIG_09-25_ Feb09.pdf (accessed July 5, 2018).

5. George D. Haddow, Jane A. Bullock, and Damon P. Coppola, *Introduction to Emergency Management*, 4th ed. (Burlington, MA: Butterworth-Heinemann of Elsevier, 2011), 336.

6. U.S. Department of Homeland Security, Office of Inspector General, "FEMA: In or Out?" February 2009, cited previously.

7. Ibid.

8. Patrick S. Roberts, *Disasters and the American State* (New York: Cambridge University Press, 2013), 121.

9. U.S. Department of Homeland Security, Office of Inspector General, "FEMA: In or Out?" February 2009, cited previously.

10. See U.S. Department of Homeland Security, "Who Joined DHS," September 15, 2015, https://www.dhs.gov/who-joined-dhs (access July 5, 2018).

11. U.S. Department of Homeland Security, Office of Inspector General, "FEMA: In or Out?" February 2009, cited previously.

12. Ibid.

13. Ibid.

14. Ibid.

15. See Lee Clarke, *Mission Improbable: Using Fantasy Documents to Tame Disaster* (Chicago, IL: University of Chicago Press, 1999).

16. U.S. Department of Homeland Security, "National Protection Framework," 2nd ed., June 2016, p. 16, https://www.fema.gov/media-library-data/1466017309052-85051ed62fe595d4ad026edf4d85541e/National_Protection_Framework2nd.pdf (accessed July 4, 2018).

17. U.S. Department of Homeland Security, "The Department's Five Responsibilities," June 8, 2009, https://www.dhs.gov/blog/2009/06/08/departments-five-responsibilities (accessed July 1, 2018).

18. Ibid.

19. See George D. Haddow, Jane A. Bullock, and Damon P. Coppola, *Introduction to Emergency Management*, 4th ed., 347–349, cited previously.

20. Shawn Reese, "Department of Homeland Security Preparedness Grants: A Summary and Issues," *Congressional Research Service*, October 28, 2016, p. 3, https://fas.org/sgp/crs/homesec/R44669.pdf (accessed July 2, 2018).

21. Lucien G. Canton, *Emergency Management: Concepts and Strategies for Effective Programs* (Hoboken, NJ: Wiley, 2007). Canton insists, "An emergency manager is first and foremost, a program manager. He or she has the responsibility for developing a strategy to guide the emergency management program and for providing oversight to ensure that the goals and objectives of that strategy are being met. This involves coordinating activities, evaluating progress, and providing technical expertise" (p. 73).

22. The World Bank, *Natural Hazards and Unnatural Disasters: The Economics of Effective Prevention* (Washington, DC: International Bank for Reconstruction and Development, 2010).

23. David Drum, "Political Animal," *Washington Monthly*, September 12, 2005, http://www.washingtonmonthly.com/archives/individual/2005_09/007104.php (accessed September 13, 2018).

24. Omri Ben-Shahar and Kyle D. Logue, "Lessons from Hurricane Harvey: Federal Flood Insurance is the Problem, Not the Solution," *Forbes*, August 30, 2017, https://www.forbes.com/sites/omribenshahar/2017/08/30/lessons-from-hurricane-harvey-federal-flood-insurance-is-the-problem-not-the-solution/2/#14e567e3614d (accessed July 5, 2018).

25. Ibid.

26. From BrainyQuote, "Jim Wallis Quotes," http://www.brainyquote.com/quotes/quotes/j/jimwallis383544.html (accessed September 13, 2018).

27. See Kathleen Tierney, *The Social Roots of Risk: Producing Disasters, Promoting Resilience* (Stanford, CA: Stanford University Press, 2014).

28. James L. Jaffe, *Financial Preparation and Recovery: Disaster Dollars* (Morrisville, NC: Lulu, 2015).

29. See Richard Sylves, *Disaster Policy and Politics*, 2nd ed. (Thousand Oaks, CA: Sage/CQ Press, 2015), 244–264.

30. Denial of government relief is something always threatened in communities with recurring flood disasters. FEMA has proposed denying post-disaster relief to homeowners flooded in the past and warned that they must buy National Flood Insurance but did not. Every time FEMA attempts to deny relief in such cases, a political intercession by the area's senators and representatives to the president results in a withdrawal of the threat. However, the National Flood Insurance Act of 2012 calls for denial of post-flood relief to those who could have purchased National Flood Insurance policies and chose not to.

31. Veoci, About Us, undated, https://www.info.veoci.com/fema-project-reimbursements?gclid=EAIaIQobChMIv4H5sarQ2AIVQ1cNCh0heAT-EAEYASAAEgL9avD_BwE (accessed July 5, 2018).

32. *Reporters Committee for Freedom of the Press*, "Anti-SLAPP Laws," Fall 2010, https://www.rcfp.org/browse-media-law-resources/digital-journalists-legal-guide/anti-slapp-laws-0 (accessed July 4, 2018).

33. Gretchen T. Goldman, Emily Berman, Michael Halpern, Charise Johnson, Yogin Kothari, Genna Reed, and Andrew A. Rosenberg, "Ensuring Scientific Integrity in the Age of Trump," *Science*, Feb 17, 2017: Vol. 355, Issue 6326, 696–698, http://science.sciencemag.org/content/355/6326/696.summary (accessed July 4, 2018).

34. Louise Comfort, Arjen Boin, and Chris Demchak, *Designing Resilience for Communities at Risk: Sociotechnical Approaches* (Pittsburgh, PA: University of Pittsburgh Press, 2010).

35. Committee on Increasing National Resilience to Hazards and Disasters & Committee on Science, Engineering, and Public Policy, the National Academies, *Disaster Resilience: A National Imperative* (Washington, DC: National Academies Press, 2012).

36. See Robert Bland, Jessica E. Short, and Simon A. Andrew, "Financial Resiliency by Local Governments to Natural Disasters," *The Future of Disaster Management in the U.S.*, Amy LePore, editor (New York: Routledge, Taylor and Francis Group, 2017), 196–199.

37. See FEMA, Resilience Directorate, Last Updated: June 7, 2018 (accessed July 5, 2018).

38. Jim McKay, "Hawaii Fallout: Mistakes Happen, but Probably Not Here: Emergency Managers Review Their Protocols after Hawaii False Alert," *Emergency Management Magazine*, January 25, 2018, http://www.govtech.com/em/disaster/Hawaii-Fallout-Mistakes-Happen-but-Probably-Not-Here.html?utm_term=Hawaii%20Fallout%3A%20Mistakes%20Happen%2C%20but%20Probably%20Not%20Here&utm_campaign=No%20Deaths%20From%20Storm%20Surge%20Last%20Year&utm_content=email&utm_source=Act-On+Software&utm_medium=email (accessed July 1, 2018).

39. Adam Nagourney, David E. Sanger, and Johanna Barr, "Hawaii Panics after Alert About Incoming Missile Is Sent in Error," *The New York Times*, January 13, 2018, https://www.nytimes.com/2018/01/13/us/hawaii-missile.html (accessed July 4, 2018).

40. Ibid.

41. Jim McKay, "Hawaii Fallout: Mistakes Happen, but Probably Not Here: Emergency Managers Review Their Protocols after Hawaii False Alert," *Emergency Management Magazine*, January 25, 2018, cited previously.

42. Ibid.

43. Ibid.

44. Adam Nagourney et al., "Hawaii Panics after Alert About Incoming Missile Is Sent in Error," *The New York Times*, January 13, 2018, cited previously.

45. Ibid.

46. Jim McKay, "Hawaii Fallout: Mistakes Happen, but Probably Not Here: Emergency Managers Review Their Protocols after Hawaii False Alert," *Emergency Management Magazine*, January 25, 2018, cited previously

47. Ibid.

48. Ibid.

49. Ibid.

50. Adam Nagourney et al., "Hawaii Panics after Alert About Incoming Missile Is Sent in Error," *The New York Times*, January 13, 2018, cited previously.

51. Ibid.

52. Ibid.

53. Dennis S. Mileti, *Disasters by Design: A Reassessment of Natural Hazards in the United States* (Washington, DC: Joseph Henry Press, 1999); Enrico L. Quarantelli, "Disaster Planning, Emergency Management, and Civil Protection: The Historical Development of Organized Efforts to Plan for and to Respond to Disasters," DRC Preliminary Paper 301 (Newark: University of Delaware, Disaster Research Center, 2000), http://udspace.udel.edu/handle/19716/673 (accessed September 13, 2018); Kathleen J. Tierney, Michael K. Lindell, and Ronald W. Perry, *Facing the Unexpected: Disaster Preparedness*

and Response in the United States (Washington, DC: Joseph Henry Press, 2001).

54. See Patrick S. Roberts, *Disasters and the American State: How Politicians, Bureaucrats, and the Public Prepare for the Unexpected* (New York: Cambridge University Press, 2013), 7–8, 145, 192.

GLOSSARY

1. The National Weather Service, Climate Prediction Center, "Background Information: The North Atlantic Hurricane Season," August 6, 2015, http://www.cpc.ncep.noaa.gov/products/outlooks/background_information.shtml (accessed July 23, 2018).

2. Google at https://www.google.com/search?q=an+algorithm+is+a+well-defined+procedure+that+allows+a+computer+to+solve+a+problem.&rlz=1C1CHWA_enUS634US641&oq=an+algorithm+is+a+well-defined+procedure+that+allows+a+computer+to+solve+a+problem.&aqs=chrome..69i57.2681j0j7&sourceid=chrome&ie=UTF-8 (accessed July 23, 2018).

3. CBS Boston, WBZ 1030 News Radio, "US Government to Seek Death Penalty in Boston Marathon Bombing Case," January 30, 2014, http://boston.cbslocal.com/2014/01/30/us-government-to-seek-death-penalty-in-boston-marathon-bombing-case (accessed September 17, 2018).

4. See U.S. Department of State, "Bureau of Political/Military Affairs," available at http://www.state.gov/t/pm (accessed September 17, 2018).

5. FEMA Careers, "Cadre of On-Call Response/Recovery," undated, https://careers.fema.gov/cadre-call-responserecovery (accessed October 8, 2018).

6. Veronica Villafañe, "Lin-Manuel Miranda Partners with Google.org for Puerto Rico Recovery $2 Million Matching Grant," *Forbes*, June 8, 2018, https://www.forbes.com/sites/veronicavillafane/2018/06/08/lin-manuel-miranda-amplifies-puerto-rico-fundraising-efforts-with-google-org-2m-matching-grant/#1b115a671035 (accessed July 24, 2018).

7. F. Henri and B. Pudelko, "Understanding and Analysing Activity and Learning in Virtual Communities," *Journal of Computer Assisted Learning* 19, no. 4 (2003): 478.

8. U.S. Department of Homeland Security, "Fiscal Year 2017 Homeland Security Grant Program," 2016, Hereafter, "DHS FY 2017 Homeland Security Grant Program, 2016." https://www.fema.gov/media-library-data/1496327128641-40d3a338eaaa2ba7679f020410ce9847/FY_2017_HSGP_Fact_Sheet_FINAL_508.pdf (accessed June 6, 2018).

9. Ibid.

10. Dhavan V. Shah, Joseph N. Cappella, and W. Russell Neuman, "Big Data, Digital Media, and Computational Social Science: Possibilities and Perils," *The Annals of the Academy of Political and Social Science*, Vol. 659, No. 1, (May 2015), 6–13. Hereafter "Shah et al., 2015."

11. Gary King, Director: Institute for Quantitative Social Science, Harvard University, Public Lecture transcribed from personal notes by Richard Sylves, "The Big Deal about Big Data: Improving National Security and Public Policy" (Washington, DC: Dirksen Senate Office Building, Room 106, May 11, 2016; 4–5:30 p.m.). (Hereafter, "King Lecture 2016.")

12. See Jack Corbett, "Nuclear War and Crisis Relocation Planning: A View from the Grassroots," Impact Assessment, 2:4, 23–33, https://www.tandfonline.com/doi/pdf/10.1080/07349165.1983.9725997 (accessed July 15, 2018).

13. Keith Smith, *Environmental Hazards: Assessing Risk and Reducing Disaster*, 6th ed. (New York: Routledge, 2013), 213. 12.

14. U.S. Department of Homeland Security, "Science and Technology: Our Work," undated, https://www.dhs.gov/science-and-technology/our-work (accessed July 24, 2018).

15. George D. Haddow and Jane A. Bullock, *Introduction to Emergency Management,* 2nd ed. (Boston: Butterworth-Heinemann, 2006), 237.

16. See Public Safety Canada, "Disaster Financial Assistance Arrangements (DFAA)," May 15, 2018, https://www.publicsafety.gc.ca/cnt/mrgnc-mngmnt/rcvr-dsstrs/dsstr-fnncl-ssstnc-rrngmnts/index-en.aspx#a01 (accessed June 12, 2018).

17. See Gavin Smith, *Planning for Post-Disaster Recovery* (Falls Church, VA: Public Entity Risk Institute, 2011).

18. Damon P. Coppola, *Introduction to International Disaster Management* (Boston: Butterworth-Heinemann, 2007), 466.

19. Committee on Increasing National Resilience to Hazards and Disasters & Committee on Science, Engineering, and Public Policy, the National Academies, *Disaster Resilience: A National Imperative* (Washington, DC: National Academies Press, 2012), 1.

20. Ryan Burke and Sue McNeil, "Toward a Unified Military Response: Hurricane Sandy and the Dual Status Commander" (Carlisle, PA: Strategic Studies Institute and the U.S. Army War College Press, 2015), 6, https://ssi.armywarcollege.edu/pubs/display.cfm?pubID=1263 (accessed July 24, 2018).

21. Ibid.

22. Ibid.

23. Federal Communications Commission, Guide, Emergency Alert System, https://www.fcc.gov/general/emergency-alert-system-eas (accessed September 17, 2018).

24. FEMA, "The Disaster Declaration Process," Last updated: 01/08/2018, https://www.fema.gov/disaster-declaration-process (accessed July 16, 2018).

25. Federal Emergency Management Agency, "History," https://www.fema.gov/about-agency (accessed October 8, 2018).

26. U.S. Department of Health and Human Services, "Emergency Support Functions," Public Health Emergencies, June 2, 2015, https://www.phe.gov/preparedness/support/esf8/Pages/default.aspx (accessed July 23, 2018).

27. Ibid.

28. National Weather Service, "Enhanced Fujita Scale," undated, https://www.weather.gov/oun/efscale (accessed July 24, 2018).

29. National Public Radio, *NPR*, "What Is Executive Privilege, Anyway?" June 28, 2007. At https://www.npr.org/templates/story/story.php?storyId=11527747 (accessed May 4, 2018).

30. Mauro F. Guillén, book review of Lee Clarke, *Mission Improbable: Using Fantasy Documents to Tame Disaster* (Chicago, IL: University of Chicago Press, 1999), Reproduced from *Administrative Science Quarterly*, March 2001 (46:1:151–153), permission of *ASQ*, https://leeclarke.com/mipages/guillen.html (accessed July 24, 2018).

31. See Public Safety Canada, "Disaster Financial Assistance Arrangements (DFAA)," May 15, 2018, https://www.publicsafety.gc.ca/cnt/mrgnc-mngmnt/rcvr-dsstrs/dsstr-fnncl-ssstnc-rrngmnts/index-en.aspx#a01 (accessed June 12, 2018).

32. FEMA, "Disaster Fraud," October 27, 2017, https://www.fema.gov/disaster-fraud (accessed July 23, 2018).

33. Jim McKay, "Hawaii Fallout: Mistakes Happen, but Probably Not Here: Emergency Managers Review Their Protocols after Hawaii False Alert," *Emergency Management Magazine*, January 25, 2018, http://www.govtech.com/em/disaster/Hawaii-Fallout-Mistakes-Happen-but-Probably-Not-Here.html?utm_term=Hawaii%20Fallout%3A%20Mistakes%20Happen%2C%20but%20Probably%20Not%20Here&utm_campaign=No%20Deaths%20From%20Storm%20Surge%20Last%20Year&utm_content=email&utm_source=Act-On+Software&utm_medium=email (accessed July 1, 2018).

34. See Jon D. Russell and Aaron Bostrom, "Federalism, Dillon Rule and Home Rule," *The American City County Exchange*, White Paper, January 2016, https://www.alec.org/app/uploads/2016/01/2016-ACCE-White-Paper-Dillon-House-Rule-Final.pdf (accessed July 15, 2018). This source also shows which states provide Dillon Rule or Home Rule powers to their sub-state governments. Different states confer different conditions on the powers they entrust to various types of local government within their respective jurisdictions.

35. The Free Dictionary, s.v. "home rule," https://legal-dictionary.thefreedictionary.com/home+rule (accessed July 15, 2018).

36. To read the Homeland Security Act of 2002 in full, see U.S. Department of Homeland Security, " Homeland Security Act of 2002," Public Law 107-296, 116 Stat. 2135, enacted November 25, 2002, https://www.dhs.gov/sites/default/files/publications/hr_5005_enr.pdf (accessed July 15, 2018).

37. Ibid.

38. Eric S. Blake and David A. Zelinsky, "National Hurricane Center, Tropical Cyclone Report: Hurricane Harvey," May 9, 2018, https://www.nhc.noaa.gov/data/tcr/AL092017_Harvey.pdf (accessed July 23, 2018).

39. Ibid.

40. World Vision, "Hurricane Irma: Facts, FAQs, and How to Help," February 14, 2018, https://www.worldvision.org/disaster-relief-news-stories/hurricane-irma-facts (accessed June 23, 2018).

41. John P. Cangialosi, Andrew S. Latto, and Robbie Berg, "National Hurricane Center, Tropical Cyclone Report: Hurricane Irma," National Hurricane Center, June 30, 2018, https://www.nhc.noaa.gov/data/tcr/AL112017_Irma.pdf (accessed July 23, 2018).

42. Ibid.

43. Robinson Meyer, "What's Happening with the Relief Effort in Puerto Rico? A Timeline of the Unprecedented Catastrophe of Hurricane Maria," *The Atlantic*, October 4, 2017, https://www.theatlantic.com/science/archive/2017/10/what-happened-in-puerto-rico-a-timeline-of-hurricane-maria/541956/ (accessed June 25, 2018).

44. Sheri Fink, "Puerto Rico's Hurricane Maria Death Toll Could Exceed 4,000, New Study Estimates," *The New York Times*, May 29, 2018, https://www.nytimes.com/2018/05/29/us/puerto-rico-deaths-hurricane.html (accessed July 23, 2018).

45. Richard J. Pasch, Andrew B. Penny, and Robbie Berg, "The National Hurricane Center Tropical Cycle Report: Hurricane Maria," April 10, 2018, https://www.nhc.noaa.gov/data/tcr/AL152017_Maria.pdf (accessed July 23, 2018).

46. Ibid.

47. Your Dictionary, "Hyperpartisanship," undated http://www.yourdictionary.com/hyperpartisanship (accessed July 24, 2018).

48. Federal Emergency Management Agency, "Federal/State Individual & Family Grant Program - Q & A," September 23, 1999, Release Number: 1292-13, http://www.fema.gov/news-release/1999/09/23/federal/state-individual-family-grant-program-q (accessed September 17, 2018).

49. Walter R. Mead, "The Jacksonian Tradition," *The National Interest* 58 (Winter 1999–2000), http://nationalinterest.org/article/the-jacksonian-tradition-939 (accessed September 17, 2018).

50. Ibid.

51. This is required under section 2006 of the Homeland Security Act of 2002, as amended (6 U.S.C. § 607). Also, law enforcement is linked to one or more core capabilities within the National Preparedness Goal.

52. David A. McEntire, *Disaster Response and Recovery* (Hoboken, NJ: Wiley, 2007), 49.

53. Ibid., 55.

54. Brenda D. Phillips and David M. Neal, "Recovery," in *Emergency Management: Principles and Practice for Local Government,* 2nd ed., eds. William L. Waugh Jr. and Kathleen Tierney (Washington, DC: ICMA Press, 2007), 208.

55. Gilbert Cruz, "Top 10 Environmental Disasters—And the Earth Cried: Love Canal," *Time,* May 3, 2010, http://content.time.com/time/specials/packages/article/0,28804,1986457_1986501_1986441,00.html (accessed September 17, 2018).

56. United States Code, V. 26, Title 42, The Public Health and Welfare, (2), "Major Disaster" (Washington, DC: Government Printing Office, 2006), 163.

57. Richard T. Sylves, "The Politics and Budgeting of Federal Emergency Management," in *Disaster Management in the U.S. and Canada,* eds. Richard T. Sylves and William L. Waugh Jr. (Springfield, IL: Charles C Thomas, 1996), 32; U.S. Government Accountability Office, *Disaster Assistance: Improvement Needed in Disaster Declaration Criteria and Eligibility Assurance Procedures. GAO-01-837* (Washington, DC: Government Printing Office, 2001), 9–15.

58. FEMA, "Emergency Support Function #6—Mass Care, Emergency Assistance, Housing, and Human Services Annex," January 2008, https://www.fema.gov/pdf/emergency/nrf/nrf-esf-06.pdf (accessed July 23, 2018).

59. See FEMA Mission Assignment Policy (FP 104-101-2), at https://www.fema.gov/media-library-data/1450099364660-fd855ba68f3189d974966ea259a2641a/Mission_Assignment_Policy.pdf (accessed September 23, 2018).

60. U.S. Geological Survey, Earthquake Hazards Program, "The Modified Mercalli Intensity Scale,"

undated, https://earthquake.usgs.gov/learn/topics/mercalli.php (accessed July 24, 2018).

61. UPSeis, Michigan Tech, "How Are Earthquake Magnitudes Measured?" undated. At http://www.geo.mtu.edu/UPSeis/intensity.html (accessed May 12, 2018).

62. Richard T. Sylves, "Federal Emergency Management Comes of Age: 1979–2001," in *Emergency Management: The American Experience: 1900–2010*, 2nd ed., ed. Claire B. Rubin (Boca Raton, FL: CRC Press, 2012), 122.

63. Keith Smith, *Environmental Hazards: Assessing Risk and Reducing Disasters*, 6th ed. (New York: Routledge, 2013), 376–378.

64. See National Research Council, *Launching a National Conversation on Disaster Resilience in America: Workshop Summary* (Washington, DC: National Academies Press, 2013); National Research Council. Disaster Resilience: A National Imperative (Washington, DC: National Academies Press, 2012); National Research Council, *Building Community Disaster Resilience through Private-Public Collaboration* (Washington, DC: National Academies Press, 2011); and National Research Council, *Increasing National Resilience to Hazards and Disasters: The Perspective from the Gulf Coast of Louisiana and Mississippi: Summary of a Workshop* (Washington, DC: National Academies Press, 2011).

65. FEMA, "The National Earthquake Hazards Reduction Program (NEHRP) Overview," August 8, 2016, https://www.fema.gov/media-library-data/1470676164637-ef214c30572785a34c044fd26e6adf32/NEHRP_Overview_080116.pdf (accessed July 15, 2018).

66. U.S. Fire Administration, "National Fire Academy," https://www.usfa.fema.gov/training/nfa/index.html (accessed September 17, 2018).

67. FEMA, "National Planning Frameworks," Last updated: June 19, 2018, https://www.fema.gov/national-planning-frameworks (accessed July 23, 2018).

68. Ibid.

69. Federal Emergency Management Agency, "National Response Framework: Third Edition," June 16, 2016, https://www.fema.gov/media-library/assets/documents/117791 (accessed October 8, 2018).

70. National Science Foundation, "About the National Science Foundation," The National Earthquake Hazards Reduction Program (NEHRP) Overview, https://www.nsf.gov/about/ (accessed July 15, 2018).

71. Ibid.

72. Christopher T. Geldart, " Anatomy of a U.S. National Special Security Event," *Domestic Preparedness*, June 7, 2017, https://www.domesticpreparedness.com/preparedness/anatomy-of-a-national-special-security-event/ (accessed October 8, 2018).

73. National Voluntary Organizations Active in Disaster, "Who We Are," http://www.nvoad.org/about (accessed September 17, 2018). National Voluntary Organizations Active in Disaster (VOAD) is a nonprofit, nonpartisan membership-based organization that serves as the forum in which organizations share knowledge and resources throughout the disaster cycle—preparation, response, and recovery—to help disaster survivors and their communities. To carry out this mission, national VOAD fosters more effective service to people affected by disaster through convening mechanisms, outreach, advocacy, and as a champion and facilitator for the application of our values and core principles. Since its founding in 1970, national VOAD member organizations have worked to assist communities affected by disasters. Over the past 42 years, the VOAD movement has grown to include 111 member organizations throughout the nation, serving in all 50 states, five territories, and the District of Columbia. Guided by the core principles of the 4Cs—cooperation, communication, coordination, and collaboration—national VOAD members provide the leadership that builds strong, resilient communities and delivers hope in times of need.

74. National Weather Service, "About NOAA's National Weather Service," http://www.weather.gov/about (accessed September 17, 2018).

75. Peter Folger, "National Earthquake Hazards Reduction Program (NEHRP): Issues in Brief," Congressional Research Service, September 20, 2018, https://fas.org/sgp/crs/misc/R43141.pdf (accessed October 8, 2018).

76. See Cory Janssen, "Network Theory," Techopedia, http://www.techopedia.com/definition/25064/network-theory (accessed September 17, 2018).

77. New normalcy is discussed in Donald F. Kettl, *System under Stress: Homeland and American Politics,* 3rd ed. (Washington, DC: CQ Press, 2014), 166.

78. NSSL The National Severe Storms Laboratory, "About NSSL," https://www.nssl.noaa.gov/about/ (accessed July 15, 2018).

79. Ibid.

80. Peter Bondarenko, "North American Free Trade Agreement," Encyclopedia Britannica, July 1, 1988 original version, https://www.britannica.com/event/North-American-Free-Trade-Agreement (accessed July 24, 2018).

81. The UNHCR spends an average of $22 million per deployment. Haddow and Bullock, *Introduction to Emergency Management,* 2nd ed., 228.

82. Kate Jastram and Marilyn Achiron, Office of the United Nations High Commissioner for Refugees, *Refugee Protection: A Guide to International Refugee Law* (Geneva, Switzerland: Inter-Parliamentary Union 2001), http://archive.ipu.org/PDF/publications/refugee_en.pdf (accessed September 17, 2018).

83. Ibid.

84. U.S. Federal Bureau of Investigation, History, Famous Cases and Criminals, "The Oklahoma City Bombing," https://www.fbi.gov/history/famous-cases/oklahoma-city-bombing (accessed October 8, 2018).

85. Homeland Security Grants. Info, "Operation Stonegarden (OPSG) Program," 2018, https://www.homelandsecuritygrants.info/GrantDetails.aspx?gid=21875 (accessed June 10, 2018).

86. Ibid.

87. Kristian Bannister, "Understanding Sentiment Analysis: What It Is & Why It's Used," January 26, 2015, *Brandwatch* at https://www.brandwatch.com/blog/understanding-sentiment-analysis/ (accessed July 23, 2018).

88. Keith Smith, *Environmental Hazards: Assessing Risks and Reducing Disasters*, 6th ed. (New York: Routledge, 2013), 146.

89. "King Lecture 2016," cited previously.

90. Problem Solving with Algorithms and Data Structures, "What Is Programming?, undated, http://interactivepython.org/courselib/static/pythonds/Introduction/WhatIsProgramming.html (accessed July 23, 2018).

91. Ibid.

92. Emergency Management Act, S.C. 2007, c. 15, Assented to 2007-06-22. An Act to provide for emergency management and to amend and repeal certain Acts. Her Majesty, by and with the advice and consent of the Senate and House of Commons of Canada, enact. Justice Laws Website, "Emergency Management Act: S.C. 2007, c. 15," Government of Canada, June 28, 2018, http://laws-lois.justice.gc.ca/eng/acts/E-4.56/FullText.html?wbdisable=true (accessed July 24, 2018).

93. Ibid.

94. Ibid.

95. Urban Studies Mid-term Review, Queens College, City University of New York, "URBST 101 Midterm Review Fall 2018 (1).docx–1," https://www.coursehero.com/file/30183317/URBST-101-Midterm-Review-Fall-2018-1docx/ (accessed July 23, 2018).

96. Governance and Social Development Resource Centre, "What is Disaster Resilience?" 2018, http://gsdrc.org/topic-guides/disaster-resilience/concepts/what-is-disaster-resilience/ (accessed July 23, 2018).

97. UPSeis, Michigan Tech, "How Are Earthquake Magnitudes Measured?" undated. At http://www.geo.mtu.edu/UPSeis/intensity.html (accessed May 12, 2018).

98. Keith Smith, *Environmental Hazards: Assessing Risks and Reducing Disasters*, 6th ed., 11. Cited previously.

99. Howard Kunreuther, "Has the Time Come for Comprehensive National Disaster Insurance?" in *On Risk and Disaster,* eds. Ronald J. Daniels, Donald E. Kettl, and Howard Kunreuther (Philadelphia: University of Pennsylvania Press, 2006), 188. See also Deborah Stone, *The Samaritan's Dilemma:*

Should Government Help Your Neighbor? (New York: Nation Books, 2008).

100. See U.S. Congress, "Disaster Relief Appropriations," Public Law 113-2, section 1110, (Washington, DC: U.S. Government Printing Office, January 29, 2013), https://www.congress.gov/113/plaws/publ2/PLAW-113publ2.pdf (accessed July 15, 2018). In precise terms, "INDIAN TRIBAL GOVERNMENT REQUESTS.—(1) IN GENERAL.—The Chief Executive of an affected Indian tribal government may submit a request for a declaration by the President that a major disaster exists consistent with the requirements of subsection (a). (2) REFERENCES.—In implementing assistance authorized by the President under this Act in response to a request of the Chief Executive of an affected Indian tribal government for a major disaster declaration, any reference in this title or title III (except sections 310 and 326) to a State or the Governor of a State is deemed to refer to an affected Indian tribal government or the Chief Executive of an affected Indian tribal government, as appropriate. "(3) SAVINGS PROVISION.—Nothing in this subsection shall prohibit an Indian tribal government from receiving assistance under this title through a declaration made by the President at the request of a State under subsection (a) if the President does not make a declaration under this subsection for the same incident." Ibid.

101. Brian Marshall and Susan L. Nasr, "How Biological and Chemical Warfare Works," *How Stuff Works,* http://science.howstuffworks.com/biochem-war3.htm (accessed September 17, 2018).

102. Smith, *Environmental Hazards,* 6th ed., 146.

103. Lucy Birmingham, "Japan's Earthquake Warning System Explained," *Time,* March 18, 2011. http://www.time.com/time/world/article/0,8599,2059780,00.html (accessed September 17, 2018).

104. U.S. Geological Survey, "Earthquake Glossary: S Wave," undated, https://earthquake.usgs.gov/learn/glossary/?term=S%20wave (accessed July 23, 2018).

105. Kristian Bannister, "Understanding Sentiment Analysis: What It Is & Why It's Used," January 26, 2015, *Brandwatch,* cited previously.

106. Phillips and Neal, "Recovery," 208.

107. Teaching Resource Center, University of California, Berkeley, "Learning: Theory and Research: Social Constructivism, Teaching Guide for Graduate Student Instructors," http://gsi.berkeley.edu/teachingguide/theories/social.html.

108. Adam Crowe, *Disasters 2.0: The Application of Social Media Systems for Modern Emergency Management* (Boca Raton, FL: CRC Press, 2012), 25, 109.

109. See FEMA, "Robert T. Stafford Disaster Relief and Emergency Assistance Act, Public Law 93-288, as amended, 42 U.S.C. 5121 et seq., and Related Authorities," February 23, 2018, https://www.fema.gov/media-library-data/1519395888776-af5f95a1a9237302af7e3fd5b0d07d71/StaffordAct.pdf (accessed July 15, 2018).

110. Ryan Burke and Sue McNeil, "Toward a Unified Military Response: Hurricane Sandy and the Dual Status Commander," 10, cited previously.

111. U.S. Department of Homeland Security, "Surge Capacity Force," September 25, 2017, https://www.dhs.gov/topic/surge-capacity-force (accessed July 23, 2018).

112. See FEMA, "Threat and Hazard Identification and Risk Assessment," Last updated, May 31, 2018, at https://www.fema.gov/threat-and-hazard-identification-and-risk-assessment (accessed October 2, 2018).

113. "King Lecture 2016," cited previously.

114. Charles Perrow, *Normal Accidents* (New York: Basic Books, 1984). See also Charles Perrow, *The Next Catastrophe: Reducing Our Vulnerabilities to Natural, Industrial, and Terrorist Disasters* (Princeton, NJ: Princeton University Press, 2011).

115. James Jay Carafano, "Catastrophic Disaster and the Future of the Military Response," *Disaster Preparedness* 1, no. 1 (Summer 2006).

116. George D. Haddow and Jane A. Bullock, *Introduction to Emergency Management,* 2nd ed. (Boston: Butterworth-Heinemann, 2006), 85.

117. See Connie M. White, *Social Media, Crisis Communication, and Emergency Management,* (Boca Raton, FL: CRC Press of Taylor & Francis Group, 2012). White's book offers many examples of Twitter's use and benefits in emergency management.

118. United Nations Office for the Coordination of Humanitarian Affairs, "About Us: The Under-Secretary-General and Emergency Relief Coordinator," www.unocha.org/about-us/headofOCHA (accessed March 8, 2014).

119. U.S. Navy, Military Sealift Command, "Ship Inventory: Hospital Ships," undated, http://www.msc.navy.mil/inventory/ships.asp?ship=74 (accessed July 23, 2018).

120. Trend Micro Inc., "The Patriot Act Revision: What Does It Mean to You? [updated]," June 5, 2015, https://www.trendmicro.com/vinfo/us/security/news/online-privacy/patriot-act-revision-underway-what-does-it-mean-to-you (accessed June 2, 2018).

121. See Michael Hirsh and James Oliphant, "Obama Will Never End the War on Terror," *National Journal Magazine*, February 27, 2014, https://www.nationaljournal.com/s/627840/obama-will-never-end-war-terror (accessed September 17, 2018). Hirsh and Oliphant write, "No one has been more aware of this probability than the president himself, who has regularly warned that America must get off a 'perpetual wartime footing,' declaring in a landmark speech last year, 'We must define the nature and scope of this struggle, or else it will define us. . . . Unless we discipline our thinking, our definitions, our actions, we may be drawn into more wars we don't need to fight, or continue to grant presidents unbound powers.'" Ibid.

122. *Virginian-Pilot*, "Timeline: The History of The Weather Channel," July 6, 2008, at http://hamptonroads.com/2008/07/timeline-history-weather-channel (accessed September 17, 2018).

MASTER BIBLIOGRAPHY

Acosta, Jim and Sophie Tatum. "Source: Trump's Puerto Rico Tweets were Response to San Juan Mayor." *CNN Politics*, October 13, 2017. https://www.cnn .com/2017/10/12/politics/donald-trump-puerto-rico-twitter/index.html.

Akter, Shahriar and Samuel Fosso Wamba. "Big Data and Disaster Management: A Systematic Review and Agenda for Future Research." *Annals of Operations Research*, August 21, 2017. https://link.springer.com/ article/10.1007/s10479-017-2584-2.

Alaniz, Ryan, Jessica Hubbard, Claire Rubin, Richard T. Sylves, and William L. Waugh Jr. "Teaching Recover: A Report for the Theory of Recovery Workshop." Powerpoint presentation, Disaster Recovery Workshop from the Center for the Study of Natural Hazards and Disasters, University of North Carolina at Chapel Hill, Chapel Hill, NC, November 2010. https://training.fema .gov/hiedu/11conf/presentations/hubbard-peri%20-%20 teaching%20recovery(2).pptx.

Albala-Bertrand, J. M. "Globalization and Localization: An Economic Approach." In *Handbook of Disaster Research*, edited by Havidan Rodriguez, Enrico L. Quarantelli, and Russell R. Dynes, 147–167. New York: Springer, 2007.

Alexander, David. *Natural Disasters*. New York: Chapman & Hall, 1993.

Alexander, David. "Rapid Adaptation to Threat: The London Bombings." In *Designing Resilience: Preparing for Extreme Events*, edited by Louise K. Comfort, Arjin Boin, and Chris C. Demchak, 143–157. Pittsburgh, PA: University of Pittsburgh Press, 2010.

Allison, Graham T. *Destined for War: Can America and China Escape Thucydides's Trap?* Boston, MA: Houghton, Mifflin, Harcourt, 2017.

Allison, Graham T. *Essence of Decision: Explaining the Cuban Missile Crisis*. Boston: Little, Brown, 1971.

Ambinder, Marc. "America's Doomsday Secrets." *The Week*, November 2, 2012. http://theweek.com/ articles/470754/americas-doomsday-secrets.

"America Is Good at Dealing with Hurricanes on the Mainland—After They Strike." *The Economist*, June 1, 2018. https://www.economist.com/graphic-detail/2018/06/01/america-is-good-at-dealing-with-hurricanes-on-the-mainland-after-they-strike.

American Civil Liberties Union. "The Militarization of Policing in America." Accessed September 10, 2018. http://www.aclu.org/militarization.

American Heritage Dictionary of the English Language, s.v. "Atomic Age," accessed July 18, 2018, https://www .ahdictionary.com/word/search.html?q=atomic+age.

American Red Cross. "Disaster Relief." Accessed September 7, 2018. https://www.redcross.org/about-us/ our-work/disaster-relief.html.

Anderson, C. V. *The Federal Emergency Management Agency (FEMA)*. New York: Nova Science Publishers, 2003.

Anderson, James E. *Public Policymaking: An Introduction*, 3rd ed. Boston: Houghton Mifflin, 1997.

Anderson, Robert and Ines Pearce. "Public Private Partnerships in Mitigation Initiatives." In *Natural Hazard Mitigation*, edited by Alessandra Jerolleman and John J. Kiefer, 68. Boca Raton, FL: CRC Press, 2013.

Anton, Thomas J. *American Federalism and Public Policy*. New York: Random House, 1989.

Arceneaux, Kevin and Robert M. Stein. "Who Is Held Responsible When Disaster Strikes? The Attribution of Responsibility for a Natural Disaster in an Urban Election." *Journal of Urban Affairs* 28 (January 2006): 43.

Arndt, Gary. "Everything You Need to Know About the Territories of the United States." *Everything Everywhere* (blog), June 27, 2013. https://everything-everywhere.

com/everything-you-need-to-know-about-the-territories-of-the-united-states/.

Arrow, Kenneth J. "The Economics of Agency." In *Principals and Agents: The Structure of Business*, edited by John W. Pratt and Richard J. Zeckhauser, 37–51. Boston: Harvard Business School Press, 1988.

The Associated Press. "Military Mission in Puerto Rico after Hurricane was Better than Critics Say but Suffered Flaws." *WTOP*, March 30, 2018. https://wtop.com/national/2018/03/military-mission-in-puerto-rico-after-hurricane-was-better-than-critics-say-but-suffered-flaws/.

Baker, Peter. "Trump Lashes Out at Puerto Rico Mayor Who Criticized Storm Response." *The New York Times*, September 30, 2017. https://www.nytimes.com/2017/09/30/us/politics/trump-puerto-rico-mayor.html.

Bannister, Kristian. "Understanding Sentiment Analysis: What It Is & Why It's Used." *Brandwatch*, January 26, 2015. https://www.brandwatch.com/blog/understanding-sentiment-analysis/.

Barber, James David. "Presidential Character." In *American Government: Readings and Cases*, edited by Karen O'Connor, 204. Boston: Allyn & Bacon, 1995.

Barnard, Chester I. *Functions of the Executive*, 30th anniversary ed. Cambridge, MA: Harvard University Press, 1968.

Barrett, James. "A Complete List of Radical Islamic Terror Attacks on U.S. Soil Under Obama." *Dailywire*, December 7, 2016. https://www.dailywire.com/news/11410/complete-list-radical-islamic-terror-attacks-us-james-barrett.

Barron, James. "The Blackout of 2003: The Overview; Power Surge Blacks Out Northeast Hitting Cities in 8 states and Canada; Midday Shutdowns Disrupt Millions." *The New York Times*, August 15, 2003.

Barry, John. *The Rising Tide: The Great Mississippi Flood of 1927 and How It Changed America*. New York: Touchstone, 1998.

Barzelay, Michael. *Breaking through Bureaucracy: A New Vision for Management in Government*. Berkeley: University of California Press, 1992.

Bea, Keith. *Federal Stafford Act Disaster Assistance: Presidential Declarations, Eligible Activities, and Funding*. Washington, DC: Congressional Research Service, 2006.

Bea, Keith. "The Formative Years: 1950–1978." In *Emergency Management: The American Experience, 1900–2010*, 2nd ed., edited by Claire B. Rubin. Boca Raton, FL: CRC Press, 2012.

Ben-Shahar, Omri and Kyle D. Logue. "Lessons from Hurricane Harvey: Federal Flood Insurance Is the Problem, Not the Solution." *Forbes*, August 30, 2017. https://www.forbes.com/sites/omribenshahar/2017/08/30/lessons-from-hurricane-harvey-federal-flood-insurance-is-the-problem-not-the-solution/2/#14e567e3614d.

"A Big Storm Requires Big Government." *The New York Times*, October 29, 2012. http://www.nytimes.com/2012/10/30/opinion/a-big-storm-requires-big-government.html?_r=0.

The Bill and Melinda Gates Foundation. "What We Do: Emergency Response, Strategy Overview." Accessed May 10, 2018. https://www.gatesfoundation.org/What-We-Do/Global-Development/Emergency-Response.

Biography. "Alexander Hamilton." Accessed March 30, 2018. https://www.biography.com/people/alexander-hamilton-9326481.

Biography. "Andrew Jackson." Accessed April 13, 2018. www.biography.com/people/andrew-jackson-9350991?page=1.

Birkland, Thomas A. *After Disaster: Agenda Setting, Public Policy, and Focusing Events*. Washington, DC: Georgetown University Press, 1997.

Birkland, Thomas A. *An Introduction to the Policy Process*, 4th ed. New York: Routledge, 2016.

Birkland, Thomas A. *Lessons of Disaster: Policy Change after Catastrophic Events*. Washington, DC: Georgetown University Press, 2006.

Birmingham, Lucy. "Japan's Earthquake Warning System Explained." *Time*, March 18, 2011. http://www.time.com/time/world/article/0,8599,2059780,00.html.

Blad, Evie. "Issues A-Z: School Shootings: Five Critical Questions." *Education Week*, February 16, 2018. http://www.edweek.org/ew/issues/school-shootings/.

Blair, William G. "John W. Macy, Jr., 69, Ex-Leader of the Civil Service Commission Dies." *The New York Times*, December 25, 1986. https://www.nytimes.com/1986/12/25/obituaries/john-w-macy-jr-69-ex-leader-of-civil-service-commission-dies.html.

Blake, Eric S. and David A. Zelinsky. *Tropical Cyclone Report: Hurricane Harvey*. Miami, FL: National Hurricane Center, 2018. https://www.nhc.noaa.gov/data/tcr/AL092017_Harvey.pdf.

Bland, Robert Jessica E. Short, and Simon A. Andrew. "Financial Resiliency by Local Governments to Natural Disasters." In *The Future of Disaster Management in the U.S.*, edited by Amy LePore, 196–199. New York: Routledge, Taylor and Francis Group, 2017.

Blankstein, Andrew and Monica Alba. "Why Do So Few California Homeowners Have Earthquake Insurance?" *NBC News*, October 17, 2014. https://www.nbcnews.com/news/investigations/why-do-so-few-california-homeowners-have-earthquake-insurance-n227711.

Blanshard, Brand. "Rationalism." *Encyclopaedia Britannica*, July 22, 2016. www.britannica.com/EBchecked/topic/492034/rationalism.

Blocker, T. Jean, E. Burke Rochford Jr., and Darren E. Sherkat. "Political Responses to Natural Hazards: Social Movement Participation Following a Flood." *International Journal of Mass Emergencies and Disasters* 9 (1991): 367–382.

Blume, Tara. "Disaster Assistance from FEMA." *KFOR*, May 25, 2013. https://kfor.com/2013/05/25/disaster-assitance-from-fema/.

Boin, Arjen, Paul 't Hart, Eric Stern, and Bengt Sundelius. *The Politics of Crisis Management: Public Leadership under Pressure*, 2nd ed. Cambridge, UK: Cambridge University Press, University Printing House, 2017.

Bolin, Robert and Lois Stanford. *The Northridge Earthquake: Vulnerability and Disaster*. London: Routledge, 1999.

Bondarenko, Peter. "North American Free Trade Agreement." *Encyclopaedia Britannica*, July 1, 1988. https://www.britannica.com/event/North-American-Free-Trade-Agreement.

Borodzicz, Edward P. *Risk, Crisis, and Security Management*. Hoboken, NJ: Wiley, 2005.

Bowman, Tom and Siobhan Gorman. "Increasing Military's Role Raises Questions." *Baltimore Sun*, September 20, 2005.

Boyd, Eugene. *American Federalism, 1776 to 1997: Significant Events*. US Embassy, January 6, 1997. https://usa.usembassy.de/etexts/gov/federal.htm.

BrainyQuote. "Disaster Quotes." Accessed June 11, 2018. https://www.brainyquote.com/quotes/neil_degrasse_tyson_531162?src=t_disaster.

BrainyQuote. "Jim Wallis Quotes." Accessed September 13, 2018. http://www.brainyquote.com/quotes/quotes/j/jimwallis383544.html.

Brinkley, Douglas. *The Great Deluge: Hurricane Katrina, New Orleans, and the Mississippi Gulf Coast*. New York: William Morrow, 2006.

Brookings Institution. *Protecting the American Homeland: A Second Look at How We're Meeting the Challenge, A Brookings Briefing*. Washington, DC: Brookings Institution, 2003. http://www.brookings.edu/events/2003/01/23defense.

Brown, Jared T., Francis X. McCarthy, and Edwin C. Liu. *Analysis of the Sandy Recovery Improvement Act of 2013*. Washington, DC: U.S. Congressional Research Service, 2013.

Brown, Jared T., Nicole T. Carter, Diane P. Horn, Sarah A. Lister, and William L. Painter. "Congressional Considerations Related to Hurricanes Harvey and Irma." *CRS Insight*, September 8, 2017. https://fas.org/sgp/crs/homesec/IN10763.pdf.

Budjeryn, Mariana, Simon Saradzhyan, and William Tobey. "25 Years of Nuclear Security Cooperation by the US, Russia and Other Newly Independent States: A Timeline." *Russia Matters*, June 16, 2017. https://www.russiamatters.org/analysis/25-years-nuclear-security-cooperation-us-russia-and-other-newly-independent-states.

Bullock, Jane A., George Haddow, and Damon P. Coppola. *Introduction to Homeland Security*, 2nd ed. Waltham, MA: Butterworth-Heinemann, 2006.

Burke, Ryan and Sue McNeil. *Toward a Unified Military Response: Hurricane Sandy and the Dual Status Commander*. Carlisle, PA: Strategic Studies Institute and the U.S. Army War College Press, 2015. https://ssi.armywarcollege.edu/pubs/display.cfm?pubID=1263.

Burns, Melinda. "When It Rains Again: Science of a Disaster." *Newsmakers with Jerry Roberts*, January 16, 2018. https://www.newsmakerswithjr.com/single-post/2018/01/16/When-It-Rains-Again-Science-of-a-Disaster.

Bush, George W. Homeland Security Presidential Directive-1. October 29, 2001. http://www.fas.org/irp/offdocs/nspd/hspd-1.htm.

Bush, George W. Homeland Security Presidential Directive-5. February 28, 2003. http://www.michigan.gov/documents/deq/deq-wb-wws-HSPD-5_268188_7.pdf.

Bush, George W. "A Week of Crisis (August 29–September 5)." Chap. 4 in *The Federal Response to Hurricane Katrina: Lessons Learned*. Washington, DC: The White House & Executive Office of the President, 2006. http://georgewbush-whitehouse.archives.gov/reports/katrina-lessons-learned/chapter4.html.

Butler, David. "Focusing Events in the Early Twentieth Century: A Hurricane, Two Earthquakes, and a Pandemic." In *Emergency Management: The American Experience 1900-2010*, 2nd ed., edited by Claire B. Rubin. Boca Raton, FL: CRC Press, 2012.

Cal Fire. "Top 20 Largest California Wildfires." Last modified January 15, 2019. https://www.fire.ca.gov/communications/downloads/fact_sheets/Top20_Acres.pdf.

Caldwell, Leigh Ann and Alex Moe. "Trump Signs Disaster Aid, and His Deal with Dems, into Law." *NBC News Politics*, September 8, 2017. https://www.nbcnews.com/politics/congress/house-passes-disaster-relief-sending-trump-sign-n799796.

California Earthquake Authority. "An Earthquake Could Happen Today." Accessed April 2, 2018. https://www.earthquakeauthority.com/.

Cameron, David and Richard Simeon. "Intergovernmental Relations in Canada: The Emergence of Collaborative Federalism." *Publius: The Journal of Federalism* 32, no. 2 (2002): 49–72. http://publius.oxfordjournals.org/content/32/2/49.short.

Cangialosi, John P., Andrew S. Latto, and Robbie Berg. *Tropical Cyclone Report: Hurricane Irma*. Miami, FL: National Hurricane Center, 2018. https://www.nhc.noaa.gov/data/tcr/AL112017_Irma.pdf.

Canton, Lucien G. *Emergency Management: Concepts and Strategies for Effective Programs*. Hoboken, NJ: Wiley, 2007.

Carafano, James Jay. "Catastrophic Disaster and the Future of the Military Response." *Disaster Preparedness* 1, no. 1 (Summer 2006).

Carter, Jimmy. "Portland, Oregon Remarks and a Question-and-Answer Session With Reporters Following an Inspection Tour of Areas Damaged by the Mount St. Helens Eruption." *The American Presidency Project*, May 22, 1980. https://www.presidency.ucsb.edu/node/252206.

Center for Responsive Politics. "Insurance Lobbying." Accessed September 4, 2018. https://www.opensecrets.org/industries/lobbying.php?cycle=2018&ind=F09

Cha, Bonnie. "Too Embarrassed to Ask: What Is 'The Cloud' and How Does It Work?" *Recode*, April 30, 2015. https://www.recode.net/2015/4/30/11562024/too-embarrassed-to-ask-what-is-the-cloud-and-how-does-it-work.

Chaudhuri, Debarshi. "Government: Response to Katrina." Mission 2010: New Orleans. Accessed April 26, 2018. http://web.mit.edu/12.000/www/m2010/finalwebsite/katrina/government/government-response.html.

Chernow, Ron. *Alexander Hamilton*. New York: The Penguin Group, 2004.

Cigler, Beverly A. "Coping with Floods, Lessons from the 1990s." In *Disaster Management in the U.S. and Canada*, edited by Richard T. Sylves and William L. Waugh Jr., 196–198. Springfield, IL: Charles C Thomas, 1996.

Clark, Charles S. "The Obama Way: Assessing the President's Management Approach." *National Journal*, August 3, 2012. https://www.yahoo.com/news/obama-way-assessing-presidents-management-approach-155437265.html.

Clark, Len Elisha. *Implementation of the National Incident Management System in New Jersey*. PhD diss., University of Baltimore, 2010. http://ubalt.worldcat.org/title/implementation-of-the-national-incident-management-system-in-new-jersey/oclc/636022706&referer=brief_results.

Clarke, Lee. *Mission Improbable: Using Fantasy Documents to Tame Disaster*. Chicago, IL: University of Chicago Press, 1999.

Clovis, Samuel, Jr. "Promises Unfulfilled: The Suboptimization of Homeland Security National Preparedness." *Homeland Security Affairs* IV, no. 3 (October 2008): 14–15. http://www.hsaj.org/?fullarticle=4.3.3.

CNN. "About CNN.com." Accessed June 7, 2018. https://www.cnn.com/2014/01/17/cnn-info/about/index.html.

CNN. "Beirut Marine Barracks Bombing Fast Facts." Accessed September 4, 2018. http://www.cnn.com/2013/06/13/world/meast/beirut-marine-barracks-bombing-fast-facts.

CNN. "Oklahoma City Bombing Fast Facts." Accessed April 26, 2018. https://www.cnn.com/2013/09/18/us/oklahoma-city-bombing-fast-facts/index.html.

Colarusso, L. M. "Air Force Told to Pick Up Noble Eagle Costs." *Air Force Times*, February 7, 2005.

Colvin, Richard Lee. "FEMA Answers Earthquake Disaster with a Blizzard of Aid Checks." *Los Angeles Times*, April 2, 1994. http://articles.latimes.com/1994-04-02/news/mn-41370_1_fema-aid.

Comfort, Louise K., ed. *Managing Disaster: Strategies and Policy Perspectives*. Durham, NC: Duke University Press, 1988.

Comfort, Louise K., Arjen Boin, and Chris C. Demchak, eds. *Designing Resilience for Communities at Risk: Sociotechnical Approaches*. Pittsburgh, PA: University of Pittsburgh Press, 2010.

Comfort, Louise K., Arjen Boin, and Chris C. Demchak, eds. *Designing Resilience: Preparing for Extreme Events*. Pittsburgh, PA: University of Pittsburgh Press, 2010.

Committee on Increasing National Resilience to Hazards & Disasters and Committee on Science, Engineering, and Public Policy. *Disaster Resilience: A National Imperative*. Washington, DC: The National Academies Press, 2012. https://www.nap.edu/read/13457/chapter/1.

Cook, Alethia H. "Towards an Emergency Response Report Card: Evaluating the Response to the I-35W Bridge Collapse." *Journal of Homeland Security and Emergency Management* 6, no. 1 (2009), Article 39.

Cooper, Robert. *The Breaking of Nations: Order and Chaos in the Twenty-First Century*. New York: Atlantic Monthly Press, 2003.

Coppola, Damon P. *Introduction to International Disaster Management*. Waltham, MA: Butterworth-Heinemann, 2007.

Coppola, Damon P. *Introduction to International Disaster Management*, 2nd ed. Waltham, MA: Butterworth-Heinemann, 2011.

Coppola, Damon P. *Introduction to International Disaster Management*, 3rd ed. Waltham, MA: Butterworth-Heinemann, 2015.

Corbett, Jack. "Nuclear War and Crisis Relocation Planning: A View from the Grassroots." *Impact Assessment* 2, no. 4 (1983): 23–33. doi:10.1080/07349165.1983.9725997.

Cornell Law School, Legal Information Institute. "Commander in Chief Powers." Accessed May 3, 2018. https://www.law.cornell.edu/wex/commander_in_chief_powers.

Cornell Law School, Legal Information Institute. "42 U.S. Code § 5121 – Congressional findings and declarations." Cornell University Law School. Legal Information Institute." Accessed September 7, 2018. http://www.law.cornell.edu/uscode/text/42/5121.

Cronin, Thomas E. "The Swelling of the Presidency." In *Classic Readings in American Politics*, edited by Pietro S. Nivola and David H. Rosenbloom, 413–426. New York: St. Martin's, 1986.

Crowe, Adam. *Disasters 2.0: The Application of Social Media Systems for Modern Emergency Management*. Boca Raton, FL: CRC Press, 2012.

Cruz, Gilbert. "Top 10 Environmental Disasters—And the Earth Cried: Love Canal." *Time*, May 3, 2010. http://content.time.com/time/specials/packages/article/0,28804,1986457_1986501_1986441,00.html.

Cumming, William R. and Richard T. Sylves. "FEMA's Place in Policy, Law, and Management: A Hazardous Materials Perspective, 1979–2003." In *Homeland Security Law and Policy*, edited by William C. Nicholson. Springfield, IL: Charles C Thomas, 2005.

Cutter, Susan L., ed. *American Hazardscapes: The Regionalization of Hazards and Disasters/* Washington, DC: Joseph Henry Press, 2001).

Daines, Guy E. "Planning, Training, and Exercising." In *Emergency Management: Principles and Practice*, edited by Thomas E. Drabek and Gerard J. Hoetmer, 164–165. Washington, DC: International City Management Association, 1991.

Daniels, R. Steven and Carolyn L. Clark-Daniels. *Transforming Government: The Renewal and Revitalization of the Federal Emergency Management Agency*. Arlington, VA: Pricewaterhouse Coopers Endowment for the Business of Government, 2000.

de Rugy, Veronica and Nick Gillespie. "The War on Hype: America's Fleecing in the Name of Security." *San Francisco Chronicle*, February 19, 2006. http://www.sfgate.com/cgi-bin/article.cgi?f=/c/a/2006/02/19/INGDDH8E311.DTL.

Dennis, Michael Aaron. "Big Science." *Encyclopedia Britannica*, November 3, 1988. https://www.britannica.com/science/Big-Science-science.

"Disaster Assistance; Factors Considered When Evaluating a Governor's Request for a Major Disaster Declaration; Final rule." *Federal Register* 64, no. 169 (September 1, 1999): 47697–47699. https://www.federalregister.gov/documents/2017/10/12/2017-22032/notice-of-maximum-amount-of-assistance-under-the-individuals-and-households-program.

Dockrill, Martin, Nick Ford, and Andrew Dlugolecki. "Market Failure and Climate Change, Coping with Climate Change Risks and Opportunities for Insurers." In *Climate Change Research Report 2009*. London: The Chartered Insurance Institute, 2009.

Downs, Anthony. "Up and Down with Ecology: The 'Issue-Attention Cycle.'" *The Public Interest* 28 (Summer 1972): 38–50.

Drabek, Thomas E. "Emergency Management and Homeland Security Curricula: Contexts, Cultures, and Constraints." Paper presented at the annual meeting of the Western Social Science Association, Calgary, Alberta, Canada, April 2007.

Drogin, Bob and David S. Cloud. "U.S. and Allies Fire Missiles at Syria in Retaliation for Suspected Poison Gas Attack." *Los Angeles Times*, April 13, 2018. http://www.latimes.com/nation/la-na-pol-trump-syria-attack-20180411-story.html.

Drum, David. "Political Animal." *Washington Monthly*, September 12, 2005. http://www.washingtonmonthly.com/archives/individual/2005_09/007104.php.

Dymon, Ude J. and Rutherford H. Platt. "U.S. Federal Disaster Declarations: A Geographical Analysis." In *Disasters and Democracy: The Politics of Extreme Natural Events*, edited by Rutherford H. Platt. Washington, DC: Island Press, 1999.

Edwards, Frances L. "Federal Intervention in Local Emergency Planning: Nightmare on Main Street." *State and Local Government Review* 39, no. 1 (2007): 34.

Edwards, Frances L. "Homeland Security from the Local Perspective." In *Homeland Security Law and Policy*, edited by William C. Nicholson, 114. Springfield, IL: Charles C Thomas, 2005.

Edwards, Frances L. and Daniel C. Goodrich. *Introduction to Transportation Security*. Boca Raton, FL: CRC Press, 2013.

Elmore, Richard F. "Backward Mapping: Implementation Research and Policy Decisions." *Political Science Quarterly* 94, no. 4 (1979/1980): 69–83.

Emergency Management Accreditation Program. "What is EMAP?" Accessed June 7, 2018. https://emap.org/index.php/what-is-emap/the-emergency-management-standard.

Emergency Management Degree Program Guide. "What Emergency Management Associations Should I Join?" Accessed June 7, 2018. https://www.emergency-management-degree.org/faq/what-emergency-management-associations-should-i-join/.

Emery, David. "What Was the Actual Death Toll from Hurricane Maria in Puerto Rico?" *Snopes*, June 4, 2018. https://www.snopes.com/news/2018/06/04/death-toll-hurricane-maria-puerto-rico/.

Encyclopaedia Britannica. "Pendleton Civil Service Act." Accessed March 30, 2018. https://www.britannica.com/topic/Pendleton-Civil-Service-Act.

Encyclopaedia Britannica. "Trust Territory of the Pacific Islands." Accessed May 13, 2018. https://www.britannica.com/place/Trust-Territory-of-the-Pacific-Islands.

Erdman, Jonathan. "2017 Atlantic Hurricane Season Among Top 10 Most Active in History." *The Weather Channel*, October 2, 2017. https://weather.com/storms/hurricane/news/2017-atlantic-hurricane-season-one-of-busiest-september.

Executive Office of the President (Donald J. Trump). "Annual Report to Congress on the White House Office Personnel." June 29, 2018. https://www.whitehouse.gov/wp-content/uploads/2018/06/07012018-report-final.pdf.

Federal Aviation Administration. "Notices to Airmen." Accessed April 15, 2018. https://www.faa.gov/air_traffic/publications/notices/.

Federal Communications Commission. "Guide, Emergency Alert System." Accessed September 6, 2018. http://www.fcc.gov/guides/emergency-alert-system-eas.

Federal Emergency Management Agency. *A Citizen's Guide to Disaster Assistance*. Washington, DC: Federal Emergency Management Agency, 1999. https://training.fema.gov/emiweb/downloads/is7unit_3.pdf.

Federal Emergency Management Agency. "The College List: Colleges, Universities and Institutions Offering Emergency Management Courses." Accessed September 4, 2018. http://www.training.fema.gov/emiweb/edu/collegelist.

Federal Emergency Management Agency. "Cost Share Adjustment for Public Assistance–Hurricane Harvey in Texas." *FEMA Fact Sheet*, September 3, 2017. https://www.fema.gov/media-library-data/1506702623604-b97 38beff09d4126ba0cac2b77944ae2/FEMA_Cost_Share_Adjustment_Fact_Sheet_508_FINAL.pdf.

Federal Emergency Management Agency. "The Declaration Process." Last modified March 1, 2018. https://www.fema.gov/declaration-process.

Federal Emergency Management Agency. "The Disaster Declaration Process." Last modified January 8, 2018. https://www.fema.gov/disaster-declaration-process.

Federal Emergency Management Agency. "Disaster Fraud." Last modified October 27, 2017. https://www.fema.gov/disaster-fraud.

Federal Emergency Management Agency. *Disaster Relief Fund: Monthly Report as of April 30, 2018*. Washington, DC: Federal Emergency Management Agency, 2018. https://www.fema.gov/media-library-data/1526358994453-ab5a4d20c8e7136da5c6ed583286ff6a/May2018Disaster ReliefFundReport.pdf.

Federal Emergency Management Agency. "Disaster-Specific Memorandum of Understanding." Accessed May 16, 2018. https://www.fema.gov/media-library-data/1416583062704-86cb8bebe23906b594ce14860d86f 8af/Disaster-Specific_MOU_updated_weblinks.pdf.

Federal Emergency Management Agency. "Emergency Management Performance Grants (EMPG) Program." Last modified June 7, 2018. https://www.fema.gov/emergency-management-performance-grant-program.

Federal Emergency Management Agency. "Emergency Support Function Annexes." Accessed May 26, 2018. https://www.fema.gov/media-library/assets/documents/25512.

Federal Emergency Management Agency. "Fact Sheet: Individuals and Households Program." Last modified May 2018. https://www.fema.gov/media-library-data/1528984381358-6f256cab09bfcbe67475 10c215445560/IndividualsHouseholdsPrograms.pdf.

Federal Emergency Management Agency. "Fact Sheet: What is FEMA's Individual Assistance Program?" Last modified February 2, 2017. https://www.fema.gov/disaster/4294-4297/updates/fact-sheet-what-femas-individual-assistance-program.

Federal Emergency Management Agency. "Federal/State Individual & Family Grant Program - Q & A." Last modified September 23, 1999. http://www.fema.gov/news-release/1999/09/23/federal/state-individual-family-grant-program-q.

Federal Emergency Management Agency. "FEMA Careers: Reservists (On-call)." Accessed May 28, 2018. https://careers.fema.gov/oncall.

Federal Emergency Management Agency. "FEMA Hazard Mitigation Grants: 404 and 406." News release no. FS 001, May 3, 2017. https://www.fema.gov/news-release/2017/05/03/4309/fema-hazard-mitigation-grants-404-and-406.

Federal Emergency Management Agency. *FEMA Manual 8600.7*, Foreword signed by James L. Witt, November 18, 1999. https://www.fema.gov/pdf/library/8600_7.pdf.

Federal Emergency Management Agency. "FEMA Registration Deadline Extended for Hurricane Sandy Survivors in N.Y." Last modified February 26, 2013. https://www.fema.gov/news-release/2013/02/26/fema-registration-deadline-extended-hurricane-sandy-survivors-ny.

Federal Emergency Management Agency. "FEMA-State Agreement–2017 Fire Management Assistance Grant Program, State of New Mexico." Signed by New Mexico's Governor on July 19, 2017. https://www.fema.gov/media-library-data/1502899392296-beca921e0be140fd7 2cade474fbf46b3/2017NewMexicoSignedFSA.pdf.

Federal Emergency Management Agency. "Fire Management Assistance Grant Program." Accessed May 21, 2018. https://www.fema.gov/fire-management-assistance-grant-program.

Federal Emergency Management Agency. "Flood Insurance Reform - The Law." Accessed April 4, 2018. https://www.fema.gov/flood-insurance-reform-law.

Federal Emergency Management Agency. "Hazus: FEMA's Methodology for Estimating Potential Losses from Disasters." Accessed September 4, 2018. http://www.fema.gov/hazus.

Federal Emergency Management Agency. "Historic Disaster Response to Hurricane Harvey in Texas." Last modified September 22, 2017. https://www.fema.gov/news-release/2017/09/22/historic-disaster-response-hurricane-harvey-texas.

Federal Emergency Management Agency. "History." Accessed October 8, 2018. https://www.fema.gov/about-agency.

Federal Emergency Management Agency. "Hurricane Maria." Last modified June 12, 2018. https://www.fema.gov/hurricane-maria.

Federal Emergency Management Agency. "Individual and Community Preparedness Division." Accessed March 30, 2018. https://www.fema.gov/individual-and-community-preparedness-division.

Federal Emergency Management Agency. "IS-634 Introduction to FEMA's Public Assistance Program, Lesson 2: Steps in the PA Process." Accessed May 3, 2018. https://emilms.fema.gov/IS634/PA0102summary.htm.

Federal Emergency Management Agency. "Mission Assignment Policy." FP104-010-2, November 6, 2015. https://www.fema.gov/media-library-data/1450099364660-fd855ba68f3189d974966ea259a2641a/Mission_Assignment_Policy.pdf.

Federal Emergency Management Agency. "National Disaster Recovery Framework." Accessed August 31, 2018. http://www.fema.gov/national-disaster-recovery-framework.

Federal Emergency Management Agency. "The National Earthquake Hazards Reduction Program (NEHRP) Overview." Last modified August 8, 2016. https://www.fema.gov/media-library-data/1470676164637-ef214c30572785a34c044fd26e6adf32/NEHRP_Overview_080116.pdf.

Federal Emergency Management Agency. "National Emergency Management System." Accessed September 10, 2018. http://www.fema.gov/national-incident-management-system.

Federal Emergency Management Agency. "National Flood Insurance Program and the Consolidated Appropriations Act of 2014." *Fact Sheet*, February 10, 2014. https://www.fema.gov/media-library/assets/documents/90829.

Federal Emergency Management Agency. "National Planning Frameworks." Last modified June 19, 2018. https://www.fema.gov/national-planning-frameworks.

Federal Emergency Management Agency. "National Qualification System." Last modified June 26, 2018. https://www.fema.gov/national-qualification-system.

Federal Emergency Management Agency. *National Response Framework*, 3rd ed. Washington, DC: U.S. Department of Homeland Security, 2016. https://www.fema.gov/media-library/assets/documents/117791.

Federal Emergency Management Agency. "National Urban Search & Rescue Response System." Accessed May 13, 2018. https://www.documentcloud.org/documents/3988843-FEMA-Urban-Search-and-Rescue-task-force-fact-sheet.html.

Federal Emergency Management Agency. "New Public Assistance Delivery Model." Accessed May 16, 2018. https://www.fema.gov/new-public-assistance-delivery-model.

Federal Emergency Management Agency. "President Donald J. Trump Amends Puerto Rico Disaster Declaration." Last modified May 24, 2018. https://www.fema.gov/news-release/2018/05/24/president-donald-j-trump-amends-puerto-rico-disaster-declaration.

Federal Emergency Management Agency. "Professional Development Series (PDS)." Last modified April 25, 2014. https://www.fema.gov/faq-details/Professional-Development-Series-PDS.

Federal Emergency Management Agency. "Public Assistance Per Capita Impact Indicator and Project Thresholds." Accessed April 30, 2018. https://www.fema.gov/public-assistance-indicator-and-project-thresholds.

Federal Emergency Management Agency. "Public Assistance: Private Non-Profit Houses of Worship." *Fact Sheet*, January 26, 2018. https://www.fema.gov/media-library-data/1518794956930-8c2ade230f1a98b484895cacf63c1940/PublicAssistancePrivateNonprofitHousesofWorshipFAQ1.pdf.

Federal Emergency Management Agency. *Public Assistance Program and Policy Guide*. Washington, DC: Federal Emergency Management Agency, 2018. https://www.fema.gov/media-library-data/1525468328389-4a038bbef9081cd7dfe7538e7751aa9c/PAPPG_3.1_508_FINAL_5-4-2018.pdf.

Federal Emergency Management Agency. *Publication 1*. Washington, DC: The Federal Emergency Management Agency, 2010. https://www.fema.gov/media-library-data/20130726-1823-25045-8164/pub_1_final.pdf.

Federal Emergency Management Agency. "Registering for Individual Assistance." Last modified September 10, 2017. https://www.fema.gov/faq-details/Registering-for-Individual-Assistance-1370032115514.

Federal Emergency Management Agency. "State/Indian Tribal Government Administrative Plan, Individual and Households Program (Other Needs Assistance)." Accessed May 16, 2018. https://www.fema.gov/media-library/assets/documents/31206.

Federal Emergency Management Agency. "Threat and Hazard Identification and Risk Assessment." Last modified May 31, 2018. https://www.fema.gov/threat-and-hazard-identification-and-risk-assessment.

Federal Emergency Management Agency. "Typed Resource Definitions Search and Rescue Resources." Accessed May 13, 2018. https://www.fema.gov/pdf/emergency/nims/508-8_search_and_rescue_resources.pdf.

Federal Emergency Management Agency. *2017 Hurricane Season After-Action Report*. Washington, DC: Federal Emergency Management Agency, 2018. https://www.fema.gov/media-library-data/1533643262195-6d1398339449ca85942538a1249d2ae9/2017FEMAHurricaneAARv20180730.pdf.

Federal Emergency Management Agency. "Understanding Individual Assistance and Public Assistance." January 15, 2018. https://www.fema.gov/news-release/2018/01/15/understanding-individual-assistance-and-public-assistance.

Federal Emergency Management Agency. "Welcome to the Assistance to Firefighters Grant Program." Accessed September 6, 2018. http://www.fema.gov/welcome-assistance-firefighters-grant-program.

Federal Emergency Management Agency. "William Craig Fugate." Accessed September 4, 2018. https://www.fema.gov/profile/william-craig-fugate.

Federal Emergency Management Agency, Emergency Management Institute. "Post-Katrina Emergency Management Reform Act." Accessed April 26, 2018. https://emilms.fema.gov/is230c/fem0101200.htm.

Federal Research Division, Library of Congress. *A Guide to Directors of Homeland Security, Emergency Management, and Military Departments in the States and Territories of the United States*. Washington, DC: Federal Research Division, Library of Congress, 2007. https://www.loc.gov/rr/frd/pdf-files/CNGR_Guide-State-Directors-Rev.pdf.

FEMA Careers. "Cadre of On-Call Response/Recovery." Accessed October 8, 2018. https://careers.fema.gov/cadre-call-responserecovery.

Fernandez, Manny. "FEMA Denied Texas Request for Full Disaster Aid, Rankling Stricken Town." *The New York Times*, June 22, 2013. http://www.nytimes.com/2013/06/23/us/fema-denies-texas-request-for-full-disaster-aid-rankling-stricken-town.html?pagewanted=all&_r=0.

Ferris, David. "How Puerto Rico became the Worst Grid Disaster." *E&E News*, April 19, 2018. https://www.eenews.net/stories/1060079499.

Fertala, Katarzyna. "EMAP Proves Invaluable as Method of Standardization for Emergency Management Programs." The University of Maryland, Center for Health & Homeland Security, July 26, 2013. https://www.mdchhs.com/emap-proves-invaluable-as-method-of-standardization-for-emergency-management-programs/.

Fink, Sheri. "Puerto Rico's Hurricane Maria Death Toll Could Exceed 4,000, New Study Estimates." *The New York Times*, May 29, 2018. https://www.nytimes.com/2018/05/29/us/puerto-rico-deaths-hurricane.html.

Firehouse News. "Rescue Teams from across Country Respond to TX." August 27, 2017. https://www.firehouse.com/rescue/news/12363165/rescue-teams-from-across-the-county-respond-to-tx.

FireServiceInfo.com. "A Little Fire Service History." Last modified June 28, 2016. http://www.fireserviceinfo.com/history.html#amfiredept.

Florida Demographics by Cubit. "Florida Counties by Population." Accessed June 25, 2018. https://www.florida-demographics.com/counties_by_population.

Florida Department of Health, Tampa Bay Health & Medical Preparedness Coalition. "Hurricane Irma After Action Report for the Tampa Bay Area." November 7, 2017. http://www.tampabayhmpc.org/wp-content/

uploads/2017/11/AAR-Hurr-Irma-9-5-thru-9-22-FINAL. pdf.

Folger, Peter. "National Earthquake Hazards Reduction Program (NEHRP): Issues in Brief." *Congressional Research Service*, September 20, 2018. https://fas.org/ sgp/crs/misc/R43141.pdf.

Formby, Brandon. "Abbott and FEMA are Using Harvey to Reinvent Disaster Response. Some Say that Makes Displaced Texans 'Guinea Pigs.'" *The Texas Tribune*, February 27, 2018. https://www.texastribune.org/series/ in-harveys-wake/.

Frances, Edwards. "Federal Intervention in Local Emergency Planning: Nightmare on Main Street." *State and Local Government Review* 39, no. 1 (2007): 31–43.

Frederickson, George and Kevin B. Smith. *The Public Administration Theory Primer*. Boulder, CO: Westview Press, 2003.

The Free Dictionary. "Home rule." Accessed July 15, 2018. https://legal-dictionary.thefreedictionary.com/ home+rule.

Frosch, Dan and Cameron McWhirter. "Five Reasons Houston Is Especially Vulnerable to Flooding." *The Wall Street Journal*, August 25, 2017. https://www.wsj.com/ articles/five-reasons-houston-is-especially-vulnerable- to-flooding-1503676480.

Fullerjan, Thomas. "A Rush to Find Survivors Amid the Mud of Southern California Enclave." *The New York Times*, January 10, 2018. https://www.nytimes .com/2018/01/10/us/montecito-mudslides-california. html.

Garret, Thomas A. and Russell S. Sobel. "The Political Economy of FEMA Disaster Payments." *Economic Inquiry* 41, no. 3 (2003): 496–509.

Gasper, John T. and Andrew Reeves. "Make It Rain? Retrospection and the Attentive Electorate in the Context of Natural Disasters." *American Journal of Political Science* 55, no. 2 (2011): 340–355.

Geldart, Christopher T. "Anatomy of a National Special Security Event." *Domestic Preparedness*, June 7, 2017. https://www.domesticpreparedness.com/preparedness/ anatomy-of-a-national-special-security-event/.

George Washington University, Milken Institute School of Public Health and University of Puerto Rico Graduate School of Public Health. *Ascertainment of the Estimated Excess Mortality from Hurricane Maria in Puerto Rico*. Washington, DC: Milken Institute School of Public Health, 2018. https://publichealth.gwu.edu/sites/default/files/ downloads/projects/PRstudy/Acertaintion.

Giles, Martin. "Six Cyber Threats to Really Worry About in 2018." *MIT Technology Review*, January 2, 2018. https://www.technologyreview.com/s/609641/six-cyber- threats-to-really-worry-about-in-2018/.

Gilmore Commission. "Fifth Annual Report to the President and the Congress of the Advisory Panel to Assess Domestic Response Capabilities for Terrorism Involving Weapons of Mass Destruction (the so-called Gilmore Commission)." *Forging America's New Normalcy: Securing Our Homeland, Preserving Our Liberty*. Arlington, VA: RAND, 2003.

Godschalk, David R., David J. Brower, and Timothy Beatley. *Catastrophic Coastal Storms: Hazard Mitigation and Development Management*. Durham, NC: Duke University Press, 1989.

Goldman, Gretchen T., Emily Berman, Michael Halpern, Charise Johnson, Yogin Kothari, Genna Reed, and Andrew A. Rosenberg. "Ensuring Scientific Integrity in the Age of Trump." *Science* 355, no. 6326 (2017): 696–698. http://science.sciencemag.org/content/355/6326/696. summary.

Governance and Social Development Resource Centre. "What Is Disaster Resilience?" Accessed July 23, 2018. http://gsdrc.org/topic-guides/disaster-resilience/ concepts/what-is-disaster-resilience/.

Government of Canada and Government of the United States of America. "Agreement between the Government of Canada and the Government of the United States of America on Emergency Management Cooperation." E105173, December 12, 2008. http://www.state.gov/ documents/organization/142916.pdf.

Graves, Jerry V., Jr. "Intergovernmental Relations and Hazard Mitigation." In *Natural Hazard Mitigation*, edited by Alessandra Jerolleman and John J. Kiefer. Boca Raton, FL: CRC Press, 2013.

Greenberg, Jon. "How Much Does the United States Contribute to the UN?" *Polifact*, February 21, 2017. https:// www.politifact.com/global-news/statements/2017/ feb/01/rob-portman/us-contribution-un-22-percent/#.

Greer, Alex. "Earthquake Preparedness and Response: A Comparison of the United States and Japan." Paper written for POSC/UAPP 656 Politics and Disaster, graduate level, University of Delaware, Newark, May 2010.

GSI Teaching and Resource Center. *Learning: Theory and Research*. Berkeley, CA: Regents of the University of California, 2016. http://gsi.berkeley.edu/teachingguide/theories/social.html.

Guillén, Mauro F. *"Mission Improbable: Using Fantasy Documents to Tame Disaster* by Lee Clarke." *Administrative Science Quarterly* 46, no. 1 (2001): 151–153. https://leeclarke.com/mipages/guillen.html.

Haas, Peter M. "Introduction: Epistemic Communities and International Policy Coordination." *International Organization* 46, no. 1 (Winter 1992): 1–35.

Haase, Thomas W. "International Disaster Resilience: Preparing for Transnational Disaster." In *Designing Resilience: Preparing for Extreme Events*, edited by Louise K. Comfort, Arjin Boin, and Chris C. Demchak, 220–243. Pittsburgh: University of Pittsburgh Press, 2010.

Haddow, George D. and Jane A. Bullock. *Introduction to Emergency Management*, 2nd ed. Waltham, MA: Butterworth-Heinemann, 2006.

Haddow, George D., Jane A. Bullock, and Damon P. Coppola. *Introduction to Emergency Management*, 4th ed. Waltham, MA: Butterworth-Heinemann, 2011.

Haddow, George D., Jane A. Bullock, and Damon P. Coppola. *Introduction to Emergency Management,* 6th ed. Waltham, MA: Butterworth-Heinemann, 2017.

Haidt, Jonathan and Sam Abrams. "The Top 10 Reasons American Politics Are So Broken." *The Washington Post*, January 7, 2015. https://www.washingtonpost.com/news/wonk/wp/2015/01/07/the-top-10-reasons-american-politics-are-worse-than-ever/?utm_term=.0e5275bb7d91.

Halligatte, Stéphane. *Natural Disasters and Climate Change: An Economic Perspective*. New York: Springer International Publishing, 2014.

Ham, Becky. "AAAS Seeks to Uphold Science's Role in Policy-making." *Science* 355, no. 6332 (March 2017): 1383–1384. http://science.sciencemag.org/content/355/6332/1383.full.

Hammond, M. C. "The *Posse Comitatus* Act: A Principle in Need of Renewal." *Washington University Law Quarterly* 75, no. 20 (1997).

Hannigan, John. *Disasters without Borders: The International Politics of Natural Disasters*. Malden, MA: Polity Press, 2012.

Hardy, Patrick. "The 15 U.S. National Planning Scenarios." *Hytrophy* (blog), April 28, 2012. http://hytropy.blogspot.com/2012/04/15-us-national-planning-scenarios.html.

Harrington, Holly. "A Message from Michael D. Brown." *Transitioning Newsletter*, March 5, 2003.

Harris, Ainsley. "How GoFundMe Is Redefining the Business of Disaster Relief." *Fast Company Newsletter*, December 8, 2017. https://www.fastcompany.com/40490985/how-gofundme-is-redefining-the-business-of-disaster-relief.

Harris, Peter. "The Worst Natural Disasters in Canadian History." *Yankler Magazine*, July 8, 2016. http://yackler.ca/blog/2016/07/08/worst-natural-disasters-in-canadian-history/.

Hartman, Chester and Gregory D. Squires, eds. *There Is No Such Thing as a Natural Disaster*. New York: Routledge, 2006.

Health Knowledge. "Social Networks and Communities of Interest." Accessed August 31, 2018. http://www.healthknowledge.org.uk/public-health-textbook/organisation-management/5b-understanding-ofs/social-networks.

Healy, Andrew and Neal Malhotra. "Myopic Votes and Natural Disaster Policy." *American Political Science Review* 103, no. 3 (2009): 387–406.

Helsloot, Ira, Arjen Boin, Brian Jacobs, and Louise K. Comfort, eds. *Mega-Crises: Understanding the Prospects, Nature, Characteristics, and the Effects of Cataclysmic Events*. Springfield, IL: Charles C Thomas Publishers, 2012.

Henri, France and Béatrice Pudelko. "Understanding and Analysing Activity and Learning in Virtual Communities." *Journal of Computer Assisted Learning* 19, no. 4 (2003): 478.

Heppard, Kurt A. and Steve G. Green. "Department of Defense Capabilities in Homeland and Transportation Security." Paper presented at the Annual Conference of the American Society for Public Administration, Denver, CO, March/April 2006.

Hernandez, Arelis R. "New Puerto Rico Data Shows Deaths Increased by 1,400 after Hurricane Maria." *Washington Post*, reprinted by the *Chicago Tribune*, June 1, 2018. http://www.chicagotribune.com/news/nationworld/ct-puerto-rico-hurricane-maria-death-toll-20180601-story.html.

Hinman, Eve E. and David J. Hammond. *Lessons for the Oklahoma City Bombing: Defensive Design Techniques.* Reston, VA: American Society of Civil Engineers, 1997.

Hinshaw, Robert E. *Living with Nature's Extremes: The Life of Gilbert Fowler White.* Boulder, CO: Johnson Books, 2006.

Hirsh, Michael and James Oliphant. "Obama Will Never End the War on Terror." *National Journal Magazine*, February 27, 2014. https://www.nationaljournal.com/s/627840/obama-will-never-end-war-terror.

Hogue, Henry B. and Keith Bea. *Federal Emergency Management and Homeland Security Organization: Historical Developments and Legislative Options.* Washington, DC: U.S. Congressional Research Service, 2006.

Holden, Emily. "Climate Change Skeptics Run the Trump Administration." *Politico*, March 7, 2018. https://www.politico.com/story/2018/03/07/trump-climate-change-deniers-443533.

Holden, Lindsey. "FEMA Approves Federal Disaster Relief Money for Montecito Mudslides." *The Tribune* (San Luis Obispo, CA), January 12, 2018. http://www.sanluisobispo.com/news/state/california/article194416414.html.

Homeland Security National Preparedness Task Force. *Civil Defense and Homeland Security: A Short History of National Preparedness Efforts.* Washington, DC: U.S. Department of Homeland Security, 2006.

HomelandSecurityGrants.info. "Operation Stonegarden (OPSG) Program." Accessed June 10, 2018. https://www.homelandsecuritygrants.info/GrantDetails.aspx?gid=21875.

HomelandSecurityGrants.info. "Urban Areas Security Initiative: Summary." Accessed June 2, 2018. https://www.homelandsecuritygrants.info/GrantDetails.aspx?gid=17162.

Huckabee, Gregory M. "Partnering with the Department of Defense for Improved Homeland Security." In *Homeland Security Law and Policy,* edited by William C. Nicholson, 164. Springfield, IL: Charles C Thomas, 2005.

Hudak, Stephen. "Trump Orders Feds to Pay More to Help Florida Cities, Counties Pay for Hurricane Irma Debris." *Orlando Sentinel*, October 4, 2017. http://www.orlandosentinel.com/news/orange/os-feds-to-pay-more-for-florida-storm-debris-20171003-story.html.

Hughes, Amanda L., Leysia Palen, and Steve Peterson. "Social Media and Emergency Management." In *Critical Issues in Disaster Science and Management: A Dialogue Between Researchers and Practitioners*, edited by Joseph E. Trainor and Tony Subbio, 349–392. Newark, DE: University of Delaware Library, Museums, and Press, 2014. http://udspace.udel.edu/handle/19716/13418.

Human Rights Campaign. "Working with the Lesbian, Gay, Bisexual, and Transgender Community: A Cultural Competence Guide for Emergency Responders and Volunteers." Washington, DC: Human Rights Campaign, 2013. https://nationalmasscarestrategy.files.wordpress.com/2013/01/emergencyresponders_-_lgbt_competency.pdf.

"Hurricane Iniki: Quick Facts about Hawaii's Most Powerful Storm." *Hawaii News Now*, September 17, 2017. http://www.hawaiinewsnow.com/story/36315106/hurricane-iniki-quick-facts-about-hawaiis-most-powerful-storm.

Husbands Fealing, Kaye, Julia I. Lane, John H. Marburger III, and Stephanie S. Shipp, eds. *The Science of Science Policy.* Palo Alto, CA: Stanford University Press, 2011.

Infoplease. "Members of the United Nations." Accessed September 11, 2018. https://www.infoplease.com/world/international-relations/members-united-nations.

Infoplease. "The Top Ten: States with Longest Coastlines." Last modified December 10, 2017. https://www.infoplease.com/top-ten-states-longest-coastlines.

International Association of Emergency Managers. "About IAEM." Accessed June 7, 2018. http://iaem.com/page.cfm? p=about/intro.

International Association of Fire Fighters. "IAFF Legislative Fact Sheet, SAFER and FIRE Grants." Accessed September 6, 2018. http://www.iaff.org/politics/legislative/SAFERFIREfactsheet.htm.

Ishida, David A. "Federal Role and Response to Disaster." Powerpoint presentation, accessed May 16, 2018. http://slideplayer.com/slide/5752941/.

Isidore, Chris. "Puerto Rico's Main Airport is Barely Functioning." *CNN Money*, September 26, 2017. http://money.cnn.com/2017/09/26/news/puerto-rico-flights/index.html.

Israel, Brett. "How Are Earthquakes Measured?" *LiveScience*, August 20, 2010. https://www.livescience.com/32779-measuring-earthquake-magnitude-richter-scale.html.

Issacharoff, Avi. "Why Did Assad Use Chemical Weapons? Because He Can." *Times of Israel*, April 8, 2018. https://www.timesofisrael.com/why-did-assad-use-chemical-weapons-because-he-can/.

Jackson, Andrew J. "The CARVER Method for Preppers." *Prepography: The Study of Self-Reliance,* January 7, 2014. http://prepography.com/carver-method-preppers.

Jaffe, James L. *Financial Preparation and Recovery: Disaster Dollars.* Morrisville, NC: Lulu, 2015.

Janssen, Cory. "Network Theory." *Techopedia*. Accessed April 13, 2018. www.techopedia.com/definition/25064/network-theory.

Japan Meteorological Agency. "The National Meteorological Service of Japan." Accessed September 6, 2018. http://www.jma.go.jp/jma/indexe.html.

Jastram, Kate and Marilyn Achiron. *Refugee Protection: A Guide to International Refugee Law.* Geneva, Switzerland: United Nations High Commissioner for Refugees, 2001. http://www.unhcr.org/publ/PUBL/3d4aba564.pdf.

Jerolleman, Alessandra and John J. Kiefer, eds. *Natural Hazard Mitigation*. Boca Raton, FL: CRC Press, 2013.

Jines, Johnny. "Best Practices for Disaster Preparedness." *Law and Order*, September 2010. http://www.hendonpub.com/resources/article_archive/results/details?id=1602.

"J.J. Watt Reveals Plans for Hurricane Harvey Funds." *Around the NFL*, October 26, 2017. http://www.nfl.com/news/story/0ap3000000867498/article/jj-watt-reveals-plans-for-hurricane-harvey-funds.

Johnson, Alex, Daniel Arkin, Jason Cumming, and Bill Karins. "Hurricane Irma Skirts Puerto Rico, Leaves 1 Million Without Power." *NBC News*, September 6, 2017. https://www.nbcnews.com/storyline/hurricane-irma/hurricane-irma-skirts-puerto-rico-lashing-it-powerful-winds-flooding-n799086.

Jones, Lucy. *The Big Ones: How Natural Disasters Have Shaped Us.* New York: Doubleday, 2018.

Kaczmarek, Michael. "U.S. Counter-terrorism since 9/11: Trends under the Trump Administration." *European Parliament Think Tank*, May 25, 2018. http://www.europarl.europa.eu/thinktank/en/document.html?reference=EPRS_BRI(2018)621898.

Kapucu, Naim, Montgomery Van Wart, Richard T. Sylves, and Farhod Yuldashev. "U.S. Presidents and Their Roles in Emergency Management and Disaster Policy 1950–2009." *Risk, Hazards, & Crisis in Public Policy* 2, no. 3 (2011): 1–34. https://onlinelibrary.wiley.com/doi/pdf/10.2202/1944-4079.1065.

Karpovich, Glen. "Professional Certification in Emergency Management." *Officer*, April 17, 2007. http://www.officer.com/article/10249956/professional-certification-in-emergency-management.

Keen, David. *Complex Humanitarian Emergencies.* Cambridge, MA: Polity Press, 2008.

Kern, Willian. *The Economics of Natural and Unnatural Disaster.* Kalamazoo, MI: W.E. Upjohn Institute for Employment Research, 2010.

Kessler, Gary C. "The Impact of Cyber-Security on Critical Infrastructure Protection." In *Critical Issues in Homeland Security*, edited by James D. Ramsay and Linda Kiltz, 237–238. Boulder, CO: Westview Press, 2014.

Kettl, Donald F. *System under Stress: Homeland Security and American Politics*, 2nd ed. Washington, DC: CQ Press, 2004.

Kettl, Donald F. *System under Stress: Homeland Security and American Politics*, 3rd ed. Washington, DC: CQ Press, 2014.

Kettl, Donald F. *System under Stress: The Challenge to 21st Century Governance*, 3rd ed. Washington, DC: CQ Press, 2014.

King, Alexandra. "San Juan Mayor: Trump's Words on Puerto Rico Are 'Utter Hypocrisy.'" *CNN Politics*, February 1, 2018. https://www.cnn.com/2018/01/31/politics/san-juan-mayor-trump-hypocrisy-cnntv/index.html.

King, Gary. "The Big Deal about Big Data: Improving National Security and Public Policy." Speech, Washington, DC, May 11, 2016.

Kingdon, John W. *Agendas, Alternatives, and Public Policies*, 2nd ed. New York: Longman, 1995.

Kitamura, Masaharu. "Extraction of Lessons from the Fukushima Daiichi Accident Based on a Resilience Engineering Perspective." In *Proceedings of the Fourth Resilience Engineering Symposium*, edited by Erik Hollnagel, Eric Rigaud, and Denis Besnard, 142–174. Sophia Antipolis, France: Resilience Engineering Association, 2011. http://books.openedition.org/pressesmines/1031.

Klebs, Robert W. and Richard T. Sylves. "The Northridge Earthquake: Memoir of a FEMA Inspector." In *Disaster Management in the U.S. and Canada*, 2nd ed., edited by Richard T. Sylves and William L. Waugh, Jr., 126–160. Springfield, IL: Charles C Thomas, 1996.

Klein, Sam. "Assessing the United States' Bioterrorism Preparation." *CIMSEC*, April 23, 2017. http://cimsec.org/assessing-united-states-bioterrorism-preparation/32137.

Kleinerman, Benjamin A. *The Discretionary President: The Promise and Peril of Executive Power*. Lawrence, KS: University Press of Kansas, 2009.

Koh, Harold. "What War Powers Does the President Have?" *Slate*, September 13, 2001. http://www.slate.com/articles/news_and_politics/explainer/2001/09/what_war_powers_does_the_president_have.html.

Kornblut, Anne E. "Pick as Acting FEMA Leader Has Disaster Relief Experience." *The New York Times*, September 13, 2005. https://www.nytimes.com/2005/09/13/us/nationalspecial/pick-as-acting-fema-leader-has-disaster-relief.html.

Kraemer, Sylvia. *Science and Technology Policy*. Piscataway, NJ: Rutgers University Press, 2006.

Kruger, Lennard G. *Assistance to Firefighters Program: Distribution of Fire Grant Funding*. Washington, DC: Congressional Research Service, 2017. https://digitalcommons.ilr.cornell.edu/cgi/viewcontent.cgi?article=2932&context=key_workplace.

Kunreuther, Howard. "Disaster Mitigation: Lessons from Katrina." *Annals of the American Academy of Political and Social Science* 604 (March 2006): 216.

Kunreuther, Howard. "Has the Time Come for Comprehensive National Disaster Insurance?" In *On Risk and Disaster*, edited by Ronald J. Daniels, Donald E. Kettl, and Howard Kunreuther, 188. Philadelphia: University of Pennsylvania Press, 2006.

Kunreuther, Howard. "Insurability Conditions and the Supply of Coverage." In *Paying the Price: The Status and Role of Insurance against Natural Disasters in the United States*, edited by Howard Kunreuther and Richard J. Roth Sr. Washington, DC: Joseph Henry Press, 1998.

Kunreuther, Howard and Michael Useem, eds. *Learning from Catastrophes: Strategies for Reaction and Response*. Upper Saddle River, NJ: Pearson Education, 2010.

Kunreuther, Howard and Richard J. Roth Sr., eds. *Paying the Price: The Status and Role of Insurance against Natural Disasters in the United States*. Washington, DC: Joseph Henry Press, 1998.

Lambright, W. Henry. *Governing Science and Technology*. New York: Oxford University Press, 1993.

Lamothe, Dan. "Maria Hit 9 Days Ago. Less than Half of the Puerto Rico National Guard is on Duty." *The Washington Post*, September 29, 2017. https://www.washingtonpost.com/news/checkpoint/wp/2017/09/29/maria-hit-9-days-ago-less-than-half-of-the-puerto-rico-national-guard-is-on-duty/?utm_term=.2858d2e18bb3.

Levenson, Eric. "3 storms, 3 responses: Comparing Harvey, Irma and Maria." *CNN*, September 27, 2017. http://www.cnn.com/2017/09/26/us/response-harvey-irma-maria/index.html.

Levin, Sam. "Questions for TSA after Reports of Laptop and Phone Searches on Domestic Flights." *The Guardian*, March 12, 2018. https://www.theguardian.com/world/2018/mar/12/tsa-surveillance-laptops-cellphones-domestic-flights.

Lexalytics. "Sentiment Analysis Explained." Accessed August 31, 2018. https://www.lexalytics.com/technology/sentiment.

Lindell, Michael K., Carla S. Prater, and Ronald W. Perry. "Building an Effective Emergency Management Organization." Chap. 3 in *Fundamentals of Emergency Management*. Washington, DC: Federal Emergency Management Institute, 2006. https://training.fema.gov/

hiedu/docs/fem/chapter%203%20-%20building%20
an%20effective%20em%20org.doc.

Lindell, Michael K., Carla S. Prater, and Ronald W. Perry. *Introduction to Emergency Management.* Hoboken, NJ: Wiley, 2007.

Lindsay, Bruce R. *Stafford Act Assistance and Acts of Terrorism.* Washington, DC: U.S. Congressional Research Service, 2017. https://fas.org/sgp/crs/homesec/R44801.pdf.

Lindsay, Bruce R. *Stafford Act Declarations 1953–2016: Trends, Analysis, and Implications for Congress.* Washington, DC: Congressional Research Service, 2017.

Lobosco, Katie, Donna Borak, and Tami Luhby. "What's New in the US, Canada and Mexico Trade Deal?" *CNN Politics,* October 1, 2018. https://www.cnn.com/2018/10/01/politics/nafta-usmca-differences/index.html.

López-Carresi, Alejandro, Maureen Fordham, Ben Wisner, Ilan Kelman, and J. C. Gaillard, eds. *Disaster Management: International Lessons in Risk Reduction, Response and Recovery.* New York: Springer, 2014.

Lynn, Laurence E., Jr. *Public Management as Art, Science, and Profession.* Chatham, NJ: Chatham House, 1996.

MacPherson, James. "Trump Denies Disaster Declaration for Dakota Access Pipeline." *U.S. News and World Report,* July 13, 2017. https://www.usnews.com/news/best-states/north-dakota/articles/2017-07-13/trump-denies-disaster-declaration-for-dakota-access-pipeline.

Magnoli, Giana. "Disaster Relief Available for Santa Barbara County Victims of Thomas Fire, Montecito Floods." *NoozHawk* (Santa Barbara, CA) Local News, January 17, 2018. https://www.noozhawk.com/article/disaster_relief_and_recovery_resources_for_thomas_fire_montecito_floods.

Maines, John. "Florida School Shooting At Stoneman Douglas High School." *Sun Sentinel,* April 2, 2018. http://www.sun-sentinel.com/local/broward/parkland/florida-school-shooting/.

Marshall, Brian and Susan L. Nasr. "How Biological and Chemical Warfare Works." *How Stuff Works,* n.d. http://science.howstuffworks.com/biochem-war3.htm.

Martin, Douglas. "Stephen H. Schneider, Climatologist, Is Dead at 65." *New York Times,* July 20, 2010. http://www.nytimes.com/2010/07/20/science/earth/20schneider.html?_r=0.

May, Peter J. *Recovering from Catastrophes: Federal Disaster Relief Policy and Politics.* Westport, CT: Greenwood Press, 1985.

May, Peter J. and Walter W. Williams. *Disaster Policy Implementation: Managing Programs under Shared Governance.* New York: Plenum Press, 1986.

McCambridge, Ruth. "Study Reveals Shocking Rise in Federal Disaster Relief Costs." *Nonprofit Quarterly,* May 23, 2013. http://www.nonprofitquarterly.org/policysocial-context/22344-study-reveals-shocking-rise-in-federal-disaster-relief-costs.html.

McCarthy, Francis X. *FEMA's Disaster Declaration Process: A Primer.* Washington, DC: U.S. Congressional Research Service, 2007.

McCreight, Robert. "Educational Challenges in Homeland Security and Emergency Management." *Journal of Homeland Security and Emergency Management* 6, no. 1 (2009): 34. http://www.bepress.com/jhsem/vol6/iss1/34/.

McEntire, David A. *Disaster Response and Recovery.* Hoboken, NJ: Wiley, 2007.

McKay, Jim. "Hawaii Fallout: Mistakes Happen, but Probably Not Here: Emergency Managers Review their Protocols after Hawaii False Alert." *Emergency Management Magazine,* January 25, 2018. http://www.govtech.com/em/disaster/Hawaii-Fallout-Mistakes-Happen-but-Probably-Not-Here.html?utm_term=Hawaii%20Fallout%3A%20Mistakes%20Happen%2C%20but%20Probably%20Not%20Here&utm_campaign=No%20Deaths%20From%20Storm%20Surge%20Last%20Year&utm_content=email&utm_source=Act-On+Software&utm_medium=email.

Mead, Walter R. "The Jacksonian Tradition." *The National Interest* 58 (Winter 1999–2000). http://nationalinterest.org/article/the-jacksonian-tradition-939.

Mehta, Amisha M., Axel Bruns, and Judith Newton. "Trust, but Verify: Social Media Models for Disaster Management." *Disasters* 41, no. 3 (2017): 549–565. https://onlinelibrary.wiley.com/doi/full/10.1111/disa.12218.

Merin, Gili. "AD Classics: The Dymaxion House/ Buckminster Fuller." *ArchDaily*, July 12, 2013. https:// www.archdaily.com/401528/ad-classics-the-dymaxion-house-buckminster-fuller.

Merriam Webster. "Martial law." Accessed June 10, 2018. https://www.merriam-webster.com/dictionary/martial%20law.

Meyer, Robinson. "What's Happening with the Relief Effort in Puerto Rico? A Timeline of the Unprecedented Catastrophe of Hurricane Maria." *The Atlantic*, October 4, 2017. https://www.theatlantic.com/science/archive/2017/10/what-happened-in-puerto-rico-a-timeline-of-hurricane-maria/541956/.

Mileti, Dennis S. *Disasters by Design: A Reassessment of Natural Hazards in the United States*. Washington, DC: Joseph Henry Press, 1999.

Mileti, Dennis S. "Opening Plenary Welcoming Speech." Speech presented at the University of Colorado Hazards Center Annual Workshop, Boulder, CO, July 2004.

Miller, Bradley N. and David L. Ranum. *Problem Solving with Algorithms and Data Structures Using Python*, 2nd ed. Portland, OR: Franklin, Beedle & Associates, 2011. http://interactivepython.org/courselib/static/pythonds/Introduction/WhatIsProgramming.html.

Miller, H. Crane. "Defense Production Act of 1950 and Homeland Security." In *A Legal Guide to Homeland Security and Emergency Management for State and Local Governments*, edited by Ernest B. Abbott and Otto J. Hertzel, 237. Lanham, MD: National Book Network, 2006.

Miranda, Lin-Manuel and Jeremy McCarter. *Alexander Hamilton: The Revolution*. New York: Grand Central Publishing, a Division of Hachette Book Group, 2016.

Miskel, James F. *Disaster Response and Homeland Security: What Works, What Doesn't*. Westport, CT: Praeger, 2006.

Mittler, Elliott. "Nonstructural Hazard Mitigation." In *Managing Disaster: Strategies and Policy Perspectives*, edited by Louise K. Comfort. Durham, NC: Duke University Press, 1988.

Mizushima, Asaho. "The Japan-US 'Military' Response to the Earthquake, and the Strengthening of the Military Alliance as a Result." *Fukushima on the Globe*, December 10, 2012. http://fukushimaontheglobe.com/the-earthquake-and-the-nuclear-accident/whats-happened/the-japan-us-military-response.

Morgan, David R. and Robert E. England. *Managing Urban America*, 4th ed. Chatham, NJ: Chatham House, 1996.

Morgan, Gareth. *Images of Organization*, updated ed. Thousand Oaks, CA: Sage, 2006.

Morin, Alexander J. *Science Policy and Politics*. Englewood Cliffs, NJ: Prentice Hall, 1993.

Morton, John Fass. *Next-Generation Homeland Security: Network Federalism and the Course to National Preparedness*. Annapolis, MD: Naval Institute Press, 2012.

Mycoff, Jason D. "Congress and Katrina: A Failure of Oversight." *State and Local Government Review* 39, no. 1 (2007): 16–30.

Nagourney, Adam, David E. Sanger, and Johanna Barr. "Hawaii Panics after Alert about Incoming Missile Is Sent in Error." *The New York Times*, January 13, 2018. https://www.nytimes.com/2018/01/13/us/hawaii-missile.html.

Nash, Rebecca M. "Predicting the Impact of Urban Area Security Initiative Funding on Terrorist Incidents in the United States." *Criminology, Criminal Justice, Law & Society* 18, no. 2 (2017): 13. https://ccjls.scholasticahq.com/article/1989.pdf.

National Academy of Public Administration. *Coping with Catastrophe: Building an Emergency Management System to Meet People's Needs in Natural and Manmade Disasters*. Washington, DC: National Academy of Public Administration, 1993.

National Action Council for Minorities in Engineering. "Types of Engineering: Discover the Different Types of Engineering Careers." Accessed May 9, 2018. http://www.nacme.org/types-of-engineering.

National Congress of American Indians (NCAI). "Homeland Security and Emergency Management." Accessed June 9, 2018. http://www.ncai.org/5_FY2018-NCAI-Budget-Request2-Homeland_Security.pdf.

National Emergency Management Association. "What is NEMA?" Accessed June 7, 2018. https://www.nemaweb.org/index.php/about/what-is-nema.

National Emergency Management Association, Emergency Management Assistance Compact. "How EMAC Works." Accessed May 22, 2018. https://www.emacweb.org/index.php/learn-about-emac/how-emac-works.

National Guard Association of the United States. "NGAUS Fact Sheet: Understanding the Guard's Duty Status." Accessed June 4, 2018. https://www.ngaus.org/sites/default/files/Guard%20Statues.pdf.

National Law Enforcement Officers Memorial Fund. "Law Enforcement Facts." Accessed May 21, 2018. http://www.nleomf.org/facts/enforcement/?mfc_popup=t.

National Research Council. *Building Community Disaster Resilience through Private-Public Collaboration*. Washington, DC: National Academies Press, 2011.

National Research Council. *Disaster Resilience: A National Imperative*. Washington, DC: National Academies Press, 2012.

National Research Council. *Facing Hazards and Disasters: Understanding Human Dimensions*. Washington, DC: National Academies Press, 2006.

National Research Council. *Geotargeted Alerts and Warnings: Report of a Workshop on Current Knowledge and Research Gaps*. Washington, DC: National Academies Press, 2013. https://www.nap.edu/read/18414/chapter/2.

National Research Council. *The Impacts of Natural Disasters: A Framework for Loss Estimation*. Washington, DC: National Academies Press, 1999.

National Research Council. *Increasing National Resilience to Hazards and Disasters: The Perspective from the Gulf Coast of Louisiana and Mississippi: Summary of a Workshop*. Washington, DC: National Academies Press, 2011.

National Research Council. *Launching a National Conversation on Disaster Resilience in America: Workshop Summary*. Washington, DC: National Academies Press, 2013.

National Research Council. *Making the Nation Safer: The Role of Science and Technology in Countering Terrorism*. Washington, DC: National Academies Press, 2002.

National Research Council, Committee on Disaster Research in the Social Sciences. *Facing Hazards and Disasters: Understanding Human Dimensions*. Washington, DC: National Academies Press, 2006.

National Science Foundation. "About the National Science Foundation." Accessed July 15, 2018. https://www.nsf.gov/about/.

National Science Foundation. "Interdisciplinary Research in Hazards and Disasters (Hazards SEES)." Accessed September 6, 2018. http://www.nsf.gov/pubs/2012/nsf12610/nsf12610.htm.

The National Severe Storms Laboratory. "About NSSL." Accessed July 15, 2018. https://www.nssl.noaa.gov/about/.

National Voluntary Organizations Active in Disaster. "VOAD Members." Accessed May 28, 2018. https://www.nvoad.org/voad-members/.

National Voluntary Organizations Active in Disaster. "Who We Are." Accessed September 7, 2018. https://www.nvoad.org/about-us/.

National Weather Service. "About NOAA's National Weather Service." Accessed September 17, 2018. http://www.weather.gov/about.

National Weather Service. "Enhanced Fujita Scale." Accessed July 24, 2018. https://www.weather.gov/oun/efscale.

National Weather Service, Climate Prediction Center. "Background Information: The North Atlantic Hurricane Season." Last modified August 6, 2015. http://www.cpc.ncep.noaa.gov/products/outlooks/background_information.shtml.

New Georgia Encyclopedia. "CNN." Accessed September 4, 2018. http://www.georgiaencyclopedia.org/articles/arts-culture/cnn.

Newsome, Brian Oliver and Jack A. Jarmon. *A Practical Introduction to Homeland Security and Emergency Management: From Home to Abroad*. Washington, DC: CQ Press, 2016.

Nicholson, William C., ed. *Emergency Response and Emergency Management Law: Cases and Materials*. Springfield, IL: Charles C Thomas, 2003.

Nicholson, William C., ed. *Homeland Security Law and Policy*. Springfield, IL: Charles C Thomas, 2005.

9/11 Commission. *The 9/11 Commission Report: Final Report of the National Commission on Terrorist Attacks upon the United States*. New York: National Commission on Terrorist Attacks Upon the United States, 2004.

NOAA National Severe Storms Laboratory. "About NSSL." Accessed September 6, 2018. http://www.nssl.noaa.gov/about.

NOAA National Severe Storms Laboratory. "Tornado Research: Basic Convective and Mesoscale Research." Accessed September 6, 2018. http://www.nssl.noaa.gov/research/tornadoes.

O'Connor, Anahad and Timothy Williams. "Scores Die in Storms across South; Tornado Ravages City." *New York Times,* April 27, 2011. http://www.nytimes.com/2011/04/28/us/28storm.html?_r=0.

O'Toole, Laurence K., Jr. and Robert K. Christensen. *American Intergovernmental Relations,* 5th ed. Washington, DC: CQ Press, 2013.

Obama, Barack. "Remarks by the President on Climate Change." Speech, Georgetown University, Washington, DC, June 25, 2013. http://www.whitehouse.gov/the-press-office/2013/06/25/remarks-president-climate-change.

"Oklahoma Tornado: President Barack Obama Visits Moore, Vows Unwavering Support." *ABC*, May 6, 2013. https://6abc.com/archive/9116779/.

Osborne, Hilary and Hannah Jane Parkinson. "Cambridge Analytica Scandal: The Biggest Revelations So Far." *The Guardian*, March 22, 2018. https://www.theguardian.com/uk-news/2018/mar/22/cambridge-analytica-scandal-the-biggest-revelations-so-far.

Ostrom, Thomas P. *The United States Coast Guard and National Defense: A History from World War I to the Present*. Jefferson, NC: McFarland & Company, Inc., 2012.

Painter, William L. *2017 Disaster Supplemental Appropriations: Overview*. Congressional Research Service, March 20, 2018. https://fas.org/sgp/crs/homesec/R45084.pdf.

Pasch, Richard J., Andrew B. Penny, and Robbie Berg. *Tropical Cycle Report: Hurricane Maria*. Miami, FL: National Hurricane Center, 2018. https://www.nhc.noaa.gov/data/tcr/AL152017_Maria.pdf.

"The Patriot Act Revision: What Does It Mean to You? [updated]." Trend Micro, June 5, 2015. https://www.trendmicro.com/vinfo/us/security/news/online-privacy/patriot-act-revision-underway-what-does-it-mean-to-you.

Perkins, Heather. "Why States Join Interstate Compacts." Council of State Governments, September 6, 2017. http://knowledgecenter.csg.org/kc/content/why-states-join-interstate-compacts.

Perrow, Charles. *The Next Catastrophe: Reducing Our Vulnerabilities to Natural, Industrial, and Terrorist Disasters*. Princeton, NJ: Princeton University Press, 2011.

Perrow, Charles. *Normal Accidents*. New York: Basic Books, 1984.

Petak, William J. "Emergency Management: A Challenge to Public Administration." *Public Administration Review* 45 (January 1985): 3.

Petak, William J. and Arthur A. Atkisson. *Natural Hazard Risk Assessment and Public Policy*. New York: Springer-Verlag, 1982.

Peters, Katherine M. and Jason Vest. "Calling in the Cavalry." *Government Executive,* October 1, 2005. http://www.govexec.com/features/1005-01/1005-01s1.htm.

Petrow, Steven. "Civilities: What Does the Acronym 'LGBTQ' Stand For?" *The Washington Post*, May 23, 2014.

Phillips, Brenda D. and David M. Neal. "Recovery." In *Emergency Management: Principles and Practice for Local Government*, 2nd ed., edited by William L. Waugh Jr. and Kathleen Tierney. Washington, DC: ICMA Press, 2007.

Phillips, Brenda D., David M. Neal, and Gary R Webb. *Introduction to Emergency Management*. Boca Raton, FL: CRC Press, 2012.

Pielke, Roger A., Jr. *The Honest Broker: Making Sense of Science in Policy and Politics*. New York: Cambridge University Press, 2007.

Pika, Joseph A. and John Anthony Maltese. *The Politics of the Presidency*, 6th ed. Washington, DC: CQ Press, 2004.

Pilkey, Orrin H. and Katherine L. Dixon. *The Corps and the Shore*. Washington, DC: Island Press, 1996.

Pine, John C. *Technology in Emergency Management*. Hoboken, NJ: John Wiley and Sons, 2007.

Pine, John C. *Technology in Emergency Management*, 2nd ed. Hoboken, NJ: John Wiley and Sons, 2018.

Plano, Jack C. and Milton Greenberg. *The American Political Dictionary*, 7th ed. New York: Holt, Rinehart and Winston, 1985.

Platt, Rutherford H., ed. *Disasters and Democracy: The Politics of Extreme Natural Events*. Washington, DC: Island Press, 1999.

Porter, David. "Hurricane Sandy Was Second-Costliest in U.S. History, Report Shows." *Huffington Post*, February 12, 2013. https://www.cbsnews.com/news/report-sandy-second-costliest-hurricane-in-us-history/.

Posner, Eric A. "Executive Decision." *The New Republic*, March 29, 2010. https://newrepublic.com/article/74041/executive-decision.

Project on Government Oversight. "Federal Contractor Misconduct Database." Accessed September 7, 2018. http://www.contractormisconduct.org.

Przybyla, Heidi M. "Trump: Hurricane Harvey Recovery Response 'a Wonderful Thing,'" *USA Today*, September 2, 2017. https://www.usatoday.com/story/news/politics/2017/09/02/trump-houston-survey-hurricane-harvey-damage/628259001/.

Public Safety Canada. "Compendium of U.S.–Canada Emergency Management Assistance Mechanisms: National-level acts, agreements, frameworks, guidance, plans, and procedures for response operations, communication and coordination, preparedness, and recovery." June 2012. https://www.dhs.gov/xlibrary/assets/policy/btb-compendium-of-us-canada-emergency-management-assistance-mechanisms.pdf.

Public Safety Canada. "Disaster Financial Assistance Arrangements (DFAA)." Last modified May 15, 2018. https://www.publicsafety.gc.ca/cnt/mrgnc-mngmnt/rcvr-dsstrs/dsstr-fnncl-ssstnc-rrngmnts/index-en.aspx#a01.

Public Safety Canada. *Guidelines for the Disaster Financial Assistance Arrangements*. Ottawa, Canada: Public Safety Canada, 2007. http://www.publicsafety.gc.ca/cnt/mrgnc-mngmnt/rcvr-dsstrs/gdlns-dsstr-ssstnc/index-eng.aspx.

Quarantelli, E. L. *Disaster Planning, Emergency Management, and Civil Protection: The Historical Development of Organized Efforts to Plan for and to Respond to Disasters*. Newark, DE: University of Delaware, Disaster Research Center, 2000. http://udspace.udel.edu/handle/19716/673.

Quarantelli, E. L. *Future Disaster Trends and Policy Implications for Developing Countries*. Newark, DE: University of Delaware, Disaster Research Center, 1994.

Queally, James and Louis Sahagun. "Death Toll from Montecito Mudslide Rises to 18." *Los Angeles Times*, January 12, 2018. https://www.latimes.com/la-lb-771-39548-la-me-montecito-mudsides-101-htmlstory.html.

Rahm, Dianne. *United States Public Policy: A Budgetary Approach*. Belmont, CA: Wadsworth, 2004.

Reese, Shawn. "Department of Homeland Security Preparedness Grants: A Summary and Issues." *Congressional Research Service*, October 28, 2016. https://fas.org/sgp/crs/homesec/R44669.pdf.

Reese, Shawn. *National Special Security Events: Fact Sheet*. Washington, DC: U.S. Congressional Research Service, 2017. https://fas.org/sgp/crs/homesec/R43522.pdf.

Reeves, Andrew. "Political Disaster? Presidential Disaster Declarations and Electoral Politics." *The Journal of Politics* 73, no. 4 (October 2011): 1142–1151. http://andrewreeves.org/sites/default/files/fema_supp.pdf.

Reeves, Andrew. "Political Disaster: Unilateral Powers, Electoral Incentives, and Presidential Disaster Declarations." *The Journal of Politics* 1, no. 1 (2009): 1–10.

Ripley, Amanda. *The Unthinkable: Who Survives When Disaster Strikes—and Why*. New York: Three Rivers Press, 2009.

Roberts, Patrick S. *Disasters and the American State: How Politicians, Bureaucrats, and the Public Prepare for the Unexpected*. New York: Cambridge University Press, 2013.

Roberts, Patrick S. "FEMA and the Prospects for Reputational Authority." *Studies in American Political Development* 20 (Spring 2006): 16.

Roberts, Patrick S., Robert Ward, and Gary Wamsley. "The Evolving Federal Role in Emergency Management Policies and Processes." In *Emergency Management: The American Experience 1900–2010*, 2nd ed., edited by

Claire B. Rubin, 247–276. Boca Raton, FL: CRC Press, 2012.

Robillard, Kevin. "10 Facts about the Katrina Response." *Politico*, October 3, 2012. https://www.politico.com/story/2012/10/10-facts-about-the-katrina-response-081957.

Rodriguez, Havidan, Enrico L. Quarantelli, and Russell R. Dynes, eds. *Handbook of Disaster Research*. New York: Springer, 2007.

Rosenthal, Uriel, R. A. Boin, and Louise Comfort. *From Crises to Contingencies: A Global Perspective*. Springfield, IL: Charles C Thomas, 2002.

Rubin, Claire B. and Irmak R. Tanali. *Disaster Time Line: Selected Milestone Events and U.S. Outcomes, 1965–2001*. Arlington, VA: Claire B. Rubin and Associates, 2001.

Rubini, Jeffrey H. "Use of Volunteers During the Deepwater Horizon Oil Spill in the Gulf of Mexico in 2010." Unpublished paper, George Washington University, Washington, DC, Fall 2011.

Russell, Jon D. and Aaron Bostrom. "Federalism, Dillon Rule and Home Rule." *White Paper*, January 2016. https://www.alec.org/app/uploads/2016/01/2016-ACCE-White-Paper-Dillon-House-Rule-Final.pdf.

Rutgers University. *Advancing Integration of Health and Community Engagement in Pre-Disaster Recovery and Resilience Planning: Opportunities for Health Impact Assessment*, New Brunswick, NJ: Rutgers, The State University of New Jersey, 2016. http://phci.rutgers.edu/wp-content/uploads/2016/07/PHCI-report-Summary-Revised.pdf.

Sadler, James A. "FEMA's Participation in State-Sponsored Non-Binding Wind versus Flood Disaster Claims Mediation Program," W-13058. Washington, DC: Federal Emergency Management Agency, 2013. https://bsa.nfipstat.fema.gov/wyobull/2013/w-13058.txt.

"Sailing the Wired Seas." *The Economist*, March 10, 2018. https://www.economist.com/news/technology-quarterly/21738088-internet-infrastructure-being-built-span-oceans-sailing-wired-seas.

Sanger, David E. "Bush Wants to Consider Broadening of Military's Powers during Natural Disasters." *New York Times*, September 27, 2005. http://www.nytimes.com/2005/09/27/national/nationalspecial/27military.html.

Scheer, Robert. *With Enough Shovels: Reagan, Bush and Nuclear War*. New York: Vintage Books, 1983.

Schmidle, Nicholas. "Getting Bin Laden: What Happened that Night in Abbottabad." *The New Yorker*, August 8, 2011. https://www.newyorker.com/magazine/2011/08/08/getting-bin-laden.

Schneider, Keith. "The Midwest Flooding: In this Emergency, Agency Wins Praise for Its Response." *New York Times*, July 20, 1993. http://www.nytimes.com/1993/07/20/us/the-midwest-flooding-in-this-emergency-agency-wins-praise-for-its-response.html.

Schneider, Saundra K. *Dealing with Disaster: Public Management in Crisis Situations*, 2nd ed. Armonk, NY: M.E. Sharpe, 2011.

Schneider, Saundra K. *Flirting with Disaster: Public Management in Crisis Situations*. Armonk, NY: M.E. Sharpe, 1995.

Schneider, Stephen H., Armin Rosencranz, Michael D. Mastrandrea, and Kristin Kuntz-Duriseti, eds. *Climate Change Science and Policy*. Washington, DC: Island Press, 2010.

Schroeder, Aaron and Gary Wamsley. "The Evolution of Emergency Management in America: From a Painful Past to a Promising but Uncertain Future." In *Handbook of Crisis and Emergency Management*, edited by Ali Farazmand. New York: Marcel Dekker, 2002.

Schuller, Mark. *Killing with Kindness: Haiti, International Aid, and NGOs*. New Brunswick, NJ: Rutgers University Press, 2012.

Seidman, Harold. *Politics, Position and Power: The Dynamics of Federal Organization*, 5th ed. New York: Oxford University Press, 1998.

Senate and House of Commons of Canada. "Emergency Management Act: S.C. 2007, c. 15." Government of Canada, June 28, 2018. http://laws-lois.justice.gc.ca/eng/acts/E-4.56/FullText.html?wbdisable=true.

Senate Committee on Governmental Affairs. *Hearing on Rebuilding FEMA: Preparing for the Next Disaster*, 103rd Cong., 1st sess., May 18, 1993, 151.

"Senate Confirms Trump's Nominee to Head FEMA." *U.S. News & World Report*, June 20, 2017. https://www.usnews.com/news/politics/articles/2017-06-20/senate-confirms-trumps-nominee-to-head-fema.

Settle, Allen K. "Disaster Assistance: Securing Presidential Declarations." In *Cities and Disaster: North American Studies in Emergency Management*, edited by Richard T. Sylves and William L. Waugh Jr., 33–57. Springfield, IL: Charles C Thomas, 1990.

Settlement.org. "What Is Canada's Political System?" Last modified July 13, 2016. https://settlement.org/ontario/immigration-citizenship/canadian-government/canadian-political-system/what-is-canada-s-political-system/.

Shafritz, Jay M., Karen S. Layne, and Christopher P. Borick. *Classics of Public Policy*. New York: Pearson, 2005.

Shah, Dhavan V., Joseph N. Cappella, and W. Russell Neuman. "Big Data, Digital Media, and Computational Social Science: Possibilities and Perils." *The Annals of the Academy of Political and Social Science* 659, no. 1 (2015): 6–13.

Shanahan, Elizabeth A., Michael D. Jones, Mark K. McBeth, and Claudio M. Radaelli. "The Narrative Policy Framework." In *Theories of the Policy Process*, edited by Christopher M. Weible and Paul A. Sabatier. New York: Westview Press, 2018.

Sibley, Robert. "Veteran Journalism Teacher Joe Scanlon Dies at 82." *Ottawa Citizen*, May 3, 2015. https://ottawacitizen.com/news/local-news/veteran-journalism-teacher-joe-scanlon-dies-at-82.

Singer, P. W. "Strange Brew: Private Military Contractors and Humanitarians." In *Disaster and the Politics of Intervention*, edited by Andrew Lakoff, 70–99. New York: Columbia University Press, 2010.

Single Audit Resource Center. "97.126 National Special Security Event." Accessed October 1, 2018. https://singleaudit.org/program/?id=97.126.

Smith, Gavin. *Planning for Post-Disaster Recovery*. Falls Church, VA: Public Entity Risk Institute, 2011.

Smith, Keith. *Environmental Hazards: Assessing Risk and Reducing Disaster*, 6th ed. New York: Routledge, 2013.

Smith, Kevin B. and Christopher W. Larimer. *The Public Policy Theory Primer*, 2nd ed. Boulder, CO: Westview Press, 2013.

Smith, Loran B. and David T. Jervis. "Tornadoes." In *Handbook of Emergency Management*, by Ronald J. Hy and William L. Waugh, 106–128. Westport, CT: Greenwood Press, 1990.

Snyder, Mike. "Disaster Victim Activists Concerned about FEMA's Fairness, Transparency." *Houston Chronicle*, January 25, 2018. https://www.houstonchronicle.com/news/houston-texas/houston/article/FEMA-grants-Harvey-victims-fairness-equity-12526374.php.

Spears, Jeffrey, Brian Robinson, and Ben Gullo, eds. *Domestic Operational Law: 2011 Handbook for Judge Advocates*. Charlottesville, VA: Center for Law and Military Operations, 2011.

Stallings, Robert A. *Promoting Risk: Constructing the Earthquake Threat*. New York: Aldine de Gruyter, 1995.

Stanford Encyclopedia of Philosophy. "Federalism." Accessed August 31, 2018. http://plato.stanford.edu/entries/federalism.

Steinberg, Ted. *Acts of God: The Unnatural History of Natural Disaster in America*. New York: Oxford University Press, 2000.

Steinbuch, Yaron. "Tropical Storm Harvey Makes Landfall in Louisiana." *New York Post*, August 30, 2017. https://nypost.com/2017/08/30/tropical-storm-harvey-makes-landfall-in-louisiana/.

Stone, Deborah. *The Samaritan's Dilemma: Should Government Help Your Neighbor?* New York: Nation Books, 2008.

Sutter, Daniel and Kevin M. Simmons. "The Socioeconomic Impact of Tornadoes." In *The Economics of Unnatural Disasters*, edited by William Kern. Kalamazoo, MI: W.E. Upjohn Institute for Employment Research, 2010.

Sylves, Richard T. "A Précis on Political Theory and Emergency Management." *Journal of Emergency Management* 2, no. 3 (Summer 2004).

Sylves, Richard T. "Budgeting for Emergency Management." In *Emergency Management: Principles and Practice for Local Government*, 2nd ed., edited by William L. Waugh Jr. and Kathleen Tierney, 299–318. Washington, DC: ICMA Publications, 2007.

Sylves, Richard T. *Disaster Policy and Politics*. Washington, DC: CQ Press, 2008.

Sylves, Richard T. *Disaster Policy and Politics*, 2nd ed. Washington, DC: CQ Press, 2015.

Sylves, Richard T. "Earthquakes." In *Handbook of Emergency Management*, edited by William L. Waugh Jr. and Ronald W. Hy, 33–34. Westport, CT: Greenwood Press, 1991.

Sylves, Richard T. "Federal Emergency Management Comes of Age: 1979–2001." In *Emergency Management: The American Experience: 1900-2010*, 2nd ed., edited by Claire B. Rubin, 115–166. Boca Raton, FL: CRC Press, 2012.

Sylves, Richard T. "Ferment at FEMA: Reforming Emergency Management." *Public Administration Review* 54 (May/June 1994): 303–307.

Sylves, Richard T. *The Nuclear Oracles: A Political History of the General Advisory Committee of the U.S. Atomic Energy Commission, 1947–1977*. Ames, IA: Iowa State University Press, 1986.

Sylves, Richard T. "Political Theory and Emergency Management." Paper presented at the FEMA Emergency Management Higher Education Conference, FEMA Emergency Management Institute, Emmitsburg, MD, June 8, 2004.

Sylves, Richard T. "President Bush and Hurricane Katrina: A Presidential Leadership Study." *Annals of the American Academy of Political and Social Science* 604 (March 2006): 26–56.

Sylves, Richard T. "Presidential Declaration of Disaster Decisions: The Case of Turndowns." In *Critical Issues in Homeland Security: A Casebook*, edited by James D. Ramsay and Linda Kiltz. Boulder, CO: Westview Press, 2014.

Sylves, Richard T. and William L. Waugh Jr., eds. *Cities and Disaster: North American Studies in Emergency Management*. Springfield, IL: Charles C Thomas, 1990.

Sylves, Richard T. and William L. Waugh Jr., eds. *Disaster Management in the U.S. and Canada,* 2nd ed. Springfield, IL: Charles C Thomas, 1996.

Sylves, Richard T. and Zoltan I. Buzas. "Presidential Disaster Declaration Decisions, 1953–2003: What Influences Odds of Approval." *State & Local Government Review* 39, no. 1 (2007): 3–15.

Tarcey, Brian. "Flooding the Ballot Box: The Politics of Disaster." *Harvard Magazine,* March–April 2004.

Taylor, Alan. "The Northridge Earthquake: 20 Years Ago Today." *The Atlantic*, January 17, 2014. https://www.theatlantic.com/photo/2014/01/the-northridge-earthquake-20-years-ago-today/100664/.

Techopedia. "Network Theory." Accessed September 17, 2018. http://www.techopedia.com/definition/25064/network-theory.

Teh, Jiah-Shin and Harvey Rubin. "Dealing with Pandemics: Global Security, Risk Analysis, and Science Policy." In *Learning from Catastrophes*, edited by Howard Kunreuther and Michael Useem, 211–234. Upper Saddle River, NJ: Pearson Education, 2010.

"10 Ways Purpose-Built Rugged Tablets Smooth the Way for Emergency Managers." Rugged Tech Talk with DT Researcher (blog), November 7, 2017. http://www.dtresearch.com/blog/10-ways-purpose-built-rugged-tablets-smooth-the-way-for-emergency-managers/.

Texas Department of Public Safety, Division of Emergency Management. "TCEQ Regional Workshop: Emergency Response Preparing for Disasters and Emergency Incidents." Powerpoint presentation, June 2, 2015. http://slideplayer.com/slide/6083987/.

Texas General Land Office, Community Development and Revitalization Program. *State of Texas Plan for Disaster Recovery: Hurricane Harvey*. Austin, TX: Texas General Land Office, 2018. http://www.glo.texas.gov/the-glo/public-information/notices/files/action-plan-final-draft-1-18-18.pdf.

Thomas, Edward A. "Natural Hazards and the Law." In *Natural Hazard Mitigation*, edited by Alessandra Jerolleman and John J. Kiefer, 146–148. Boca Raton, FL: CRC Press, 2013.

Thomas, Lauren. "Here's What It's Like to Be a Home Improvement Retailer in the Midst of a Hurricane." *CNBC*, September 14, 2017. https://www.cnbc.com/2017/09/14/what-its-like-to-be-a-home-improvement-retailer-during-a-hurricane.html.

Tierney, Kathleen J. "Recent Developments in U.S. Homeland Security Policies and Their Implications for the Management of Extreme Events." In *Handbook of Disaster Research*, edited by Havidan Rodriguez, Enrico L. Quarantelli, and Russell R. Dynes. New York: Springer, 2007.

Tierney, Kathleen J. *The Social Roots of Risk: Producing Disasters, Promoting Resilience*. Stanford, CA: Stanford University Press, 2014.

Tierney, Kathleen J., Michael K. Lindell, and Ronald W. Perry. *Facing the Unexpected: Disaster Preparedness and Response in the United States*. Washington, DC: Joseph Henry Press, 2001.

"Timeline: The History of The Weather Channel." *The Virginian-Pilot*, July 6, 2008. http://hamptonroads.com/2008/07/timeline-history-weather-channel.

Toft, Brian and Simon Reynolds. *Learning from Disasters*. Waltham, MA: Butterworth-Heinemann, 1994.

Tsui, Ed. "Initial Response to Complex Emergencies and Natural Disasters." In *Emergency Relief Operation*, edited by Kevin M. Cahill, 32–54. New York: Fordham University Press, 2003.

Twigg, David K. *The Politics of Disaster: Tracking the Impact of Hurricane Andrew*. Gainesville: University of Florida Press, 2012.

Twigg, John. *Corporate Social Responsibility and Disaster Reduction*. London: Benfield Greig Hazard Research Centre at University College London, 2001. http://drr.upeace.org/english/documents/References/Topic%20 7-Preparedness-%20Early%20Warning,%20Planning,%20 Monitoring%20and%20Evaluation/Twigg%202001%20 CSR%20and%20disaster%20management.pdf.

U.S. Agency for International Development. *At Freedom's Frontiers: A Democracy and Governance Strategic Framework*. Washington, DC: U.S. Agency for International Development, 2005.

U.S. Agency for International Development. "Bureau for Democracy, Conflict and Humanitarian Assistance." Accessed September 11, 2018. http://www.usaid.gov/who-we-are/organization/bureaus/bureau-democracy-conflict-and-humanitarian-assistance.

U.S. Agency for International Development. *Fragile States Strategy*. Washington, DC: U.S. Agency for International Development, 2005.

U.S. Agency for International Development. "Home-Reports and Data-Budget," Last modified March 21, 2018. https://www.usaid.gov/results-and-data/budget-spending.

U.S. Agency for International Development. *Policy Framework for Bilateral Aid, Implementing Transformational Diplomacy through Development*. Washington, DC: U.S. Agency for International Development, 2006.

U.S. Agency for International Development, Office of U.S. Foreign Disaster Assistance. "Organization Chart." Accessed September 11, 2018. http://www.usaid.gov/who-we-are/organization/bureaus/bureau-democracy-conflict-and-humanitarian-assistance/office-us.

U.S. Army Corps of Engineers. *The U.S. Army Corps of Engineers: A Brief History*. Accessed September 10, 2018. http://www.usace.army.mil/About/History/BriefHistoryoftheCorps/Introduction.aspx.

U.S. Army Corps of Engineers, Office of History. *The History of the U.S. Army Corps of Engineers*. Stockton, CA: University Press of the Pacific, 2004.

U.S. Census Bureau. "Census Bureau Reports There Are 89,004 Local Governments in the United States." August 30, 2012. https://www.census.gov/newsroom/releases/archives/governments/cb12-161.html.

U.S. Census Bureau. "Quick Facts: Florida." Accessed June 25, 2018. https://www.census.gov/quickfacts/fact/table/fl/PST045217.

U.S. Census Bureau. "Quick Facts: Puerto Rico." Accessed June 25, 2018. https://www.census.gov/quickfacts/fact/table/pr/PST045217.

U.S. Centers for Disease Control and Prevention. "2014–2016 Ebola Outbreak in West Africa." Last modified December 27, 2017. https://www.cdc.gov/vhf/ebola/outbreaks/2014-west-africa/index.html.

U.S. Central Intelligence Agency. "Field Listing: Broadcast Media." *World Fact Book*, Broadcast Media by Country. Accessed September 28, 2018. https://www.cia.gov/library/publications/the-world-factbook/fields/2213.html.

U.S. Congress. "Disaster Relief Appropriations." Public Law 113-2, section 1110. Washington, DC: U.S. Government Printing Office, January 29, 2013. https://www.congress.gov/113/plaws/publ2/PLAW-113publ2.pdf.

U.S. Congress. House. *Making Further Supplemental Appropriations for the Fiscal Year Ending September 30, 2018, for Disaster Assistance for Hurricanes Harvey, Irma, and Maria, and Calendar Year 2017 Wildfires, and for Other Purposes*. HR 4667. 115th Congress, 2nd sess. Introduced in House December 18, 2017. https://www.congress.gov/bill/115th-congress/house-bill/4667.

U.S. Congressional Research Service. "National Special Security Events: Fact Sheet." Accessed October 1, 2018. https://www.everycrsreport.com/reports/R43522.html.

U.S. Congressional Research Service. "Staffing for Adequate Fire and Emergency Response: The SAFER Grant Program." Accessed May 12, 2018. https://www.everycrsreport.com/reports/RL33375.html.

U.S. Customs and Border Protection. "CBP Hosts DHS' 15th Anniversary Event." Last modified March 12, 2018. https://www.cbp.gov/newsroom/spotlights/cbp-hosts-dhs-15th-anniversary-event.

U.S. Department of Health and Human Services. "Emergency Support Functions." Public Health Emergency, June 2, 2015. https://www.phe.gov/preparedness/support/esf8/Pages/default.aspx.

U.S. Department of Homeland Security. "About DHS." Accessed May 15, 2018. https://www.dhs.gov/about-dhs.

U.S. Department of Homeland Security. *Best Practices for Incorporating Social Media into Exercises: Social Media Working Group for Emergency Services and Disaster Management and DHS S&T First Responders Group*. Washington, DC: U.S. Department of Homeland Security, 2017. https://www.dhs.gov/sites/default/files/publications/Best-Practices-Incorporating-Social-Media-Into-Exercises-508%20.pdf.

U.S. Department of Homeland Security. *The Department's Five Responsibilities*. Washington, DC: U.S. Department of Homeland Security, 2009. https://www.dhs.gov/blog/2009/06/08/departments-five-responsibilities.

U.S. Department of Homeland Security. "FEMA Leadership Organizational Structure." *FEMA Organizational Chart in March 2018*. Washington, DC: Federal Emergency Management Agency, 2018. https://www.fema.gov/media-library/assets/documents/28183.

U.S. Department of Homeland Security. *FY 2006 Homeland Security Grant Program: Program Guidance and Application Kit*. Washington, DC: U.S. Department of Homeland Security, 2005. http://link.library.in.gov/portal/Department-of-Homeland-Security-DHS-fiscal-year/mDv0NJrUiY4/.

U.S. Department of Homeland Security. "Homeland Security Act of 2002." Public Law 107-296, 116 Stat. 2135, enacted November 25, 2002. https://www.dhs.gov/sites/default/files/publications/hr_5005_enr.pdf.

U.S. Department of Homeland Security. "Homeland Security Presidential Directive 7: Critical Infrastructure Identification, Prioritization, and Protection." Accessed September 6, 2018. http://www.dhs.gov/homeland-security-presidential-directive-7.

U.S. Department of Homeland Security. *National Protection Framework*, 2nd ed. Washington, DC: U.S. Department of Homeland Security, 2016. https://www.fema.gov/media-library-data/1466017309052-85051ed62fe595d4ad026edf4d85541e/National_Protection_Framework2nd.pdf.

U.S. Department of Homeland Security. "National Response Framework." January 2008. http://www.fema.gov/pdf/emergency/nrf/nrf-core.pdf.

U.S. Department of Homeland Security. "National Response Plan." December 2004. https://fas.org/irp/agency/dhs/nrp.pdf.

U.S. Department of Homeland Security. "National Terrorism Advisory System." Accessed September 25, 2018. https://www.dhs.gov/national-terrorism-advisory-system.

U.S. Department of Homeland Security. "Presidential Policy Directive/PPD-8: National Preparedness." Accessed August 31, 2018. http://www.dhs.gov/presidential-policy-directive-8-national-preparedness.

U.S. Department of Homeland Security. "Science and Technology: Our Work." Accessed July 24, 2018. https://www.dhs.gov/science-and-technology/our-work.

U.S. Department of Homeland Security. "State Homeland Security and Emergency Services." Last modified March 21, 2017. https://www.dhs.gov/state-homeland-security-and-emergency-services.

U.S. Department of Homeland Security. "Surge Capacity Force." Last modified September 25, 2017. https://www.dhs.gov/topic/surge-capacity-force.

U.S. Department of Homeland Security. "Weapons of Mass Destruction." Accessed April 29, 2018. https://www.dhs.gov/topic/weapons-mass-destruction.

U.S. Department of Homeland Security. "Who Joined DHS." Last modified September 15, 2015. https://www.dhs.gov/who-joined-dhs.

U.S. Department of Homeland Security. "Written testimony of FEMA Administrator Brock Long for a Senate Committee on Homeland Security and Governmental Affairs hearing titled 'FEMA: Prioritizing a Culture of Preparedness.'" April 11, 2018. https://www.dhs.gov/news/2018/04/11/written-testimony-fema-administrator-senate-committee-homeland-security-and.

U.S. Department of Homeland Security, Federal Emergency Management Agency. *Budget Overview, Fiscal Year 2018 Congressional Justification.* Washington, DC: DHS, 2017.

U.S. Department of Homeland Security, Federal Emergency Management Agency. "Fiscal Year 2016 Emergency Management Performance Grant Program (EMPG)." Notice of Funding Opportunity (NOFO), 2016. https://www.fema.gov/media-library-data/1455571902574-a84f5a1b2f450795a70cce1f5ee7b967/FY_2016_EMPG_NOFO_FINAL.pdf.

U.S. Department of Homeland Security, Federal Emergency Management Agency. "Fiscal Year 2018 Emergency Management Performance Grant (EMPG) Program." Notice of Funding Opportunity (NOFO)–Key Changes, 2017. https://www.fema.gov/media-library-data/1526578708333-010b3bbbeb00201b3b133a0366913696/FY_2018_EMPG_Key_Changes_FINAL_508.pdf.

U.S. Department of Homeland Security, Homeland Security National Preparedness Task Force. *Civil Defense and Homeland Security: A Short History of National Preparedness Efforts.* Washington, DC: U.S. Department of Homeland Security, 2006.

U.S. Department of Homeland Security, Office of Inspector General. "Component: Federal Emergency Management Agency (FEMA)." Accessed September 7, 2018. http://www.oig.dhs.gov/index.php?option=com_content&view=article&id=25&Itemid=38.

U.S. Department of Homeland Security, Office of Inspector General. *FEMA: In or Out?* Washington, DC:

U.S. Department of Homeland Security, 2009. https://www.oig.dhs.gov/assets/Mgmt/OIG_09-25_Feb09.pdf.

U.S. Department of Homeland Security, Office of Inspector General. Opportunities to Improve FEMA's Public Assistance Preliminary Damage Assessment Process. OIG-12-79, May 2012, 9.

U.S. Department of Homeland Security, Ready.gov. "Plan Ahead for Disasters." Accessed May 28, 2018. https://www.ready.gov/voluntary-organizations-active-disaster.

U.S. Department of Justice, Office of Justice Programs, Bureau of Justice Statistics. "National Sources of Law Enforcement Employment Data." Revised October 4, 2016. https://www.bjs.gov/content/pub/pdf/nsleed.pdf.

U.S. Department of State. "Bureau of Political/Military Affairs." Accessed September 17, 2018. http://www.state.gov/t/pm.

U.S. Department of State. "Going the Distance: The U.S. Tsunami Relief Effort 2005: Americans Respond to Tragedy." Accessed September 25, 2018. https://www.hsdl.org/?view&did=773838.

U.S. Department of State and U.S. Agency for International Development. *FY 2007–2012 Department of State and USAID Strategic Plan.* Washington, DC: U.S. Department of State, 2007. http://www.state.gov/s/d/rm/rls/dosstrat/2007.

U.S. Department of State and U.S. Agency for International Development. *Security, Democracy, Prosperity—USAID-State Strategic Plan, Fiscal Year 2004–2009.* Washington, DC: U.S. Department of State, 2003.

U.S. Department of the Treasury, Resource Center. *Terrorism Risk Insurance Program, Overview.* Accessed May 2, 2018. http://www.treasury.gov/resource-center/fin-mkts/Pages/program.aspx.

U.S. Federal Bureau of Investigation. "Oklahoma City Bombing." Accessed October 8, 2018. https://www.fbi.gov/history/famous-cases/oklahoma-city-bombing.

U.S. Fire Administration. "National Fire Academy." Accessed September 17, 2018. https://www.usfa.fema.gov/training/nfa/index.html.

U.S. Fire Administration. "National Fire Department Registry Quick Facts." Last modified May 15, 2018. https://apps.usfa.fema.gov/registry/summary/.

U.S. Geological Survey. "Earthquake Glossary: S Wave." Accessed July 23, 2018. https://earthquake.usgs.gov/learn/glossary/?term=S%20wave.

U.S. Geological Survey, Earthquake Hazards Program. "Earthquake Notification Service." Accessed May 10, 2018. https://earthquake.usgs.gov/ens/.

U.S. Geological Survey, Earthquake Hazards Program. "The Modified Mercalli Intensity Scale." Accessed July 24, 2018. https://earthquake.usgs.gov/learn/topics/mercalli.php.

U.S. Government Accountability Office. *Disaster Assistance: Improvement Needed in Disaster Declaration Criteria and Eligibility Assurance Procedures.* Washington, DC: Government Printing Office, 2001.

U.S. Government Accountability Office. *Federal Disaster Assistance: Individual Assistance Requests Often Granted but FEMA Could Better Document Factors Considered.* Washington, DC: GAO, 2018. https://www.gao.gov/products/GAO-18-366.

U.S. Government Accountability Office. *Federal Emergency Management Agency: Additional Planning and Data Collection Could Help Improve Workforce Management Efforts.* Washington, DC: GAO, 2015. https://www.gao.gov/assets/680/671276.pdf.

U.S. Government Accountability Office. *2017 Disaster Contracting: Observations on Federal Contracting for Response and Recovery Efforts.* Washington, DC: GAO, 2018.

"US Government to Seek Death Penalty in Boston Marathon Bombing Case." *CBS Boston*, January 30, 2014. http://boston.cbslocal.com/2014/01/30/us-government-to-seek-death-penalty-in-boston-marathon-bombing-case.

U.S. House of Representatives, House Committee on Public Works and Transportation, Subcommittee on Water Resources and the Environment. *Midwest Floods of 1993: Flood Control and Floodplain Policy and Proposals.* Hearing statement of Harold L. Volkmer, 103rd Cong., 1st sess., 1993, serial number 103-57, 241.

U.S. House of Representatives, House Subcommittee on National Security, Emerging Threats, and International Relations, Subcommittee on Energy Policy, Natural Resources and Regulatory Affairs. *Statement of James L. Witt.* 108th Cong., 2nd sess., March 24, 2004.

U.S. National Weather Service, National Oceanic and Atmospheric Administration. "The Enhanced Fujita Scale (EF Scale)." Accessed May 12, 2018. https://www.weather.gov/oun/efscale.

U.S. Navy's Military Sealift Command. "Hospital Ships." Accessed July 23, 2018. http://www.msc.navy.mil/inventory/ships.asp?ship=74.

U.S. Nuclear Regulatory Commission. "The Near-Term Task Force Review of Insights from the Fukushima Dai-ichi Accident, Recommendations for Enhancing Reactor Safety in the 21st Century." 1–82, July 12, 2011.

U.S. Senate. "Glossary Term: Rescission." Accessed April 19, 2018. https://www.senate.gov/reference/glossary_term/rescission.htm.

U.S. Senate, Senate Committee on Governmental Affairs. *Hearing on Rebuilding FEMA: Preparing for the Next Disaster.* 103rd Cong., 1st sess., May 18, 1993, 151.

U.S. Small Business Administration. "About the Office of Disaster Assistance." Accessed May 6, 2018. https://www.sba.gov/offices/headquarters/oda/about-us.

U.S. Small Business Administration. "Home and Property Disaster Loans." Accessed May 6, 2018. https://www.benefits.gov/benefits/benefit-details/1503.

UN General Assembly. "Under-Secretary-General for Management Briefs Fifth Committee on Financial Situation; Says Regular Budget Position Weaker Now Compared to Last Year." May 18, 2007. http://www.un.org/News/Press/docs/2007/gaab3800.doc.htm.

UNICEF. "Putting Children First All Over the World." Accessed September 11, 2018. https://www.unicefusa.org/mission.

UNICEF. "UNICEF in Emergencies." Accessed September 11, 2018. http://www.unicef.org/emergencies.

United Nations High Commissioner for Refugees. "States Parties to the 1951 Convention Relating to the Status of Refugees and the 1967 Protocol." Accessed September 11, 2018. http://www.unhcr.org/protect/PROTECTION/3b73b0d63.pdf.

United Nations, Office for the Coordination of Humanitarian Affairs. "About Us: The Under-Secretary-General and Emergency Relief Coordinator." Accessed March 8, 2014. www.unocha.org/about-us/headofOCHA.

United Nations, Office for the Coordination of Humanitarian Affairs. "ReliefWeb." Accessed September 11, 2018. http://reliefweb.int/disasters.

United States Trade Representative, Executive Office of the President. "Canada: U.S.-Canada Trade Facts." Accessed June 11, 2018. https://ustr.gov/countries-regions/americas/canada.

UPSeis, Michigan Tech. "How Are Earthquake Magnitudes Measured?" Accessed May 12, 2018. http://www.geo.mtu.edu/UPSeis/intensity.html.

UShistory.org. "The Declaration of Independence." Accessed June 8, 2018. http://www.ushistory.org/declaration/document/.

van Munster, Rens. "Securitization." *Oxford Bibliographies*, June 26, 2012. http://www.oxfordbibliographies.com/view/document/obo-9780199743292/obo-9780199743292-0091.xml.

van Um, Eric and Daniela Pisoiu. "Effective counterterrorism: What have we learned so far?" Economics of Security Working Paper 55. Berlin, Germany: Economics of Security, 2011. https://www.diw.de/documents/publikationen/73 /diw_01.c.386651.de/diw_econsec0055.pdf.

Veoci. "About Us." Accessed July 5, 2018. https://www.info.veoci.com/fema-project-reimbursements?gclid=EAIaIQobChMIv4H5sarQ2AIVQ1cNCh0heAT-EAEYASAAEgL9avD_BwE.

VI Now. "Hurricanes Irma & Maria." Accessed June 27, 2018. http://www.vinow.com/gallery/hurricanes-irma-maria/.

Victor, Daniel. "Hurricane Andrew: How The Times Reported the Destruction of 1992." *The New York Times*, September 6, 2017. https://www.nytimes.com/2017/09/06/us/hurricane-andrew-florida.html.

Villafañe, Veronica. "Lin-Manuel Miranda Partners with Google.org for Puerto Rico Recovery $2 Million Matching Grant." *Forbes*, June 8, 2018. https://www.forbes.com/sites/veronicavillafane/2018/06/08/lin-manuel-miranda-amplifies-puerto-rico-fundraising-efforts-with-google-org-2m-matching-grant/#1b115a671035.

Vock, Daniel C. "The Pact Changing How Governments Respond to Disaster." *Governing*, March, 2018. http://www.governing.com/gov-emergency-management-local-federal-fema-states.html.

Wachtendorf, Tricia. "When Disasters Defy Borders: What We Can Learn from the Red River Flood about Transnational Disasters." *Australian Journal of Emergency Management* 15, no. 3 (2000). https://ajem.infoservices.com.au/items/AJEM-15-03-09.

Waldo, Dwight. *The Administrative State*. New York: Ronald Press, 1948.

Walker, David B. *The Rebirth of Federalism: Slouching toward Washington*. Chatham, NJ: Chatham House, 1995.

Walker, David B. *The Rebirth of Federalism: Slouching toward Washington*, 2nd ed. New York: Chatham House, 2000.

Walsh, Donald W., Hank T. Christen Jr., Graydon C. Lord, and Geoffrey T. Miller. *National Incident Management System: Principles and Practice,* 2nd ed. Sudbury, MA: Jones & Bartlett, 2012.

Walt, Vivienne. "Greenwald on Snowden Leaks: The Worst Is Yet to Come." *Time*, October 14, 2013. http://world.time.com/2013/10/14/greenwald-on-snowden-leaks-the-worst-is-yet-to-come/#ixzz2i24YfwWd.

Wamsler, Christine. *Cities, Disaster Risk, and Adaptation*. New York: Routledge, 2014.

Wamsley, Gary L. "Escalating in a Quagmire: The Changing Dynamics of the Emergency Management Policy Subsystem." *Public Administration Review* 56 (May/June 1996): 235–244.

Wamsley, Gary L., Aaron D. Schroeder, and Larry M. Lane. "To Politicize Is NOT to Control: The Pathologies of Control in Federal Emergency Management." *American Review of Public Administration* 26, no. 3 (1996): 263–285.

Ward, Peter D. *The Flooded Earth: Our Future in a World without Ice Caps*. New York: Basic Books, 2010.

Warrick, Joby. "FBI Investigation of 2001 Anthrax Attacks Concluded; U.S. Releases Details." *Washington Post*, February 20, 2010. http://www.washingtonpost.com/wp-dyn/content/article/2010/02/19/AR2010021902369.html.

Waugh, William L., Jr. *Living with Hazards, Dealing with Disasters: An Introduction to Emergency Management*. Armonk, NY: M.E. Sharpe, 2000.

Waugh, William L., Jr. "Terrorism, Homeland Security, and the National Emergency Management Network." *Public Organization Review* 3 (December 2003): 373–385.

Waugh, William L., Jr. and Richard T. Sylves. "Organizing the War on Terrorism." *Public Administration Review* 62 (September 2002): 145–153.

Waugh, William L., Jr. and Ronald John Hy, eds. *Handbook of Emergency Management*. Westport, CT: Greenwood Press, 1991.

Weible, Christopher M. and Paul A. Sabatier, eds. *Theories of the Policy Process*, 4th ed. Boulder, CO: Westview Press, 2018.

Weinberger, Matt. "Why Amazon's Echo Is Totally Dominating—And What Google, Microsoft, and Apple Have to Do to Catch Up." *Business Insider*, January 14, 2017. http://www.businessinsider.com/amazon-echo-google-home-microsoft-cortana-apple-siri-2017-1.

Weiner, Eric. "What Is Executive Privilege, Anyway?" *NPR*, June 28, 2007. https://www.npr.org/templates/story/story.php?storyId=11527747.

Weiss, Daniel J. and Jackie Weidman. "Disastrous Spending: Federal Disaster-Relief Expenditures Rise Amid More Extreme Weather." Center for American Progress, April 29, 2013. http://www.americanprogress.org/issues/green/report/2013/04/29/61633/disastrous-spending-federal-disaster-relief-expenditures-rise-amid-more-extreme-weather.

Wellerstein, Alex. "The Hawaii Alert Was an Accident. The Dread It Inspired Wasn't." *The Washington Post*, January 16, 2018. https://www.washingtonpost.com/news/posteverything/wp/2018/01/16/the-hawaii-alert-was-an-accident-the-dread-it-inspired-wasnt/?utm_term=.3a2789320c2b.

Westfall, Catherine. "Rethinking Big Science: Modest, Mezzo, Grand Science and the Development of the Bevalac, 1971–1993," *Isis* 94 (March 2003): 32.

Weston, Liz Pulliam. "Rethinking Your Stance on Earthquake Coverage: Rethinking Your Stance on Earthquake Coverage." *The Los Angeles Times*, December 18, 2017. http://www.latimes.com/la-homeauto-story1-story.html.

White, Connie M. *Social Media, Crisis Communication, and Emergency Management*. Boca Raton, FL: CRC Press of Taylor & Francis Group, 2012.

White, Gilbert F., Wesley Calef, James W. Hudson, Harold M. Mayer, John R. Sheaffer, and Donald J. Volk. "Changes in Urban Occupancy of Flood Plains in the United States." Research Paper 57, Department of Geography, University of Chicago, 1958.

The White House. "White House Internship Program: Presidential Departments." Accessed October 1, 2018. https://www.whitehouse.gov/get-involved/internships/presidential-departments/.

The White House, Office of the Press Secretary. "Ongoing Response to Hurricane Sandy." November 15, 2012. http://www.whitehouse.gov/the-press-office/2012/11/15/ongoing-response-hurricane-sandy.

Willingham, A. J. and Saeed Ahmed. "Mass shootings in America are a serious problem -- and these 9 charts show just why." *CNN*, November 6, 2017. https://www.cnn.com/2016/06/13/health/mass-shootings-in-america-in-charts-and-graphs-trnd/index.html.

Winkler, Jurgen R. "Political Culture: Political Science." *Encyclopedia Britannica*, May 4, 2018. https://www.britannica.com/topic/political-culture.

Winsor, Morgan. "US Virgin Islands in Ruins from Hurricane Maria." *ABC News*, September 29, 2017. https://abcnews.go.com/International/us-virgin-islands-ruins-hurricane-maria/story?id=50178300.

Wise, Charles R. "Organizing for Homeland Security." *Public Administration Review* 62 (September 2002): 131–144.

Wise, Charles R. and Rania Nader. "Organizing the Federal System for Homeland Security: Problems, Issues, and Dilemmas." *Public Administration Review* 62 (September 2002): 44–57.

Witt, James Lee. "Military Role in Natural Disaster Response." *Disaster Preparedness* 1, no. 1 (Summer 2006).

Witt, James Lee and James Morgan. *Stronger in the Broken Places: Nine Lessons for Turning Crisis into Triumph*. New York: Times Books, 2002.

Wood, Adrian, Raymond Apthorpe, and John Borton, eds. *Evaluating International Humanitarian Action*. London: Zed Books, 2001.

Wood, David. "National Guard Increases Sandy Response, Sends Reinforcements to NY, NJ." *Huffington Post*, November 1, 2012. http://www.huffingtonpost.com/2012/11/01/national-guard-sandy-ny-nj_n_2060249.html.

Woodward, Bob. *FEAR: Trump in the White House*. New York: Simon & Schuster, 2018.

The World Bank. *Natural Hazards and Unnatural Disasters: The Economics of Effective Prevention.* Washington, DC: International Bank for Reconstruction and Development, 2010.

World Food Programme. "Overview." Accessed September 11, 2018. http://www1.wfp.org/overview.

World Nuclear Association. "Fukushima Accident." Accessed September 6, 2018. http://www.world-nuclear.org/info/Safety-and-Security/Safety-of-Plants/Fukushima-Accident.

World Population Review. "Population of Cities in Texas (2018)." Accessed June 23, 2018. http://worldpopulation review.com/states/texas-population/cities/.

World Vision. "Hurricane Irma: Facts, FAQs, and How to Help," Last modified February 14, 2018. https://www.worldvision.org/disaster-relief-news-stories/hurricane-irma-facts.

Wright, Deil S. "Models of National/State/Local Relations." In *American Intergovernmental Relations*, edited by Laurence J. O'Toole Jr., 59. Washington, DC: Congressional Quarterly, 1985.

Wright, Deil S. *Understanding Intergovernmental Relations*, 3rd ed. Pacific Grove, CA: Brooks/Cole, 1988.

Yee, Vivian and Alan Blindermarch. "National School Walkout: Thousands Protest Against Gun Violence Across the U.S." *The New York Times*, March 14, 2018. https://www.nytimes.com/2018/03/14/us/school-walkout.html.

YourDictionary. "Hyperpartisanship." Accessed July 24, 2018. http://www.yourdictionary.com/hyperpartisanship.

Zeller, Tom. "U.S. Nuclear Plants Have Same Risks, and Backups, as Japan Counterparts." *New York Times*, March 13, 2011. http://www.nytimes.com/2011/03/14/world/asia/14industry.html?ref=global-home&_r=0.

INDEX